# The Blue-Collar Bible Scholar

*Reader's Guide to the New Testament*

# Blue-Collar Bible Scholar

*Reader's Guide to the New Testament*

JOEL EDMUND ANDERSON

McGahan

The Blue Collar Bible Scholar's *Reader's Guide to the New Testament*

Copyright © 2023 by Joel Edmund Anderson

All rights reserved. No part of this publication may be reproduced, stored in a retrieval system, or transmitted in any form or by any means—electronic, mechanical, photocopy, recording, or any other—except for brief quotations in printed reviews, without the prior permission of the publisher.

Unless otherwise indicated, all Scripture quotations are from The ESV® Bible (The Holy Bible, English Standard Version®), © 2001 by Crossway, a publishing ministry of Good News Publishers. Used by permission. All rights reserved."

McGahan Publishing House | Lynchburg, Tennessee

www.mphbooks.com

Requests for information should be sent to:

info@mphbooks.com

ISBN 978-1-951252-29-8 (Hardcover)

## DEDICATION

For Dr. Gordon Fee, who passed on October 25, 2022.

I was an admiring student of his at Regent College and completely revered the man. The Holy Spirit walked into the room when Dr. Fee taught his classes. It is because of him that I decided to dedicate my life to Biblical Studies.

# CONTENTS

**PREFACE** ........................................................................................... 9

**INTRODUCTION** ............................................................................ 15

**THE SYNOPTIC GOSPELS** ........................................................... 35

    THE GOSPEL OF MARK .......................................................... 41

    THE GOSPEL OF MATTHEW ................................................. 83

    THE GOSPEL OF LUKE ......................................................... 133

**THE BOOK OF ACTS** .................................................................. 175

**THE LETTERS OF PAUL** ............................................................ 211

    GALATIANS ............................................................................ 217

    I/II THESSALONIANS ............................................................ 235

    I CORINTHIANS .................................................................... 245

    II CORINTHIANS ................................................................... 268

    ROMANS ................................................................................. 285

    PHILIPPIANS ......................................................................... 319

    EPHESIANS ............................................................................ 327

    COLOSSIANS ......................................................................... 341

    PHILEMON ............................................................................. 353

    TITUS ........................................................................................... 357

    I TIMOTHY ................................................................................ 363

    II TIMOTHY .............................................................................. 373

**THE GENERAL LETTERS** ............................................................**379**

    HEBREWS .................................................................................. 381

    JAMES ......................................................................................... 403

    I PETER ....................................................................................... 415

    II PETER ..................................................................................... 430

    JUDE ........................................................................................... 437

**THE WRITINGS OF JOHN** ...........................................................**443**

    I/II/III JOHN ............................................................................. 445

    THE GOSPEL OF JOHN ........................................................ 461

    REVELATION .......................................................................... 507

# PREFACE

My love of the Bible began when I was in grade school, when I was given an illustrated Bible. The illustrations weren't childish cartoons of "kiddie Bibles," but neither were they the kind of over-the-top illustrations you find in superhero comic books. This illustrated Bible just had realistic-looking characters and it focused on the entire story of the Old and New Testaments. That illustrated Bible was my Bible up through junior high, and it taught me the overall story of the Bible from beginning to end—not decontextualized snippets, but the overarching biblical narrative. It captured my imagination, drew me into the biblical world, and cultivated my love of the biblical story.

As I got older, I began to realize that not everyone really knew the biblical story. Even for those who grew up in church, knowledge of the Bible tends to be limited to a few isolated Sunday school stories. There really isn't much knowledge of the history of the biblical world. Let's face it, of us don't really *read* the Bible anyway, because when we try, we simply can't make sense of it. And the reason we can't make sense of it is because not only have we not been taught how to read the Bible, but we actually have been taught to treat the Bible badly—solely as a devotional book for our quiet time, and nothing more. Instead of reading the Bible as a narrative whole, we tend to treat it like a grab bag in which we rummage around for a few inspirational treasures that we can easily apply to our daily lives.

Now, there is certainly nothing wrong with devotional reading of the Bible—that's a good thing to do. The problem, though, is that without a knowledge of the depth of the biblical story and the richness of the biblical world, you simply are going to be missing a whole lot of what is going on in the Bible, the result being that your Bible reading will inevitably be rather superficial at best.

Perhaps that is the wrong way to put it, though. It sounds too negative. Let's flip it around and put a positive spin on it and say that if you take the time to learn just a *little bit of the history of the biblical world* and a *little bit of the literary creativity of the biblical authors*, you are going to see things that you've never seen before. It will be like switching from an old 20-inch black and white television to a wide-screen television in high definition. Everything will be clearer and will make more sense.

But there really is more to it than that, and so my little analogy can only go so far. The fact is there is no magic pill and no single book you can read that will make everything clear all at once. In that respect, learning to read the Bible in its historical and literary contexts isn't as simple as turning on a HD television. In fact, the Bible isn't "simple" at all. It really is an entire world that you can (and should) spend your life exploring. The key is to be given a decent enough map and travel guide so that you can explore the biblical world.

As strange as it may sound, if you want to get more out of the Bible, you have to initially forget that you're reading the **Holy Bible**. When you begin reading it, come to it as you would any other book and just read it to understand it. Don't try to immediately come up with a personal "life application." For that matter, forget about "you" altogether. The Bible isn't there to cater to *your needs*. It is an entire world that invites you in and challenges you to explore it. Granted, it is a big challenge to try to get a grasp of biblical history, and it is also a big challenge to gain an appreciation for the way the biblical authors wrote their works. But the fact is, ignorance of the history and literary creativity of the Bible leads to an ignorance of the message of the Bible.

Therefore, I think it is tremendously beneficial to try to come to the Bible with no presuppositions about it—just read it and try to understand it. Come ready to wrestle with it. I've found that when you approach the Bible that way, that is when you will truly appreciate it as the inspired work that it is. If you come to it already thinking, "This is *inspired*," you're going to be too afraid to really wrestle with it, and your *stated belief* of its inspiration won't really match with your *experience* of reading it. You may say it is inspired, but most of it will seem dry, confusing, or boring. But if you dare to forget it is inspired, and you just jump into the ring and wrestle with it, I believe it will come alive for you and you'll find yourself wrestling with a text truly inspired by God. It won't be a stated presupposition, but an experienced reality.

I've taught Biblical Studies at both the high school and college level for about 25 years, and even though I love the academic study of the Bible, it has always bugged me that academic textbooks on the Bible tend to be way over the heads of most people. On top of that, they tend to be really dry. I think I know the reason why. It is because most scholars who end up writing academic books on the Bible have spent most of their careers at the academic level. So, when they write introductory textbooks on the Bible that are supposed to be *introductions to the Bible*, they don't really write for people at the *introductory level*. Instead, they write in a way that will impress other academics, and that means they spend most of their time writing about all the academic debates and controversies scholars like to obsess over.

The fact is, though, students taking an Old or New Testament Introduction course simply aren't ready for that. Chances are their knowledge of the Bible probably doesn't go much beyond Sunday sermons, Sunday school, and perhaps a group Bible study. For that matter, that's about the level of knowledge about the Bible most Christians have, period. To use an analogy, the problem with most academic introduction books to the Bible is that they are like a training program for runners who want to compete in the Olympics. But not everyone wants to compete in the Olympics. Most just want to be able to go for a jog in the park, enjoy the scenery, and get in better shape, but they don't really know where to begin. In that respect, most Christians don't want to become full-time scholars. They simply want to make sense of what they read in the Bible so they can apply it to their lives in a more substantial way. They just don't know where to begin, and most introduction books are over their heads.

That is the problem I want to address in this book. From the time I started my first graduate program at Regent College in 1995, I have always wanted to be able to take what I learned at the graduate level in Biblical Studies and make it available and understandable to Christians who are never going to get a college degree in Biblical Studies. That is why I chose to work my way through two master's programs and a PhD program while teaching Bible at the high school level for sixteen years. At every step of the way, I would try to take what I had learned and make it understandable to teenagers. Believe me, that can be quite the challenge. For the most part, though, I think I was quite successful. I now teach at the college level, and a lot of what I use in my introduction courses was actually developed in my high school Bible classes.

The aim of this book is simply to open the door to the biblical world (and the various "countries" within it) and provide a survey of the land by pointing out the major landmarks and features, so to speak, and enough of a biblical map/travel guide so that you can get your bearings and start navigating and exploring the biblical world yourself. I want to provide just enough **historical background information** to get you firmly established in the time period of a particular biblical book, and enough **literary guidance** with each biblical book to help you interpret and appreciate what is being said and how it is being communicated to the original audience of that particular biblical book. After all, it is important to remember that the books in the New Testament were not directly written to us in the modern world, but rather to very real people and communities who lived back in the first century. Therefore, it is extremely important to understand what each book in the New Testament meant *back then* before we try to figure out what it means to us *now*.

In short, whether you are a high school or college student talking a New Testament Introduction course or just an everyday Christian who simply wants to understand the New Testament better, I hope this book helps you help to become a good reader of the New Testament. And hopefully, in the process of wrestling with the inspired message of the Bible and trying to understand it better in its original context, the Holy Spirit will "guide you in all truth," both in your individual reading and also as you share your thoughts with other Christians.

**A "How to" Guide**

There are a number of things I want to make clear regarding what is in this book, as well as how you should use it. Remember, this is a **reader's guide** to the New Testament, not a substitute for reading the New Testament. Therefore, I would suggest the following reading strategy. Let's use the Gospel of Mark as an example:

First, read my introductory comments on Mark and take a look at the story chart I made to act as a visual map to help understand Mark as a whole. Skim through the chart and take note of every episode you think you are familiar with. For example, "Oh, I see the Prologue in 1:1-15 is about Jesus' baptism and temptation in the wilderness. I know about that. That sounds familiar." Or perhaps, "I thought the gospels began with the birth of Jesus in Bethlehem, with shepherds and Wise Men., but I don't see them in Mark. Where are they?"

Second, before you read my walkthrough section, open your Bible and read through Mark's Prologue in 1:1-15, and, perhaps in a notebook, under the heading, **Mark 1:1-15**, bullet-point any observations or questions you have: What are the Old Testament verses that Mark quotes? What are we told about John the Baptist? What's up with the dove coming out of heaven? Write down anything that stands out to you.

Third, after that, read my walkthrough section on Mark's Prologue. Perhaps there is something in there that will have answered one of your questions. Perhaps I will have pointed out something you hadn't noticed before.

Fourth, go back, re-read Mark 1:1-15 and try to see the whole episode unfold in light of what you've learned.

Finally, as should be obvious, don't stop there. Let what you learned inform your reading and contemplation of these biblical books from here on out.

Now, you don't have to do that with every single episode. Perhaps you want to read the second section in Mark (1:16-2:12) all the way through, and then read that section in my walkthrough. However you do it, the trick is to (1) read the biblical passage first, on your own, noting any questions you may have, then (2) read the corresponding walkthrough section to get more informed about that passage, and then (3) re-read the biblical passage and let it speak to you as contemplate it.

There are a few more things about my *Reader's Guide* that I want to highlight. First, one thing I've come to see as incredibly important as I've studied and taught the New Testament is the impact that the **Jewish War of AD 66-70** had on the early Christian Church, and how that shows up almost everywhere in the New Testament. Unfortunately, most people are wholly ignorant of what happened during the Jewish War and how impactful it was, not only on Christianity, but on Judaism as well. In particular, although the Synoptic Gospels covered the ministry of Jesus that took place roughly between AD 27-30, they weren't written until around AD 70. Mark was probably the first Gospel written, perhaps in the 60s, with Matthew and Luke being written sometime in the 70s or 80s. Therefore, at the time these Gospels would have first been read, the Jewish War was either unfolding or had just happened. That is going to have a huge impact on many things you read in the Gospels. I do the best I can to show how the New Testament writings would probably have been read in light of the events of the Jewish War. Believe me, it makes a huge difference.

Secondly, I sometimes discuss a keyword or phrase in Greek that is of particular interest when it comes to proper interpretation. Since most people reading this book are not fluent in New Testament Greek, I simply transliterate the word into English.

Thirdly, I purposely did not put a lot of footnotes in this *Reader's Guide*. The historical background details I discuss at the beginning of each New Testament book can be found in almost any New Testament commentary. Still, I want to note that the book I probably most relied on for the historical background was *The New Testament in Antiquity*, by Gary M. Burge and Gene L. Green. In my opinion, it is one of the best New Testament Introduction books out there.

Finally, as you read this book, you will notice that the illustrations are done in my own handwriting—and are admittedly a little "rough"! The reason I wanted to do it like that is that I want to emphasize how doing simple, rough drawings and visuals helps the learning process. My illustrations cover some New Testament passages. If you find them helpful, draw your own illustrations for other passages. You'll be amazed at how much better you understand something, and much easier it will be to remember something, if you take the time to draw silly, even messy, little illustrations to help understand any given passage.

The goal of this *Reader's Guide* is to help you wrestle with the Bible so that you become a better reader of it and will therefore be in a better and more informed position to truly apply it and let it challenge your life. So, go ahead, start with the introduction. Don't skip over it. It will give a much-needed overview, not only of the New Testament, but also of the Old Testament and the intervening time period that led up to Jesus and the early Church.

# INTRODUCTION

If you want to understand the New Testament, you have to know a little bit of history and you have to be a good reader of literature, because the New Testament is not only about **historical events**, but much of it comes in the form of a **story**. On one hand, you have to know about the historical events that led up to the New Testament times in the first century, as well as the events in the first century themselves, if you want to better understand the writings of the New Testament. Without that historical context, you are simply going to miss a lot of what the New Testament really is about. To use an example from American history, it would be like reading the Gettysburg Address with no knowledge of the Civil War, or the Declaration of Independence without any understanding of the American Revolution. On the other hand, you have to make sure you're reading the books of the New Testament correctly. By that, I mean you have to understand each book's genre and literary characteristics. You don't want to read a parable as if it is commandment, and you want to be able to tell the difference between when the author uses a metaphor and when he is making a historical claim.

Now, much of what you will read in the walkthrough sections will help you become a better reader of the Synoptic Gospels and Acts. Here in the introduction, though, I want to give you a foundational understanding of the larger historical backdrop regarding (1) the Old Testament story that leads into the New Testament, (2) the events of the **Intertestamental Period** (the roughly 400 years between the last events in the Old Testament and the life of Christ in the New Testament) that have a huge impact on first century Judaism, (3) the world of the first century, both the Roman Empire and the various Jewish sects within **Second Temple Judaism** (basically, the different Jewish groups in the first century), and (4) the prevailing Jewish expectations regarding "the end times" (what scholars call the Jewish Eschatological Hope).

## I. WHAT IS THE NEW TESTAMENT?

The New Testament is a collection of writings that contain the earliest testimony of the first century early Church. If you want to get an idea of what the earliest Christians believed, taught, and proclaimed, you need to read the New Testament. Although the actual ministry of Jesus Christ happened around AD 27-30, the writings we have in the New Testament were written anywhere between AD 48 and AD 95. Perhaps the easiest way to get a grasp on what is in the New Testament is to break it down into four categories: (1) *The Letters of Paul*, (2) *The*

*General Letters* (Hebrews, James, I/II Peter, Jude), (3) *The Synoptic Gospels and Acts*, and (4) *The Writings of John*. The reason they are listed in that order has to do with when they were written.

## The Letters of Paul

It may sound surprising, but the letters of Paul are actually the earliest New Testament writings we have. Even though the Synoptic Gospels are obviously about the life of Jesus around AD 27-30 (and therefore those events precede Paul), they weren't actually written until around AD 70-80.

The Apostle Paul was a Pharisee and one of the earliest persecutors of the "Jesus movement" in Judea after Pentecost. He had a life-changing experience on his way to Damascus to arrest Jesus followers who were known at that time as **The Way**. He claimed he had encountered the resurrected Christ, and that experience changed the course of his life. He became the apostle to the Gentiles. The letters he wrote are the earliest New Testament documents we have, written from around AD 48-64. The thing to remember about Paul's letters is that they are **occasional letters**. That means they were written to address specific issues that arose in those specific churches at that specific time. Therefore, Paul was not writing systematic theology, but was essentially applying the core Gospel message concerning Jesus' death, resurrection, and the outpouring of the Holy Spirit to the real-life situations his churches were confronting. In that sense, he was "writing theology on the fly."

## The General Letters

The writings of Hebrews, James, I/II Peter, and Jude clearly address very Jewish concerns. Although there isn't any general scholarly agreement on the issues of their authorship and time of writing, Church Tradition does, in fact, claim a first century origin. And if James, Peter, and Jude really wrote those letters (Hebrews is anonymous), that means all of these writings would be dated before AD 70 and the destruction of Jerusalem. That would place them as written in the same time period as when Paul was writing his letters.

## The Synoptic Gospels and Acts

The Synoptic Gospels and Acts can be a bit tricky to grasp. As I mentioned earlier, although the Synoptic Gospels are about the life and ministry of Jesus in AD 28-30, they were written a good 35-50 years later, around the time of the Jewish War of AD 66-70. This does not mean the authors of the Synoptic Gospels simply made up their stories. They were actually compiling what the early Church had been proclaiming about Jesus from the very beginning. Mark and Matthew are, in fact, considered **historical biographies** (focusing on the life and ministry of Jesus), and Luke-Acts is a **historical monograph** (focusing not just on Jesus, but also the growth of the early Church over roughly a thirty-year time span). They collected what the early Church had proclaimed and taught about Jesus during those previous 35-50 years and arranged that material into their respective Gospels. The Book of Acts is a continuation of Luke, and it covers roughly the 30 years between Pentecost (AD 30) to Paul's imprisonment in Rome (AD 60-62). It is the work that gives us a glimpse into the earliest times of the early Church. Generally speaking, Mark is believed to have been written first, possibly in the late 60s. Matthew and Luke were written shortly after that, during the 70s-80s, with Acts, the second volume of Luke-Acts, also written around that time.

### The Writings of John

The last of the New Testament writings are the writings of John: The Gospel of John, I/II/III John, and Revelation. They are believed to have been written at some point in the 90s, about 20-25 years after the destruction of Jerusalem. Although it focuses on the ministry of Jesus, the Gospel of John is not laid out in the same way as the Synoptics at all. It has different material and an altogether different flavor. This is because the situation between Christians and Jews in the 90s was considerably different than it was before AD 70. Before AD 70, Christianity was still seen to some extent as a Jewish, or Jewish-related, sect. Despite its acceptance by a growing number of Gentiles, its ties to Jerusalem were still strong.

After the Jewish War of AD 66-70, though, Christianity was, for all intents and purposes, seen as distinct from Judaism. The Book of Revelation is generally dated to the time of the Roman Emperor Domitian, around AD 95. Even though it is **apocalyptic literature**, it still needs to be read and understood within the context of what the Church was going through in the late first century during that first empire-wide persecution of Christians by Domitian. I/II/III John are short letters John wrote to his community that emphasize many of the same themes found in his Gospel.

## II. THE OLD TESTAMENT STORY

You will never fully understand or appreciate the New Testament if you don't first understand the Old Testament. Granted, if you've ever looked at the Old Testament, you already know it is quite massive. That is why I've included this section. It will not only provide the basic Old Testament themes that will help you understand the New Testament better, but it will also help you understand the Old Testament itself. The fact is, if you don't know your Old Testament, you're going to miss a whole lot in the New Testament.

**Genesis 1-11**

Genesis 1-11 sets the stage for the entire story of God's involvement in ancient Israel, the life of Christ, and the early Church. If you don't get the main themes of Genesis 1-11, you're going to miss a whole lot in the Old and New Testaments. After the initial creation narrative in Genesis 1, the first thing we are told about human beings is found in 1:26-27, where God declares that Mankind is created **in God's image**. In the ancient Near East, this was **idol language**. An idol represented the deity, and it was believed that wherever the image of that god was, the deity was somehow present. Now, one of the key commandments in the Old Testament was that the Israelites were not to worship other gods and were not to worship **the images of other gods**, because they **themselves were the image of the true God**.

As strange as it may sound, human beings were fashioned to be "idols" of YHWH, the God of Israel. "YHWH" (pronounced *Yahweh*) is the traditional way God's name is given in the Old Testament. It is the name that God gave Moses at the burning bush in Exodus 3, and it means "I Am." In any case, the point of being made in God's image (being "idols" of YHWH) meant that human beings were to be His representatives in the world. That is what the image of God language is about: **human beings are to make God's presence known in the world through bearing God's image and practicing God's justice, mercy, love, and compassion in the world**.

In Genesis 1-2, therefore, we are told that Adam (human beings) has a two-fold task as God's image-bearer: (A) To rule over the beasts, and (B) To take care of the garden. Thus, he was to be **God's co-regent** who ruled God's creation, **God's priest** who sanctified God's creation, and **God's custodian** who took care of God's creation. He was to be a **servant-king** and a **holy custodian** who exercised God's authority in the world through serving.

Of course, beginning in Genesis 3, that is not what happens. Because of Adam's choice, mankind no longer reflects God's image in the world and all creation is plunged into corruption, sin, and death. That is the stage that Genesis 1-11 lays out: **God's creation is good and human beings are made in God's**

**image, but because of sin, both human beings and the creation itself are in bondage to corruption and death.** So, the question becomes, "How is God going to make good on His promise in Genesis 3:16, when He says that the 'offspring of the woman' would eventually 'crush the head of the serpent'"?

### Abraham and the Covenant

The answer begins with the narrative of Abraham. In it, we find that YHWH, the Creator God, chooses to work through Abraham to redeem His creation by entering into a **covenant** with him. A covenant is like a contract, where two parties enter into a relationship with each other for a certain purpose. In His covenant with Abraham, in exchange for Abraham putting his faith in YHWH, YHWH makes three promises: (1) **"I will make your name great"**—We can see this when Abram's name is changed to Abraham; (2) **"I will make you into a great nation"**—We see this beginning at Sinai and the forming of the Hebrews into a nation; and (3) **"Through that nation, all nations will be blessed"**—This is the part of YHWH's promise that doesn't get fully answered in the Old Testament. It is, though, answered in the New Testament: Through Christ and the outpouring of the Holy Spirit, the Gentiles are brought in to become part of the people of God.

### Moses, the Exodus, and the Covenant

The second part of YHWH's promise to Abraham begins to be fulfilled during the Exodus, when the Hebrews encounter YHWH on Mount Sinai and He forms them into a nation, so that they would be able to be a light to the Gentiles. To use Genesis language, Israel was essentially to be the "true Adam," the true humanity who reflected God's image in a world full of idolatrous beasts. It is here where we really notice a fundamental theme in the Old Testament: **You become like what you worship**. If you worship YHWH, the true Creator God in whose image you were made, you become more like God and become a true human being who reflects that image by practicing justice, mercy, love and compassion. By contrast, if you worship idols who may have eyes and ears, but cannot really see or hear, and who are often fashioned in the image of beasts, you become like that idol. You become spiritually blind and deaf, and you become like a violent beast ruled by its passions and instincts who practices injustice, violence and evil.

### The Problem in the History of Israel

Israel, though, failed horribly to be a "light to the Gentiles," in that they didn't reflect God's image to the rest of the world. Instead, they turned to idols and reflected the beastly images of the Gentile world. The result ultimately was the

**Babylonian Exile**, when they finally suffered the consequences of breaking the Mosaic covenant. Israel was supposed to be like Adam who ruled the beasts, but with the exile, Israel became ruled by those very beastly Gentile nations. Everything was turned upside down. The Mosaic covenant had been broken and it seemed that God's covenant promises to Abraham had failed. Yet, in the midst of Israel's failure, many of the prophets (Jeremiah 31:31-33) promised there would be a **New Covenant**, not like the Mosaic Covenant, that would fulfill God's promises to Abraham.

### The Faithful Exilic Remnant

Among those in Judah who were sent into the Babylonian Exile, there was a **faithful remnant** who stayed faithful to the covenant, and who, though imperfect, ended up being that "light to the Gentiles" that the unfaithful nation had failed to be. This is the message of Daniel 1-6. Although the faithful remnant suffered because of the sins of the nation of Israel, it was nevertheless a light to the Gentiles while in exile and it was further refined within the fires of exile. This faithful remnant is identified with the Suffering Servant of Isaiah 40-55, who not only suffers on behalf of the nation, but who also is a light to the Gentiles.

### The Hope of the Post-Exilic Jewish Community

When the Jews returned from exile, they saw themselves as the refined remnant and they hoped for a resurrection of their nation that would include a new temple being rebuilt, and a new king who would rule over the nations. The hope was that they could be that "true Adam" who would be a light to the Gentile nations and rule over the Gentile beasts. They saw the Promised Land sort of like Eden in the Genesis story. Thus, the Exile was like the expulsion of Adam and Eve from Eden, and the return from the Exile was like a resurrection of God's people and a return to Eden.

### What Will this Resurrected People of God Look Like?

Things didn't turn out the way the returned exiles had hoped, though. The new temple didn't compare to Solomon's temple, a new king/messiah never came, Gentile nations continued to rule over them, and much to their dismay, there was still injustice and evil within the Jewish community. They didn't seem to be as refined and purified as they thought they were. On top of that, there was the question regarding how they should relate to foreigners in their midst. When they had returned from Exile, they encountered people in the land who were the descendants of Israelites who had intermarried with foreigners. These were the people who later became known as the Samaritans. As far as the returning exiles were concerned, they were idolatrous half-breeds.

So, what were the returned exiles supposed to do? The reason they had gone into exile was because they failed to be God's people and had let themselves be corrupted by Gentiles and paganism. Therefore, what we see at the end of the Old Testament period is the post-exilic community wrestling with this issue. On one hand, there was the view of Ezra and Nehemiah that said they should kick out the foreigners so that they wouldn't be lured back into pagan idolatry and instead be a pure race of Jews.

On the other hand, there was the view of many prophets like Isaiah and Zechariah who said that when YHWH resurrected His people and brought about the promised New Covenant, somehow Gentiles would "get in" and become part of God's people. The later prophets also looked forward to a future Day of YHWH and proclaimed that when the Messiah came, there would be conflict and some in Judah, as well as some Gentiles, would reject him. Afterwards, though, both faithful Jews and Gentiles would come together and worship YHWH. God's "salvation plan" that had been first hinted at in Genesis 3 (the woman's offspring would eventually defeat the serpent and his offspring), had then implemented with Abraham in the Abrahamic covenant, and slowly unfolded throughout the history of Israel, would finally be brought to its fulfillment.

## III. THE INTERTESTAMENTAL PERIOD

The **Intertestamental Period** refers to the 400-year period between the close of the Old Testament and the birth of Jesus Christ. Most Christians are unaware of this period, but it is important to get a general grasp of it because it is the world into which Jesus was born. Jesus was not born during the Exodus, or the time of David and Solomon, or the time of the Babylonian Exile. His world was significantly shaped by events of the Intertestamental Period, and that is why we must take a brief glimpse at the two most significant events of that period: The **Maccabean Revolt** and the rise of the **Roman Empire**.

The Maccabean Revolt happened in the 160s BC. For the previous 150 years or so, the entire region, along with most of the known world, had been **Hellenized** due to the military campaigns of Alexander the Great (356-323 BC). He brought Greek learning and culture to every land he conquered, from Egypt in the south to India in the east. When Alexander died, his empire was divided up among his generals. The Antigonids ruled Macedonia, the Ptolemies ruled Egypt, Libya, and Palestine, and the Seleucids ruled Syria and Persia. For about 100 years, there was relative peace in Palestine, and Jerusalem became a Temple State, governed by a high priestly aristocracy.

Yet in 198 BC the Seleucids took over Palestine when the king, Antiochus the Great, gained support from the Jews because he promised tax relief and relative freedom. Many Jews were enamored with Greek culture, but Antiochus the Great didn't force it on them. He largely left the Jews to their own affairs and customs. When his son, Antiochus Epiphanes, came to power in 175 BC, things dramatically changed because Antiochus Epiphanes was determined to not only force Greek culture on the Jews, but to eradicate Judaism altogether. He wanted his kingdom to be united under one religion, with himself being worshipped as a god.

He first succeeded in playing two rival Jewish aristocratic families—the **Oniads** and the **Tobiads**—against each other in order to gain more power. The Oniads were the descendants of the Zadokite line since the time of David and were in charge of the high priesthood. The Tobiads, though, wanted to gain control of the priesthood. Both families promised Antiochus Epiphanes a variety of things so that he, a pagan ruler, would appoint one of their own to be the high priesthood in the Temple of YHWH. When it was all said and done, a Tobiad was given the high priesthood, and Antiochus Epiphanes got an increase in taxes, regular tribute, a Greek Gymnasium built in Jerusalem, and the Jewish citizens of Jerusalem to be called **Antiochenes**.

Then in 169 BC, after an unsuccessful military campaign in Egypt, Antiochus Epiphanes, in desperate need of money, plundered the Temple. This was a sacrilege to observant Jews. But he wasn't done. He then ordered that a statue of himself as Zeus Olympius be set up in the Temple in Jerusalem, that altars be erected all over Palestine, and that Jews must sacrifice swine to him as Zeus. On top of that, he made it a crime for any Jew to take part in any Jewish tradition, ceremony, sacrifice, Sabbath, or circumcision. Any Jew who did so would be punished by death.

Inevitably, a revolt began in the small Jewish town of Modein, when a Jewish man named **Mattathias Maccabees** not only killed a Jew who was making the pagan sacrifice, but also the army officer who was sent to enforce the new anti-Jewish laws. He tore down the pagan altar, and along with his five sons, started a guerrilla war against Antiochus Epiphanes. After Mattathias died, **Judas**

Maccabees took over the Jewish liberation movement, and by 164 BC he won a truce with Syria. Antiochus Epiphanes withdrew from the area and Judas Maccabees rode in triumph into Jerusalem and proceeded to cleanse the Temple. It is the victory over Antiochus Epiphanes and Judas Maccabees' cleansing of the Temple that is celebrated in the Jewish holiday called **Hanukkah**.

After Judas Maccabees died in 161 BC, his brother **Jonathan** became the political, religious, and military leader of the Jews. Ironically, he was appointed high priest by Alexander Balas, the new Seleucid ruler. Seven years later, in 145 BC, a new Syrian ruler arrested and killed Jonathan, but then in 142 BC, Judea became an independent state, and **Simon**, Jonathan's brother, became ruler and high priest (142-134 BC). This began a short period in which the Maccabean family, known as the **Hasmonean rulers**, ruled over Judea. It was during the Hasmonean dynasty that we find the first mention of **Pharisees** and **Sadducees**.

The next ruler, **John Hyrcanus** (134-104 BC) supported the Sadducees and destroyed the Samaritan Temple on Mount Gerizim (the mountain to which the Samaritan woman referred in John 4). When **Alexander Jannaeus** became ruler and high priest (103-76 BC), this marked the beginning of the end of the Hasmonean Dynasty. There was a civil war between the Sadducees and the Pharisees, and 50,000 Jews died. In a barbaric act, Alexander Jannaeus had 800 Pharisees crucified and executed their families in front of them as they lay hanging on their crosses. After Alexander Jannaeus died, **Salome Alexandria**, his widow, took over the throne (76-67 BC) and made peace with the Pharisees, who came to be the power behind the throne. She made her son, **Hyrcanus II** (a Pharisee) the high priest, and made her other son, **Aristobulus II** (a Sadducee) the head of the army. When Salome died, they became co-rulers and ruled from 67-63 BC.

In 63 BC, the Roman general **Pompey** took control over Judea and made it a Roman province. He took Aristobulus II to Rome as a prisoner and made Hyrcanus II his vassal high priest. Shortly after that, **Julius Caesar** named **Antipater** as the Procurator of Judea, and Antipater appointed his two sons as governors: **Phasel** was the governor of Judea; and **Herod** was the governor of Galilee. After Antipater died, Herod put down an insurrection in Galilee. Rome was so impressed with his ability to control the populace, it expanded Herod's territory to Samaria. But in Judea, **Antigonus**, a son of Aristobulus II, killed Phasel, took control of Judea, then captured Hyrcanus II and cut off his ears. This prevented him from serving as high priest, because it was not allowed for anyone with any kind of physical deformity to serve as high priest. Antigonus then became both the high priest and king of Judea. In fear for his life, Herod fled to Rome and appealed to Caesar for help. In return, Caesar declared Herod was the king of Judea, and in 37 BC Herod invaded Judea with Rome's help, captured Jerusalem, and executed Antigonus. This man came to be known as **Herod the Great**, and he ruled from 37-4 BC.

Herod, though, proved paranoid about being assassinated. During his reign, he ended up killing his uncle Joseph, his brother-in-law, his trusted aide and eldest son Antipater, Hyrcanus II, his wife Mariamne, two of his sons by Mariamne…and all the boys two years and younger who were living in Bethlehem (in an attempt to kill a potential rival king named Jesus!). Still, he was also a great builder. He built various fortresses like the Herodium, Masada, Machaerus, as well as the port at Caesarea. He also rebuilt Samaria, completely renovated the Temple, and built palaces in Jerusalem and Jericho.

## IV. FIRST CENTURY HISTORY

All that gets us to the doorstep of the first century, when all the events in the New Testament take place. Now, even though most people have heard of Jesus, Peter, Paul, and many other New Testament figures, and know a number of New Testament events (Jesus' ministry, crucifixion, and resurrection, Paul's conversion and missionary journeys), when it comes to actually plotting those people and events on a coherent timeline, most people are at a loss and tend to just lump everything together as "back then." But that really isn't a good thing to do. After all, try to understand the various events of the 20$^{th}$ century without a basic historical framework that shows how certain events led to other events, and how certain people at certain times made choices that changed the course of the 20$^{th}$ century. You won't understand why 9/11 happened if you don't understand what happened during the Gulf War of the early 1990s, and you won't understand why that happened if you don't understand the Iran-Iraq crisis of the 1980s, and so on.

Needless to say, the ability to plot out the major events of any given century on a basic timeline will go a long way to helping you understand, not only the specific events and people of that century, but also the overall historical flow of that century. With that said, over just the next few pages, here is a bird's-eye overview of the New Testament events of the first century, set against the backdrop of the Roman Emperors of that century.

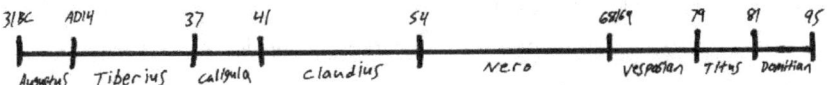

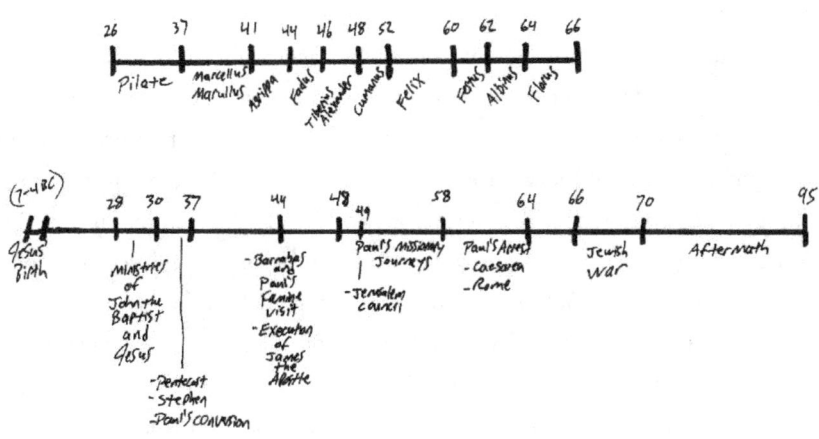

## Augustus (31 BC– AD 14)

There were two key things that happened in the reign of Augustus that directly relate to New Testament history. First, Jesus was born in Bethlehem somewhere between 6-4 BC. How could Jesus be born in 6 years before Christ, you may ask? The answer is simple: The medieval monk who set the Christian calendar got some of his numbers wrong). His birth happened during the later years of Herod the Great, who died in 4 BC.

The second thing concerns Augustus' empire-wide census, which took place in AD 6, when Quirinius was the governor of Syria. Luke places Jesus' birth during the time of this census, while at the same time placing the angel Gabriel's announcements to both Zechariah and Mary in the days of Herod. This creates an obvious chronological problem: How could Jesus be born both in the days of Herod and at the time of Caesar's census? That problem is discussed in the Luke Section, but in terms of understanding the unfolding events in Judea in the first century, Caesar's census can almost be considered the lighting of the revolutionary fuse that eventually resulted in the Jewish Revolt of AD 66-70. For in AD 6, a certain revolutionary zealot named Judas the Galilean led an initial Jewish revolt against Rome in reaction to Caesar's census. The zealots' view was that only YHWH was king, therefore it was a blasphemy against God Himself if any other earthly ruler attempted to take a census of God's people. Even though Judas' revolt was crushed by Rome, that revolt in AD 6 marked the beginning of a revolutionary movement in Judea that continued to spread until the entire region exploded in revolution in AD 66-70.

**Tiberius** (AD 14–37)

It was during the reign of Tiberius that all the events of the Gospels, beginning with the arrival of John the Baptist, as well as the first few chapters in Acts, happened. Not only that, but it was during this time (AD 26-36) that Pontus Pilate was the Roman prefect of Judea. From what we can tell, the entire ministry of John the Baptist lasted a little more than a year or two (AD 27-28), and that means that the entire ministry of Jesus, which overlapped John the Baptist a little, lasted only about three years (AD 28-30). Jesus' crucifixion happened on the eve of Passover of AD 30 (April 7th in our calendars) and thus the outpouring of the Holy Spirit at Pentecost would have happened in late May of that year. Initially, for the first couple of years, the "Jesus movement" (not yet known as "Christianity") seemed to have thrived, at least among the populace of Jerusalem. At some point, though, after Stephen's martyrdom (Acts 6-7), the Sanhedrin (the main Jewish legal authority Rome allowed to oversee Jewish affairs) unleashed the first sustained persecution against Jesus' followers, causing many of them to leave Jerusalem, and by doing so, to take the Gospel to people beyond the borders of Judaism. It was during that time that Philip established the church in Samaria (where Peter confronted Simon the magician), shared the Gospel with the Ethiopian eunuch, and eventually settled in Caesarea.

At some point in AD 33, a zealous Pharisee named Saul was given authority by the Sanhedrin to travel up to Damascus to arrest certain followers of Jesus and to bring them back to Jerusalem for trial. On his way to Damascus, though, Saul encountered the resurrected Jesus and was struck blind for three days. He was taken into Damascus, where a follower of Jesus named Ananias came to him, restored his sight, after which Saul became a follower of Jesus as well. Saul then traveled to Arabia for about three years, then came back to Damascus around AD 36, but when his life was threatened by the provincial governor under King Aretas of Nabatea, he escaped Damascus and went back to Jerusalem for the first time since he had left on his mission from the Sanhedrin. All in all, he was in Jerusalem for fifteen days, during which time he met with the apostles who were still there. Yet, since his life was threatened in Jerusalem as well, they made sure to get him out of

Jerusalem, and he eventually made his way back to Tarsus. With that, we don't know a lot about Saul (who went by Paul in the Greek-speaking world) for the next ten years or so.

**Caligula** (AD 37–41)

After Tiberius died, Caligula became the new emperor of Rome. He was a megalomaniac who had threatened to erect a statue of himself as a god in the Temple of Jerusalem. As things turned out, he died before that had actually happened. In any case, the only notable incident in the New Testament that happened during this time (although it might have happened in the last year or so of Tiberius) was Peter's encounter with Cornelius in Acts 10-11, where God had revealed to Peter that he should accept Gentiles who put their faith in Christ and are baptized in the Holy Spirit.

**Claudius** (AD 41–54)

During Claudius' reign, only a few things are known to have happened in relation to the early Church. First, Claudius named Herod Agrippa to be King of Judea (AD 41-44). It was also during Herod's reign that Barnabas travelled to Tarsus to convince Saul to help him establish and build up the church in Antioch, where the term **Christians** was first used to describe the followers of Jesus (Acts 11:25-29). Then, at some point in AD 42, Barnabas and Saul went to Jerusalem with some famine relief that the Christians in Antioch had sent to help those in Jerusalem. Yet it was also during this time (again, probably AD 42) that Herod arrested both James and Peter. He executed James, yet Peter miraculously escaped from prison before Herod could execute him too, and "went off to another place" (Acts 12:1-18). After the death of the apostle James, and Peter's move out of Jerusalem, James the brother of Jesus became the leader of the Christian community in Jerusalem.

Agrippa died in AD 44 of worms (Acts 12:19-24) and a few years later, in AD 47-48, Barnabas and Saul (now using his Roman name Paul) set out on their first missionary journey through Cyprus and the province of Galatia (southern Turkey), where they established a number of Gentile Christian churches. Shortly after the conclusion of that first missionary journey, though, the debate over whether or not Gentile Christians had to get circumcised and officially become Jews came to a head, and that led to the Jerusalem Council (AD 49-50), when it was formally decided that Gentile Christians did not have to become Jews in order to be considered part of God's people.

It should come as no surprise to find out that it was during this time in AD 49 that Claudius issued the **Edict of Claudius** and expelled all Jews from Rome because they were fighting with each other over a man named *Chrestus* and were creating public disturbances. It is believed that this **Chrestus** was a reference to **Christ**. Because of his edict, Aquila and Priscilla, two Jewish-Christians in Rome, moved to Corinth, where they met the Paul during his second missionary journey (AD 50-52) and helped him establish the Church there.

**Nero** (AD 54–68)

During Nero's reign, a number of watershed moments in the life of the early Church took place. First, it was early in Nero's reign that Paul had his third missionary journey (which really amounted to him primarily living in Ephesus for about three years).

Second, in AD 58 Paul travelled to Jerusalem in order to deliver his collection from his Gentile churches to those who were needy in Judea. He hoped this collection would help bridge the divide between the Jews and his Gentile converts, and in so doing, serve to bring his Jewish brothers to repentance and their acceptance of Jesus and the Gospel. Unfortunately, that did not happen. Shortly after Paul arrived in Jerusalem, a mob tried to kill Paul, and he was actually saved when the Roman garrison in Jerusalem, arrested him and eventually held him in Caesarea for about two years. His initial arrest in AD 58 happened while Felix was governor of Judea (AD 52-60), but it was during the governorship of Festus (AD 60-62) that Paul made his appeal to Caesar. He was then taken to Rome and put under house arrest for two more years as he waited to get his case heard. According to Church tradition, he was acquitted sometime in AD 62, then travelled to Spain for a time.

Third, around the same time Paul was acquitted, Festus died suddenly, and Nero appointed Albinus to be the next governor of Judea. Yet before he could make his way to Judea, the Sanhedrin arrested and killed James, the brother of Jesus and the head of the Jerusalem Church. With the death of James, a man named Simeon (possibly a cousin of Jesus) became the next leader of the dwindling Christian community in Jerusalem.

Fourth, a couple of years after that, the great fire of Rome in AD 64 sparked Nero's persecution of Christians in the vicinity of Rome. It is believed at this time, somewhere around AD 65-68, that not only was Paul re-arrested and beheaded, but that Peter was also arrested and crucified upside down.

Fifth, in AD 66 the Jewish Revolt began when priests in the Temple in Jerusalem refused to make any more sacrifices on behalf of Caesar, and the Jewish zealot Menelaus attacked and took the fortress of Masada and then marched to Jerusalem and slaughtered the Roman garrison stationed there. It was around that time that Simeon and the small Christian community in Jerusalem fled Jerusalem to Pella (in modern day Jordan) to get out of harm's way when the Roman legions would inevitably show up. As expected, Nero dispatched the Roman general Vespasian to crush the revolt. Yet after Nero died in AD 68, Vespasian travelled to Rome to be crowned emperor in AD 69 and left his son Titus in charge of the campaign.

**Vespasian** (AD 69–79) and **Titus** (AD 79-81)

Early on in Vespasian's reign, his son Titus crushed the Jewish revolt and brought an end to the Jewish War in AD 70, when he destroyed Jerusalem and burned the Temple to the ground. For all intents and purposes, it was the Jewish War that signaled the clear "divorce" between what was to become known as Rabbinic Judaism and Christianity. From AD 30-70, the "Jesus movement" was seen as an odd Jewish messianic movement that was reaching out to Gentiles, while not requiring Gentile believers to become Jews. By doing so, it created a growing rift with traditional Judaism. With the destruction of the Temple, though, that "divorce" was finalized, with the Pharisees transforming Second Temple Judaism into Rabbinic Judaism, from which modern Judaism stemmed, and the "Jesus movement" becoming Christianity, a clearly different religion from Judaism.

**Domitian** (AD 81-96)

When Vespasian died, Titus became the new emperor, but died a few years later and was succeeded by his brother Domitian. Since the Book of Acts ends with Paul's first imprisonment in Rome, we simply do not know much of anything about the early Church during the 70s and 80s. But we do know a little bit about the Church during Domitian's reign. Domitian not only required everyone to hail him as a god, but also launched the first empire-wide persecution of the Christians. This is when John wrote Revelation while exiled on the island of Patmos (just off the coast of Asia Minor) to seven small churches in that area.

## V. OVERVIEW OF FIRST CENTURY JUDAISM

With all that said, when it comes to Judaism in the first century, you really have to be able to distinguish between the different "brands" of Judaism. First, there was the Judaism of the **Essene community** at Qumran. They had set up their own community out in the Judean desert, away from their fellow Jews, because they viewed the Temple priesthood as hopelessly corrupt. They rigorously practiced Jewish purification codes and waited for God to act through some cosmic apocalyptic event. Aside from a brief mention of the Essenes by the Jewish historian Josephus, we really didn't know much about them until 1947, when the Dead Sea Scrolls were discovered. The Dead Sea Scrolls essentially was the library of the Essene community, consisting of both their own copies of Old Testament texts, as well as the rules and regulations unique to their community.

Second, there was the Judaism of **Herod** and the **Sadducees of the Temple priesthood**. They compromised with Rome, built fortresses, palaces, and renovated the Temple so they could keep power over the Jewish population and get along with their political overlords. They may have had power, but most Jews viewed them as sell-outs.

Third, there was the Judaism of the **Pharisees**. They were so committed to keeping the Torah (the Jewish Law given by YHWH to Moses that outlined the terms of YHWH's covenant with Israel) that they even made up their own "oral tradition" of rules that would ensure that the Torah was kept. They believed that if they could show God they were devoted to the Torah, that when God sent His Messiah and redeemed Israel, they would be rewarded as being truly righteous, not like their fellow Jews, whom they felt weren't as devoted to the Torah as they were.

Fourthly, there was the Judaism of the **Zealots**—the Sicarii. They were basically the militant religious extremists of first century Judaism. They thought that since there was no king but God, any submission to Rome was unacceptable. Therefore, they would engage in terrorist activities in an attempt to spark a holy war against Rome.

Finally, there was the **Jesus movement**, which would eventually become the distinct religion of **Christianity** after AD 70. Before the Jewish War, though, the Jesus movement was still considered to be part of Judaism, no matter how strained the relationship might be.

Of course, there were many Jews who fell somewhere between these options. Many Pharisees, for example, were part of the Sadducee-led Sanhedrin and tried to work in some way with Rome. Other Pharisees leaned more toward the zealot side of the spectrum. Still others, like Paul, were followers of Christ. In any case, the Jews of Jesus' day were very much divided in their opinions concerning how to live as God's chosen people in the midst of foreign nations.

Despite these differences, though, all Jews traditionally held certain things in common. The observance of **Sabbath** and the **Jewish food laws** served to mark Jews off from their Gentile neighbors. In fact, many Jews who lived throughout the Roman Empire were vegetarians because virtually all meat sold in the marketplaces of the Roman Empire had been butchered by pagan priests in pagan temples. The Jewish understanding of the **Promised Land** was also central to Jewish belief. In fact, the mere presence of Roman soldiers in the Promised Land deeply offended the Jews because it was the land that YHWH Himself promised to them. There was also the **Temple**, the place where YHWH would dwell when He came back to redeem His people from foreign oppression. Although many Jews saw the Temple at that time as tainted because it was built by Herod, a puppet of Rome, it was still as a symbol of national pride. Finally, there was the **Torah**, which became central to the Jews after the destruction of Solomon's Temple in 587 BC. Despite the differences among the Jewish sects, these five "identity-markers" held them together. They encapsulated the Jewish worldview in the first century.

If you understand that, then you'll easily see why the emergence of the Jesus movement during that first generation between AD 30-70 was so controversial. It called into question all of the common practices of traditional Judaism.

## VI. THE JEWISH ESCHATOLOGICAL HOPE

Given all that, the Jewish worldview of the first century had certain expectations regarding what would happen when the Kingdom of God arrived. They viewed themselves as living in the **old age**—the present, evil age that was dominated by sin, sickness, death, foreign oppression, and ultimately Satan. They looked forward to a coming **Messianic new age** when God would establish the Kingdom of God and redeem all of creation.

Therefore, their "end times" **eschatological hope** was that YHWH would raise up His Messiah (a king from the line of David) who would (a) defeat the Romans, (b) cleanse the Temple so that YHWH's presence could once more dwell with His people, (c) restore the kingdom of Israel, and (d) establish the Kingdom of God, which would be marked by the resurrection of the dead. The righteous dead would rise up and rule in God's Kingdom, while the unrighteous dead would receive their full punishment for trampling down God's people. All that would mark the arrival of the **Age to Come**.

Until then, the Jews would continue to keep Sabbath, maintain Jewish food laws, offer sacrifices in the Temple, observe the Torah, and resist the Roman occupation of their land. They were convinced that the source of evil in the world was the beast-like pagan nations, so they avoided contact with them at all costs. These were the things they felt it was necessary to do to ensure that they were counted as the righteous ones who would inherit the Age to Come. To be clear, Jews didn't believe they would "go to heaven" when they died. They had the eschatological hope that although they were going to die, that when the Messiah comes, the great turn of the ages would happen all at once. He would establish the Kingdom of God, renew all creation, usher in the Age to Come, and they would be resurrected and would have a place in that Kingdom of God and New Creation in the Age to Come. Thus, their eschatological hope looked like this:

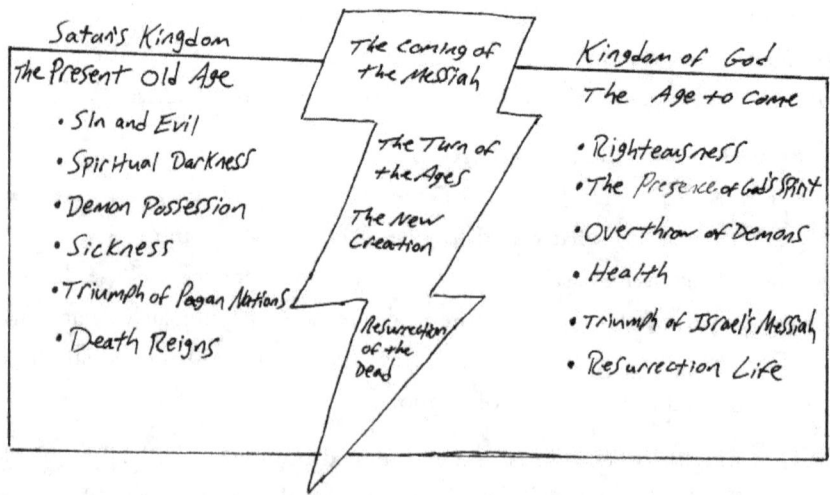

The Christian Gospel, though, declared that the long awaited Jewish eschatological hope had happened, or more properly had begun to happen, in a way that nobody was expecting. In light of Jesus' resurrection, the Christian Gospel declared that the Messiah *had come*, that the resurrection of the dead *had happened in him*, and that the Kingdom of God and the New Creation *had broken into the present evil age* but *had not yet* been fully consummated. Thus, **the Kingdom of God was already here, but not yet fully realized,** and in this interim time, through the power of the Holy Spirit, the Church has been sent by the resurrected Jesus to proclaim the arrival of the Kingdom and offer salvation to those who turn to Christ. Thus, the Christian eschatological understanding essentially looked like this:

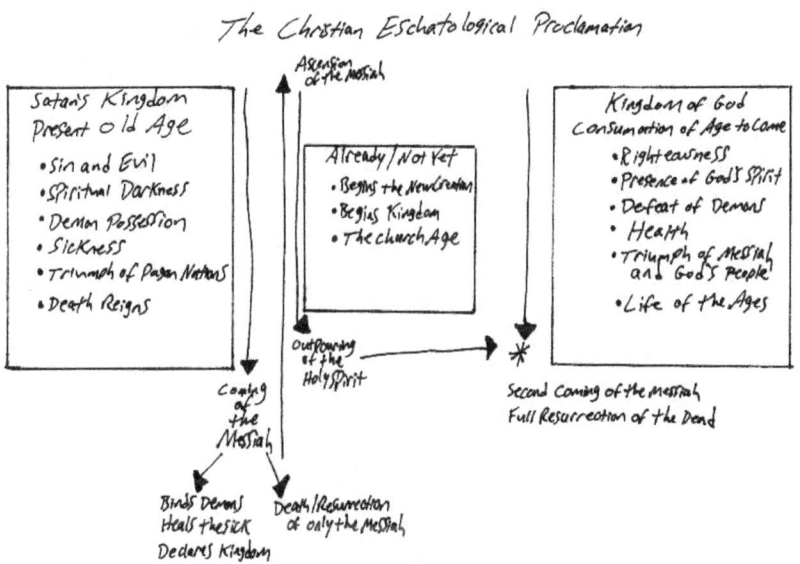

# AN OVERVIEW OF THE SYNOPTIC GOSPELS

## Histories or Literary Works? Yes! Both!

The Synoptic Gospels are Matthew, Mark, and Luke. In terms of genre, they are **ancient historical biographies** that highlight the public ministry of Jesus. Therefore, they are about real historical people and events—they are **histories**. That is why it is important to understand them within the historical context of first century Judaism and early Christianity within the Roman Empire. That being said, they are not written as *modern histories*. They are not trying to be "objective" or tell of that history from some sort of detached perspective. They clearly want to convince their readers that Jesus was the Jewish Messiah and risen Lord, and that his followers, the Church, had been sent out into the world to share his Gospel.

Even though they are histories, though, they are not written like textbooks, and they aren't necessarily trying to be chronologically accurate with every detail of Jesus' life. Instead, they are shaping the historical events of Jesus' life and ministry into a coherent story and are thus **creative literary works**. The Gospel writers freely rearranged the material and used a certain amount of artistic license in the way they present their stories. What this all means is that, while we can be confident that the Synoptic Gospels are telling about real historical people and events, we also need to realize they are giving us more of a creative portrait painting of Jesus and the early Church than an actual snapshot.

## The Synoptic Problem (...not *really* a "problem," though)

The reason Matthew, Mark, and Luke are called the Synoptic Gospels is because their content is all very similar. It is so similar that it is quite clear that Matthew and Luke incorporated large sections of Mark into their own gospels. In fact, over 75% of Mark's material is also in Matthew and Luke. For that matter, almost 25% of Matthew and Luke is identical to each other, while 20% of Matthew is unique to Matthew and 35% of Luke is unique to Luke. Scholars call this the **Synoptic problem** and speculate that Matthew and Luke got their extra material from another source they call "Q." Whether or not "Q" was an actual document, though, is pure speculation. It is obvious that Matthew and Luke put into their works material that isn't in Mark, but that is as far as we can take it. For that reason, we can probably talk about "Q *material*," but we should be hesitant to speak of "Q" as if it were an actual *document*. It is purely hypothetical.

In any case, it is generally agreed that all three Synoptic Gospels were written during the 60s-80s in the first century. That means all three reflect what the early

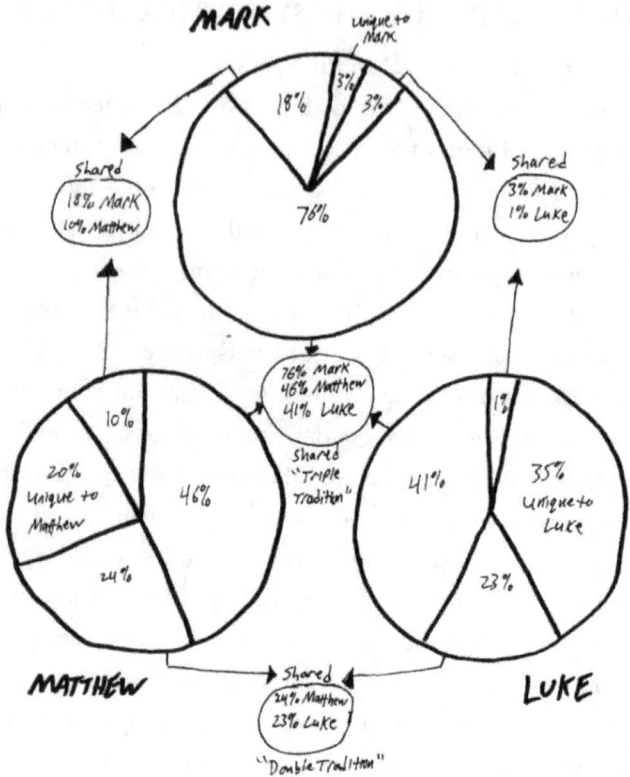

The Synoptic "Situation"

first century Church was proclaiming about the life, ministry, death, and resurrection of Jesus. In that sense, no matter where Luke and Matthew got their extra material from, it is ultimately irrelevant to the fact that the material in all three Synoptic Gospels reflects the first century witness and proclamation of the early Church concerning Jesus.

With all this common material, it shouldn't be surprising to find that Matthew, Mark, and Luke all share the same basic storyline and similar themes. In all three Synoptics, Jesus first steps on the public scene when he is baptized by John the Baptist. He then begins and continues his ministry in Galilee for a good portion of each respective Gospel. There is then a section where he travels to Jerusalem for Passover, and that is followed by the events of the Passion Week leading up to his crucifixion and resurrection.

### Some Really Big Things Common to All Three Synoptics

Before we get into the specifics of each Gospel, it would be best to highlight a number of basic themes, concepts, and points of emphasis that Mark, Matthew, and Luke all share.

### The Kingdom of God/Kingdom of Heaven

This means God's rule on earth, but it has to be understood within the context of first century Judaism. Ever since the Jews returned from the Babylonian exile in 539 BC, their expectation was that they would return to the *Promised Land*, rebuild the *Temple*, again have a *Davidic king (Messiah)*, and through him, YHWH would establish the kingdom of Israel as the dominant nation to rule all nations. Specifically, in the first century, since the Jews viewed Rome as their oppressor, they believed that when God's kingdom was established, that the Messiah would defeat Rome. Therefore, when Jesus began his ministry, proclaiming that the **Kingdom of God** was near, *that was what most Jews were expecting would happen.* Of course, Jesus' version of the Kingdom of God proved to be something quite different. The big enemy wasn't Rome, but rather the kingdom of Satan, and shockingly, Jesus said that Satan didn't just have his grip on Rome, but also the Jews as well.

### The New Exodus and the New Creation

All three Synoptic Gospels tell the story of Jesus against the of the Old Testament story of Israel to show that he is the fulfillment of God's purposes for Israel. In doing that, the two biggest allusions to the Old Testament have to do with the **Exodus story** and the **Creation story**. First, they present salvation in Christ as a **New Exodus**, not from slavery in the physical land of Egypt, but from the corruption and death of this present age. Second, they present salvation in Christ as a **New Creation**, not just a new life in a literal piece of Promised Land, but the new, resurrection life of the Age to Come.

### The Messiah, the Temple, and Conflict with the Temple Authorities

Not only was Jesus' proclamation of the Kingdom of God different from the traditional Jewish expectation of it, but so was his understanding of the **Messiah's relationship to the Temple**. The Jews were looking for a Messiah who would *cleanse the Temple* and fight Israel's enemies, namely Rome. But not only did Jesus not lead a revolt against Rome, when he came to Jerusalem, *picked a fight with the Temple authorities instead.* He didn't "cleanse" the Temple, but rather condemned it and prophesied that it would be destroyed. Historically speaking, this is what gets Jesus ultimately crucified.

### The Son of Man/The Son of God

It may sound odd, but the title **Son of God** is not a title that emphasizes his divinity. Rather, it is a royal title that designates the Messiah, the Davidic king. By contrast, the title used to emphasize Jesus' divinity is **Son of Man**. It is taken from **Daniel 7:13-14**, where "one like the Son of Man" ascends to sit at the right hand of God to rule. This is the title that Jesus uses mostly for himself.

### The Day of the Lord/The Coming of the Son of Man

In the Old Testament, the **Day of the Lord** was any time YHWH would bring His wrath and judgment upon the enemies of His people and bring salvation and vindication for His people. In Hebrew, it was literally referred to as the **Day of YHWH**, and it was often described with **cosmic upheaval language** (the sun going dark, the moon turning to blood, the stars falling from the sky), as if to say, "When YHWH acts, it is going to be an earth-shattering event!" In addition, in Daniel 7 there is an apocalyptic vision of **one like the Son of Man coming on the clouds of heaven**, a messianic figure who ascends to heaven and is given the authority of God after the defeat of the "little horn" who had oppressed God's people.

In the Synoptic Gospels, though, Jesus takes these two images of the Day of YHWH and the Coming of the Son of Man and gives them a shocking re-interpretation in the Olivet Discourse (Mark 13, Matthew 24, Luke 21). The Old Testament Day of YHWH became the **Day of Christ and the coming of the Son of Man**, when God's wrath would come *upon Jerusalem* because the Jews had rejected Jesus as their Messiah and had persecuted his followers, God' true people. Since the Synoptics were all written around the time of the Jewish War of AD 66-70, when Jerusalem and the Temple were destroyed, we should realize that those events were probably the impetus for the writing of the Synoptics. They were the testimony of the early Church, and they were written to show that what Jesus had prophesied had indeed come to pass: God had brought His wrath on Jerusalem, had vindicated both Jesus as the Messiah and the Church as His people.

### Life of the Ages/Eternal Life

If you are like me, whenever you read the phrase, **eternal life**, in the New Testament, you think in general terms of "forever," and for some reason think of outer space. The actual Greek phrase, though, literally means the **Life of the Ages** and it reflects the Jewish and Christian eschatological hope for God's purposes. The hope was that when the Messiah comes and establishes the Kingdom of God, the old, corrupt age of sin and death would be over, and a new Messianic Age would be ushered in. The Gospel proclamation, both here in the Synoptic Gospels and the entire New Testament, is that through Christ's death and resurrection, the Kingdom of God and the **Life of the Ages** has broken into the present, old age, and through the power of the Holy Spirit, was in the midst of transforming things from the inside out. Simply put, when the Gospels talk of "eternal life," they aren't talking about an over-generalized "forever" and outer space. They are talking about the transformative and incorruptible life of the Kingdom of God and the new Messianic Age that is made available to those who put their faith in Christ.

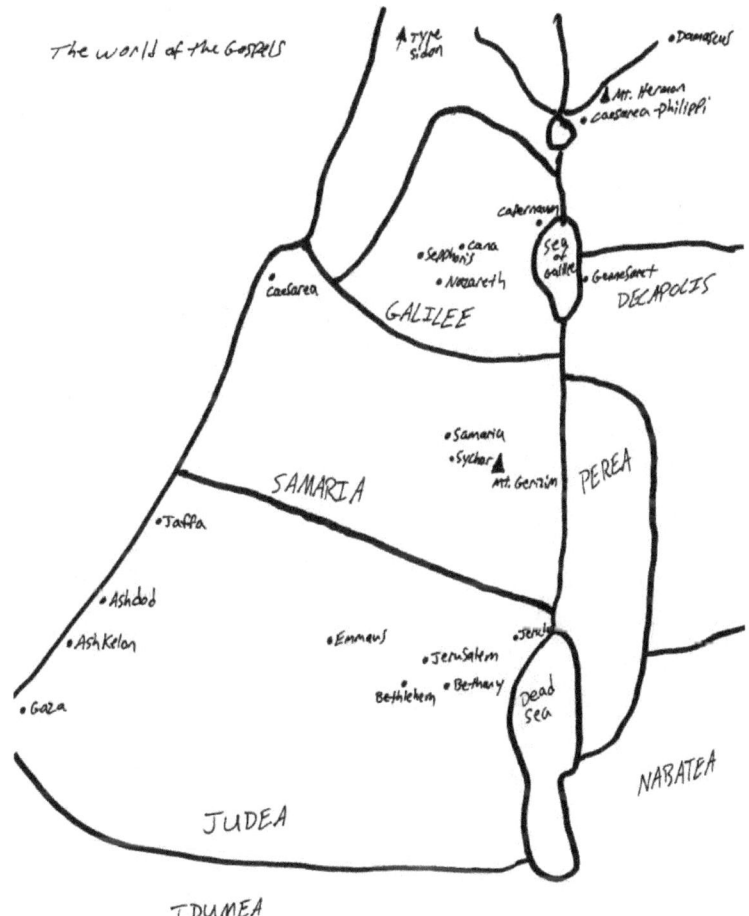

# THE GOSPEL OF MARK

**Time of Writing**: Although the life and ministry of Jesus took place around AD 28-30, Mark was probably written either sometime in the 60s, shortly before the destruction of Jerusalem in AD 70, or in the decade after Jerusalem's destruction.

**Authorship**: There is nothing in the Gospel that claims Mark was the author, but Papias, the early 2nd century bishop of Hierapolis, says Mark wrote his Gospel while in Rome in the mid-60s, while he was with Peter, shortly before Peter's martyrdom.

## The Big Things to Know in Mark
A. **Jesus' Miracles**: More properly speaking, they are "dynamic deeds" that serve as evidence of the power of the Kingdom of God to overcome the satanic powers of this present age.
B. **The Kingdom of God's Welcome Mat**: The Kingdom of God is about reaching out to the undesirables: prostitutes, tax-collectors, "sinners," and even Gentiles.
C. **If You Ain't Last, You Won't Be First**: To be great in the Kingdom of God means becoming a servant to others in this present age.
D. **The Real Enemies**: Jesus seemingly regards the power of Rome as irrelevant, and instead constantly runs into conflict with the Jewish religious leaders: Pharisees, Sadducees, and the Temple establishment.
E. **The Prophecy of the Temple's Destruction**: Jesus prophesies that because the religious establishment rejects him as the Messiah and will choose instead to embrace Jewish revolution against Rome, that Jerusalem and the Temple will be destroyed within a generation. That event will mark the *Day of the Lord* in the vein of the Old Testament prophets, but it will not signal the end of the age.
F. **Jesus' Crucifixion is "Passover 2.0"**: The original Passover celebrated the Exodus out of bondage in Egypt. Jesus' *Passover 2.0* celebrates a new Exodus out of bondage in this present age.
G. **Jesus' Resurrection and the New Creation**: Jesus' resurrection is evidence of the Kingdom of God's power over death. It marks the beginning of a new creation.

## The Gospel of Mark: Story Chart

|  | | | | | | |
|---|---|---|---|---|---|---|
| **The Prologue (1:1-15)** | **1:1-15** Baptism/Temptation of Jesus — *The Kingdom of God is Near* | | | | | |
| **Early Ministry: Attraction (1:16-2:12)** | 1:16-20 *Sea* Calling the First Disciples | 1:21-28 *Synagogue* Demon-Possessed Man | 1:29-34 Simon's Mother-in-Law | 1:35-39 *Galilee* Healings; Casting out of Demons | 1:40-45 Healing of a Leper | 2:1-12 Healing of the Paralytic |
| **Early Ministry: Conflict (2:13-3:19)** | 2:13-17 *Sea* Calling of Levi | 2:18-22 *Question* Fasting | 2:23-28 *Question* Working on the Sabbath | 3:1-6 *Synagogue* Healing Withered Hand on the Sabbath | 3:7-12 *Sea* People: Galilee Jerusalem Idumea Decapolis | 3:13-19 *Mountain* Jesus Chooses Twelve Apostles |
| **Question of Kingdoms (3:20-5:20)** | 3:20-35 Beelzebub Controversy | 4:1-34 *Kingdom of God in Parables* | | 4:35-41 Jesus Calms the Sea | 5:1-20 Demoniac of the Gerasenes | |
| **Kingdom to the Jews (5:21-6:56)** | 5:21-43 Woman/ Jarius' Daughter | 6:1-13 Nazareth and Jewish Villages | 6:14-46 Herod-John Jesus-5,000 | 6:47-52 Jesus Walks on the Water | 6:53-56 Healing in Gennesaret | |
| **Kingdom to the Gentiles (7:1-8:13)** | 7:1-23 Tradition of the Elders | 7:24-37 Tyre Sidon | 8:1-10 Jesus-4,000 | 8:11-13 To Pharisees: "No Sign!" | | |
| **Do you see the Kingdom clearly? (8:14-9:32)** | 8:14-21 Yeast of Pharisees and Herod | 8:22-26 2x Healed Blind Man *Bethsaida* | 8:27-9:1 Peter's Confession *Caesarea Philippi* | 9:2-13 Transfig-uration | 9:14-29 Down the Mountain Jesus Heals a Boy | |

## Gospel of Mark | 43

**Galilee to Jerusalem (9:30-10:52)**

| 9:30-37 Who is the Greatest in the Kingdom? | 9:38-50 Who is Part of the Kingdom? | 10:1-12 Teaching on Divorce | 10:13-16 Kingdom of God is for Little Children |
|---|---|---|---|
| 10:17-31 The Rich Young Man | 10:32-34 Jesus Predicts His Death | 10:35-45 The Request of James and John | 10:46-52 Doorstep of Jerusalem Blind Bartimaeus |

**11:1-11 Un-Triumphal Entry**

**Jerusalem Opposition (11:1-13:37)**

| 11:12-26 Fig Tree Temple Action | 11:27-33 Jesus' Authority Questioned | 12:1-12 Parable of the Vineyard | 12:13-37 Round of Questions | 12:38-44 Jesus Condemns Scribes |
|---|---|---|---|---|

**13:1-37 Olivet Discourse**

**Last Supper to Resurrection (14:1-16:20)**

| 14:1-11 Jesus Anointed at Bethany | 14:12-31 Passover Last Supper | 14:32-52 Arrest at Gethsemane |
|---|---|---|
| 14:53-72 Before the Sanhedrin | 15:1-20 Before Pilate | 15:21-47 Crucifixion Death and Burial |

**16:1-20 The Resurrection**

## A Walkthrough of Mark

The Gospel of Mark is the earliest (and shortest) of the Synoptic Gospels. Maybe the biggest difference between Mark and the other two Synoptic Gospels is that Mark doesn't have an infancy narrative about Jesus. Instead, within the first 15 verses, Mark gives (a) a brief introduction in which he packs together allusions and partial quotes of **Isaiah 40:3**, **Genesis 1:1**, **Exodus 23:20**, and **Malachi 3:1**, and (b) a short prologue in which he rushes through Jesus' baptism and his temptations in the wilderness. From there, Mark continues to speed through the entire ministry and life of Jesus.

That is why the Gospel of Mark is traditionally represented by a **lion**. In Mark's Gospel, Jesus is constantly on the prowl, either stalking his prey or constantly growling at his disciples over their lack of faith and their failure to understand what he is doing. Nevertheless, although it is the shortest of the four Gospels, the literary structure and artistry used in Mark is beautiful in its simplicity. On top of that, even though Mark doesn't quote the Old Testament nearly as much as Matthew, Mark is filled with Old Testament allusions and imagery that helps tell the story of Jesus against the larger backdrop of God's purposes in the life of Old Testament Israel. With that, let's take a journey through Mark's Gospel and get a lay of the land.

### 1. The Prologue (1:1-15)

Mark 1:1-15 acts as a prologue and lays out a number of themes that run all throughout Mark: **The Kingdom of God**, **the New Exodus**, **the End of Exile**, and **the New Creation**. Basically, Mark explains who Jesus is by using a whole lot of creation language from Genesis and a whole lot of exodus language from Exodus.

Although Mark doesn't quote the Old Testament as Matthew, his story about Jesus clearly is rooted in the Old Testament story and is presented as the culmination of the Old Testament story. The very first words of his Gospel, *"The beginning of the Gospel,"* echo the creation story in Genesis 1: *In the beginning*. By doing this, Mark is telling us that the Gospel about Jesus is ultimately **a re-creation story**: In Jesus, God is bringing about the **new creation**. In addition, Mark also identifies Jesus with the royal titles of the **Messiah** and the **Son of God**. By doing so, he is saying that Jesus is the long-awaited king of Israel through whom God would redeem both His people and the entire creation.

Mark really kicks off his Gospel, though, with a double quotation of **Isaiah 40:3** and **Malachi 3:1**, as well as an allusion to **Exodus 23:20**, that serve to bring Jesus and his ministry into focus through the lens of the Exodus. Both Isaiah 40:3 and Malachi 3:1 depict the return from the Babylonian Exile as a **new Exodus** in which God would send some sort of prophetic messenger (or angel), as Exodus 23:20 states, who would prepare the way for the Kingdom of God and protect them in the wilderness. Put all that together, Mark's message gives us a big slap in the face within the first few verses: *Jesus is the long-awaited* **king of Israel** *who will lead God's people through the* **new Exodus**, *bring about the* **end of their exile**, *and establish the* **Kingdom of God**. *Through Him, God's* **new creation** *has come.*

With that, Mark then shifts to John the Baptist, the messenger who prepares the way for Jesus, literally in the **wilderness** of Judea. John's description of wearing a leather belt and eating locusts and wild honey is a clear allusion to Elijah in **Malachi 4:5-6**, who will come *before* the **Day of the Lord**. Since the coming of Jesus marks the coming of the Day of the Lord, John the Baptist is that Elijah-like messenger who prepares the way for it. John's baptizing in the Jordan River has further echoes of the end of the Exodus, for that was the very river that Joshua and the Israelites crossed over into the Promised Land. Thus, by going out into the wilderness to be baptized by John in the waters of the Jordan, the Jews were essentially re-enacting the Exodus. They were going into the wilderness, passing through the waters, and then re-entering the Promised Land.

Therefore, when Jesus comes to be baptized by John, he does so as a Jew who is waiting for the Kingdom of God. Of course, when he is baptized, we see he is a little more than just your typical Jew. For when he comes up out of the water, Mark quotes **Psalm 2:7** when telling us what the voice from heaven says: *"You are my Son, the Beloved. With you, I am well-pleased."* Psalm 2 is a royal psalm that celebrates the enthronement of the Davidic king. So, when the voice from heaven quotes Psalm 2:7, it couldn't be any clearer: **Jesus is the Messiah**. That puts his baptism in a different light, for as the Messiah, Jesus is the representative of all God's people. Thus, his baptism isn't just for him alone—it is on behalf of all God's people. It is through his work that this new Exodus will come about.

Then there is Mark's description of the **heavens being torn apart** and the **Spirit came down like a dove** when Jesus comes out of the water. Matthew and Luke simply say that the heavens were "opened," but Mark's description is a bit more violent. The reason is that Mark is giving us a subtle allusion specifically to **Isaiah 64:1** and its larger context of **Isaiah 63:7-64:12**. In that passage, the prophet is thinking back to God's salvation of the Hebrews during the Exodus, when He sent His **Holy Spirit** among them, brought them **through the wilderness** and **through the sea**. The prophet then prays in Isaiah 64:1 for God to "tear the heavens open" again and come down to save His people by His Holy Spirit. Let's be clear: *He is praying for a new Exodus.* Thus, by alluding to this passage, Mark is saying that in Jesus, the long-awaited hope that God would return to His people to save them has finally come to pass and the new Exodus has begun.

In addition, by saying that the Holy Spirit descended in the form of a dove, Mark makes the subtle allusion to a new creation as well. Just as **God's Spirit** hovers over the **waters** at the beginning of creation, and just as **Noah's dove** goes back and forth over the **waters**, looking for evidence of a new creation after the flood, here we see the **Holy Spirit in the form of a dove** as Jesus comes up out of the **waters**—the new creation is at hand. Finally, there is the brief mention of Jesus being thrown into the wilderness by the Spirit to be tested by Satan for 40 days. Matthew and Luke elaborate on the temptations more than Mark, but for our purposes, we need to see that Mark is once again making an allusion to the Exodus in his effort to explain the significance of who Jesus is. As the Messiah, Jesus is Israel's representative, and so he symbolically does what Israel did in the Exodus. Israel passed through the waters of the Red Sea, went into the wilderness for 40 years, and then crossed the Jordan River to inherit the Promised Land. Jesus also passes through the waters of his baptism, then after spending 40 days in the wilderness, he (obviously) crosses back over the Jordan River into the Promised Land, goes to Galilee and begins proclaiming that the Kingdom of God is near. Thus, if you know your Old Testament, it is pretty clear what Mark is saying in his prologue: **Jesus is the long-awaited Messiah who is bringing about the New Exodus into the Kingdom of God and the New Creation.** *(The illustration below was actually done by Rikk Watts, a professor of mine at Regent College back in the 1990s. It was this illustration that got me in the habit of drawing illustrations to help me understand any given passage).*

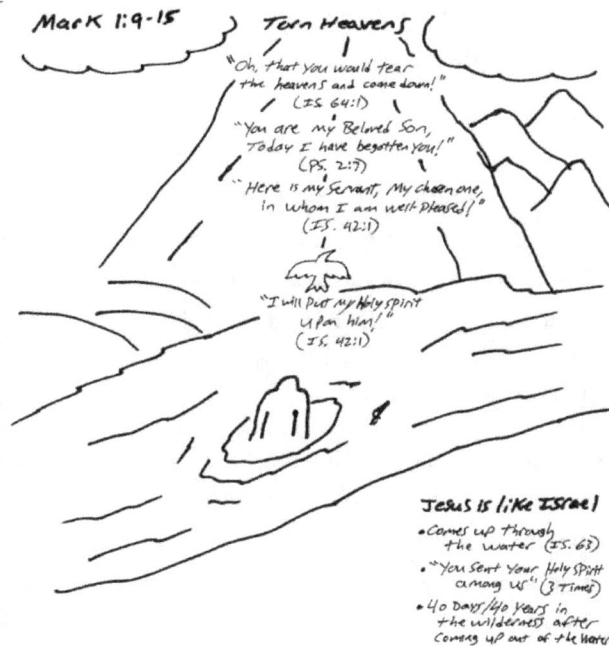

## The Early Ministry of Jesus: Attraction (1:16-2:12)

After the prologue, the next section in Mark focuses on Jesus' early ministry in where he gains a following and calls his disciples. As he preaches in the synagogues and performs various miracles, there is growing interest by his fellow Jews. At this point in his ministry, there isn't any mention of resistance or hostility to Jesus.

In the **first episode (1:16-20)**, Jesus is by the sea where he calls his first disciples (who were fishermen) and tells them in an ironic fashion that from now on they would be "fishers of men."

In the **second episode (1:21-28)**, Jesus casts out a demon from a man in the synagogue in Capernaum. The shocker here can be seen when you keep in mind that the Jews who were waiting for the Kingdom of God viewed themselves as living in the Old Age, and therefore believed that when the Messiah came, he would overthrow the rule of Satan and demonic Rome. But what we learn here is that the "demon-problem" wasn't just happening with Rome—*it was happening within the Jewish synagogue as well.* In any case, the demon recognizes Jesus and even calls him, "The Holy One of God." We have to remember that at this point no one was thinking that Jesus was God yet. Jesus tells the demon to shut up and not reveal who he really was. One final note here is that the people realized Jesus was teaching with a unique kind of **authority**. Whereas other scribes and rabbis would base their teaching on the authority of older, established rabbis, Jesus spoke on his own authority.

In the **third and fourth episodes (1:29-34; 1:35-39)**, Jesus continues to demonstrate the power of the Kingdom of God by healing Simon Peter's mother-in-law, as well as many others who were sick, and casting out demons from those Jews living in Capernaum. Jesus then goes throughout Galilee, proclaiming the Gospel, healing people, and casting out demons. All of this would be seen as signs that the Kingdom of God was at hand.

In the **fifth episode (1:40-45)**, Jesus heals a leper and tells him not to tell anyone that Jesus was the one who healed him. He then tells him to go show himself to a priest to bear witness, not only to his healing, but to the fact that the Kingdom of God was at hand, for healings and exorcisms were seen as a sign of God's Spirit at work in the bringing of salvation. Why didn't Jesus want his fellow Jews to know he was the Messiah yet? Perhaps it is because that even though Jesus was the Messiah, his fellow Jews simply had a wrong expectation regarding what the Messiah would do. They were hoping for a political Messiah who would defeat the demonic forces of Satan by defeating Rome. But Jesus' war, so to speak, wasn't really with Rome—it was with the demonic forces of Satan that were at work not only in the Gentile world, but within the Jewish people as well. So, Jesus had to show what the Messiah's mission truly was before he revealed himself to be, in fact, the Messiah. In any case, up to this point, there has been nothing but positive reaction to Jesus.

In the **sixth episode (2:1-12)** things begin to change when, before, Jesus heals the paralytic, he says, "Child, your sins are forgiven." The scribes object to this because only God could forgive sins. They see that by claiming to forgive the paralytic's sins, Jesus is claiming to have the same authority as God. Jesus responds to their objection by telling the paralytic to get up and walk. By doing this, he shows that his ability to *physically heal* people serves as proof of his *spiritual authority* to forgive sins. So, who is this guy? A clue can be seen when Jesus calls himself the **Son of Man**. By doing so, he is making an allusion to **Daniel 7**, in which a figure *like the Son of Man* ascends to the *Ancient of Days* (God) and is given all dominion and power after the evil beasts from the sea (the Satanic-empowered kingdoms of the world) are destroyed. The Son of Man is thus both a **Messianic figure** and the

**embodiment of the people of God**. By calling himself the Son of Man, Jesus is declaring that not only is he the Messiah, but that he has all the power and authority of God Himself.

### The Early Ministry of Jesus: Conflict (2:13-3:19)

It is this claim to forgive sins that sets off the conflict between Jesus and certain Jewish leaders, particularly scribes and Pharisees. They take issue with Jesus' ambivalent attitude toward their oral tradition and interpretation of the Torah. We see this conflict grow over in the next section of Mark.

In the **first episode (2:13-17)**, Jesus, again by the sea, calls Levi, a tax collector for Rome, to follow him then goes so far to eat with Levi, along with other tax collectors and "sinners." Everything about this would be offensive, not just to Pharisees, but to most Jews, because tax collectors were viewed as traitors to their people. Worse yet, to share a meal with someone indicated a public acceptance of that person. The Messiah was supposed to fight against Rome, not ask people who collaborated with Rome to be in his movement and then openly share a meal with those kinds of people. Yet here Jesus is, doing that very thing.

The Pharisees' objection to **Jesus eating with sinners** is also something that needs to be explained. For the Pharisees, *sinner* wasn't a general term describing everyone. It was a specific insult directed to any fellow Jew who was not as devoted to obeying the Torah as they were. The Pharisees were convinced that the reason God hadn't returned to His people yet was because they weren't yet fully devoted to the Torah. Therefore, not only were the Pharisees obsessed with the keeping of Torah, but they also made extra rules to make sure they didn't break the actual laws in the Torah. This was known as the **oral tradition**. Therefore, in the Pharisees' minds, *they weren't sinners*. Jews who weren't as devoted as the Pharisees were. What Jesus tells them in 2:17 is that he was the kind of Messiah who was going to call and save the kind of sinners that they self-righteously condemned.

In the **second episode (2:18-22)**, there is more conflict. The Pharisees, along with some of John the Baptist's disciples, ask Jesus why he and his disciples don't fast. Jews fasted in anticipation of the Kingdom of God, often described as a **wedding banquet**. Basically, the thinking was, *"Fast now, and celebrate when the Kingdom of God comes."* Jesus responds by equating himself with a **bridegroom** and his disciples as the attendants and is thus saying that the Kingdom of God has arrived and now is the time to celebrate. The shocker, of course, is that Jesus was celebrating the Kingdom of God by eating with tax collectors and sinners—all the wrong kind of people! Jesus then hints of a coming time when he would no longer be around and says that is the time when his followers would, in fact. This foreshadows his eventual death, resurrection, and ascension.

Jesus goes on to talk about how one doesn't put **new wine into old wineskins** or sew a **new piece of cloth onto an old garment**. Simply put, he is saying that now that he has come as the Messiah to usher in the Kingdom of God, the old religious traditions of the Mosaic covenant weren't going to be adequate. They had served their purpose, but a whole new reality was at hand. Now that the new covenant had come, the old covenant had been rendered obsolete.

In the **third episode (2:23-28)**, there is another conflict between Jesus and the Pharisees. The Pharisees object to the fact that Jesus' disciples are picking some heads of grain off the stalks to eat them on the Sabbath. According to their oral tradition, taking heads of grain off stalks is considered to be work, and therefore a violation of the commandment to not work on the Sabbath. Jesus responds by pointing out that David, while fleeing from Saul, ate the Bread of the Presence in the tabernacle that only priests were allowed to eat (**I Samuel 21**). He ends by saying that he, the Son of Man, is Lord of the Sabbath and that, "The Sabbath was created for man, and not man for the Sabbath." Simply put, the purpose of Sabbath was to give people a break from their work, not to be an extra rule to obsess over.

In the **fourth episode (3:1-6)**, there is another conflict between Jesus and the Pharisees. They are in the synagogue, and there is a question over whether or not healing the withered hand of a man constituted working on the Sabbath. Jesus responds by asking if it is allowed in the Torah to do good or evil, to save a life or destroy a life, on the Sabbath? His point is that it doesn't matter if it takes place on the Sabbath or not: *doing good is always good; doing evil is always evil.* He then proceeds to heal the man's hand. The Pharisees then team up with the **Herodians** (supporters of King Herod) to find a way to destroy Jesus. Already early on in Jesus' ministry, he is being targeted by both **religious** and **political authorities**.

In the **fifth episode (3:7-12)**, Jesus is again by sea with his disciples, healing people, casting out demons, and prohibiting the demons from telling who he was. We are also told that people were coming from everywhere to follow him: Galilee, Judea, Jerusalem, Idumea, the other side of the Jordan, Tyre and Sidon. Jesus is not just attracting Jews from Galilee and Judea. He is attracting people from outside the Jewish people as well.

The **sixth episode (3:13-19)** concludes the opening two sections about Jesus' early ministry in Galilee when he goes up a mountain and formally chooses **twelve apostles** from among his larger group of disciples. The make-up of the twelve is striking: Judea and Galilee, fishermen, tax-collectors, zealots, even a Canaanite. (Incidentally, a **disciple** is a student of a teacher who puts himself under the tutelage and discipline of the teacher, whereas an **apostle** is chosen by the teacher to help him in his ministry and spread his teaching). Not only does Jesus send them out to proclaim his teaching, but he gives him his **authority** to cast out demons.

His choosing of the twelve apostles also echoes the story of the Exodus, where Moses had led the Hebrews through the waters of the **Red Sea** to **Mount Sinai** so that the **twelve tribes** could become the people of God. Here we see Jesus, having been **by the sea** when he had called his disciples, now bringing them to **a mountain** to call **twelve apostles**. The message is clear: *Jesus is forming a new people of God. He is reconstituting Israel, not around the Torah, but around himself and his own authority.* Not surprisingly, such an act is bound to create even more controversy among the Jewish people, specifically the Jewish leaders.

### The Beelzebub Controversy to Transfiguration (3:20-9:29)

Mark 3:20-9:29 is an intricate literary unit that is constructed in four sections (see the story chart). It begins with the Beelzebub Controversy, in which we are confronted with a basic question: *"What kingdom is Jesus working for? The kingdom of Satan or the Kingdom of God?"* For the rest of the unit, Mark slowly answers that question, and so much more. The four sections unfold in the following manner: (A) *A Question of Kingdoms* (3:20-5:20), where Jesus teaches and demonstrates what the Kingdom of God is about; (B) *The Kingdom to the Jews* (5:21-6:56), where Jesus offers the Kingdom of God to his fellow Jews; (C) *The Kingdom to the Gentiles* (7:1-8:13), where Jesus offers the Kingdom of God to Gentiles; and (D) *Do You See the Kingdom Clearly?* (8:14-9:29), where Jesus challenges his disciples to understand the nature of the Kingdom of God (which they don't *really* get yet).

### Question of Kingdoms (3:20-5:20)

After Jesus' action on the mountain, where he reconstitutes Israel around himself, the next question about his movement is, "What kingdom is Jesus bringing about?" In the **first episode** in this section **(3:20-35)**, the Beelzebub controversy, the scribes accuse Jesus of working for Beelzebub's kingdom (Beelzebub is another name for Satan). The action unfolds in a chiastic fashion. As you can see with my **theological cheeseburger** illustration to the right, a **chiasm** is a literary device that lays the content of a literary unit out in a very specific way: the beginning and end of the unit parallel each other (the top and bottom bun), the second and second-to-last part of the unit parallel each other (the cheese and the lettuce), and the middle of the unit (the burger) is the real "meat" of the passage. A chiasm can be more or less complex, but that is basically how it is laid out. In terms of the Beelzebub controversy, the "theological cheeseburger" of a chiasm is laid out in the following way:

In the "top bun," we are told that some of Jesus' relatives think he's crazy.

In the "cheese," we are told the scribes accuse Jesus of casting out demons by the power of Beelzebub (he's working for Satan's kingdom).

In the "meat" of the passage, Jesus lays out the nature of his ministry. He responds by saying if he was working for the kingdom of Satan, then casting out demons would be a pretty dumb way to build up Satan's kingdom! Instead, he explains he is **binding the strong man**, meaning he is actually binding the power of Satan so that Satan's "house" (the world) could be plundered. Basically, Jesus is bringing about the Kingdom of God and is breaking Satan's grip on the world.

In the "lettuce," Jesus accuses the scribes of blaspheming the Holy Spirit and saying it is the unforgivable sin. They were witnessing the Holy Spirit in action, freeing people from the bondage of Satan, and they rejected God's work as being Satanic. By doing so, they had slandered God.

In the "bottom bun," the episode ends by highlighting Jesus' relationship with his family, who are outside, wanting to see him. Jesus comments that anyone who does the will of God is part of his family. In the Kingdom of God, the people of God will not be defined along ethnic or family lines.

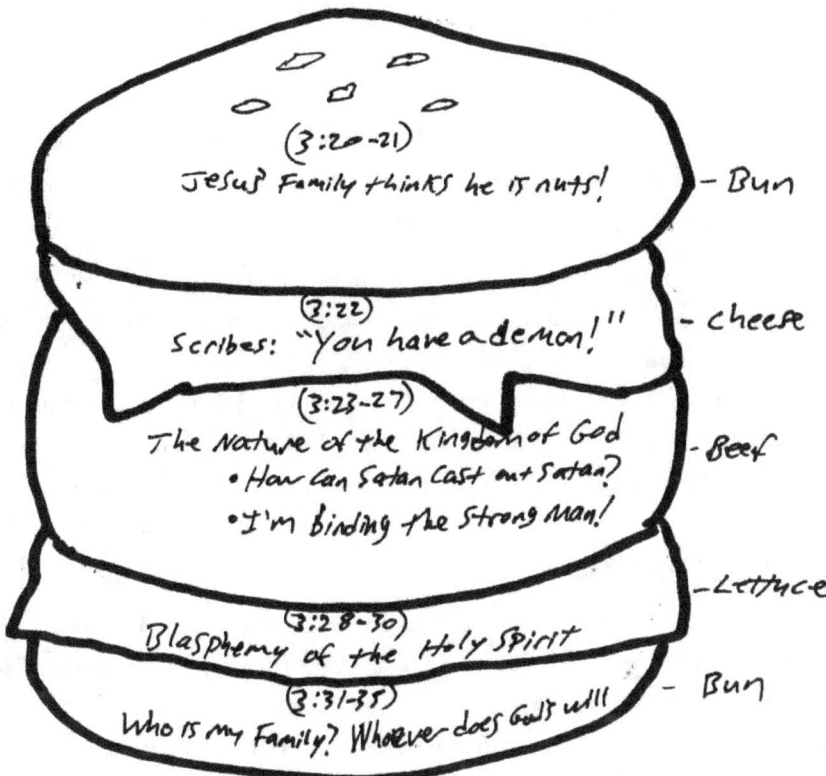

If Jesus is bringing about the Kingdom of God, then what is that going to look like? In the **second episode (4:1-34)**, Jesus gives a number of parables that hint at the kind of kingdom he was bringing. The main parable is the **Parable of the Sower**, where a man sows seed on four different kinds of ground—**by the path, on rocky ground, among the thorns,** and **in good soil**—only the seed in the good soil takes root, grows, and flourishes. He then tells the crowd, *"Whoever has ears, let him hear!"* When the Twelve ask him privately why he speaks to the crowds in parables, Jesus refers to **Isaiah 6:9-10**, where God tells Isaiah that his prophetic message will fall on deaf ears because the people of Judah were idolators. They were like their idols, in that they had eyes and ears, but could spiritually see or hear. Therefore, his parables will reveal who his true followers are. His true followers will hear and understand what Jesus is saying about the Kingdom of God, but those Jews who have made things like the Torah (or political power) into their own idol will be blind and deaf to his message of the Kingdom of God.

When Jesus explains the Parable of the Sower to the Twelve, it becomes clear that it is about the different responses people have to Jesus' kingdom declaration: the seed sown on the soil by the path gets snatched up by Satan before it has the chance to take root; the seed in the rocky soil initially sets down some roots, but they don't go deep enough to withstand any kind of hardship; the seed in the thorns tries to grow, but it gets choked out by the cares of the world; and the seed in the good soil takes root, grows, and flourishes.

The rest of the episode contains a number of cryptic parables about the Kingdom of God: (A) **A lamp** needs to be put on a lampstand; (B) **The standard you place on others** will be the standard that will be placed upon you; (C) The Kingdom of God is like **seed thrown on the ground grows up all on its own**, though nobody really knows how it does so; and (D) The Kingdom of God is like **a tiny mustard seed** that grows to be the largest of all the garden herbs. We are told that although Jesus would explain these in private to his disciples, he wouldn't explain them to the crowds.

In the **third episode (4:35-41),** Jesus gets into a boat with his disciples to cross the Sea of Galilee and stills the storm at sea. The episode is an allusion to the story of Jonah. The key difference is that, whereas Jonah tells the sailors that God had sent the storm because he was running away from God and that the only way to get the storm to stop would be to throw him into the sea, Jesus instead does a very God-like thing and commands the wind and sea to be still. By doing something only God can do, Jesus shows that he's more than just a prophet. He is somehow equal to God Himself. The disciples, though, don't really get it yet and ask, "Who is this man?"

The **fourth episode (5:1-20)** is continues the stilling of the storm episode, for just as Jonah ended up in Nineveh after his storm adventure, Jesus also goes to the Gentile region of the **Gerasenes**. The allusion to Jonah doesn't just tell us something about Jesus (that he does things only God can do), but it also tells us something about the nature of the Kingdom of God—it is going to go to the Gentiles as well.

We are told that the demoniac Jesus confronts was *unable to be bound*. As we learned in the Beelzebub Controversy, Jesus has come to *bind the strong man*. The demon calls Jesus the **Son of God the Most High**, and when Jesus asks the demon its name, it says its name is **Legion**. Most Jews were hoping for a political

Messiah who would come and drive out the *Roman legions*, but Jesus is showing that he has come to drive out, not Roman legions, but the *legions of Satan*. The fact he sends the demons into a herd of pigs that rush over the bank into the sea further emphasizes this very thing. Pigs were considered unclean by the Jews, and the sea (although here literally the Sea of Galilee) carried with it the imagery of the Sea of Chaos and Sheol. Jesus, so to speak, is sending the demons back to hell.

The people of the Gerasenes end up telling Jesus and his disciples to go back to where they came from, and the formerly demon-possessed man, now sane, spreads the news about Jesus throughout the Gentile region of the Decapolis. By doing so, he is "sowing the seeds" of a future harvest among the Gentiles.

### A. The Kingdom of God to the Jews (5:21-6:56)

Jesus and his disciples get back in the boat and return to Jewish territory. This signals the beginning of the next section in the larger *Question of Kingdoms* unit. In this section, the focus is on Jesus' Kingdom of God work among the Jews. Some accept it, some don't.

The **first episode (5:21-43)** is really a double-episode involving Jesus' healing of Jarius' daughter and his healing of a woman suffering from a continual menstrual hemorrhage. It has a much simpler chiastic structure than what we saw in the Beelzebub Controversy. That is why I call this more of a **theological burger**. It begins, in the "top bun," with Jarius coming to Jesus to ask him to heal his daughter. On his way to heal Jarius daughter, in the "meat" of the passage, Jesus encounters a woman suffering from a menstrual hemorrhage. The episode ends in the "bottom bun" with Jesus getting to Jarius' house and raising his daughter from the dead. The reason the episode is set up like this is to draw a parallel between Jarius' daughter and the woman with the hemorrhage. This parallel is made by the use of a number of repeated words:

Jarius asks Jesus to come and **heal** his daughter, and Jesus tells the woman that her faith has **healed** her. Actually, the Greek word translated as "heal" is *sozo*, which literally means **save**. It is a shame most translations have "heal," because although Jesus does heal both Jarius' daughter and the woman, his physical healing is seen as bringing about a foretaste of God's eventual salvation of the entire material world, for salvation involves the redemption and healing of our bodies as well.

The woman has been suffering her condition for **twelve years**, and Jarius' daughter was **twelve years old**. The number twelve is also significant in that it is the number of the twelve tribes of Israel.

Not only does Jarius ask Jesus about his **daughter**, but Jesus addresses the woman as **daughter**.

Finally, Jesus tells the woman that her **faith** has healed/saved her, and when he gets to Jarius' house and finds out his daughter had died, Jesus tells Jarius to **have faith**.

So, what's the point? According to the Torah, both the woman with the menstrual flow and the corpse were ritually unclean. Both were thus cut off from the life of the community of God's people. By physically healing the woman and raising Jarius' daughter, Jesus was also restoring both of them to the larger community of Israel (hence the number twelve). Jesus was bringing healing and restoration to the people of Israel—he was bringing the Kingdom of God to the Jews.

The **second episode (6:1-13)** highlights the mixed results Jesus gets when he takes his message of the Kingdom of God to his fellow Jews. He returns to Nazareth only to be rejected by his own people. They see him as nothing more than a carpenter's son. Because of their lack of faith, he is unable to do any miracles among them. Jesus then sends out his disciples in pairs to the surrounding Jewish villages to proclaim the Kingdom of God and give them an opportunity to repent. Jesus gives them **authority** over the unclean spirits and tells them to stay where they are welcomed, but to "shake the dust from their feet" wherever they are not welcomed. Again, the expectation is that some will accept Jesus' message, and some won't.

The **third episode (6:14-46)** is another double-episode involving both Herod's beheading of John the Baptist and Jesus' feeding of the 5,000. To fully understand both, one must read them in light of each other. In the first part, we are told the events that led to Herod's killing of John the Baptist. Herod had arrested John because John had publicly condemned his marriage to Herodias, the former wife of his brother Philip, as a violation of the Torah. On his birthday, though, Herodias' daughter, at the instigation of Herodias, pressures Herod into beheading John and bringing his head in on a platter.

That gruesome story serves as a contrast to Jesus in the next part of the episode. After getting news about John the Baptist, Jesus takes his disciples into the wilderness to get away, but a great crowd follows them. When Jesus sees them,

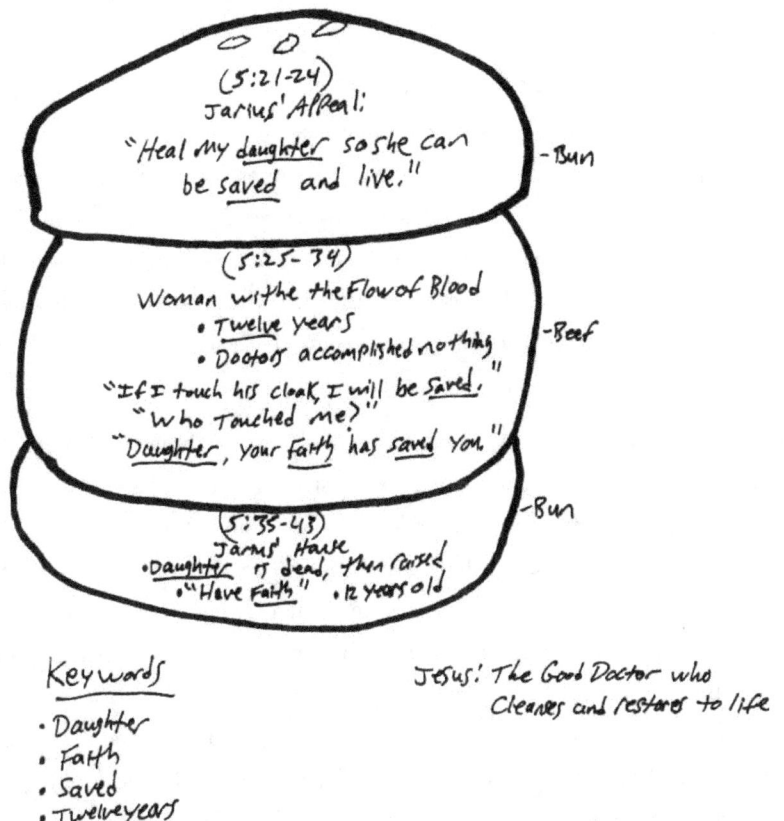

Mark says he has compassion on them *"because they were like sheep without a shepherd"* (an allusion to **Zechariah 10:2**) He then proceeds to feed 5,000 people with just two fish and five loaves of bread. The comment about *sheep without a shepherd* is key to understanding both parts of this episode, for the kings of Israel were often called the **shepherds** of God's people. In light of that, the contrast between Herod and Jesus becomes clear: Herod is a **bad shepherd** who slaughters and devours God's flock, whereas Jesus is the **good shepherd** who cares for and feeds his flock.

Obviously, Herod and his guests didn't actually dine on John's head, but the imagery of John's head on a platter serves as a contrast to Jesus' feeding of the 5,000. As for the feeding itself, it echoes the miraculous feeding of the Hebrews in the wilderness during the Exodus that involved the manna. The fact that **twelve baskets** of leftovers were collected emphasize the relationship to the twelve tribes of Israel. Once again, the story of Jesus as the Messiah and his bringing the

Kingdom of God is set against the backdrop of the Exodus. In Jesus, the new Exodus has come.

The **fourth episode (6:47-52)** involves another scene with the disciples in a boat during a storm at sea. Jesus isn't with them because he stayed behind on the mountain to pray. In the middle of the storm, he comes **walking on the sea** to the disciples, and Mark tells us that Jesus was intending to *pass them by*. The disciples are afraid it is a ghost, so Jesus reassures them it is him and gets into the boat. Mark then tells us that the disciples still didn't understand because they weren't able to put everything together concerning the feeding of the 5,000. So, what is going on?

First, as we saw when Jesus stilled the storm, Jesus is shown as having the power only God has. Whether it is the creation story or the stories of Noah and Jonah, the sea depicts the powers of evil and chaos, and throughout the Old Testament YHWH is described as having power over the Sea of Chaos. **Job 9:8** even describes YHWH as the one who "treads upon the waves of the sea." Therefore, when Jesus walks upon the sea is showing he is doing something that only God Himself can do. Secondly, as far as Jesus intending to *pass them by* is concerned, it is an allusion to the two scenes in **Exodus 33:19-23** and **I Kings 19:11-13** in which YHWH *passes by* Moses and Elijah respectively on Mount Sinai, allowing them to get a glimpse of His glory. To *pass by* means to reveal His glory. Jesus wasn't trying to outrun the boat. He was intending to reveal his glory to his disciples, just as YHWH revealed His glory to Moses and Elijah. But since the disciples were afraid, Jesus *didn't reveal his glory to them*. That would have to wait. We aren't told what the feeding of the 5,000 has to do with the disciples' lack of understanding—that answer, too, has to wait until later.

The **fifth episode (6:53-56)** parallels the pattern seen earlier in 4:35-41 and 5:1-20. There is an episode at sea where Jesus does what only God can do, but the disciples don't understand. That is followed by an episode where Jesus demonstrates his power in Gentile territory. After trying to reveal who he is and having the disciples again failing to understand in 6:47-52, Jesus is once again on the other side of the Sea of Galilee, in Gentile territory, where further healings occur. The Gospel of the Kingdom is offered to Jews, but it is also going to move out into the Gentile world.

## B. The Kingdom of God to the Gentiles (7:1-8:13)

The third section in 3:20-9:29 follows the same literary pattern as the second section, but the focus here is on Jesus' interactions with the Gentile world. It is important to take notice of the geographical cues in Mark's Gospel. After we are told of his healings in Gennesaret (6:53-56), we are not told that he got into the boat yet to go back over into Jewish territory. That doesn't happen until the end of this section, in 8:13. This section happens in Gentile territory.

In the **first episode (7:1-23)**, some Pharisees and scribes from Jerusalem object to the fact that Jesus' disciples do not ceremonially wash their hands when eating food from the marketplace. Although it was not commanded in the Torah, it did violate the oral tradition of the elders. In response, Jesus quotes **Isaiah 29:13** and accuses them of actually violating the Torah by keeping to their oral tradition. For even though the Torah says to honor one's father and mother, the Pharisees and scribes encouraged people to give the money that would have gone to help their needy parents as a **corban gift** to them instead. Jesus then, by virtue of his own authority, says that the Jewish food laws are irrelevant in terms of righteousness. It isn't what goes into your mouth that defiles you, but rather what comes out of your mouth.

The **second episode (7:24-37)** highlights Jesus' interaction with Gentiles in Tyre and Sidon. In Tyre, Jesus casts a demon out of the daughter of a Syrophoenician woman. At first, Jesus comes across as harsh when he refuses the woman's request and says that the *children* (Jews) should be fed before the *dogs* (Gentiles) are fed. But as the episode unfolds, we see something else going on. When Jesus says that the *children* should be fed before the dogs are, he uses the standard word *teknon*. When the woman responds, though, she uses the word *paidon* to describe the Jews, which is more of an affectionate term, like *dear children*. She acknowledges the Jews as the people of God, but she still asks Jesus to cast the demon from her daughter. Not only does Jesus grant her request, but Mark makes sure to refer to the woman's daughter as a *paidon* as well to show that when the Gospel of the Kingdom goes out to the Gentile world, the old racial distinctions become irrelevant. After that, while in Sidon and the Decapolis, Jesus heals a deaf and mute man, who then spreads the word about the Kingdom even more among Gentiles.

In the **third episode (8:1-10)**, while still in Gentile territory, Jesus performs a second feeding, this time of 4,000 people. As with the first feeding in Jewish territory, Jesus feeds the 4,000 *in the wilderness* with only a little *bit of bread and a few fish*. But this time, the disciples pick up **seven baskets** of leftovers, as opposed to twelve baskets with the feeding of the 5,000. Jesus and the disciples then get into the boat and go to Dalmanutha. It is significant to note that Jesus is doing the same thing among Gentiles that he is doing among Jews.

The **fourth episode (8:11-13)** that concludes this *Question of Kingdoms* section is brief, but quite telling. Presumably when they are in Dalmanutha, some Pharisees demand that Jesus give them a **sign from heaven**. Jesus, though, tells them that he isn't going to give a sign to **this generation**, and proceeds to get into the boat with his disciples and go to the other side of the lake, back into Jewish territory. What is ironic is that the Pharisees' demand for a "sign from heaven" comes not only on the heels of so many healings and casting out of demons on the part of Jesus, but specifically right after Jesus' miraculous feeding of the 4,000, which was the second miraculous feeding in little over a chapter. The further irony is that both feedings echo the miraculous feeding in the wilderness during the Exodus, where YHWH sends the people of Israel *bread from heaven*. So, why does Jesus say they'll get no sign? Because a sign from heaven has been given, *twice already*, and the Pharisees are simply unable to recognize it because they have made the Torah into an idol and are showing themselves to have eyes that don't see and ears that don't see what Jesus is doing.

### D. Do You See the Kingdom Clearly? (8:14-9:29)

The fourth section within 3:20-9:29 serves as the climax where we see whether or not the disciples are able to finally clearly see who Jesus is and what the Kingdom of God is all about.

In the **first episode (8:14-21)**, as they are coming back from Dalmanutha, Jesus challenges his disciples by warning them about the **yeast of the Pharisees and the yeast of Herod**. The disciples think he's talking to them about them forgetting to bring actual bread for the trip home. Jesus' response to their thick-headedness takes us all the way back to 4:1-34, when he explained why he spoke in parables. He asks them if their heart is calloused and if they **have eyes that can't see and ears that don't hear**. Even after Jesus reminds them that they had picked up twelve baskets of leftovers after the feeding of the 5,000 (in Jewish territory) and seven baskets after the feeding of the 4,000 (in Gentile territory), the disciples still don't understand what he is getting at. It actually is quite simple. The twelve baskets represent the twelve tribes of Israel, and the seven baskets represent the full number of Gentiles who will become part of the reconstituted people of God in Christ. This is what the Kingdom of God is going to look like. It is going to include both Jews and Gentiles who come together under the Messiahship of Jesus himself. Therefore, the disciples should reject the versions of the kingdom that the Pharisees and Herod are pushing.

Of course, the disciples don't really get it yet, and this is what the **second episode (8:22-26)** illustrates in the story of the twice-healed blind man in Bethsaida. On the surface, the episode seems odd. Jesus heals the blind man, but his vision is still blurry, and he says the people look like trees. So, Jesus touches his eyes a second time, and it is then that his vision is fully restored. So, what is the point of this episode? The answer begins to unfold in the very next episode.

The **third episode (8:27-9:1)** is Peter's confession at Caesarea-Philippi, a city in northern Galilee, at the base of Mount Hermon. Jesus first asks his disciples who people think he is, and they say John the Baptist, Elijah, or a prophet. When Jesus asks them who they think he is, Peter says, "You are the Messiah!" *Peter sees that Jesus is the Messiah.* Yet right after that, for the first time in Mark's Gospel, Jesus tells them that **he must suffer, be rejected by Jewish religious leaders, and be killed—but that he would then rise up three days later**. Peter, though, openly rebukes Jesus for saying this. Jesus responds **by calling Peter Satan** and telling him that his mind isn't set on the things of God, but rather the things of men. Jesus then calls the crowd together and tells them that the cost of being his disciple will require them taking up their cross and following him, and that if they are too ashamed to do that, then the Son of Man will be ashamed of them when he comes in the glory of his Father.

It becomes clear that although Peter and the disciples *see that Jesus is the Messiah*, they do not yet *see clearly what kind of Messiah he is.* Hence, Peter and the disciples are like the twice-healed blind man. They are expecting a Messiah who would establish the Kingdom of God through force, yet Jesus is going to be a Messiah who will establish the Kingdom of God through suffering, death, and resurrection, and who calls his disciples to follow his sacrificial example. Obviously, the disciples don't really get this yet—*they don't see clearly yet.* The episode ends with Jesus telling the crowd there at that time (around AD 30), some who were standing there would not taste death until they see the Kingdom of God having come in power. How could that be true, since we are now in the 21st century and that hasn't happened yet? The answer is that if you think that, you're reading the text wrong. What Jesus is talking about takes place in the next episode.

The **fourth episode (9:2-13)** is of the Transfiguration. It brings Jesus' Galilean ministry to a close and serves as the climax to this larger literary unit of *A Question of Kingdoms*. Six days after Peter's confession, Jesus takes Peter, James, and John upon a **high mountain** where he is transfigured before them, and they see him talking with **Moses** and **Elijah**. To be clear, Mark does not name the mountain, but given the fact that Peter's confession in the previous episode took place in Caesarea-Philippi, many scholars reason that the mountain in question is Mount Hermon (although others believe it was Mount Tabor, a mountain slightly southwest of the Sea of Galilee).

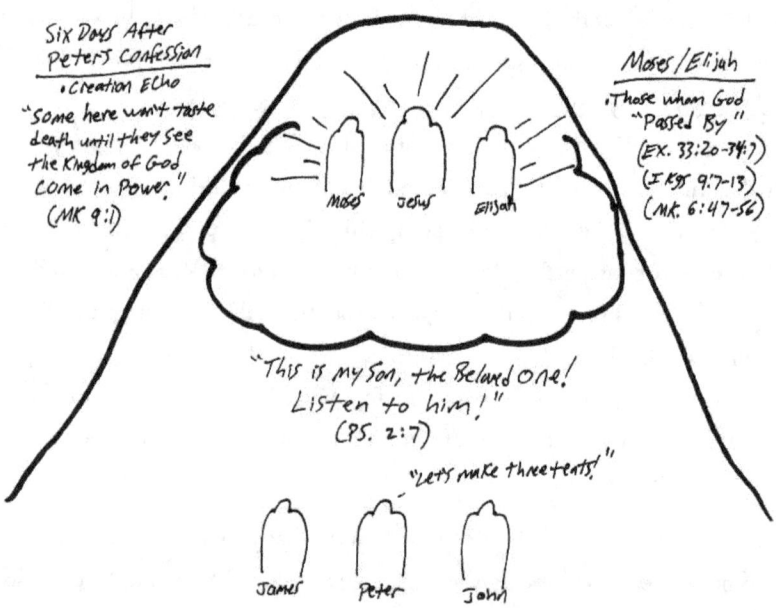

In any case, there is the obvious question: **Why Moses and Elijah?** First, Moses and Elijah represent the Torah and the Prophets, both of which bear witness to Jesus. Second, this connects back to where Jesus walked on the sea and intended to "pass by" and reveal his glory to the disciples but didn't because they were too afraid. Here, though, *Jesus finally passes by the disciples and reveals his glory to them.* Third, the fact this takes place on a high mountain is an allusion to Mount Sinai, where YHWH "passed by" both Moses and Elijah. Fourth, Jesus words at the end of the previous episode now make sense: Peter, James, and John are the "some standing here" who would catch a glimpse of the Kingdom of God coming in power.

In any case, after Peter's nonsensical suggestion to build three tents, a cloud overshadows them all and for only the second time in Mark's Gospel (the first one being at Jesus' baptism) God speaks, once again, with an allusion to **Psalm 2:7**: *"This is my son, the Beloved One. Listen to him!"* It is as if God is pleading with the disciples and saying, "Look at everything he's done and told you! Don't you get it yet? *Open your ears and listen to him!"*

On the way down the mountain, Jesus orders them not to tell anyone what they had seen until **the Son of Man has risen from the dead**. In true disciple-like fashion, they don't get it and argue with themselves what "rising from the dead" could mean. When they ask him about the scribes saying that Elijah had to precede the coming of the Messiah (a reference to **Malachi 4:5-6**), Jesus tells them that Elijah had already come first (in the figure of John the Baptist). By saying this, Jesus was really making a claim about himself—he really was the Messiah.

In the **fifth episode (9:14-29)**, once they come down the mountain, they encounter a man who had taken his son who had an unclean spirit to some of Jesus' disciples, but they were not strong enough to cast it out of the boy. After showing his frustration with those followers, Jesus casts the spirit out from the boy. Once again, various elements from a number of earlier episodes can be seen:

1. Jesus' disciples weren't *strong enough*, just as the people in the Gerasenes weren't *strong enough* to bind the demoniac of the tombs, but Jesus does prove himself to be strong enough to *bind the Strong Man*.
2. Jesus *has compassion* on the man and his son, just as he *had compassion* on the people who were like sheep without a shepherd.
3. The deed was able to be done because of the *man's faith*, just as in the story of the woman with the menstrual flow and Jarius' daughter (and unlike the faithlessness of the people of Nazareth).
4. The specific healing involved *deafness and dumbness*, just as with the deaf and dumb man in Sidon.

After this was over, Jesus' disciples ask him in private why they weren't able to cast out the spirit. He tells them that such work can only come about through prayer.

### 5. The Transition: From Galilee to Jerusalem (9:30-10:52)

With the Galilean ministry ended, this next major section in Mark marks the transition from Jesus' Galilean ministry to the Passover in Jerusalem during which

Jesus will be arrested and crucified. Now that the disciples have acknowledged him to be the Messiah, yet don't yet see clearly what kind of Messiah he is, Jesus spends the trip to Jerusalem trying to hammer his version of the Kingdom of God into their heads so that they can finally clearly see the true nature of the Kingdom of God.

The **first episode (9:30-37)**, even though Jesus tells his disciples for a third time that he was going to be arrested and killed but that he would rise up three days later, they still hold to their incorrect notions of what it means to be great in the coming kingdom. So, Jesus turns their notion of greatness on its head by saying, *"If one wants to be first, he must become last of all and a slave to everyone."* Then he brings a child before them and say that to receive a child was to receive him, and to receive him was to receive "the one who sent me" (God). The politics of the Kingdom of God are not like the politics of the kingdoms of the world. In the Kingdom of God, true greatness is found in the ones who are last, who are slaves, who are weak as children.

In the **second episode (9:38-50)**, Jesus also has to correct their wrong notions regarding who is "in" and "out" of the Kingdom. When his disciples tell him that they tried to stop someone who was not in their group who was casting out demons in Jesus' name, Jesus tells them that anyone who wasn't against them was actually for them and anyone who does something good in the name of the Messiah was to be welcomed. Once again, he gives an example of children to explain to his disciples that if they prevent someone from doing something good in the name of Jesus, they were going to cause people to be confused and to stumble in their faith. He then makes a number of hyperbolic statements about how it would be better to lose a body part that scandalizes you (be it a hand, or foot, or eye) and enter the Kingdom of God lame than to keep those body parts and end up in **Gehenna**.

Gehenna was a literal place outside the walls of Jerusalem that was known as the Valley of Hinnom in the Old Testament. The valley was considered cursed because it had been the place where child sacrifices were conducted. It subsequently became essentially a garbage dump where the city's garbage was burned up. That image of the constant fires burning up the garbage eventually became symbolic of judgment and eternal punishment (what we would call "hell" today). To be clear, though, in Jewish thought, there was a difference between Sheol and Gehenna. Sheol was simply the grave, where *everyone* ended up when they died, whereas the literal garbage dump of Gehenna was symbolic of God's punishment of the wicked. This is thus associated with the **Lake of Fire** in Revelation 20.

In the **third episode (10:1-12)**, Jesus has a debate with the Pharisees over the issue of divorce in which he corrects their misunderstanding as to why divorce was allowed in the Torah. Jesus tells them that the only reason that rule was in the Torah was because of their hard-heartedness. In reality a man and wife become "one flesh," and should not be separated. Divorce might be necessary for a variety of reasons, but divorce is never "good" just because it is in the Torah.

When his disciples ask him about this in private, Jesus expands on his answer and tells them if someone gets divorced and then marries another, that person still is committing adultery. We must be clear on what Jesus is saying, though. He isn't saying that if a husband and wife get divorced, and then ten years later the man happens to meet another woman and gets remarried, that he is committing adultery. He is addressing the way some were using the divorce law in the Torah to justify their own bad behavior. If a married man saw another woman he wanted to marry, he would divorce his wife for the sole purpose of marrying the other woman and would justify it by claiming divorce was allowed in the Torah. In light of that, Jesus is simply saying that if you divorce your spouse *because you already have someone else lined up*, you're still effectively committing adultery.

In the **fourth episode (10:13-16)**, Jesus once again uses the illustration of little children to teach what the Kingdom of God is like. Just as he said in both 9:36-37 and 9:42, Jesus says that one cannot enter the Kingdom of God unless one receives it like a little child.

The **fifth episode (10:17-31)** involves Jesus' interaction with a rich young man who asks Jesus what he has to do to inherit eternal life. The term **eternal life** can be misleading here, though, because the actual Greek term means the **Life of the Ages**, and it is related to the Jewish hope of the coming Kingdom of God. Therefore, the young man wasn't asking some nebulous concept of living forever, but rather about the specific hope of the coming Messianic Age, when God would fulfill his promises to Abraham, bless all nations, redeem all creation, and defeat sin and death. Jesus first refers the young man to the commandments, but when he tells Jesus he's kept them ever since his youth, Jesus then tells him he should sell all he has, give his money to the poor, and then follow Jesus. The young man doesn't take Jesus up on his offer, though, because he preferred his worldly wealth to any treasure in Heaven.

In response, Jesus tells his disciples that it is easier for a camel to pass through the eye of a needle than for the rich to enter the Kingdom of God. When the disciples then ask who is able to be saved, Jesus says with men, no one is able, but with God anything is possible. When Peter then points out that they had, in fact, left everything to follow him, Jesus reassures them that even though they would soon suffer persecution, they would receive a hundred times more in the **Coming Age, the Life of the Age**. He then reiterates what he has said earlier: *many who are first will be last, and those who are last will be first*. Jesus' point in all this is that all too often the rich and powerful *of this age* are so attached to the riches and power **of this age**, that they are completely unwilling to give it up, even for the sake of the Kingdom of God. Conversely, those **in this age** who are willing to give up everything and endure persecution for the Kingdom of God will be the ones who will receive much more in the coming age than they ever gave up in this present age.

In the **sixth episode (10:32-34)**, as Jesus is leading his disciples to Jerusalem, we learn that the disciples are terrified of what might happen. For the fourth time since Peter's confession, Jesus them that he is going to be handed over to the chief priests and scribes who will condemn him to death, and that he will be killed by the Gentiles. He, though, will be raised up after three days. The disciples still don't clearly see what Jesus is telling them.

So, in the **seventh episode (10:35-45)**, Jesus again has to correct the wrong notions his disciples have regarding the Kingdom of God. When James and John ask Jesus if they can be seated on his right and left when he comes in his glory (presumably they had in mind some prime political positions of power), Jesus once again turns everything on its head. He first asks them if they think they can *drink from the cup* he is going to drink and *be baptized with his kind of baptism*. They tell him "Yes," but it is pretty obvious they were thinking in terms of doing what it takes to gain political power. What Jesus is actually referring to is his literal suffering and death. So, Jesus tells them that they most certainly would *drink from his cup* and *be baptized with his baptism* (meaning they would, indeed, suffer for the Kingdom), but that it wasn't up to him to decide who will be at his right and left hand in his glory.

What Jesus is talking about and what James and John think he's talking about are two different things. Just like Peter at his confession, they realize that Jesus is the Messiah, but their idea as to what kind of Messiah he is and what kind of Kingdom of God he is going to bring isn't quite clear yet. They too are like the twice-healed blind man before the second touch from Jesus. When the other disciples get mad about their request, Jesus brings them all together and again tries to teach them about the nature of the Kingdom of God. It wasn't like other kingdoms, where rulers lord their authority over their subjects. In the Kingdom of God, the way to greatness is the way of servanthood. This is what he came to do: to serve and to give his life as a ransom for many, and if they are going to be great in his Kingdom, that is what they must do as well.

The **eighth episode (10:46-52)** concludes the section in which Jesus makes his way to Jerusalem. As Jesus and his disciples pass through Jericho (a city about 15 miles east of Jerusalem), they encounter a blind beggar named Bartimaeus. He calls Jesus **Son of David** (a messianic royal title) and begs Jesus to have mercy on him. When Jesus asks him what he wants, he replies, *"I want to see."* Jesus heals him, tells him his faith has saved him, and Bartimaeus proceeds to follow Jesus on the way to Jerusalem. This episode needs to be understood in the context of the episodes involving the twice-healed blind man and Peter's confession. In those episodes, the disciples were like the twice-healed blind man, in that they *saw* Jesus was the Messiah, but didn't yet *see clearly* what kind of Messiah he was. Here, Bartimaeus *clearly sees immediately* and continues to follow Jesus on the way to Jerusalem, where Jesus will suffer and die. He, too, represents the disciples. When they get to Jerusalem, they are going to *clearly see* that Jesus is the kind of Messiah who will suffer, die, and rise again.

### 6. The Confrontation in Jerusalem (11:1-13:37)

The next section in Mark covers chapters 11-13, when Jesus comes to confront the Jewish religious leaders and temple priests in Jerusalem. These chapters explain what led to Jesus eventually being arrested and crucified. It is important to notice that everything in this section is connected to the Temple in some way, shape, or form. From here on out, the two main things that dominate the Passion narrative are **(1) Jesus' claim of Messiahship** and **(2) Jesus' opposition to the Temple establishment**.

The **first episode (11:1-11)** is the so-called "Triumphal Entry" that happened on Palm Sunday. In reality, it is anything but that. In fact, the entire point of the episode is to turn the Jewish hopes of a "triumphal entry" of their Messiah on their head. They wanted the Messiah to **(a) confront and defeat Rome, (b) enter Jerusalem in triumph**, and **(c) cleanse the Temple**. Everything in this episode highlights those Jewish messianic hopes and expectations.

First, Jesus rides down from the **Mount of Olives on a donkey**, an obvious allusion to **Zechariah 9:9** (*"Behold, your king is coming to you; righteous and having salvation is he, humble and mounted on a donkey, on a colt, the foal of a donkey"*) as well as the apocalyptic text in **Zechariah 14:4**, in which YHWH Himself stands on the Mount of Olives and wages war with the nations. Second, the Jews welcome Jesus by **laying down their cloaks and waving palm branches**. This is what they did when Judas Maccabees entered Jerusalem in triumph after successfully driving out the evil Seleucid king Antiochus Epiphanes IV. Judas Maccabees entered Jerusalem and then proceeded to cleanse the Temple of the idols that Antiochus Epiphanes had put there. Third, the Jews were singing **Psalm 118:25-26**: *"Hosanna! Blessed is he who comes in the name of the Lord!"* Psalm 118 was an enthronement psalm that celebrated the establishment of a new king of Israel. The word "Hosanna" literally means, "Save us!" It is pretty clear that the crowds thought Jesus was the kind of Messiah who was going to defeat Rome and reestablish the kingdom of David.

Yet, with all that build up and expectation, Mark tells us that Jesus went into Jerusalem, went to the Temple…but then left and went back to Bethany, because it was getting late. Talk about an anticlimactic letdown. What's going on? Jesus isn't going to be the kind of Messiah the Jews were expecting. For the next few days, he's going to show himself to be something quite different, beginning the next day.

The **second episode (11:12-26)** takes place the next day, on Monday. Although it is often referred to as Jesus *cleansing the Temple*, he does no such thing. That is what the Jews were hoping he would do. He doesn't cleanse it, *he condemns it*.

The episode is laid out in yet another chiastic fashion. It begins with him leaving Bethany and cursing a fig tree because it had produced no figs. Jesus then proceeds to the Temple *and trashes the place*. As he is doing that, he quotes **Jeremiah 7:11**: *"My house will be called a house of prayer for all nations,"* and then accuses them of turning the Temple into a hideout for **lestai**. Some translations translate this as "robbers," but the fuller meaning of this word is to designate **zealots** and **revolutionaries** who would rob the rich on the highways in order to fund their revolution. Just like Jeremiah did six centuries earlier, Jesus condemns the Temple for being corrupt and for failing to be what it was originally intended to be—a place where people *from all nations* would come and worship the God of Israel. Instead, the Temple had become a nationalistic symbol *against the nations*. In fact, within 40 years, the Temple would literally become the headquarters of the zealot leaders during the Jewish Revolt against Rome in AD 66-70. We must be clear here: **Jesus' prophetic condemnation of the Temple is why the chief priests and scribes immediately start looking for a way to destroy him. Instead of saying Rome was the enemy, Jesus was saying that they, the Temple leaders, were the problem**.

The episode ends the next morning, on Tuesday. When Jesus and his disciples pass by the same fig tree, they find it completely withered. Jesus then tells them to have faith in God, and that if anyone who acts in faith and tells *this mountain* to be thrown *into the sea*, without doubting in his heart, it would happen. He then goes on to say that if they forgive others, God will forgive them, but if they don't forgive others, God will not forgive them. It becomes obvious that the fig tree represents the Temple. Just as the fig tree is cursed and withers because it wasn't producing literal fruit, so too is the Temple condemned for not producing spiritual fruit. And, 40 years later in AD 70, the Temple is eventually destroyed. Concerning Jesus' comments regarding *this mountain* and *the sea*, we should see them as a reference to the eventual destruction of Temple Mount. Jesus is telling his disciples that if they too proclaim that the Temple will one day be destroyed, it will happen. And that is what happened in AD 70.

The **third episode (11:27-33)** takes place later on that day, when Jesus goes back to the Temple and is confronted by the chief priests, scribes, and elders. They ask him by whose **authority** was he doing these things. Jesus responds to the elders by saying he'll answer their question if they first tell him whether or not John the Baptist was a true prophet. This question backs them into a corner. If they say John was a prophet, Jesus will ask why they don't believe him, because John had baptized Jesus and acknowledged who Jesus was. But if they say John wasn't a prophet, the crowds will get mad, because they did consider John to be a prophet. So, just like spineless politicians, they claim they didn't know. In response, Jesus tells them that he won't give an answer to them either. Of course, by bringing up John in the first place, Jesus really had given an answer—John was the forerunner, and Jesus was the one greater than John who would baptize in the Holy Spirit. Thus, Jesus' authority comes from God.

The **fourth episode (12:1-12)** happens that same day in the Temple, when Jesus tells the crowd the **Parable of the Vineyard** which directly condemns the chief priests. The parable isn't hard to figure out: (1) The owner of the vineyard is **God**, (2) The vineyard is **Israel**, (3) The tenants whom the owner put in charge of the vineyard are the Jewish leaders, namely the **chief priests**, (4) The servants of the owner whom the tenants abuse and kill are the **past prophets**, and (5) The owner's son whom they kill in order to try to take the inheritance of the vineyard for themselves is **Jesus**. The message of the parable is clear: The leaders of Israel have always been against God and have always persecuted God's prophets. And because they are going to kill him too, when God does return, He will destroy them and the Temple and "give the vineyard to others," namely the Kingdom of God will be extended to the Gentiles.

Jesus then quotes **Psalm 118:22-23**, the very psalm the crowds were singing when he came into Jerusalem: *"The stone that the builders rejected has become the cornerstone."* The imagery of **builders** and the **cornerstone** puts Jesus' condemnation of the Temple into an even starker light. Jesus is saying he is the Messiah (the cornerstone), but the Jewish leaders (the builders) have rejected him, and that is why the Temple will be destroyed. Still, he is the cornerstone of God's new Temple, and the reconstituted people of God will be built around him. (Incidentally, the Temple during Jesus' day was in the midst of a massive renovation that only was completed shortly before the outbreak of the Jewish War in AD 66. So, at the time of Jesus' confrontation with the Jewish leaders, there was literal building going on in the Temple). In any case, the chief priests know full well that the parable was directed at them, and so they want to arrest Jesus. The problem is that if they arrest him in public, the crowds will riot. So, they decide to try to damage Jesus' reputation instead.

|  | Question | Response |
|---|---|---|
| 12:13-17 | **Pharisees/Herodians:** Taxes to Caesar? | **Jesus:** Picture on the money? Pay it…but give to God what's God's. |
| 12:18-27 | **Sadducees:** Whose wife will this woman be in the resurrection? | **Jesus:** No marriage in the resurrection. |
| 12:28-34 | **Scribe:** What is the greatest commandment? | **Jesus:** Love God and love your neighbor. |
| 12:35-40 | **Jesus:** How can the Messiah only be David's descendant, when David calls him "Lord"? | **Crowd:** Amazement |

The **fifth episode (12:13-37)** is about the attempt by the Jewish leaders to damage Jesus' reputation. The **Pharisees and Herodians** ask him whether or not the Torah permits Jews to **pay taxes to Caesar**. If Jesus says they should pay taxes to Caesar, he will anger many of his followers, but if he says they shouldn't pay taxes to Caesar, he could be arrested by Rome on charges of revolting against Rome. Jesus responds by essentially saying, "If Caesar's face is on the money, then pay him what is his, but taxes aren't really the important issue here. The real issue is whether or not you give to God what belongs to God."

The **Sadducees** then question Jesus about the **future resurrection**. They denied the resurrection because it had clear political connotations. It was the belief that when the Kingdom of God is established, righteous Jews who died fighting the oppressors of God's people would be resurrected and live in God's new creation. Since the Sadducees were Jewish aristocrats who got their power and influence from Rome, though, they taught against the idea of a future resurrection. In any case, their question about a woman who marries seven brothers is meant to mock the idea of a resurrection: Whose wife would she be in the resurrection? In response, Jesus says there will be no marriage in the resurrection because people will be raised whole and complete, and therefore marriage will be unnecessary. Jesus then ends his answer by alluding to what God tells Moses at the burning bush, *"I AM the God of Abraham, Isaac, and Jacob,"* and emphasizing that God *is* the God of Abraham—present tense. Abraham might be physically dead, but he is still alive in God. He might not yet be made complete—that will happen in the resurrection, but he (like everyone else) isn't truly "dead and gone," for God is the God of the living.

The third question comes from a **scribe** who asks Jesus what the **greatest commandment** is. Jesus gives a two-part answer. The first part is the **Shema** from **Deuteronomy 6:4-5**: *"Love the Lord with all your heart, soul, mind, and strength."* Then Jesus says there is an equally important second commandment: *"Love your neighbor as yourself."* These two commandments are more important than all offerings or sacrifices, for they describe the very goal the Torah. If you love God and love your neighbor, you've fulfilled the Torah. The scribe sees that Jesus has answered correctly, and in response, Jesus tells the scribe that he wasn't too far from the Kingdom of God.

It is now Jesus' turn to ask a question of his own. His question deals with the **identity of the Messiah**. The Messiah was called the "son of David" because would be a descendent in the line of David. Jesus, though, quotes **Psalm 110:1**, where David writes, *"The Lord* (YHWH) *said to my Lord* (who is that?), *'Sit at my right hand, until I put your enemies under your feet.'"* He then points out that if the one who sits at God's right hand is the Messiah, and yet David calls the Messiah *his Lord*, then how can the Messiah merely be a descendant of David? Jesus is not only implying that he really is the Messiah in the line of David, but he's saying he is a lot more than what the Jews were expecting. **He shares the throne of God; he sits at God's right hand; he has the authority and power of God; he is the Son of God Himself.**

The **sixth episode (12:38-44)** consists of Jesus contrasting the pride of the scribes with the humility of a poor widow. He says that all the scribes wanted was adulation and praise in the synagogues, marketplaces, and feasts, but even though they would make long prayers to impress people, in reality they "devour widows' houses." They put on a religious show, while at the same time actively destroy the weakest of God's people. They claim to love God, but they hate their neighbor, and because of that, they will receive the greater condemnation. By contrast, Jesus points out a poor widow who, unlike the rich who put large sums of money into the Temple treasury, was able to put in only two copper coins. Jesus says that she has given more than any of them. What they gave was essentially leftovers—they didn't need it anyway. But the widow gave all she had—her offering, therefore, was much more valuable in the eyes of God.

The **seventh episode (13:1-37)** is the **Olivet Discourse**, the climax of Jesus' confrontation with the Temple establishment. It is incredibly important to understand because not only does it highlight the reason why Jesus gets arrested and crucified, but it also gives us a clue as to why Mark's Gospel was written in the first place. Now what makes the Olivet Discourse so hard to understand is that it is full of apocalyptic imagery, and most people simply have no idea how to interpret it. Now, the setting of the episode is straightforward. As they are leaving the Temple, Jesus' disciples are marveling at the buildings on the Temple Mount. Jesus, though, tells them that they would soon be destroyed. Then, once they get to the Mount of Olives opposite of the Temple, Peter, James, and John ask Jesus when it would happen and what would signal it was about to happen. Everything in the Olivet Discourse is directed to answering that question: *"When will the Temple be destroyed?"*

Two additional things need to be kept in mind, though, that will impact how the Olivet Discourse is understood. First, we need to read it through two historical lenses: (A) **Passover in AD 30**, when Jesus prophesied the Temple's destruction, and (B) **The year AD 70**, when the Temple was, in fact, destroyed by the Romans at the end of the Jewish War. Related to this is the fact that the Gospel of Mark was written around the time the Temple was destroyed, possibly in the years leading up to its destruction. What this means is that when Mark wrote his Gospel, what he was emphasizing here in the Olivet Discourse is that the Temple's destruction had been prophesied by Jesus 40 years prior: what Jesus said would happen was happening.

Secondly, the Olivet Discourse is going to be hard to understand if one doesn't understand what the **Day of the Lord** is. The Old Testament prophets spoke of the Day of the Lord (literally the **Day of YHWH**) as the times within history when God acted to **bring judgment** upon the oppressors of His people and to **vindicate and save** His people, Israel. The prophets used metaphorical language of the undoing of the created order (stars falling from the skies, earthquakes, the sun going dark, the moon turning to blood) to describe the Day of the Lord in order to emphasize that when God would act, it would be an "earth-shattering" event, so to speak.

During the Intertestamental Period, though, writers took those parts in Old Testament prophecy and created a new genre of **apocalyptic writing** to emphasize their conviction that they were living in the **Old Age** and that an **Ultimate Day of the Lord** would happen when He would bring an end to the current, corrupt Old Age and then re-create a **New Age**. This "turn of the ages" would happen when the Messiah would come, defeat the forces of evil, cleanse the Temple, redeem God's people, and then usher in that New Messianic Age and the Kingdom of God.

Here in the Olivet Discourse, though, Jesus uses that apocalyptic language but turns everything on its head. The oppressors of God's people aren't Rome, but rather the Temple establishment itself, and God's people isn't ethnic Israel, but rather the followers of Jesus. Hence, here in the Olivet Discourse, Jesus says that God's judgment and wrath is going to come upon Jerusalem because its Jewish leaders are guilty of persecuting both Jesus and his followers. On the Day of the Lord (which is now the **Day of Christ**), Jerusalem will suffer God's wrath and the followers of Jesus will be vindicated.

With that laid out, we can now look at the specifics of the Olivet Discourse. Jesus begins in **13:5-13** by warning his disciples about the coming Jewish War that will lead to the Temple's destruction: *false messiahs, wars, rumors of wars, earthquakes,* and *famines*. He tells them that in the lead up to the war that they would suffer at the hands of both Jewish and Gentile leaders. Still, he says that "the end won't happen yet" and that it would just be the beginning of *birth pangs*. He is thus making a distinction between the prophetic meaning of the Day of the Lord *within history* (the Jewish War when God brings His wrath upon the Temple), and the apocalyptic meaning of the Ultimate Day of the Lord that signals *the turn of the ages*.

Then in **13:14-27**, Jesus first alludes to **Daniel 9:27**, **11:31**, and **12:11** and tells his disciples that when they see the **Abomination of Desolation standing where it should not**, those in Judea should escape to the hills because horrible suffering would soon come upon Jerusalem. (Mark then inserts his own remark that the reader should understand what that is about—another indication that he intended this passage to be read in light of AD 70). Jesus then uses more apocalyptic imagery to describe what would happen in those days: *"The sun and moon will no longer give light, the stars will fall from the sky, the powers in heaven will be shaken, and then the Son of Man will come on the clouds with great power and glory, and he will send out his angels to gather his chosen ones from throughout the world."*

In the original context of Daniel, the Abomination of Desolation was a reference to the events around 170-160 BC, when Antiochus Epiphanes tried to wipe out Judaism and even erected a giant idol of himself in the Holy of Holies in the Temple. That idol was an abomination that desolated the Temple. Therefore, ever since the Maccabean Revolt, the Abomination of Desolation was a phrase that denoted the desecration of the Temple. Scholars debate over what specifically Jesus could be referring to in the mid-first century:

(1) Caligula planning to put a statue of himself in the Temple

(2) Titus walking into the Holy of Holies before it burned down, or

(3) The abominations that Jewish zealots committed in the Temple courts during the Jewish War.

Whatever it was, one this is clear: Jesus was telling his disciples that when they see things have gotten so bad in Jerusalem that its destruction is inevitable, they needed to get out of there, because suffering and wrath is coming.

The *cosmic upheaval apocalyptic language* further emphasizes God's bringing His judgment against the oppressors. This time, though, shockingly the oppressor is Jerusalem. The *Son of Man coming on the clouds* is an allusion to **Daniel 7**, where a Messianic figure *ascends to heaven* to be invested with the glory and power of God. Simply put, it is about how he, along with the people of God he represents, will be vindicated when the oppressors of God's people are judged. Put all that together and we get this: **Jesus is telling his disciples that Jerusalem is going to be destroyed because Jerusalem's leaders will reject and kill Jesus, will continue to persecute Jesus' followers, and will embrace the way of zealotry and revolution against Rome. They will show themselves to be the oppressors of God's people, and Jesus and his followers will be vindicated as the true people of God. Still, even though the destruction of Jerusalem is to be seen as the Day of the Lord within history, the ultimate end—that ultimate Day of the Lord—is still yet to come.**

In **13:28-37**, Jesus charges his disciples to stay awake and watch for when these things start to happen, because it would happen within a generation. When it actually happened, Mark did what so many disciples of the Old Testament prophets had done. He collected the teachings and accounts of Jesus' life that had been shared for 40 years and put them in his Gospel to serve as a testimony that Jesus was a true prophet and the true Messiah. When seen in this light, a major part of the message of Mark's Gospel is just this: **It is happening! What Jesus prophesied about has come to pass! This destruction of Jerusalem and the Temple has happened because the Jewish people have rejected Jesus as their Messiah and they've been persecuting his followers for the past 40 years.**

### 7. From the Arrest to the Resurrection (14:1-16:20)

The final section in Mark focuses on what happened to Jesus during the end of the Passion Week, from the time of Jesus' anointing at Bethany and the Last Supper up through his arrest, crucifixion, burial, and resurrection.

The **first episode (14:1-11)** takes place on Wednesday, two days before Passover. The chief priests and scribes are looking for a way to kill Jesus, but they are afraid if they arrest him in public that it might start a riot among the common people. Jesus, though, is not currently in Jerusalem. He is in Bethany, in the house of **Simon the leper**. When a woman comes in and pours out an entire jar of perfume on Jesus' head, the disciples argue that the perfume could have been sold and the money given to the poor. Jesus, though, defends the woman and says that she has **anointed his body for burial**.

The thing to note is that the word **Messiah** means "anointed one." While most Jews were hoping for a Messiah who would be anointed *to conquer and rule through force*, Jesus is pointing out he is a different kind of Messiah. He hasn't come to be anointed to rule a political kingdom. He has come to be *anointed for burial*. It is as this point that Judas Iscariot goes to the chief priests to hand Jesus over. We can only assume that when Judas finally realized that Jesus wasn't going to be the kind of Messiah he was hoping for, it was then that he decided to betray him.

The **second episode (14:12-31)** takes place on Thursday night, the night before the Jews actually celebrated Passover. It seems, therefore, that Mark is using a bit of artistic license. He identifies the Last Supper with the actual Passover meal and goes out of his way to mention it was the day the Passover Lamb was sacrificed, so he could portray Jesus as the Passover Lamb. Indeed, the entire Last Supper is replete with **Exodus** and **Passover** symbolism in order to emphasize the significance of Jesus' upcoming death. His sacrificial death will bring about the **New Exodus**, not from Egypt, but from the Old Age. Not only is Jesus a different kind of Messiah, but he is also a **new Passover Lamb**. He gives a new meaning to the Passover meal by reinterpreting the bread and wine as his own body and blood of the new covenant. From that point on, when his followers celebrate Passover, they are to celebrate *his sacrifice* that brings about the New Exodus and establishes the New Covenant and the Kingdom of God.

Jesus also tells his disciples he knows one of them is planning to betray him to the chief priests. After quoting **Zechariah 13:7**: (*"I will strike down the shepherd and the sheep will be scattered"*) he tells them that all of them are going to desert him, but after his is raised up, they are to meet him in Galilee. When Peter insists that he would never abandon him, Jesus tells him that not only will he abandon him, but that before that very night is through, Peter would deny three times that he even knew him.

The **third episode (14:32-52)** tells of Jesus' arrest in the garden of Gethsemane, just outside of the walls of Jerusalem, on the other side of the Kidron Valley. Once there, he takes Peter, James, and John, and tells them to stay awake and keep watch while he goes off to pray alone. The command to **keep watch** echoes what Jesus told his disciples at the end of the Olivet Discourse in 13:33-37. Not surprisingly, they fail to stay awake and keep watch while Jesus goes off three times by himself to pray and to ask Father that this "cup" be taken away from him. Each time Jesus comes back from praying, he finds his disciples sleeping.

After the third time, Jesus says, "The hour has come! The Son of Man is being handed over into the hands of *sinners*!" Remember, the Pharisees called Jews who didn't keep the Torah and their oral tradition "sinners." Here, Jesus is using the term to describe the Jewish religious leaders of the Sanhedrin, for we are told that

Judas comes, not with Roman soldiers, but with the Temple guard, sent by the Sanhedrin. They are the ones who arrest Jesus, not Rome.

After Judas identifies Jesus with a kiss, someone draws a sword and cuts off the ear of the slave of the high priest. Jesus stops this person and then asks the Temple guard why they were arresting him in the middle of the night, as if he were **some kind of revolutionary**. We already know the answer. The chief priests didn't want to arrest him during the day because they were afraid of the crowds. They wanted to get him out of the way before anyone really knew what was happening. After Jesus gives himself up, all the disciples desert him and flee. The episode ends, though, with a very curious comment about a **young man** who was wearing a linen garment who initially followed Jesus. When the guard tried to seize him, though, somehow his linen garment came off and he fled, naked. This seems an odd thing to mention. The answer will be made clear before Mark's Gospel is done.

In the **fourth episode (14:53-72)**, the scene that night shifts from Gethsemane to the illegitimate night trial in the Sanhedrin that had been arranged as a way to get rid of Jesus in the middle of the night, before the larger populace had any idea what had happened. Their goal was to get Jesus condemned and up on the cross by the break of day, so that by the time people woke up and found out what had happened, everything would already be taken care of. The account of the trial is bracketed by what was happening with Peter who had followed Jesus and was hanging out in the courtyard. The trial itself consisted of false accusations against Jesus that would justify condemning him to death. The problem was that the testimonies of the people they brought forth to accuse Jesus were contradictory.

Still, it was clear their main problem with Jesus was that he spoke against the Temple, which he clearly did. In addition, it is worth noting that he was accused of saying he would demolish the Temple that was *made by human hands* and that after three days he'd build a new Temple that was *not made by human hands*. Throughout the Old Testament, idols were described as "being made by human hands." By contrast, something that is made "not by human hands" is a reference to a work of God. So, when Jesus says this, not only is claiming equality with the Father, but he is also saying the Temple had effectively become an idol, for it was "made by human hands." The Temple that Jesus would build, as it made clear throughout the rest of the New Testament, is the Church, the reconstituted Israel centered around Jesus as the Messiah, the body of Christ.

When the high priest eventually asks Jesus, "Are you the Messiah, the Son of the Blessed One?" Jesus' answer guarantees his condemnation. Not only does he answer with a definitive "yes," but he then quotes **Daniel 7:13** and says the high priest would **"see the Son of Man sitting at the Right Hand of the Power [God] and coming on the clouds of Heaven."** Given the context of both Daniel 7 and Jesus standing before the high priest, not only is Jesus affirming that he is the Messiah, but he is saying the high priest is the equivalent of Antiochus Epiphanes. That is what sealed Jesus' fate. As soon as he said that the Sanhedrin accused him of blasphemy and condemned him to death. Back in the courtyard, three different times people recognize Peter as a disciple of Jesus, and just as Jesus told Peter earlier that night, Peter denied him all three times.

In the **fifth episode (15:1-20)** the scene shifts to the trial before Pilate, the Roman governor the next morning, when the Sanhedrin attempts to frame Jesus and get him executed as quickly as possible, before the rest of the city finds out. The big thing to note is how the chief priests completely change their accusations against Jesus. During the night trial, they accused Jesus of **speaking against the Temple** and **claiming to be the Messiah**. Since Pilate would not have cared about such religious squabbles, they change their accusation before Pilate and say that Jesus had claimed to be the **King of the Jews**, a political accusation that Pilate couldn't ignore. Anyone who claimed to be a king was a threat to Caesar who must be killed.

Pilate, though, sees the charges brought against Jesus were trumped up, so he makes an offer to the crowd from the Sanhedrin. He was willing to release to them either Barabbas, a revolutionary, or Jesus, whom Pilate (probably mockingly) calls the *King of the Jews*. The fact they choose a revolutionary over the King of the Jews is an illustration as to why Jerusalem and the Temple were eventually destroyed. Jesus has just condemned the Temple as a hideout for revolutionaries a few days earlier, and here the Temple authorities were, choosing a revolutionary and rejecting Jesus as the Messiah.

Even though Pilate sees that the charges against Jesus were false, he capitulates to their demands and has Jesus crucified anyway. We can only speculate, but Pilate probably saw Jesus as just a worthless Jewish peasant anyway. The Roman soldiers do what they usually did with anyone who was being crucified on the charge of claiming to be a king, and thus a threat to Caesar. They go out of their way to mock and degrade the person. Jesus is **flogged**, dressed in a **purple robe**, made to wear

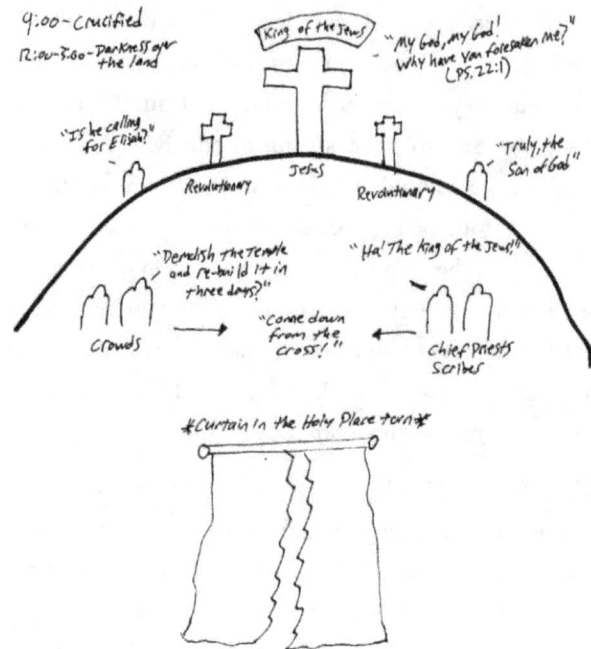

**a crown of thorns**, and then is hailed by the Roman soldiers as the **King of the Jews**. After that degrading scene, he is then taken to be crucified.

The **sixth episode (15:21-47)** involves Jesus' crucifixion, death, and burial. His cross is carried by **Simon of Cyrene** up to a hill just outside Jerusalem called **Golgotha**. The reason why the Romans crucified people just outside the city walls was to send a message to the people that if anyone crossed the Romans, the Romans would nail them up on a cross. This is also why they wrote **King of the Jews** above Jesus on his cross. It was the official charge for which he was being crucified. Jesus was crucified at 9 am in the morning, a mere three hours from the time the chief priests had taken him before Pilate. The Sanhedrin's plan worked. They got Jesus condemned and crucified before most of the people of Jerusalem had gotten their day started.

Jesus was crucified with two other **revolutionaries**. Despite all of his warning against going the way of revolution, the Sanhedrin had successfully gotten Jesus crucified as a revolutionary. He was crucified for being the kind of revolutionary Messiah that the Jews longed for, yet he refused to be. Not surprisingly, the people there (presumably from the Sanhedrin) mock Jesus for claiming to destroy and rebuild the Temple in three days, while the chief priests and scribes mock him for claiming to be the Messiah. The issues of **Temple** and **Messiah** have dominated Mark's narrative ever since Jesus rode into Jerusalem.

Mark says that **darkness came over the land** from about noon to 3 pm. He doesn't explain this, and he doesn't claim there was an eclipse. Whatever natural occurrence might have happened, we shouldn't miss the significance of the imagery of the darkness of evil and the coming death of Jesus. At 3 pm, Jesus cries out from the cross and quotes **Psalm 22:1**: *"My God, my God, why have you forsaken me?"* To understand what is going on, one must look back and look at the original context of Psalm 22. In this case, although Psalm 22 *begins* with the psalmist wondering why it seems God has forsaken him, *by the end of the psalm*, we find out that God hasn't forsaken him. In fact, the psalmist is now declaring the glory of God among His people. The psalm *begins* in despair but *ends* in vindication. Given that, Jesus' cry can be seen in a whole new light. In the midst of his suffering, he is declaring that God will vindicate him. He's essentially saying, "You all think that God has forsaken me, but I know how the psalm ends! Check back in three days!"

After Jesus is given a drink of bitter wine, he cries out and dies. At that moment, the **curtain in the Holy Place** was ripped in two, from top to bottom. The tearing of the curtain symbolizes that, because of Jesus' sacrificial death, God has done away with the barrier between Himself and humanity and has opened the way to reconciliation. It is also interesting to note that after Jesus dies, the first person in Mark's Gospel to declare that Jesus was the "Son of God" is a **Roman centurion**. Being a pagan, he probably was saying that Jesus proved himself to be the "son of a god." But even that declaration spoke more truth than even he realized, for one of Caesar's titles was that of being the "son of a god." Thus, Mark highlights the centurion's comment to show that Jesus, not Caesar, is the true Son of God.

The man who asks Pilate for Jesus' body in order to bury it was **Joseph of Arimathea**, a member of the Sanhedrin. Clearly, not everyone in the Sanhedrin had agreed with what the high priest had orchestrated the night before. Joseph and the women wrap up the corpse, put it in a tomb, and have the stone rolled in front of it. It is interesting to note that whereas Jesus' parents were Joseph and Mary, among the people who were there to bury him was another Joseph, and Mary of Magdala and Mary of Joses.

The **seventh episode (16:1-20)** tells of the resurrection of Jesus. The earliest manuscripts we have of Mark end with Mark 16:8, with the women fleeing from the tomb in fear. That doesn't mean that Mark's Gospel actually ended without any actual resurrection appearances. It just means that the earliest copy of Mark that we have cuts off abruptly and doesn't have the ending that the other copies do. The longer ending is that of 16:9-20, which contains a brief account of Jesus' resurrection appearances that are reported in Matthew and Luke.

In Mark 16:1-8, the women go to the tomb to anoint Jesus and prepare the body for burial because they did not have time to do it on Friday evening. When they get to the tomb, they see the stone had been rolled away and a **young man clothed in a white garment** sitting there. It is clearly an angelic figure, but Mark describes this angelic figure as a "young man" in order to draw a literary connection between the angel at the tomb and the young men who fled naked in Gethsemane. Just as Jesus' ordeal began with his arrest and a young man fleeing naked, now Jesus' triumph over death at his resurrection is declared by a "young man clothed in white" who tells the women not to fear because Jesus had been raised. After inviting them to check out the tomb for themselves, he tells them to go tell Peter and the rest of the disciples that Jesus is going to meet them in Galilee. The women, though, just flee and don't tell anyone initially.

Mark 16:9-20 contains a shorter version of the resurrection accounts in Matthew and Luke: Mary goes to the others, but they don't believe her. Jesus appears to two of his followers in the country, they go back to tell the rest, but the rest still don't believe it. Jesus finally appears to all of them together and chews them out for not believing the initial resurrection claims. He sends them out to the world to proclaim the Gospel and gives them the power and authority to heal the sick and cast out demons. He is then taken up into Heaven to sit at the right hand of God, and they go out to proclaim the Gospel.

# THE GOSPEL OF MATTHEW

**Time of Writing**: Although the events of the life and ministry of Jesus took place roughly between AD 28-30, the Gospel of Matthew was probably written shortly after the Gospel of Mark. Most scholars think it was written sometime during the 70s-80s, after the Jewish War, probably in either Palestine or Syria.

**Authorship**: Although nothing in the gospel itself claims Matthew was the author, the early Church Father Papias, the early 2nd century bishop of Hierapolis, tells us that Matthew wrote the gospel in the "Hebrew dialect" or "Hebrew style."

## The Big Things to Know in Matthew
In addition to sharing the same "big things" as in Mark, Matthew has a few unique points of emphasis:

**Fulfillment of Old Testament Prophecy**: One of the distinct things in Matthew is his constant quoting of Old Testament passages and his proclamation that Jesus "fulfilled" these prophecies. It is important to realize, though, that when Matthew says "fulfilled," he doesn't mean it in a simplistic sense that "That prophet back then made a *prediction* about Jesus, and the Jews held on to it for *700 years or so*, and then Jesus came, and that prediction came to pass." Rather, Matthew is pointing to specific events in the Old Testament story and is then saying that God's actions and salvation that were partly seen in those Old Testament events had now found their culmination (and "fulfillment") in Christ. If I can put it this way, Matthew is pointing to those past Old Testament events and says, "Jesus is like that, *but bigger!*"

> **A. Jesus, Not Herod**: Matthew takes the time, both in his infancy narrative as well as in other places, to emphasize that Jesus, not Herod, is the true King of the Jews. Herod is simply a pretender. Jesus is the long-awaited Davidic Messiah.
>
> **B. Jesus as the New Moses**: One of the main images of Jesus that Matthew emphasizes is that of a teacher, namely, as a new Moses who brings to completion the entire Old Testament story. Matthew shows this in five distinct and unique teaching sections. The very first one, the Sermon on the Mount (Matthew 5-7) purposely portrays Jesus as "Moses 2.0," who goes up a mountain, teaches about the Torah based on his own authority. As "Moses 2.0," Jesus is reconstituting the People of God, no longer constituted around the Torah, but rather around his own authority and status as the Messiah. The other teaching passages in Matthew are found in Chapters 10, 13, 18 and 24-25.

## The Gospel of Matthew: Story Chart

|  | | | | | |
|---|---|---|---|---|---|
| **Infancy Narrative (1:1-2:23)** | 1:1-17 The Genealogy of Jesus | 1:18-25 Joseph's Dream | 2:1-12 The Magi Visits Jesus | 2:13-23 Herod's Slaughter of the Innocents | |
| **Early Ministry (1) (3:1-4:25)** | 3:1-17 John Baptizes Jesus Mk 1:1-11 | 4:1-11 40 Days in the Wilderness Mk 1:12-13 | 4:12-17 Jesus Begins Ministry Mk 1:14-15 | 4:18-22 Calling First Disciples Mk 1:16-20 | 4:23-25 Healings Casting Out Demons Mk 1:35-39 |
| **Sermon on the Mount (5:1-7:29)** | 5:1-16 True Israel | 5:17-48 True Torah | 6:1-18 True Righteousness | 6:19-34 True Treasure | 7:1-14 True Searching | 7:15-28 True vs. False People of God |
| **Early Ministry (2) (8:1-9:34)** | 8:1-4 Leper Cleansed Mk 1:40-45 | 8:5-13 Healing the Centurion's Servant | 8:14-17 Healing Peter's Mother-in-Law Mk 1:29-34 | 8:18-22 Scribe and Disciple Turn Back | |
| | 8:23-27 Jesus Calms the Sea Mk 4:35-41 | 8:28-9:1 Demoniacs of the Gadarenes Mk 5:1-20 | 9:2-8 Healing the Paralytic Mk 2:1-12 | 9:9-13 The Calling of Matthew Mk 2:13-17 | |
| | 9:14-17 Question about Fasting Mk 2:18-22 | 9:18-26 Daughter and Bleeding Woman Mk 5:21-43 | 9:27-31 Two Blind Men Healed | 9:32-34 Healing Mute The Pharisees' Accusation | |
| **Growing Tensions (9:35-12:21)** | 9:35-10:42 Jesus Chooses/Sends out the Twelve Mk 3:13-19/Mk 6:7-13* | 11:1-19 John the Baptist's Question | 11:20-30 Jesus Condemns Cities My Yoke is Easy | | |
| | 12:1-8 Grain Fields on the Sabbath Mk 2:23-28 | 12:9-14 Synagogue: Withered Hand Mk 3:1-6 | 12:15-21 My Servant the Beloved One Isaiah 42 | | |

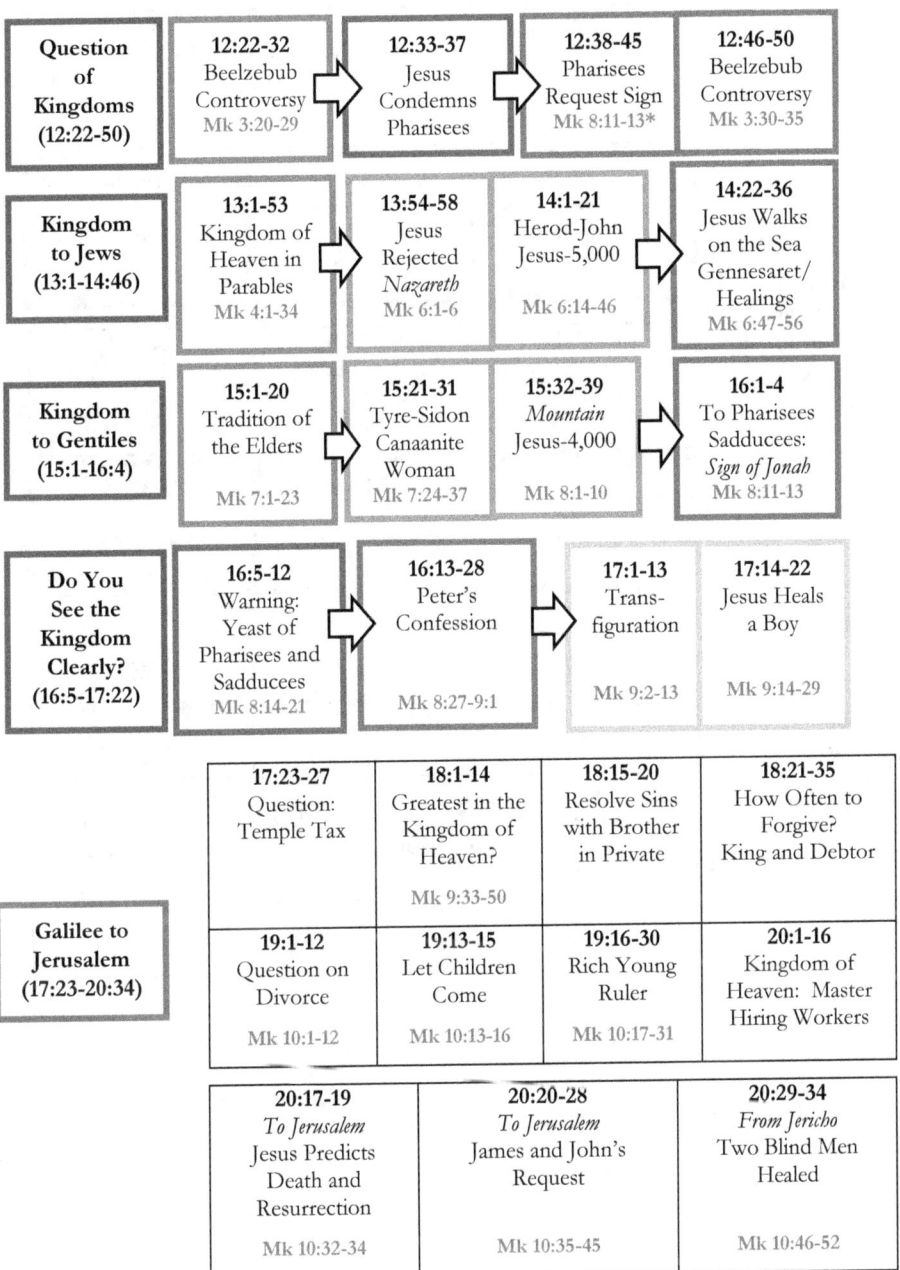

| | | | |
|---|---|---|---|
| **Conflict in the Temple (21:1-25:46)** | 21:1-11 Un-Triumphal Entry  Mk 11:1-11 | 21:12-22 Temple Condemned Fig Tree  Mk 11:12-26 | 21:23-27 Chief Priests Questions Authority  Mk 11:27-33 |
| | 21:28-32 *Parable* A Man and His Two Sons | 21:33-46 *Parable* The Vineyard | 22:1-14 *Parable* Wedding Banquet  Mk 12:1-12 |
| | 22:15-46 Round of Questions  Mk 12:13-40 | 23:1-39 Jesus vs Leaders Lament over Jerusalem | 24:1-51 Olivet Discourse  Mk 13:1-37 |
| | 25:1-13 *Parable* Ten Virgins | 25:14-30 *Parable* Servants and Talents | 25:31-46 *Parable* Sheep and the Goats |
| **Last Supper to Resurrection (26:1-28:20)** | 26:1-16 Anointed at Bethany  Mk 14:1-11 | 26:17-35 Last Supper  Mk 14:12-31 | 26:36-56 Arrest-Gethsemane  Mk 14:32-52 |

| | | | |
|---|---|---|---|
| 26:57-75 Before the Sanhedrin  Mk 14:53-72 | 27:1-31 Before Pilate  Mk 15:1-20 | 27:32-66 Crucifixion Death Burial  Mk 15:21-47 | 28:1-20 Resurrection  Mk 16:1-20 |

## A Walkthrough of Matthew

The Gospel of Matthew essentially is Mark 2.0—the revised and expanded version. It keeps Mark's overall literary structure but re-arranges and expands a few episodes and adds a few unique episodes. That being said, Matthew still has a flavor all its own. Matthew quotes much more directly from the Old Testament and emphasizes the fulfillment of prophecy a whole lot more than Mark. Also, Matthew includes more teaching material than Mark. That is why the Gospel of Matthew is traditionally depicted with *a man with a teaching staff*. Matthew also includes an infancy narrative about Jesus that Mark does not include. Perhaps a more minor point is that instead of the term *Kingdom of God*, Matthew uses the term *Kingdom of Heaven*.

### 1. The Infancy Narrative (Chapters 1-2)

A common feature in many ancient historical biographies is that of a short infancy narrative at the beginning of the biography to serve as an introduction to the person of whom the biography is about and to lay out certain major themes the author is going to focus on in the course of the biography. Both Matthew and Luke also use this convention in their works. Matthew's infancy narrative, therefore, lays out some of the basic theological themes about Jesus that he will emphasize in the course of his Gospel.

The **first episode (1:1-17)** is Matthew's genealogy of Jesus, traced through the kings of Israel, back through David, and all the way back to Abraham. Matthew's point is that Jesus is the Messiah, the King of Israel. Matthew points out there were fourteen generations from Abraham to David, from David to the Babylonian Exile, and from the Exile to the birth of Jesus, totaling six "sevens" from the time of Abraham to Jesus—a subtle allusion to the six days of the creation story. Just as on the seventh day, God "rests" as king and begins to rule, Matthew is saying is that with the coming of Jesus, God's reign/rest has begun.

Most interesting, though, is the fact that, in addition to Mary, Matthew mentions only four women in Jesus' genealogy: **Tamar**, **Rahab**, **Ruth**, and **the wife of Uriah the Hittite** (**Bathsheba**). There are two reasons for this. First, the fact that Mary had got pregnant out of wedlock was obviously a scandal. Matthew, though, makes sure to show that God has a history of using women who had engaged in questionable sexual behavior in order to bring about His purposes. Tamar had dressed up like a prostitute and had sex with her father-in-law Judah; Rahab was a prostitute in Jericho; Ruth had "uncovered the feet" (often a euphemism for exposing one's private parts) of Boaz as he was sleeping in order to get him to agree to marry her; and Bathsheba had committed adultery with David. Still, all these women were still nevertheless held in high honor in Judaism.

Second, all four women were Gentiles: Tamar was a Canaanite, Rahab was a Canaanite, Ruth was a Moabite, and Bathsheba was connected to the Hittites. Matthew's point is that Gentiles are found within the genealogy of the Messiah, and that they will be included in God's Kingdom that Jesus is establishing.

The **second episode (1:18-25)** is that of the angel's birth announcement to Joseph to reassure him to not divorce Mary, but to instead go through with the marriage because Mary had conceived by the power of the Holy Spirit. He tells Joseph to name the child **Jesus**, because the name means "salvation." It is at this point that Matthew gives us his first of many **fulfillment passages**, when he says that the birth of Jesus fulfilled was what spoken through the prophet **Isaiah 7:14**: *"Look! The young maiden (virgin) will conceive and give birth to a son, and they will call his name, 'Emmanuel.'"* He then notes that "Emmanuel" means "God is with us."

Before we go any further in Matthew, we need to clarify just what Matthew is doing with his many fulfillment passages, when he quotes from the Old Testament. In short, he was not saying these verses were **predictions** that the Old Testament prophets had said and that the Jews had held on to for 500-700 years or so. When Matthew is claiming an Old Testament passage was "fulfilled," he wants his readers to go back to the original context of that passage, understand what it meant in the original context, and then interpret the particular event in the life of Jesus in light of that passage, for Matthew is using that passage to emphasize just who Jesus was.

In the case of **Isaiah 7:14**, that verse is part of the larger section of **Isaiah 7-12**, where Isaiah confronts King Ahaz about his unfaithfulness to YHWH during the **Syro-Ephraimite Crisis**, when the kingdoms of Israel and Syria were threatening the kingdom of Judah around 745 BC. Instead of heeding Isaiah's advice to put his faith in YHWH, Ahaz chose to call on the help of Assyria, the major superpower in the region. In response, Isaiah tells Ahaz that his unfaithfulness would lead to Judah being oppressed by Assyria, but that his son Hezekiah would be faithful, and because of his faithfulness, *God would be with us* and would save Judah from Assyrian oppression. Therefore, given the fact that in the original context, Isaiah 7:14 is about the birth of Hezekiah, we can see that Matthew is saying that *Jesus was like Hezekiah, but bigger.* Hezekiah was a king through whom God worked to achieve salvation from Assyria, whereas Jesus is the Messiah-King through whom God will work through to achieve salvation from sin and death.

One final thing that needs to be addressed is the virginity of the woman in Isaiah 7:14. In its original context, the Hebrew word **almah** does, in fact, mean nothing more than "young woman" not necessarily "virgin." The *almah* of Isaiah 7:14 was understood to have gotten pregnant just like any other woman, through sex. There is another Hebrew word, **betulah**, that specifies a virgin, and that is not used in Isaiah 7:14. When the Hebrew Bible was translated into the Greek Septuagint, *almah* was translated with the Greek word **parthenos**, which could mean just "young woman," or also "virgin." Since Matthew was quoting from the Septuagint, this gave him a perfect opportunity to use Isaiah 7:14 for two purposes: (1) To emphasize Jesus' Messiahship (*like Hezekiah, but bigger*), and (2) To argue that Mary, although she may have been thought to have conceived out of wedlock, was nevertheless a virgin.

| OT Quotations in Matthew's Infancy Narrative ||
|---|---|
| **Matthew's Quote** | **OT Allusion** |
| (1:23): The virgin will give birth to a son, Emmanuel | **Isaiah 7:14**: During Syro-Ephraimite Crisis—prophesied birth of Hezekiah |
| (2:5): A prince to come out of Bethlehem | **Micah 5:2**: A prophecy of a future Davidic king |
| (2:14): Out of Egypt, I called my son | **Hosea 11:1**: Looked back at the Exodus, and the failure of Israel to be faithful to YHWH |
| (2:18): Rachel weeping for her children—they are no more | **Jeremiah 31:15**: Looks back at Rachel to describe the grief of women who lost their sons during the exile |
| (2:23): He will be called a Nazarene | **Isaiah 11:1 (?)**: A wordplay on the Hebrew word *nezer* (branch) |

The **third episode (2:1-12)** tells about the visit of the magi to Bethlehem during the reign of King Herod. They were astrologers from "the east" (perhaps Babylon) who came to pay homage to whom they thought was a newborn king of the Jews—that is why they went to Jerusalem first, where King Herod was. We should not interpret this as if **kings from the east** came to **worship** a king of the Jews as if he were God-in-the-flesh. We also should not think they literally followed a moving star that came to stop over a manger scene in Bethlehem. It is more likely they had seen the specific star sign considered to be the star sign of the king of Israel, a conjunction of Jupiter and Venus within the constellation of Pisces. This specific star sign was seen three different times in 7 BC, and many consider that this was probably the "star" that the magi had seen.

As a side note, since Herod died in 4 BC, scholars generally date the birth of Jesus somewhere between 7-4 BC. It might sound odd to say that Jesus was born *before Christ,* but this is because the medieval monk who established the Christian calendar miscalculated and was off by about six years. In any case, once the magi get to Jerusalem and inquire about a newborn king of the Jews, Herod consults with the Jewish scribes. They refer him to **Micah 5:2**, which says the Messiah was to be born in Bethlehem, the hometown of King David. Herod sends the magi off, tells them to report back to him, but when they arrive in Bethlehem and find Jesus, they are warned in a dream not to go back to Jerusalem. So, they return home by another route.

From the perspective of the magi, they went pay homage to an earthly Jewish king. But when seen against the backdrop of the Old Testament story, Matthew is making an allusion to a theme found throughout the Old Testament prophets and psalms, that Gentile kings would come to bow down before the king of Israel and to worship YHWH, the God of Israel (**Psalm 72:10-15**). Thus, here at the opening of his Gospel, Matthew gives us an instance of where Gentiles are coming to bow down to Jesus the Messiah, and in doing so, are worshipping the God of Israel.

The **fourth and final episode (2:13-23)** of Matthew's infancy narrative is that of Herod's killing of the baby boys in Bethlehem. Joseph flees with Mary and Jesus into Egypt after an angel warns them in a dream that Herod was going to try to kill the child. They stay in Egypt until Herod dies. When they return, Matthew quotes **Hosea 11:1**: *"Out of Egypt I have called My Son."* In its original context, **Hosea 11:1-11** looks back to the Exodus, when YHWH brought Israel (His "son") out of Egypt, and then condemns Israel for turning its back on YHWH by going after idols, and thus failing to be the light to the Gentiles that He wanted them to be. By saying that Hosea 11:1 was fulfilled in Jesus, Matthew is saying that Jesus succeeds as God's Son where Israel failed as God's "son."

After Herod orders the baby boys two years old and younger in Bethlehem be killed (something that was entirely in his character to do), Matthew quotes **Jeremiah 31:15**: *"A voice is heard in Ramah, full of weeping and mourning! Rachel is weeping for her babies, and she doesn't want to be comforted, because they are no more!"* In its original context, Jeremiah is lamenting the upcoming Babylonian exile and alluding to the death of Rachel from **Genesis 35**, when she is comforted by being told that she had given birth to Benjamin, even though she herself was dying. That happened near Ramah, on the road to Bethlehem. In Jeremiah's day, though, it was from Ramah that the Babylonians were deporting the Jewish captives into exile. Jeremiah flips the scene of Rachel's death on its head by using Rachel as a symbol for the mothers of Judah during Nebuchadnezzar's deportation who wept for the loss of their children who were taken into exile.

Nevertheless, in the very next verse, **Jeremiah 31:16**, YHWH gives a word of comfort by assuring "Rachel" that her children will one day return from exile. Matthew is thus equating the **reign of Herod** with that of the **Babylonian Exile**. Just as with Babylon, Herod's actions send Jesus into sort of exile into Egypt. Still, Jeremiah 31:16 promises there will be a return from exile, and that is precisely what happens in Matthew 2:19-23, when Joseph returns to the land of Israel and settles in Nazareth of Galilee.

Matthew ends his infancy narrative with a fifth fulfillment passage, only this time, it isn't a quotation. Matthew simply says their settling in Nazareth fulfilled what was spoken by the prophets: *"He will be called a Nazarene."* The only problem is that there is no verse in the Old Testament that says that. It is likely that Matthew is engaging in a bit of a word play with the word **Nazareth** and what is said in **Isaiah 11:1**: *"There will come forth a shoot from the stump of Jesse, and a branch from his roots will bear fruit."* The Hebrew word that is translated as "branch" is **nezer**. Thus, Matthew begins and ends his infancy narrative with references to the messianic prophecies of Isaiah 7-12. In their original context, they were about King Hezekiah being faithful to YHWH and YHWH saving the people of Israel from Assyrian oppression. Matthew, though, presents Jesus as a **new Hezekiah**, in that he is the ultimate King of Israel who succeeds where Israel fails and whose faithfulness will bring about salvation from the oppression of sin and death itself.

## 2. The Beginning of Jesus' Ministry (Chapters 3-4)

Matthew proceeds to follow the sequence of events in **Mark 1:1-39** over the course of his next two chapters, while expanding upon what Mark laid out in his Gospel. The **first episode (3:1-17)** covers John the Baptist and the baptism of Jesus. Matthew associates John with the *voice crying out in the wilderness* of **Isaiah 40:3**, evoking the idea of a **New Exodus** and the **final end of the Exile**. He also associates John the Baptist with the Elijah-figure of **Malachi 4:5**, who would come before the **Day of YHWH** to cleanse God's people before His judgment falls upon the land.

John preaches a message of repentance, declares the Kingdom of Heaven is near, but envisions it as being a time of judgment and wrath directed against the Jewish religious leaders, whom he calls **offspring of serpents**. Ever since **Genesis 3:15**, as seen in those early genealogies of Genesis 1-11, the enemies of God's people were seen as *the offspring of serpents* who would eventually get crushed by the *offspring of the woman*. That is what is shocking about his declaration of the coming Day of YHWH: John redefines who the people of God are when he tells the Jews that being mere descendants of Abraham is worthless if they don't produce fruit worthy of repentance. If they don't repent, they will be counted as the offspring of the serpent and will suffering God's wrath. That is why John speaks of the axe being at the root of the trees, and every tree that doesn't produce fruit being thrown into the **fire of God's wrath**. Thus, John's vision of the coming Messiah is one who will baptize in the **Holy Spirit and in fire** and who will clean out the threshing floor. John clearly expects the coming one to usher in the Day of YHWH and separate repentant Jews from unrepentant Jews.

When Jesus shows up to be baptized, John doesn't feel worthy to baptize Jesus. Jesus, though, insists it is necessary to "fulfill all righteousness," meaning that since Jesus is the Messiah who represents Israel as the people of God, his baptism is a baptism on behalf of Israel. When Jesus comes out of the water, the Spirit of God comes down like a dove and a voice from heaven says, *"This is my Son, the Beloved One! I have approved of him!"* This is a combination of **Psalm 2:7** and **Isaiah 42:1-4**. Not only do we find the clear declaration of Jesus being the Messiah and God's Son in Psalm 2:7, but we also have allusions to the **Exodus** (Israel coming through the Red Sea) as well as **creation** (God's Spirit, in the form of a dove, being over the waters). The point is clear: **Jesus is the Messiah who will bring God's people through a New Exodus and who will bring about the New Creation.**

The **second episode (4:1-11)** is that of Jesus' three temptations in the wilderness. Again, the episode has clear allusions to the wilderness wanderings in Exodus. Satan tempts Jesus in three ways: (1) He tempts Jesus to turn stones into bread, (2) He tempts Jesus to throw himself off the Temple and have the angels catch him, and (3) He tempts Jesus to bow down and pay homage to him in order to receive all the kingdoms of the world. With each temptation, Satan tries to get Jesus to essentially become a self-serving Messiah who is willing to "sell his soul," so to speak, in order to satisfy his own desires, impress people with his own greatness, and to eventually gain political power, just like any other power-hungry political leader.

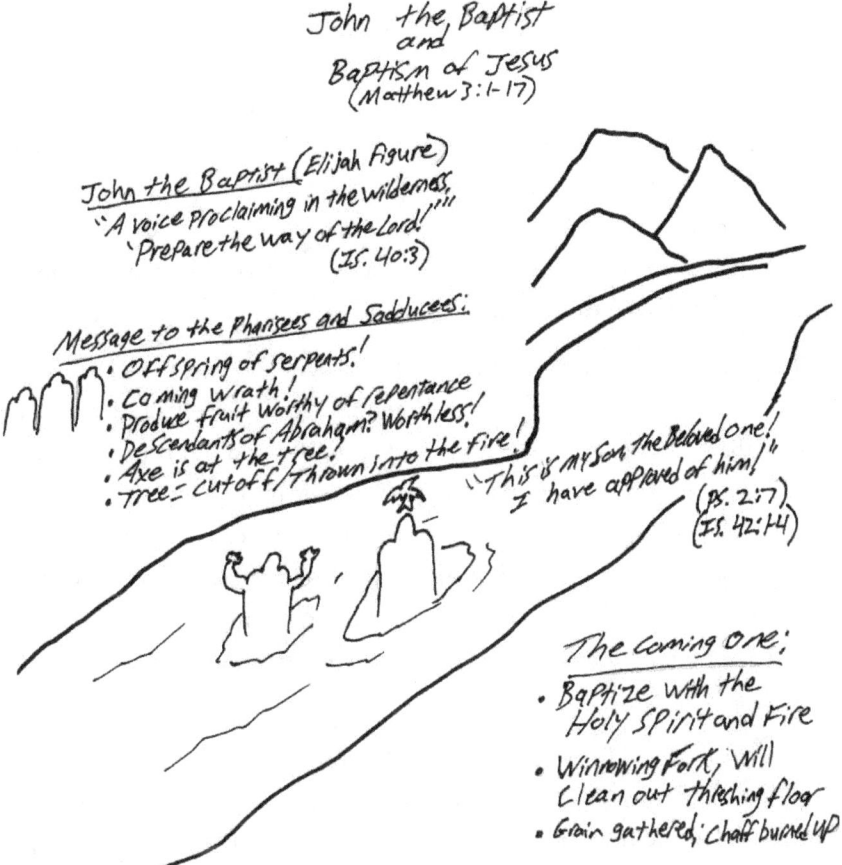

Jesus, responds each time by quoting from Deuteronomy: (1) **Deuteronomy 8:3** recalls the time the Hebrews complained about not having enough to eat and were then fed with manna in the wilderness. (2) **Deuteronomy 6:16** recalls the time when the Hebrews complained about not having enough water and were then given water from the rock. (3) **Deuteronomy 6:13** recalls the time when the Hebrews worshipped the golden calf at Mount Sinai. What this shows is that Jesus, as the Messiah, is tempted in three specific ways Israel was tempted in the wilderness during the Exodus, and yet **Jesus the Messiah succeeds where Israel failed; Jesus the Messiah proves himself to be faithful, where Israel had proved herself to be unfaithful.**

In the **third episode (4:12-17)**, Jesus returns to Galilee and starts to proclaim the **Kingdom of Heaven is near.** Matthew mentions it is the region of the Old

Testament tribes of Zebulun and Naphtali so that he can quote a sixth fulfillment passage, **Isaiah 9:1-2**. Once again, it is from the larger section of Isaiah 7-12, where Isaiah prophesied about the birth of Hezekiah, about how he would be faithful to YHWH, and about how YHWH would work through him to save the remnant of Judah from Assyrian oppression. The larger passage of **Isaiah 9:1-7** goes on to say that **a child is born, and a son is given**, who will sit on David's throne and establish peace and justice for God's people. Once again, *Jesus is like Hezekiah, but bigger*. He has come to save God's people, not from Assyrian oppression, but of Satanic oppression and death itself.

The **fourth episode (4:18-22)** tells of Jesus calling his first disciples, Simon, Andrew, James, and John. They are all fisherman, so when Jesus calls them, he tells them they will become "fishers of men." The **fifth and final episode (4:23-25)** acts as summary statement of the general activity of Jesus' early Galilean ministry. He goes throughout Galilee, proclaiming the Gospel of the Kingdom, healing the sick, and casting out demons. Jesus' reputation soon extends beyond the region of Galilee, so that not only are people from Judea and Jerusalem coming to see him, but also people from the Gentile regions of Syria and the Decapolis as well.

### 3. The Sermon on the Mount (Chapters 5-7)

At this point in Matthew's Gospel, Matthew dramatically diverges from Mark's Gospel, in that he inserts the large section of teaching material known as the **Sermon on the Mount**. In reality, this section is probably a collection of various things Jesus taught during his ministry in Galilee. The reason it is presented as a single sermon has to do with yet another allusion to the Exodus. Having gone through the waters and then out into the wilderness for 40 days and nights, Jesus now begins to gain followers. He then goes **up a mountain** and starts critiquing and reinterpreting **the Torah**. *Jesus is presented as a new Moses*, the prophet of **Deuteronomy 18:15-19** who comes after Moses. The content of the Sermon on the Mount is wide-ranging, but it boils down to two things: (1) What it means to be the true people of God, the true Israel; and (2) Jesus demonstrating his authority over the Torah itself.

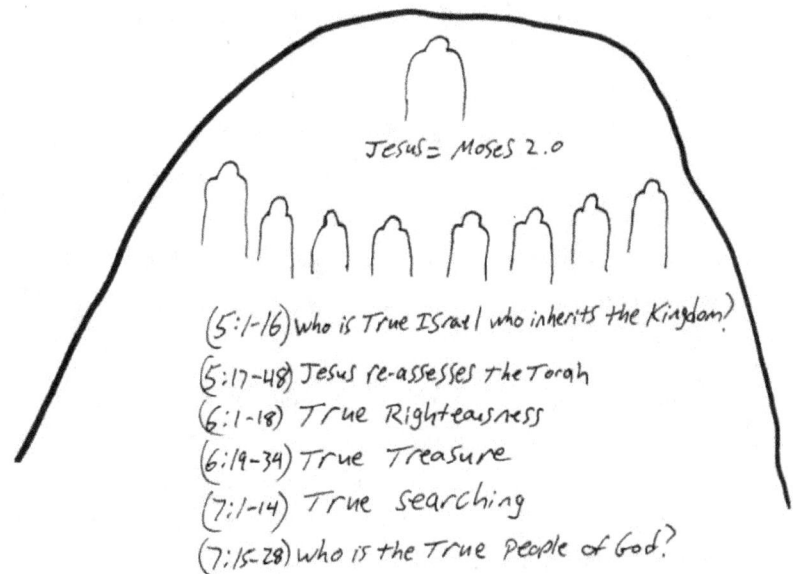

In the **first part of the Sermon on the Mount (5:1-17)**, Jesus focuses on what the true people of God—**True Israel**—looks like. In the *Beatitudes* of 5:1-12, Jesus describes the people of God as being the ones who are poor in spirit, who mourn, who are meek, who hunger and thirst for righteousness, who are merciful, who are pure in heart, who make peace, and who are willing to be persecuted for the sake of righteousness. Contrary to the growing calls for zealotry, Jesus says the way to inherit the Kingdom of Heaven isn't through armed revolution, but rather through striving for peace and righteousness, and being willing to be persecuted for it. He then continues in 5:13-16 to say that the whole purpose of God choosing Israel to be His people was so that they could be a **light to the Gentiles** and the **salt of the earth**.

We shouldn't overlook the threat of impending judgment in Jesus' words when he says if the salt loses its flavor, it's good for nothing and will be trampled upon. He's telling his fellow Jews that if they fail to be the kind of people God wants for His people, they will be trampled. This is what would later happen in AD 70, when Rome destroyed Jerusalem and the Temple.

In the **second part (5:17-48)**, Jesus, by his own authority, reinterprets the Torah in a way that gets to the heart of what the true Torah really is all about. In this sense, he says he came to fulfill the Torah. The Torah was the covenant the law code and constitution that defined Israel under the Mosaic covenant so that it could be God's light to the Gentiles. Israel failure to be faithful to the Torah, though, revealed a deeper problem that went beyond the Torah. So, when Jesus says he has come to fulfill the Torah and Prophets, he is saying that he has come to do what the Torah failed to do: *To create a people for God's Name who would actually be that light to the Gentiles.*

That means, though, that Torah observance doesn't bring true righteousness. That is why in 5:21-32 Jesus points out that even if one never commits murder or adultery, and even if one follows the Torah's rules for divorce, that doesn't mean that person is righteous. That person still hates, still lusts, and may have divorced his wife because he already has in mind the next woman he wants to marry. In 5:33-37, Jesus says a truly righteous person doesn't need to take an oath. In 5:38-42, he talks about how sometimes *pursuing justice is not always the best way to combat evil*. And in 5:43-48, Jesus says it is not enough to love your neighbor and hate your enemy, because ultimately, your enemy is your neighbor. Therefore, you should love your enemy and pray for him. That is what **true Torah observance** looks like.

In the **third part (6:1-18)**, Jesus focuses on how **true righteousness** goes beyond the legalistic self-righteousness of the scribes and Pharisees, whom he routinely calls **hypocrites**. True righteousness means *giving to the poor in secret* (6:1-4) and *praying in secret* (6:5-8), not doing them in public, like the hypocrites do, in order to call attention to yourself. Jesus then gives the example of the **Lord's Prayer** (6:9-15) as a way to emphasize what the essential aspects of prayer are: Reverence for God the Father; Praying for the coming Kingdom and for God's will to be done; Asking God to provide for us, to forgive us, and to save us from the Evil One. Jesus then says that you will only be forgiven by God if you too forgive others. Finally, Jesus addresses fasting and says that when one fasts, one shouldn't call attention to oneself, like the hypocrites do (6:16-18).

In the **fourth part (6:19-34)**, Jesus contrasts **worldly treasure** the hypocrites go after with the **true treasure of heaven** that true followers should strive for (6:19-24). Ultimately, there are only *two kinds of treasure* and only *two lords*: **God** or **Mammon**. The pursuit of earthly treasures makes one become a servant of wealth (or Mammon) and it will result in corruption. The pursuit of heavenly treasures makes one become a servant of God and it will result in the Kingdom of God. Jesus then talks about how one shouldn't worry about one's material existence, because as long as one is seeking for the Kingdom of God and pursuing true righteousness, one can be assured that God will provide what is needed.

In the **fifth part (7:1-14)**, Jesus develops that theme of seeking God's Kingdom to further emphasize what **true seeking** looks like. He first talks about how, since you will be judged according to the same standard you judge others, you should take a look at yourself and address your own faults first (7:1-6). At the same time, sometimes it isn't worth **throwing your pearls before swine**, because some people are just bad people. Even if you are right about that person's faults, confronting that person won't do any good, and it might drag you down into their filth as well.

Instead, Jesus encourages people be the kind of people who search, knock, and ask (7:7-12). Instead of going around offering advice and help to people who don't want it, just be the kind of person who asks for advice and help from others. This is what the **Golden Rule** is about. Whatever you want other people to do for you, you should do for them. Treat others the way you want to be treated. That is ultimately what the Torah and Prophets are all about. Jesus then talks about which path one should choose in life (7:13-14): **The way of the narrow gate and narrow street**, which is the way of tribulation that leads to life, or **the way of the broad street**, which, though is the easy way, leads to destruction.

In the **sixth part (7:15-28)**, Jesus comes back to his original focus on what it means to be **True Israel** (the true people of God), and proceeds to contrast it with, we can say, **false Israel**. He first warns about wolves in sheep's clothing and talks about knowing a tree by its fruit (7:15-20). In the context of the Sermon on the Mount, it seems obvious that the "wolves" are hypocritical religious leaders who portray themselves as godly, but in reality, destroy people's lives. Jesus also warns about cutting down any tree that doesn't produce fruit and throwing it into the fire, thus echoing John the Baptist's words in Matthew 3.

Related to this is what Jesus says in 7:21-23, that not everyone who says, "Lord! Lord!" will enter the Kingdom of Heaven. Interestingly, Jesus calls those who don't do the will of his Father in Heaven **workers of lawlessness**, the antithesis of the Torah. Thus, Jesus is saying that these wolves, these fruitless trees, the people who don't do God's will are actually doing **anti-Torah deeds**. The irony is that the focus of Jesus' criticisms throughout the Sermon on the Mount has been the **scribes and Pharisees**—the religious groups who supposedly revere the Torah the most are the worst offenders of breaking the Torah.

Jesus concludes with contrasting images of the **house on the rock** and the **house on the sand** (7:24-27). This too is a veiled criticism of the Jewish religious leaders, and specifically of the Temple. Jesus and his teachings are the foundation for a new Temple, and those who follow his teachings will be in the "house" that withstands the floodwaters of God's judgment that will come upon Jerusalem. By contrast, those who following the teachings of the scribes and Pharisees will perish along with the "house" that is built on the sand, the Temple itself. With that, Matthew tells us in 7:28-29 that the crowds were astounded by the **authority** with which Jesus taught. By the end of the Sermon on the Mount, two things are clear: (1) Jesus is the New Moses who has the authority to reinterpret the Torah, and (2) Jesus has set himself up in direct contrast to the religious authorities of his day, namely the scribes and Pharisees.

### 4. Jesus' Early Ministry in Galilee (Chapters 8-9)

Matthew 8-9 re-works a number of episodes from the early chapters of Mark and then adds four new episodes to flesh out a bit more of Jesus' early Galilean ministry. In the **first episode (8:1-4)**, Jesus heals a leper and then tells the man to show himself to a priest and give the proper offering that Moses had directed as a means of bearing witness.

The **second episode (8:5-13)** is unique to Matthew. While in Capernaum, a Roman centurion asks Jesus to come to heal his servant. Yet he does not feel he is worthy enough to have Jesus even come to his house, so he appeals to **Jesus' authority**. He knows Jesus has the authority to just command a healing and have it done without him ever going there. Jesus responds to this show of faith by a Gentile by telling the Jewish crowd that he hasn't seen such faith in all of Israel. He then says that **many will come from the east and west** (Gentiles) and be welcomed along Abraham, Isaac, and Jacob in the Kingdom of Heaven. Not only that, but Jesus then says that the **sons of the kingdom** (some Jews) will be thrown out of the Kingdom, into outer darkness, where there will be weeping and gnashing of teeth. Jesus then gives the word and the centurion's servant is healed that very hour.

The **third episode (8:14-17)** is of Jesus healing of Peter's mother-in-law. Matthew then speaks of Jesus' healings as being a fulfillment of **Isaiah 53:4**: *"He took our sicknesses and removed our diseases."* In its original context, the **Suffering Servant** of Isaiah 53 was understood to be the restored remnant of God's people who suffered during the Babylonian exile but then came out as the purified people of God by whom God would heal His people. Of course, the returned exiles continued to have their problems. Therefore, just as with the other fulfillment passages, Matthew is saying that Jesus is fulfilling those Messianic hopes and is doing what Israel has failed to do.

The **fourth episode (8:18-22)** is also unique to Matthew. When a scribe comes and tells Jesus he wants to follow him, Jesus tells him that even foxes have holes and birds have nests, but the Son of Man has no place to lay his head. Another disciple also says he wants to follow him but wants some time to bury his father. Jesus responds by telling him if he really wants to follow him, he is to let the dead bury the dead. As harsh as those responses are, Matthew is emphasizing the cost of following Jesus—it is a hard life.

The **fifth episode (8:23-27)** is about Jesus calming the wind and sea. The entire episode echoes the **story of Jonah**, with the key difference being that Jesus doesn't calm the sea by being thrown into it (because he isn't rebelling against God), but rather displays an authority over the wind and sea that only God has. Still, the disciples do not yet understand who Jesus really is, even though it is obvious that he is a lot more than just a prophet. He's doing things that only God can do.

In the **sixth episode (8:28-9:1),** Jesus and the disciples cross over to the east side of the Sea of Galilee and go into Gentile territory, where they encounter two demoniacs in the region of the **Gadarenes** (Mark calls it the Gerasenes). When the demoniacs encounter Jesus, the demons acknowledge he is the Son of God and beg Jesus that if he was going to cast them out of the men, to send them into a herd of swine. Jesus complies and sends them into the swine, who then run off the cliff and into the sea. The men were restored, but the people of the region ask Jesus to leave the region. It is worth noting that in Matthew's episode, there are two demoniacs, whereas in Mark, there was just one.

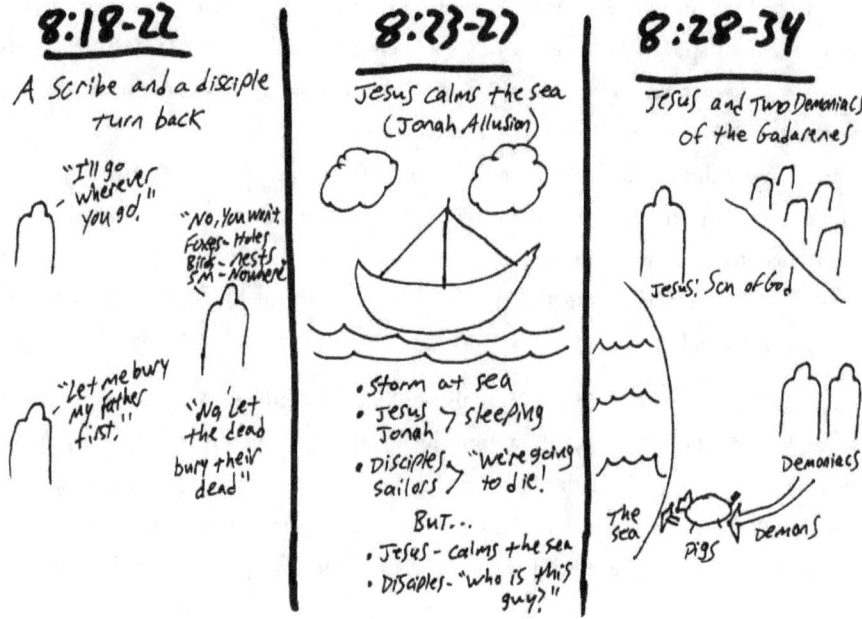

Rather than a contradiction, this is an example of the creative freedom the Gospel writers had in composing their Gospels. Matthew has a tendency to do things in twos. In 8:5-13, Jesus said that Gentiles will enter the Kingdom of Heaven while some Jews will be kicked out. Then in 8:18-22, we see *two Jewish men* who end up not following Jesus, whereas here in 8:28-9:1, we see Jesus casting demons out of *two Gentiles*. Thus, it is likely that Matthew has two demoniacs in this episode to act as a narrative contrast to the two Jewish men of 8:18-22.

In the **seventh episode (9:2-8)**, Jesus heals a paralytic, only after he tells him that his sins are forgiven. It is this claim to forgive sins that creates more conflict with the scribes, for they insist that only God has the authority to forgive sins. In response to that objection, Jesus then heals the paralytic in order to provide physical proof that he has the spiritual authority to forgive sins.

The **eighth episode (9:9-13)** tells of Jesus calling Matthew the tax-collector to be his disciple (Mark uses the name Levi). The scandal, of course, is that the Messiah is accepting of Jews who were considered traitors to their own people by collecting taxes for Rome. When the Pharisees object to him eating with such "sinners," Jesus says he has come as a doctor to minister to those who are sick, and then tells the Pharisees to learn what **Hosea 6:6** means: *"I desire mercy, not sacrifice."* This emphasizes the theme we've seen thus far in Matthew: Jesus, as the New

Moses, is pointing to something more important than just following the letter of the Law (Torah).

In the **ninth episode (9:14-17)**, John the Baptist's disciples ask Jesus why his disciples don't fast like them and the Pharisees. Jesus tells them that the time to fast is not when the bridegroom is here, but after the bridegroom has left. The reason for fasting was in anticipation of God's Kingdom. Jesus is saying that he, the Messiah, is the bridegroom, so now was time to celebrate. He then gives the images of *new wine in old wineskins* and *new cloth on an old garment* to emphasize the inevitable discontinuity with the coming of the Messiah and the God's Kingdom. Now that the long-awaited Kingdom has come, the old categories laid out in the Torah and Jewish customs become irrelevant. If something is new, you don't cram it into that which is old.

In the **tenth episode (9:18-26)**, Jesus is asked by a Jewish leader to come and raise his daughter who had just died. On the way there, a woman with a perpetual menstrual flow reaches out to touch Jesus' garment and is immediately healed. Jesus continues to the leader's house and raises his daughter from the dead. The message in both cases is that Jesus' healing of the woman and raising of the dead girl aren't just physical healings. They both restore each one back to the community of Israel.

The **eleventh episode (9:27-31)** tells about Jesus healing two blind men. As is Matthew's tendency in his Gospel, we once again see things come in pairs, like the two men who turn back from following Jesus and the two demoniacs in Gentile territory. Here, the two men cry out to Jesus, *"Son of David, have mercy on us!"* By calling him **Son of David**, it is clear the two blind men acknowledge him to be the Messiah. Jesus responds by healing them, but then tells them not to tell people what he did for them. They go and tell about it anyway.

The **twelfth episode (9:32-34)** is unique to Matthew and involves Jesus healing a mute man who was also demon-possessed. Jesus casts out the demon, and it is at that time that the Pharisees begin to accuse Jesus of casting out demons by the leader of demons (Satan). As we will see, this foreshadows the same accusation in Matthew's version of the Beelzebub controversy in 12:22-32.

### 5. Early Ministry: Growing Tensions (9:35-12:21)

In the next section of Matthew, we see the growing tensions, or at least the mixed reactions, between Jesus and many of his fellow Jews. The **first episode (9:35-38)** acts as a hinge episode, in that it summarizes the previous section and serves as a jumping off point for this section. Matthew tells us Jesus travelled throughout Galilee, proclaiming the Gospel of the Kingdom and healing the sick. He saw the Jews were like **sheep without a shepherd** (echoing Old Testament passages like **Zechariah 10:2**) and he told his disciples that the **harvest is great** but there were too few workers.

This sets the stage for the **second episode (10:1-11:1)**, where Jesus first chooses his twelve apostles, then sends them out to proclaim the Kingdom to their fellow Jews, staying where they are welcomed and moving on when they are rejected. He tells them they are going out as sheep among wolves, so they had better be "clever as serpents," and yet "innocent as doves." Nevertheless, they should expect ill-treatment by their fellow Jews, but they won't finish going through all the towns of Israel **before the Son of Man comes**. To be clear, this is not a reference to the **second coming**. At this point in Matthew, it is rather obscure, but as we will see later on in the Olivet Discourse of Matthew 24, such language is related to Jesus' prophecy about the Temple's destruction.

In any case, Jesus tells them he hasn't come to bring peace, but a sword, meaning he know that his proclamation of the Kingdom was bound to create division among his fellow Jews: some will accept it, while others will reject it. Jesus then tells his disciples that they must be willing to **take up their cross** if they are to follow him, and that if they lose their lives for his sake, that they will find it.

In the **third episode (11:2-19)**, John the Baptist sends a message to Jesus while in prison. Was he, in fact, the **Coming One**, or was there going to be someone else? Jesus responds by alluding to **Isaiah 61:1-2**, a passage in which the prophet says the Spirit of YHWH is upon him and that he has been **anointed** to preach the Gospel to the poor, heal the sick, release prisoners, and proclaim liberty, the year of YHWH's favor, and **the day of vengeance of God.** Jesus thus tells John that confrontation and wrath is coming, but first he is bringing the Gospel to the poor and needy.

Jesus then says that John the Baptist was, in fact, the Elijah of **Malachi 3:1**, the forerunner of the Coming One. When Jesus says, *"From the days of John the Baptist until now, the Kingdom of Heaven has been violently attacked, and the violent ones are seizing it away by force,"* he is drawing a line in the sand with his fellow Jews. He is the Coming One who is proclaiming the Kingdom of Heaven, but groups who oppose him, be they Pharisees, Sadducees, chief priests, scribes, or zealots, are the **violent ones** who are actually attacking the Kingdom. When John the Baptist came, they attacked him for being demon-possessed, and when Jesus came, they accused him of being a drunk who associates with the wrong people. Because John and Jesus challenged the Jewish religious establishment, they were both slandered and eventually killed.

The **fourth episode (11:20-30)** stems from the previous episode. Since John the Baptist's declared that God's wrath was coming, so we can assume that the reason why he was asking Jesus if he was the Coming One, was because he was wondering if Jesus would ever bring that "axe to the tree." Here is where Jesus begins to do just that by condemning Chorazin, Bethsaida, and Capernaum for being cities that will suffer God's wrath because they rejected his proclamation of the Kingdom. He goes so far to say that on the **Day of Judgment**, cities like Sodom and Gomorrah will have it easier than those cities in Israel who did not repent. Jesus speaks of the **infants** among Israel who had been wearied and burdened by the **violent ones** and appeals to them to take **his yoke** and be discipled by him in order to find rest, as opposed to the yoke of the violent ones that will bring about God's wrath.

After that, we find in the **fifth episode (12:1-8)** a confrontation between Jesus and the Pharisees over whether or not it was okay for his disciples to pick heads of grain on the Sabbath to eat. The Pharisees want to impose a heavy yoke on people, whereas Jesus' yoke is lighter. Jesus responds to the Pharisees' objection by giving the examples of (1) David eating the Bread of the Presence that only the priests were allowed to eat (**I Samuel 21**), and (2) the priests performing their priestly functions in the Temple on the Sabbath. If both of those examples are deemed okay, then it is even more okay for Jesus' disciples to pick the head of grain on the Sabbath because Jesus and his proclamation of the Kingdom is greater than the Temple. In light of that, Jesus again alludes (as he has already done in 9:13) to **Hosea 6:6** (*I desire mercy not sacrifice*) and claims that he, the Son of Man, is the Lord of the Sabbath.

In the **sixth episode (12:9-14)**, Jesus heals a man with a withered hand on the Sabbath. When the Pharisees again object to Jesus working on the Sabbath, Jesus tells them that if someone had a sheep that had fallen in a well on the Sabbath, that person would lift it up out of the well and no one would mind. Therefore, no one should have a problem with his healing on the Sabbath because human beings are more valuable than sheep. Doing good is not a violation of the Torah. In response, the Pharisees show themselves to be the "violent ones" Jesus spoke about in 11:20-30 by deciding to try to destroy him.

The **seventh episode (12:15-21)** acts as another summary statement in which Matthew gives another fulfillment passage when he says that Jesus' healings and his conflict with the Jewish religious leaders are a fulfillment of **Isaiah 42:1-4**. The Servant is called the Beloved One in whom God is well-pleased and on whom God has put His Spirit. This also echoes the voice from Heaven at Jesus' baptism. In addition, Isaiah 42:1-4 speaks of the Servant proclaiming justice to the Gentiles and of the Gentiles putting their hope in him. This passage not only summarizes the mounting conflict between Jesus and the Jewish religious leaders, but it also sets the stage for the next major section in Matthew.

### 6. Beelzebub Controversy to the Transfiguration: (12:22-17:22)

Matthew 12:22-17:22 closely follows Mark 3:20-9:29, beginning with the **Beelzebub Controversy** and climaxing with the **Transfiguration**. Just like in Mark, the basic question is laid out in the Beelzebub Controversy: *"What kingdom is Jesus working for? The kingdom of Satan or the Kingdom of Heaven?"* And, just like in Mark, the unit unfolds in four different sections that go to the heart of that initial question: (A) *A Question of Kingdoms* (**12:22-50**), where Jesus teaches and demonstrates what his Kingdom is about; (B) *The Kingdom to the Jews* (**13:1-14:46,** )where Jesus offers the Kingdom to his fellow Jews; (C) *The Kingdom to the Gentiles* (**15:1-16:4**) where Jesus offers the Kingdom to Gentiles; and (D) *Do You See the Kingdom Clearly?* (**16:5-17:22**), where Jesus challenges his disciples to understand the nature of the Kingdom.

#### A. Question of Kingdoms (12:22-50)

As will become obvious to anyone who compares Matthew and Mark, there are a number of alterations in Matthew throughout the entire literary unit. Our task here, though, is to provide an overview of what Matthew presents. The first section here of a *Question of Kingdoms* is presented as a single encounter between Jesus and the Pharisees. Matthew begins in the same way Mark does, in that the **first episode (12:22-32)** is that of the **Beelzebub Controversy**. As people see Jesus' healings, they wonder if he really could be the Son of David (the Messiah). The Pharisees, though, claim that he only casts out demons by the power of Beelzebub. Jesus responds by pointing out the absurdity of such an accusation, for if Satan casts out Satan, he is destroying his own kingdom. Instead, Jesus says he is casting out demons by the power of the Spirit of God and is thus **binding the Strong Man**. Thus, his power over Satan shows that the Kingdom of Heaven has come.

Therefore, the Pharisees' attributing the power of God *to Satan* amounts to blasphemy of God's Holy Spirit.

Jesus continues his condemnation of the Pharisees in the **second episode (12:33-37)** by echoing many of the things John the Baptist said Matthew 3:7-12. He says the Pharisees are rotten trees that produce rotten fruit, and he even calls them the **offspring of vipers**. Jesus then ends with a warning about how the words that come out of a person's mouth reveal what is in that person's heart and how each person will be judged accordingly on the Day of Judgment.

In the **third episode (12:38-45)**, the Pharisees respond by demanding a sign that he is, in fact, casting out demons by the Spirit of God, and not Beelzebub. Jesus says only an evil and adulterous generation asks for a sign and that the only sign they'll get is the **sign of Jonah**. He goes on to say that both the men of Nineveh and the Queen of Sheba would rise up on the Day of Judgment to pronounce judgment on that generation, because both of them responded respectively to Jonah and Solomon (something similar to what he said in 11:20-30). He then says that he is greater than both Jonah and Solomon, and still "this generation" would reject him (something similar to what he said in 12:1-8). Now, even though the "sign of Jonah" equates Jonah's three days and nights in the belly of the sea monster with Jesus' three days and nights in the tomb, the other aspect of the "sign of Jonah" is that the message of the Kingdom was going to be taken to Gentiles as well as Jews.

In any case, Jesus then equates that evil generation to a man who has had an unclean spirit cast out of him, and who is cleaned up and set in order, like a house. That unclean spirit, though, gets seven other unclean spirits to "take the house back" and re-possess him, the result being that the man is now worse off than he was before. In light of the Beelzebub Controversy, the point shouldn't be missed: Jesus is casting out demons, but by rejecting him, the Pharisees and this evil generation will soon find themselves even more in the grip of demonic forces than before.

With that, the **fourth episode (12:46-50)** brings the section to a close by telling us that when Jesus' family come to see him, he says that anyone who does the will of his Father in Heaven is his family. In the Kingdom of Heaven that Jesus is bringing, the old divisions between Jew from Gentile, or even family members from non-family members, are being erased.

### B. The Kingdom to the Jews (13:1-14:46)

In the next section, Jesus now takes the Kingdom to his fellow Jews. The **first episode (13:1-53)** consists of parables Jesus tells regarding the Kingdom of Heaven. The first is the **Parable of the Sower** (13:1-23), where the Sower sows seed on four types of soil: by the path, among the rocks, among the thorns, and in good soil. Only the seeds that fell on the good soil took root, grew strong, and prospered. When his disciples ask him privately why he speaks in parables, Jesus quotes **Isaiah 6:9-10**, where God tells Isaiah that the people of Judah would not listen to him because they were like the idols they worshipped, *spiritually blind and deaf*. His point is those who are truly seeking God will understand the parables, but those who are spiritual idolators will be blind and deaf to what he's saying, and thus will condemn themselves.

Jesus then tells the **Parable of the Weeds** (13:24-30) in which he compares the Kingdom of Heaven to a field in which a man has sown seed, but whose enemy has snuck in and sowed weeds in the same field, causing the wheat and the weeds to grow up together. Instead of uprooting both the wheat and weeds, the man chooses to let them grow up together. Then, at harvest time, he gathers them both, separates them,

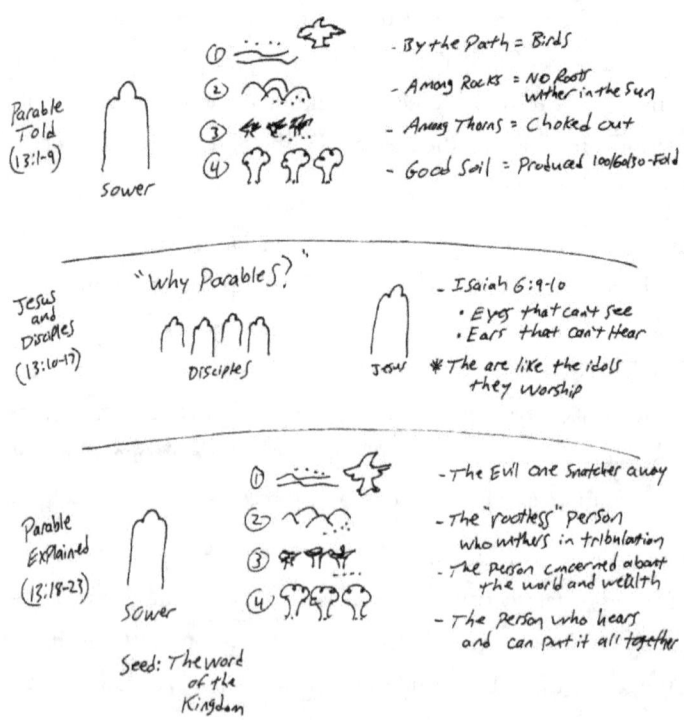

and then burns up the weeds while storing the grain. Jesus explains the parable is in 13:36-43: The man who sowed the good seed is the **Son of Man** (Jesus) and his enemy is the **devil**. The harvest is the **consummation of the age**.

Now, parables like this one need to be seen through two different lenses at the same time. The reason why goes back to what was discussed in the introduction concerning the Jewish eschatological hope, and how that hope was tweaked by Jesus and his proclamation of the Kingdom. At the risk of being too simplistic, the Jewish expectation was that when the Messiah would come, that would signal the end of the **old age**, when the enemies of God's people are defeated, and the immediate arrival of the **new Messianic age**, when the Kingdom of Heaven is fully established in the new creation. The Christian proclamation, though, originating in the teachings of Jesus himself, was that there would be an interim period between the end of the **old age** and the **consummation of the new creation**, when the forces of evil are defeated for good, and there is a new Heaven and Earth.

As we will see in the Olivet Discourse in Matthew 24, it seems quite clear that the destruction of Jerusalem and the Temple in AD 70 signaled the end of the "old age," shockingly declaring that God's wrath had come upon Jerusalem because the Jews had rejected Jesus as the Messiah and had thus shown themselves to be, not God's people, but the enemies of God's people, namely the followers of Jesus. But that event in history did not signal the ultimate consummation of the new creation—it merely foreshadowed it. The ultimate consummation of the new creation is still yet in the future, but the destruction of the Temple signaled the end of God's working through the Jewish people as a nation.

With all that said, the Parable of the Weeds can be seen in two ways: (A) being fulfilled in the events of the Jewish War of AD 70, when Jerusalem and the Temple were burned up and there was no longer any confusion between Christians and Jews, the "wheat from the weeds," so to speak; and (B) being seen as a foreshadowing of the ultimate consummation of the age, when the new creation will be fully established and the forces and evil and death will be done away with for good.

In the rest of the episode, Jesus also describes the Kingdom of Heaven as a *mustard seed* and as *yeast* (13:31-33), as well as a *treasure hidden in a field*, a *pearl of great price*, and a *net thrown in a sea* that catches a wide range of fish—after the catch is made, only then do the fishermen separate the good and bad fish. They all emphasize different aspects of the Kingdom. It starts small but grows great, it is invaluable, and it will all be sorted out at the consummation of the age.

In the **second episode (13:53-58)**, Jesus returns to Nazareth, only to be rejected by his hometown. They reject him because he was known to them as the carpenter's son. They knew him growing up, so they can't see how he could be anything special. Because of their lack of faith in him, Jesus does not do many miracles there.

The **third episode (14:1-21)** is a dual-episode involving the stories of Herod's beheading of John the Baptist and Jesus' feeding of the 5,000. Herod had been pushed by his wife Herodias to arrest John because John had publicly condemned their marriage as a violation of the Torah, on account that Herodias had been married to Herod's brother Philip. Still, Herod did not want to kill John because he thought John was a prophet. He is tricked by his stepdaughter and wife to behead John and bring his head in on a platter during Herod's birthday celebration. Thus, Herod, the king of the Jews, is presented as a **bad shepherd** who slaughters God's flock. In contrast to that, Jesus is presented as a **good shepherd** (the true King of the Jews) who cares for and feeds God's flock. The fact that this miraculous feeding happens out in the wilderness is a further echo of the miraculous feeding in the wilderness during the Exodus.

After that, the **fourth episode (14:22-33)** tells the story of Jesus walking on the sea. He had sent the disciples ahead to cross over the sea in the boat, while he remained on the mountain to pray. In the middle of the storm, though, Jesus comes walking on the sea to them. When the disciples see this, they think he is a ghost, but Peter calls out to Jesus and asks, if it really is him, if he could come out to him, walking on the waters. Jesus tells him to come, and at first Peter does, but he soon loses faith and starts to sink. Jesus then grabs hold of him and they both get into the boat. There are two points to the episode: (A) Jesus is doing things only God can do, and (B) Peter's attempt, although it eventually fails, nevertheless is a genuine attempt to step out in faith and follow Jesus.

The **fifth episode (14:34-46)** is brief, but important. Once they cross the sea, they are in Gentile territory again, where Jesus does further healings. Not only is this again emphasizing the notion that the Kingdom will be extended to Gentiles as well, but it also sets the stage for the next section.

### C. The Kingdom to the Gentiles (15:1-16:4)

This entire section takes place in Gentile territory. We know this because in 14:34-36 Jesus has crossed the Sea of Galilee from Jewish territory into Gentile territory, and there is no mention of him returning to Jewish territory yet. What transpires in this section, therefore, is essentially a mirror image of the previous *Kingdom to the Jews* section that emphasize the notion that Jesus is taking the Kingdom to Gentiles as well.

We see how this would be a conflict with his fellow Jews in the **first episode (15:1-20)**, where the Pharisees and scribes object to the fact that Jesus and his disciples do not wash their hands before eating and thus are breaking the oral tradition of the elders. The Pharisees and scribes see this as an issue of purity. By not observing the oral tradition of the elders, especially while among the Gentiles, Jesus and his disciples were allowing themselves to be defiled.

Jesus responds by saying that their own oral tradition actually encourages people to break the Torah and gives the example of how the Pharisees actually encourage people to break the Torah when they say it is okay to take money that should go to taking care of one's parents and instead give it to them as a gift to God. Thus, although they give the impression that they are devout and religious, in reality they are hypocrites who encourage the violation of the Torah. After that, Jesus then says that it isn't eating certain food that defiles someone, but rather what comes out of a person's mouth that defiles him. By saying this, Jesus was saying that the Jewish food laws that were there to make a distinction between Jews and Gentiles were now irrelevant.

In the **second episode (15:21-31)**, Jesus travels to Tyre and Sidon, where he encounters a Canaanite woman who begs him to heal her daughter from demonic oppression. He first challenges her by giving the standard Jewish view of Gentiles and telling her that he has come to the lost sheep of Israel and that it wouldn't be right to take food meant for God's children (Jews) and give it to dogs (Gentiles). When she responds that even dogs are allowed to eat the crumbs that fall from the children's table, Jesus marvels at her faith and heals her daughter. That act of healing makes it clear that in the Kingdom, Gentiles will experience healing as well.

In the **third episode (15:32-39)**, Jesus feeds 4,000 people in Gentile territory. The entire episode mirrors his feeding of the 5,000 in Jewish territory. Both happen **by the sea** and **on a mountain**. In both episodes, Jesus **has compassion** on the people and feeds the crowd with some bread and fish. The one difference is that this time the disciples collect **seven baskets** of leftovers, whereas they collected **twelve baskets** after the feeding of the 5,000. Once again, Jesus is doing among the Gentiles the same thing he had done among the Jews. The Kingdom is going out to the Gentiles, and they will be brought in to be part of God's people.

In the **fourth episode (16:1-4)**, after the miraculous feeding, some Pharisees and Sadducees ask Jesus for a sign from heaven a second time. Once again, after accusing them of being an evil and adulterous generation who is unable to read the **signs of the times**, Jesus tells them that the only sign they will get is **the sign of Jonah**. This is not simply a reference to Jesus' death and resurrection. It is also a sign that the Kingdom of Heaven is going to go out and include Gentiles, for Jonah ended up going to Nineveh, where God extended His grace and salvation to Gentiles.

### D. Do You See the Kingdom Clearly? (16:5-17:22)

This fourth section within the literary unit of 12:22-17:22 brings the entire thing to its climax and makes crystal clear just whose kingdom Jesus is working for. The **first episode (16:5-12)** takes place on the boat ride back to Jewish territory, when Jesus warns his disciples about the **yeast of the Pharisees and Sadducees**. The disciples think Jesus is talking about not bringing enough bread, so Jesus has to spell it out them what he is talking about by reminding them of the amount of bread that was picked up at both the feeding of the 5,000 (12 baskets) and the feeding of the 4,000 (7 baskets). At that point, the disciples realize that he was warning them about the **teaching of the Pharisees and Sadducees**. Jesus was teaching that the Kingdom would be extended beyond the Jews to Gentiles as well. By contrast, the Pharisees and Sadducees taught that Jews had to keep the Torah and offer sacrifices at the Temple in order to keep themselves distinct from the Gentiles.

The **second episode (16:13-28)** is of Peter's confession at Caesarea Philippi. After Jesus asks the disciples who other people think he is, he then asks them who they think he is. It is at that point that Peter says, *"You are the Messiah, the Son of the Living God,"* Jesus responds with, *"Blessed are you, Simon* **son of Jonah!***"* and he tells Peter, *"Upon this rock I will build my church, and the gates of Hades will not be able to stand against it."* Jesus also tells Peter that he will be given the keys of the Kingdom of Heaven, and whatever he binds or loosens on earth with be bound and loosened in Heaven. Jesus is speaking about how the Church is built upon the testimony and truth that Jesus is the Messiah. As for the **binding and loosing** talk, we should think back to the beginning of 12:22-17:22, to the Beelzebub Controversy, where

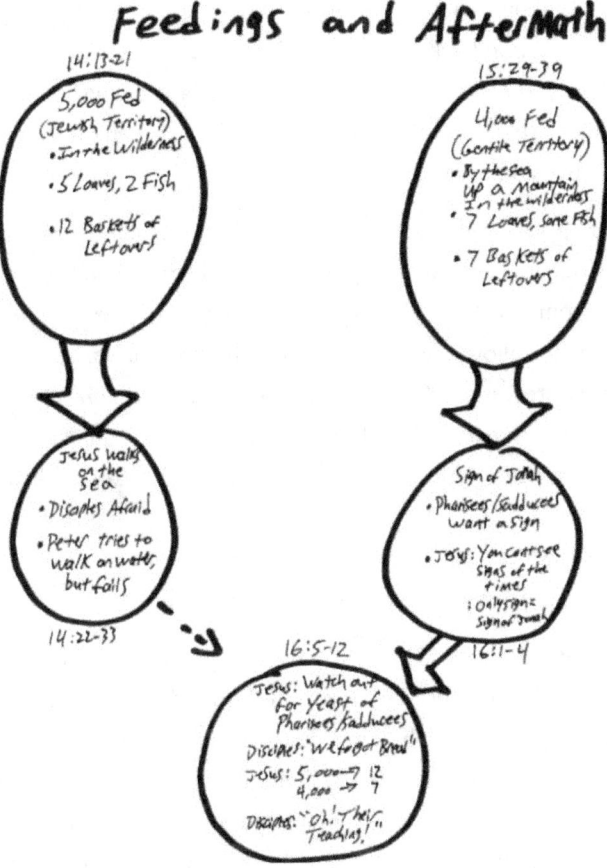

Jesus says that he is **binding the Strong Man** and thus loosening Satan's grip on this world. Thus, Jesus is saying that his Church will have the same authority as Jesus himself.

Finally, it is curious that Jesus calls Peter **son of Jonah** because we know from **John 21:15-17** that Peter's father was named John. If we consider this in the context of this larger section of 12:22-17:22, though, it makes sense. The **sign of Jonah** was both a reference to the future death and resurrection of Jesus, as well as a comment on the nature of the Kingdom, namely that it is going be extended to Gentiles. So, when Peter says that Jesus is the Messiah, it seems that he gets what the sign of Jonah is about.

It turns out, though, that Peter doesn't really get it yet, for as soon as Jesus starts telling his disciples that he was going to suffer at the hands of the elders, chief priests, and scribes, and that he was going to be killed but would raise up in three days, Peter actually rebukes Jesus. Jesus responds with, *"Get behind me, Satan,"* again, an interesting connection back to the Beelzebub Controversy. In any case, Jesus is telling Peter that by objecting to Jesus' mission, Peter is setting himself up as his adversary. If Peter really thinks Jesus is the Messiah, he's going to have to let Jesus be the kind of Messiah he was meant to be.

This is what Jesus emphasizes for the rest of the episode. To oppose him is to align oneself with Satan and following him mean picking up your cross and being willing to give your life for the sake of the Kingdom. The way to inherit the Kingdom will me to follow Christ and suffer with him. And this brings us back to the Beelzebub Controversy: *Whose kingdom will you choose to work for?* The episode ends with the often-misunderstood statement by Jesus that there were some standing there at the time with him would not taste death until they saw the Son of Man coming in his Kingdom. Jesus is not talking about his future second coming. He is saying that some of them will get a clear glimpse of him in his glory—and they do, as we will see in the final episode in this section.

The **third episode (17:1-13)** that culminates the larger section of 12:22-17:22 is that of the **Transfiguration**, the decisive response to question first brought up in the Beelzebub Controversy. The Transfiguration takes place six days after Peter's confession and is thus a subtle allusion to Genesis 1: *it is the beginning of a new creation.* Jesus takes Peter, James, and John, up a mountain, and it is there where they witness Jesus in glory, along with Moses and Elijah. A voice comes out of Heaven and says, *"This is my Son, the Beloved One, in whom I am well-pleased...listen to him!"* Not only is this a quote of **Psalm 2:7**, but it echoes what the voice from heaven said at Jesus' baptism as well. It is as if God is saying to them, "Hey! Like I said earlier! This is my Beloved Son! *Listen to him! Stop trying to rebuke him when he tells you something you don't want to hear!"*

In the **fourth episode (17:14-22)**, on their way down from the mountain, Jesus again tells them not to tell anyone what they saw until after he had risen from the dead. This is the second time he tells them about his future suffering, death, and resurrection. When they ask him about Elijah coming first, he tells them that John the Baptist was Elijah, the messenger who was to come to prepare the way for the Messiah, but that most of the Jews didn't realize it. By saying this, Jesus is saying that he is the Messiah. Once they returned to the crowds, when Jesus finds out that his followers were unable to cast out the demon from a young boy, he rebukes their lack of faith and heals the boy himself.

## 7. From Galilee to Jerusalem (17:23-20:34)

Now that the disciples have been given a glimpse of Jesus' glory, the next section transitions from Galilee to Jerusalem. It is time for him to begin to make his way to Jerusalem. All along the way, Jesus continues to teach his disciples about the nature of the Kingdom.

In the **first episode (17:23-27)**, while Jesus is still in Capernaum, he tells his disciples for a third time that he will be handed over, killed, and be raised up three days later. After that, Peter is asked by the Temple tax-collectors if Jesus pays the two-drachma tax. Peter says he does, but then goes to ask Jesus about it to make sure. In response, Jesus asks him a question: *Do kings get taxes from their sons or from others?* The answer is obvious. The subjects pay taxes, sons don't. Jesus' point is that he is the Son of God, and therefore doesn't have to pay the Temple tax. Nevertheless, he tells Peter to go fishing and to open the mouth of the first fish he catches. When he does, he will find a two-drachma coin in its mouth, and that Peter is to pay the Temple tax with that coin.

In the **second episode (18:1-14)**, Jesus teaches his disciples that whoever humbles himself like a little child will be the greatest in the Kingdom of Heaven. Jesus then warns his disciples not to cause any of these *little ones* to stumble. He isn't necessarily talking about literal children, but rather those who are immature in the faith. That is why Jesus then says that it would be better to gouge out an eye (or cut off a hand or foot) and to enter the Kingdom of Heaven lame than to cause someone to stumble in their faith and then be thrown into Gehenna with two eyes, hands, and feet. (Gehenna was understood to be the place of punishment). Jesus then gives the example of a shepherd leaving the 99 sheep to go find the one lost sheep in order to emphasize how important it is for him to seek and save the lost sheep and the *little ones* of the world.

The **third episode (18:15-20)** is a continuation of the previous episode. Here, Jesus tells his disciples what to do if a someone sins against them. First, go in private to try to hash things out, and if that doesn't work, bring two or three others to talk to him. If that still doesn't work, speak to the **entire church** about it. If he still won't listen, it is at that point the person should be treated like a "Gentile or tax-collector," meaning they are to have nothing to do with him. Jesus then re-emphasizes what he said at Caesarea Philippi. Whatever they bind or loose on earth will be bound and loosed in Heaven, for if two can come to an agreement, it will be done for them by the Father in Heaven. He says that wherever two or three are gathered in his name, he will be there with them.

It is worth noting that the Greek word for "church" is **ekklesia**. That is the word used in the Septuagint (the Greek translation of the Hebrew Bible) to translate the Hebrew word **qahal**, which is used to designate Israel as God's special people. In that sense, in the Old Testament, Israel was the "church" of YHWH. Given that, it seems that Jesus was telling his disciples how to deal with problem with their Jewish brothers within the people of God. Still, given the fact that Jesus was re-constituting the people of God around himself as the Messiah, we should realize that he is now referring to his own movement, and not the Jewish community as a whole, as the Church, the **ekklesia**, the **qahal** of God.

In the **fourth episode (18:21-35)**, the disciples ask Jesus how many times they are to forgive someone if that person continues to sin against them. When Peter asks if it should be seven times, Jesus responds by saying it should be **seventy-seven times**, meaning there shouldn't be a limit. If you're keeping tabs on the number of times you supposedly forgive someone, that shows you haven't really ever forgiven that person. To illustrate his point, Jesus tells the story of a king who forgives a servant's large debt, only to find that very servant has turned around and refused to forgive a small debt of a fellow servant. In response, the king tells the evil servant that since he was shown mercy by the king, he should have shown mercy to his fellow servant. Then the king throws the evil servant in jail until he is able to pay off his large debt. Jesus' point is simple: The reason why you should forgive others of their sins is because God has forgiven you of yours.

In the **fifth episode (19:1-12)**, the Pharisees question Jesus about whether or not the Torah allows for divorce. Jesus refers to **Genesis 1:27** and **2:24** and says that when two people get married, they become **one flesh** and therefore (ideally) shouldn't be separated. Therefore, just because the Torah provided a legal means of divorce, that doesn't make divorce a good thing. The problem is that some men would divorce their wives for any reason in order to marry someone else, and claim it was okay because the Torah allowed for divorce. Jesus says if you do that, then you're still committing adultery in God's eyes. When the disciples say it might be better to not get married in the first place, Jesus says a celibate life (being a eunuch) isn't for everyone. Some men just never want to marry, some have been literally castrated, and some purposely choose to stay celibate for the sake of the Kingdom.

There is then a brief **sixth episode (19:13-15)** where Jesus welcomes the little children who want to see him and reminds his disciples that it is for the sake of the little children that the Kingdom of Heaven has come. This is followed by the **seventh episode (19:16-30)**, where a rich young man asks Jesus what he must do to inherit **eternal life**. More properly, we should understand it as the **Life of the Ages**, because the young man asking about the life of the *coming Messianic age*. Jesus mentions keeping the commandments, which the young man says he has always kept. So, Jesus tells him if he wants to be **perfect**, he should sell all he has and give the money to the poor. Now, the Greek word translated here as "perfect" doesn't mean some sort of static state of perfection, but rather attaining *full maturity* and growing into the fullness of Christ, and thus being a human being who truly is in God's image and likeness.

In any case, the young man refuses to give away all he has, so he leaves, and Jesus notes how hard it is for the rich to enter the Kingdom. When Peter points out that they have left everything to follow him, Jesus reassures them that in the **Coming Age**, those who have left everything for his sake will receive a hundred-fold, the first will be last, and the last will be first. In 19:28, Jesus calls this "coming age" the **Rebirth**, and says that is when the Son of Man will sit on his throne of glory, with the disciples also sitting on twelve thrones, judging the twelve tribes of Israel.

In the **eighth episode (20:1-16)**, Jesus tells a parable in which he equates the Kingdom of Heaven to a man who hires workers to work in his vineyard. He goes out and hires men at 9 am, noon, 3 pm, and 5 pm. At the end of the day, the man decides to pay all the workers for a full day's work. When the men who were hired at 9 am complain that it wasn't fair, the man says it was fair because he paid them what he promised them. They were just angry that he chose to be extra generous to the later workers. His generosity does not make him an evil and unjust person. The parable thus illustrates something about the nature of the Kingdom of Heaven. Everyone who chooses to respond to God's call will receive a full reward, no matter when they end up responding to God. The first will be last and the last will be first, *but all will receive a full reward.*

In the **ninth episode (20:17-19)**, as they get closer to Jerusalem, Jesus tells his disciples for a fourth time that he is going to be handed over to the chief priests and scribes, they are going to pass judgment on him and call for his death. Then they will hand him over to the Gentiles, who will mock, whip, and crucify him. Still, as he has said before, he will raise up on the third day.

In the **tenth episode (20:20-28)**, the mother of James and John asks Jesus if her sons could sit on his right and left hand in his kingdom. She wants her sons to have positions of power in what she thinks will be an earthly kingdom. Jesus asks them if they think they'll be able to drink from the cup he drinks, and they respond in the affirmative. So, Jesus says, "Yes, you really are going to drink from my cup (meaning, you're going to be killed too)! But I don't choose who will be on my right and left hand." When the other disciples get mad about their request, Jesus tells them all that they still have it all wrong. The Kingdom of Heaven isn't about getting political power and authority to beat others into submission and making them serve you. That is the way of the world. The Kingdom of Heaven is about becoming a servant and willingly being last. Then for a fifth time, Jesus uses his own upcoming death to show that his whole mission as the Messiah, as the Son of Man, is to give his life as a ransom for many.

The **eleventh episode (20:29-34)** takes place right outside of Jericho. As he does throughout his Gospel, Matthew has an episode involving two men. Here, he tells us that two blind men approach Jesus, call him **Son of David**, and ask him to heal them. Jesus takes pity on them, heals them, and they immediately follow him…to Jerusalem.

### 8. Confrontation in Jerusalem (21:1-25:46)

This section involving Jesus' confrontation with the Jewish religious leaders in Jerusalem largely parallels Mark, but Matthew includes a few new episodes of his own. The **first episode (21:1-11)** is that of what is commonly called the "Triumphal Entry," but it is anything but that. The Messianic hopes of the Jews in the first century was that the Messiah would defeat the oppressing power of Rome, then ride into Jerusalem in triumph and cleanse the Temple. Although the episode is set up as if those hopes will be realized, Jesus ends up doing none of them, *because the Kingdom he is bringing is not like the kingdom his fellow Jews were hoping for.*

It begins with having all the hallmarks of fulfilling the Jewish hopes. Jesus rides into Jerusalem on a donkey and Matthew says it was a fulfillment of **Zechariah 9:9**: *"Say to the daughter of Zion, Look! Your king is coming to you! Humble and riding upon a donkey, on the young colt of a beast of burden!"* The crowds are singing **Psalm 118** and Matthew quotes **118:25-26**: *"Hosanna, Son of David! Blessed is the one coming in the name of YHWH! Hosanna in the highest heaven!"* Clearly, the expectation is of a political king who would defeat Rome, cleanse the Temple, and re-establish the Davidic kingdom.

The **second episode (21:12-22)** describes what Jesus actually does when he makes it to the Temple that day. Instead of cleansing it, Jesus disrupts the place and trashes it. As he is overturning tables, he quotes **Isaiah 56:7**, *"My house will be called a house of prayer,"* and alludes to **Jeremiah 7:11**, *"but you have made it into a hideout for revolutionaries!"* In his day, Jeremiah prophesied that the Temple would be destroyed by Babylon. By quoting Jeremiah, Jesus is making it clear that he, too, is prophesying that the Temple would soon be destroyed (as it turns out, by Rome). Even though most translations have "den of robbers," the Greek word **lestai** is a reference to zealot revolutionaries. This prophesy of the Temple's destruction came to pass 40 years later, during the Jewish War of AD 66-70, when zealots rebelled, took of Jerusalem, and made the Temple their base of operations while Rome came and destroyed both the city and Temple.

Keeping with a theme throughout his Gospel, Matthew highlights the fact that not only was Jesus healing the blind and lame in the Temple, but also that children were saying, "Save us, Son of David!" When the chief priests and scribes object to this, Jesus quotes **Psalm 8:2**, *"From the lips of children, you have ordained praise."*

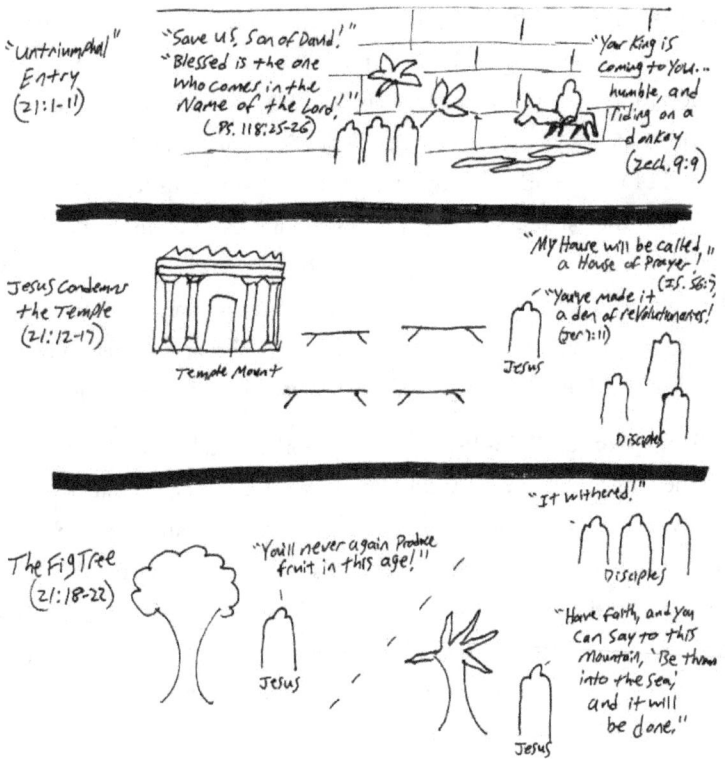

The next morning, Jesus curses and withers the fig tree near Bethany because it wasn't bearing fruit. The connection between the fig tree and Temple is clear. Like the fig tree, the Temple has failed to bear fruit and therefore will be destroyed. Jesus then tells his disciples that if they have faith and this **this mountain** to be thrown in the sea, that it would happen. "This mountain" is a reference to the Temple Mount. Clearly, as the testimony in the Gospels show, Jesus' followers did, in fact, to declare the Temple's destruction to their fellow Jews up until the time of the Jewish War.

The **third episode (21:23-27)** takes place when Jesus goes back to the Temple that day. The chief priests confront Jesus and ask him who gave him the authority to do what he was doing. Jesus asks them whether or not they think John the Baptist came from heaven and was thus a true prophet. They realize if they say he was a prophet, Jesus will ask them why they don't believe him (because he said Jesus was the Coming One); but if they say he wasn't a prophet, they will anger the crowds who considered John a prophet. Being political animals, they side-step the question and say they don't know. So, Jesus tells them he won't answer their question either.

In the **fourth episode (21:28-32)**, Jesus proceeds to tell a parable in which a man told both of his sons to go out and work in his vineyard. The first son initially said, "No," but ended up going out and working anyway, whereas the other son initially said, "Yes," but ended up not going out to work. When Jesus asks the chief priests which son did the will of the father, they say, "The first one." So, Jesus tells them that tax-collectors and prostitutes are going to get into the Kingdom before they do, because even though they initially weren't doing the will of God, after they heard John the Baptist, they repented and ended up "working in the vineyard," so to speak, by following Jesus. By contrast, the chief priests, who claimed they were faithful vineyard workers, didn't accept John the Baptist and were obviously not accepting Jesus.

In the **fifth episode (21:33-46)**, Jesus tells another parable, the **Parable of the Vineyard**. The vineyard owner is God, the vineyard is Israel, the farmers are the chief priests and Pharisees, the servants are the prophets, and the son is Jesus. Because the farmers beat and killed the owner's servants and then killed his son, Jesus says that when the owner comes back, he will destroy those farmers and give the vineyard to others. This is a clear condemnation of the Temple establishment. Jesus is saying when God comes back—when the **Day of the Lord** comes—they will be destroyed, and the vineyard will be given to the Gentiles. When one considers that Matthew was written shortly after Jerusalem and the Temple were destroyed in AD 70, it becomes obvious that the original audience would have realized that what Jesus said here had just happened.

The episode ends with Jesus quoting **Psalm 118:22-23**: *"The stone that the builders rejected has become the chief cornerstone. This is the Lord's doing, and it is marvelous in our eyes!"* This is the very Psalm the crowds were singing when they welcomed him into Jerusalem as the Messiah. Jesus is pointing out that the Messiah would, in fact, be rejected by the "builders," namely the chief priests, but that he would be the foundation for a new Temple (the Church). By contrast, those who side with the chief priests will be crushed along with the Temple when it is destroyed. Like I mentioned in Mark, it is interesting to note that at this time the Temple was in the midst of major renovations. So, there was literal building going on in the Temple when Jesus said this. In any case, the chief priests and Pharisees begin to search for a way to arrest him. They had to find a way to do it in secret, away from the crowds, though, because Jesus has the crowds on his side.

In the **sixth episode (22:1-14)**, during the same time, Jesus tells another parable, the **Parable of the Wedding Banquet**. A king prepares a wedding banquet for his son and sends out invitations, only to find that some invitees ignore the invitation and go about their business, while others outright reject the invitation by insulting and killing the king's servants. So, the king sends his soldiers to destroy the murderers and burn their city to the ground. In the parable, the king is God, the son is Jesus, the wedding banquet is the Messianic banquet celebrating the Kingdom, and those who reject the invitation are the chief priests and Pharisees. As with the previous parable, the point is clear: Jerusalem will be destroyed because it has rejected Jesus as the Messiah.

There is still more to the parable. After burning down their city, the king sends his servants to invite those outside of the city (Gentiles). The servants go out and gather everyone they find, both good and bad people. One man, though, isn't dressed in a wedding garment, so he is bound and thrown out into outermost darkness, *where there is weeping and gnashing of teeth*. Jesus ends his parable by saying, "Though many are called, few are chosen." His point is that although the Gospel of the Kingdom will go out to the Gentiles, not all will get in, just as not all Jews will get in. Incidentally, regarding the comment about *outer darkness* and *weeping and gnashing of teeth*, Jesus isn't talking in terms of the ultimate destiny of people going to hell. He is speaking in terms of the Kingdom. Although it will be offered to both Jews and Gentiles, those who reject Jesus will be left out of the Kingdom.

In the **seventh episode (22:15-46)**, various Jewish leaders ask Jesus some questions trip him up. The **Pharisees** ask about **paying taxes to Caesar**, and Jesus says that if Caesar's image is on the money, then they should pay him what it his. What is more important, though, is to pay to God what belongs to Him. The **Sadducees** ask about the **resurrection**, and Jesus says that there will be no need for marriage in the age to come, and that those who are faithful to God aren't really dead anyway. A **scribe** asks about the **greatest commandment**, and Jesus says that the greatest commandment is to love God, and along with that there is a second one, to love your neighbor as yourself. Together they summarize the entire intent of the Torah. **Jesus** then asks them about the **identity of the Messiah** by quoting **Psalm 110:1**. Jesus' point is that the Messiah is a lot more than just a descendant of David, because David himself calls him "Lord." Thus, Jesus is saying that not only is he the Messiah, but he is actually greater than David, in some sense on par with God Himself.

|  | Question | Response |
|---|---|---|
| 22:15-22 | **Pharisees**: Taxes to Caesar? | **Jesus**: Pay it…but give to God what's God's. |
| 22:23-33 | **Sadducees**: Whose wife will this woman be in the resurrection? | **Jesus**: No marriage in the resurrection. |
| 22:34-40 | **Scribe**: What's the greatest commandment? | **Jesus**: Love God and love your neighbor. |
| 22:41-46 | **Jesus**: How can the Messiah only be David's descendant, when David calls him "Lord"? | **Crowd**: Nobody dared to respond |

The **eighth episode (23:1-39)** takes up the entire chapter. In it, Jesus openly condemns the Pharisees and scribes as religious hypocrites, and openly laments over the coming destruction of Jerusalem. The Pharisees and scribes love their reputations but practice a kind of legalism that places more burdens on suffering people. Because they have the Torah, they don't feel compassion is necessary. In fact, they actually prevent people from entering the Kingdom of Heaven. They only succeed in making people more into the **sons of Gehenna** like they are (23:1-15). They are blind guides who pressure people into giving more gold and gifts in order to get greater blessings (23:16-22). They are all about outward appearances of religiosity, but neglect justice, mercy, and faith, and thus are filthy and dead inside. They may honor the prophets, but the fact is that it was their own ancestors who persecuted and killed the prophets. That is why "all this," meaning his prophecy about the destruction of Jerusalem and the Temple, *will come upon this generation* (23:23-36).

Jesus ends with a lament over Jerusalem in 23:37-39. He calls it the city that killed the prophets and says that even though he had longed to gather the children of Jerusalem to himself, like a hen gathers her chicks under her wings to shelter them from harm, he knows they will reject him. Because of that, the Temple would soon be destroyed. He then says they will no longer see him until they say, *"Blessed is the One who comes in the Name of YHWH"*—**Psalm 118:26**, the very psalm the crowds had sung when he entered Jerusalem a few days earlier. The problem then was that they had the wrong understanding of what kind of Messiah he was. They were hoping for a nationalistic, political king who would fight the Gentiles and cleanse the Temple, but Jesus was the kind of Messiah who picked a fight with the Temple establishment and said the Temple was so corrupt that it was deserving of judgment. When that happened, the Kingdom would go out to the Gentiles. So, until they see what kind of Messiah the "One coming in the Name of YHWH" really is, they will not see Jesus again.

The **ninth episode (24:1-51)**, the **Olivet Discourse**, takes up an entire chapter. It takes place on the Mount of Olives, which overlooks the Temple. After Jesus again tells his disciples the Temple would be torn down, they ask him when it would happen and what **the sign of his coming at the close of the age** would be. The Greek word translated as "coming" is **parousia**. It denotes the arrival of a king after a great victory, where the people go out to welcome him into the city as its rightful king. Thus, the disciples are asking Jesus: (1) When his *parousia* would happen, (2) When the Temple would be destroyed, and (3) When would he come to Jerusalem in victory to be enthroned as the rightful king of Israel and usher in the Messianic Age? Jesus' answer, although confusing to us in the 21st century, makes perfect sense when understood in light of the events of the Jewish War of AD 66-70.

In 24:3-14, Jesus warns his disciples of **false messiahs** and **wars** (zealot leaders who would claim to be sent by God to revolt against Rome). He warns about **famines** and **earthquakes** (during the siege of Jerusalem, a devastating famine took place within Jerusalem, causing countless civilians to die of starvation). He also warns his disciples about being **tortured** and **killed** and being **hated by all nations** (as the books of Acts tells us, from AD 30-66, followers of Jesus were indeed persecuted, tortured, and killed, both by the Temple establishment and Roman authorities as well).

In 24:15-31, when Jesus tells his disciples that when they see the **Abomination of Desolation standing in the holy place**, they should flee to the hills, he is alluding to **Daniel 9:26-27** and **12:10-11**. In its original context, it was referring to the abomination that Antiochus Epiphanes set up in the Temple to defile it. By Jesus' day, the term "Abomination of Desolation" had essentially become a term that described any monumental sacrilege to the Temple. Therefore, when seen in light of the Jewish War of AD 66-70, Jesus is likely referring to the desolation that the Jewish zealots themselves did in the Temple courts during the war. In fact, Josephus repeatedly emphasizes that, because of the zealots, "the House of God is full of *abominations*." Therefore, Jesus is telling his disciples that when they see the handwriting on the wall and see the abominations of the Zealot "false messiahs," they should realize the destruction of Jerusalem was immanent, give up their hope that the Jewish nation would embrace Jesus' message, and *abandon Jerusalem*, because it would soon suffer God's wrath and be destroyed by Rome.

This helps explain the odd verse, *"Wherever there might be a corpse, it is there the vultures will gather."* The Greek word translated as "vultures" is **aetoi**, which can also mean "eagles." It is possible that Jesus is prophesying about both the carnage the Zealots would bring upon Jerusalem, and how the Roman armies under the emblem of the Roman Eagle would "feast" upon them. Hence, *aetoi* might carry a double meaning of both the Roman Eagle and vultures who feast on corpses.

Jesus makes is clear, though, in 24:27-29, that the **parousia of the Son of Man** would not happen at the time of the Jewish War. It would happen *after* that time of tribulation. At this point, he gives what can be called "cosmic upheaval" language to describe his prophecy of Jerusalem's destruction: the sun will go dark, the moon won't give its light, the stars will fall from the sky, and the very powers in Heaven will be shaken. This is Old Testament prophetic language that describes the **Day of YHWH**, when God would bring His wrath upon His enemies and salvation for His people. Shockingly, Jesus is saying that Jerusalem had become God's enemy and would suffer God's wrath.

This brings us to 24:30-31, where Jesus talks about the **sign of the Son of Man** coming to light in Heaven, and about how all the tribes of the earth would mourn and see *"the Son of Man coming on the clouds of heaven."* This is a reference to

**Daniel 7:13-14**, where the Son of Man ascends to heaven after great tribulation and suffering of God's people. The image of "coming on the clouds of heaven" is thus **vindication language** that describes the Messiah and his people being victorious over the God's enemies. So, in addition to saying that Jerusalem will be destroyed because the Jewish nation will reject him as their Messiah, Jesus is also saying that both he and his followers would be vindicated once everything Jesus had prophesied happens. This helps us make sense of Jesus' comments about the Son of Man *"sending out his angels to gather his elect from the four winds"* (24:31). The word **angelos** means a royal messenger who does the king's business. Therefore, it seems Jesus is saying that with the destruction of the Temple, his followers would be his royal messengers to the Gentile nations to spread the Gospel, and to "gather his elect" from among both Jews and Gentiles.

The rest of 24:32-51 consists of Jesus telling his disciples to stay alert and remain faithful. He first uses the illustration of a fig tree: just like when you see its leaves are green you know summer is near, so too, Jesus says to his disciples, when they see "these things" starting to happen, they should know that "it is at the gates." The fact that Jesus says, *"this generation will not pass away until all these things happen"* (24:34), firmly roots his prophecy of the Temple's destruction to within that generation.

He then equates the coming of the Son of Man to **the days of Noah**, indicating that Jerusalem's destruction will come suddenly and catch many people unprepared. Some will be taken away to be slaves or die in the colosseum, and some will be left among the ruins of Jerusalem. Jesus then ends with an analogy of servants who are left in charge of their Lord's household while he is gone. The wicked servant doesn't think the Lord is coming anytime soon, so he treats his other servants horribly. When his Lord returns, though, he will be caught unprepared and will be cut to pieces and thrown out with the **hypocrites**, where there will be **weeping and gnashing of teeth**, meaning cast out of the Kingdom, along with the Pharisees and scribes. Jerusalem and the Temple would soon be destroyed, so the disciples had better be ready when it happens.

In the **tenth episode (25:1-13)**, while still on the Mount of Olives, Jesus tells the **Parable of the Ten Virgins** in order to give further teaching regarding what is to come. In the parable, Jesus equates the Kingdom of Heaven to ten virgins who go out to meet the coming bridegroom. Five brought enough oil for their lamps in case of a long wait, while five did not. The was a long wait, and they all fell asleep.

When the bridegroom finally comes, they all wake up, but the five foolish virgins don't have any oil left and their lamps are going out. The five sensible virgins don't have enough to give them, so they have to go off and buy more oil. In the meantime, the bridegroom comes, and the five sensible virgins go in with him to the wedding banquet. When the five foolish virgins show up, they are locked out of the wedding banquet.

The meaning of the parable is fairly obvious: Jesus is the bridegroom, and the virgins represent the Jews, including his own followers. The foolish virgins are those who don't see what is coming, whereas the sensible ones do. The coming of the bridegroom is the Coming of the Son of Man and the subsequent Messianic wedding banquet in the Kingdom of God. Those who aren't prepared, who haven't understood the "signs of the times" of which Jesus spoke about in the Olivet Discourse, will find themselves locked out of God's Kingdom and the Messianic wedding banquet.

In the **eleventh episode (25:14-30)**, Jesus gives a second parable, the **Parable of the Talents**, which focuses on the behavior of certain servants when their Lord comes back. The servant who was given five talents earns an additional five talents and is rewarded by being put in charge of many things and allowed to "enter into the joy" of his Lord. The servant who was given two talents earns an additional two talents and is rewarded in the same way. The servant who was given one talent and who buried it in the ground because he clearly didn't like his Lord angers his Lord by just giving it back. So, his talent is taken and given to the servant who has ten talents, and he is thrown out into **outer darkness**, where there is **weeping and gnashing of teeth**. This is the sixth time the phrase "weeping and gnashing of teeth" is found in Matthew (8:12; 13:42, 50; 22:13; and 24:51). Each time, the place of "weeping and gnashing of teeth" is outside of the coming Kingdom, outside of the coming Messianic wedding banquet of the bridegroom, and outside of the joy of the Lord.

In the **twelfth episode (25:31-46)**, Jesus tells the story of the *Sheep and the Goats* to tell about what will happen when the Son of Man "comes in his glory." In the Olivet Discourse, Jesus prophesied about the destruction of the Temple and his and his followers' vindication as the true people of God. But he said "the end" wouldn't happen at that time. There would be an interim time between the Temple's destruction and final consummation of God's Kingdom, when he'd send his messengers out among the nations to gather the elect. Therefore, what Jesus says in the story of the Sheep and the Goats should be easy to understand.

When he comes in his glory as King of all creation, he will separate the nations, like a shepherd separates the sheep from the goats. The sheep will inherit the Kingdom because they cared for the *least of these* with whom the Son of Man identifies himself: the poor, the sick, the needy, the imprisoned, and the foreigner. The goats, though, are cast out into the fire prepared for the devil and his angels because they refused to care for the least of these, and by extension, the Son of Man. At the consummation of the age, when God's Kingdom arrives in full, the determining factor between those who inherit the Kingdom and those who are cast out is based on how they treated the "least of these"—they very kind of people whom Jesus has been saying throughout the Gospel that the Kingdom has come for.

### 9. From the Last Supper to the Resurrection (26:1-28:20)

The final section takes us from Jesus' anointing at Bethany all the way through to his resurrection. The **first episode (26:1-16)** begins with Jesus again telling his disciples that he was soon going to be handed over to be crucified. It turns out that the chief priests and elders were, in fact, conspiring to do that very thing. Then, while in Bethany, at the house of **Simon the leper**, a woman pours a jar of expensive oil over Jesus' head, and the disciples object and say that the oil could have been sold and the money given to the poor. Jesus defends the woman and says that she has anointed his body for burial. Given the fact *Messiah* means "anointed one," her action takes on added significance, for the Jewish expectation was for the Messiah to be anointed to conquer his enemies, but here Jesus is saying that he is a Messiah who is anointed to suffer and die. At this point, Judas decides to go to the chief priests with an offer to hand Jesus over to be arrested. Perhaps it was then that Judas realized Jesus was not going to be the kind of conquering Messiah he was hoping for.

The **second episode (26:17-35)** tells about the **Last Supper**. Jesus first instructs his disciples to go into the city to make preparations, and then at the meal, Jesus tells them he knows one of them there is going to betray him. When Judas asks Jesus if it will be him, Jesus responds, "You've said it." Jesus then focuses on the bread and the cup, equating his body with the bread and the cup with the blood of the covenant and says he will not drink of it again until the day when he will drink it with them in the Kingdom. By doing this, Jesus is re-interpreting the traditional Passover meal to center around his own sacrifice.

While the Passover meal signaled the beginning of the Mosaic covenant around which Old Testament Israel was built, the Last Supper declares that Jesus' sacrifice signals the beginning of the New Covenant around which the reconstituted people of God will be built. Jesus and the disciples then go out to the Mount of Olives, where he tells them they will all fall away from him that night, and that it will be a fulfillment of **Zechariah 13:7**: *"Strike the shepherd and the sheep will be scattered."* Still, he reassures them that they will all see him in Galilee once he is raised. When Peter says he will never do that, Jesus tells him that he will deny him three times before the cock crows.

The **third episode (26:36-56)** is that of **Jesus' arrest in Gethsemane**. Once there, Jesus takes Peter, James, and John to one part Gethsemane and tells them to keep watch while he goes off to pray. Yet during the three times he goes off to pray that this cup be taken from him, they all fall asleep. Judas then shows up with a group from the chief priests and elders and he kisses Jesus to signal whom they are to arrest. At that point, one disciple takes a sword and cuts off the ear of the servant of the high priest, but Jesus tells the disciple to put the sword away because whoever takes up the sword will be killed by the sword. He further says that he could call twelve legions of angels to protect him, but it was necessary for all this to happen.

Given the fact that Matthew was written shortly after the destruction of Jerusalem in AD 70, we can see Jesus' words here as have extra significance to the original readers: *those who take up the sword will die by the sword*. This is exactly what had happened to the Jews during the Jewish revolt. In any case, Jesus asks the Temple police why they didn't arrest him in broad daylight, when he was teaching in the Temple. We already know the answer. If they did that, the crowds would have rioted. In any case, Jesus then lets himself be taken and the disciples all flee.

In the **fourth episode (26:57-75)**, the scene shifts to the **illegal night trial before the Sanhedrin**, while Peter is in the courtyard. The Sanhedrin produces witnesses who accuse Jesus of saying he would destroy **the Temple** and raise it up in three days. Then, when the high priest asks Jesus if he is **the Messiah**, Jesus affirms that he is, and then quotes **Daniel 7:13** and tells them that they will see the **Son of Man coming on the clouds of heaven and seated at the right hand of God**. By doing this, Jesus is actually telling the high priest that he is in the position of the little horn of Daniel 7, who would have been understood to be the infamous Antiochus Epiphanes. Not surprisingly, the Sanhedrin accuses him of blasphemy and beats him. Jesus has given them just what they wanted—an excuse to kill him. Jesus not only claimed to be the Messiah, but because he also dared to say that the Temple establishment, *and not Rome*, were the enemies of God, the Sanhedrin wanted him dead. Meanwhile, Peter is busying denying Jesus three times while in the courtyard. The cock crows, Peter remembers what Jesus had told him, and runs off in shame.

In the **fifth episode (27:1-31)**, the Sanhedrin reconvene the next morning to formally agree to what they had already decided during the night and then take Jesus to Pilate. Before **Jesus' trial before Pilate** begins, we are told that Judas regrets betraying Jesus, so he goes to the chief priests and tells them he has sinned. Ironically, the chief priests really don't care, so he throws the 30 silver coins he received for betraying Jesus into the Temple and goes out and hangs himself. In a further ironic twist, the chief priests realize they can't put the money they used to pay Judas to betray Jesus into the Temple treasury because it was "blood money." So, they use the money to buy the Potter's Field so it could be used as a burial site for foreigners.

Matthew says the field became known as the **Field of Blood**, and that it fulfilled what was spoken by Jeremiah, even though the verse Matthew quotes is really a conflation of **Jeremiah 32:6-15** and **Zechariah 11:12-13**. The upshot of using these passages is twofold: (1) Matthew is equating the Sanhedrin with the bad shepherds in Zechariah 11; and (2) Matthew is nevertheless tying the field they buy to the prophetic action of Jeremiah in his purchase of the field to signal the hope of new life after the "death" of the exile.

In any case, when the chief priests take Jesus to Pilate, they know he would not care about any religious accusation involving the Temple or a Messiah, so they decide to make a political accusation against Jesus. They tell Pilate that Jesus had claimed to be the **King of the Jews**. Any claim to kingship would be viewed as a threat to Caesar and it would bring about a quick execution. Pilate, though, sees the accusation as a trumped-up charge, so he tells the crowd that the chief priests had assembled there that he will release either Barabbas the revolutionary or Jesus the supposed Messiah. They choose Barabbas and insist that Jesus be crucified. When seen in the light of both Jesus' ministry, as well as the realities of the Jewish War of

AD 66-70, the choice is telling. They chose a revolutionary over their Messiah, and by doing so, they brought destruction upon Jerusalem.

Pilate releases Barabbas and sends Jesus off to be flogged, during which the Roman soldiers dress him up in a **scarlet robe**, put a **crown of thorns** on his head and **a cane in his hand**, and mockingly hail him as the **King of the Jews**. After that, they lead Jesus to be crucified. In the midst of all this, Matthew tells us that Pilate's wife had sent him a message to have nothing to do with Jesus' execution because he was, in fact, innocent. That is why Pilate publicly washes his hands and says he was innocent of Jesus' blood. In response to that public act, the crowd from the chief priests take responsibility for it and say that Jesus' blood would be upon them and their children. It is vital to note that this crowd was not all of Jerusalem, but rather the crowd assembled by the Sanhedrin. The reason they had the night trial and then brought Jesus to Pilate at the break of day was precisely because they wanted to avoid the populace altogether. The fact that it is the Sanhedrin who admits to getting Jesus crucified thus fits into what Jesus has been saying all along. Matthew puts the blame squarely on the chief priests and Sanhedrin. Yes, both Judas and Pilate knowingly played a part in the whole thing, but the guilt (the blood-money, the blood upon their heads) is put squarely on the Sanhedrin.

The **sixth episode (27:32-66)** tells us of **Jesus' crucifixion, death, and burial**. Jesus' cross is carried by **Simon of Cyrene**, and Jesus is crucified at **Golgotha**, where the Roman soldiers divide his garments by casting lots. The charge on his cross is "King of the Jews," and he is crucified with two **lestai** (revolutionaries) on either side of him. The crowd mocks him for what he said about the **Temple**, while the chief priests, scribes, and elders mock him for claiming to be the **Son of God** and the **King of Israel**. Darkness comes over the land from about noon to 3 o'clock, at which time Jesus cries out with the first verse of **Psalm 22**.

Many people think that is the moment in time God the Father turned away from Jesus, because all the world's sin was put upon Jesus, but we need to consider that Matthew is doing something else. As we've already noted, whenever Matthew quotes from the Old Testament, he is inviting the reader to go back to the original context and consider that original context in light of what is going on in his Gospel. In this case, when one reads Psalm 22, although it certainly begins with the speaker feeling that God has forsaken him, by the end of the psalm, it becomes clear that God hasn't forsaken him, but indeed has saved and vindicated him. Jesus knows how Psalm 22 ends, and he is making a declaration on the cross that even though it seems God has forsaken him, he knows he will be vindicated (as it turns out, three days later)!

In any case, some think he is crying out for **Elijah** to save him, but it is then that Jesus breathes his last. When that happens, the **curtain in the Temple** is torn in two, from top to bottom, and the centurion acknowledges that he was the Son of God. **Joseph of Arimathea** gets permission to bury Jesus, and he and Jesus' women followers wrap his body in linen and put it in a new tomb. All of that emphasizes the following: (A) The Sanhedrin successfully got Jesus crucified before most of Jerusalem knew about it; (B) Jesus was officially executed as a zealot revolutionary, even though he was no such thing; and (C) The real reason Jesus got crucified was because he claimed to be the Messiah, and said that the Temple establishment was the real problem and the Temple would be destroyed because they would make it into a symbol for the revolution. Nevertheless, there were some in the Sanhedrin, like Joseph of Arimathea, who clearly disagreed with what the Sanhedrin had done.

The oddest part of this episode, of course, is Matthew's description in 27:51-53 of an **earthquake**, of the **tombs being opened**, and of the **bodies of those who had "been asleep" (dead) being raised and then appearing to many in the holy city** after Jesus had been raised. As odd as these verses may sound, they actually do make sense when read in light of the traditional Jewish apocalyptic worldview regarding God's coming Kingdom. In short, the Jews were expecting that when the Messiah came to establish God's Kingdom, the old creation would suffer upheaval and be swept away, there would be the resurrection of the dead, and that would signal **the end of the old age** and **the beginning of the Messianic New Age**, in which the Messiah would reign in God's Kingdom in the new creation—and they expected it to happen in one fell swoop.

The Christian worldview, no doubt rooted in the death and resurrection of Jesus, took that Jewish expectation and tweaked it. The Christian proclamation is that all of what the Jews were expected *had happened, but only in part*, and that there would be an interim time before God's Kingdom, the new creation and new age comes in full. That is what Matthew is emphasizing here with the mention of the earthquake, the rocks splitting apart, and the resurrection of some of the dead. It is his creative way to drive that point home: **The resurrection life of the Kingdom of God and the Age to Come had invaded the present age. The old was being done away with and new resurrection life had come.**

At the end of the episode, the chief priests and Pharisees convince Pilate to have a guard put at the tomb, because they are afraid that Jesus' followers might try to steal the body and claim he was resurrected. The reason why Matthew mentions this is because three days after Jesus' crucifixion, his followers did start to claim that he had resurrected from the dead and that they had seen him and were witnesses to the resurrection. No doubt one of the accusations made to try to discredit that claim was that they had simply stolen the body. That is why Matthew includes these verses. He is pointing out that Jesus' followers couldn't have stolen Jesus' body because the Sanhedrin had made sure that there was a Roman guard at the tomb.

The **seventh and final episode (28:1-20)** is that of the **resurrection**. Matthew tells us there was an earthquake, that an angel came down from heaven and rolled away the stone, and that the guards were so afraid that they became like dead men. This sounds very similar to those odd verses in 27:51-53, where there is an earthquake and some of the dead are raised after Jesus' resurrection. Whether or not there were two earthquakes (one at his crucifixion and another at his resurrection) or whether both passages really are describing the same earthquake (after all, 27:53 says that the dead of the other people were raised *after* Jesus' resurrection), we need to consider what Matthew is doing here. The bottom line in both of these passages is that **with the crucifixion and resurrection of Jesus, the life of the Messianic age and Kingdom of God has invaded this present old age.**

In any case, the women then go to the tomb after the Sabbath and find the stone has been rolled away. They are then told by an angel that Jesus had been raised. After they look in the tomb, the angel tells them to go tell Jesus' disciples that he will see them in Galilee. As the women go to tell the disciples, the guards go tell the chief priests what had happened. The Sanhedrin decides to pay them off and tells them to say that the disciples came and stole the body while they were sleeping. If Pilate got word of it, they would cover for the soldiers and keep them out of trouble. Matthew then adds an editorial note and says that that story was still circulated among the Jews up to the time of his writing (in AD 70-80).

Matthew ends by saying that when Jesus appeared to the disciples in Galilee, some worshipped, but some still doubted. To be clear, they couldn't have doubted he was alive. Perhaps they doubted whether or not he was really the Messiah, or they doubted what their mission really was to be. Maybe they still were having a hard time accepting that Jesus was now telling them to go out and **make disciples of all nations**. In any case, Jesus tells them to baptize in the name of the Father, the Son, and the Holy Spirit (clearly a Trinitarian understanding of God), and then tells them that he will be with them until the **consummation of the age**, thus highlighting the early Christian worldview of the "already/not yet" of the two ages. The followers of Jesus, as the reconstituted people of God, the Church, have a mission to take the Kingdom of God out to the Gentile world while still living in this present, old age. The full end of this present age, the consummation of the Kingdom of God, and the dawn of the new Messianic age is still to come.

Until it does come, though, Jesus has sent his followers on a mission. He is the Messiah, the King, and we are his royal messengers who are to go out to the four corners of the earth, proclaim his Kingdom to the Gentiles, and to gather followers from all nations.

# THE GOSPEL OF LUKE

**Time of Writing**: The Gospel of Luke was probably written around the same time as Matthew, sometime during the 70s-80s, after the Jewish War. That being said, there is some speculation that it was written earlier than that. Given the fact that Acts doesn't record Paul's death, some speculate that Paul hadn't been martyred yet when Luke had written Acts. If that is the case, then logic dictates that Luke's Gospel must have been written before Acts. That is why some speculate that Luke-Acts may have been written in the mid-60s.

**Authorship**: According to Church tradition, Luke the physician and missionary partner with the Apostle Paul wrote both the Gospel of Luke and the Acts of the Apostles. Whereas Matthew had a decidedly Jewish audience, Luke's audience is most certainly Gentile.

### The Big Things to Know in Luke
In addition to sharing the same "big things" as in Mark, Luke has a few unique points of emphases:

A. **Luke's Historical Rooting of His Gospel**: Luke takes extra care to root his story in the history of both the Roman Empire and the Temple Priesthood. In his infancy narrative, he points out that the angel Gabriel's appearance to both Zechariah and Mary took place *in the days of Herod*. He also sets the birth of Jesus during the time of *Augustus' census decree*, while Quirinius was the governor of Syria. And he has the beginning of John the Baptist's ministry dated to the *15th year of Tiberius*, when Pilate was the governor of Judea, Herod was tetrarch of Galilee, Philip was tetrarch of Ituraea and Trachonitis, and Lysanias was tetrarch of Abilene, during the high priesthood of Annas and Caiaphas.

B. **Jesus, Not Caesar**: From the beginning of his infancy narrative and all the way through his Gospel, Luke makes it a point to emphasize that the true ruler of the world wasn't Caesar, but rather Jesus.

C. **The Work of the Holy Spirit**: More so than either Mark or Matthew, Luke emphasizes the role of Holy Spirit, not only throughout the life and ministry of Jesus, but also throughout the life and ministry of the early Church in Acts. What Luke is trying to emphasize is the continuity between the work of Christ and the mission of the early Church.

**D. Jesus' Teachings and Parables**: Even though the Gospel of Matthew portrays Jesus as a Moses-like teacher, it is Luke that contains the greatest number of parables. Matthew certainly contains its fair share of parables, but they are all over the place in Luke. The purpose of the parables is to subversively teach about the Kingdom of God in such a way that those who are spiritually blind and deaf because of their own kind of idolatry won't be able to truly grasp what Jesus is teaching, but those who are truly seeking the Kingdom of God will understand what Jesus is saying.

## The Gospel of Luke: Story Chart

| | | | | |
|---|---|---|---|---|
| **Infancy Narrative (1:1-2:52)** | 1:1-4 Dedication to Theophilus | 1:5-25 Birth of John the Baptist Foretold | 1:26-38 Birth of Jesus Foretold | 1:39-56 Mary Visits Elizabeth |
| | 1:57-80 Birth of John the Baptist | 2:1-21 Birth of Jesus | 2:22-40 Jesus Presented in the Temple | 2:41-52 12-Year-Old Jesus in the Temple |
| **Beginning of Jesus' Ministry in Galilee (3:1-6:49)** | 3:1-22 John the Baptist<br><br>Mk 1:1-11<br>Mt 3:1-17 | 3:23-38 The Genealogy of Jesus | 4:1-13 Temptations of Jesus<br><br>Mk 1:12-13<br>Mt 4:1-11 | 4:14-15 Jesus Begins Ministry<br><br>Mk 1:14-15<br>Mt 4:12-17 |
| | 4:16-30 Jesus Rejected at Nazareth<br><br>Mk 6:1-6<br>Mt 13:54-58 | 4:31-37 *Capernaum* Synagogue Unclean Spirit<br><br>Mk 1:21-28 | 4:38-44 Simon's Mother-in-Law<br><br>Mk 1:29-39<br>Mt 8:14-17<br>Mt 4:23-25 | 5:1-11 *Lake Gennesaret* Jesus Calls First Disciples<br><br>Mk 1:16-20<br>Mt 4:18-22 |
| | 5:12-16 Jesus Cleanses a Leper<br><br>Mk 1:40-45<br>Mt 8:1-4 | 5:17-26 Jesus Heals a Paralytic<br><br>Mk 2:1-12<br>Mt 9:2-8 | 5:27-32 Jesus Calls Levi<br><br>Mk 2:13-17<br>Mt 9:9-13 | 5:33-39 Questions About Fasting<br><br>Mk 2:18-22<br>Mt 9:14-17 |
| | 6:1-5 Working on Sabbath<br><br>Mk 2:23-28<br>Mt 12:1-8 | 6:6-11 Withered Hand on Sabbath<br><br>Mk 3:1-6<br>Mt 12:9-14 | 6:12-16 Jesus Calls the Twelve<br><br>Mk 3:13-19<br>Mt 10:1-4 | 6:17-49 Sermon on the Plain<br><br>Mt 5:3-12, 38-42<br>Mt 7:1-5, 24-27 |

Gospel of Luke | 135

| | | | | |
|---|---|---|---|---|
| | 7:1-10<br>Jesus Heals Centurion's Servant<br><br>Mt 8:5-13 | 7:11-17<br>Jesus Raises Widow's Son<br>*Nain* | 7:18-35<br>John the Baptist's Question<br><br>Mt 11:1-19 | 7:36-8:3<br>Simon the Pharisee's House<br><br>Mk 14:1-11*<br>Mt 26:1-16* |
| **Further Galilean Ministry (7:1-9:62)** | 8:4-21<br>*Parable of Sower*<br>Mk 4:1-34<br>Mt 13:1-53<br><br>Jesus' Family<br>Mk 3:31-34<br>Mt 12:46-50 | 8:22-25<br>Jesus Calms the Storm<br><br><br><br>Mk 4:35-41<br>Mt 8:23-27 | 8:26-39<br>Demoniac of the Gerasenes<br><br><br><br>Mk 5:1-20<br>Mt 8:28-9:1 | 8:40-56<br>Jarius' Daughter Woman with Blood Flow<br><br>Mk 5:21-43<br>Mt 9:18-26 |
| | 9:1-17<br>The Twelve/ Herod/ Jesus-5,000<br><br>Mk 6:14-46<br>Mt 14:1-21 | 9:18-27<br>Peter's Confession<br><br><br>Mk 8:27-9:1<br>Mt 16:13-28 | 9:28-36<br>Trans-figuration<br><br><br>Mk 9:2-13<br>Mt 17:1-13 | 9:37-45<br>Jesus Heals Boy/ Foretells Death<br><br>Mk 9:14-29<br>Mt 17:14-23 |

| | | |
|---|---|---|
| | 9:46-50<br>Who is the Greatest?<br><br>Mk 9:33-50<br>Mt 18:1-14 | 9:51-62<br>*To Jerusalem*<br>Rejection in Samaria<br>Foxes Have Holes |

| | | | | | |
|---|---|---|---|---|---|
| | 10:1-24<br>The 70<br>Woe to Cities<br><br><br><br>Mt 11:20-24 | 10:25-37<br>*Parable*<br>Good Samaritan | 10:38-42<br>Mary and Martha | 11:1-13<br>The Lord's Prayer<br><br><br>Mt 6:5-18<br>Mt 7:7-11 | 11:14-36<br>Beelzebub Controversy /Sign of Jonah<br><br>Mk 3:20-35<br>Mt 12:22-45 |
| **Journey to Jerusalem (2) (14:1-17:10)** | 11:37-54<br>Jesus Denounces Pharisees and Scribes<br><br>Mt 15:1-9 | 12:1-12<br>Jesus Warns the Crowds<br><br><br><br>Mk 8:14-21<br>Mt 10:26-33 | 12:13-34<br>*Parable*<br>Rich Fool<br><br><br><br>Mt 6:19-34 | 12:35-48<br>Keep Watch Faithful Servants<br><br><br>Mt 24:42-51 | 12:49-59<br>Interpret the Times<br><br>Mt 10:34-36<br>Mt 16:2-3<br>Mt 5:25-26 |
| | 13:1-9<br>*Parable*<br>The Barren Fig Tree | 13:10-17<br>Healing a Disabled Woman | 13:18-21<br>Mustard Seed/ Leaven<br><br>Mt 13:31-33 | 13:22-30<br>Narrow Door<br><br><br>Mt. 7:13-14 | 13:31-35<br>Lament Over Jerusalem<br><br>Mt 23:37-39 |

| | | 14:1-24<br>*Pharisee's House:*<br>Healing on Sabbath<br>*Parables:* Wedding Feast, Great Banquet<br><br>Mt 22:1-14 | 14:25-35<br>*Call to Discipleship:*<br>The Cost of Discipleship<br><br><br><br>Mt 10:38-39 |
|---|---|---|---|
| **Journey to Jerusalem (2) (14:1-17:10)** | | 15:1-32<br>*Pharisees Object to Tax-Collectors/Sinners*<br>*Parables:* Lost Sheep, Lost Coin, Prodigal Son<br><br>Mt 18:12-14 | 16:1-13<br>*Jesus to the Disciples*<br><br>*Parable:* The Dishonest Manager<br><br>Mt 6:24 |
| | | 16:14-31<br>*Pharisees' Love of Money*<br>Torah and Kingdom<br>Rich Man and Lazarus | 17:1-10<br>*Jesus to the Disciples*<br>Scandals and Obedient Slaves<br><br>Mt 18:6-7 |

| | 17:11-19<br>Jesus Cleanses Ten Lepers | 17:20-37<br>Kingdom of God Among You | 18:1-17<br>*Parables*<br>Persistent Widow;<br>Pharisee/Tax-Collector | 18:18-30<br>Rich Young Ruler<br><br>Mk 10:17-31<br>Mt 19:16-30 |
|---|---|---|---|---|
| **Journey to Jerusalem (3) (17:11-19:27)** | 18:31-34<br>Jesus Foretells His Death<br><br>Mk 10:32-34<br>Mt 20:17-19 | 18:35-43<br>*To Jericho*<br>Jesus Heals Blind Beggar<br><br>Mk 10:46-52<br>Mt 20:29-34 | 19:1-10<br>*Jericho*<br>Jesus and Zacchaeus | 19:11-27<br>Parable of the Ten Minas |

| Jesus at Jerusalem Temple (19:28-21:38) | 19:28-44 Un-triumphal Entry  Mk 11:1-11 Mt 21:1-11 | 19:45-48 Jesus Trashes the Temple  Mk 11:12-26 Mt 21:12-22 | 20:1-8 Questioning Jesus' Authority  Mk 11:27-33 Mt 21:23-27 |
|---|---|---|---|
| | 20:9-18 Parable of the Wicked Tenants  Mk 12:1-12 Mt 21:33-46 | 20:19-44 Taxes to Caesar; Resurrection; Messiah as the Son of David  Mk 12:13-40 Mt 22:15-46 | 20:45-21:4 Warning about Scribes/Widow's Offering  Mt 23:1-39 Mk 12:41-44 |
| | | 21:5-38 Olivet Discourse Mk 13:1-37/ Mt 24:1-51 | |
| Last Supper to Resurrection Appearances (22:1-24:53) | 22:1-6 Plot to Kill Jesus Judas Agrees to Betray Jesus  Mk 14:10-11 Mt 26:14-16 | 22:7-38 *Passover* Last Supper Jesus Foretells Peter's Denial  Mk 14:12-31 Mt 26:17-35 | 22:39-53 *Mount of Olives* Judas' Betrayal Jesus is Arrested  Mk 14:32-52 Mt 26:36-56 |
| | 22:54-71 *Night Trial to Daybreak* Jesus Mocked Peter's Denial  Mk 14:53-72 Mt 26:57-75 | 23:1-25 *Morning* Before Pilate, Herod, Pilate  Mk 15:1-20 Mt 27:1-31 | 23:26-56 Crucifixion Death Burial  Mk 15:21-47 Mt 27:32-66 |
| | 24:1-12 The Resurrection of Jesus  Mk 16:1-20 Mt 28:1-20 | 24:13-35 The Road to Emmaus | 24:34-53 Jesus Before the Disciples Ascension of Jesus |

## Walkthrough of Luke

The easiest way to describe Luke's Gospel is that whereas Matthew basically takes Mark and expands on it while keeping the same basic narrative structure as Mark, Luke takes parts of Mark, parts of Matthew, and some parts unique to Luke, and puts them together to construct a very different narrative structure. Also, Luke's audience is distinctly Gentile, which is why he does not include too many quotations or allusions from the Old Testament. According to Church tradition, Luke's Gospel is often represented with an ox, because in Luke, not only does Jesus take his time to get places (like Jerusalem), but he is presented as bearing others' burdens more than in Matthew or Mark.

As a small editorial note, since so many episodes in Luke are similar to that of both Mark and Matthew, and since I've already covered them in Mark and Matthew, I do not spend as much time with them here in Luke. Therefore, I suggest looking back at those parallel passages in Mark and Matthew from time to time as you read through Luke.

### 1. Luke's Infancy Narrative (Chapters 1-2)

Like Matthew, Luke also has an infancy narrative. Luke's infancy narrative, though, is completely different than that of Matthew. Luke begins his Gospel with a **short dedication (1:1-14)** in which he addresses someone named **Theophilus**. Luke says he has set down an "orderly account" of the life and ministry of Jesus so that Theophilus might have certainty regarding the things he has been taught regarding the faith. The name *Theophilus* means "Loved by God," so it could be the name of a specific person, or it could be a more general term Luke uses to address new believers within the Church.

The **first episode (1:5-25)** is that of the angel Gabriel's birth announcement to Zechariah the priest while he was serving in the Temple during the days of King Herod of Judah. Despite the fact that Zechariah and his wife Elizabeth were old and Elizabeth barren, Gabriel tells Zechariah that they would have a son. The birth announcement is similar to that of Samson's mother in **Judges 13** and Hannah in **I Samuel 1**. Not only do all three accounts involve a barren woman, but they all declare that the child (Samson, Samuel, and John) is to be a Nazirite from birth, never to drink wine or strong drink. Gabriel further tells Zechariah that John will be filled with the **Holy Spirit** from the time he is born and will go out in the **spirit** of **Elijah** to prepare a people for the Lord. Zechariah, though, doesn't believe that it is possible for Elizabeth to conceive, and so he doubts Gabriel's word. As a consequence, he is struck dumb until the time of John's birth. After his time in the Temple was up, he goes back home to Elizabeth and soon she conceives. She then keeps herself hidden for five months.

In the **second episode (1:26-38)**, the scene shifts to Nazareth, where Gabriel makes a second birth announcement to Mary during the sixth month of Elizabeth's pregnancy. Gabriel tells Mary she is going to become pregnant and give birth to a son whom she is to name Jesus, and that he is going to be called the **Son of the Most High**, will be given the **throne of David**, and will have a kingdom that will never end. The announcement is thoroughly messianic: *Jesus will be the promised king of Israel through whom God would restore Israel.* Unlike Zechariah, Mary doesn't express doubt, but rather asks how it would happen, given that she was a virgin. Gabriel tells her that the **Holy Spirit** will come over her and it will be through the power of the Most High that it would happen. He then refers to the child to be born as the **holy one** and says he will be called the **Son of God**. There actually is a double meaning going on with the terms *Son of the Most High* and *Son of God*. On one hand, they were applied to the king of Israel who was adopted as the "God's son" when he took his throne. But as Luke proceeds in his Gospel, it becomes clear that Jesus is the Son of God on a much deeper level.

In the **third episode (1:39-56)**, Mary visits Elizabeth, and when Elizabeth hears Mary's greeting at the door, we are told that she was **filled with the Holy Spirit** and the baby in her womb leapt for joy. It is at this point that Mary gives what is known as **Mary's Magnificat**, a praise song that echoes various themes found throughout the psalms and other passages in the Old Testament, particularly that of God caring for and exalting the lowly while bringing down the arrogant and powerful. She clearly understood that her son would be the Messiah who would fulfill the hopes of Israel and would save them. Of course, how that would eventually play out and what Mary herself probably expected will prove to be two different things.

The **fourth episode (1:57-80)** is that of the birth of John the Baptist. When he is born, everyone is shocked when Elizabeth says his name would be John, because everyone expected him to be named after his father. When Zechariah confirms in writing that this is to be the case, he is **filled with the Holy Spirit** and his speech is restored. Zechariah then launches into a praise song of his own that centers on the messianic hopes of the Jews at that time. He mentions God raising up a **horn of salvation** from the **House of David**, seeing it in terms of freedom from their enemies. He also mentions **God's covenant with Abraham** and says his son will be a **prophet of the Most High** who will prepare the way for the coming Messiah. The episode ends by telling us that John grew up, was **strengthened in the Spirit**, and remained in the **wilderness** until he began his public ministry to Israel. The image of the wilderness evokes the notion of the Exodus wanderings as well as the wilderness of the exile.

The **fifth episode (2:1-21)** is that of the birth of Jesus. Luke tells us that Joseph and Mary were originally living in Nazareth but had to travel to Bethlehem to register for the first census by Caesar Augustus, while Quirinius was the governor of Syria. The problem, though, is that Quirinius was the governor of Syria from AD 6-12 and Caesar's first census happened in AD 6. Yet Matthew clearly says that Jesus was born before the death of Herod the Great (4 BC). On top of that, Luke himself says in 1:5 that Gabriel gave his announcement to Zechariah *in the days of King Herod*. That would clearly imply that John and Jesus were born during the days of King Herod as well. So how could Jesus have been born during the days of King Herod, before 4 BC, and also be born during the census of Caesar Augustus in AD 6?

There is a huge amount of scholarly debate about this, but the easiest and most logical way to make sense of this chronological problem is to consider the possibility that Luke is exercising a certain amount of creative license here and has placed Jesus' birth during the time of Caesar's census because he wants to contrast Jesus' Lordship with that of Caesar. What Luke is doing is something akin to what movie directors do when they make a movie about a historical figure. Sometimes they move a few historical details around in order to highlight certain themes they want to emphasize in their telling of the story. In any case, Matthew and Luke do agree on one key point: **Jesus was born in Bethlehem but grew up in Nazareth.**

Luke's mention of the shepherds coming to visit Jesus also serves to further highlight his contrast between Jesus with Caesar. While lowly shepherds visit Israel's Messiah laying in a feeding trough, Caesar is busying exercising his lordship. Not only does this picture emphasize the humbleness of the Messiah, but it also highlights the association of the king of Israel with shepherds. David was a lowly shepherd in Bethlehem before he became king, and Jesus, the Messiah, was visited by the shepherds of Bethlehem at his birth.

The **sixth episode (2:22-40)** is that of the presentation of the baby Jesus in the Temple. Here, we are told the reactions of an old man named **Simeon** and a prophetess named **Anna**. The **Holy Spirit** had revealed to Simeon that he would not die before he had seen the Messiah of the Lord. When Simeon sees the baby Jesus, he holds him in his arms and gives was is known as **Simeon's Song**, where he says that Jesus is the **salvation of God**, the **light to the Gentiles**, and the **glory of Israel**. Simeon also tells Mary that Jesus will cause the **falling and rising** of many in Israel, that he will be **a sign of opposition** that reveals the thoughts of many hearts, and that **a sword would pierce her own soul** as well. He realizes that with the coming of the Messiah, the true intentions of many in Israel will be revealed. There is also the 84-year-old prophetess named **Anna**, who had been married for seven years, but who had then been a widow ever since. She too tells people there in the Temple about Jesus. After Jesus' dedication in the Temple, Joseph takes Mary and Jesus and returns to Nazareth in Galilee, where Jesus grows up and is filled with wisdom and the grace of God.

In the **seventh episode (2:41-52)**, it is twelve years later. Joseph, Mary, and Jesus are back in Jerusalem for Passover. When it is over, they leave to go back to Nazareth, but soon realize they left Jesus behind. When they go back to Jerusalem, they find Jesus in the Temple, talking with the rabbis. When they tell him they've been worried sick, Jesus says, *"Didn't you know that I must be in my Father's House?"* Luke says they didn't understand what he meant. This indicates that although they believed he was to be the Messiah they didn't yet fully understand who he really was. The entire episode of Jesus in the Temple is a foreshadowing of his death and resurrection. The fact he is **twelve years old** equals the twelve tribes of Israel. His parents not being able to find him **after Passover** foreshadows Jesus being in the tomb after Passover. And their finding him in the **Temple after three days of searching** foreshadows his death, resurrection, and laying the foundation of the new Temple, the Church.

### 2. The Beginning of Jesus' Ministry in Galilee (3:1-6:49)

The next section in Luke covers Jesus' early ministry in Galilee, from the ministry of John the Baptist and Jesus' baptism to Jesus' calling of his twelve apostles. The **first episode (3:1-22)** is that of the baptism of Jesus. Luke begins, though, by placing the beginning of John's ministry during the 15th year of

**Tiberias Caesar**, when **Pilate** was the governor of Judea, when **Herod** was the Tetrarch of Galilee, **Philip** was the Tetrarch of Iturea and Trachonitis, and **Lysanias** was the Tetrarch of Abilene, during the high priesthood of **Annas** and **Caiaphas**. Since Tiberias became Caesar in AD 14, that puts the beginning of John's ministry at AD 28.

As with Mark and Matthew, Luke identifies John as the *voice crying out in the wilderness* of **Isaiah 40:3-5**. John's message is one of coming wrath and the **Day of YHWH**. He tells the crowds that they are **offspring of vipers** and says that God's axe was ready to cut down every tree that wasn't bearing fruit. When they ask him what they should do, he tells them that if they want to be spared from God's wrath, they are to share their garments and food with those in need. He also tells tax-collectors not to cheat people and soldiers not to harass or extort people. When some say they think he might be the Messiah, John makes clear he is not. He only baptized in water, but there would be a **Coming One** who would baptize in the **Holy Spirit** and fire and would "clean out the threshing floor" and burn up the chaff with an unquenchable fire. John's message is clear: **The coming Messiah was going to purify Israel, and in the process, purge it of the unfaithful.**

Herod, though, has imprisoned John for speaking out against his marriage to his brother's wife, but not before John baptized Jesus. Luke tells us that at Jesus' baptism, Heaven was opened, the Holy Spirit came down in the form of a dove, and a voice from Heaven said, *"You are my Beloved Son! I am well-pleased with you!"* (A quotation from **Psalm 2:7**).

After that, Luke gives us the genealogy of Jesus in the **second episode (3:23-38)**. Although it traces Jesus' lineage through Joseph, just like in Matthew, Luke's genealogy is vastly different. To make sense of this, we need to realize that neither Matthew nor Luke was trying to give a "historically accurate" genealogy akin to an *Ancestry.com* report. Rather, they were doing Christology with their genealogies, not strict history. Matthew's audience is Jewish, and one of the main themes he emphasizes in his Gospel is that Jesus is the **Jewish Messiah, the King of the Jews**. Therefore, his genealogy goes through the kings of Judah and ends with Abraham, the father of the Jews. Luke's audience is Gentile, though, so he isn't just going to emphasize that Jesus is the Jewish Messiah. He is going to emphasize that Jesus is **Lord of all humanity**. Therefore, he doesn't trace Jesus' genealogy through the kings of Judah because that was irrelevant for his audience. Instead, he takes things all the way back to Adam to emphasize that Jesus is Lord of all.

The **third episode (4:1-13)** covers Jesus' temptations in the wilderness. After his baptism, Jesus is led by the Holy Spirit into the wilderness for **40 days** to be tested by the Devil. The number **40** is always associated with either the judgment of God or the threat of God's judgment (Noah's flood for 40 days and nights and Israel in the wilderness for 40 years, for example). Here, Jesus is tempted to (1) turn stones to bread, (2) worship the Devil in exchange for all the kingdoms of the world, and (3) throw himself off the Temple and be saved by angels. In each case, Jesus rebukes the Devil by quoting **Deuteronomy 8:3, 6:13** and **6:16**, each one referencing a time during the Exodus where Israel failed to be faithful to God. The point here is clear: **Jesus goes to the wilderness and is tempted just like Israel, but he succeeds in being faithful to God whereas Israel had failed.** Therefore, he proves himself to be the true Son of God.

The **fourth episode (4:14-15)** transitions back to Galilee, where Jesus then begins his ministry. Once again, Luke emphasizes the role of the Holy Spirit when he says Jesus returned to Galilee **in the power of the Spirit**. Interestingly, Luke doesn't have Jesus proclaiming, *"Repent! The Kingdom of God is near."* Luke simply has Jesus to back to Galilee to start teaching in their synagogues. The reason for this is because the term "Kingdom of God" has clearly Jewish messianic overtones that Luke's Gentile audience would not have picked up. Therefore, Luke has chosen not to use it.

In the **fifth episode (4:16-30)**, Jesus goes back to the synagogue in Nazareth and formerly begins his ministry when he takes the scroll of the prophet Isaiah, reads **Isaiah 61:1-2** where it says, *"The Spirit of the Lord is upon me…"* and declares that the passage is fulfilled in him. Isaiah 61:1-12 is a very significant passage, for in its original context, set after the Babylonian Exile, it prophetically looks forward to when YHWH would fully restore the returned exiles from Babylon. They had returned from exile in 539 BC and hoped that God would pour out His Spirit upon them, that they would have a glorious rebuilt Temple, a Davidic king, and that they would be free of foreign oppression. None of that really happened. Although physically out of Babylonian Exile, the Jews still viewed still in "exile" of the old age.

Passages like Isaiah 61 looked forward to that time when God would bring about that promised full restoration by means of an **anointed one** (Messiah) upon whom God would put His Spirit. So, when Jesus declares that Isaiah 61 is being fulfilled in him, he is claiming that he, in fact, is the long-awaited Messiah. The people of Nazareth are outraged, because after all, they knew him growing up. He was just the son of Joseph, and therefore didn't seem like "king material." Jesus' remarks about **Elijah** and **Elisha** are also telling. Both men had continual conflicts with the leaders of the northern kingdom of Israel, and both men had gone and revealed the glory and power of the God of Israel to **Gentiles**. Therefore, what Jesus is saying is that not only does he know his own people are going to reject him, but that the Gospel will eventually go out to the Gentile world. When they then try to throw him over a cliff, he somehow manages to get away.

The **sixth episode (4:31-37)** takes place in the synagogue in Capernaum and involves Jesus casting a demon from a man in the synagogue. The unclean spirit knows who Jesus is, the **Holy One of God**, Jesus tells the unclean spirit to shut up, and then he casts the spirit out of the man. The response from the people there is one of amazement, and they marvel at his authority. Already, we are seeing mixed reaction from his fellow Jews. Those in Nazareth reject him, while some in Capernaum accept him.

The **seventh episode (4:38-44)** is that of Jesus healing Peter's mother-in-law. That evening, Jesus heals more people and casts out more demons. Whenever the demons try to shout out, *"You are the Son of God!"* Jesus silences them. Interestingly, although in the parallel passage in Mark we are told that Jesus goes about preaching and healing throughout the synagogues of *Galilee*, Luke says Jesus went throughout the synagogues of *Judea*, even though Capernaum is in Galilee. (Perhaps Luke the historian wasn't really good at geography!).

The **eighth episode (5:1-11)** tells us about Jesus calling his first disciples. He is teaching the crowds by the Sea of Galilee and uses Simon's boat to get out into the water as he is teaching. After he is done, he tells Simon, along with James and John, to take the boat out for a catch. Despite having caught nothing all night, they let down their nets and haul in a massive catch of fish. Jesus then tells them that they will now be catching men, and so they leave their nets to follow him. Thus, the entire story of the **great catch of fish** essentially serves as a metaphor for Jesus telling them that they would become "fishers of men."

In the **ninth episode (5:12-16)**, Jesus cleanses a leper and tells him not to tell anyone what he has done for him. Instead, Jesus tells the man to go show himself to the priest and offer up the offering for cleansing that Moses designated in the Torah to bear witness to them.

In the **tenth episode (5:17-26)**, Jesus heals a paralytic whose friends had lowered through the roof. Before he heals him, though, Jesus tells him that his sins are forgiven. Immediately, the scribes and Pharisees object to this because only God was able to forgive sins. So, in order to show that he has authority to forgive sins, Jesus tells the paralytic to take up his mat and go home, which he then does.

In the **eleventh episode (5:27-32)**, Jesus calls Levi the tax-collector to follow him and be a disciple. Levi follows Jesus and gives a banquet for him, but the Pharisees object to Jesus eating with "tax-collectors and sinners." In response, Jesus says that it is the sick who need a doctor, not those who are healthy, and that he hasn't come to call the righteous to repentance, but rather the sinners to repentance.

In the **twelfth episode (5:33-39)**, some Pharisees and some of the disciples of John the Baptist ask Jesus why his disciples don't fast. Jesus says the wedding guests should celebrate with feasting when the bridegroom is with them, and that the time to fast will be when he is taken away from them. This further clarifies his eating with tax-collectors and sinners. He is the bridegroom, and because they have repented, they are the wedding guests. Therefore, it is time to celebrate. Jesus then talks about pouring new wine into new wineskins, not old ones, and sewing a new piece of cloth onto a new garment, not an old one. Both examples stress the discontinuity between the Old Covenant that was centered on the Torah and the New Covenant that is centered on himself. There is no longer any need to continue with the practices of the Old Covenant that anticipated the Kingdom of God, because the Kingdom has now arrived.

In the **thirteenth episode (6:1-5)**, the Pharisees question Jesus about why his disciples "worked" on the Sabbath when they picked heads of grain. Jesus refers to David eating the Bread of the Presence, even though the Torah says only the priests were allowed to eat it (**I Samuel 21**), and then declares that he, the Son of Man, is Lord of the Sabbath.

In the **fourteenth episode (6:6-11)**, the Pharisees and scribes are looking to see if Jesus would heal on the Sabbath so they could have an accusation against him. Jesus brings a man with a withered hand in front of everyone and asks them what the Torah allows to be done on the Sabbath: Good or evil? Saving a life or destroying a life? With the answer being obvious, Jesus then heals the man's withered hand. It is then that the Pharisees start discussing with each other what to do about Jesus.

In the **fifteenth episode (6:12-16)**, Jesus goes up a mountain and chooses twelve apostles from among the larger group of his disciples and then sends them to the surrounding Jewish towns to proclaim his teaching.

The **sixteenth episode (6:17-49)** is a section of teaching material commonly known as the **Sermon on the Plain**. It is essentially a truncated version of Matthew's **Sermon on the Mount**. We should realize that what is presented both in Matthew and here in Luke was probably not a single sermon Jesus gave at one point in time. Instead, we should see that both Matthew and Luke probably have compiled numerous things Jesus had preached and taught over the course of his ministry and have fashioned them into their respective "sermons" in their own works.

Whereas the *Sermon on the Mount* was addressed to his fellow Jews, in Luke's *Sermon on the Plain*, Jesus teaches not only his disciples, but also huge crowds that come from Judea, Jerusalem, Tyre and Sidon. The sermon begins with the Beatitudes (6:20-23) as well as a number of Woes (6:24-26), in which Jesus is saying that the Kingdom of God is for those who are currently poor, hungry, crying, and hated, whereas those who are currently rich, satisfied, laughing, and loved already have their reward, and will eventually get what is coming to them. He then speaks about loving your enemies (6:27-36) and says it is easy to love those who love you and to do good things to those you know will do the same for you, but if you love your enemies, pray for them, turn the other cheek, and give without expecting anything in return, **then you will be Sons of the Most High**. It is interesting to note that is how Gabriel describes Jesus in the birth announcement to Mary in Luke 1:32.

After that, Jesus then emphasizes that you will be judged the by same standard by which you judged others and will be forgiven to the same extent you forgive others (6:37-42). To illustrate this, Jesus gives the **parable of the blind leading the blind**. If neither one can see, both will fall into a pit. Therefore, instead of judging others and looking to get that speck out of other people's eyes, you should first take the log out of your own eye. Only then will you be able to see clearly enough to even begin to help the other people get the speck out of his own eye…and avoid falling into a pit. Related to this is Jesus' analogy of a tree being known by is fruit (6:43-45): A good man will produce "good fruit," whereas a bad man will produce "bad fruit."

He ends with yet another analogy to illustrate the two kinds of people who listen to him (6:46-49). Those who listen and put his words into action are like those who build a house on a solid foundation, whereas those who don't do what Jesus says are like those who build a house without any foundation at all. When the river flooded, the house with the solid foundation wasn't shaken, whereas the house without a foundation collapsed.

### 3. Further Galilean Ministry (7:1-9:62)

The next section in Luke is composed of a host of various episodes (some found in Mark and Matthew, some unique to Luke) that further describe Jesus' Galilean ministry. The **first episode (7:1-10)** is that of Jesus healing the servant of a centurion who is sick and about to die. The centurion sends some of the elders of the Jews to Jesus to vouch for him and to ask Jesus on his behalf. Jesus agrees to go with the elders to the centurion's house, but on the way, they are stopped by some of the centurion's friends to just ask Jesus to say the word for the servant to be healed. Jesus marvels at the centurion's faith and says he hasn't found that much faith in Israel. He then gives the word, and the servant is healed.

The **second episode (7:11-17)** is unique to Luke. It takes place in Nain, a small town in Galilee, where Jesus and the disciples come across a funeral process of a young man whose mother was a widow. Jesus tells her not to cry, touches the coffin, and tells the dead man to get up, which he does. The people who witness it are convinced that Jesus is a great prophet and that God had visited His people. Once again, though, despite the fact that Nain is a town in Galilee, Luke tells us that word spread about Jesus *throughout Judea* and the entire surrounding district.

In the **third episode (7:18-35)**, some of John the Baptist's disciples come and ask Jesus if he is truly the Coming One. Jesus affirms he is by alluding to **Isaiah 61**, the same passage he read in Nazareth in 4:16-30. After they leave, he tells the crowds no one born of a woman was greater than John and quotes **Malachi 3:1** to say that John was the messenger about which Malachi prophesied. Luke then draws a distinction between those who acknowledged John to be righteous and the Pharisees and scribes who had refused to be baptized by John. They are the ones Jesus is referring to when he condemns "the men of this generation" of accusing John of having a demon and then him of being a glutton, a drunkard, and a friend of tax-collectors and sinners. In response to those accusations, Jesus says, "Wisdom is made righteous by *all her children*."

The **fourth episode (7:36-8:3)** takes place in the house of a Pharisee named Simon who had invited Jesus to have a meal in his home. While there, a woman with an alabaster jar of perfume shows up, crying, and she washes Jesus' feet with her tears and anoints his feet with the perfume. The Pharisee is offended by this because he sees her as a "sinner." We are not told what he means by that, but given the fact that Jesus is routinely criticized for associating with tax-collectors and prostitutes, it is possible this woman had been a prostitute.

Jesus responds by asking the Pharisee a hypothetical question involving two men in debt to a moneylender, one for 500 denarii and the other for 50 denarii. If both debts are forgiven, which man will be more grateful and love the man who forgave their debt more? When the Pharisee answers that it would be the man who owed the 500 denarii, Jesus tells him that he's right, and then draws a parallel between the Pharisee and the woman. Although she probably had a greater "debt of sin," she was clearly repentant and treated Jesus with much more honor and love that the Pharisee, who obviously felt his "debt of sin" wasn't that great. Jesus then tells the woman her sins are forgiven and that she can go in peace.

Luke ends the episode by mentioning some of the names of the women who accompanied Jesus during his ministry as he proclaimed the Kingdom of God: Mary Magdalene, Joanna the wife of Chuza (whom Luke points out was the steward of Herod), and Susanna.

In the **fifth episode (8:4-21)**, Jesus tells the **Parable of the Sower**, where seed is sown on four different types of ground: off the path, rocky ground, among thorns, and good soil. The only soil where the seed was able to take root and flourish is the good soil. When the disciples ask Jesus about it, and why he speaks in parables, Jesus first quotes **Isaiah 6:9-10**, where, in its original context, God tells Isaiah that the reason why the people of Judah were not going to listen to him is because they are spiritually blind and deaf, just like the idols they worshipped. Hence, the purpose of the parables is to determine who are the true worshippers of God and who are essentially idolaters. After he explains the parable to them, he talks about putting a lamp on a lampstand so it can shine the light into the darkness. That is what his parables are doing. They are "bringing to light" what is in people's hearts. The episode ends with Jesus being told that his mother and brothers came to see him but weren't able to get to him because of the crowd. In response, Jesus says that his mother and brothers are those who hear and do the Word of God.

The **sixth episode (8:22-25)** happens on another day. When Jesus and his disciples get in a boat to go to the other side of the lake, a storm rises up and threatens to destroy the boat. The disciples wake Jesus up and tell him they are all going to die, but Jesus then orders the wind and sea to calm down, and when they do, he asks the disciples where their faith is. Their response is to ask themselves, "Who is this guy?" They do not fully understand who Jesus is at this point. They thought he was the Messiah, but they weren't expecting to see him do things only God can do.

The **seventh episode (8:26-39)** piggybacks off the previous episode and takes place in the Gentile region of the Gerasenes, where Jesus encounters a demoniac who cannot be bound, who was living among the tombs. When he sees Jesus, he addresses him as the **Son of God the Most High** and begs Jesus not to torment him. When the demon tells Jesus his name is **Legion**, we are told that they beg Jesus not to send them into **the abyss**, namely the Sea of Chaos (basically, hell—the abode of demons). Jesus sends them into a herd of swine, and the herd immediately runs off the cliff and drowns in the sea. The entire episode essentially shows Jesus' power over demons and his ability to send them back to hell. The people of the Gerasenes, though, beg Jesus to leave, and as he leaves, he tells the former demoniac to go home and tell people what God had done for him. Hence, the early seeds of the Gospel among Gentiles are sown.

The **eighth episode (8:40-56)** is a dual-episode involving both Jarius' request for Jesus to heal his daughter and an anonymous woman being healed from her menstrual hemorrhage. It begins with Jarius, a leader in the synagogue, coming and asking Jesus to come to his house to heal his daughter. On the way there, a woman with a menstrual flow for twelve years touches Jesus' garment and is healed. When Jesus stops and asks who touched him, she comes forward and he tells her that her faith has saved her. He then proceeds to go Jarius' house to find the daughter dead. After he goes into the room with her father, mother, Peter, James and John, Jesus raises her up.

The **ninth episode (9:1-17)**, really comes in four parts. First, Jesus sends the Twelve out with the authority to heal sicknesses, cast out demons, and to proclaim the Gospel (9:1-6). They are to stay where they are welcomed and leave where they are rejected. Second, Herod the Tetrarch thinks Jesus might be John the Baptist risen from the dead, while others think he might be Elijah or another one of the prophets of old (9:7-9). After that, the twelve apostles return and report to Jesus what they had accomplished (9:10-11). Jesus then withdraws with them to Bethsaida, yet crowds continued to follow him, so he continued to minister to them. When it was getting late, the disciples ask Jesus to disperse the crowd because they are all out in the wilderness and there isn't enough food for everyone. At that point, Jesus proceeds to feed the 5,000 with five loaves and two fish. Afterwards, the disciples pick up twelve baskets of leftovers.

The **tenth episode (9:18-27)** is that of Peter's confession. Unlike Mark and Matthew, though, Luke doesn't specify that it took place at Caesarea Philippi. Jesus asks his disciples who people think he is, and they tell him various answers: John the Baptist, Elijah, or one of the prophets. When he asks them their opinion, Peter steps forward and says, "You are the Christ of God." Jesus first tells them not to tell anyone, and then tells them that he was going to be rejected by the chief priests, elders, and scribes, he was going to be killed, but he was going to rise again on the third day. Interestingly, though, unlike Mark and Matthew, Luke doesn't include Peter's rebuking of Jesus, or Jesus' telling Peter to "Get behind me, Satan." He does though proceed to tell his disciples about the cost of discipleship, and that the only way to save one's life will be to lose it for his sake. After that, Jesus tells them that some of them standing there would not taste death before they see the Kingdom of God. That statement leads directly into the next episode.

The **eleventh episode (9:28-36)** is that of the Transfiguration. Eight days later after Peter's confession, Jesus takes Peter, James, and John up a mountain and they see him transfigured and talking with Moses and Elijah. Luke tells us that the appearance of Jesus' face changed, and his clothes became dazzling white. Simply put, it is Peter, James, and John who get a glimpse of the Kingdom of God before they taste death. Interestingly, Luke tells us that Moses and Elijah were speaking to Jesus about his **departure that he was about to accomplish in Jerusalem**.

The Greek word translated as "departure" is actually **exodus**. On one hand, the reference is to Jesus' upcoming death in Jerusalem, but on the other hand, it gives an extra wrinkle to the significance of Jesus' death. The Exodus was a story about release from bondage and the journey to freedom in the Promised Land.

Jesus' death also marks the beginning of the release from the bondage of death itself and the journey to the ultimate Promised Land—the New Creation. The fact that Peter suggests they make three tents for them is in and of itself another allusion to the Exodus. Still another Exodus echo is seen in the cloud that overshadows them. After the voice says, *"This is my Son, my Chosen One! Listen to him!"* the disciples look up to find Moses and Elijah had gone.

The **twelfth episode (9:37-45)** takes place the next day, when Jesus casts a demon out form a boy after the boy's father tells Jesus that his disciples had not been able to do so. Jesus then calls them a *faithless generation* and tells the man to bring the boy to him. As they do, the demon throws him to the ground, he starts convulsing, but Jesus rebukes the spirit, heals the boy, and give him back to his father. Jesus then again tells his disciples that he is going to be betrayed, but they didn't understand and were too afraid to ask him about it.

In the **thirteenth episode (9:46-50)**, the disciples are arguing about who would be the greatest in the Kingdom of God. When Jesus hears them, he brings out a little child and tells them that whoever welcomes a little child welcomes him and the one who sent him, and thus whomever is the least among them will be the greatest in the Kingdom of God. When John tells Jesus that they tried to stop someone from casting a demon out in his name because that person wasn't with them, Jesus tells him not to do that, because "whoever isn't against you is for you."

The **fourteenth episode (9:51-62)** marks the transition from Jesus' Galilean ministry to his journey to Jerusalem. On the way there, Jesus and the disciples pass through a Samaritan village but are not welcomed there. In response, James and John ask Jesus if they should call down fire from heaven to consume the town. Yet Jesus rebukes them and they move on. Later, Jesus encounters a man who says he wants to follow him, but Jesus tells him that although foxes have holes and birds have nests, he, the Son of Man, has no place to lay his head. Another man tells Jesus he wants to follow him, but he wants to first go bury his father. Jesus tells him to let the dead bury their own dead. When a third man wants to first say goodbye to his family, Jesus says that no one who "puts a hand to the plow" but then looks back is fit for the Kingdom of God.

## 4. The Journey to Jerusalem: Part 1 (10:1-13:35)

The next ten chapters of Luke consist of a slow journey to Jerusalem. Even though I have broken these chapters up into three sections, Luke 10-19 really is one entire section. The length of this journey toward Jerusalem is astounding, given that Mark takes all of one chapter to get to Jerusalem and Matthew takes only three.

In any case, the **first episode (10:1-24)** tells us of Jesus sending out 70 of his disciples to the cities in which he was about to travel. Jesus says the harvest is great, but the workers are few, and tells them they are being sent out as sheep among wolves. He tells them to stay where they are welcomed and move on from where they are rejected, for the cities that reject them will be worse off than Sodom on **Judgment Day**. As I mentioned in my comments on Matthew 11, in light of the fact that Luke (like Matthew) was written shortly after the Jewish War of AD 66-70, we have to at least consider that Jesus' words here would have been interpreted by the original audience as prophetically referring to the coming war, in which Rome would march through Galilee and Judea and eventually destroy Jerusalem. Simply put, in the immediate context, Judgment Day was a reference to the Jewish War.

With that, Jesus launches into a condemnation of Chorazin, Bethsaida, and Capernaum for rejecting him, even though he had done many dynamic deeds in them. The 70 eventually return to tell Jesus of their success, and that even demons were subject to them. Jesus says he saw Satan fall like lightning from heaven and that they should rejoice that their names had been written in heaven. Then Jesus thanks the Father that He had revealed the Gospel to "infants" and not to the learned and wise and tells his disciples that just as the Father had sent him, so now does he send them. He also tells his disciples that they have been blessed to see things that the prophets of the past had only been able to hope for.

In the **second episode (10:25-37)**, a scribe asks Jesus what he must do to inherit the **Life of the Ages** (eternal life) and make sure he gets to "get in" the new Messianic Age. Jesus tells him that it comes down to loving God and loving your neighbor. This, as we learn elsewhere, is considered the summation of what the Torah is all about. When the scribe asks, "Who is my neighbor?" Jesus then tells the **Parable of the Good Samaritan**. In the parable, a man gets mugged on the road to Jericho, not just by a band of **lestai** (not "robbers," but *revolutionaries*) and is left to die. Both a priest and a Levite see him there, ignore him, and pass on. It is a hated Samaritan who sees him there, binds his wounds, takes him to an inn, and pays his expenses until he recovers. Thus, the key to inheriting the Life of the Ages is to love God and love your neighbor—and your neighbor is anyone who is in need of help, even if it someone from a people group you hate.

The **third episode (10:38-42)** tells us a little about Jesus' friendship with Mary and Martha. Luke tells us that whenever Jesus would visit them, Mary would **sit at his feet** to listen to him, while Martha busied herself serving everyone. When she complains to Jesus, he tells her not to let herself be distracted by so many things, and that the only thing necessary was to do what Mary was doing. Incidentally, to "sit at the feet" of a rabbi was understood to be in a privileged position of a disciple who was taught by a rabbi. So, here we see Mary being allowed to "sit at the feet" of Jesus and learn from him, along with his male disciples.

The **fourth episode (11:1-13)** consists of Jesus teaching his followers about praying. He gives them the **Lord's Prayer** as an example and encourages them to be persistent in their prayers and requests to God, because He is more willing to grant their requests than any friend or family member. The Father, Jesus says, is more than willing to give the Holy Spirit to anyone who asks Him.

The **fifth episode (11:14-36)** tells us of the **Beelzebub Controversy**. In Luke, some people accuse Jesus of using the power of Beelzebub to cast out demons, while others ask him for a sign from Heaven. Jesus responds to the accusation by saying that idea is preposterous—**a house divided** against itself cannot stand. Rather than using the power of Beelzebub, Jesus says he's binding Beelzebub (the strong man). Also, apparently there were other Jewish exorcists at the time, and so Jesus asks the accusing crowd that if they say he is using the power of Beelzebub, then would that imply that "their sons" who are casting out demons also using the power of Beelzebub? The question is meant to be absurd.

Still, Jesus' deeds are different than the deeds of the other Jewish exorcists. He says that if he is casting out demons by **the finger of God** (thus implying he is doing just that), then the Kingdom of God has come. Simply put, his casting out of demons serves as the sign that the long-awaited Kingdom had come. God, through the work of Jesus, had invaded Satan's turf. By contrast, although he doesn't say that the other Jewish exorcists are using the power of Beelzebub, he does say that their efforts to confront demonic forces will prove to be ineffective and self-defeating. That is the point of Jesus' comments in 11:24-26 about the spirit getting seven other spirits to retake the "house" out of which he's been cast out. Finally, when a woman telling Jesus that his mother is blessed for having given birth to him, he says that whoever hears and obeys the Word of God is the one who is truly blessed.

After that, Jesus then addresses the demand for a sign from Heaven by telling them that the only sign they will be given is the **sign of Jonah**. In Luke, though, Jesus makes no mention of Jonah being in the belly of the sea monster for three days and nights. Here, the focus is on the response of both the Ninevites to Jonah and the Queen of the South's response to Solomon. In both examples, the Kingdom of God is seen as being extended to Gentiles. With that, Jesus then speaks about how a lamp is to be put on a lampstand, so that all could see its light, and how one's entire body should be full of light. When considered in the context of the sign of Jonah, it would seem that these verses take on a meaning of being **a light to the Gentiles**.

In the **sixth episode (11:37-54)**, Jesus openly condemns the Pharisees and scribes. It begins when a Pharisee, having invited Jesus to a meal, was shocked that Jesus didn't wash his hands before a meal. To be clear, this was in reference to ceremonial washing for religious reasons. In response, Jesus accuses the Pharisees of hypocrisy and says the outside of their cup is clean, but the inside is full of greed and evil. He goes on and says they pay their tithe but neglect executing justice, and even though they love places of honor, they really are nothing more than unmarked graves.

When the scribes stick up for the Pharisees and tell Jesus that he is insulting them as well, Jesus then turns his attention to them and accuses them of loading people up with burdens (regulations and rules) that they themselves don't even touch. He says that not only do they build tombs to honor the very prophet who were killed by their fathers, but they have actually made people dumber (taken away the key of knowledge) when it comes to being able to understand the will of God. As a result, both the scribes and the Pharisees begin to hold a grudge against Jesus and start attacking him every chance they can get.

The **seventh episode (12:1-12)** continues to highlight Jesus' conflict with the Pharisees. Here, he warns his disciples about the **yeast of the Pharisees** (which Luke says is their **hypocrisy**). Jesus then talks about how whatever is said in the darkness will eventually come to light. He talks about not being afraid of those who can kill the body, but rather only of the one who has the authority to throw you into **Gehenna** (the place of punishment of the unrighteous—basically what we would consider hell). At the same time, they should not be afraid of God because He cares for them. He then tells his followers that if they confess him before men, then he, the Son of Man, will confess them before the angels of God, but if they deny him, then he will deny them. Still, if someone speaks against him, the Son of Man, that person still can be forgiven, but whoever blasphemes the Holy Spirit can never be forgiven. Therefore, Jesus tells them that when they are dragged in front of rulers and authorities that they shouldn't be worried about what to say because the Holy Spirit will reveal to them what to say at that time.

In the **eighth episode (12:13-34)**, Jesus tells the **Parable of the Rich Young Fool** in response to a dispute two brothers were having over their inheritance. In actuality, the next three episodes all have that as their setting. In the parable, a man owns a field and then builds a bigger barn to store all his crops. He thinks that since he has all his crops stored up, he can sit back and enjoy life, not realizing that he was going to die that very night. The point of the parable is simple: don't spend your life greedily obsessing over "stuff." Jesus then extends the parable by launching into a short discourse on not worrying about material things. He tells his disciples to look at how God cares for the ravens and the lilies and then realize that they are worth much more to God then mere birds and flowers. He then tells them to sell what they have and store up treasures in Heaven.

The **ninth episode (12:35-48)** really is a continuation of the previous episode. Here, Jesus admonishes his disciples to stay prepared and alert for the **coming of the Son of Man,** which he describes as coming of a lord to his wedding feast. His servants are to stay awake and watch for him, so they can welcome him when he comes. After that, Jesus then gives the analogy of servants who are placed in charge of the house until their master returns. The faithful servants, Jesus says, will be blessed when the master returns, but the wicked servant will be punished and beaten when the master returns.

The **tenth episode (12:49-59)** contains Jesus' concluding comments to the two brothers who were arguing over their inheritance. In 12:49-53, right after talking about the faithful and unfaithful servants, Jesus now says that he has come to set fire to the land and has come, not to bring peace, but rather a sword—not simply division among the Jews, but even division within households. Thus, what began as division among brothers over a question of their inheritance has evolved into a talk about seeking heavenly treasures and about division among faithful and unfaithful servants who will be thus rewarded or beaten by their master when he returns (the coming of the Son of Man). After that, in 12:54-59, Jesus talks about the importance of interpreting the signs of the times and uses the analogy of resolving a legal matter with one's opponent before the case is taken before the judge and lose your case.

If we put all this together, we see that Jesus is equating the **coming of the Son of Man** in 12:35-40, the **return of the master** in 12:41-43, and **going before the judge** in 12:54-59 with the coming judgment coming upon Israel in the form of the Jewish War of AD 66-70. Thus, Jesus is saying that in light of the coming judgment, his fellow Jews must put their affairs in order before it happens and get ready.

The **eleventh episode (13:1-9)** needs to be read in light of what Jesus has just said about impending judgment. Someone brings up the news about the Galileans whom Pilate had killed and then had their blood mixed with their sacrifices. Jesus responds by bringing up another incident involving 18 people who died when the tower in Siloam fell on them and says that neither those Galileans nor those 18 people were any worse sinners than other people in Galilee and Jerusalem. So, unless they repent, they will be destroyed too. He then tells a short parable about a man who planted a fig tree that wasn't producing fruit. The man wants to cut it down but is convinced by the gardener to wait one more year to see if the gardener could save the tree and get it to produce fruit. If it still didn't produce fruit after a year, then he would cut it down.

It is pretty clear that Jesus' call to repentance is said in the hope that his fellow Jews would avoid coming judgment (which would have been understood to be the events of the Jewish War of AD 66-70). In Luke, this seems to be a major component of Jesus' ministry. He prophesied that God's judgment was coming upon Israel and was calling his fellow Jews to repent and put their faith in him and in his offering of the Kingdom of God, so that they could be spared God's judgment. He knew, though, that such a choice between his offering of the Kingdom and that of the Pharisees and scribes would undoubtedly bring division among the Jewish people.

The **twelfth episode (13:10-17)** involves Jesus healing a disabled woman on the Sabbath in the synagogue. When he does, the head of the synagogue objects that Jesus had "worked" on the Sabbath. In response, Jesus gives the example of untying an ox or donkey and leading it to water on the Sabbath, and says that if it is acceptable to do that, then what is so wrong about "untying" a woman from her physical bondage on the Sabbath? That response creates division within the synagogue, with those who opposed Jesus being put to shame while others go away rejoicing over what Jesus was doing.

The **thirteenth episode (13:18-21)** is a brief episode in which Jesus likens the Kingdom of God to a mustard seed that grows into a tree and yeast that works its way through a batch of dough. Here, in Luke, though, these verses are divorced from that context entirely, and quite frankly, don't really seem to fit in with any of the surrounding context in Luke 13.

In the **fourteenth episode (13:22-30)**, when someone asks Jesus if only a small number would be saved, Jesus tells people to try to come in through the **narrow gate** and says that once the **head of the house** (the Lord) locks the gate, those still outside might beg to be let in, but he will call them **workers of unrighteousness** and will say never knew them. Those who are left outside will then weep and grind their teeth when they see those coming from all around the world (Gentiles) to sit at the table in the Kingdom of God, eating with Abraham, Isaac and Jacob. Jesus then ends by saying, *"The last will be first, and the first will be last."* In the context of the previous two chapters in Luke, the focus here is clearly on imploring his listeners to enter into the Kingdom of God before it is too late, as well as the implication that somehow Gentiles will be welcomed into the Kingdom of God while some Jews are left out and rejected as unrighteous.

In the **fifteenth episode (13:31-35)**, some Pharisees warn Jesus that Herod was looking to kill him. Jesus tells them to tell Herod he's going to keep casting out demons and healing people "today and tomorrow" and on the **third day** will complete his work (foreshadowing his resurrection). He also says it isn't possible for a prophet to die outside of Jerusalem (quite a condemnation of Jerusalem!). Jesus is basically saying, *"We all know that it has always been Jewish leaders in Jerusalem who are hostile to God's prophets and who kill them!"* In light of that, and in light of what he knows is coming, Jesus laments over Jerusalem, calling it a **killer of prophets**. He says he wants to protect the children of Jerusalem from danger, but he laments that "your house" (the Temple) would be left desolate (again, a prophetic reference to the eventual destruction of the Temple in AD 70). He ends by saying Jerusalem would not see him until it says, *"Blessed his the one who comes in the Name of the Lord."* This last comment foreshadows when Jesus comes into Jerusalem during the so-called "triumphal entry," when the crowds actually quote that line from **Psalm 118:26**.

## 5. The Journey to Jerusalem: Part 2 (14:1-17:10)

This next section in Jesus' journey to Jerusalem is constructed in a way that shows a stark contrast between the religious hypocrisy of the Pharisees and the poor, needy, and repentant tax-collectors and sinners. Throughout this contrast, there is the constant call to true discipleship. The section is set up in the following manner: (1) The Pharisees are contrasted with either the *poor and needy* or *tax-collectors and sinners*; (2) Jesus tells a parable that addresses the issue at hand; and (3) Jesus then issues a challenge to his followers and disciples regarding true discipleship.

The **first episode (14:1-24)** takes place in the house of a Pharisee and involves Jesus healing a man with dropsy, even though it was on the Sabbath. When some guests object, Jesus says that since they would pull their own ox, or son even, out of a well, even if it were on the Sabbath, it was also okay to heal someone on the Sabbath. He then notices that the guests were vying to be seated at the places of honor. Just earlier in Luke 11:43, Jesus already condemned the Pharisees for seeking the seat of honor in the synagogues. In any case, Jesus takes the opportunity to tell the people there that if they are invited to a **wedding banquet**, they should voluntarily sit at the last place. Then, if the host moves them up to a better seat, they will then be honored. The point is simple: **humble yourself, and you will be later exalted; exalt yourself, and you'll be sure to be humbled**.

Jesus then tells his host that whenever he prepares a banquet, he shouldn't invite his friends, family, or rich associates, but rather the poor, the crippled, the lame, and the blind, because they are truly the "least of these." Even though they won't be able to repay him, he will be repaid in the **resurrection of the righteous**. This implies the coming of the Kingdom of God and the dawning of the Messianic Age, which was often seen in terms of the great **Messianic Wedding Banquet**.

We need to see that Jesus isn't just saying, "Be nice to poor people and there will be 'jewels in your crown'!" He is telling them that the blessing and glory in the Messianic Age is reserved for those who, in this age, reach out and honor the poor, needy, and lowly. If you spend your time in this age vying for your own honor and neglecting the poor and needy, you will be humbled in the Age to Come. Or to put it another way, if you invite the poor and needy to your own table whenever you have any kind of banquet, you will have your reward in the resurrection, in the Messianic Age, at the great Messianic Wedding Banquet.

When someone there clearly gets his allusion to the future Wedding Banquet in the Kingdom of God, Jesus then proceeds to tell the **Parable of the Great Banquet**, in which a man prepares a banquet for his son and then invites many people, only to find out that they make excuses and don't come. So, the man is filled with wrath, and proceeds to send his servant out to invite the poor, crippled, blind, and lame. When there still is more space available, he sends his servant out to the highways to invite anyone, so the banquet hall would be filled. The man then says that none of those who were originally invited will taste his banquet.

In the context of the episode, this parable is shocking. The focus of Jesus' comments has been on inviting the poor who can't repay you, so that you will be rewarded in the Kingdom of God. There is, if you will, a positive emphasis. But the Parable of the Great Banquet is rather ominous, in that its focus at the end is that those who didn't accept the original invitation will never get it. It is clear that the banquet in this parable is not just a regular old banquet. It really is about that great eschatological Messianic Wedding Banquet in the Kingdom of God.

In the **second episode (14:25-35)**, Luke mentions some of the things Jesus would regularly tell the crowds who followed him, like that unless they hated their own family or weren't willing to take up their cross, they couldn't be his disciples. To flesh out this idea of "counting the cost," Jesus gives two examples: (1) a man who sets out to build a watchtower but doesn't figure out the cost ahead of time, and (2) a king who goes to battle before figuring out a good strategy to win. In both cases, not counting the cost before committing to the work runs the risk of failing. Thus, Jesus is saying, "If you're going to follow me, you had better realize what you're going to be in for—*it's going to be hard!*" Jesus then ends by talking about how if salt loses its taste, then it is good for nothing and is bound to get thrown out.

The **third episode (15:1-32)** once again involves Jesus confronting the Pharisees and scribes who were complaining that Jesus wasn't just welcoming tax-collectors and sinners, but that he was eating with them as well. In 14:1-24, Jesus challenged the Pharisees about welcoming the **poor and needy**, and here he is challenging them about welcoming **tax-collectors and sinners**. It is almost as if they were thinking, "Well, okay, fine, the poor and needy—it would be good to help them, *but tax collectors?*" In short, Jesus' response is, "Yes, even tax-collectors and sinners!"

To illustrate this, Jesus puts forth three parables. The first two—the **Parable of the Lost Sheep** and the **Parable of the Lost Coin**—are pretty self-explanatory. The lost sheep/lost coin that is found represents a sinner who repents, and the shepherd who finds the lost sheep and the woman who finds the lost coin represents both God and the angels in Heaven. Jesus says they rejoice and celebrate when a sinner repents. This relates to Jesus eating with tax-collectors and sinner in that by sharing a meal with them, he is celebrating their repentance, and the ordinary meal thus becomes illustrative of the future **Messianic Wedding Banquet**.

It is the **Parable of the Prodigal Son**, though, that drives this point home even more. The **young prodigal** represents the tax-collectors and sinners, the **father** represents God, and the **older son** represents the Pharisees and scribes. When the prodigal son comes home, the father celebrates by throwing **a banquet** for him. The older son, though, (the one who keeps all the rules) is bitter that the father has thrown a celebratory banquet for the lowlife prodigal son and refuses to join in on the banquet. The father begs the older son to come in and join the celebration, because the younger son had been dead, and was now alive; he had been lost, but now was found.

The reason why Jesus doesn't say what the older son chose to do, is the parable acts as a direct challenge (and invitation) to the Pharisees and scribes to join Jesus in celebrating the Kingdom with tax-collectors and sinners. When seen in light of the previous chapter, that choice takes on eschatological importance. Jesus is celebrating the Messianic Banquet with tax-collectors and sinners who repent and is telling the Pharisees and scribes that if they don't accept their invitation to the celebration, they're never going to get in. If they don't humble themselves enough to associate with the "wrong kind of people," they're going to miss out on the whole thing.

In the **fourth episode (16:1-13)**, coming off the heels of his challenge to the Pharisees and scribes, Jesus now addresses his disciples and tells them the **Parable of the Dishonest House Steward**. In the parable, a rich man tells his dishonest house steward that he is going to lose his job because he was wasting the rich man's possessions. Since he knows he would soon be out of a job, the house steward goes about currying favor with his lord's debtors by giving them a discount on what they owed. That way, once he was out of a job, they would be inclined to help him out because he gave them a break. When the rich man found out what the house steward had done, he congratulated him on his shrewdness. The house steward may have been dishonest, but he wasn't a fool, and he found a way to ensure his survival after he got fired.

Jesus ends the parable by saying, *"The sons of this age are shrewder than the sons of light are to their own generation."* This odd saying is the key to understanding the point of the parable. The **sons of this age** are simply people like the house steward in the parable—people in this world who are smart enough to ensure their survival after they are caught doing something wrong. The **sons of light** are Jews like the Pharisees and scribes. For the previous two chapters, the issue has been their aversion to show charity and cut some slack to the poor and needy and to tax-collectors and sinners, the kind of people who have "racked up debt," so to speak.

Therefore, in light of all that, Jesus is saying here that the Jewish religious leaders would soon lose their position as leaders of God's people because they have refused to show charity to the poor and needy and have refused to celebrate with Jesus when tax-collectors and sinners repent. They have shown themselves to be not only unrighteous, but also quite stupid from a practical standpoint. Jesus' comment in 16:9 about being welcome into the **eternal homes** when the wealth of the unrighteous fails echoes what he said in 14:14 about being repaid in the resurrection of the righteous. But since this is something the Pharisees and scribes are unwilling to do, Jesus emphasizes that no one can serve both God and money.

The **fifth episode (16:14-31)** takes us back to comments about the Pharisees and builds off of Jesus' words about serving God and money. Luke tells us that the Pharisees were **lovers of money** and were making fun of Jesus for saying what he said. Jesus first responds by telling them that even though they put their righteous acts on display in order to get praise from men, in reality, God knows the wickedness in their hearts. He then says that there are those trying to violently force their way into the Kingdom of God, but that nothing in the Torah will fall unless Heaven passes away.

Given the context, Jesus is saying the Pharisees are in opposition to his bringing of the Kingdom even though his Kingdom is the fulfillment of the Torah. Thus, by opposing him, the Pharisees are opposing the Torah, for the whole purpose of the Torah is to get people to love God, love their neighbor, and bring God's blessing to the nations. As far as Jesus' final comment in 16:18 regarding divorce, remarriage, and adultery is concerned, though, it seems oddly out of place, given the context.

Jesus continues by telling the **Parable of the Rich Man and Lazarus**. It fits right in with what Jesus has been saying in chapters 14-16. In the story, there is a rich man who fails to care for and feed Lazarus, a poor, sickly man at his gate. When both eventually die, Lazarus ends up in Abraham's bosom, while the rich man ends up in torment in Hades. Even then, the rich man sees Lazarus as nothing but a lowly slave and asks Abraham to send Lazarus to him to give him some water. Abraham tells him it is impossible to do because the chasm is too wide. Given that reality, the rich man then asks Abraham to send Lazarus to his brothers who were still alive to warn them (and to presumably tell them they should care for the poor and needy!). Abraham tells him they have Moses and the Prophets to tell them that. When the man objects and says if someone came back from the dead to tell them to care for the poor, then they would listen, Abraham says, *"If they don't listen to Moses and the Prophets, they won't listen even if someone comes back from the dead."*

This parable sums up everything that chapters 14-16 are addressing. The rich man represents the Pharisees and scribes who object to Jesus' teaching to care for the poor and his celebrating with repentant sinners. But Jesus is insistent: If you care for the poor and needy *now*, and if you celebrate with repentant sinners *now*, you will be rewarded in the resurrection of the righteous, welcomed into their eternal homes, and will celebrate in the Messianic Wedding Banquet. But if you neglect the poor and needy *now*, and if you refuse to celebrate with repentant sinners *now*, not only will you miss out on the Messianic celebration, but you will find yourself in darkness and torment.

The **sixth episode (17:1-10)** concludes this section with Jesus addressing his disciples about true discipleship. He tells them that scandals will come but the one who brings the scandals will suffer judgment, and that they should forgive anyone who repents, no matter how often they may sin. When they ask him to increase their faith, he says if they had the faith of a mustard seed, they'd be able to tell a mulberry tree to be planted in the sea, and it would obey. Jesus finishes by talking about a servant who does his job. He won't eat and drink until he cleans himself up and serves his master first. Furthermore, the master isn't going to fawn over the servant for just doing his job. This is how the disciples should see themselves, as servants. Just in case they might start getting a big head because they care for the poor and needy, just in case they might be tempted to look at the Pharisees and say, "Look at them! They aren't doing what they should be doing, *but we are! We are so great for doing this!*" Jesus is reminding them, "Hey, you're just doing what you should be doing all along! Don't get a big head! The reward comes later. For now, just do your job as a servant."

### 6. The Journey to Jerusalem: Part 3 (17:11-19:27)

Jesus and his disciples continue to Jerusalem. In the **first episode (17:11-19)**, they pass through Samaria and Galilee, when ten lepers come out of a town and ask Jesus for mercy. Jesus tells them to go show themselves to the priests, and on the way to the priests, the lepers are cleansed. Despite that, only one man comes back to thank Jesus, and that man was, of all people, a Samaritan. The picture is striking in that Jesus, the Jewish Messiah, is extending salvation and the Kingdom of God to foreigners. He is being the light to the nations.

In the **second episode (17:20-37)**, the Pharisees ask Jesus when the Kingdom of God was coming. It is important to note that Jesus' response here in Luke is found in the Olivet Discourse of **Mark 13:14-23/Matthew 24:17-41**, where Jesus is speaking of the Temple's destruction and the coming of the Son of Man. That should tell us that those three things (the **Temple's destruction**, the **coming of the Son of Man**, and the **coming of the Kingdom of God**) were all seen in connection with each other on some level. In any case, Jesus says that the Kingdom of God wouldn't come in a way that can be observed, but rather that it was already among them.

He then talks about the **day of the Son of Man** and the **day of the revelation of the Son of Man**, using cosmic upheaval language associated with the **Day of YHWH** in the Old Testament. Jesus equates this "day" with the destruction of **Noah's flood** and the destruction of **Sodom** in Lot's day. Jesus' point is that people won't see the destruction coming, and when it does come, they should flee. He says one will be taken and one will be left, and ends with the strange phrase, *"The vultures will gather where there is a corpse,"* implying that death is coming on that day.

Given the connection to the Olivet Discourse in Mark and Matthew, it seems that Jesus is saying two essential things: (1) The Kingdom of God isn't going to come in the way they are expecting (the establishment of a literal earthly kingdom); and (2) Instead, of vindication, they should expect coming judgment and wrath, most likely a reference to the Jewish War of AD 66-70.

The **third episode (18:1-17)** consists of two parables that Jesus would often tell his followers. The **Parable of the Widow and the Unjust Judge** (18:1-8) is one Jesus would tell to encourage his followers to pray at all times and not get tired.

In it, a poor widow badgers an unjust judge until he gets so sick of her that he grants her justice just so she won't bother him anymore. Therefore, if a persistent widow can get justice from an unjust judge, how much more quickly will those who pray to God, who is righteous and just, get justice? Jesus ends the parable with a curious statement: *"When the Son of Man comes, will he find any faith in the land?"* We must remember that throughout the Gospels, the coming of the Son of Man is closely associated with the Temple's destruction. It seems, therefore, that in this parable, Jesus is telling his followers to keep praying for God's justice, because it will come quickly in the form of the coming of the Son of Man, when God's wrath will come upon the enemies of His people, which shockingly will prove to be the Jewish nation, hence the destruction of the Temple.

In the **Parable of the Pharisee and the Tax-Collector** (18:9-14), Jesus again illustrates the difference between self-righteous religious hypocrites who show no mercy to the poor and needy, and repentant sinners whom Jesus has welcomed into the Kingdom. Two men go to the Temple to pray. The Pharisee's prayer is self-congratulatory and self-righteous, amounting to, "Thank you, God, that I am so great, not like *that* scumbag!" The tax-collector's prayer is full of repentance and admission of his sin. Jesus says that he, not the Pharisee, will be justified and made righteous.

The point is simple. Those who humble themselves will be exalted, and those who exalt themselves will be humbled. To illustrate that, Jesus welcomes little children to come to him as he tells his disciples that the Kingdom of God is for them, meaning for those who are lowly and humble. Whether it is repentant sinners, poor widows, or little children, the Kingdom of God is for *those kinds of people*, not the rich, powerful, self-congratulatory, and self-righteous religious hypocrites.

In the **fourth episode (18:18-30)**, a rich young man asks Jesus what he must do to inherit the **Life of the Ages**, so Jesus tells him to keep the commandments. When he says he has kept them, Jesus then tells him to sell his possessions and give the money to the poor—and then he'll have **treasure in Heaven**. The man leaves because he does not want to give up his possessions. Jesus' point, one that has been a constant theme since 14:1-6, is that it is hard for the rich to enter into the Kingdom of God, but those who have given up everything to follow him will be rewarded in the **Age to Come**. Therefore, the challenge to those who are rich and religious is to reach out to the poor and needy and celebrate the Kingdom with repentant sinners.

The **fifth episode (18:31-34)** is a short episode in which Jesus, on the doorstep of Jerusalem, reiterates to his disciples that when they get to Jerusalem, he is going to be arrested, beaten, and killed, but after three days he will rise again. In true disciple-like fashion, the disciples didn't get what he was talking about.

In the **sixth episode (18:35-43)**, as they are getting near Jericho, a blind beggar calls out to Jesus, calling him the **Son of David**, and begs him for mercy. When Jesus asks him what he wants, he says he wants to see again, so Jesus heals him, and he receives his sight. Once again, this is illustrative of the constant theme since 14:1-6 that emphasizes extending mercy and charity to the poor and needy.

The **seventh episode (19:1-10)** is the story of Jesus eating at the house of Zacchaeus the tax-collector in Jericho. As before, when Jesus eats at his house, people object precisely because Zacchaeus is a tax-collector and sinner. Yet it is precisely because Jesus chooses to eat with him that Zacchaeus repents and announces that he will give one half of his property to the poor and will pay back anyone he has cheated four times over. In response, Jesus announces that salvation has come to Zacchaeus' house, that he too is a **son of Abraham**, and that this is precisely why the Son of Man came: **to seek and save the lost**. That phrase hearkens back to the three parables involving the lost sheep, the lost coin, and the Prodigal Son in Luke 15, where there is celebration because what was lost has been found.

The **eighth episode (19:11-27)** consists of Jesus telling the **Parable of the Ten Minas**. Luke tells us that as Jesus was getting closer to Jerusalem, that some people were expecting the Kingdom of God to immediately appear. As was made obvious in the second episode in 17:20-37, Jesus has already said that the Kingdom was not going to appear in the way they were expecting. Instead, **the day of the revelation of the Son of Man** would bring about judgment. That is the same sentiment we see here Luke 19:11-27. In the parable, a nobleman goes to a distant country **to receive a kingdom** and gives ten minas to ten of his servants and tells them to conduct business while he is away.

His citizens, though, hate him so much that they send a representative after him to tell him they didn't want him to rule over them. Once he receives his kingdom, he returns and calls three of his servants to see what they have done with the money he had given them. The first two show him the profit they made, so he gives them charge over various cities. The third servant, though, gives his one mina back to the nobleman. He simply had stored the mina in a cloth and didn't do anything with it, because he knew the king was a harsh man and would just take whatever the servant made with it anyway. The king calls him a wicked servant and takes the one mina away. After that, he calls those who didn't want him to rule over them **his enemies** and orders that they be brought in and **slaughtered in his presence**.

It is a shocking ending but given Jesus' response to the Pharisees' question about the coming of the Kingdom of God in 17:20-37, the ending of this parable make sense. Like in 17:20-37, Jesus turns the tables on those who were looking for the coming of an observable Kingdom of God in the near future, and essentially says, *"You're expecting a conquering kingdom, but you're going to get judgment and wrath because you will reject me as the king."* And this would have been seen as being fulfilled in the events of the Jewish War: God's wrath and judgment had come upon the Jews for their rejection of Jesus as the Messiah.

### 7. Jesus at Jerusalem vs. Temple Establishment (19:28-21:38)

Jesus' confrontation with the Jewish religious leaders comes to a head when he arrives in Jerusalem for Passover. The section begins with the **first episode (19:28-44)** about the so-called "triumphal entry" into Jerusalem on what we call Palm Sunday. Jesus sends two of his disciples to get a young donkey for him to ride upon and then comes into Jerusalem with people spreading their garments on the road before him and shouting out **Psalm 118:26**: *"Blessed is the king who comes in the name of the Lord!"* As Jesus was coming into Jerusalem, some of the Pharisees objected to what the crowds were saying and called upon Jesus to rebuke them. In response, Jesus says, *"If they stay silent, the very rocks will cry out!"* As he is coming into the city, Jesus then laments over Jerusalem and says that since Jerusalem was blind to the peace he was offering and "didn't know the time of your visitation," it would at some point be besieged and destroyed. It is unmistakable: Jesus comes to Jerusalem, prophesying its destruction. It is front and center in his confrontation with the Temple establishment during that week.

In the **second episode (19:45-48)**, Jesus' action in the Temple is quick and direct. He goes into the Temple courts, throws out those who were doing business in it, and then quotes **Isaiah 56:7** *("My House will be a house of prayer")* and **Jeremiah 7:11** *("You've made it into a den of revolutionaries")*. It is clearly a prophetic action in which Jesus, just like Jeremiah did 600 years earlier, condemns the

Temple for its corruption and prophesies its destruction. Because of this action, the chief priests, scribes, and other religious leaders began seeking to destroy Jesus, but they are too afraid to do anything in front of the crowds, because the crowds were backing Jesus.

In the **third episode (20:1-8)**, the chief priests, scribes, and elders confront Jesus and ask him by whose authority he was doing these things, he says he will answer their question if they first tell him if the baptism of John the Baptist was from heaven or from men? They say they don't know because they realize that if they say from heaven, Jesus will ask why they didn't believe John (because John had said Jesus was the Coming One). But if they say from men, then the people will turn against them, because everyone considered John to be a prophet. Since they refuse to give an answer, Jesus says he won't tell them by whose authority he was doing those things. It was already obvious. His authority came from God.

The **fourth episode (20:9-18)** is that of Jesus telling the **Parable of the Vineyard** in the Temple courts. In the parable, a man plants a vineyard, rents it out to farmers, and goes on a journey. Whenever he sends a servant back to collect the revenue, the farmers either beat up or even kill the servant. Finally, when the man sends his son, the farmers decide to kill the son so they could have the **inheritance of the vineyard** for themselves. Given that, Jesus then says that when the lord of the vineyard returns, he is going to destroy those farmers and give the vineyard to others. When some people object, Jesus then quotes from **Psalm 118:22**, the very psalm that was sung upon his entrance into Jerusalem: *"The stone that the builders rejected has become the chief cornerstone."*

The chief priests and scribes realize the parable was directed toward them. They were the farmers, and the vineyard was the people of God. Jesus was saying that he was the son, that they were going to kill him, and because of that God was going to destroy them and give the leadership of His people to others. Therefore, because they view him as a threat, they plot to catch him somehow, away from the people, and hand him over to Pilate the governor.

The **fifth episode (20:19-44)** involves a series of questions and answers between Jesus and the religious leaders in the Temple. First, the **chief priests and scribes** ask Jesus about paying **taxes to Caesar**, to which Jesus says, "If his face is on the money, then yes. But you need to give to God the things that are God's." Then, the **Sadducees** ask Jesus about the **resurrection**, specifically whose wife would a woman be if she married seven brothers in this life. Jesus responds by saying that there will be no marriage in the resurrection and that God is not the God of the dead, but of the living. **Jesus** then asks a question of his own: **How can the Messiah be just the son of David**, since in **Psalm 110:1** David himself wrote, "YHWH said to *my* lord, 'Sit at my Right Hand until I make your enemies a footstool for your feet'"? Jesus' point is simple: He is the Messiah, but he is a whole lot more than just a descendant of David. He is actually above David and shares authority and equality with God Himself.

In the **sixth episode (20:45-21:4)** Jesus then warns the crowds about the scribes and says that even though they love to be noticed and praised and take the places of honor at banquets, they are guilty of oppressing the poor, and will receive a greater judgment. Jesus then points out a certain widow in the Temple who threw in a mere two pennies into the treasury and says she threw in more than all of the rich people could ever give, precisely because she gave, despite her need.

The **seventh episode (21:5-38)** is the **Olivet Discourse**, and it concludes the section involving Jesus' confrontation with the Temple establishment. In it, Jesus prophesies the destruction of the Temple. Luke, though, strips away most of the allusions to the Old Testament prophecies and apocalyptic images in Mark and Matthew, because he is writing for a Gentile audience, and they would not have understood them. In that respect, Luke's version is actually easier to follow. It begins with Jesus telling the disciples that the Temple will at some point be destroyed. When they ask when that will happen and what will be the sign that it will happen, Jesus begins by saying there will be wars and insurrections first, but before that happens, they themselves will be persecuted by both Jews as well as Gentiles and everyone will hate them.

At this point, where both Mark and Matthew speak of the **Abomination of Desolation,** Luke strips away the mystery and simply says, *"When you see Jerusalem surrounded by armies, know that her destruction is near."* This is a clear reference to the destruction of Jerusalem in AD 70. Jesus tells them that when they see this coming, they had better get out of Jerusalem because that will be the time **God's wrath** comes upon Jerusalem. Wrath was always something God brought upon the enemies of His people. So, Jesus makes it clear that by rejecting him and persecuting his followers, Jerusalem had become the enemies of God's people (whereas his followers were the true people of God), and thus was going to suffer God's wrath.

Jesus then says Jerusalem will be **trampled by the nations** and uses apocalyptic cosmic upheaval imagery that denotes the **Day of YHWH**, when God brings wrath upon His enemies and vindicates His people. And *that* is what Jesus associates with the **coming of the Son of Man on the clouds**. The Jews might be looking for a visible Kingdom of God, but what they are going to get is the coming of the Son of Man when God brings His wrath upon Jerusalem and destroys the Temple. Thus, the Day of YHWH of the Old Testament is transformed into the **Day of Christ** in the New Testament. Jesus ends his discourse by giving the example of a fig tree. When the fig tree begins to put out leaves, you know summer is near. Similarly, he tells his disciples that when they see these things start to happen, that Jerusalem's destruction is at hand. Therefore, they are to stay alert and watch for it. His emphasis that **this generation would not pass away** until they saw the destruction of Jerusalem is further indication that what Jesus is talking about was, in fact, AD 70.

### 8. From the Last Supper to the Resurrection (22:1-24:53)

The final section of Luke's Gospel takes us from the Last Supper, through the arrest, trials, crucifixion, death, and burial of Jesus, to the post-resurrection appearances. The **first episode (22:1-6)** tells us about Judas Iscariot agreeing to betray Jesus. There is no indication as to why Judas agrees to betray Jesus. All we are told is that he met with the chief priests and scribes and that they paid him some money to orchestrate a time when the crowds weren't around when they could arrest him.

The **second episode (22:7-38)** is that of the **Last Supper**. Jesus first sends Peter and John to make preparations for Passover. At the Last Supper, Jesus tells them that he won't eat this Passover meal again until it is fulfilled in the Kingdom of God. He then establishes the practice of the bread and wine and tells them that from now on they are do this in memory of him. At that point, Jesus tells them that one of them is going to betray him. When the disciples, once again, start arguing about who will be the greatest in Jesus' kingdom, Jesus tells them that the one who is greatest in the Kingdom of God must be a servant and must follow his example, and he even tells Peter that he will deny him three times before the end of that night.

After that, Jesus then reminds the disciples about the instructions he had given to them back in 9:1-6 (when he sent out the twelve) and in 10:1-24 (when he sent out the 70) regarding not to take anything with them. *Now*, he says, it is time to take a purse, a bag, and even buy a sword, because everything was about to come to its fulfillment, and he was going to be counted among the transgressors. When they produce two swords, he says it is enough, and they proceed to Gethsemane. Jesus is essentially telling his disciples, *"You'd had better get prepared, because they're going to come after you too from now on."* He isn't so much telling them to go pick a fight with anyone, as he is telling them they had better prepare to be attacked and hunted down as "transgressors," precisely because they are his followers.

The **third episode (22:39-53)** shifts to the **Garden of Gethsemane** and the arrest of Jesus in the middle of the night. While there, Jesus tells his disciples to keep watch while he goes off to pray, during which time Jesus sweated drops of blood. The disciples, though, all fall asleep, and when Jesus comes back to wake them up, Judas arrives with a crowd to betray Jesus with a kiss. One of the disciples strikes off the ear of the servant of the chief priest. Jesus, though, tells him to put the sword and away and then heals the servant's ear. It seems that this disciple had taken Jesus' comments about the two swords in 22:35-38 to mean Jesus was encouraging them to strike back immediately. Nevertheless, Jesus tells him to put his sword away and makes it clear that was not what he meant.

In the **fourth episode (23:54-71)**, Jesus is brought **before the high priest in the middle of the night**, while Peter is out in the courtyard, denying he even knows Jesus. He is accused of being Jesus' disciple three different times and denies it every single time. When the cock crows, he leaves, bitterly weeping over his denial. As that was happening, Luke tells us that Jesus was being ridiculed and beaten inside. It is at daybreak that the Sanhedrin convenes, together with the chief priests and scribes, and Jesus is asked if he is the Messiah. He replies in the affirmative and goes on to allude to both **Daniel 7:13-14**, which talks about the Son of Man coming on the clouds up to the Ancient of Days to be given dominion over all, and **Psalm 110:1**, a messianic psalm which speaks of God establishing the throne of the king by having him sit at the right hand of God. Essentially, Jesus is saying, "Yes, I am the Messiah, and I will be given authority by God *over you*." This is all the Sanhedrin needs to justify them taking him to Pilate and trying to get him killed.

The **fifth episode (23:1-25)** is Jesus' **trial before Pilate**. The Sanhedrin brings Jesus before Pilate and accuses him of misleading the Jews, trying to prevent paying taxes to Caesar, and claiming to be a king. Pilate questions Jesus and finds there is no basis to the charges. When the chief priests mention Jesus had come from

Galilee, Pilate tries to sluff the whole thing off into Herod's lap and sends Jesus to Herod, who was in town for Passover. When before Herod, the chief priests make their accusations against Jesus, but Jesus refuses to even speak to Herod, so after mocking him and putting a fine robe on him, Herod sends Jesus back to Pilate. In an attempt to placate the Sanhedrin, Pilate ends up scourging Jesus, and then offers to release either Jesus or Barabbas, a murderer and revolutionary. The crowd from the Sanhedrin, though, chooses Barabbas and demands Jesus be crucified. Pilate finally agrees and sends Jesus to be crucified.

The **sixth episode (23:26-56)** is that of the **crucifixion, death, and burial of Jesus**. Luke tells us that **Simon of Cyrene** carried Jesus' cross to **Golgotha**, and that on the way to Golgotha, Jesus addresses the women who were weeping for him. He tells them not to weep for him, but rather for their children, because the days were coming when barren women will be called blessed. He then says, *"If they do this while the wood is green, what will happen when it is dry?"* He is saying that if the Jews are crucifying him now, when there was still hope the Jews might repent and accept the Messiah, what is going to happen when that hope is gone? The answer has been obvious throughout Luke's Gospel: **Destruction is soon coming upon Jerusalem**.

Once at Golgotha, while he is being crucified with two other criminals (Luke uses the actual Greek word for *criminals*, and not *revolutionaries*), Jesus says, "Father, forgive them, for they don't know what they are doing." The soldiers offer him sour wine, cast lots for his clothing, and put the inscription **King of the Jews** on his cross, signifying the crime for which he was being executed. The rulers (Jewish leaders), the soldiers, and even one of the criminals mock Jesus for claiming to be the Messiah, the King of the Jews. Interestingly, unlike in Mark and Matthew, there is no mention of the Temple. In any case, the other criminal admits that he and the other criminal deserve their punishment but says that Jesus is clearly innocent. He then asks Jesus to remember him when he **comes into his kingdom**. Jesus tells the man that he will be with him in paradise that very day.

From noon until 3 pm, darkness comes over the land, and then at 3:00 pm, Jesus cries out, "Father, into your hands I commit my spirit," and the curtain in the Temple is split in two. At that point, the centurion overseeing the crucifixion says, "Truly, this man was righteous." After Jesus dies, a member of the Sanhedrin named **Joseph of Arimathea** comes forward to ask Pilate for the body so he could bury Jesus in a new tomb.

The **seventh episode (24:1-12)** takes place on Sunday morning, when **Mary Magdalene**, **Joanna**, and **Mary the mother of James** discover the empty tomb. They encounter an angel who tells them that Jesus has risen from the dead. They go tell Jesus' disciples, and although some don't believe it, Peter runs to the tomb, finds it empty, with only the linen cloth left. He then goes home, not sure to make of what had happened.

In the **eighth episode (24:13-35)**, the scene shifts to two unnamed disciples of Jesus walking from Jerusalem to **Emmaus**, a small town about seven miles outside of Jerusalem, later that day. Jesus shows up and ends up walking and talking with them the entire time, yet they don't recognize that it is Jesus. When he asks them what they are talking about, **Cleopas** says that Jesus was a prophet from Nazareth whom they hoped would be the one to redeem Israel, but who had run afoul of the Temple priesthood, so they had him arrested and got him crucified. Now, three days later, some of the women followers were claiming they encountered angels who told them that Jesus was risen from the dead, and they just didn't know what to think.

At that point, Jesus tells them that this was what the prophets had said must happen all along: **the Messiah had to suffer and die before he entered into his glory**. For the rest of the walk to Emmaus, Jesus proceeds to teach them from Scripture just what he was talking about. Once they get to Emmaus, the two disciples invite Jesus to have a meal with them, and in the course of the meal, when Jesus breaks the bread and gives it to them, their eyes are opened, and they recognize him. But at the same time, he simply vanishes. So, they get up and go back to Jerusalem to tell the rest of the disciples what had happened.

As odd as this resurrection account may be, it nevertheless gives us a glimpse of what the early believers claimed. It is clear they claimed Jesus was literally, physically resurrected, and that it wasn't just some sort of vision or dream. At the same time, there was a new aspect to his physicality. Somehow, he had the ability to just appear and disappear. In addition, they claimed the proclamation regarding how Jesus fulfilled the Scriptures came to them *directly from the resurrected Jesus himself*. This cannot be emphasized enough. None of the disciples, indeed none of the Jews, were expecting the Messiah to suffer and die. Yet from the very beginning of the Church, part of the Gospel claim was that the Scriptures taught that the Messiah must suffer and die, and that Jesus fulfilled these Scriptures. Where did they get this new interpretation? Their answer was clear: from the resurrected Jesus himself.

The **ninth and final episode (24:36-53)** happens later that evening, back in Jerusalem, when the two disciples go back and tell the other disciples what had happened. As they were talking, Jesus appears in their midst and says, "Peace to you!" Some fear he might be a ghost, so he proves to them he really is there in the flesh by telling them to touch him and to notice the scars in his hands and feet. He even asks them to give him something to eat. They give him some broiled fish and he eats it in front of them. Then he tells them that not only did he tell them all this had to happen, but that it all happened to fulfill the Torah of Moses, the prophets, and the psalms. He then proceeds to teach them from Scripture how the Messiah had to suffer, die, and rise on the third day, and how repentance and the forgiveness of sins was to be proclaimed in his name to all nations, beginning in Jerusalem. He says they are witnesses to everything and that they are to stay in Jerusalem until they are **clothed with power from on high**. After this, Jesus leads them out to Bethany, where he is taken up into heaven. The disciples then go back into Jerusalem and continually worship God in the Temple.

It has been noted that Luke's ending is quite different than Matthew's ending. Here, Luke has Jesus ascend to heaven right outside of Bethany, seemingly shortly after his resurrection. Matthew, though, has Jesus meet the disciples back in Galilee at a later time, and he doesn't even mention the ascension at all. So, what's going on? The easiest answer is to see that the Gospel writers, although telling about historical events, were still nevertheless presenting those historical events in a format of a story and were thus free to shape the events in such a way that fit in with their particular narratives. As far as Matthew is concerned, after his infancy narrative, he begins the story of Jesus' ministry in Galilee. So, he brings his Gospel back full circle, with Jesus and his disciples back in Galilee and Jesus telling them to go out into the world and make disciples of all nations.

With Luke, though, we have to remember that it is really only part one of a two-volume work, with part two being the Book of Acts. In Acts 1:8 we find a thesis statement that charts the course for the entire narrative of Acts. Jesus tells his disciples that they will be his witnesses in **Jerusalem, Judea, Samaria**, and to the **ends of the earth**. Like a bullseye with concentric circles around it, Luke presents the early Church as beginning in Jerusalem, and then gradually expanding throughout the known world, with the story ending with Paul in Rome. That's the narrative flow to Acts. Therefore, for the sake of the narrative of Luke-Acts, Luke has just decided it was unnecessary to mention the disciples went back to Galilee for a time before they returned to Jerusalem for Pentecost fifty days later. He just keeps them in Jerusalem and then opens Acts with the events at Pentecost in Acts 2.

Since the disciples were from Galilee and only came to Jerusalem with Jesus for Passover, it is entirely plausible that they initially went back to their homes in Galilee and then returned to Jerusalem for Pentecost. Sure, it certainly is possible that they stayed in Jerusalem from Passover to Pentecost, like Luke says, but it doesn't really matter. There are literary reasons for the decisions of both Luke and Matthew, and the bottom line is that they were in Jerusalem during Passover when Jesus was crucified and resurrected, and they were in Jerusalem during Pentecost when the Holy Spirit was poured out upon them.

# THE BOOK OF ACTS

**Time of Writing**: Acts is *Part 2* to the Gospel of Luke's *Part 1* and was probably written around the same time in the 70s or 80s. Still, it is odd that Acts takes us up to Paul's first imprisonment in Rome, around AD 60-63, and doesn't tell us the result of that imprisonment. Eusebius records that Paul was released, went to Spain, and then later got re-imprisoned in Rome, where he was beheaded during Nero's persecution of Christians following the great fire of Rome in AD 64. That could suggest that Acts, as well as Luke, was written before Paul was initially released, thus placing both Luke and Acts in the early 60s.

**Authorship**: Luke the Physician, who was a frequent partner with Paul on his missionary journeys. Luke is mentioned in Romans 16:21, Colossians 4:14, Philemon 1:23, and II Timothy 4:11.

### The Big Things to Know in Acts
A. **Jesus as God's Servant**: In the early chapters of Acts, the apostles routinely refer to Jesus as *God's Servant* and the necessity of his suffering. This reflects an early re-interpretation of the Suffering Servant songs in Isaiah 40-55 and a fusing it with the identity of the Messiah. Simply put, in Judaism, the Messiah was to come *after* the suffering of God's servant, Israel. The apostles now declared that the Messiah was to suffer *as* God's Servant *on behalf of* God's people.
B. **The Work of the Holy Spirit**: As in Luke's Gospel, here in Acts Luke continues to emphasize the role of the Holy Spirit in the spreading of the Gospel, first in Jerusalem, but soon beyond the borders of the Jewish world itself.
C. **Hellenists and Hebrews**: The basic distinction is that *Hellenists* are Jews who live throughout the Greek-speaking Roman Empire, whereas *Hebrews* are Jews who are native to the land of Israel.
D. **God-Fearers and Proselytes**: *God-Fearers* are Gentiles who observe Jewish customs and attend synagogue, but who are not circumcised and thus do not become Jewish. *Proselytes* are Gentiles who have actually converted to Judaism and have undergone circumcision.
E. **A Slow-Growing Divorce**: Going hand-in-hand with chronicling the growth of the first century Church in the Gentile world, Luke also emphasizing the slow but steady "divorce" within Judaism between Jesus' followers who were moving and reaching out to the Gentile world and the more traditional form of Judaism that did not approve of that Gentile mission. This "divorce" was pretty much finalized after AD 70, after which Christianity and Rabbinic Judaism were clear two distinct religions, but Acts shows how in the 35-40 years between Pentecost and the Jewish War this "divorce" was steady but sure.

## Acts Story Chart

|  | | | | |
|---|---|---|---|---|
| **Prologue (1:1-26)** | 1:1-5<br>Introduction to Theophilus | 1:6-11<br>The Ascension of Jesus | 1:12-26<br>Choosing Matthias | |
| **The Early Church in Jerusalem (2:1-5:42)** | 2:1-41<br>Pentecost Peter's Speech | 2:42-47<br>SUMMARY<br>*Fellowship of the Believers* | 3:1-26<br>Lame Beggar Peter's Speech | 4:1-31<br>Peter and John before the Sanhedrin |
| | 4:32-35<br>SUMMARY<br>*Everything in Common* | 4:36-5:11<br>Ananias and Sapphira | 5:12-16<br>SUMMARY<br>*Signs and Wonders* | 5:17-42<br>Apostles Arrested and Freed |
| **Start of Persecution (6:1-8:3)** | 6:1-7<br>Choosing Seven Deacons | 6:8-15<br>Stephen Seized | 7:1-53<br>Stephen's Speech | 7:54-60<br>The Stoning of Stephen | 8:1-3<br>Saul Ravages the Church |
| **Early Movement Beyond Jerusalem (8:4-11:30)** | 8:4-25<br>*Samaria*<br>Philip and Simon the Magician | | 8:26-40<br>*Gaza*<br>Philip and Ethiopian Eunuch | |
| | 9:1-25<br>*Damascus*<br>Conversion of Saul | | 9:26-31<br>*Jerusalem*<br>Paul meets the Apostles | |
| | 9:32-43<br>*Lydda/Joppa*<br>Peter Heals Aeneas and Restores Dorcas | | 10:1-48<br>*Joppa/Caesarea*<br>Peter Preaches to Cornelius | |
| | 11:1-18<br>*Jerusalem*<br>Peter Reports to the Church | | 11:19-30<br>*Antioch*<br>Church in Antioch Barnabas and Saul | |
| **Persecutions in Jerusalem (12:1-25)** | 12:1-19<br>*Jerusalem*<br>James Killed Peter Imprisoned/Rescued | | 12:20-25<br>*Caesarea*<br>The Death of King Herod | |

# Book of Acts | 177

| Paul's First Missionary Journey (13:1-15:35) | 13:1-12<br>Paul and Barnabas in Cyprus | 13:13-52<br>Paul and Barnabas at Antioch in Pisidia | 14:1-7<br>Paul and Barnabas at Iconium | 14:8-28<br>Paul and Barnabas at Lystra; Return to Antioch | 15:1-35<br>The Jerusalem Council |
|---|---|---|---|---|---|
| **Paul's Second Missionary Journey (15:36-18:23)** | 15:36-41<br>*Antioch*<br>Paul and Barnabas Separate | 16:1-5<br>*Derbe/Lystra*<br>Timothy joins Paul/Silas | 16:6-10<br>*Troas*<br>Macedonian Call | | |
| | 16:11-40<br>*Philippi*<br>Conversion of Lydia Paul/Silas in Jail | 17:1-9<br>*Thessalonica*<br>Paul/Silas Flee in the Midst of Conflict | 17:10-15<br>*Berea*<br>Timothy/Silas Stay Paul Goes to Athens | | |
| | 17:16-34<br>*Athens*<br>Mars Hill | 18:1-17<br>*Corinth*<br>Paul with Aquila and Priscilla | 18:18-23<br>*Antioch*<br>Paul Returns | | |
| **Paul's Third Missionary Journey (18:24-20:38)** | 18:24-28<br>*Ephesus*<br>Apollos in Ephesus | 19:1-41<br>*Ephesus*<br>Paul and the Riot | 20:1-38<br>Paul in Philippi, Troas, and Miletus | | |
| **Paul in Jerusalem and Caesarea (21:1-26:32)** | 21:1-16<br>Paul in Jerusalem | 21:17-26<br>Paul Visits James | 21:27-36<br>*Temple*<br>Paul Arrested | 21:37-22:29<br>Paul's Speech to the People | 22:30-23:11<br>Paul Before the Sanhedrin |
| | 23:12-35<br>Plot to Kill Paul; Paul Sent to Felix | 24:1-27<br>*Caesarea*<br>Paul Before Felix | 25:1-12<br>Festus Paul Appeals to Caesar | 25:13-27<br>Paul Before Agrippa and Bernice | 26:1-32<br>Paul's Defense Before Agrippa |
| **Paul's Journey to Rome (27:1-28:31)** | 27:1-12<br>Paul Sails to Rome | 27:13-38<br>The Storm at Sea | 27:39-44<br>The Shipwreck | 28:1-10<br>Paul in Malta | 28:11-31<br>Paul in Rome |

## A Walkthrough of Acts

Luke's focus in his Gospel is obviously on the life of Jesus. In Acts, the focus is on roughly the first 30 years of the early Church, from the time of Pentecost in AD 30 to the time just before the outbreak of the Jewish War of AD 66-70. There are two major themes in Acts: (A) **The expansion of the Church**: from its birth in Jerusalem to throughout the Roman Empire, and (B) **The activity of the Holy Spirit** in the life of the early Church.

### 1. Prologue (1:1-26)

The first section is comprised of three episodes that transition from Luke's Gospel to the narrative of Acts. It begins with Luke's introduction to Theophilus **(1:1-5)** in which he tells Theophilus that Jesus had appeared to and taught the apostles about the Kingdom of God for a period of 40 days after his resurrection. He then told them to wait in Jerusalem for the promise of the Father, which would be the outpouring of the **Holy Spirit**. Jesus even reminds the apostles of John the Baptist's words in **Luke 3:16** regarding the coming baptism of the Holy Spirit.

The next episode **(1:6-11)** tells us about the ascension of Jesus. Even after the resurrection, the apostles still don't quite get what the Kingdom of God was all about, for they ask Jesus if he was now going to finally reestablish the Kingdom to Israel. Jesus, though, tells them of a different agenda. He tells them that they are going to receive power when the Holy Spirit comes upon them, and that they are going to be his witnesses throughout the world. It is here in **Acts 1:8** that we find the basic thesis statement to the entire book of Acts that traces out the geographical progression in the book. The story of the Church was to start in Jerusalem, then expand out to Judea, Samaria, and eventually to the entire world. Jesus is then taken up into Heaven and two men in white clothing (angels) tell the apostles that Jesus would eventually return in the same way in which they saw him go into Heaven. Luke's point is that there was a distinct time when the apostles knew the resurrected Jesus had left them.

The next episode **(1:12-26)** tells of how the apostles decided to replace Judas Iscariot. The significance of having **twelve apostles** is that it portrays this new Jesus movement as **reconstituted Israel**, the **true people of God**, centered around the death and resurrection of **Jesus as the Messiah**. It is at this point that Luke tells what had happened to Judas. According to Luke, Judas had bought a field with the money he got for betraying Jesus but had fallen over somehow to where his body burst open, and his intestines spilled out. Because of that, the field became known as the **Field of Blood**. There is no real way to harmonize Luke's account of Judas' death with that of Matthew. That being said, both Matthew and Luke agree that Judas was dead shortly after his betrayal of Jesus and that there was a field in Jerusalem called the Field of Blood that it was in some way connected to Judas.

In any case, the qualification for the person to replace Judas is that he had to have been with them since the beginning of Jesus' ministry and had to have been a witness to the resurrection. The final two candidates are **Joseph** (who was also known as both Barsabbas and Justus), and **Matthias**. It is Matthias who ends up being counted among the Twelve. With that, the loose ends of the Gospel of Luke are now tied up, and the door opens to a new chapter in the life of the Jesus movement, namely, the beginning of the early Church, beginning with the outpouring of the Holy Spirit at Pentecost.

### 2. The Early Church in Jerusalem (2:1-5:42)

The next four chapters in Acts give us a glimpse of what was going on in Jerusalem during the early days of the Jesus movement. At this point, we should still see this as a movement *within Judaism*. In fact, for the first thirty years or so, the Jesus movement wasn't seen as completely distinct from Judaism. That is why the issue of whether or not Gentiles should get circumcised and keep the Torah is so prominent in Acts and Paul's letters. That controversial issue, though, doesn't really start coming up in Acts until later. In these early chapters, the focus is solely on the growth of the early Church in Jerusalem and its conflicts with the Temple establishment.

The **first episode (2:1-42)** is the **Day of Pentecost**, which takes place 50 days after Passover and celebrates the firstfruits of the harvest. Having Pentecost be the birth of the Church is fitting, for the first believers can be considered the firstfruits of the full harvest of people of God. Luke tells us that the Holy Spirit was poured out on the original believers as they experienced a **violent rushing wind** and **tongues of fire**. It was then that they were filled with the Holy Spirit and began to speak in different languages, so that the Jews who had come from around the Roman Empire to Jerusalem for Pentecost would be able to hear the Gospel in their own language. That is important to remember, for on the Day of Pentecost the audience in Jerusalem consisted of Jews and proselytes. This was something that initially happened *within Judaism*.

When some accuse the believers of being drunk, Peter stands up and speaks to the crowd. He tells his fellow Jews the significance of what was happening by quoting **Joel 2:28-32**, which prophesies that in the **last days** God would **pour out His Spirit on all flesh**, and that this would happen **before the Day of YHWH**. The standard Jewish expectation was that the Messiah would come, God would pour out His Spirit on the Jews, and *then* the Day of YHWH would happen where the Jews would be vindicated as God's people and their Gentile enemies would suffer judgment. Yet Peter tells them the Messiah *had come*, that they *had rejected* and *killed* him, but that God *had resurrected* him. Thus, the coming Day of YHWH would be the coming **Day of Christ**, who is the Lord. To underscore the notion of the Messiah's resurrection, Peter quotes **Psalm 16:8-11**, in which it says that the **Lord's Holy One** will not see decay and tells the crowd that it was prophetically about the resurrection of Jesus the Messiah, and that he and his fellow disciples were all witnesses to it. Not only was he resurrected, but he was now exalted at the right hand of God. To underscore this, Peter quotes **Psalm 110:1** (*"Sit at my right hand, until I make your enemies your footstool"*).

Peter makes it clear that **Joel 2:28-32** was being fulfilled that day, and that day signaled the *beginning of the last days*. God *had poured out His Spirit*, not on the nation of Israel as a whole, but rather upon the followers of Jesus, the crucified and resurrected Messiah, and was available to anyone who repented and was baptized in the name of Jesus the Messiah. Peter exhorts his fellow Jews to turn to God before the Day of YHWH happened, so they could avoid God's judgment. About 3,000 Jews repented and were baptized that day and they dedicated themselves to the **teaching of the apostles**, the **fellowship**, to the **breaking of bread** and to **prayer**. Pentecost was now a celebration of the firstfruits of a future harvest of believers.

The **second episode (2:43-47)** gives a brief snapshot of the life of the early Church in Jerusalem. There are signs and wonders, everyone is united in the faith, and believers share their property and possessions and hold everything in common. Still, they regularly meet in the Temple (the very one Jesus had already prophesied would eventually be destroyed). We are told that they have **grace from all the people**, meaning that initially they were well-received by their fellow Jews. In fact, more and more Jews are joining them and being saved every day.

The **third episode (3:1-26)** takes place in the Temple precincts. Peter and John are in the Temple at 3:00 in the afternoon, (the very time of the day Jesus had died on the cross). It is there they encounter a beggar who had been lame from birth. When he asks for money, Peter heals him **in the name of Jesus of Nazareth, the Messiah**. This healing quickly attracts a crowd, setting the stage for Peter's second sermon. He makes it clear that the lame beggar was healed by the power of God in the name of Jesus and then proceeds tell them that even though they had handed Jesus over to Pilate and had him put to death, that God had raised him up and that the followers of Jesus were all witnesses to his resurrection.

During his sermon, Peter also calls Jesus **God's Servant**, the **Holy and Righteous One**, as well as the **Author (or Originator) of Life**. The fact that he presents Jesus as the Messiah and as God's Suffering Servant obviously brings up echoes of the **Suffering Servant in Isaiah 40-55**. In its original context, the Suffering Servant was understood to be the Jews who had been refined in the exile to become the purified remnant of Israel, and who were then able to be God's faithful servant and a light to the Gentiles. Of course, the returning exiles failed to be God's faithful servant and light to the Gentiles. Thus, by identifying Jesus with the Suffering Servant, Peter is declaring that Jesus succeeded where Israel had failed.

In any case, Peter calls upon his fellow Jews to repent and turn to Jesus as the resurrected and glorified Messiah, so that the **times of refreshing** could come from the Lord, and so that He could send Jesus the Messiah to them. Peter tells them that Jesus was to remain in Heaven until the **time of restoration of all things** that God had spoken about through His prophets had come to pass. This alludes back to God's original promise to Abraham, that through the great nation that will come from him (Israel), God would bless all nations. The blessing of all nations was the endgame of God's covenant with Abraham. So here, the "restoration of all things" is the long-awaited blessing of all nations and the redemption of all creation. The "times of refreshing," though, is the hope for the purification of sinful Israel so that it could finally be that "light to the nations" through whom God would bless all nations. Basically, Peter is saying to his fellow Jews, "Repent and turn to Jesus, the resurrected Messiah, so that you can be refreshed as God's people and so that through you, God can finally fulfill the covenant with Abraham and bless all nations."

Peter also says Jesus is the **prophet like Moses** mentioned in **Deuteronomy 18:15-16** and tells the crowd that all the prophets had spoken about the very things that were currently happening at that time. Therefore, since God had raised His Servant Jesus from the dead, the offer of repentance was open to them so they could finally be the **offspring of Abraham** through whom God would bless all nations.

The **fourth episode (4:1-31)** tells of Peter and John's confrontation with the Temple establishment, who obviously do not approve of what Peter and John are telling the crowd in the Temple. They arrest Peter and John, put them in prison for the night, and bring them up in front of the Sanhedrin the next day. Just like Jesus told his disciples in the Olivet Discourse in **Luke 21:12-15**, Peter and John find themselves hauled up before the authorities. Peter, though, is *filled with the Holy Spirit* and proceeds to tell the Sanhedrin that the lame man was healed in the name of the Messiah, Jesus of Nazareth. They know full well who Jesus was—they had framed him and handed him over to Pilate to be crucified! Despite that, Peter tells them God had raised him up. He then quotes **Psalm 118:25-26** and tells them (just like Jesus told them when he confronted them in the Temple shortly before his crucifixion) they are the builders that rejected Jesus, but that Jesus had become the chief cornerstone. Salvation was to be found in no one else.

The Sanhedrin continues to threaten Peter and John, but they insist they will continue to speak about Jesus. In the end, the Sanhedrin releases them. When Peter and John go back to their fellow believers, they offer a prayer to God that truly is astounding. They quote **Psalm 2:1-2**, a psalm talks about how **the nations** rebel against YHWH and His Messiah. Here, though, they attribute this *to the Sanhedrin*, and are thus equating them (along with Herod and Pilate) with the rebellious nations who plot against YHWH and His Messiah. The lines of demarcation between God's people and everyone else have been redrawn. As they are praying, they are filled with the Holy Spirit and continue to speak the Word of God with boldness.

The **fifth episode (4:32-35)** is simply a summary statement of the early Church in Jerusalem. We are told that there is a unity among all the believers and that the apostles are bearing witness to the resurrection of the Lord Jesus with great power. People also are giving the apostles money so they can distribute it to anyone in need. Simply put, they start their own welfare program and charity.

The **sixth episode (4:36-5:11)** Barnabas sells a field and gives the proceeds to the apostles. After that, Ananias and Sapphira do the same thing, only they keep some of the proceeds for themselves, but give the impression that they had given the apostles all the proceeds. Peter confronts them about their deception and God strikes both of them down. As a result, a great fear comes over the entire Church. The sin of Ananias and Sapphira is that they **lied to the Holy Spirit** and **tested the Spirit of the Lord**. It was the lying and the deception, not the keeping of some of the money, for which they are held accountable.

The **seventh episode (5:12-16)** is another summary statement of the early Church in Jerusalem. The apostles continue to do many signs and wonders and the early believers continue to meet regularly in the Temple, at the Portico of Solomon. Even though their fellow Jews are hesitant to associate with them, they still hold them in high esteem and bring out their sick in the streets in hopes of getting them healed when Peter would walk by and his shadow would fall upon them. Whether or not that literally happened in that exact way isn't the point. What Acts is conveying is that Peter and the apostles were healing people, and because of that, many Jews would bring their sick out to Peter and the apostles in hopes of getting healed.

The **eighth episode (5:17-42)** tells of another attempt by the Sanhedrin to intimidate the Church in Jerusalem. The high priest, along with the Sadducees, arrests the apostles and throws them in prison. Yet that night, an angel frees them and they are back in the Temple preaching the next morning. When the Sanhedrin calls for them to be brought from the jail, they are told that the apostles aren't there, even though the jail was secured. When they find out the apostles are back in the Temple, teaching the people, the Temple guard goes and brings the apostles before the Sanhedrin. The Sanhedrin asks the apostles why they keep teaching about Jesus, even though they had been told to stop. The Sanhedrin then accuses the apostles of trying to "bring the blood of this man upon us." The irony is that the Sanhedrin was, in fact, responsible for Jesus' arrest. They were the ones who conspired to get Pilate to crucify him. The bottom line is that they are being exposed, and they don't like it.

In any case, the apostles, led by Peter, refuse to back down and reiterate the message they have been proclaiming: (1) The Sanhedrin was responsible for getting Jesus killed, (2) God raised Jesus from the dead and exalted him to His Right Hand, therefore (3) Jesus is both Leader and Savior and offers repentance and forgiveness of sins to Israel, and (4) They are witnesses to this, as is the Holy Spirit, whom God has given to all who obey Him. The Sanhedrin is so infuriated that they want to kill the apostles, but a respected Pharisee named **Gamaliel**, though, convinces them not to do it. After making reference to **Theudas** and **Judas the Galilean**, two previous Jewish revolutionaries who had risen up but were soon crushed, Gamaliel tells the Sanhedrin that if the apostles are truly from God, then not only would they not be able to stop them, but they would end up opposing God Himself. But if they aren't from God, they'd soon fail, just like previous movements that had failed.

So, the Sanhedrin beats the apostles, but lets them go, and the apostles continue to meet in the Temple and teach the Gospel of Jesus the Messiah.

### 3. The Beginning of Persecution in Jerusalem (6:1-8:3)

In this section we are told of the spark that ignited the first full-out persecution of the early followers of Jesus in Jerusalem. The result of it was that the Gospel was taken out to primarily Jewish communities beyond the borders of Judea. The **first episode (6:1-7)** begins by telling us about a problem in the early Church in Jerusalem and the apostles attempt to address it. The **Hellenist Jews** (Greek-speaking Jews from outside Judea) in Jerusalem complained to the Twelve that their widows were being overlooked in the daily ministry and that the **Hebrew Jews** (Jews native to Judea) were getting preferential treatment. Although this was still an "inner-Judaism" problem, the Hellenists were discriminated against because they were viewed as being "contaminated" by the Gentiles to a degree. The Twelve choose seven men to be deacons to oversee everything and make sure everything was fair.

What is shocking is who these seven deacons are. We find in 6:5 that they all have **Greek names**. Not only that, but one of them, Nicolaus, is a **proselyte** from Antioch. To the point, the seven deacons are Hellenists...and one was originally a Gentile. Such a move no doubt angers some native-born Jews. This is what sparks the first real persecution of the Jesus movement. In any case, Luke does tell us in 6:7 that a large number of priests joined the movement and became obedient to the faith.

The **second episode (6:8-15)** tells of the arrest of Stephen, one of the seven deacons. In his description of Stephen, Luke tells us he was **full of faith and the Holy Spirit**, **full of grace and power**, and did **great wonders** and signs among the people. He had gotten into a debate with some men from the **Synagogue of Freedmen**, Hellenistic Jews in Jerusalem who clearly were not followers of Jesus. Because they can't beat him in a debate, they get some people to accuse him of speaking against Moses and God. Then they haul him up in front of the Sanhedrin and accuse him of **speaking against the Temple** and **speaking against Moses**. Specifically, they say Stephen proclaimed Jesus had prophesied the Temple would be destroyed and had advocated changing the customs Moses had given the Jews.

The **third episode (7:1-53)** tells us of Stephen's trial before the Sanhedrin. After he is accused of speaking against the Temple and speaking against Moses,

Stephen defends himself by recounting the stories of the Patriarchs (7:1-16), the Exodus (7:17-37), and as well as the wilderness wanderings, the golden calf incident, and their idolatry once they entered the Promised Land (7:38-43). He then points out that God had given Moses directions to make the **Tent of Witness** and that even after Israel had come into the Promised Land, up until the time of David, they had kept the Tent of Witness. But when David wanted to build a **Temple**, God told him *He never asked for one*, but *Solomon had built one anyway* (7:44-47).

After that, Stephen then launches into the thing that gets him killed. He first quotes **Isaiah 66:1-2**, where God says He didn't need a Temple, and tells them that God does not live in houses **built with human hands**. Throughout the Old Testament, things that are referred to as being made "by human hands" *are idols*. In the context of Stephen's speech, he is saying that the Jews had made the Temple into an idol. He also accuses the Jews of being a **stiff-necked people**. By calling them that, he is alluding to the golden calf incident and echoing a constant theme throughout the Bible: *You become like what you worship*. Israel was called "stiff-necked" because they were like the golden calf they worshipped, so therefore they get a yoke put on them to force them to do what they are supposed to do.

Stephen further insults them by saying they have **an uncircumcised heart and uncircumcised ears**. They may have officially gotten circumcised and formally obeyed the Torah on that command, but physical circumcision means nothing if one does not remain faithful to God by practicing justice, righteousness and mercy. Thus, he accuses them of **always fighting against the Holy Spirit** and being just like their rebellious, idolatrous ancestors who made the golden calf, worshipped idols, and constantly rebelled against Moses. Not only that, but they had murdered Jesus, the **Righteous One**, just like their ancestors killed the prophets. This is what got Stephen killed.

The **fourth episode (7:54-60)** tells of the execution of Stephen. The people at the trial before the Sanhedrin are so enraged that they drag Stephen outside the city and stone him to death. Stephen, though, filled with the Holy Spirit, looks up into Heaven and says that he sees Jesus, the Son of Man, standing at the Right Hand of God. This is an allusion to both **Psalm 110:1** and **Daniel 7:13-14**, as well as to what Jesus told the high priest at his trial before the Sanhedrin in **Luke 22:69**. Even as he is being stoned, Stephen continues to testify that Jesus was, in fact, the Messiah, the Son of Man who had been vindicated and glorified by God. He then asks the Lord Jesus to receive his spirit (just like Jesus had asked the Father to receive his spirit) and asks the Lord not to hold this sin of stoning him against his executioners (just like Jesus had asked the Father to forgive his executioners). Near the end of the episode, we are told that a certain Saul participated in the stoning of Stephen. This is the event that inspired him to begin persecuting the early believers.

The **fifth episode (8:1-3)** briefly tells us that after Stephen's death, a great persecution of the Church begins in Jerusalem. Everyone except the apostles is forced to flee Jerusalem and go throughout Judea and Samaria. While Stephen is buried and mourned, Saul begins to harass the Church and drag believers off to prison. This brief episode launches us into the next major section in Acts, where the Gospel begins to go beyond Jerusalem, not only into Samaria, but to Gentiles as well.

### 4. Early Movement Beyond Jerusalem (8:4-11:30)

The next section in Acts is laid out almost as four dual episodes involving Phillip, Saul, Peter, and then a final one highlighting the Church in both Jerusalem and Antioch. The **first dual episode (8:4-25/8:26-40)** primarily focuses on the **work of Phillip**. Philip goes to the city of Samaria to proclaim Christ and perform dynamic deeds among the Samaritans (8:4-25). There is a certain man named **Simon** who was a magician considered to have the power of God. When he sees the deeds that Philip was doing, he comes to the faith and gets baptized. Since the apostles were still considered to be those in positions of authority, they send Peter and John as overseers to pray with the new believers so that they could receive the Holy Spirit. In any case, Simon the magician runs into conflict with Peter when he offers Peter money so that he could receive the Holy Spirit and have that kind of authority and power. Peter rebukes Simon, says his heart is not right with God, and calls him to repent of his wickedness. We never hear about Simon the magician again, but Church tradition claims that Simon fell away from the faith and actually began a number of heresies that plagued the early Church for quite some time.

After that, as Philip is traveling on the road that goes down from Jerusalem to Gaza, he encounters an **Ethiopian eunuch**, an official of Queen Candance, who was returning home after having gone to Jerusalem to worship (8:26-40). Presumably, he was either a Jew or a proselyte to Judaism. Philip hears him reading from **Isaiah 53:7-8**, from the famous Suffering Servant song. When he asks Philip who the passage is about, Philip, beginning with this passage, proceeds to tell the eunuch the Gospel of Jesus.

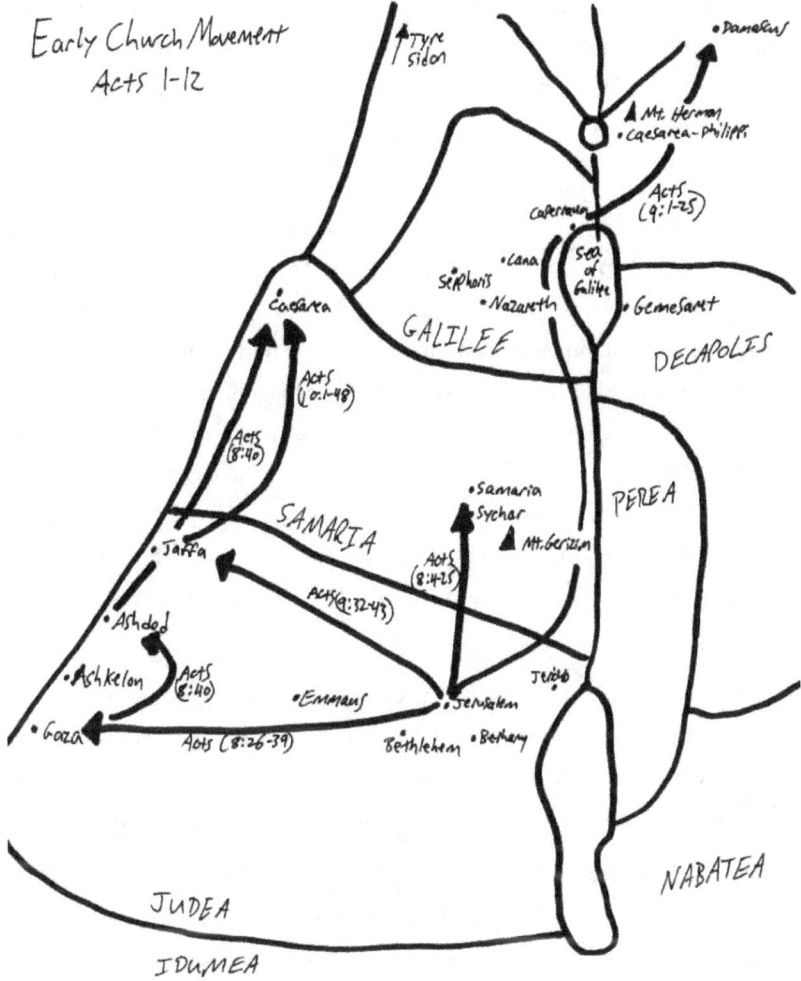

We need to remember that the early Christians used these Old Testament prophecies in such a way as to point to that original context and fulfillment and then show how Jesus was like that, *but bigger*. The original Suffering Servant was faithful Israel who came out of the Babylonian Exile, through whom God promised to work to bring about his ultimate salvation of the world. That salvation plan was fulfilled through the suffering, death, and resurrection of Jesus.

In any case, the eunuch decides he wants to get baptized. After Philip baptizes him, we are told that the Spirit carries Philip away to Ashdod and that eunuch never saw him again. We do not have to think that Philip was magically teleported away. We can just take it to mean that he was called to move on. Philip continues to proclaim the Gospel until he comes to Caesarea. It is worth noting how this episode contrasts with the episode involving Simon the magician. Simon's offering money to Peter revealed that *his heart* was not right with God, whereas here, Philip specifically tells the eunuch that he could get baptized if he believed with *all his heart*.

The **second dual episode (9:1-25/9:26-31)** focuses on the **conversion of Saul**, which likely happened around AD 34-35. At this point in Acts, since he is still among the Jews, he is known by his Hebrew name, Saul. Luke starts using his Hellenistic name, Paul, in Acts 13:4, during his first missionary journey. Here, we are told that Saul is going from Jerusalem to the synagogues of Damascus to find any Jews who were followers of Jesus. On the way there, he encounters the risen Jesus, is blinded, and is then taken into Damascus. A believer named Ananias is then told by the Lord in a vision to visit Saul, because Saul had been chosen to take the name of Jesus (the Gospel) to the Gentiles. Ananias goes to Saul and prays for him, and Saul recovers his sight and is filled with the Holy Spirit (9:1-25).

Since this is such a crucial event in the early Church, we need to make sure we note a number of things. First, in 9:2 the early Jesus movement was known as **The Way**, which probably goes back to what John the Baptist's proclamation in Luke 3:4 about preparing the **way of the Lord**, which in itself is a reference to **Isaiah 40:3-5**, which is all about the New Exodus and the coming out of Exile.

Second, although Saul's encounter here in Acts 9 differs a bit from his later accounts of it in Acts 21:6-11 and 26:12-18, all three accounts agree on the essential elements of the encounter: (1) Saul encountered a bright light, (2) he heard the voice of Jesus, (3) the men with him didn't comprehend what was happening, and (4) he was struck blind and led into Damascus. To be clear, even though Saul didn't witness the physical, resurrected body of Jesus, he did encounter Jesus in some way. At the same time, as is obvious in the rest of Acts as well as Paul's letters, Paul was convinced that Jesus physically rose from the dead, for that is what resurrection means. To put it in another way, Paul realized he wouldn't have encountered Jesus on the Damascus Road in the way he did if Jesus had not been first resurrected.

Third, the impact of the Damascus Road encounter cannot be overstated. Saul, Pharisee who zealously kept Torah, was convinced that what he was *fighting against God's enemies*. He saw the followers of Jesus as blasphemers who claimed a crucified criminal was the Messiah. What he realized on the Damascus Road, though, was that he was actually *fighting against God and His people*, and by doing so, *he had made himself God's enemy*. Despite his keeping Torah, despite the righteousness he thought he had gained by keeping Torah, he was still not only a sinner, but was an enemy of God. The Torah had not truly made him righteous. The only way he was to become righteous was going to be because of the unmerited mercy and grace of Christ, and that is why we find in his letters his insistence that Torah observance could never make one righteous.

Fourth, we are told then when Ananias healed Saul, that something like scales fell off his eyes. It is possible that even though Saul recovered his sight, that he still was left partially blinded, and that poor eyesight was the "thorn in Paul's side" that he talks about in **II Corinthians 12:7**, where he says it was given to him to keep him humble. Also, **Galatians 4:13-15**, he tells the Galatians that when he came to them with a physical ailment, they would have "torn out their own eyes" for him if they could. Finally, in **Galatians 6:11**, where Paul would have written the last few lines in his own hand to authenticate the letter, he makes the passing comment, "Look at what large letters I make with my own hand!" All this implies that Paul's thorn in his side might have been poor eyesight that was a result of his Damascus Road encounter with Christ.

In any case, Saul starts proclaiming Jesus is the Messiah in the Jewish synagogues in Damascus and winning debates with the Jews of Damascus who didn't accept Jesus as the Messiah. Soon the Jews in Damascus plot to kill Saul, so the believers sneak Saul out of the city by lowering him over the wall in a large basket. Even though members of *The Way* were not yet known as "Christians," and were still seen as a sect within Judaism, they were already being seen as distinct enough to where Luke differentiates them from "the Jews."

From there, Paul goes to Jerusalem, but he can't initially get near the disciples because, quite frankly, they don't trust him yet. Barabbas, though (probably the same Barabbas from Acts 4:36, the one who sold his field), reaches out to Saul and introduces him to the apostles (9:26-31). Later on, it is Barabbas who helps Saul establish the Church in Antioch. Paul ends up staying in Jerusalem for a short time and even debates with the Hellenists. When it becomes evident that his life is in danger, the apostles take him to Caesarea and then back to his hometown of Tarsus.

As a historical point, here in Acts, it seems that Paul *immediately* goes to Jerusalem after leaving Damascus, placing this episode sometime around AD 34-

35. Paul himself, though, says in **Galatians 1:18** that after Damascus, he went to Arabia for a time, then back to Damascus, and then, *three years later*, he went to Jerusalem. That thus placing his return to Jerusalem around AD 36-37.

The **third dual episode (9:32-43/10:1-48)** focuses on **Peter and his encounter with the Gentile world**. It begins in 9:32-43 with Peter first going to Lydda, a small town between Joppa on the Mediterranean coast and Jerusalem, where he heals a man named Aeneas, who had been paralyzed. Peter then goes on to Joppa, where a disciple named Tabitha had gotten sick and died. So, Peter goes there and raises her from the dead.

This begins the second part of the dual episode in 10:1-48. While in Joppa, Peter is contacted by **Cornelius**, a Roman centurion living in Caesarea. Luke tells us he was a godly man who "feared God," thus suggesting he was a **God-fearer**, a Gentile who worshipped the God of Israel, but who did not get circumcised to become a Jew. Also, it is interesting to note that Caesarea has been mentioned already, both in Acts 8:40 (where Phillip travelled to after his encounter with the Ethiopian eunuch) and Acts 9:30 (where Paul had stopped on his way back to Tarsus). In any case, God tells Cornelius to send for Peter, who was staying at the house of **Simon the leather worker** (10:1-8). If for no other reason than to point out a bit of coincidence, the last time we saw Peter, he was in Samaria, in conflict with another **Simon, the magician**.

The episode shifts back to Joppa in 10:9-23, where Peter is praying on the roof when he receives a vision from God. Three times he sees a giant sheet filled with unclean animals and hears God telling him to kill and eat, and three times Peter refuses because they are unclean. Each time, a voice from Heaven tells him that if God has cleansed the animals, then they are not unclean to eat. Peter, though, doesn't understand the vision. At that time, Cornelius' servants arrive at the house, and the Holy Spirit tells Peter to go down and welcome them. They tell him about Cornelius, about how he fears God and is well-respected by the Jews of Caesarea, and about the vision of the angel that Cornelius had. And so, Peter agrees to go with them.

Peter meets Cornelius in Caesarea in 10:23-48. Once there, Peter understands the vision. He should not call any man unclean, even if that man is a Gentile. After Cornelius and Peter talk, Peter says that he now understands that God welcomes even Gentiles who fear Him, and thus does not show favoritism. Peter then tells

Cornelius and the other Gentiles there that Jesus is both the Christ (Jewish Messiah) and Lord of all (a title attributed to Caesar). He tells them about Jesus' healing ministry by the power of the Holy Spirit, about how the Jews in Jerusalem had him killed, about how God raised him from the dead, and how he and the other apostles personally witnessed this and that they had seen Jesus and ate and drank with him after his resurrection.

While Peter is telling them about Jesus, the Holy Spirit falls upon everyone there and *Gentiles receive the Holy Spirit*. Once they do, Peter has them baptized in the name of Jesus Christ. Since baptism was seen as entrance into the group, Peter is following God's lead and welcoming Gentiles into the community of faith, thus acknowledging that it was the reception of the Holy Spirit that marked off who the people of God were. Whether or not they were circumcised was irrelevant.

The **fourth dual episode (11:1-30)** then focuses on the Church in two different places: **Jerusalem** (11:1-18) and **Antioch** (11:19-30). Back in Jerusalem, Peter explains his actions to the community. When the **circumcision group** takes issue with Peter going to uncircumcised Gentiles and eating with them, Peter responds by telling what had happened and concluding that if God gave the Gentiles the same Holy Spirit that He gave Jewish believers, who was he to say no to God? The rest of the Jewish believers agree with Peter and end up glorifying God. We must remember that at this time, there still was not yet a clear-cut distinction between Judaism and Christianity. The early believers in Jerusalem were Jews living among their fellow Jews. That is why many of them still felt that the main identity markers of Judaism (circumcision, food laws, Torah observance) still applied.

So, when Peter goes back to Jerusalem to explain what had happened in Caesarea, we shouldn't assume that he went back and reported to "the Church," as if it were a completely separate entity outside of Judaism. Rather, we need to realize that Peter goes back to Jerusalem and responds to criticisms *within the Jewish community* of which the followers of Jesus were a part. That is why we should see the "circumcision group" as Jews who objected to Peter eating with uncircumcised Gentiles, and *some of those Jews* were also part of the Jesus movement. Why? Because this issue regarding Gentiles being part of the people of God was being challenged among the Jews at the time. It wasn't an issue that had been fully resolved yet. In fact, by doing what he did, Peter was bringing up the issue for the first time. How would it play out? That is what we find in the rest of Acts.

Meanwhile, the Church was continuing to spread outside of Judea, even as far as Antioch. Still, the Jewish believers still only shared the Gospel primarily with their fellow Jews, be they Hebrew-speaking Jews, Greek-speaking Jews (Hellenists), or proselytes to Judaism. As they did with Samaria, the Church in Jerusalem sends Barnabas to Antioch to teach and guide the community in the faith of the apostles. Barnabas first goes and gets Saul from Tarsus to come help him build up the Church in Antioch. It was in Antioch that the term **Christian** was first used. The distinction between Jew and Christian was beginning to be made clearer. Still, at this point, it still was seen as largely a Jewish sect.

Around this time, a prophet named **Agabus** had come to Antioch from Jerusalem and had prophesied that there would be a great famine. This famine happened sometime during the reign of Claudius, who was emperor from AD 41-54. And so, at some point, the Church in Antioch sent Barnabas and Saul with famine relief to those living in Judea. Given the fact that Acts 12 tells us that it was around that time that Herod Agrippa beheaded the apostle James, we can generally assume the famine relief happened around AD 44.

### 5. More Persecution in Jerusalem (12:1-25)

This short section, which really is a dual episode in and of itself, signals the conclusion of Luke's focus on the early Church in Jerusalem. King Herod Agrippa begins to persecute some in the Church and actually kills the apostle James, the brother of John, one of the "big three" among Jesus' original disciples (12:1-18). When he sees this pleases the Jews of Jerusalem, he arrests Peter as well and plans to execute him too. An angel, though, somehow frees Peter from prison, and Peter goes to the house of Mary, the mother of John Mark, where a number of believers were gathered to pray for him. Initially they don't believe the maid Rhoda when she tells them Peter was at the gate, but eventually they go to the gate and find him there. He tells them to tell James and "the brothers" what had happened, and then "went to another place." The next morning, when Herod is told Peter had somehow escaped, he has the guards executed instead.

Herod's beheading of James and his imprisonment of Peter probably happened in the spring of AD 44. This helps us form a general historical timeline regarding the events here in Acts 1-12. If Pentecost happened in AD 30, the stoning of Stephen must have happened within a year or so of that, fairly early on. Soon after that, Saul began his persecution of the followers of Jesus, yet had his experience on the Damascus Road probably sometime in AD 34-35. He briefly spent some time in

Jerusalem three years later, roughly around AD 36-37, before moving to Tarsus. That means that, according to Acts, the events regarding Peter and Cornelius, as well as the growth of the Church in Antioch, happened sometime between AD 37-44.

It is worth noting that is the first mention of **John Mark**. He was obviously a native of Jerusalem, and he ends up travelling with Paul and Barnabas on their missionary journeys. Also, the **James** that Peter mentions in Acts 12:17 is **James the brother of Jesus**, who became the leader of the Jerusalem Church after the apostles left the city, as we see Peter doing at the end of this episode. Finally, after this episode, Peter largely disappears from Acts, with the exception of him being back in Jerusalem for the Jerusalem Council in Acts 15.

In 12:19-25, Luke tells us about the death of Herod Agrippa in Caesarea, which happened in the summer of AD 44. Luke tells us that God struck him down because, when the people there hailed him as a god, he accepted the praise and didn't give glory to the true God. Luke even tells us the gory details of his body being eaten by worms. Josephus tells us that he suffered pains in both his heart and abdomen. The episode ends by telling us that the Word of God continued to grow and that Barnabas and Saul, after completing their mission of famine relief, returned to Antioch, bringing along John Mark.

### 6. Paul's 1st Missionary Journey/Jerusalem Council (13:1-15:35)

Acts 13 begins a change in the narrative of Acts, where the focus shifts from Peter and the Church in Jerusalem to Paul and his missionary journeys. Here in Acts 13-15, we are told of the first missionary journey of Barnabas and Paul, as well as the fallout of that journey in terms of the conflict that had to be addressed at the Jerusalem Council. Paul's first missionary journey took place somewhere around AD 48-49, and the Jerusalem Council probably happened shortly after that, in AD 49-50.

In the **first episode (13:1-12)**, Paul and Barnabas, along with John Mark, journey from **Antioch** through the island of **Cyprus**, beginning in the town of Salamis and ending in Paphos. From now on, Luke refers to Saul by his Greek name, Paul. Also, as a side note, Luke mentions that **Manaen**, one of the members of the Church in Antioch, was a close friend of Herod the Tetrarch. In any case, with every town to which they travel, they first go to the Jewish synagogue and proclaim Jesus to the Jews there. In Paphos, they run into a confrontation a Jewish prophet named Bar-Jesus, or **Elymas**, while Paul is trying to speak with **Sergius Paulus** the proconsul. When Elymas tries to convince Sergius not to listen to Paul,

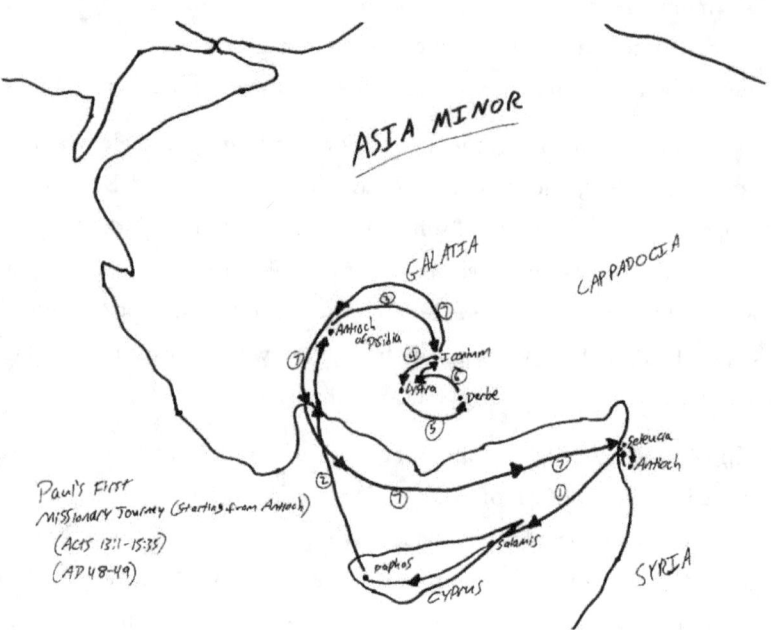

Paul is filled with the Holy Spirit and rebukes Elymas. He calls him the **Son of the Devil** and says he would become blind for a time. Elymas instantly loses his sight and has to be led out. As a result, the proconsul comes to the faith.

In the **second episode (13:13-52)**, as Paul and Barnabas leave Cyprus and travel into **Asia Minor**, John Mark leaves them and goes back to Jerusalem. Paul and Barnabas continue to **Antioch in Pisidia**, where they first go to the synagogue to proclaim Jesus to the Jews. Paul speaks of the history of Israel, from the time of the Exodus to John the Baptist, and then tells them about Jesus' crucifixion, death, and resurrection, and how the rulers in Jerusalem got Pilate to have Jesus crucified, but God raised him from the dead, and he appeared to his followers for a time, and that they were witnesses to the resurrection. Paul declares that Jesus is the Messiah who rose from the dead, that forgiveness of sins is found in him, and that righteousness cannot come through the Torah, but only through him.

A number of Jews and proselytes follow after Paul and Barnabas and the next week, an even greater crowd shows up to listen to Paul. Some of the Jews, though, are jealous of Paul and Barnabas and start to badmouth them. In response, Paul and Barnabas quote **Isaiah 49:5** (*"I have made you a light to the Gentiles"*) and say that since they were rejecting their message, that they would take it to the Gentiles. As a result, the Jews would incite people to persecute Paul and Barnabas wherever they went, and so they decide to move on to Iconium.

In the **third episode (14:1-7)**, the same pattern of events plays out when Paul and Barnabas get to **Iconium**. They initially speak in the synagogue, win over some Jews and Gentiles, but other "disobedient Jews" reject Paul and Barnabas and end up harassing the Gentiles who had come to the faith. Ironically, the disobedient Jews end up allying themselves with other non-believing Gentiles in an attempt to harass and even kill Paul and Barnabas. The line of demarcation was no longer **Jew vs. Gentile**, but now **Disobedient Jew/Pagan Gentile vs. Believing Jew/Believing Gentile**. Eventually, Paul and Barnabas move on to Lystra and Derbe.

In the **fourth episode (14:8-28)**, when Paul and Barnabas arrive in **Lystra**, they find no Jewish population there. Therefore, when they heal a man who had been lame from birth, the pagans there think Paul and Barnabas are Zeus and Hermes and start to worship them. Paul and Barnabas, though, tell them to turn from their idols, accept the Gospel, and to turn to the Living God who created everything. They make little headway, though, and when the Jews from Antioch and Iconium show up, they incite the pagan crowd to stone Paul outside the city. Somehow, Paul survives, and they go on to **Derbe**, where they are able to bring some people to the faith.

After that, Paul and Barnabas pass back through Lystra, then Iconium, then Antioch to encourage the new believers in those cities and to appoint elders for each of the new Christian communities. They also tell the new believers that it is *necessary to enter into the Kingdom of God through tribulation and suffering*. If Christ was indeed the Suffering Servant, and the Church was the body of Christ, suffering was to be expected. They then return home to Antioch of Syria.

The **fifth episode (15:1-35)** tells of the Jerusalem Council in AD 49-50 that took place shortly after Paul and Barnabas' first missionary journey. It is one of the most pivotal events in the life of the early Church, for it conclusively dealt with the issue regarding whether Gentiles who had accepted Christ had to become Jews in order to be part of the people of God. One of the tricky things about the Jerusalem Council involves working out a coherent timeline of events that includes the things Paul mentions in Galatians that Luke doesn't mention in Acts. In Galatians, Paul gives the following timeline of his Christian life: (A)After his conversion in

Damascus (AD 34), he was in Arabia for three years; (B) Then he stopped by Jerusalem (around AD 36) for fifteen days, where he visited with Peter and James; (C) He then went back to Tarsus in the region of Syria and Cilcia; (D) About fourteen years later (AD 49-50), he went to Jerusalem with Barnabas and Titus to lay out privately before the leaders of the Church what he and Barnabas had been doing among the Gentiles.

We need to consider Acts 15 in light of that timeline Paul gives in Galatians. When we do, we realize that everything seems to fit rather nicely. In Acts 15:1-2, we are told that some Jews from Judea had encroached on Paul and Barnabas' churches that had established in Asia Minor during their first missionary journey and started pressuring the Gentiles who had come to the faith that they had to get circumcised according to the Torah and effectively become Jews. Therefore, when Paul and Barnabas went to Jerusalem fourteen years later, we can assume this was *after* their first missionary journey. The private meeting Paul speaks about in Galatians, though, probably was not the Jerusalem Council here in Acts 15, for the Jerusalem Council was clearly a public forum.

Therefore, Paul and Barnabas, along with Titus, probably swung by Jerusalem on their way home after their first missionary journey to meet privately with James, Peter, and John, let know what they had just done among the Gentiles, and to make sure they were okay it. The apostles approved and Paul and Barnabas went back to Antioch. Shortly after that, as Paul relates in Galatians 2:11-14, Peter went up to Antioch to visit the Church there and initially interacted with the Gentile believers. But when some "pro-circumcision" Jews who were connected to James showed up, Peter pulled back from eating with the Gentile believers, and this put pressure on the other Jews, even Barnabas, to pull back as well.

Hence, the controversy regarding Gentile believers getting circumcised and whether or not Jewish believers should share table with them was an issue that came to a boiling point *after the first missionary journey*. Even though Paul and Barnabas had initially gotten an "unofficial okay" from Peter, James, and John (this is what Paul alludes to in Galatians 2:1-10), there had been no official decision on the matter. After all, the early believers were Jews, but they were faced with the fact that some Gentiles had accepted Jesus and had received the Holy Spirit as well. So, what do you do with them? Do they have to become Jews? If they don't get circumcised, how should Jewish believers interact with them?

That is why Jews from Jerusalem started going around to Paul's churches and telling the Gentile believers they had to get circumcised and become Jews. And that is why even some of the Jewish believers (like Peter and like those around James) balked at actually sharing table with Gentile believers. That is why there had to be an official decision made by the Church leadership in Jerusalem. This is precisely what we find in Acts 15.

The episode here is straightforward. Some Pharisees insist Gentile believers must get circumcised and be ordered to keep the Torah. Paul then makes his case and says has been called by God to take the Gospel to the Gentiles, and since the Gentile believers have received the Holy Spirit, there is no difference between Gentiles and Jews. Therefore, what is the sense in forcing Gentiles to live like Jews when Jews themselves can't keep the Torah perfectly and therefore can't be made righteous by it? After that, James recalls Peter's encounter with Cornelius and alludes to **Amos 9:11-12**, which talks about God *"rebuilding the tent of David"* so that the Gentiles can seek Him and call upon His Name.

The Church then decides that the only thing they should require of Gentile believers was for them to stay away from pagan idolatrous practices: idols, fornication (as in temple prostitution related activities), and eating blood or anything that had been strangled. They write an official letter, send it by the hand of Judas and Silas, and send them off with Paul and Barnabas back to the Church in Antioch. This decision by the Jewish believers in the Church in Jerusalem was just another instance that led to the eventual divorce between Judaism and Christianity. When the Jewish-Christians began to accept Gentile-Christians as equals in the faith, this caused the Jews who did not accept Jesus as the Messiah to further conclude that the Jewish followers of Jesus were polluting Judaism by their acceptance of Gentiles.

### 7. Paul's 2nd Missionary Journey (15:36-18:32)

Shortly after the Jerusalem Council, Paul and Barnabas decide to revisit the churches they had established during their first missionary journey, possibly to given them the official decision of the Jerusalem Council in person. This second missionary journey happened during the years of AD 50-52. In the **first episode (15:36-41)**, though, Paul and Barnabas decide to part ways because they disagree whether or not they should take John Mark along with them. Since John Mark had left on them during their first missionary journey, Paul is against it. So, Barnabas takes John and goes to Cyprus, where Paul and Barnabas had gone in Acts 13:4-12,

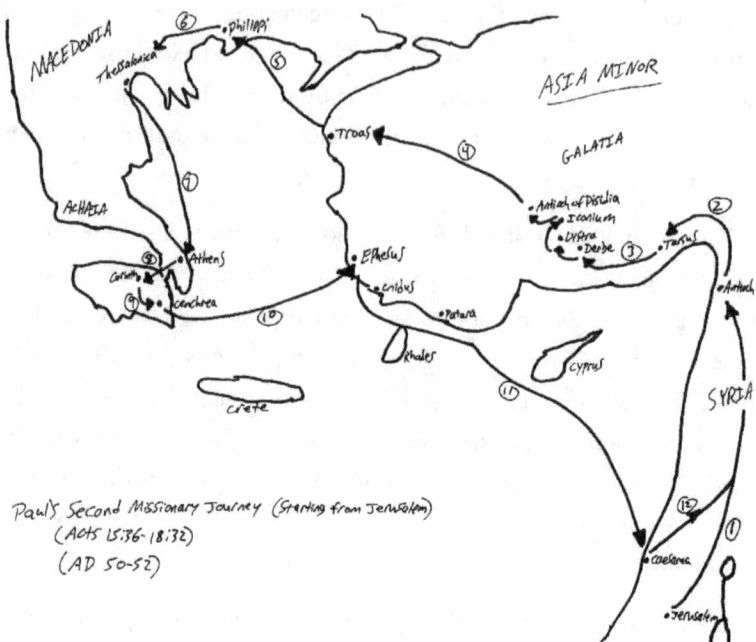

Paul's Second Missionary Journey (Starting from Jerusalem)
(Acts 15:36-18:32)
(AD 50-52)

and Paul takes Silas and goes through Syria and Cilicia, where they had gone in Acts 13:13-14:21.

The **second episode (16:1-5)** takes place in **Derbe**, where Paul and Silas meet **Timothy**, the son of a Jewish woman of the Christian faith and a Greek father. Timothy was a believer, but since his father was Greek, he had not been circumcised. Paul ends up circumcising Timothy to appease the Jews of the region. This might seem like an odd thing for Paul to do, given the fact he was so adamantly against Gentile believers being forced to get circumcised. The difference here was that Timothy was Jewish on his mother's side. Paul was against Gentiles getting circumcised because it sent the message that faith in Christ wasn't enough and made circumcision and Torah observance a requirement for being part of the people of God. Timothy, on the other hand, already was ethnically Jewish. Hence, circumcision was a cultural thing for Jews. The Jews of the region would have seen Timothy as already part Jewish but not circumcised, so Paul circumcised Timothy in order to have that not be an obstacle to the Jews. He had no problem with Jews getting circumcised, because that was part of being a Jew. But Paul wanted to make sure that everyone knew that salvation wasn't dependent on becoming a Jew.

The **third episode (16:6-10)** tells of another pivotal point in Church history. Paul's original purpose on his second missionary journey was to revisit the churches in the region of Galatia (central Turkey) that were established during the first missionary journey. After that, Paul and Silas made unsuccessful attempts to travel to the region of Asia (western Turkey) and the region of Bithynia (northern Turkey). They ended up travelling all the way to **Troas**, a city on the coast of the Aegean Sea in what is in the northwest corner of Asia (Turkey). In Troas, Paul has a vision of a Macedonian man asking him to come to Macedonia (northern Greece). Paul and Silas then go into Macedonia.

In the **fourth episode (16:11-40)**, Paul and Silas travel from to **Samothrace**, then **Neapolis**, and finally to **Philippi**. On the Sabbath, they go out by the river to look for a place of prayer because there wasn't a bit enough Jewish community there to have a synagogue in the city. Philippi was a thoroughly Gentile city. It is by the river that they meet **Lydia**, a Greek businesswoman from Thyatira, who after listening to Paul and Silas, comes to the faith and invites them to stay at her house. Since there were no actual church buildings at that time, the early Church communities would often meet in people's houses, and many times, as it happened in Philippi, it was prominent Christian women like Lydia who opened their houses for the meetings.

A short time after that, Paul and Silas are involved in a confrontation with the Philippian city leaders after they had cast a divining spirit (the **spirit of Python**) from a servant-girl who was being used by some men to make money telling fortunes. Once the spirit was cast out, the girl could no longer tell fortunes, and that meant her owners were out of business. So, they have Paul and Silas seized and dragged before the city officials. They accuse Paul and Silas of being Jews who were stirring up trouble by promoting the practice of illegal customs for Romans. Simply put, Jews preaching that there is only one God, and that Jesus was Lord over all would not sit too well with pagans in a Roman colony like Philippi that had a tremendous amount of loyalty for Caesar.

The city officials beat Paul and Silas and throw them into prison without a trial. That night there is an earthquake, and the prison is so damaged that the prisoners could have escaped. The jailer thinks the prisoners had escaped, so he prepares to commit suicide because he assumes he'd probably be killed anyway for letting them escape. Paul and Silas tell him, though, that everyone is still there. In response, the jailer and his entire family come to the faith and are baptized.

The next day, the city officials decide to release Paul and Silas, but Paul and Silas refuse to leave the prison and proceed to inform the city officials that they were actually Roman citizens. Since the city officials had beaten them and thrown them in jail without a trial, they had violated Roman law. So, Paul and Silas essentially stick it to the city officials by telling them that the only way they'd leave the prison would be if they personally came down to the prison and apologize to them in public. The city officials did so, and then kindly asked Paul and Silas to leave the city.

The **fifth episode (17:1-9)** finds Paul and Silas in **Thessalonica**, another city in Macedonia. They go to the synagogue in the city and, for three weeks, talk with the Jews there about how the Scriptures taught that it was necessary for the Christ to suffer and rise from the dead, and that Jesus was, in fact, the Christ who had suffered and risen from the dead. As elsewhere, some Jews and some Gentile God-fearers come to the faith, but other Jews become jealous and start stirring up trouble among the pagan Gentiles of Thessalonica for Paul and Silas. The mob fails to find Paul and Silas, but they catch a man named **Jason**, a Gentile believer in whose house the Christians were meeting and haul him up in front of the city officials. They accuse Jason of harboring traitors to Caesar and accuse Paul and Silas of causing trouble throughout the empire, opposing the decrees of Caesar, and claiming that Jesus was a king (and hence a threat to Caesar). This causes quite the uproar, but after posting bail, Jason and the Christians with him are let go. Because of the tense situation, Paul and Silas move on to Berea, another city in Macedonia.

The **sixth episode (17:10-15)** finds Paul and Silas in **Berea**. They first go to the local synagogue to share the Gospel message with the Jews, and the Jews in Berea welcome Paul and Silas' message and many Jews come to the faith, as well as several Gentiles. But then, some Jews come from Thessalonica and start causing trouble for them. So, Paul gets on a boat and goes to Athens, while Timothy and Silas stay behind in Berea.

In the **seventh episode (17:16-34)**, Paul visits **Athens** and is astounded at the number of idols in the city. He spends time in the local synagogue, talking with the Jews and Gentile God-fearers, but also spends time in the Agora, debating with Stoic and Epicurean philosophers and speaking about the Gospel of Jesus and his resurrection. The Athenian philosophers had never heard of the Gospel before, and so they invite Paul to speak to them at **Mars Hill**. Paul begins his talks by calling their attention to the altar in Athens that was dedicated to the **unknown**

**god** and proceeds to tell them that unknown god was the creator of the universe and that He didn't live in temples and didn't need pagan priests to attend to Him. Paul quotes from both the **Latin poet Virgil** and the **Greek poet Aratus** to argue that the unknown God was not only near to human beings, in their very beings, but that human beings are actually the **offspring of God Himself**. Because of that, it was foolish to worship idols in pagan temples.

Paul then tells them that God and long overlooked such ignorance, but now was the time to repent of their idolatry because God would soon judge the world through Christ, a man who rose from the dead. As soon as Paul makes the claim that Jesus was bodily resurrected from the dead, the philosophers there begin to make fun of him. After all, the Greeks viewed the body and the material world as dirty and second-rate compared to the "pure" **World of Immaterial Forms**. Human beings were spirits trapped in a material body, and so to die was to "shed the mortal coil." Why would anyone want such second-rate material stuff to come back? Of course, the Jewish worldview saw the created order as good and believed God would eventually redeem and transform the material world. The resurrection, therefore, was an affirmation of the goodness of creation and God's determination to redeem it. In any case, there were some there who ended up coming to the faith, among whom was a man named **Dionysius the Aeropagite**, as well as a woman named **Damarius**.

In the **eighth episode (18:1-17)**, Paul makes his way to **Corinth** and teams up with fellow tent-makers **Aquila and Priscilla**, who had recently moved from Rome to Corinth in AD 49, when Emperor Claudius issued his **Edict of Claudius**, in which he expelled all Jews from Rome because they were fighting with each other over a man named **Chrestus**. It is possible that this "Chrestus" is a reference to Christ, and that the controversy over whether Jesus was indeed the Messiah (the Christ) caused such an uproar among the Jewish community in Rome that Claudius just decided to kick them all out of the city. It was also at this time that Silas and Timothy finally come down from Macedonia and meet up with Paul again. As was his routine, Paul spends time the synagogue in Corinth, sharing the Gospel to both Jews and Gentiles alike. When the Jews reject what he has to say, he declares that he would now go to go the Gentiles. He then literally goes next door, to the house of a God-fearer named **Titius Justus**, to start the Church in Corinth. Interestingly, **Crispus**, the leader of the synagogue, comes to the faith and is baptized, as well as several other Corinthians.

Paul lives in Corinth for a year and a half. Yet when **Gallio** becomes the new proconsul of Achaia (Greece), the Jews haul Paul into court and accuse him of trying to get people to worship God in a way contrary to the Torah. Gallio doesn't care about any of it, so he kicks them all out, but not before he had **Sosthenes**, *the leader of the synagogue*, seized and beat up right in front of the judgment seat.

In the **ninth episode (18:18-23)**, Paul makes his way back to **Antioch**. Aquila and Priscilla leave with him from Corinth as far as **Ephesus**. On the way, in **Cenchreae** (a town just east of Corinth), Paul cuts his hair because of an oath he had taken. He then stays in Ephesus for a few days to talk with the Jews in the synagogue, but he insists on leaving, even after they ask him to stay. He tells them that he would come back if he could. He leaves Aquila and Priscilla in Ephesus and makes his way to Caesarea, and then back to Antioch.

### 8. Paul's Third Missionary Journey (18:24-20:38)

Paul's third missionary journey covers just over two chapters in Acts. In some ways, it is hard to call it a journey because he basically moves to **Ephesus** and lives there for two years. In the **first episode (18:24-28)**, we are told that **Apollos**, a Jew from Alexandria, who had been "instructed in the way of the Lord," had moved to Ephesus and began to teach about Jesus, but only knew about the baptism of John. It seems he had knowledge of the life and ministry of Jesus but had missed the events of Pentecost and the baptism of the Holy Spirit. Aquilla and Priscilla (who had stayed in Ephesus after Paul went back to Antioch) instruct him further in the Way of God and he eventually moves on to Achaia (Greece) and helps the churches there.

The **second episode (19:1-41)** tells us about Paul's time in Ephesus while Apollos is in Corinth. Once back in Ephesus, Paul encounters twelve men there who, like Apollos, had only heard about the baptism of John. After Paul tells them that Jesus was the one who came after John, they are baptized in the name of the Lord Jesus and immediately the Holy Spirit comes upon them, and they begin to speak in tongues and prophesy. Paul ends up living in Ephesus for two years. He begins teaching in the synagogue, but when the Jews eventually reject him, he moves to the lecture hall of **Tyrannus**. During those two years, Paul heals the sick and casts out evil spirits. At one point, **seven sons of a Jewish priest named Sceva** try to cast out an evil spirit from a man "in the name of the Jesus whom Paul proclaims," even though they weren't believers. The demon-possessed man

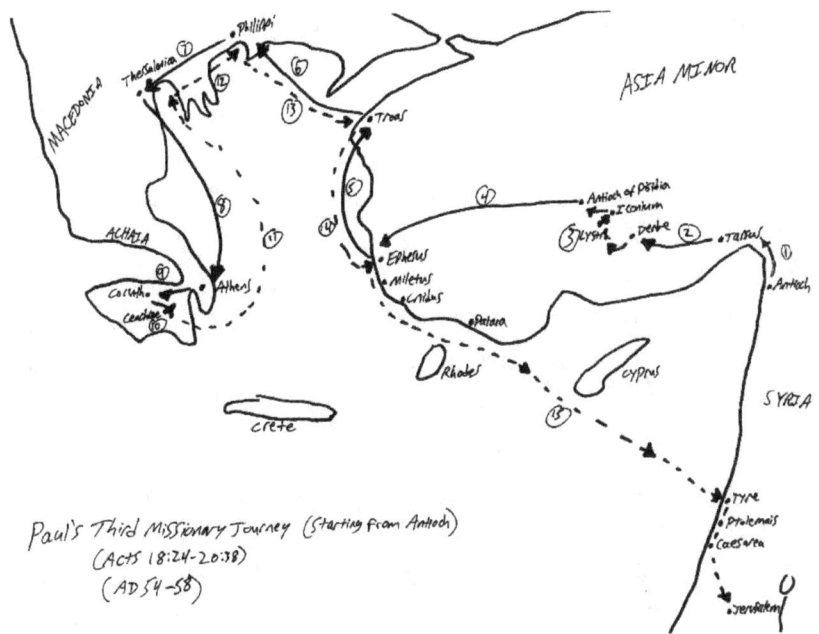

Paul's Third Missionary Journey (Starting from Antioch)
(Acts 18:24-20:38)
(AD 54-58)

proceeds to attack them. Paul's ministry is so successful that many come to the faith and end up burning their pagan magic books.

Eventually, Paul decides he wants to travel back to Macedonia, Achaia, then to Jerusalem, and hopefully to Rome at some point. This foreshadows the events to come at the end Acts. He sends **Timothy** and **Erastus** ahead to Macedonia but decides to stay a bit longer in Ephesus. If he had left Ephesus, he would have missed the great riot of Ephesus that was sparked by Demetrius the silversmith and his fellow artisans. Because there were so many people coming to the faith, the idol business was losing customers and the artisans were not making any money. They were also afraid that the **Temple of Artemis** would eventually lose its prestige. So, they start a riot in Ephesus, grab two of Paul's companions, **Gaius** and **Aristarchus**, and drag them into the theater. Paul wants to go in and address the mob, but he is persuaded not to go. Eventually, a city clerk convinces the mob not to do anything rash, but rather to take their concerns through the proper legal channels. The riot subsides and the people go home.

In the **third episode (20:1-38)**, Paul is about to set sail back to Syria, but when he finds out about a plot by some Jews against him, he travels instead to Troas. As Paul stops in Philippi, Luke uses "we" once again, suggesting that Luke was accompanying Paul at this time. Luke adds that Paul spent Passover in Philippi.

Once in Troas, we are told of a young man name **Eutychus** who had fallen asleep during one of Paul's talks and had fallen out of the window. He was thought to be dead, but Paul reassures everyone that he was alive and going to be fine. From Troas, Paul begins to make his way to Jerusalem to celebrate Pentecost. On his way there, Paul decides he doesn't want to stop in Ephesus, but does want to meet with the church elders of Ephesus one last time, so he invites them to meet him in Miletus. When they meet up, Paul tells them he is going to Jerusalem and expects trouble. They will never see him again. He also tells them they should expect tribulations, trouble, and challenges in the Ephesian church as well. Then, after encouraging them to stay dedicated to serving the Church, Paul makes his way to Jerusalem for Pentecost.

### 9. Paul in Jerusalem and Caesarea (21:1-26:32)

This section in Acts focuses on Paul when he returns to Jerusalem in AD 58. The **first episode (21:1-16)** tells us of Paul's trip from Miletus to Jerusalem. While in Tyre, the Christians there tell Paul that the Spirit was telling him that he should not go to Jerusalem. Paul, though, insisted on going. In **Caesarea**, Paul stays with **Philip the Evangelist** (one of the seven deacons the apostles had chosen in Acts 6) and his four daughters (who were prophetesses). This was the same Philip who had gone to Samaria and who had witnessed to the Ethiopian eunuch in Acts 8. At that point, we were told that Philip had gone to Caesarea, and as we find here in Acts 21, he ended up living there for a time. While still in Caesarea, a prophet named **Agabus** comes from Jerusalem and tells Paul that the Holy Spirit was telling Paul that if he went to Jerusalem, he'd be arrested and handed over to the Gentiles. Paul still insists on going. Once back in Jerusalem, Paul is a guest of a man named **Mnason of Cyprus**, who was an original disciple.

In the **second episode (21:17-26)**, when Paul meets with James and the other elders of the Jerusalem Church, they tell him that the Jews there had been told he was teaching apostasy from Moses and was telling Jews in Gentile lands that they should not circumcise their children or observe Jewish customs. Even though this wasn't true, it was clear Paul's reputation in Jerusalem was quite bad. James tells Paul to go to the Temple with four other Jewish-Christians to go through the rite of purification and to pay for them to have their head shaved (which was part of the rite). James tells him that if he does this, the Jews will realize what they had been told about him wasn't true, and that Paul was still a Torah-observant Jew. Paul agrees and then goes to the Temple to go through the rite of purification.

In the **third episode (21:27-36)**, when the seven-day rite of purification was almost over, some Jews from Asia (modern-day Turkey, where Paul had done much of his missionary work), recognize Paul and seize him. They accuse Paul of speaking against the Jews, the Torah, the Temple, and of even bringing Greeks into the Temple. They had seen **Trophimus**, a Greek Christian from Ephesus, with Paul earlier in the city and assumed Paul had brought him into the Temple. As a result, Paul is dragged out of the Temple and beaten. He only survives because the Roman cohort in Jerusalem come in, get Paul, and bring him to their barracks.

The **fourth episode (21:37-22:29)** tells us of Paul's speech to the mob after he convinces the Roman tribune to let him speak to them. When the tribune realizes that Paul spoke Greek, he asks Paul if he was the revolutionary leader known as **the Egyptian** who stirred up a revolt with 4,000 assassins in the wilderness. When Paul says he was just a Jew from Tarsus, the tribune allows Paul to speak to the mob.

Paul's speech consists of him giving his personal testimony: he was a Jew, born in Tarsus, raised in Jerusalem, a student of Gamaliel, and originally a persecutor of *The Way*. On his way to Damascus to arrest more members of *The Way*, he encountered Christ, was struck blind, and was led into the city. He received his sight back and was baptized when Ananias visited him. When he came back to Jerusalem, while he was worshipping in the Temple, he fell into a trace and heard Jesus tell him to get out of Jerusalem and to go to the Gentiles. As soon as he mentioned going to the Gentiles, though, the crowd goes crazy and tries to attack Paul again. The tribune brings Paul back into the barracks and orders that he be flogged and questioned as to what he did to cause them to fall into such an uproar. When Paul informs the tribune that he is a Roman citizen from birth, the tribune backs off. If he was going to find out the reason for the uproar, he would have to take another track.

The **fifth episode (22:30-23:11)** takes place the next day, when the tribune brings Paul before the Sanhedrin. As soon as Paul begins to address the Sanhedrin, the **high priest Ananias** orders some people to strike Paul. In response, Paul calls him a "whitewashed wall" and berates him for breaking the Torah by ordering to have him struck. When they tell Paul that Ananias was the high priest, Paul apologizes, for it was also written that one should not speak evil of a ruler of the people. In any case, Paul proceeds to divide the Sadducees and the Pharisees on the council by saying he was a Pharisee, and that the reason he was on trial was because he held to the hope of the resurrection of the dead. The mention of the resurrection has exactly the effect Paul hoped. The Pharisees and Sadducees start to have a violent confrontation with each other, so much so that the tribune must forcibly remove Paul and bring him back to the barracks. That night, presumably in a vision, the Lord tells Paul that he is going to testify in Rome.

The **sixth episode (23:12-35)** recounts the circumstances that led to Paul being taken out of Jerusalem to Caesarea. It turns out that 40 Jews had made a vow that they wouldn't eat until they had killed Paul. They go to the Sanhedrin, tell them to request a meeting with Paul again so that they could ambush and kill him when he came. Somehow, Paul's nephew finds out about the plot and goes to tell both Paul and the tribune about it. The tribune, whose name was **Claudius Lysias**, arranges for Paul to be transferred to Caesarea in the middle of the night. He sends a letter to **Felix the governor**, explains the situation, and tells why Paul was being transferred. Felix then agrees to hear Paul's case once his accusers arrive from Jerusalem. Until then, Paul is placed under guard in the residence of Herod.

In the **seventh episode (24:1-27)**, Ananias the high priest goes to Caesarea, along with some of the elders of the Sanhedrin and an attorney whose name was **Tertullus**, to bring a number of accusations against Paul. They tell Felix that Paul was a pestilence, that he stirred up discord among the Jews every place he went, that he was a ringleader of **the Nazarenes**, and that he tried to desecrate the Temple. Paul responds by telling Felix he had just arrived in Jerusalem twelve days earlier, and that he wasn't causing any kind of disturbance in the Temple or in any synagogue. He was a faithful Jew, was a member of *The Way*, and held to the hope of a coming resurrection. What he was doing in the Temple was making alms and sacrifices for the nation of Israel, without any disturbance whatsoever. On top of that, if anyone were to bring accusations against him, it ought to the Jews who were in the Temple at the time, not Ananias and the elders of the Sanhedrin.

Being familiar with *The Way*, Felix decides to delay the hearing until Lysias the tribune could return. Paul is kept under guard but given a certain amount of freedom and was allowed to have his own people look after him. A few days later, Felix brings his wife **Drusilla**, who happened to be Jewish, to listen to Paul talk about the faith in Christ Jesus. For some reason, as Paul is discussing righteousness, self-control, and the coming judgment, Felix becomes afraid, cuts the meeting off, and leaves. Apparently, he was hoping Paul would give him a bribe to rule in his favor, but obviously, Paul didn't offer a bribe. In any case, Felix never hands down a decision, and the result is that Paul is just left under guard in Caesarea for two years. Eventually, **Festus** succeeds Felix as the governor of Judea.

The **eighth episode (25:1-12)** takes place three days after Festus arrives in Judea, when he goes up to Jerusalem to meet the high priests and other leading Jews. Since they still had hopes of ambushing and killing Paul, they ask Festus to send Paul to Jerusalem. Festus, though, says Paul would stay in Caesarea and they would need to go there to bring charges against Paul. Ten days later, that is exactly what they do. They lay out their case before Festus but fail in proving any of their charges against Paul. For his part, Paul insists that he hadn't sinned against the Torah, the Temple, or Caesar. Since Festus wants to garner favor with the Jewish leaders, he asks Paul in open court if he'd be willing to go to Jerusalem to stand trial. Paul will have none of it. He knows if he is taken to Jerusalem, he'd be killed. So, he asserts his right as a Roman citizen to appeal to Caesar himself and insists on being sent to Rome.

The **ninth episode (25:13-27)** takes place a few days later. Before Paul is sent to Rome, **King Herod Agrippa** and his wife **Bernice** come to Caesarea to greet Festus. During their talk, when Festus tells Agrippa Paul's case, Agrippa says he would like to listen to Paul. So, the next day, Paul is brought in to talk to Agrippa and Bernice. Festus says the official reason for the audience was so that Agrippa might listen to Paul and then help Festus write something to Caesar regarding the reason for sending Paul to Rome.

The **tenth episode (26:1-32)** tells us about Paul's speech before Agrippa. He tells Agrippa that he was a Jew, a Pharisee even, who believed in the resurrection of the dead. Initially, he was a persecutor of the followers of Jesus, but on his way to Damascus, he encountered Jesus, who told Paul that He had chosen him to be a servant and a martyr for the Gospel to take the Gospel to the Gentiles. That was why the Jews in Jerusalem had arrested him in the Temple. Paul tells Agrippa that both the prophets and Moses not only spoke of the suffering, death, and resurrection of the Messiah, but they also spoke of how the Gospel would then be proclaimed to the Gentiles. Festus tells Paul he was insane, but Paul insists that wasn't true and says Agrippa knew the prophets fairly well and could attest to what he was saying. When Agrippa says he thinks Paul is trying to convert him, Paul basically says, "Absolutely." Interestingly, both Festus and Agrippa agree that Paul had done nothing wrong and that he could have been set free if he hadn't appealed to Caesar.

## 10. Paul's Trip to Rome (27:1-28:31)

The final section in Acts is the account of Paul's journey to Rome. The **first episode (27:1-12)** tells of the first leg of the voyage to Rome, from **Caesarea** up to the city of **Lasea**. The trip by boat went by means of hugging the coast all the way up to what is modern day Turkey, along its southern coast down, then crossing over to **Crete** and hugging its southern coast. Given that winter was coming, Paul warns the centurion (whose name was **Julius** of the Imperial cohort) that the sea was bound to get rough and that if they continue, they'd risk losing the ship and even dying. Julius, though, decides to try to get around the western edge of Crete to a harbor near the town of **Phoenix**. That turns out to be a bad mistake.

The **second episode (27:13-44)** tells of the storm at sea that forces the ship off course until it eventually shipwrecks on the island of **Malta**. As they were trying to get around the western edge of Crete, a strong wind called **Euraquilo** blew the ship out in the Adriatic Sea, where they were adrift for fourteen days. When some of the soldiers attempt to abandon ship, Paul tells them if they didn't stay in the boat, they wouldn't survive. Finally, the night before they run aground, Paul encourages everyone to eat some food and reassures them that they would all survive. The next morning, the ship gets caught on a reef, and the soldiers and prisoners end up swimming to shore. The soldiers are going to kill the prisoners so they wouldn't escape, but since Julius wants to save Paul, he orders them not to kill any of the prisoners.

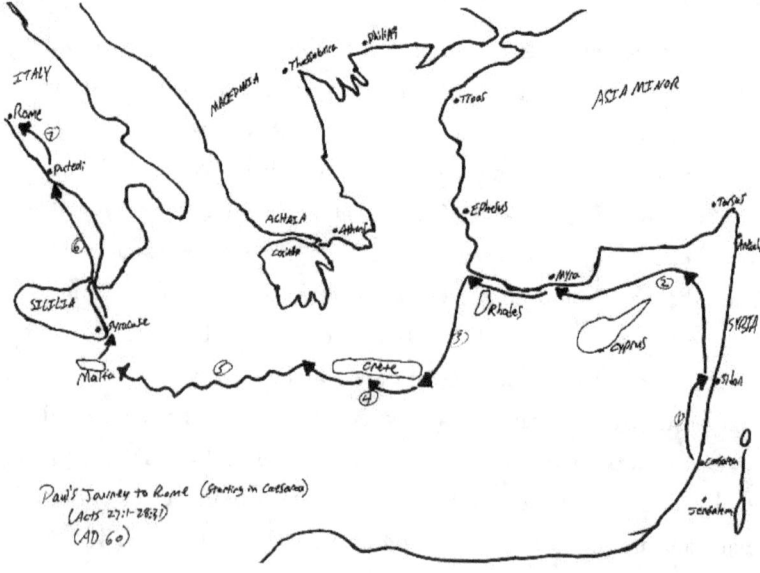

Paul's Journey to Rome (Starting in Caesarea)
(Acts 27:1-28:31)
(AD 60)

The **third episode (28:1-10)** tells of what happened on Malta, an island off the southern tip of Italy. The people of Malta take care of them, but when Paul gets bitten by a viper, the people assume he is a murderer of some sort and is getting what he deserves. Amazingly, Paul shakes off the snake and keeps doing what he was doing. This causes the people to change their minds about Paul. He wasn't a murderer; he must be a god! In any case, while on Malta, Paul heals the father of a prominent man on the island of Malta named **Publius**.

In the **fourth episode (28:11-31)**, Paul arrives in Rome three months later. Once in Rome, Paul is allowed to stay by himself, with only a soldier to guard him. One of the first things he does in Rome is to call for the leading Jews of the city so he could tell them his side of the story, just in case the Jews from Judea had spread rumors about him. The Jews of Rome, though, tell Paul they hadn't been told anything about him. In fact, they would like to hear what Paul had to say about his particular sect. Some Jews in Rome accept what Paul says and come to the faith, whereas some did not. Just as had happened in so many other cities Paul had visited, there was a disagreement that sprang up among the Jews.

The Book of Acts ends with Paul addressing the Jews in Rome who had rejected the Gospel by quoting **Isaiah 6:9-10** (the same passage Jesus quoted when explaining to his disciples why he spoke in parables) and telling them that salvation was being sent to the Gentiles. Isaiah 6:9-10 is part of the call of Isaiah to be a prophet, where God tells Isaiah he is going to prophesy to the people of Judah, but they weren't going to listen to him because they were idolators. The more he prophesied to them, the more blind and deaf they would become, because they were just as blind and deaf as the idols they worshipped. The fact that Paul quotes Isaiah 6:9-10 here is telling. He is saying that the Jews who rejected Christ were effectively still idol-worshippers. They may not have been worshipping literal idols at this time, but they had made things like the Temple and the Torah into idols. Therefore, they were blind and deaf to what God was doing through Jesus Christ.

The Book of Acts comes to an abrupt ending. Luke tells us that Paul spends two years in Rome, proclaiming the Kingdom of God, but doesn't tell us about Paul's trial before Caesar or about anything else. According to Church tradition, Paul was cleared of the charges against him and eventually travelled to Spain for a time. It was later that he was re-arrested and eventually beheaded in Rome, at some point after AD 64, during Nero's persecutions of Christians in Rome following the great fire of Rome.

# AN OVERVIEW OF THE LETTERS OF PAUL

Understanding the letters of the Apostle Paul can be a challenge. In reality, most people don't *really read* Paul's letters. Instead, they basically cherry pick certain verses to memorize or put on display as inspirational quotes. Yet if you ask most people what Paul is arguing in, let's say, in Galatians, or Ephesians, or Philippians, you're going to get a lot of blank stares. Why? Because, like I just said, Paul is a challenge. Theologically speaking, he is on a whole different level than most people.

To use a guitar analogy, when it comes to Christian theology, you might be able to strum out a few chords and sing a song or two. Paul, though, is like Jimi Hendrix or Eric Clapton. When you listen to them, your mind is blown. What you're hearing is amazing, *but you really have no idea what Hendrix and Clapton are doing.* Now, with a lot of focus, practice, and yes, study, not only will you get a lot better at playing the guitar, but you'll be able to better understand the techniques and styles of Hendrix and Clapton as well. You'll be able to grow from just, "I like what I hear," to "I understand what they are doing and how they are making the music." The same goes for understanding Paul's letters.

## The Three (no, four!) Worlds of Paul

We are going to be looking at the letters he wrote during the 15-20-year period of his missionary travels described in **Acts 13-28**. Knowing that history will serve as the foundation for understanding Paul's letters. We will be able to plug each of his letters into the points in time in which he wrote them, and that will give us a historical context for each letter. That will help us understand *who he is writing to* and *why he is writing his letter.*

That being said, there is something else that needs to be covered up front, before we get into any of the specifics of Paul's letters. To do this, I'm going to borrow a little bit from the New Testament scholar N.T. Wright's presentation of Paul, which I found to be tremendously helpful. In order to understand Paul, you have to understand that he really grew up in *three different worlds.*

- (1) He grew up within the time of **Second Temple Judaism**. More specifically, he was a **Pharisaic Jew**. Both of these things shaped his entire religious outlook and life.
- (2) He was also a **Hellenistic Jew** who grew up outside of Judea and was therefore part of the **Hellenistic world of Greek culture**. To understand the significance of this a bit better, it would be like if you were *Hispanic* and your family was *Catholic*, but you grew up in *Alabama*. You would very much take

pride in your Hispanic heritage and your Catholic faith would no doubt shape your worldview, but at the same time, you would grow up in a particular southern culture, and chances are you'd be either a die-hard Auburn fan or a die-hard Alabama fan. Simply put, **your heritage** might be Hispanic, **your faith** might be Catholic, but **the culture** in which you grew up would be fanatical about college football.

- (3) Finally, Paul was also an actual citizen of the **Roman world**. Again, to use my analogy, even if you were a Hispanic Catholic living in Alabama, if you were also an official American citizen, that would give you certain rights and privileges that undocumented workers, illegal aliens, or foreigners with temporary work visas simply don't have. The fact that Paul was an official Roman citizen gave him certain privileges and rights as well.

Having said that, we should also acknowledge that Paul was part of a fourth world that came to define him most of all:

- (4) Being a Christian, Paul was a member of **the early Church, the family of Jesus the Messiah, the true People of God**. Paul may have grown up a Pharisaic Jew, but his encounter with the resurrected Jesus on the Damascus Road caused him to re-evaluate everything, and that change completely affected how he interacted with those first three worlds of Judaism, Hellenistic culture, and the Roman world. That is the dynamic we are seeing as we read his letters: *How does the Gospel speak and relate to first century Judaism, to Hellenistic culture, and to the Roman world?*

**Five Key Items in Jewish Self-Understanding**

Now Paul was a zealous Pharisaic Jew, steeped in Second Temple Judaism. After his Damascus Road encounter, though, Paul became part of the **Jesus movement** known as **The Way**, which, at that time, was *still considered to be a movement within Judaism*. Still, the fact of Jesus' resurrection from the dead caused Paul to completely re-think and re-evaluate the fundamental tenets of Judaism and to re-interpret them in light of Jesus as the long-promised Messiah.

To be clear (again, borrowing heavily from N.T. Wright), whether one was a Sadducee, Pharisee, Essene, Zealot, or any other kind of Jew at the time, all Jews basically held five things in common that went straight to the heart of their identity and self-understanding as Jews.

- (1) They were the **children of Abraham** who inherited God's **promises to Abraham** in the Abrahamic Covenant that (a) He would raise a great nation from Abraham (the Jews), and that (b) they would be His chosen people through whom (c) He would bring blessing to all nations.
- (2) They defined themselves as a people by means of the **Torah that God had given them at Mount Sinai**. The Torah spelled out how that great nation

promised in the Abrahamic Covenant were to live and conduct themselves, and in so doing, be a "light to the nations."

- (3) Within the Torah, there a number of **identity markers** prescribed for them, as God's chosen people, to do to mark themselves off as distinct from the pagan nations around them: the *Sabbath*, the *Food Laws*, and *Circumcision*.
- (4) There was the **Promised Land**, the land that God had promised to give to Abraham's descendants. The Jews considered it to be God's special piece of real estate, and they believed that when God sent His Messiah, it would be the place he established his kingdom from which he would rule the nations.
- (5) There was the **Temple**, the physical place where God's Presence would dwell with His people. I say *would* because in the first century, the Jews understood that at that time God's Presence *wasn't dwelling in the Temple*. He had abandoned the Temple at the time of the Babylonian Exile and had allowed Nebuchadnezzar to destroy it. When they returned from exile, the Jews had rebuilt the Temple, and in the first century, King Herod had engaged in a massive renovation of the Temple, but it was still somewhat problematic in most Jews' eyes because God's Presence had not yet returned to it. In addition, the guy renovating the Temple was an Idumean—basically a half-breed Jew who had gotten his power from the oppressive Roman Empire.

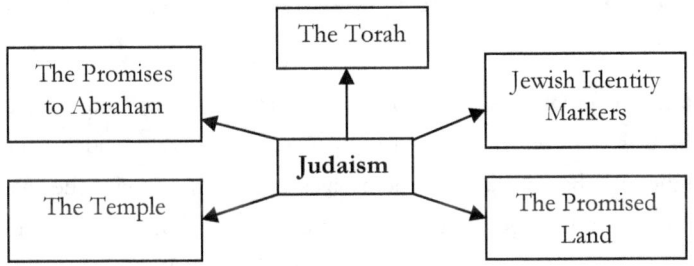

**Jewish Expectations and Paul's Gospel**

Those five things largely defined what it meant to be a Jew and a member of God's people who would eventually bring blessing to all nations. Of course, the Jews knew full well by looking at their own history that they had acted like anything but God's holy people. This caused them to both look back at their history in a certain way to understand the problem, and to look forward to the future in anticipation of how God would fix things in order to fulfill His covenant promises to Abraham. Again, to borrow from N.T. Wright, we can lay things out with three propositions.

- (1) The Jews looked back to **God's covenant with Abraham** as the general blueprint God was going to use to accomplish three things: (1) Save all people

and bring blessing to all nations, (2) Deal with sin and evil within His good creation, and (3) Remake Man in His image.
- (2) The Jews looked back at their history as God's chosen people (**that great nation from Abraham**) and realized they had not been the kind of people they were supposed to be. Instead of living as God's image-bearers for the world, they ended up being sinful idol-worshippers, just like the pagan nations around them. That is why God abandoned the Temple and let them be taken into exile, outside of the Promised Land.
- (3) Nevertheless, through the prophets, God had continued to promise that *somehow* He would restore them as His people and use them to fulfill those three things He promised to do in His covenant with Abraham.

So how would God do that? After the Jews returned from the exile, they came back to the Promised Land and they rebuilt the Temple, but they never felt fully restored. And if they weren't fully restored, they wouldn't be able to be God's People through whom He would accomplish His purposes. Therefore, the prevailing Jewish expectation was that at some point in time, God would send His Messiah who would overthrow their enemies and cleanse the Temple so that God's Presence would return. When that happened, God would pour out His Spirit on His people and they would be empowered to bless all nations by means of the Messiah's rule.

But they had to wait for God to act, and that led to another question: **"What's the hold up?"** As far as the Pharisees were concerned, God hadn't returned because the Jews had not proven themselves truly worthy. Once they were able to show God that they were truly committed to the Torah, once they showed themselves to be righteous in His sight, then God would send His Messiah, His Presence would return to them, and He would finally fully restore them and fulfill the covenant. Since Paul was a Pharisee, that was pretty much his view as well. Yet, his encounter with the resurrected Jesus caused him rethink everything.

Paul came to realize that the fulfillment of God's covenant was not achieved through those five tenets of Jewish identity. Instead, it was fulfilled in the death and resurrection of Christ. Christ defeated the power of sin and death through his death and resurrection. Then, beginning at Pentecost, God had poured out His Spirit on His people...*and His people were not defined by those five tenets of Jewish identity*. Instead, they identified themselves as the people of Jesus Christ who had been empowered by the Holy Spirit to live a whole new kind of existence that involved Jews and Gentiles living together in a new creation with Christ as their Messiah and Lord.

Therefore, Paul preached that the death and resurrection of Jesus had marked *the fulfillment of the Mosaic Covenant*, in that God had used the Jews to bring about the promised Messiah. Now that the Messiah had come, *the Torah and the Mosaic Covenant had served its purpose.* Like a road sign that points you to a certain city, once you get to the city, you don't need the road sign anymore. That is why Paul spends so much time arguing with his fellow Jews about Torah observance. They want to hang on to the road sign, and Paul is saying it was no longer needed.

Still, since the Gospel is all about bringing Jews and Gentiles together in Christ, that presents a whole new set of challenges. How do you "translate" a Gospel so firmly planted in Judaism, to a thoroughly pagan world? How does it speak to the Hellenistic culture in the Roman world? How does it challenge the ideology of Roman imperialism? It's pretty easy *to say*, "Through Christ, God will bring blessing to all nations." It is quite another thing to *understand exactly how that is going to happen*. It's quite another thing to *get to work putting that blessing into action*. That is the sort of thing we see Paul is trying to work out in his letters to the new churches he had established throughout the Roman world.

## Chronology of Paul's Letters

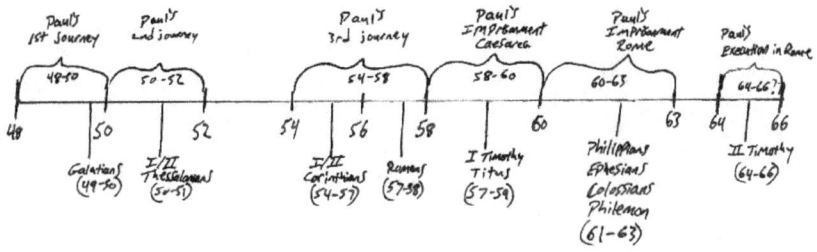

**Galatians**: Probably written shortly after the end of Paul's first missionary journey, yet before the Jerusalem Council (AD 49-50)

**I/II Thessalonians**: Written from Corinth, during Paul's 18-month stay on his second missionary journey (AD 52-53)

**I Corinthians**: Written from Ephesus, during Paul's third missionary journey (AD 54-57)

**II Corinthians**: Written somewhere in Macedonia during Paul's third missionary journey, on his way to Corinth (AD 56-57)

**Romans**: Written from Corinth, during near the end of Paul's third missionary journey (AD 56-57)

**I Timothy**: Written at some point after Paul left Ephesus, to Timothy who was back in Ephesus (Possibly AD 57-59 or sometime between his first and second imprisonment in Rome, AD 63-64?)

**Titus**: No one knows for sure when Paul wrote his letter to Titus. Its similarities to I Timothy suggest either AD 57-59 or AD 64-65 as well

**Philippians**: Written while under house arrest in Rome (AD 61-63)

**Colossians**: Written while under house arrest in Rome (AD 61-63)

**Philemon**: Written while under house arrest in Rome (AD 61-63)

**Ephesians**: Written while under house arrest in Rome (AD 61-63)

**II Timothy**: Possibly written during Paul's second imprisonment in Rome, shortly before his death (AD 64-66?)

# GALATIANS

**Time of Writing:** After Paul's first missionary journey, at some point before the Jerusalem Council (AD 49-50)

## History of Galatia/Paul in Galatia

Galatians isn't addressed to a church in a specific city, but rather to the churches Paul and Barnabas established in the province in what is today central Turkey, where they went on their first missionary journey (Act 13-14): Antioch Pisidia, Iconium, Lystra, and Derbe. Paul and Barnabas first travelled through Cyprus, then went up into Galatia. During their journey, they encountered opposition from most of the Jews in the province, especially when they reached out to Gentiles, brought many of them to faith in Christ, and told the Gentile believers they didn't have to get circumcised and become Jews. It is this issue that becomes a major controversy in the early decades of the Church.

## The Debate over the Writing of Galatians

There is a scholarly debate regarding when Paul wrote Galatians. The **Northern Galatia theory** argues that Paul wrote Galatians during his third missionary journey, somewhere between AD 54-57, to churches in the northern region of Galatia that he must have visited during his second missionary journey (AD 51-52). Therefore, it argues that Paul's visit to Jerusalem in Galatians 2:1-10 must be a reference to the Jerusalem Council in Acts 15. The problem with this theory is if that is the case, then why was circumcision such a contentious issue with these churches if Paul had visited them *after* the Jerusalem Council had already decided that Gentiles didn't need to get circumcised? Besides, we simply have no knowledge of Paul establishing any churches in northern Galatia.

The **Southern Galatia theory** argues that Paul wrote Galatians shortly after the conclusion of his first missionary journey to the cities of south Galatia (Acts 13-14), yet before the Jerusalem Council (Acts 15), which took place somewhere between AD 49-50. It further argues that Paul's Jerusalem visit that he mentions in Galatians 2:1-10 was his visit to Jerusalem to deliver famine relief around AD 42 (Acts 11:27-30). This would explain why circumcision was an issue in Galatians—the Jerusalem Council had not yet made a formal decision on it.

I find the Southern Galatia theory much more plausible, but with one exception. I do not think it makes sense that Paul's visit to Jerusalem in 2:1-10 is a reference to his famine relief visit in Acts 11:27-30. Paul had not yet gone on his first missionary journey, and thus had not yet established primarily Gentile churches. Therefore, the issue of, "Should Gentile believers get circumcised?" would not have come up yet in AD 42. It makes more sense to see Paul's visit in 2:1-10 as indication that he and Barnabas visited Jerusalem *after* their first missionary journey, *before* they went back to Antioch, so they could privately meet with James, Peter, and John, tell them what they had just done, and see if they approved, which they did.

This would make sense for two reasons. First, as Galatians 2:1 clearly says, this private meeting happened 14 years after Paul's initial meeting with the apostles shortly after his conversion, which would have been around AD 36. There is no way that a famine relief visit in AD 42 would be considered 14 years later. Second, this also helps us make sense of Peter's actions in Antioch (2:11-14) after the private meeting. Since Paul's meeting with them was private, the Church as a whole had not yet taken an "official stance" on the issue of whether or not Gentile believers should be circumcised. It was that dust-up between Paul and Peter in Antioch, as well as the fact that some Jews had gone to Paul's churches in Galatia and had started pressuring Gentile believers to get circumcised, that precipitated the calling of the Jerusalem Council in Acts 15. This conflict is what is mentioned in Acts 15:1-2.

## The Big Things to Know in Galatians
A. **The Heart and Soul of the Gospel**: It is faith and the work of the Spirit that produces righteousness.
B. **Torah Observance is Worthless**: Submitting to strict adherence to the Torah and doing outward signs (like circumcision) accomplishes nothing in terms of righteousness. Insisting on Torah observance is, in fact, antithetical to the Gospel.
C. **Two Kinds of Existence**: When it comes down to it, there are only two ways to live your life. Living **according to the flesh** is to live by the rules of this present age, to be enslaved to your passions, and to produce divisiveness wherever you go. Living **according to the Spirit** is to live out the Spirit-empowered life of the Age to Come here in this present age, to live a God's children, and to produce healing and reconciliation.

## Literary Map: Galatians

| | | 1:1-5<br>The Greeting | | |
|---|---|---|---|---|
| **Paul's Background<br>(1:6-2:14)** | 1:6-10<br>Curses on those who<br>Pervert the Gospel | | 1:11-2:14<br>Conversion/Calling<br>Confrontation in Antioch | |
| **Faith or Torah?<br>(2:15-3:20)** | 2:15-21<br>*Righteousness<br>By Faith or<br>Through<br>Torah?* | 3:1-5<br>*The Spirit<br>By Faith or<br>Through<br>Torah?* | 3:6-14<br>*Abraham's<br>Faith<br>Torah<br>Curse* | 3:15-20<br>*Will<br>Covenant<br>Offspring<br>Promise* |
| **Slaves or Sons?<br>(3:21-5:12)** | 3:21-4:7<br>*Purpose of<br>Torah<br>Slaves or<br>Sons?* | 4:8-20<br>*Paul v.<br>Judaizers* | 4:21-5:1<br>*Hagar/Slave<br>Torah<br>v.<br>Sarah/Child<br>Spirit* | 5:1-12<br>*Circumcision<br>is Slavery* |
| **The Flesh vs. The Spirit<br>(5:13-6:10)** | 5:13-26<br>Works of the Flesh<br>Fruit of the Spirit | | 6:1-10<br>Fulfilling the Law of<br>Christ<br>Flesh vs. Spirit | |
| | | 6:11-18<br>Final Warning and Benediction | | |

## A Walkthrough of Galatians

### 1. The Greeting (1:1-5)

Paul begins his letter with the kind of greeting he uses in most of his letters, making reference to God the Father and Jesus Christ. Here in Galatians, he immediately makes a point to emphasize that his apostleship came specifically from Jesus Christ and God the Father, and not from anyone else. This indicates one of the main issues Paul deals with in Galatians. His apostleship was questioned by some Judaizers who had gone to his predominately Gentile churches and had started telling the Gentile Christians that they had to become Jews to be part of the people of God and that Paul didn't have any apostolic authority to do what he was doing.

Paul also emphasizes it is through the death and resurrection of Christ that has made it possible for us to be saved from the **present evil age**. This reflects a Christian version of the traditional Jewish worldview of that time. Essentially, the Jews viewed themselves as living in the **old age** that was ruled by Satan, and they believed that when the Messiah came, God would pour out His Spirit on His people, defeat their oppressors, and usher in the **new Messianic age**—and the turn of the ages would happen all at once. Early Christians, like Paul, added a wrinkle to that expectation. They said the Messiah had come and, shockingly, the Jews had rejected him. He was crucified and died, but then was resurrected and ascended to heaven. He would return in the future to usher in the new Messianic age, but until then, they were all living **in between the times**. They were still living in the old age, but God had poured out His Spirit on Christ's followers, and the Church was commissioned to go throughout the Gentile world to gather Gentiles into God's people, so that they could be saved from the coming destruction of the old age.

### 2. Paul's Background (1:6-2:14)

Paul wastes no time getting right to the point. In the **first part (1:6-10)** to this section, he directly addresses the fact that the Gentile Christians in Galatia were being told by certain **Judaizers** coming in from the outside that they had get circumcised and submit to Torah observance if they were to truly become a part of God's people. Not only were these Judaizers telling them they had to become Jews, but they were bad-mouthing Paul. They claimed he didn't get his Gospel from any of the original disciples and that the only reason he told them they didn't have to obey the Torah was because he was trying to win their approval. Paul is livid. He tells them that those Judaizers are perverting the Gospel of Christ and that anyone who preaches a different Gospel than the one he preached to the Galatians *should be cursed* (or *damned*). As for the accusation that he was just trying win the approval of men, Paul says it is an idiotic accusation, because the fact is that his preaching of the Gospel of Christ routinely gets both Jews and pagans mad at him.

Paul then launches into a bit of an autobiography in his **second part (1:11-2:14)**, from the time he was converted up to the time of his confrontation with Peter in Antioch, in order to answer the charge of the Judaizers that he wasn't a true apostle because he wasn't commissioned by any of the original twelve apostles. In this section, Paul makes three points: (A) He got his Gospel *from Christ himself*, (B) Even though he had minimal contact with the apostles, *they supported him* and agreed that Christ had sent him to the Gentiles, and (C) He *had to call out Peter for waffling on this issue* regarding Gentiles being part of the people of God, even after Peter agreed Paul was right.

As for the specifics of this section, Paul points out that initially was a zealous persecutor of the "Church of God," but that when he encountered the risen Christ (around AD 34-35), he had revealed to Paul that he was to take the Gospel to the Gentiles. After that happened, instead of immediately going to Jerusalem to consult with the original apostles, he went off to Arabia for a time and then returned to Damascus. It was only *three years later* that Paul went back to Jerusalem (AD 36), and he was only in Jerusalem for *fifteen days*, during which he met only with Peter and James. He then moved back to his hometown of Tarsus, and later Antioch.

*Fourteen years later* (circa 49 AD) he went back to Jerusalem with Barnabas and Titus to meet privately with James, Peter, and John to make sure they were in agreement with his work among the Gentiles (this would be after his first missionary journey). Paul points out that even though there were some "false brothers" who had a problem with what Paul and Barnabas were doing, James, Peter, and John had no problem with it. They acknowledged that just as Peter had been entrusted with being an apostle to the Jews, Paul had been entrusted with being an apostle to the Gentiles. Evidently, these "false brothers" pressured Titus, who was a Gentile Christian, to get circumcised, but Paul insisted that shouldn't be done.

> **Paul's Timeline Chart**
> *Galatians 1:11-2:10*
>
> **AD 34**: Paul's Damascus Road Conversion
> **AD 34-36**: Paul in Arabia (3 years)
> **AD 36**: Paul returns to Jerusalem (15 days)
> **AD 42**: Famine relief visit to Jerusalem
> **AD 48-49**: Paul's first missionary journey
> **AD 49**: Private visit with James, Peter, and John in Jerusalem
> **AD 49**: Galatian controversy/Paul's confrontation with Peter in Antioch (occasion for the letter to the Galatians), leading to…
> **AD 49-50**: Jerusalem Council

At some point, though, after that private meeting in Jerusalem, Peter made his way up to Antioch and was freely interacting and eating with the Gentile Christians there. But when some men from Jerusalem who were affiliated with James showed up in Antioch, Peter backed away from the Gentile Christians, and this actually caused some other Jewish Christians (even Barnabas) to follow suit and to separate themselves from the Gentile Christians. When that happened, Paul openly confronted Peter on his hypocrisy and argued that the very point of the Gospel is that salvation is made possible through faith in Christ and not through doing the works of the Torah. Peter knew this full well from his experience with Cornelius in Acts 11, but for some reason, he capitulated to those Judaizers in Antioch, and by doing so, ended up humiliating and belittling his Gentile Christian brothers by implying they really aren't good enough, effectively regulating them to the status of second-class citizens in the Kingdom of God. By doing this, he created division among the believers.

### 3. Faith or Torah? (2:15-3:20)

After that brief autobiography, Paul begins the actual argument of Galatians regarding the Christian faith. His basic point is this: *Torah observance cannot make one righteous, only faith in Christ can.* Now, it is important to realize that Jews did not believe they had to keep the Torah *in order to get saved.* They viewed themselves as saved already: YHWH had saved them out of Egypt and called them to be His chosen people, and only then did He give them the Torah. Therefore, Jews saw the Torah as something God's people did *because they were saved*, not *in order to get saved.* Thus, keeping Torah made you a better, more righteous person. It is what marked you out as being different from the rest of the sinful world. *Sinners didn't keep Torah;*

*God's people kept Torah.* That's how you could tell who was and who wasn't part of God's people.

But Paul's own experience on the Damascus Road showed him that one could zealously observe the Torah and yet still be God's enemy and even, in his case, be a persecutor of God's people. Not only had his Torah observance not made him righteous, but he wasn't even saved. It was then that he realized the only thing that could save him was also the only thing that could make him righteous—and that was the faithfulness of Christ and his subsequent faith in Christ to, in fact, make him righteous. Therefore, this realization changed everything for Paul. **If all his Torah observance didn't make him righteous, if, despite his Torah observance, he found himself a sinner and God's enemy, if his salvation and righteousness was entirely dependent on God's mercy and Christ's faithfulness…then his situation before his encounter with Christ on the Damascus Road was no different than any Gentile sinner.**

When it came to salvation and righteousness, Torah observance didn't help one bit—*it was entirely irrelevant.* It might mark out who is a Jew, but that means nothing in terms of righteousness. Since that was the case, trying to force Gentiles who had been saved through faith in Christ to submit to the Torah completely undermined what the Gospel was all about. It was telling them that Torah observance was the key to being made righteous—*but it wasn't. It contributed nothing.* Therefore, insisting on Torah observance only brought division and conflict. That is what lies at the heart of 2:15-3:20.

In the **first part (2:15-21)** of this section, Paul begins by contrasting Jews with Gentile sinners. "Sinner" here primarily refers to anyone who doesn't keep the Torah. The Pharisees called many of their fellow Jews "sinners" because they didn't keep the Torah to the extent the Pharisees did. All Paul is doing here is making the obvious distinction that Jews (at least in theory) strive to keep the Torah and Gentiles don't, because Gentiles aren't Jews. Despite that, Paul insists that even though Jews *have the Torah* and *do the works of Torah,* doing those works of Torah *doesn't make anyone righteous.* That is why he says that he and his fellow Jews who had put their faith in Christ know full well that keeping Torah doesn't make one righteous. Only the faithfulness of Christ makes them righteous.

This leads to what Paul says in 2:17: *"If in our seeking to be made righteous in Christ, we are found to be sinners too, does this mean Christ is a slave of sin? No way!"* Paul is simply saying that he and his fellow Jewish Christians know full well that righteousness is only found in Christ, and that means they've also realized that they are sinners, just like Gentiles, even if they observe Torah. What that doesn't mean is that the Gospel of Christ promotes sin. Or to put it another way, not observing Torah doesn't make you a sinner—you're a sinner either way, whether you keep Torah or not. The problem, as Paul articulates in 2:18-21, lies in what the Judaizers were trying to do. After all, the work of Christ has shown the Torah to be irrelevant in terms of righteousness, and thus as "torn down" the Torah as a requirement for righteousness. Therefore, for the Judaizers to try to "build it up" again and force Torah observance on Gentiles, they are showing themselves to be the transgressors, because they are going against Christ.

That is why Paul says in 2:19-21 that he "died to the Torah through the Torah." The Torah effectively condemned him as a sinner and "crucified" him because he couldn't, in fact, keep it perfectly. It was that death that opened the door to new life found in Christ. Thus, even though he is still living "in the flesh" (meaning the current age in which sin and death reign), he is living by the faithfulness of Christ. If the Torah could have achieved righteousness, the Christ would have died for nothing. What would have been the point? Why bother with faith in Christ if doing the works of Torah could do the trick?

Given that, Paul really lets the Galatian Christians have it in the **second part (3:1-5)**. He expresses his frustration with them possibly allowing themselves to be pressured by the Judaizers by calling them foolish (literally "morons"). He then asks a basic question that sets up the second half of the letter: Did they receive the Spirit **because they responded to Paul's message about faith,** or did they receive the Spirit **because they started doing the works of Torah**? Since it is obvious that Torah observance had nothing to do with their receiving of the Spirit, Paul asks them why would it be necessary to start doing the works of Torah when it was obvious *that they didn't work* when it came to becoming righteous?

It should be noted that in 3:2-3 Paul seems to be equating the **works of Torah** with **the flesh**. When Paul talks about "the flesh," he's not talking about our literal bodies, but rather about the current "old age" in which sin and death reign. Thus, he is lining up the works of Torah with an "old age" way of doing things. Simply put, the works of Torah is an "old age thing" that brings death, whereas faith in Christ is a "new messianic age thing" that brings life and righteousness. Therefore, Paul is asking the Galatians, *"Now that you've been given a taste of the life of the age to come, why would you want to go backwards and embrace something that typifies the death of the old age?"*

In the **third part (3:6-14)**, in order to "flesh" this out even more, Paul sets up a contrast between **Abraham** and the **Torah**. Paul first points out that it was *Abraham's faith* that God counted as righteousness, obviously not *his keeping of Torah* (because the Torah didn't even exist yet). Therefore, Paul argues, what is good for Abraham is good for everyone. In this sense, it is those who share the faith of Abraham who are the **true sons of Abraham**, not ethnic Jews who observe Torah. That was God's plan all along: *Through Abraham all Gentiles would be blessed.* The blessing that was to come through Abraham to the Gentiles was by means of faith, not the works of Torah.

If that is the case, though, what about Jews who observe Torah? Shockingly, Paul says that anyone who submits to trying to do the works of Torah *is actually under a curse*—and he quotes from the Torah to prove it! **Deuteronomy 27:26** says that anyone who doesn't continually do everything in the Torah is under a curse. Paul argues that the curse is being impelled to try to do something that is impossible, namely achieve righteousness through Torah observance. The more one tries, the more one fails, and the further away one gets from true righteousness. It's like running on a treadmill to try to get to the Grand Canyon—you'll never get there, and you'll die on that treadmill.

Christ, though, rescues us from the curse of the Torah by becoming a curse for us. Given the overall context of 2:15-3:20, we need to realize that when Paul says, "Christ rescued *us* from the *curse of the Torah*," that he is specifically referring to Jews like himself who came to faith in Christ, and not Gentiles who were never "under the Torah" to begin with. Paul is saying he was saved by Christ from that curse of feeling he had to keep doing the Torah in order to become righteous, even though he knew full well that it couldn't.

In addition, when Paul says Christ "became a curse for us," he is getting that from, of all places, the Torah: **Deuteronomy 21:23** says that anyone who is hung on a tree is cursed. So, what Paul is doing is tying Jesus' crucifixion on a cross of wood to the tree mentioned in Deuteronomy 21:23, hence, suffering the ultimate curse of death. Yet, by raising from the dead by the power of the Spirit, Christ opens the door to being made righteous through faith. Paul's point is that the blessing of Abraham that was to come to the Gentiles was always going to be through faith.

In the **fourth part (3:15-20)**, Paul wraps up the section of 2:15-3:20 by teasing out his point concerning Abraham and the Torah from 3:6-14 in regard to faith and blessing coming to the Gentiles. To do this, Paul engages in a wordplay in 3:15-16. The Greek word for "covenant," **diatheke**, is also the same word for "will," as in a last will and testament, where a person grants his inheritance to someone. Paul says that when a man's will (*diatheke*) is made and ratified, it can't be changed by anyone. In the same way, when God made his covenant (*diatheke*) with Abraham, God's promises in that *diatheke* were made to Abraham and **his offspring**. The Greek word for "offspring," Paul points out, is *singular*, not *plural*. So, when it says that through Abraham's "offspring" all Gentiles would be blessed, Paul says that "offspring" is a reference to Christ, for it is through Christ that blessing comes to the Gentiles.

Then in 3:17-18, Paul mentions the giving of the Torah at Sinai was a good 430 years after God made His *diatheke* with Abraham. Therefore, the giving of the Torah doesn't change the promises in the original *diatheke* God made to Abraham. The promise in the Abrahamic *diatheke* that God would bless all Gentiles through faith, and that this promise would come through Abraham's "offspring" was always in effect—the Torah cannot nullify that original *diatheke*. The inheritance of blessing going out to the Gentiles through Abraham's offspring by means of faith still stands. The Torah doesn't negate God's *diatheke* with Abraham.

If that is the case, what was the point of Torah in the first place? That is what Paul answers in 3:19. The Torah's purpose was never to make anyone righteous. Its purpose was to point out sin. Its purpose was, in effect, to point out the problem that the ultimate offspring of Abraham (Christ) was going to remedy *through faith*.

### 4. Sons or Slaves? (3:21-5:12)

In the next major section, Paul picks up from his example of Abraham the themes of **sonship** and **slavery** and further develops them to further sketch out the fundamental difference between two modes of existence. A person either lives according to **the old age and the old mode of existence**, which is characterized by slavery and division (and he squarely puts the Torah in this camp), or one lives **by faith and the new mode existence** that is characterized by the life of the Spirit.

In the **first part (3:21-4:7)**, Paul continues to elaborate on the question, *"If Torah can't produce righteousness, then what's the purpose of Torah?"* Paul first points out that although the Torah doesn't nullify God's promises to Abraham, that doesn't mean it is against them. Simply put, the Torah's job isn't to fulfill those promises. It has a different job. Its job, so to speak, is that of a governess, or nanny, if you will. Like a nanny, the Torah told people, "No, that behavior is bad! Stop it!" When people, like the children that they are, misbehave anyway, the Torah exacted discipline in order to not only *guard* people from further harm, but also to *train* them and grow them up to mature adults. Discipline actually protects people from greater harm and hopefully trains people to choose to do the right thing on their own. The goal of the Torah, as that of a nanny, is to grow the child up to where he is an adult who doesn't need a nanny anymore. Paul argues that now that Christ has come and that faith that leads to righteousness and maturity has been made available in Christ, there simply is no more need for a nanny. The Torah had a job to do, it did it, and now its job is over.

Paul then picks up on the sonship imagery from his previous comments about Abraham and says that *through faith* in Christ, believers are all *sons of God*—it doesn't matter if they are Jew or Greek, slave or free, male or female—they are all in the same boat. They are all *offspring of Abraham* because they are all one in Christ Jesus, who is, if you will, the *ultimate offspring of Abraham*. And because they are *sons*, they are also *heirs* according to the *promise* God made to Abraham. Paul then teases out the metaphor even more and says that even though one might be a son and an heir, until that son comes of age, *that kid is going to need a nanny*! God may be the king, you might be His son who is bound to inherit His kingdom, but as long as you're still a child, you are going to be put under the care of certain guardians whom you have to obey.

Interestingly, at this point in 4:3, Paul says that people were in servitude to the **elements of the world**. These "elements" are equated with idols or other worldly authorities who enslave people. Therefore, it is shocking to see Paul applying that term *to the Torah* to a certain degree. Although it acts as a guardian/nanny, it still is another manifestation of the idolatrous "elements of the world." In any case, whether it is being under the authority of the Torah or other elements of the world, Paul says you are no different than a *slave*. It is only once you come of age and reach maturity that you will "recover the rights of sons" (4:5) and no longer be under the authority of the nanny. With the coming of Christ, that has happened. You're not a slave; you're not a "son in training" who is no different than a slave; you've come of age and have now taken your place next to your father the king.

Given that situation, in the **second part (4:8-20)**, Paul makes a personal appeal to the Galatian believers and expresses his fear that they might succumb to the pressure of these Judaizers, agree to get circumcised, and start trying to keep the Torah. He reminds them that they used to worship idols but were now set free in Christ. If they submit to Torah, they would be allowing themselves to be enslaved to the same "weak and basic elements of the world" all over again—only instead of being enslaved to an idol, they'd be enslaved to the Torah. He notes with shock that they were already participating in some Jewish practices by observing days, months, seasons, and years.

Paul then recalls when he had first come to them with some sort of **weakness in the flesh** (4:12-16). He says they took care of him and would have readily "torn out their own eyes" and given them to him if possible. He says they treated him like an angel, like Christ himself even. Clearly the Galatian believers and Paul loved each other, and Paul was hoping that his stern letter to them wouldn't ruin that. This reference, along with his comments about his huge handwriting in 6:11, indicates that his "thorn in the flesh" that he mentions in **II Corinthians 12:7** was, in fact, some sort of problem with his eyesight. Given the fact he was blind for three days after his Damascus Road experience, it is possible that after he recovered his sight that he still was left partially blinded. In any case, Paul ends this part by telling them that the only reason the Judaizers were pressuring them to submit to the Torah wasn't because of some zeal for God, but rather because they were just zealous to promote themselves.

Paul then goes back in the **third part (4:21-5:1)** to tease out his Abraham example by focusing on the two main women in Abraham's life: Sarah his wife, who gave birth to Isaac, and Hagar the slave woman, who gave birth to Ishmael. Paul says that Hagar's son Ishmael was born **according to the flesh**, meaning according to the natural way. Hagar was young and fertile and when Abraham had sex with her, she conceived, because that's what normally happens. By contrast, Sarah's son Isaac was born **according to the promise**. Sarah was barren and couldn't conceive, but because God was going to make good on His promise to Abraham, He caused her to conceive and give birth to Isaac—he was, in effect, a "miracle baby."

| Hagar | Sarah |
|---|---|
| 1. Slave woman | 1. Free woman |
| 2. Ishmael: According to the Flesh | 2. Isaac: According to the Promise |
| 3. Sinai Covenant | 3. New Covenant |
| 4. Gives birth to slavery | 4. Gives birth to freedom |
| 5. Present day Jerusalem | 5. The Jerusalem Above |

Paul says that since Hagar was a **slave** who gave birth to Ishmael, **according to the flesh**, she represents **Mount Sinai** and the **Mosaic covenant**, and hence, the **Torah**. Since these Judaizers from Jerusalem were pushing the Torah on the Galatian believers, Paul says Hagar also represents **Jerusalem**. Bottom line, the Judaizers were *slaves to the Torah* and they were trying to *enslave* the Galatian believers to the Torah as well. By contrast, Sarah was a **free woman** who gave birth to Isaac, **according to God's promise**. She represents, not the present Jerusalem enslaved to the Torah, but rather the **Jerusalem above**, where there is freedom. That means that they, the Galatian Christians, were free children of the promise, like Isaac, and that the Judaizers were slave children of the flesh who were bullying them, just like Ishmael picked on Isaac. Therefore, just like Abraham drove out both Hagar and Ishmael and said they would have no part in his inheritance, Paul tells them they need to do the same with the Judaizers—reject them and kick them out, because those Judaizers will have no part of the inheritance that is in Christ.

In the **fourth part (5:2-12)** of the section, Paul makes another personal appeal to the Galatians not to succumb to circumcision by using a stark wordplay in 5:4 when he says that the Gentile believer who gets circumcised (which involves a **cutting off of the foreskin**) is effectively **cut off from Christ** and is obligated to keep the entire Torah. To do that is to say, "Faith in Christ isn't enough. I need to do the works of Torah in order to become righteous." To do that is to become enslaved to the Torah and to reject the freedom that is in Christ through faith.

After expressing his certainty that the Galatian believers will do the right thing and not listen to the Judaizers, Paul turns his attention to the Judaizers and says something that most translations do their best to tone down. In 5:12, Paul says he wishes that those who were trying to circumcise the Galatian believers would just castrate themselves or emasculate themselves. The Greek is even more graphic. Paul essentially says, "I wish those who want to circumcise you would just cut their entire sex organ off!"

## 5. The Flesh vs. The Spirit (5:13-6:10)

Here in the final section of Galatians, Paul sums up his entire argument by outlining the two modes of existence one can live by. You are either going to live **according to the flesh** or **according to the Spirit**. One is the way of freedom, while the other is the way of slavery. One is the way of love and unity, while the other is the way of dissention and division.

In the **first part (5:13-16)**, Paul talks about the difference between these two ways of living. He begins by emphasizing that freedom in Christ is not about being free to do whatever you want—or as Paul puts it, **taking opportunity in the flesh**. It actually means the **freedom to become slaves**, not to the Torah, but **to one another through love**. Paul then *quotes the Torah* and argues that the whole point of the Torah is to "love your neighbor as yourself." This notion comes directly from Jesus, when he was questioned by the scribes in the Temple as to what the greatest commandment was. He responded by giving two commandments, to love God and to love your neighbor as yourself, and then saying they summed up the entire Torah.

Paul then proceeds to contrast the two ways of life. One will either walk in the flesh or walk in the Spirit—there can be no middle ground because they are completely opposed to each other. It is important to realize here that Paul redefines what sin is. From a Jewish perspective, you were a sinner if you didn't keep Torah. Here, though, Paul states that a sinner is one who lives according to the flesh. Not only that, but Paul actually lines up the Torah

| Works of the Flesh | Fruit of the Spirit |
|---|---|
| • Fornication | • Love |
| • Impurity | • Joy |
| • Obscene Behavior | • Peace |
| • Idolatry | • Long-suffering |
| • Sorcery | • Kindness |
| • Feuding | • Generosity |
| • Strife | • Faithfulness |
| • Jealousy | • Humility |
| • Anger | • Self-control |
| • Selfish Ambition | |
| • Divisions | |
| • Factions | |
| • Rivalries | |
| • Drunkenness | |
| • Carousing | |
| *DO THAT STUFF, and no Kingdom of God for you* | *Nothing in the Torah against these things* |

on the side of the flesh when he says in 5:18, *"If you are led by the Spirit, you are not under the Torah."* It's not that the Torah itself is bad, but the kind of people who need to be subjected to the Torah *are selfish and sinful people of the flesh*. With that, Paul then gives a list of things he considers to be **works of the flesh**. His reason for labeling them as **works of the flesh** is related to his warnings about submitting to the **works of Torah**. All the things he mentions have to do in one way or another with things that create division, dissension, and hostility, thus the defining characteristic of people who live according to the flesh is one of fostering division—and that was precisely what the Judaizers were doing.

In contrast to the works of the flesh, Paul then lists the **fruit of the Spirit**. Everything in the list emphasizes behaviors that contribute to unity and community, the polar opposite of the works of the flesh. When Paul says that there is no "law" (Torah) against these things, Paul makes that important distinction between what *the goal of Torah* was (to love God and love your neighbor as yourself) and what insistence on submitting to *the works of Torah* leads to, namely factions and divisions.

After outlining these two ways of life, Paul reminds the Galatian Christians that if they are in Christ Jesus, then they have already **crucified the flesh** and exhorts them to live by the Spirit and to reject the "fleshly" temptation to become conceited and jealous of one another. The reason he says this is because that is the very thing the Judaizers were trying to inject when they pressured the Gentile believers to submit to Torah. By telling them, "Oh, that's great that you've come to faith in Christ, but *if you were really righteous,* you'd start observing Torah, because *that is what really separates the men from the boys,*" the Judaizers were essentially setting up a kind of caste system in the Christian community.

In the **second part (6:1-10)** of this section, Paul ends with some general exhortations that further illustrate just what the fruit of the Spirit looks like in practical ways. In fact, Paul says when one tries to restore someone caught up in some kind of transgression in the "Spirit of gentleness" and helps bear that person's burdens, that is how one "fully observes the *Torah* of Christ!" Paul also emphasizes personal accountability within the community, once again playing off the idea of "works." You are responsible for *your own work*, your own righteousness, and your own faith journey, not anyone else's. He then ends with emphasizing once more the utter incompatibility between the flesh and the Spirit by saying that you reap what you sow. If you sow *in the flesh* (and this would include Torah observance), you are going to reap *corruption*. If you sow *in the Spirit*, you are going to reap *eternal life*, or more accurately, the **Life of the Age**.

### 6. Final Warning and Benediction (6:11-18)

The last section of the letter was probably written by Paul's own hand. He would have dictated most of his letters but would have then added a personal note in his own handwriting at the end of his letters to authenticate that the letter was really from him—they would have recognized his handwriting. As we noted earlier, Paul's comment about how big his letters are hints at the fact that his "thorn in the flesh" was probably really poor eyesight, possibly a result of his Damascus Road experience. In any case, Paul puts down in his own handwriting one final condemnation against the Judaizers. The only reason they are preaching circumcision and Torah observance is because they don't want to be persecuted for the cross of Christ.

This interesting comment tells us that these Judaizers obviously had accepted Jesus as the Messiah. At this point in the history of the Church, there were a number of issues (like Torah observance) that obviously had not yet been hammered out. These Judaizers clearly thought Jesus was the promised Messiah, but they did not accept Paul's Gospel that he preached to the Gentiles. They clearly thought that although the Gentiles could "get in" to be a part of God's people through faith in Christ, but that then they had to actually become Jews and submit to the Torah, because the Jews were the people of God, and doing the Torah is what God's people did. Nevertheless, they were blind to the new thing that God was doing through Paul, and Paul refused to give an inch in this regard because the very heart of the Gospel was at stake. He was insistent that circumcision or uncircumcision was completely irrelevant when it came to faith in Christ and righteousness. As he says, the only thing that matters is a new creation.

In the last few verses, Paul says two more things that deserve mention. In 6:16, when he says, "May peace and mercy be upon those who "walk by this rule," he is putting forth his Gospel as the definition of what the Christian faith is, as opposed to the "rule" of Torah observance that the Judaizers were attempting to establish. Thus, Paul is saying, "Those who put their faith in Christ aren't bound to that rule of Torah observance. They are bound to the Torah of Christ, which is the way of faith and the way of walking in the Spirit." This is why Paul then essentially gives a redefinition of Israel when he says that those who are bound to the Torah of Christ are the Israel of God—not the Judaizers who were insisting Gentiles had to become Jews to be part of Israel.

After that bombshell, Paul ends his letter with a comment that would make Clint Eastwood proud: "From now on, no one had better cause me any more trouble! I carry the marks of Jesus on my body!" Translation? "Don't mess with me, punk! I've been through too much to be intimidated by a few Judaizers who are obsessed with circumcising a few Gentile believers!"

# I/II THESSALONIANS

**Time of Writing:** Paul's Second Missionary Journey (AD 50-51)

### The History of the City/Paul in Thessalonica

The city of Thessalonica was founded in 316 BC by Cassander, the king of Macedonia, who named the city after his wife, Thessaloniki (the half-sister of Alexander the Great). In 168 BC, Rome conquered Macedonia, divided it up into various districts, and made Thessalonica the capital of the 2$^{nd}$ district. In 149 BC, when Andriscus revolted against Rome and tried to re-establish the Macedonian monarchy, Thessalonica sided with Rome, and after Rome put down the revolt, it made Thessalonica the capital of the entire region of Macedonia.

In 44 BC, after the assassination of Julius Caesar, civil war broke out between Brutus/Cassius and Octavian/Mark Antony. Thessalonica sided with Octavian and Mark Antony, and after their victory, Thessalonica was rewarded with the honor of becoming a *free city*. No Roman troops were garrisoned there, and Thessalonica was allowed to govern itself according to its own traditional laws and customs.

By 31 BC, there was another civil war between Octavian and Mark Antony. Thessalonica supported Octavian, and when he defeated Mark Antony, Thessalonica celebrated his victory by (A) establishing a cult to honor the goddess Rome and (B) building a temple of Caesar that honored both Julius Caesar and Octavian, who was now known as Augustus Caesar. All this is to say what should now be obvious: Thessalonica really loved Caesar and were deeply loyal to Rome.

Paul's time in Thessalonica is recorded in **Acts 17:1-9**. After the Jerusalem Council in AD 49-50, Paul, Timothy, and Silas went on a second missionary journey where they re-visited the churches Paul established on his first missionary journey. Then they established more churches in Macedonia and Greece. When he reached Thessalonica, Paul first preached in the synagogue and attracted some Jews, along with many Gentile God-fearers. Yet the Jews who rejected Paul's message got jealous that he was attracting a following, so they convinced the pagan citizens that Paul was trying to subvert Rome. They arrested some of the Thessalonian Christians, but Paul was able to flee the city during the night. Nevertheless, they accused Paul of causing trouble, defying Caesar's decrees, and claiming that there was another king other than Caesar. Since it was illegal to predict the death of an emperor, Paul's proclamation of Jesus as king was seen as possibly an attempt to renew the monarchy of Macedonia.

Paul, Silas, and Timothy went to Berea, and from there, travelled down to Athens. After a short stay there, Paul sent Timothy back to Thessalonica to see how the Thessalonian Christians were doing. Paul meanwhile went to Corinth to wait for Timothy's return. When Timothy came to Corinth and gave Paul the good news that they were standing firm in their faith, despite being harassed, it was then that Paul wrote I Thessalonians. A short time later, when news came from Thessalonica that the persecution had gotten worse, Paul wrote II Thessalonians.

### The Big Things to Know About I/II Thessalonians

A. **Staying Faithful Amidst Persecution**: Given the reality of what happened in Thessalonica, and of Paul having to leave them, Paul makes it a point to encourage the Thessalonian believers to stay faithful, despite the current tribulation they were going through. Paul tells that that those who follow Christ should expect tribulation and should expect to suffer on behalf of Christ.

B. **The Parousia of Christ/The Day of the Lord**: *Parousia* is mostly translated as "coming," and most assume Paul is talking about Jesus' "second coming," which obviously hasn't happened yet. But, if we try to consider Paul's comments in the context of the first century, and against the backdrop of Jesus' words in the Olivet Discourse (Mark 13, Matthew 24, Luke 21), we should see that the early first century Church associated the *Coming of Christ/Day of the Lord* in some way with the destruction of the Temple, which happened in AD 70.

### Literary Map: I Thessalonians

|  | 1:1-10 Greeting/Thanksgiving |  |
|---|---|---|
| **Personal Remarks (2-3)** | 2:1-16 Paul defends his ministry and recalls persecution | 2:17-3:13 Paul's concern for them His sending of Timothy |
| **Encouragement and Teaching (4:1-5:11)** | 4:1-12 Encouragement to stay faithful to his teaching | 4:13-5:11 The Parousia of Christ The Day of the Lord |
|  | 5:12-27 Final Instructions and Benediction |  |

## A Walkthrough of I Thessalonians

### 1. Greeting and Thanksgiving (1:1-10)

As in most of his letters, Paul begins with a greeting and some sort of thanksgiving that also serves as sort of an introduction regarding what he will be addressing in his letter. After greeting them in clear trinitarian language (God the Father, the Lord Jesus Christ--God's Son, and the Holy Spirit), Paul begins with reminding the Thessalonian Christians about his time with them, about how he, Silas, and Timothy conducted themselves honorably among them, and about how they had received the Gospel with joy, even in the midst of affliction (presumably the events that happened in Thessalonica that are recorded in Acts 17:1-9). The fact Paul mentions that they turned from idols to the true God in 1:9 tells us that the church in Thessalonica was primarily Gentile.

Paul also talks about the **tribulation** (Greek word, *thlipsis*) they had endured as Christians and reassures them that they will be rescued from God's coming **wrath** (Greek word, *orgay*). These two words are consistently used throughout the New Testament to describe **the tribulation that Christians go through** and **God's wrath that will come upon those who have inflicted tribulation on God's people**. Simply put, Christians endure *thlipsis*, but will be saved from God's coming *orgay*.

Paul then praises them for their faith as they wait for God's Son (Jesus) from Heaven. This is referred elsewhere in the New Testament as the **Coming of Christ**. The Greek word for "coming" is *Parousia*, and it signifies the coming home of a victorious king after a great victory to be welcomed and honored as the rightful king. This "Coming of Christ" is also referred to as the **Day of Christ** or the **Day of the Lord**. It has its roots in the Old Testament understanding of the **Day of YHWH**, when the enemies of God's people receive judgment and wrath, and God's people are vindicated and glorified. We will see how Paul applies all that to the current situation facing the Thessalonian Christians.

### 2. Personal Remarks (2:1-3:13)

In Acts 17:1-9, we learn that Paul had to get out of Thessalonica when trouble started brewing in the city. The reason Paul wrote this letter was because he was worried that the Christians there might think he was a charlatan. Therefore, in this **first part of this section (2:1-16)**, Paul defends his ministry and reminds them of what he did while he was with them. He mentions his time in Philippi and reminds them that he worked for a living while he was with them and that he didn't take and charity because he didn't want to be a burden to them. He goes on to describe his relationship with them in terms of both a nurse taking care of her children and a father caring for his children. He was no conman. He truly cared about them.

He goes on and points out that they were currently experiencing the same thing that the Jewish Christians in Judea were experiencing, in that they, too, were suffering for their faith at the hands of their own countrymen. Paul further notes that those Jews in Judea were not only persecuting Jewish Christians, but they were trying to prevent Paul from speaking to the Gentiles. Because of that, Paul says that they would eventually **suffer wrath**. This is significant, because wrath is what the enemies of God were to suffer on the **Day of the Lord/*Parousia* of Christ**.

Paul then continues in the **second part of this section (2:17-3:13)** to explain that he had wanted to return to them shortly, but that Satan had prevented him from doing so. Whatever that means, the bottom line is that Paul tells them that he wanted to come back but wasn't able to right way. Still, he wants them to know that they are his glory, joy, and "crown of boasting" before the Lord Jesus at his **Coming (Parousia)**.

In any case, because he couldn't go back himself, Paul sent Timothy back to them while he stayed in Athens in order to see how they were doing, to encourage them, and to remind them that Paul had told them ahead of time to expect to suffer tribulation. Needless to say, Paul was overjoyed when Timothy returned to tell him they were standing strong in the faith in the midst of their tribulations and were hoping to see Paul again. Therefore, despite his own tribulation, Paul tells them that simply knowing that they were standing firm was a huge encouragement to him and that he couldn't wait to see them again.

### 3. Encouragement and Teaching (4:1-5:11)

Being the pastor that he is, Paul then takes some time in the **next part (4:1-12)** to encourage them to stay faithful and to hold to the teachings he passed on to them from Jesus. Paul first tells them to avoid fornication and "control their own vessels." Although this is applicable to Christians at all times and situations, we need to remember just how rampant sexual immorality and perversion in the pagan world and such practices were linked to idolatry and even celebrated and promoted in pagan temples. Therefore, Paul was telling them to avoid something that was seen as part of the fabric of basic pagan society.

So, when Paul tells them that they weren't called to impurity, but to holiness, he is telling them that they are to set themselves apart from the surrounding pagan society in this regard. In contrast to that kind of life, Paul encourages them to live quiet lives, to work hard, to mind their own business, and not get caught up in the pagan culture around them. He tells them to live Christ-like lives and be worthy examples to their pagan neighbors. In short, they are to be a light to the Gentiles.

Paul then takes some time in the **next part (4:13-5:11)** to teach them more regarding the coming ***Parousia* of Christ**. Due to the influence of modern-day dispensationalists, I Thessalonians 4:13-18 is one of the most misunderstood passages in Paul's letters, if not the entire New Testament. If we consider it within the context of I Thessalonians, it is actually fairly simple to understand. Paul begins by addressing their concern about what will happen to Christians who have died before Christ's *Parousia*. Paul tells them that at Christ's *Parousia* those who have died will be resurrected, just like Christ had been resurrected, and they will not miss out on the new creation. This passage, therefore, is about *Christ's coming*, not about a *secret rapture that precedes his coming*, in which believers on earth will be taken away to heaven for seven years, while the rest of the world suffers during a single "great tribulation."

We, though, need to understand that Paul is using a number of metaphors to describe Christ's *Parousia*. First of all, in the ancient world, during a *parousia* of a victorious king, the people of the city would leave the city, go out to welcome him on the road, and then escort him back into the city in celebration. Therefore, all Paul is saying is that at the *Parousia* of Christ, those who have died will be resurrected and those who are alive will join them as they all go out and welcome Christ as the conquering king of the new creation. Paul's talk about being "up in the clouds" is metaphorical language. When Christ comes from heaven, heaven is

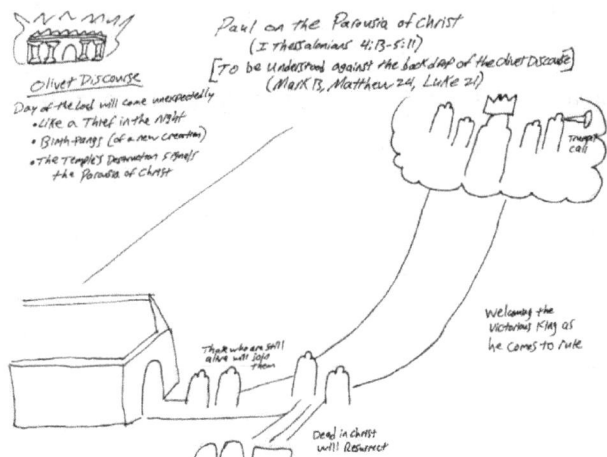

metaphorically "up there." So, when believers go out to welcome him, the metaphorical image is
> to go "up there" to welcome him back to earth as its rightful king.

Paul continues his discussion about the *Parousia* of Christ in 5:1-11 by echoing the words of Jesus in Matthew 24:43 in the Olivet Discourse: *The Day of the Lord will come unexpectedly, like a thief in the night.* Paul also gives a little jab at Rome when he says that sudden destruction will come while some are saying "peace and security." Rome's version of peace and security, Paul says, is not true peace and security. He also uses the imagery of **birth-pangs** to describe the Day of the Lord. This imagery is used throughout the Bible to denote the pain and suffering that coincides with the "birth" of new life: the old creation is going to suffer birth-pangs when the new creation is born on the Day of the Lord, at the *Parousia* of Christ.

Playing off the imagery of a thief in the night, Paul then calls the believers **children of the day**, and contrasts them and their behavior with the behavior of the implied **children of the night**. After that, he brings things back around to the original concern he addressed in 4:13-18 and encourages them by telling them that Christians, whether they are awake (currently alive) or asleep (have died), will all live in Christ and are not destined for God's wrath.

### 4. Final Instructions and Benediction (5:12-27)

Paul ends his letter by giving some practical instructions. He tells them to respect church leaders, be at peace, work hard, encourage each other, seek to do what is good, avoid evil, and to not "quench the Spirit," among other things. He prays that their spirit and soul be kept blameless until the *Parousia* of Christ. Clearly, with all the talk of Christ's *Parousia*, Paul obviously expected it to happen soon. So, what might he be referring to? We'll expand on that a bit in the walkthrough of II Thessalonians.

**Literary Map: II Thessalonians**

| 1:1-12 |
|---|
| Greeting |
| Thanksgiving |

| 2:1-12 | 2:13-17 | 3:1-5 | 3:6-12 |
|---|---|---|---|
| The Day of Christ hasn't come yet | Encouragement to stand firm in the faith | Paul's Prayer request | Call to imitate Paul: Work hard Don't be idle |

## A Walkthrough of II Thessalonians

II Thessalonians was probably written shortly after the first letter. In it, Paul attempts to clarify a few things from I Thessalonians regarding the ***Parousia* of Christ** and the End Times in general. Although it is tempting to impose our modern assumptions onto the text, we must try to understand what Paul meant in the original context of II Thessalonians. Namely, what did this mean to the early Christians living in the Roman Empire around AD 52?

In the **first section (1:1-12)**, Paul begins his letter with a greeting and an initial thanksgiving in which he introduces what he is going to discuss in the letter. He mentions their growing faith in the midst of **tribulations** and persecution and looks forward to the **Day of the Lord/Parousia of Christ**, when those who are persecuting them will suffer God's **wrath**, while they themselves will be glorified. This is standard Old Testament language regarding the **Day of YHWH**, now applied to the **Day of Christ**: *Wrath and destruction on God's enemies and glorification and salvation of God's people who have suffered tribulation.*

In addition to things like the Day of Christ and the Day of the Lord, Paul also refers to this coming Parousia of Christ as the **Revelation of the Lord Jesus**. All of these seem to be referring in some way to the same thing. This teaching regarding the Parousia of Christ was obviously so central to the early Church, that if it didn't happen in their lifetime, it is highly doubtful that Christianity would have survived, let alone thrive and continue to grow as it did. The fact that the early Christians retained these writings that spoke of the Parousia of Christ happening within a generation is a pretty good indication that they felt that *did happen*, and these writings bore witness to the fact that what Jesus said would happen, what Paul spoke about would happen, did, in fact happen. So, what happened? To what did this talk of the Parousia of Christ refer? We will tease this out in the next section.

In the **second section (2:1-12)**, Paul elaborates a bit more about the coming Day of the Lord. He wanted them to know, contrary to what some in of them had heard, Christ had not come yet. Paul is telling them, there in AD 52, that the Parousia of Christ had not yet happened. He then proceeds to go into detail about some things that will precede Christ's Parousia:

- The **rebellion** must happen first and **the man of lawlessness** (whom Paul calls the **son of destruction**) must be revealed.
- This **lawless one** will raise himself over every so-called god or object of worship and will sit in the Temple of God and declare himself to be God.
- Paul tells the Thessalonians he had already told them about all this and that they already know **what is restraining** this lawless one until he is revealed. When he is revealed, whoever is restraining him will be out of the way.
- The **mystery of lawlessness** was already at work, even in AD 52.
- When the Lord Jesus appears at his *Parousia*, he will kill this lawless one with the breath of his mouth.
- The *parousia* **of the lawless one** will be by the activity of Satan and will be accompanied by false signs and wonders that deceive people so that they refuse "to love the truth and be saved."
- The result will be that those who reject the truth and take pleasure in unrighteousness will be destroyed.

So, what is all that about? Let's start with Jesus' own words in the Olivet Discourse (Mark 13, Matthew 24, Luke 21), when he prophesies about the Jewish War of AD 66-70 and the eventual destruction of the Temple in AD 70. In doing so, he uses the standard Old Testament Day of YHWH language to describe things. Therefore, it seems that Paul's talk of the Parousia of Christ and the Day of the Lord clearly echoes Christ's prophecy about the Temple's destruction. Given that, we should consider that part of the early Christian proclamation in the years leading up to the Jewish War was that Christ had prophesied Jerusalem and the Temple would be destroyed because the Jews had rejected him as the Messiah and had embraced zealotry and revolution against Rome. Thus, the wrath that comes upon God's enemies will, surprisingly come upon Jerusalem, because the Jewish leaders had made themselves God's enemies by killing the Messiah and persecuting God's people, now understood to be the Church, the followers of Jesus.

Therefore, if the passages about the Parousia of Christ and the Day of the Lord are indeed early Christian teachings that came from Jesus' own prophecy regarding the Temple's destruction within a generation, we can make some educated guesses regarding the particulars of what Paul says here in 2:1-12. The **rebellion** would seem to be a reference to the Jewish rebellion that sparked the Jewish War in AD 66. The **man of lawlessness**, though, is a bit murkier. It is interesting to note that the Greek word for "lawlessness" is *anomias*, obviously the opposite of *nomos*, which not only means "law," but also the Greek word used for "Torah." Therefore, it is possible Paul believed this **man of *anomias***, this **son of destruction**, was in some way connected to Judaism. The fact he says this man would sit in the Temple of God when he exalts himself to the level of a god seems to connect this person to the Jerusalem priesthood.

As for who is restraining this "man of *anomias*," what the "mystery of *anomias*" is, and the fact that the *parousia* of this "man of *anomias*" is the activity of Satan and will be accompanied by false signs and wonders that deceive people—all this can be connected with the Jewish War of AD 66-70. In the years leading up to the Jewish War, there was a considerable uptick in Jewish unrest and an increasing push by Jewish zealots to rebel against Rome. The Temple priesthood tried to tap down on the ever-growing zealot movement, but in AD 66 a certain priest named Eleazar put a stop to all sacrifices on behalf of foreigners to YHWH. By doing so, he openly defied Rome by breaking the agreement between the Temple priesthood and Caesar, that instead of offering sacrifices to Caesar, they would offer a sacrifice on behalf of Caesar to YHWH.

At that same time, various Jewish zealot leaders succeeded in taking over the city and slaughtering the Roman garrison stationed in the city, further igniting the revolt against Rome. By the end of the war, the various zealot leaders ended up fighting with each other and terrorizing the people of Jerusalem while Rome besieged the city. At one point, one of the zealot leaders who had taken control of the Temple complex dressed himself in royal robes and presented himself as a king. Eventually, Rome destroyed the city and the Temple, slaughtered the zealots and sent most of the population into slavery.

The long and short of all this is that it is plausible that Paul's teaching concerning the Parousia of Christ, both here and in the rest of his letters, was essentially that the Jews were going to revolt against Rome, that Rome was going to destroy the city and Temple, and that event would signal the Parousia of Christ, vindicating him as both Lord and Messiah, vindicating the believers who had been subject to tribulation by both the Jews and Rome, and it would signal the destruction of those Jews who had made themselves out to be the enemies of God and His people. This is what Jesus prophesied would happen in the Olivet Discourse, this is what the first-generation Church preached that it would happen, and this is what did happen.

In light of the expectation of the coming Parousia of Christ, Paul gives thanks for the Thessalonian Christians in the **third section (2:13-17)**. He calls them the firstfruits of salvation and says that they will obtain that future glory of the Lord Jesus Christ. Therefore, he encourages them to stand firm in the faith and hold fast to the **traditions** they received. Traditions here refer to the apostolic teaching Paul passed on to them, whether through his letters or other writings, or through preaching.

Paul then makes a prayer request in the **fourth section (3:1-5)**. He asks them to pray for the spreading of the Gospel and protection from not only evil men, but ultimately from the Evil One as well. In the **fifth section (3:6-12)**, Paul gives some practical instructions. He calls them to imitate him, in that he worked hard for a living while he was with them. He tells them to stay away from people who are lazy and quite frankly look to mooch off of others. Basically, he encourages them to stay busy and not be busybodies. Finally, in the **sixth section (3:13-18)**, Paul gives his final instructions and a benediction. He tells them that if anyone isn't adhering to what they had been taught, they shouldn't have anything to do with that person. Paul emphasizes that they shouldn't treat that person like an enemy, but rather should warn him like a brother.

# I CORINTHIANS

**Time of Writing:** During Paul's 3rd Missionary Journey (AD 54-56)

### History of the City/Paul in Corinth

Originally, Corinth was an ancient Greek city that got destroyed by Rome in 146 BC. It was re-founded as a Roman colony in 44 BC by Julius Caesar. By AD 52 it had become the third leading city in the Roman Empire, behind only Rome and Alexandria. It was a rich and cosmopolitan city, due to its status as a port city that got rich off of trade. It was also a very immoral city, with 26 pagan temples. It was the ancient equivalent of New York, Los Angeles, and Las Vegas all rolled into one.

Paul came to Corinth during his second missionary journey (Acts 18:1-17), after he had fled from Thessalonica and spent some time in Athens. He spent 18 months in Corinth and established a church there with the help of Aquila and Priscilla, fellow Jews and fellow tentmakers who had been expelled from Rome by Emperor Claudius in AD 49. As was his custom, Paul first preached at the local synagogue in Corinth every Sabbath and attracted a number of Jews, as well as Gentile God-fearers Yet when most of the Jewish population rejected his message, Paul declared that he would take the Gospel to the Gentiles. Later, when Gallio became the new proconsul of Achaia (the southern part of Greece), the opposing Jews brought charges against Paul. Gallio, though, kicked all of them out, calling it a "Jewish problem."

### The Issue of Letters

If you read I/II Corinthians closely, you'll see that there really aren't just two letters in play. In I Corinthians 5:9-11, Paul makes reference to an earlier letter he wrote to the Corinthian church that we no longer have. That one is believed to have been written sometime in AD 52. Our I Corinthians was actually Paul's second letter to Corinth—it was in response to some questions they sent to Paul (while he was staying in Ephesus around AD 54 during his third missionary journey) by the hand of some of Chloe's household (I Corinthians 7:1). The next time Paul visited Corinth, though, there was some trouble, and that prompted him to write a third letter (AD 55)—an angry "letter of tears" (II Corinthians 2:3-4) that is lost to us. II Corinthians was actually Paul's fourth letter, written while he was in Macedonia in AD 56.

## The Big Things to Know about I Corinthians

A. **The Wisdom in Christ vs. The Wisdom of the World**: Christians value a different kind of wisdom than what the world values. Christian wisdom is found in Christ's crucifixion and a Christian's self-sacrifice, whereas the world's wisdom is found in self-aggrandizing philosophy and the self-promotion in academia.

B. **Nobody Likes You**: Paul's message to Christians is simple: Stop trying to impress groups who will never like you. Greek philosophers think you are stupid and Jewish legalists find you offensive, so stop trying to kiss up to them.

C. **How to Live Like a Christian in a Pagan World**: It is really hard to live a Christ-like life in a thoroughly unchristian culture. You're not going to fit in.

D. **Renouncing Your Rights in the Name of Love**: Being a Christian isn't about demanding your "rights." It means self-sacrificial love, even at the expense of your "rights" sometimes.

E. **Church Order and Spiritual Gifts**: Church is not a free-for-all, and it isn't about doing whatever you want to do. It is about reflecting the image of God as Church Body. That means displaying a sense of order, so that the Holy Spirit can speak through the diversity of gifts of the members of the Church. Everything is to be done with the goal of building up the Church.

F. **The Resurrection—It's a Big Deal**: Christ physically rose from the dead and thus displayed a power that defeated death itself. That changes everything. If Christ didn't really resurrect from the dead and defeat death, then nothing in Christianity makes sense.

Letters of Paul – Corinthians | 247

## Literary Map: I Corinthians

|  | | | | |
|---|---|---|---|---|
| **Greeting (1:1-9)** | 1:1-9 Greeting/Thanksgiving | | | |
| **Church Divisions (1:10-4:7)** | 1:10-17 Church Divisions | 1:18-31 Christ: Wisdom and Power of God | 2:1-16 Christ Crucified: Wisdom and Spirit of God | 3:1-4:7 Church Divisions |
| **Church Problems (4:8-6:20)** | 4:8-21 Paul Chastises the Corinthians | 5:1-13 Sexual Immorality in the Church | 6:1-11 Lawsuits Among Believers | 6:12-20 Visiting Prostitutes |
| **Marriage Advice (7:1-7:40)** | 7:1-16 Principles for Marriage | 7:17-24 Live as You are Called | 7:25-40 The Unmarried and Widowed | |
| **Idol Food Temple Feasts (8:1-11:1)** | 8:1-13 Food Offered to Idols | 9:1-27 Paul Surrenders His Rights | 10:1-11:1 Sharing Table in Pagan Temples | |
| **Church Worship (11:2-14:40)** | 11:2-16 Head Coverings | 11:17-34 Lord's Supper | 12:1-31 Spiritual Gifts | 13:1-13 Faith, Hope, Love | 14:1-40 Prophecy, Tongues, Orderly Worship |
| **Resurrection (15:1-58)** | 15:1-19 The Resurrection of Christ | 15:20-34 The Resurrection of the Dead | 15:35-49 The Resurrection of the Body | 15:50-58 Mystery: Victory Over Death |
| **Final Matters (16:1-24)** | 16:1-4 The Collection for the Saints | 16:5-18 Travel Plans Final Instructions | 16:19-24 Final Greetings | |

## A Walkthrough of I Corinthians

### 1. The Greeting and Thanksgiving (1:1-9)

Paul opens his letter with a greeting in 1:1-3, in which we learn that **Sosthenes** is with Paul at the time of the writing of the letter. In the thanksgiving in 1:4-9, Paul says that the Corinthian believers have been enriched in **knowledge** and that he prays they won't be lacking in any **gracious gift**. He then encourages them to wait for **the revelation of our Lord Jesus Christ**. When that happens, Paul says that Jesus will **strengthen them to the end**, namely on **the Day of our Lord Jesus Christ**. Paul's mention of their **knowledge** comprises one of the points Paul is going to make in his letter. Although knowledge is good, they have let their knowledge become a source of division. His prayer regarding them not lacking any **gracious gift** also foreshadows his comments on Spiritual gifts. His comment regarding them being **strengthened to the end** isn't just some overgeneralized nicety. The Greek word there is *telos*, and it carries with it a meaning of bringing something to full maturity and consummation. It is used throughout the New Testament in relation to the other thing Paul mentions: **The Revelation and Day of the Lord Jesus Christ**.

### 2. Church Divisions (1:10-4:7)

In the first major section of I Corinthians, Paul addresses the problem of the brewing divisions that were beginning to happen in the Corinthian church. In the **first part (1:10-17)**, Paul tells them that there shouldn't be any divisions among them and that they should all be of the same mind. The divisions were caused when people started to identify themselves to various leaders like Paul, Apollos, Cephas (Peter), and even Christ, over and against the others. Perhaps they had been baptized by different people, and that is why Paul mentions that, aside from Crispus, Gaius, and Stephanas, he didn't personally baptize any of them. Paul then says his job is simply to preach the Gospel, even though he doesn't do it with eloquent words or "wisdom."

In the **second part (1:18-31)**, Paul elaborates on how the Gospel of Christ that he preaches doesn't "fit in" with either Greek philosophy or Judaism. It is important to remember that in the mid-50s, Christianity was a very new thing and people were trying to figure out what it was: Was it a new kind of philosophy? Was it just a Jewish sect? Paul's answer is simple: *It's neither*. It wasn't a Jewish sect; in fact it was **a scandal to the Jews**. And it wasn't a new kind of philosophy, in fact it was considered to be **foolish to Greek philosophers in Athens**. To tease out what Paul is saying, we need a visual:

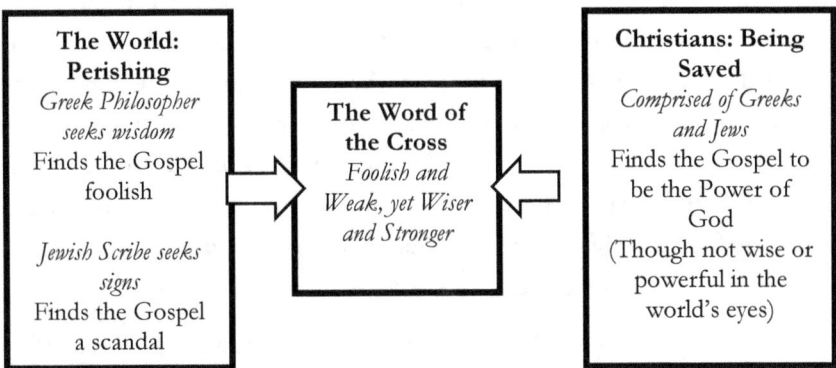

Ultimately, the Gospel is about *how salvation comes through the crucifixion, death, and resurrection of Christ*. On one side, there is the perspective of **the world**, which includes the views of both **Greek philosophy** and **Judaism**. On the other side, there is the perspective of **Christians**. Paul's point to the Corinthian believers, therefore, is that the Gospel of Christ seems absolutely moronic to those in the world, but it is the dynamic power of God to Christians. Therefore, they shouldn't be getting big heads by treating the various Christian leaders as if each one was a competing philosophical school. Simply put, Paul tells them, *"Hey, nobody likes you! Everyone thinks you are idiots! So, stop acting like them and don't boast like them! You need to remember that you are foolish and weak in their eyes, but God's foolishness and weakness is still wiser and stronger than they are."*

It is important to understand what Paul is doing. In the **old age** of Judaism in which he grew up, the division was between Jews and Gentiles. With the coming of Christ, though, the **new Messianic age** had begun and the line of demarcation had been redrawn to where Christians, be they Jew or Gentile, were on one side, and those who reject the Gospel, be they Jew or Gentile, were on the other side. Greek philosophers and Jewish scribes might have different reasons for rejecting the Gospel, but the bottom line is that they reject it and thus show themselves to be enemies of the cross. Therefore, Paul wants the Corinthian Christians to realize they are never going to win the approval of either Greek philosophers or Jewish scribes.

In the **third part (2:1-16)**, Paul focuses on how God's power seems like weakness to the world. He starts by reminding them that when he first shared the Gospel with them, it wasn't with **lofty words or wisdom**, meaning he didn't engage in some sort of philosophical-sounding rhetoric. He simply **preached Christ crucified** and demonstrated the **power of the Spirit**. Of course, Paul says what he preached to them **really was wisdom to those who are mature** (a reference to what he said in 1:8). Simply put, Paul is saying that truly mature people will realize that the Gospel contains God's wisdom, even though the **leaders of this age** think it is foolishness and reject it. Ironically, the reason why those self-professed wise philosophers and scribes rejected the Gospel was because *they didn't understand it—they were too thick-headed to get what God was doing.*

By contrast, Paul says Christians have received the Spirit of God, and it is that Spirit that has revealed to them the **mystery of the Gospel**, namely that salvation has come through the crucifixion and resurrection of Christ. Therefore, these two different reactions to the Gospel reveals two different kinds of people. On one hand, there is the **soulish person** of 2:14 (most translations have "natural person") who doesn't have the Spirit of God and thus isn't able to understand what God is doing through Christ. On the other hand, there is the **person of the Spirit** of 2:15 who truly understand what God is doing through Christ. Most translations have "spiritual person," but Paul isn't referring to people who are just generally considered to be "spiritual." He is specifically referring to Christians who have the Spirit of God. He then emphasizes that God has given His Spirit so that people who put their faith in Christ can understand the teachings of the Spirit, and those who have the **Spirit of God** have the **mind of Christ**.

In the **fourth part (3:1-4:7)**, Paul comes back to directly addressing the issue of the divisions that were going on in the Corinthian church. Paul begins with a little bit of a jab at them by saying that he couldn't speak to them as if they were *fully mature people of the Spirit*. Instead, he had to speak to them as *people of the flesh*, as *babies in Christ*. And how does he know they aren't mature people of the Spirit? Because there were divisions among them. In their attempt to emulate the "wisdom of the age," they've shown themselves to still be "living in the flesh."

Paul then tries to help them understand the roles of the various Christian leaders that they were dividing themselves over by using two analogies. First, he says they are like **God's field**. He "planted the seeds" of the Gospel in Corinth and Apollos then "watered the field," but ultimately God is the one who causes things to grow. Paul and Apollos weren't rivals. They were fellow laborers in God's field to grow people up in the faith. Second, Paul says they are **God's building**. He "laid the foundation" of the church in Corinth and someone else (be it Apollos, Peter, or anyone) then "built upon that foundation." The foundation of the Church is Jesus Christ, and what is built upon that foundation is up to the various other teachers (builders) in the Church. The quality of their work will eventually be revealed "in fire" (times of testing). The builder whose work stands up will be paid accordingly. By contrast, the builder whose work gets burned up, although he will still be saved, will still suffer the loss of his efforts.

Since Paul has used the analogy of God's building, he can't help but extend the analogy to include the **Temple**. The Temple in Jerusalem was essentially God's building—the House of YHWH. That was where the Spirit of God dwelled throughout much of the Old Testament. Of course, Jesus ended up condemning that Temple and prophesying that it would be destroyed within a generation. The **true Temple of God** was **his body**, and his body was **the Church**. Therefore, Paul tells the Corinthian Christians that they themselves, as a Church body, were the **living, breathing Temple of God**, and that **the Spirit of God dwelled in their midst**. Paul is not talking about *individual believers* at this point, but rather the *corporate body of Christ*. Since the Church as a whole was the Temple of God in which the Spirit of God dwelled, they were to work toward unity, and they should reject division.

Paul ends this section by pointing out the cause of their divisions is their own bigheadedness and their attempts to be "wise" in the world's eyes. Paul then gives them some much-needed advice: *If they are trying to be wise in a way that philosophers and scribes would be impressed with, then they need to become a fool in their eyes so that they can truly become wise in God's eyes.* Besides, allowing themselves to be divided over Paul, Apollos, or Peter is just plain dumb, because, as Paul says, all three of them belong to the Church in Corinth, and the Church in Corinth belongs to Christ, and Christ belongs to God! Bottom line, Paul is saying, *"God has given you everything you need, and we all are here to serve you! So, don't act like foolish, immature brats and fight with each other!"*

### 3. Church Problems (4:8-6:20)

In the next section, Paul turns his attention to specific issues that were going on in the Corinthian church. He begins in the **first part (4:8-21)** by taking them down a few notches because they had gotten rather arrogant about how wise they were. One needs to realize that 4:8-13 is filled with sarcasm from start to finish.

After all, Paul was an **actual apostle** through whom God had worked great deeds in the Spirit and who had suffered immense persecution on behalf of Christ. They, though, because of their arguing and divisions, were proving themselves to be immature Christians. Paul, therefore, feels he needs to put them in their place by essentially saying, *"Oh, we apostles are such fools! Look at us how much we get beaten and persecuted! We are just garbage! But not you guys! Look at how wise you all are! You all are so well off, and you haven't suffered at all for Christ! Good for you!"*

Then in 4:14-21, Paul eases up a bit and tells them, *"I'm not trying to shame you. I'm just worried about you. After all, I founded the church in Corinth, so you're like my own kids!"* Nevertheless, like a parent who will be coming home soon, he issues them a stern warning, *"Hey, I'm going to be coming to Corinth soon, so it is really up to you whether or not it is going to be a good visit or whether or not I'm going to have to come with a wooden spoon and spank you like little children!"* With that, Paul then gets to the issues at hand.

In the **second part (5:1-13)**, we learn that there was a young man in the Corinthian church who was having sex with his father's wife and that the church wasn't doing anything about it. Paul's rebuke in 5:1-5 is swift and harsh. He says that even the pagans find such behavior to be perverse! Apparently, though, they are so arrogant that they don't think it is that big of a deal! He then tells them to **hand that man over to Satan for the destruction of the flesh**. He is not saying they are to condemn him to hell, but rather that they should kick that guy out of their church body and not let him participate in the life of the church until he learns his lesson and repents. If he wants to live like a pagan, then kick him out to live with the pagans. Hopefully, he'll realize the mistake he made and repent of his sin. Then he can be welcomed back.

Paul then emphasizes in 5:6-8 that the church has the responsibility to deal with the sin among its members. If they don't, then that person's sin is going to eventually affect the entire church body, just like a little leaven works its way through the entire dough. Paul then extends the metaphor by connecting it to **Passover**: Christ is the Passover lamb who was sacrificed for their sin, and their job is to then celebrate Passover by purging themselves of the leaven of sin and wickedness. Paul clarifies, though, that when he told them they weren't to associate with fornicators, he didn't mean that they shouldn't have anything to do with non-Christians who engage in sinful behavior like idolatry and fornication. He meant that they shouldn't have anything to do with someone who *claims to be a Christian*, but who then *continues living in sin like the pagans*. Let God judge those outside the Church, but it is the Church's responsibility to deal with those in the Church.

In the **third part (6:1-11)**, Paul addresses the fact that there were some Corinthian Christians who were suing each other and taking each other to court. Paul scolds them about this and wonders why Christians would ask pagans to settle their disputes? Again, he takes a jab at their self-professed wisdom by asking, *"Aren't any of you **wise enough** to deal with this?"* Just as their divisions showed, so too their inability to deal with this issue shows that for all their boasting, they really aren't as wise and mature in Christ as they think they are. Paul then says that if you feel a Christian brother cheated you, it would be better to just let yourself be cheated than to take him to court, because kind of "justice" one will get in a pagan court is not going to be the kind of justice that characterizes the Kingdom of God.

Paul then proceeds to give a kind of "list" of people who would never inherit the Kingdom of God. Most of the list is straightforward, but, given our modern sensibilities, a few comments must be made regarding a couple of them. In 6:9, most translations translate the Greek words **malakoi** and **arsenokoitai** as something like *male prostitutes* and *homosexuals*. In the ancient world, though, no one identified themselves as a "homosexual." The term was coined only in the 19th century and is used to define our modern concept of "sexual orientation." In the ancient world, any kind of sexual act for the purpose of pleasure was seen as acceptable. Sexual libertinism was the moral code of the day. Paul, though, is clearly condemning that mindset, and he lines up same-sex sexual activity in the same category as adultery and visiting prostitutes. He is not, though, talking about the modern notion of "orientation." He's talking about *specific actions* considered to be sexually immoral.

In the **fourth part (6:12-20)**, Paul addresses the issue of whether or not Christians should go see prostitutes. That might seem like a ridiculous question. After all, what kind of Christian needs to be told *not to go to prostitutes?* Remember, though, ancient Greco-Roman culture was very different from ours. As odd as it sounds, back in the first century pagan Roman Empire, going to temple prostitutes was a commonly accepted thing. Given that mindset, Paul is specifically addressing a question they had sent to him regarding Christian freedom, namely, if there was freedom in Christ and "everything is permitted," and if Gentile Christians were not under the Torah, then was going to temple prostitutes wrong? If "the stomach is for food, and food for the stomach," then isn't the purpose of sex to give pleasure to the body? Simply put, if it is "just sex," then what's the harm?

Paul responds by saying, "Yes, everything is permitted, but that doesn't mean everything is good for you," and when it comes to sex, sex isn't "just sex." It unites people on a deep level to where they become "one flesh." Therefore, since a Christian's body is part of the body of Christ (the Church), he shouldn't unite his body to the flesh of a temple prostitute dedicated to a pagan god. To do so is to sin, not only against your own body, but against the body of Christ—the Church. Paul's comment that "your body is the Temple of the Holy Spirit" should be taken in these two ways, both an individual believer's body, and the Church as a whole, as the body of Christ. Since a believer's individual body is part of the body of Christ (the Church), and since the body of Christ is the Temple of the Holy Spirit, then no one should be visiting pagan temple prostitutes.

### 4. Marriage Advice (7:1-40)

The next section is an extension of the previous section. Here, Paul shares his thoughts on marriage. In the **first part (7:1-16)**, Paul answers some questions the Corinthians had regarding whether or not it was a good thing for husbands and wives, even though they were married, to abstain from sex. Paul tells marriage partners not to deprive their spouse of sex (or else their spouse is going to be tempted to go fornicate with those pagan temple prostitutes!). That being said, if both spouses agree to abstain from sex for a short time as a spiritual exercise, so they can devote themselves to prayer, that's okay, but don't abstain from sex for too long, or else you are going to be tempted to go to those pagan temples. Paul wants to make it clear, though, that he is just giving advice and he isn't commanding them to abstain for a time for prayer. Still, he says that he wishes everyone was like him, a gifted celibate who never married and was evidently not really tempted to have sex. Since that wasn't the case, though, Paul says it is good to get married and be devoted to your spouse.

When it comes to unmarried men and widows, Paul says that although he personally thinks it is best to be like him, if someone's sexual urges were just too strong, it would be better to get married and have an outlet for one's sexual urges than to let them get out of control. On the topic of divorce, Paul makes it clear that what he says is a command from the Lord: A Christian should not divorce a Christian spouse—that's a bad thing. But if someone divorces anyway, that person should at least stay unmarried, or else try to reconcile with his/her spouse. Yet in the case where a Christian is married to a non-Christian, Paul gives his personal opinion: If the unbelieving spouse wants to stay married, then the Christian should not seek a divorce. Maybe that unbelieving spouse will eventually "become holy" and come to the faith. If the unbelieving spouse seeks a divorce, though, Paul says that the Christian should agree to it.

In the **second part (7:17-24)**, Paul tries to sum up what he has been trying to say concerning all these situations: If you are a Christian, you should try to stay in the situation of life you were in when you came to Christ. If you were circumcised (Jewish), don't get uncircumcised and renounce your Judaism. If you were an uncircumcised Gentile, don't think you have to become Jewish. If you're a slave, then don't try to rebel because you are now "free in Christ" (although Paul says, "But if you have the opportunity to become a free man, take it!"). When it gets right down to it, Paul's advice is simple: *Just be a Christian in whatever situation you find yourself in.*

In the **third part (7:25-40)**, Paul gives some advice to unmarried people and widows. His personal opinion to young women boils down to this: It is probably better to stay unmarried, but if you get married, you're not sinning—that's okay. But realize that *marriage is a lot of work*. If you are single, you are freer to do the Lord's work, but if you are married, you will have a family to take care of. There is a lot of speculation as to what Paul means in 7:26 about the **impending crisis**, in 7:29 about the **time being short**, and 7:31 about **the present form of the world passing away**. When considered in the light of Paul's various references to the Day of the Lord, as well as Jesus' own words in the Olivet Discourse regarding the Temple's destruction and the Coming of the Son of Man, it would seem that Paul is reflecting that early Church proclamation that Jesus' prophecy about the destruction of the Temple and Jerusalem would bring about such a cataclysmic upheaval in the world, that everything would be radically different. Thus, the "impending crisis" very well could be referring to the coming Jewish War and the eventual destruction of Jerusalem.

Paul ends his remarks by once again emphasizing that it is best to stay single but getting married isn't a sin and actually is still a good thing. A woman is bound to her husband as long as he is alive, even if they get divorced, but she is free to remarry once he dies. But if she does remarry, she should only remarry "in the Lord"—probably meaning to another Christian. Still, Paul thinks it would be better to stay single.

## 5. Idol Food and Temple Feasts (8:1-11:1)

In the next section, Paul addresses the Corinthian Christians' questions regarding whether it was okay to eat food from the marketplace and whether or not it was okay to go to pagan temples and have community meals.

In the **first part (8:1-13)**, Paul addresses the issue of eating meat from the marketplace. Jews who lived throughout the Roman Empire often were vegetarians because they refused to eat the meat that was sold in the marketplaces of pagan cities. The reason for this is because all the meat that was sold in the marketplace had come from the pagan temples. Pagan priests were essentially the "holy butchers" of the ancient world, and they would send any meat that wasn't used in the temple rituals out to the market to be sold in public. In the eyes of the Jews, that meat was "idol food," and therefore they refused to eat it. The question facing the Corinthian Christians was simple. Should they do the same thing as the Jews? After all, that meat really had been offered to idols. Still, to Gentiles, meat in the marketplace was just meat. So, what did Paul think?

Paul decides to address this issue by referring to the Corinthians' *knowledge*. Although knowledge is a good thing, it can easily make a person arrogant. By contrast, *love* is more important because love always seeks to build up other people. Given that, Paul says that *knowledge* tells us that, yes, there is only one God, the Father, and one Lord, Jesus Christ. Therefore, Christians *know* that idols are simply idols of things that don't really exist. So, the meat that had been offered in pagan temples to pagan idols really wasn't offered to any god that really existed. *Knowledge tells us that it is just meat*. Eating it really shouldn't be a big deal.

Still, some people don't have that knowledge and thus have a "weak conscience." Maybe it's former pagans who were now Christians, or possibly Jews, who just couldn't shake the fact that the meat in the marketplace *was idol food*. Given that reality, Paul tells those who do realize it is just meat that they shouldn't let their *knowledge* act as a *stumbling block* to those who have a weak conscience on this issue. If it really is just meat, and if it really is no big deal to eat it, then it also isn't a big deal *not to eat it* when you are with people with a weak conscience. If you choose to flaunt your *knowledge* in front of those people form whom it still is a big deal, you run the risk of causing them to stumble, and you aren't acting in *love* and you are actually sinning against Christ because you are not showing consideration for the weaker brother.

In the **second part (9:1-27)**, Paul holds himself up as an example of the very thing he is encouraging the Corinthian Christians to do. He first points out that despite the fact that he *is free*, that he is *an apostle*, that he's *actually seen Jesus*, and that he is the one who *actually founded the Church in Corinth*, he has chosen not to use any of that "street cred," so to speak, for his own advantage. He *could have* gotten married, but he chose not to do so. He and Barnabas *could have* had them basically pay their salary, but they chose to work for a living. The reason being that they didn't want anything to hinder the spreading of the Gospel. By analogy, a **soldier** has the right to get paid by the army, a **shepherd** has the right to the milk of the flock, a **sower** has the right to reap the harvest, and a **priest in the Temple** has the right to get a portion of the sacrifice offered to God. But Paul has chosen not to take advantage of his rights as an apostle., because he doesn't want to have anything hinder the spreading of the Gospel.

To drive the point home, he stresses that even though he is *free* to do whatever he wants, he has chosen to *become a slave* in order to win more people to the Gospel. Therefore, when he is with his fellow Jews, he respects their Torah observance and won't eat meat from the marketplace. When he is with Gentiles, he doesn't let the Torah become an obstacle, so if they offer him meat from the marketplace, he'll eat it. He simply won't let inconsequential things become an obstacle to the Gospel. Then, using the athletic analogy of **running a race**, Paul says that if you want to win the prize of the victor's wreath, you have to train hard and be self-disciplined. The big difference for a Christian, of course, is that whereas a victor's wreath one might win in a race will eventually wither, the "wreath of salvation" that a Christian will win is imperishable.

In the **third part (10:1-11:1)**, Paul turns his attention to the issue of whether it was okay to go to the pagan temples and eat community meals in them. Paul's answer is an unequivocal "No!" It is important to realize that although pagan temples were places of worship and sacrifice, they were also essentially community centers. If you were a blacksmith, for example, you were part of a blacksmith guild, and that guild, instead of a patron saint, would have a *patron god*. Whenever your guild had get-togethers or community meals, they took place in the temple of that particular god. So, the Corinthian Christians wanted to know whether or not it was okay to go to those community meals that took place in pagan temples.

To answer their question, Paul gives the example of the Israelites who came out of Egypt during the Exodus and points out that although the Israelites were led out of Egypt by the power of God, most of them ended up dying in the wilderness because they did things that displeased God. He specifically refers to **Numbers 25**, when the Israelites participated in the orgy-filled worship of the Baal of Peor and then suffered God's judgment. He also refers to **Numbers 21**, when many Israelites were killed by serpents because they complained and rebelled against Moses. Again, even though those Israelites were saved from Egypt, most of them died in the wilderness because they displeased God by participating in pagan worship and practices.

Paul then addresses why it was forbidden to eat meals in pagan temples. To make his point, Paul refers to the practice of communion, where the drinking of the cup and the eating of the bread indicates that you are part of the fellowship of the body and blood of Christ. Therefore, even though pagan gods don't really exist, the fact is that, in reality, *the real power behind those false gods is demonic.* That is why you simply cannot drink from the cup and eat at the table of the Lord and then go off and have pagan meals at the table of demons.

Paul ends by clarifying everything he has said: *You are free to do anything and eat anything from the marketplace, but not everything is profitable and not everything builds up others.* If something causes a brother to stumble in the faith, then you should refrain from doing so, out of love for that weaker brother. You are free to eat anything, but if it becomes apparent that someone can't get over the fact that the food is "temple food," then it is best not to eat it. Do everything for the glory of God, but do your best not to offend Jews, Gentiles, or your fellow Christians.

### 6. Church Worship Instructions (11:2-14:40)

In the next section, Paul turns his attention to some of their questions regarding Church worship. In the **first part (11:2-16)**, Paul addresses the issue regarding husbands and wives in the midst of worship. What makes it a hard passage to understand is that it really is connected to the cultural norms of ancient Rome, and most of us simply have no frame of reference to interpret what Paul is saying. To make sense of what Paul is saying, we should keep in mind two things. First, Greco-Roman culture was very patriarchal, with women being subjugated to men. Second, in that culture, it was thought that a person's hair contributed to their fertility. Long hair on a woman made her more fertile, whereas long hair on a man made him less potent. Therefore, it was the general custom for women to have long hair and for men to have short hair. And since a woman's long hair was consider a sexual organ, women were expected to wear head coverings.

Thus, Paul is addressing the issue of how men and women worship in light of those cultural norms. The long and short of his comments is that he is redefining those culture norms in light of the Gospel and Christ's relationship with the Church. Thus, the husband is the head of the wife, like Christ is the head of the Church. Therefore, the reason why a Christian man shouldn't cover his head in worship isn't because of sexual potency concerns, but because he represents Christ. And the reason why a Christian woman should cover her head in worship isn't because of fertility concerns, but because she represents the Church and the covering represents the head of the Church, Christ. That being said, nobody really understands Paul's comment in 11:10 about a woman covering her head "because of the angels." Nevertheless, despite all that, Paul makes it clear in 11:13, 16 that his churches don't have any set custom regarding head-coverings and that the Corinthian church can figure it out for themselves. Simply put, Paul is talking about social mores, not morals.

In the **second part (11:17-34)**, Paul addresses the way the Corinthians were abusing the Lord's Supper. When the early Church celebrated the Lord's Supper, *they had an actual meal.* Within the context of that meal, the cup of wine and the bread held special significance, but it still was a meal that believers would come together to celebrate. Knowing that makes it easier to understand the problem Paul is addressing. When they came together to celebrate the Lord's Supper, they all brought their own food, but then proceeded to eat their own food without sharing it with the poor Christians among them who didn't have much to eat. Because of that, the Lord's Supper had turned into an occasion of humiliation for Christians who were not well off. That is why Paul comes right out and tells them that they were not really celebrating the Lord's Supper at all.

Paul then emphasizes what the bread and cup symbolize. The bread represents *Christ's body*, and Christ's body is *the Church*. The cup represents the *new covenant* in his blood. Taking part in the Lord's Supper thus celebrates his death until he comes. Therefore, they are to celebrate that new covenant *as a Church body who shares in the meal*, not as individuals who gorge themselves on their own food. That is why Paul says that anyone who eats and drinks without *discerning the body*—meaning the Church body—eats and drinks judgment on himself. He isn't talking about introspection into your own life regarding any unconfessed sins before you take communion. He is saying that anyone who goes to the Lord's Supper and doesn't share his meal with other people in the body of Christ, namely the poor who don't have any food, then that person is bringing judgment upon himself because he is undercutting the entire point of the Lord's Supper. **You can't celebrate the body of Christ by letting others in the body of Christ go hungry.**

In the **third part (12:1-31)**, Paul addresses the issue of Spiritual gifts—the specific "giftings" that have been bestowed on believers by the Holy Spirit once they have become Christians. That is why he prefaces his comments in 12:1-3 by reminding them they didn't have these things when they were pagans led astray by idols. In any case, Paul lists a wide range of various Spiritual gifts. As he does, though, he makes it a point to emphasize that it is the *same Spirit* who gives them all, and that the purpose of all of them is for the *common good*.

In fact, that's the point of the entire chapter: *No matter what Spiritual gift you have, the purpose of that gift is to build others in the body of Christ up.* Just as there are different body parts in a body, so are there different individuals in the Church body, and just as all those different body parts work together in the body, so are different individuals with different Spiritual gifts to work together with other individuals in the Church body for the building up of the Church as a whole. It doesn't matter if one is a Jew, Greek, slave, or free—*it's all one body*. It doesn't matter if your Spiritual gift is more visible or not as noticeable—*every body part and every Spiritual gift matters.*

Paul ends his comments by emphasizing that all these gifts should be done in the context of love. Not everyone has the same Spiritual gifts, and though it is perhaps a natural feeling to want the more "glamorous" gifts (like speaking in tongues), the most important thing is the "Spirit" in which they are done, namely of love.

In the **fourth part (13:1-13)**, Paul then focuses on the importance of doing those Spiritual gifts in the context of love within the Church. His point is simple: *It doesn't matter what Spiritual gift you have—if you exercise that gift without love for others, if your aim isn't to build other believers up, then your gift is going to be largely useless.* Paul then says that the reason why it is so important to do things in a Spirit of love is that *love is the thing that lasts into the ages*. Love is what is going to take us from this old age of sin and death and into the new Messianic Age of resurrection life. With the death and resurrection of Jesus and the outpouring of the Holy Spirit, Christians have been given a taste of the future Kingdom of God, but it is only a taste. We *already* have a glimpse of that age to come, but that age to come *hasn't come in full yet*.

This is what Paul's talk about *presently* "looking through a dirty mirror" and "knowing in part," but *then* "seeing face to face" and "knowing fully" is getting at. To use a movie analogy, Paul is saying that the current gifts of the Spirit are like teaser trailers to the blockbuster movie that has yet to come out. When the movie hits the big screen, no one is going to need the trailers anymore. Their purpose is to heighten our hope and expectation of when the full move arrives. Therefore, what is important is that people use their Spiritual gifts to build others up, because when the movie drops, we'll all want to be in the theater together.

In the **fifth part (14:1-40)**, Paul addresses orderly worship in the Church, especially in relation to **prophesying** and **speaking in tongues**. Apparently, worship in the Corinthian church tended to get out of control. Again, Paul stresses the ultimate goal should be for the *building up of the Church body*. He first says that prophesying is better and more beneficial than speaking in tongues because a prophecy spoken in a language the hearers understand will encourage them and build them up, whereas a word spoken in tongues only benefits the speaker…unless, of course, that word spoken in tongues is interpreted, so that the Church body could understand! If that happens, then speaking in tongues is just as beneficial as a prophetic word, for both would then encourage and build up the Church body. That is what Paul is getting at when he talks about **praying with the Spirit** (speaking in tongues) and **praying with the mind** (speaking in an understandable language).

He then gives specific instructions on how to manage people who speak in tongues and prophesy during a Church meeting but starts with some confusing comments in 14:22-25. First, he says that **speaking in tongues** is a sign *for those not of the faith*, but then he says if an unbeliever comes in an hears everyone speaking in tongues, he will think they are all out of their minds. Then he says that **prophesying** is a sign *for believers*, only to turn around and say if an unbeliever comes in and hears people prophesying, he will be convicted and acknowledge that God is really among them. We can make better sense of this if we first consider Pauls' comments in 14:26-31, where he stresses the importance of orderly worship. First, he says if someone speaks in tongues in a Church meeting, they should wait until the Spirit gives someone the interpretation. If there is no interpretation, then the one speaking in tongues should stay quiet. Secondly, he says that if there is more than one person who has a prophecy to share, then they should take turns and do it in an orderly way.

In light of that, Paul's comments in 14:22-25 make more sense. Speaking in tongues might be a sign to the unbeliever that something different is going on in the Church, but unless there is an interpretation, and especially if people are getting so swept up in the excitement to where everyone is shouting out at the same time, that unbeliever is going to think that they are all crazy. The disorderliness of it all will turn him away. Similarly, if different people speak out and prophesy all at the same time, the whole thing will be chaotic, and no one will get anything out of it. Therefore, Paul says, for the building up of other believers and for the opportunity for an unbeliever to acknowledge God's power, *do everything in an orderly manner so that people can understand what is being said and what is going on.*

Paul's final comments in the chapter tend to be some of the most controversial passages in the Bible, particularly because of 14:34-35: *"women should be silent in the churches. For they are not permitted to speak, but should be subordinate, as the law also says. If there is anything they desire to know, let them ask their husbands at home. For it is shameful for a woman to speak in church."* The problem with those two verses is that there is a compelling textual argument that they were not part of Paul's original letter. The sentiment doesn't even fit with Paul's other comments earlier in chapter 11 about *women praying and prophesying in Church.*

If we realize these verses aren't part of the original letter, and then read the passage without them, the sentiment flows together and fits in with the overall point Paul is making about orderly worship. In 14:32, Paul says that prophets should exercise control of the spirit of prophecy, and then, beginning in 14:33, he says, "For God isn't about disorder, but of peace, just like in all the churches of the holy saints. Or did the Word of God come from you? Or has it reached only you?" Paul is stressing that all the other churches strive for order during their worship, and that orderly worship is, in fact, a command from the Lord. Therefore, the Corinthian church was wrong to let their worship devolve into a chaotic free-for-all that not only wasn't really building anyone up but was making themselves look like insane people in the eyes of their pagan neighbors.

### 7. The Resurrection (15:1-58)

In the final section, Paul discusses the resurrection of Christ. He breaks his comments up into four parts. To understand the **first part (15:1-19)**, you first must realize that in the Greco-Roman world, pagans viewed the material world as bad and second-rate, and believed our physical bodies were little more than prison-houses to our non-material spirits. Thus, death was when our spirits would finally "shed this mortal coil" and be free from crude matter. Given that, the Jewish concept of resurrection, and the Christian proclamation that Jesus was physically resurrected from the dead, would just sound weird. So, even though the Corinthian believers had accepted the Gospel and Paul's preaching that Christ was raised from the dead, they apparently were still a bit foggy as to what that really meant and hadn't grasped the full implications of Paul's preaching of Christ's resurrection. Therefore, Paul has to clarify what those implications of Christ's resurrection were.

Paul begins with the fundamental Christian claim: **Jesus Christ really physically died, he really was buried in a tomb, and he really physically rose from the dead, and by doing so, defeated death itself**. Numerous people personally witnessed the fact the formerly dead Jesus had come back to life in a real, physical body: Peter, Jesus' inner circle, over 500 other followers, his brother James, "all the apostles," and finally Paul himself. He emphasizes that because apparently some Christians in Corinth were interpreting Jesus' resurrection in more "Greek" terms, like he wasn't literally raised from the dead in a physical sense, but rather in some kind of "spiritual" sense, and therefore Christians won't literally be resurrected, but will somehow join Christ in some non-material existence.

Paul responds by saying, over and over again, that if there isn't a literal, physical resurrection of the dead, then Christ hasn't been literally, physically resurrected. And if he hasn't been resurrected, then he hasn't defeated death. And if he hasn't defeated death, that means that when you die, there is no hope for you—you're going to stay dead. The Christian hope is that you will be physically resurrected, just like Christ was, that death will be defeated, and that there will be a new creation, a new, transformed *physical creation* empowered by the Holy Spirit. If Christ wasn't physically resurrected, then the entire Christian Gospel is a sham.

In the **second part (15:20-34)**, Paul goes on to explain the theological significance of the resurrection by contrasting Adam and Christ. **Adam** represents **natural humanity** that succumbs to death, and **Christ** represents the **new humanity**, empowered by the Spirit, living by the power of resurrection. Paul's point is that in our natural state "in Adam" we all die, but those who are "in Christ" will be made alive with Christ in the resurrection. But there is an order to it all:

Christ first, Christians later on at his coming (*Parousia*), and then eventually all of creation at the end (the *telos*).

To be clear, the Coming of Christ (*Parousia*) is not the coming of the new creation (the *telos*). It is the beginning of his reign in a still corrupt world. Eventually, though, there will come the new creation, when Christ, after putting all enemies, even death, under his feet will hand everything over to the Father, and then God will be all in all. Paul's comments about people being baptized on behalf of the dead is simply a mystery. Nobody is really sure what he is talking about. His overall point, though, is simple: **If there is no resurrection of the dead, then his entire ministry is worthless, and Christianity is a sham.**

In the **third part (15:35-49)**, Paul talks more about the actual resurrection of the body and answers the question, *"What exactly will be resurrected? What will the resurrected body look like?"* Paul says that the resurrected body isn't going to be just like the old body, but at the same time it isn't going to be a non-material body. He then uses the analogy of a seed being buried in the ground and then a plant eventually growing out of the ground from that seed. Our natural body is like the seed. It is going to die, just like a seed is planted in the ground, but when Christ comes and the full resurrection happens, that "seed" will sprout up as a plant, that plant being a resurrected body, empowered by the Spirit. Paul then teases out this analogy by contrasting the natural body that dies with the resurrected body that will be raised. He associates the **natural body** with **mortality**, **dishonor**, and **weakness**, and associates the **resurrected body** with **immortality**, **honor**, and **dynamic power**.

Most translations have the contrast as between the **natural body** and the **spiritual body**. The problem with that is it gives the impression to most people that the contrast is between a physical body and a non-material spiritual body, because in our modern mindset, we take "spiritual" to mean something akin to

| Old Humanity in Adam | New Humanity in Christ |
|---|---|
| • All die | • All are made alive |
| • "Planted" | • "Raised up" |
| • Mortality | • Immortality |
| • Dishonor | • Glory |
| • Weakness | • Dynamic Power |
| • "Soulish" Body | • Spiritual Body |
| • First Adam = Living Soul | • Last Adam = Life-Making Spirit |
| • From the Dust | • From Heaven |
| • Humanity in the image of the one from dust | • Humanity in the image of the one from Heaven |

some sort of ghost-like "spirits" floating around in heaven. This is not what Paul means. What is translated as "natural" is actually **soulish**—and that simply describes human beings in their original state. In **Genesis 2**, God forms the man from the dust, breathes into his nostrils, and the man becomes *a living soul*. In our day, we tend to conflate "soul" and "spirit" to mean the same thing: that non-material essence within our physical bodies. That is not what Paul means. Biblically speaking, you don't *have a soul*; you *are a soul*. And, as Paul makes clear, the *soulish body* will "naturally" run down and die. It is like a children's toy that runs on batteries, but the batteries are bound to run out. The contrast Paul makes, when he talks about a "spiritual" body probably should be written as a *Spiritual body*, as in the resurrected physical body that is empowered by God's Spirit, and thus is like a toy whose batteries never run down.

After that, Paul once again draws a contrast between Adam (mortal humanity) and Christ (resurrected humanity). **Adam**, the "first man" was a living being who came from the dust, whereas **Christ**, the "last man" became a life-making Spirit who was from Heaven. Hence, humanity in its natural/soulish state "bears **the image** of the one from dust" (Adam), whereas the resurrected humanity in its Spirit-empowered state will "bear **the image** of the one from Heaven" (Christ).

In the **fourth part (15:50-58)**, Paul finishes up his comments about the resurrection by focusing on what resurrection signifies—**the ultimate defeat of death itself**. To be clear, when Paul says, "Flesh and blood cannot inherit the Kingdom of God," he is not contrasting the *material* world with a *non-material, spiritual* world. He is contrasting that which empowers the physical body and material world. To use my earlier analogy, he is contrasting batteries that run down (soulish body) and batteries that never run down (Spirit-empowered body). Hence, humanity that hasn't died and been resurrected cannot inherit the Kingdom of God. Eternal life comes *through* death and out the other side. You won't have the plant if the seed doesn't first die. The apple seed has to "die" first and then grow into an apple tree before it will produce apples. Flesh and blood won't inherit the Kingdom of God; the apple seed cannot produce apples.

Paul ends by talking about **the mystery** and refers to Christ's coming with the imagery of a trumpet call. When that happens, the dead will be resurrected, the mortal will be clothed with the immortal, and death will be defeated. Paul then says something that sounds rather odd: "The sting of death is sin, and the power of sin is *the Torah*" (most translations have "law"). Paul will expand on this in Romans, but basically what he is getting at is that since people are naturally sinful, as soon as you put forth a rule that says, "Doing this or that is wrong," the sin nature within us *naturally wants to try to do that forbidden thing*. When death and sin is defeated, then there will be no need for the Torah.

### 8. Final Matters (16:1-24)

At the end of the letter, in **16:1-4**, Paul mentions the collection for the saints, his attempt to get his Gentile churches to contribute money to help the Jewish churches back in Judea. Paul's hope was that it would serve as a way to reconcile the Jewish and Gentile churches, and to essentially be a witness to his fellow Jews. Unfortunately, as we know from the Book of Acts, Paul's efforts to bridge the gap between the Gentile churches and the Jews in Judea ultimately failed. When he finally made his way back to Jerusalem to deliver the gift in Acts 21, he was attacked by his fellow Jews and ended up being imprisoned for a time in Caesarea and Rome.

In **16:5-18**, Paul tells the Corinthians about his upcoming travel plans. He is currently in Ephesus and plans to stay there until Pentecost because of some kind of opportunity there. He then plans to travel through Macedonia and eventually come and see them after that, possibly even staying with them in Corinth over the winter. He also tells them if Timothy comes to see them, that they should treat him with respect. He also tells them he wanted Apollos to come to see them, but that Apollos didn't have the time to see them at the moment. Still, he was hoping to come to see them at a later day. Paul then encourages them again to do everything in love and to respect the authority of Stephen and his household because they had devoted themselves to the ministry from the very beginning. He also lets them know that Stephanas, Fortunatos, and Achaicus (presumably people from the church in Corinth who were sent to see him) have made it and that has been a great encouragement to him. After that, in **16:19-24**, Paul tells them that the churches in Asia (modern Turkey), send their greetings, along with Aquila and Prisca.

| SUMMARY OF ISSUES IN I CORINTHIANS ||
|---|---|
| The Issue | Summary of Paul's Response |
| (5:1-13) Man having sex with his father's wife | He wants to live worse than a pagan? Kick him out of the church, and hopefully he'll repent! |
| (6:1-11) Christians taking each other to court | Christians shouldn't appeal to pagans to solve their problems! |
| (6:12-20) Christians are seeing prostitutes | You belong to Christ! Your body is the Temple of the Holy Spirit! No seeing pagan temple prostitutes! |
| (7:1-16) Christian Marriage | Martial sex is good—be there for each other; Marriage is better than frustrated lust; If an unbelieving spouse wants out—let it happen. |
| (7:17-40) Christian Singleness | Given the current situation, probably better to stay single, but it's okay to get married. |
| (8:1-13) Idol Food from the Marketplace | It's just food—it's okay to eat, but don't flaunt your freedom in front of someone who has a problem with it. |
| (10:1-11:1) Eating Meals in Pagan Temples | Absolutely not! Satan is ultimately behind pagan temples, so no eating at his table! |
| (11:2-16) Head Coverings and Male-Female Worship | We see men and women in light of Christ and the Church, not according to Roman standards. How you navigate being Christians living in Roman culture on this issue is up to you. |
| (11:17-34) The Lord's Supper | If you're not sharing your food at the Lord's Supper with the poor among you, you're making a mockery of the Lord's Supper! |
| (12:1-31) Spiritual Gifts | Everyone has different Spiritual gifts. Whatever gift you have, use it to build up the Church. |
| (14:1-40) Prophecy, Tongues During Worship | Christian worship should not be a chaotic mess. Things should be done in an orderly way, or people will think you are nuts! |

# II CORINTHIANS

## The Big Things to Know about II Corinthians

A. **The Gospel—It's All About Reconciliation and New Creation**: There will always be conflicts and challenges within the Church and between Christians. The power of the Gospel makes reconciliation possible when those conflicts and challenges arise.

B. **Living out the Age to Come, here in this Present Age**: Here in the present age, we are always going to have to deal with divisions, disappointment, and conflicts. Our calling as Christians is to live out the Gospel and display that resurrection power that makes reconciliation and healing possible, if only in part in the present age.

C. **If You're Going to Boast, Boast in Weakness**: The heart of the Gospel is that Christ's crucifixion is the key to defeating death. Therefore, the only things a Christian should boast or take pride in are the weak things in his/her life, for it is in a Christian's weaknesses and defeats that the power of Christ can be displayed.

## Literary Map: II Corinthians

| | 1:1-11 Greeting/Blessing | | |
|---|---|---|---|

| | 1:12-2:4 | 2:5-11 | 2:12-17 |
|---|---|---|---|
| **Travelogue (1:12-2:17)** | Paul's Change of Plans | Forgive the Sinner | Led in Triumph in Christ |

| | 3:1-18 | 4:1-18 | 5:1-10 |
|---|---|---|---|
| **New Covenant (3:1-5:10)** | Ministers of the New Covenant | Treasure in Clay Vessels | Our Heavenly Dwelling |

| | 5:11-21 | 6:1-10 | 6:11-7:1 | 7:2-16 |
|---|---|---|---|---|
| **Reconciliation (5:11-7:16)** | New Creation | Day of Salvation is Here | Temple of the Living God | Paul's Joy Wronged No One |

| | 8:1-24 | 9:1-15 |
|---|---|---|
| **The Collection (8:1-9:15)** | Encouragement to Give Commendation of Titus | The Collection for Jerusalem |

| | 10:1-17 | 11:1-15 | 11:16-33 | 12:1-10 | 12:11-21 |
|---|---|---|---|---|---|
| **Paul's Ministry Defense (10:1-12:21)** | Paul Defends His Ministry | Paul vs. False Apostles | Paul's Sufferings as an Apostle | Paul's Thorn in the Flesh | Paul's Concern for Corinthian Church |

| | 13:1-14 Final Warnings/Greetings | |
|---|---|---|

## A Walkthrough of II Corinthians

Before we get into II Corinthians itself, it is necessary to sketch out the historical background that led to the writing of II Corinthians. The reason to do this is simple: I Corinthians is actually Paul's second letter to the Church in Corinth, and II Corinthians is probably his fourth letter, and maybe even contains a fifth. If we just look closely at what Paul said in both I/II Corinthians, here's what we learn:

(1) After Paul founded the Church in Corinth and left, **I Corinthians 5:9-11** tells us that he wrote a letter to them. This is a letter we do not have. I Corinthians, thus, is Paul's second letter to them.
(2) After the writing of I Corinthians, apparently some **Judaizers** had made their way to Corinth, had claimed to be **super-apostles**, and were slandering Paul. When Paul made a surprise visit to Corinth, things got pretty ugly and there was some sort of confrontation between Paul and the ringleader of the super-apostles. It was so tense that Paul decided to quickly leave.
(3) Paul ended up going back to Ephesus, where he wrote his third letter to Corinth (mentioned in **II Corinthians 2:3-4** and **7:8-12**) and sent it by the hand of Titus. It was a very harsh letter in which he rebuked them. We don't have this third letter either. The plan was for Titus to deliver the letter, gauge the Corinthians' reaction, and to pave the way for Paul's third visit. Titus was then to go through Macedonia and meet up with Paul in Troas.
(4) Back in Ephesus, though, Paul experienced some kind of trial in which he thought he might die. After God spared him, he set off for Troas to meet up with Titus. When Titus wasn't there, Paul went into Macedonia to find him. When he did find him, Titus told Paul that the Corinthians had been hurt by the letter but admitted they had done wrong and wanted to reconcile.
(5) At that point, Paul wrote a fourth letter, our II Corinthians. That being said, some scholars believe that **II Corinthians 10-13** might be yet a fifth letter, or possibly the harsh third letter.

We need to keep all that in mind when we read II Corinthians, for that is the context in which it was written. Paul had written an angry letter, and when he heard that the Corinthians had responded well to it, he sat down to write a letter that reflected his relief that they were wanting to reconcile with him after that harsh visit.

### 1. Greeting and Blessing (1:1-11)

Paul's greeting is his standard greeting. In it, he mentions that Timothy is with him, and he addresses his letter not solely to the Church in Corinth, but also to all the Christians in Achaia (Greece). The greeting is followed by a blessing and thanksgiving in which Paul focuses on encouragement in the midst of tribulation. In fact, he refers to encouragement ten times and suffering/tribulation seven times in 1:3-7 alone. Paul's "thesis statement," if you will, is this: *God the Father encourages us in the midst of our tribulations because it is in our sufferings that we share in the sufferings of Christ.* After that, Paul tells the Corinthians about the specific tribulation that he had experienced in Ephesus. He says he thought he was going to die and that he realized all he could do was put his trust in God who is the one who raises the dead, and who did, in fact, save them. Paul then thanks them for their prayers.

### 2. Travelogue (1:12-2:17)

Paul then gives them a recap of his recent travels. In the **first part (1:12-2:4)** of this travelogue, he recounts the events that had led up to the writing of the letter. (These are the events that are briefly outlined above). Paul insists that, despite their confrontation, he had acted with the sincerity of God. Then in an attempt to further reconciliation, he tells them that they are his boast and he is theirs. Simply put, he's saying, "We're all in this together." He reemphasizes what he said in I Corinthians, that he didn't preach with **fleshly wisdom**, but rather with the **grace of God**. And, as he said in I Corinthians 13, he says he hopes they will come to a full understanding, just like they had understood in part, **on the Day of our Lord Jesus**.

He goes on to say that his original plan was to visit them on his way to Macedonia, then to come back through Corinth after his visit to Macedonia, and have them send him off to Judea, presumably with the collection he was planning to take to Judea. But since that initial visit was so contentious, Paul quickly left and then wrote the angry letter (letter #3) that we do not have (2:1-4).

In the **second part (2:5-11)** of this section, Paul makes an appeal for full reconciliation and forgiveness, not only between him and the Corinthian Christians, but specifically with the certain man who evidently was at the center of blow-up. Paul encourages the Corinthians to forgive this man, so that he wouldn't become swallowed up in the pain that he caused. The real problem isn't this man. The one ultimately behind the contention and division is Satan himself, whose intentions are always to foster division. Therefore, to refuse to reconcile would be to let Satan win, and that would have more lasting and more damaging consequences for the Church than the initial conflict.

In the **third part (2:12-17)** of the section, Paul returns to the details of what had happened. When he didn't find Titus in Troas, he went into Macedonia to look for him. At this point in 2:14-16, Paul throws out some vivid imagery to describe how he views his own ministry, that of a **triumphal procession**. In ancient Rome, when there was a military victory for the empire, there was often a triumphal procession (victory parade) in Rome to celebrate the victory. The victorious general would include items and booty taken in the war, as well as hosts of prisoners led in chains throughout the streets of Rome, which were filled with fragrances and incense that commemorated the victory. The prisoners were led to the temple of Jupiter and then ceremonially killed. Depending on who you were, that fragrant incense was either a good thing or a bad thing—if you were a Roman citizen, that fragrant incense said, "You are victorious! Long live Rome!" But if you were a prisoner, that fragrant incense said, "You are doomed!"

Paul takes all that and applies it to himself and his fellow evangelists. In his analogy, though, **he is being led in Christ by God the victorious king in a triumphal procession parade**. So, in that sense, he is like a prisoner. But then he turns around and equates himself **with the fragrant aroma** that would be filling the streets, and then says that those who are being saved (Christians) are the ones who "smell Paul's aroma" and celebrate life, whereas those who are being destroyed (unbelievers) are the ones who smell only the stench of coming death. Simply put, Paul's point is that there is no in-between when it comes to the Gospel. Either people will accept it and celebrate life, or people will reject it and get only death.

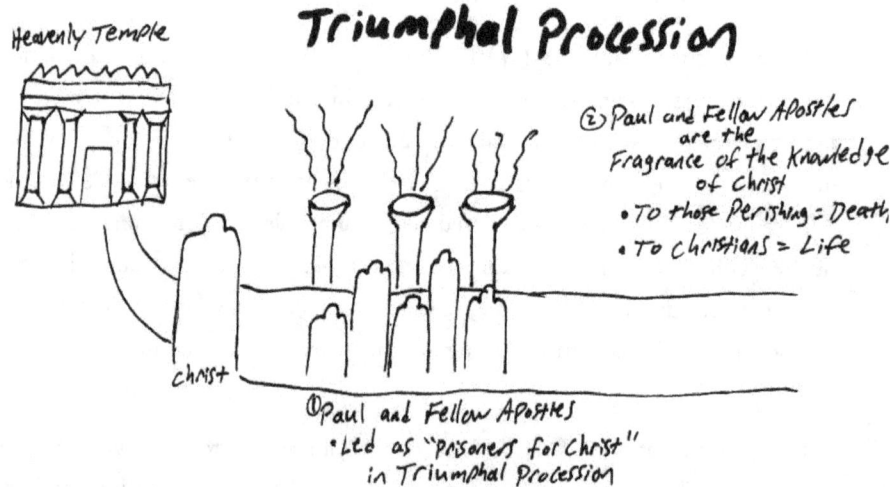

### 3. The New Covenant (3:1-5:10)

In this next section, Paul highlights the significance of the **New Covenant** by making a number of analogies to the Old Testament. In the **first part of the section (3:1-18)**, Paul begins by addressing what the so-called "super-apostles" who had encroached onto Paul's territory had done. They had bad-mouthed Paul to the Corinthian believers and had had shown them some *letters of recommendation* from some religious authorities in Jerusalem. Whoever they were, they were telling the Corinthians that they should listen to them, not Paul.

Paul responds with a truly Spirit-inspired argument in which he draws a clear distinction between the **New Covenant in Christ** and the **Judaism of the Old Covenant**. He says he doesn't need letters of recommendation from Jerusalem because *the Church in Corinth is his recommendation letter* that verifies his authority as an apostle of Christ. Then, by alluding to **Jeremiah 31:31-33** (which speaks of a New Covenant, unlike the Mosaic Covenant), he tells them they are a letter that is *written on his heart*. They, the Church in Corinth, are a **letter of Christ** that was written *with the Spirit of the Living God, not on "tablets of stone" but on "tablets of fleshly hearts."*

As Jeremiah said, the problem with the Old Covenant is that although the Torah was written on stone tablets, it was never "written on the hearts" of the Israelites—they never had a true "change of heart." Even though they had the Torah, they still continued to sin, and because they did, they fell under the judgment of the Torah and died. But the New Covenant would indeed be "written on their hearts," and they would be truly changed by the Spirit of God and they wouldn't fall under the judgment of the Torah anymore. This is what Paul is emphasizing. He doesn't need letters of recommendation from "Old Covenant Jerusalem" because *he is a minister of the New Covenant Jeremiah prophesied about*. The fact that they, Gentile Christians, had received the Spirit of God is all the proof Paul needs to legitimize his ministry.

Paul then goes so far to call the Old Covenant a **ministry of death** that was carved in letters on stone. Because the people's hearts weren't changed, they continued to sin and break the Torah, and the consequence of breaking the Torah was death. Paul then points out that when Moses came down from Sinai, he covered his face with a veil because his face was shining from beholding the glory of God, even though eventually that glory faded from his face. Even though the Old Covenant was a "ministry of death," it was still so glorious that the Israelites couldn't even look on Moses' face until that glory faded.

By contrast, Paul says the **ministry of the Spirit** of the New Covenant will bring about a lasting glory that will never fade. Paul then elaborates on Moses' veil and says the reason Moses had to put a veil over his face was because the Israelites' minds were still dull and hardened, meaning they were still idolatrous and sinful in their thinking. That "veil," Paul says, is still over the hearts of the Israelites whenever the Torah of Moses is read in public. They simply cannot see the thing to which the Torah had always been pointing—Christ. Yet when one comes to the Lord, that "veil" is taken away.

| TWO MINISTRIES/TWO COVENANTS ||
| *Mosaic Covenant* | *New Covenant* |
| --- | --- |
| Written on tablets of stone | Written on tablets of the heart by God's Spirit |
| The basis for the Judaizers' letters of recommendation | A letter of Christ, written on the hearts of the apostles/Paul's own letter of recommendation |
| The Letter (of the Torah) Kills | The Spirit gives Life |
| A Ministry of Death | A Ministry of the Spirit |
| There was *some glory* in the Ministry of Condemnation | *How much more glory* is there in the Ministry of Righteousness |
| A Veil of the Old Covenant | The veil is removed in the New Covenant<br>With unveiled faces:<br>(1) We reflect the glory of the Lord<br>(2) We are transformed into his image |

Interestingly, we can see Paul's trinitarian thinking in this passage. The Greek word in the Septuagint used to refer to YHWH is **Kurios**. Paul, though, is using *Kurios* to refer both to Christ and to the Spirit and says that wherever the *Spirit of the Kurios* is, there is freedom. Freedom from what? The Old Covenant! If we put all that together, we can see that Paul is saying this: *When one comes to the Lord Jesus, one is returning to YHWH. And the Spirit of the Lord Jesus/YHWH gives us freedom from the Old Covenant. When that happens, the "veil" is taken off our faces so that we (unlike Moses!) can reflect the glory of the Lord…who is YHWH…and Christ, and so that we can be transformed by the Spirit* **into the image of God, who is Christ.** Those who accept the Gospel and worship Christ will become like what they worship—namely, true human beings created in God's image who can clearly see and hear, and take part in, the glory of Jesus Christ.

In the **second part (4:1-18)**, Paul further clarifies the nature of his ministry. In 4:1-6, continues to contrast his ministry with the "veil" that anyone who rejects the Gospel has. He says his ministry of the Gospel brings the truth *to light*, and that those who reject the Gospel do so because their minds have been blinded to the light of the Gospel by the **god of this age**. He is the one who essentially blindfolds them with a "veil" to prevent them from seeing the light of the Gospel that reveals the glory of Christ, who is the image of God. The "god of this age" is Satan himself, who uses idols to blind people to the truth, be they literal pagan idols or the Torah itself, which the Jews have effectively turned into an idol.

Then, in 4:7-12, Paul compares Christians' present glimpse of the future glory in Christ here in the old age to **treasure in clay vessels**. Just as clay vessels are fragile and will eventually be smashed, so too is it inevitable for Christians to suffer and die. Yet, it is by suffering and dying that Christians are united with Christ in his suffering and death, so that that very new life and glory can eventually come about. This is what leads Paul to talk about the importance of the resurrection in 4:13-18. Even though suffering and death in this age is inevitable, Christians shouldn't be discouraged, and in fact should continue to rejoice and give glory to God, because the resurrection of Christ guarantees the resurrection of those who accept the Gospel and who put their faith in him. Suffering and death in this age is only temporary.

They may wear down the "outer man," but they have the effect of renewing the "inner man," so that, after death puts our mortal bodies in the ground, the resurrection life that is in Christ will raise us up in our resurrected bodies that are able to the "eternal weight of glory." If we can allude to C.S. Lewis' book, *The Great Divorce*, our current natural bodies are not solid enough to bear the true glory of Christ in the new creation. They must go through death and resurrection to be made solid enough to do that.

In the **third part (5:1-10)**, Paul brings his entire train of thought back to yet another image from the Old Testament—that of **the tabernacle in the wilderness**. He likens our mortal bodies to a tent, and then says even if it is torn down, that Christians have an **eternal house in Heaven** not made with hands. This image of a tent is obviously a reference to the wilderness wanderings during the Exodus, where God's people lived in tents for 40 years, and where God Himself "lived in a tent" with them in the tabernacle. Once the Israelites established themselves in the Promised Land, the tabernacle was replaced with the Temple, which was eventually destroyed when Nebuchadnezzar had taken the Jews into exile. Even though in Paul's day Herod's Temple was still standing, Jesus had prophesied that it would be destroyed within a generation—and that is something that the early Christians continued to proclaim. It would be destroyed because the Jews had turned the Temple into an idol, just like they had done with the Torah.

So, by likening our mortal bodies to a temporary tent and then speaking of an eternal house in Heaven that is *not made with hands*, Paul is saying that our mortal bodies, indeed, everything in this current age of corruption and death, even the Temple itself, is going to die and get torn down. The only "building" that will last is the one that God makes—*one that is not made with human hands*. That is why Paul likens the Christian experience in this old age to having treasure in clay vessels, to groaning in labor pains, and to longing to be fully-clothed in the glory of Christ in Heaven. We have been given a taste of the Age to Come, but we are still experiencing the fragility and pain of the current old age. So, even though our current "home" may be in our mortal bodies within this present age, we are to continue to walk by faith in anticipation of eventually being at home with the Lord in the New Creation that will come about when Christ is fully revealed in glory and the final resurrection happens, when we will all appear before the Judgment Seat of Christ, when we will be repaid for what we have practiced in this "tent" of a body in the present age and old creation.

### 4. Reconciliation (5:11-7:16)

In many ways, this section is a continuation of the previous section, although there is clearly a different emphasis. In this section, Paul turns his attention to what all that means in light of the recent dust-up between him and the Corinthian believers. Simply put, if the New Covenant is all about reconciling God and mankind in Christ, then it is incumbent on them to reconcile with each other. This is what he emphasizes in the **first part (5:11-21)**. The essence of his appeal is crystalized in 5:14-15: *Since Christ has died for all, and since we have all died in him, the life we live now is to be lived in the love of Christ, and that means that we live for others and not ourselves—and that means striving to reconcile with each other.*

He continues in his appeal for reconciliation when he says that even though they are still living in **the old age**, they no longer live **according to the flesh**, both of which are characterized by corruption, death, and division. Now that they are in Christ, they no longer live according to that old way of existence. Instead, they live the life of the **New Creation**, which is characterized by the empowerment of the

Spirit and the ministry of reconciliation, while still living in the old age. This reconciliation has been made possible through the death and resurrection of Christ. So, just as God did not hold our trespasses against us so that we could be reconciled to Him, Paul wants the Corinthians to know that he isn't holding any grudges against them either, and that he simply is encouraging them to reconcile themselves to God. Simply put, reconciliation is the evidence that the New Creation has taken root within the old age.

In the **second part (6:1-10)**, Paul equates their reconciliation with each other to the **Day of Salvation** mentioned in **Isaiah 49:8**: *"At an acceptable time I listened to you, and on the day of salvation I helped you."* That verse is part of a larger section of Isaiah 40-55 that emphasizes how God had redeemed Israel from the Babylonian Exile for the purpose of being *a covenant to the peoples*. In the same way, Paul says that the Corinthians have been redeemed from the bondage of their pagan idolatry and have been reconciled to God for the purpose to bring about the reconciliation of the world to God. But in order for that to happen, they must first reconcile themselves with Paul, so that there won't be any stumbling blocks to anyone coming to the faith. Paul reminds them that throughout his ministry, he has gone out of his way to make sure that no one could find any fault with him. He has endured beatings, slander, and hardship in order to do whatever he can to bring about reconciliation in Christ to the world. Therefore, in light of their conflict, as a minister of the New Covenant, he is offering them reconciliation with himself on a silver platter—all he wants them to do is to take it.

In the **third part (6:11-7:1)**, Paul makes a further contrast between the "super-apostles" and their Torah-based "ministry of death" and his own ministry of the Spirit that brings reconciliation. In doing so, he focuses on two images. The first one is that of being **unequally yoked** with the unfaithful. Paul says that there can be no partnership between **righteousness and lawlessness, light and darkness, Christ and Beliar, the faithful and the unfaithful,** and **the Temple of God and idols**. Although it is tempting to see the reference to "idols" and assume Paul is warning against associating with paganism, we need to realize that the entire focus of the letter thus far has been on dealing with the conflict that had been caused by the Judaizing "super-apostles" who had challenged Paul's legitimacy as a minister of the New Covenant. We should therefore realize that the unequal yoke Paul is warning them against isn't between his Gospel and paganism, but rather between his Gospel and the version of the Gospel that the "super-apostles" were pushing.

Throughout the New Testament, the use of the term **yoke** is used to contrast Jesus' teaching and the Gospel with traditional Jewish teaching. Jesus encouraged people to take his yoke upon them, not that of the Pharisees (**Matthew 11:29-30**). At the Jerusalem Council, Peter says that they should not put the *yoke* of Torah observance on Gentile Christians (**Acts 15:10**). Paul himself, in **Galatians 5:1**, tells Gentile Christians that they are free in Christ and should not *submit to a yoke of slavery*, namely Torah observance. Therefore, it should be obvious that the *unequal yoke* Paul is talking about here is the same thing—either the freedom that comes with the *yoke of Christ* or the slavery that comes with the *yoke of the Torah*.

If we understand this, we should see Paul's contrast to be even more shocking, for not only is he drawing a clear distinction between the Gospel and traditional Judaism, but he is equating the traditional Judaism of the "super-apostles" with lawlessness, darkness, Beliar, unfaithfulness, and idolatry! The Greek word translated as *lawlessness* is **anomos**, which is the antithesis of **nomos**, which is the word used to refer to the Torah. Thus, *anomos* could easily be understood something akin to being "anti-Torah." Thus, Paul is saying that the "super-apostles" who are pushing Torah observance on the Corinthian Christians are actually the *anti-Torah ones* because they are against the *Torah of Christ*. They are the unfaithful ones because they are being unfaithful to Christ. They are the ones associated with Beliar (or Satan) because they are pressuring the Corinthian Christians to be unfaithful to Christ. That is why Paul equates them with idolatry. They are setting up Torah observance as an idol that puts an unequal yoke on Gentile Christians. For Paul, the line of demarcation is no longer *pagan Gentile vs. Torah observant Jew*. It is now *those who are faithful to Christ vs. those who are unfaithful to Christ*. That means idol-worshipping Gentiles and Jews who insist on Torah observance are now in the same boat.

This is why Paul then uses **Temple imagery** to emphasize his contrast between the faithful and the unfaithful. He is telling the Corinthian Christians that they, the Church, are the true **Temple of the Living God**. The true God doesn't live in any one of the 26 pagan temples in Corinth, and He doesn't dwell in the Temple in Jerusalem anymore. His Spirit dwells in the Church. Paul then quotes from **Leviticus 26:12** (where God promises to dwell among His people) and **Isaiah 52:11** (where God calls the faithful remnant to come out from Babylon). His point is simple: The Church is the Temple of the Living God where God's Spirit dwells, so don't have anything to do with the idolatry of "Babylon" and the ways of "the flesh," of which (shockingly) traditional Judaism has shown itself to be a part.

In the **fourth part (7:2-16)**, Paul expresses his joy that the Corinthians had, in fact, taken his harsh letter to heart, repented, and expressed their desire to reconcile with him. He admits that he can sometimes get a bit too bold with them, but he wants them to know that he boasts about them everywhere he goes and that he is overjoyed that, despite their conflict, that they are reconciling with each other. He again apologizes to them if his harsh letter had caused them any pain, but then says he really isn't sorry about it because they had responded the way he hoped they would.

His comment in 7:10 is worth noting, for it to the heart of the choice everyone has when conflict arises. One can either step back and repent of anything one has done to cause the conflict (Godly grief), and thereby make it possible for reconciliation and salvation to happen, or one can dig one's heels in (worldly grief), further the conflict, and in doing so, eventually bring about death. Conflicts are always going to arise, but how we respond to them will determine if they result in salvation or death.

Paul ends by praising the Corinthian Christians for their eagerness to reconcile with him and their determination to let Paul know they really were innocent of causing whatever conflict that had occurred. We don't know exactly what happened, but it seems that those "super-apostles" had come to Corinth and had stirred up the misunderstanding and conflict between Paul and the Corinthian believers. Paul's harsh letter had actually helped clear the air and gotten everything out in the open. In any case, Paul then brags about how great Titus had been through all of it and tells the Corinthians that he had told Titus that he knew that they were going to react well to his harsh letter.

### 5. The Collection (8:1-9:15)

In the next section, Paul addresses the collection ("the grace and fellowship of the ministry for the holy saints") he was raising to help the Church in Judea. In the **first part (8:1-24)**, Paul encourages the Corinthian Christians to contribute generously to his fundraising efforts to help the believers in Judea, even telling them about how generous the believers in Macedonia had been, despite the fact that they were going through tribulations themselves. He then tells them that he is sending Titus back to Corinth so that they could complete what the Macedonian believers started. He doesn't want to come across like he is ordering them to give, though.

Of course, he wants them to give, but he wants them to give freely, by their own choice. Still, it is obvious that he is putting *a little pressure* on them to give. After all, he can't help but point out that, unlike the believers in Macedonia or Judea, the Church in Corinth isn't currently experiencing hardship or tribulation. Therefore, perhaps the reason why they are in such a good position is so that they could be in a position to shore up the collection to help those who are in need.

Paul then tells them that he will be sending Titus and another person ("the brother" in 8:18) back to them to help in the logistics of the collection. After vouching for both Titus and this other "brother," Paul can't help but put a *little more pressure* on them to give when he reminds them that he had bragged to all the other churches about how generous they were, and he really hopes that when Titus comes to collect the money for the believers in Judea that they prove him right!

In the **second part of the section (9:1-15)**, after telling them that he doesn't need to write anymore about the "ministry for the holy saints" (the collection), Paul proceeds *to write more about the collection of the saints!* He tells them that since he had been bragging about how generous they were going to be, he didn't want to come to them right away with some of the Macedonian believers, because if the Corinthians didn't have their gift for the collection ready to go, he would feel a little embarrassed and it would just look bad all around. If that happened, and *then* the Corinthians got their gift ready, it would look like they were being pressured to do it...but Paul knows they really want to give and he doesn't want them to look bad. That is why he is sending Titus ahead to get the Corinthians' gift for the collection ready to go as soon as Paul gets there.

Again, he puts some friendly pressure on them to give generously by telling them if they sow sparingly, they will reap sparingly. Still, Paul reiterates everyone should just give whatever they feel led to give, even though he can't help but re-emphasize again if they generously give to help supply the needs of others, that they will reap a "harvest of righteousness." In fact, the collection for the saints really is like the priestly service in the Temple. Not only do priests render service for the needs of people, but they also offer up thanksgiving to God. The bottom line is that when you help others in need, you are also giving thanks to God and glorifying Him.

### 6. Paul Defends His Ministry (10:1-12:21)

Given the way II Corinthians 9 ends, with Paul and the Corinthians reconciled and talking about taking a collection to help the struggling believers in Judea, it seems like a good conclusion to the letter. That is what makes II Corinthians 10-13 a bit odd, for in these chapters, Paul is (again) defending his ministry against the accusations made by the so-called "super-apostles." He goes so far as to call them false prophets. This is why some believe that II Corinthians 10-13 might actually be the "harsh letter" that would have been Paul's third letter. We cannot know for sure, but given the tone of these chapters, it certainly isn't out of the realm of possibility. Whatever the case, we have to understand these chapters in the context of the conflict with the "super-apostles." They were flaunting their own letters of recommendation and belittling Paul's ministry by saying he didn't have the proper "credentials" to be an apostle. In his attempt to defend his ministry, Paul knows he can't get dragged into a bragging contest. Nevertheless, he is faced with the challenge of *sort of bragging* about his qualifications to be an apostle, while at the same time saying that the kind of qualifications he shares with the super-apostles really don't matter that much. Instead, he needs to highlight the kind of "qualifications" that really do matter.

Paul begins in the **first part (10:1-18)** by stressing that even though he and his ministry partners *walk in the flesh*, that they are not *walking according to the flesh*. In other words, Paul is saying that although he is still living here in the old age, he does not conduct his life in the "old age" kind of way. That's what the "super-apostles" are, in fact, doing when they sow division in the Corinthian Church. Paul says they are "waging war" with *the weapons of the flesh*. By contrast, Paul says that he is in the business of *tearing down arguments* that hinder the knowledge of God and doesn't care to flaunt his credentials.

He then stresses the importance of Christian unity by pointing out that when the "super-apostles" claim that he (and the Corinthian believers) don't belong to Christ as much as them, that *they are, in fact, the ones who are causing division*. Paul admits that his letter might be coming off as a bit harsh, but they know full well that he never seems to be that harsh in person. That being said, he says he will be as harsh as his letters if the situation calls for it. He then says that he won't compare himself to those super-apostles who are commending themselves. Instead, he says he is going to let his personal relationship with them be all the credentials they need. This is what he means by "not boasting beyond limits," which is a subtle jab at the "super-apostles." After all, they were essentially encroaching on Paul's turf and trying to discredit him in the very church he started by appealing to commendations from outside of Corinth.

In the **second part (11:1-15)**, even though Paul has just said he won't compare himself to those "super-apostles," he realizes he has to address them somehow. So, even though he says up front that he realizes that to do so is to engage in a bit of foolishness, he does so anyway. He says that since he feels like a husband to the Church in Corinth, having established it, he views the "super-apostles" as the serpent who tempted Eve. They are leading the Corinthians away from total devotion to Christ by proclaiming "another Jesus." Therefore, Paul warns them against receiving **another spirit** or **another gospel** than the one they had accepted from him.

In any case, Paul comes right now and says he is not inferior to the "super-apostles" in any way, shape, or form. He might not speak as well as they do, but that doesn't mean he is inferior in the knowledge of the Gospel. In fact, he went out of his way to make sure there were no obstacles for the Corinthians to receive the Gospel. He reminds them that he "humbled himself" when he came to Corinth and even made it a point not to let them pay him in any way. He took support from his other churches so that the Corinthians didn't have to support him at all. That way, he could literally say he offered the Gospel to them as a gift.

The reason he brought up the fact that he humbled himself and had preached the Gospel to the Corinthians for free was because evidently that was something that these "super-apostles" *weren't doing*. By contrast, they were all about commending themselves and charging people to hear their message. So, when they told the Corinthians that Paul wasn't like them, Paul is responding with, "You're darn right, I'm not like them!" He goes so far to say that not only are they not "super-apostles," but they are, in fact, **false apostles** and **dishonest workers** who are disguising themselves as apostles of Christ. He then goes even further by equating them with Satan who disguises himself as an angel of light.

In the **third part (11:16-33)**, Paul is clearly getting worked up. It is as if he is saying, *"They like to boast about themselves, do they? Well, alright then! Let's boast! I know I'm coming across as a fool here, but let's go!"* With that, Paul proceeds to do something quite creative. Since the Judaizers where pressuring Gentile believers to submit to the Torah, that would include getting circumcised *in the flesh*. We've already seen that Paul has equated that with *walking according to the flesh* and *waging war according to the flesh*. Therefore, since the "super-apostles" insisted on boasting about his own credentials *in the flesh*, Paul decides to do a little boasting himself regarding his own credentials "in the flesh."

Not only does he have the same "Jewish credentials" they have, but his flesh has literally suffered severe beatings, imprisonments, shipwrecks, and many other tribulations. Simply put, he's not going to boast about his *circumcision in the flesh*. He'll only boast about the *tribulations his flesh has endured for the sake of the Gospel*. On top of that, there is the pressure he feels for caring for all the churches he has founded. He then remembers probably the first instance of his life being in danger for the sake of the Gospel when he had to escape from Damascus in a basket shortly after his conversion in order to avoid being arrested and killed.

In the **fourth part (12:1-10)**, Paul then "boasts" about the visions and revelations he has had. He shifts to the third person, though, when talking about a revelatory, mystical experience he had fourteen years earlier (which would place it around AD 42). He doesn't go into any detail as to what he experienced, but he is insistent that the experience was real and obviously had a major impact on his life.

In any case, he then says that it was because of these visions and revelations, God gave him a **thorn in the flesh** to keep him humble and keep him from becoming arrogant because of his visions. He says he prayed to God three times to remove it, but God told him that His grace was enough, and His power was made perfect in weakness. No one knows for sure what Paul's thorn in the flesh was, but many believe it was some sort of poor eyesight or partial blindness, stemming from his initial Damascus Road encounter with the resurrected Jesus. Paul then says that if he is going to really boast about anything, it is going to be about his own weakness, be it his sufferings, trials, or "thorn in the flesh"—for it is in those weaknesses that the power of Christ is most evident.

In the **fifth part (12:11-21)**, Paul makes a final appeal to the Corinthians to have nothing to do with the "super-apostles." Not only is he not inferior to them in any way, but the signs and acts of power that he had done while in Corinth are all the "credentials" he needs. He then again reminds them that he went out of his way to make sure he wasn't a financial burden to them at all, and sarcastically says "Please forgive me for this wrong!" After that, Paul proceeds to tell them that he is planning to come to see them for a third time, and that he still won't be a burden to them and will make sure he pays all his own expenses. After all, since he founded the Church in Corinth, he is like their father, and children shouldn't have to care for their father, but rather the other way around. He also points out that Titus and "the brother" also didn't take advantage of them when Paul sent them to Corinth.

Paul then contemplates his upcoming visit to Corinth and fears that it might be a difficult visit, although he hopes it isn't.

### 7. Final Warnings and Greetings (13:1-14)

Paul ends his letter with a bit of a threat in **13:1-4**. After reminding them that it will be the third time that he comes to them, he seems to hint that if those who had caused the initial conflict still were going to try to fight, he was ready, willing, and able to fight. His comment in 13:1 about how any accusation should be backed up by at least two or three witnesses seems to suggest that he is telling anyone who wants to accuse him of anything, that they had better have actual proof of any real wrongdoing on his part. And then, in 13:2-4, he issues the threat: *"If you doubt that I'm really speaking for Christ, challenge me when I get there, and you'll see the power of Christ on full display!"*

In **13:5-10**, Paul encourages the Corinthians to examine themselves to see if they are truly "in the faith." Given the fact that there had been a conflict with these "super-apostles," it seems Paul is basically saying, "Take stock in what you really believe and who you really want to align yourselves with." Finally, **13:11-14** is the part of the letter that Paul would have written with his own hand in order to authenticate the letter as truly coming from him. In it, he once again encourages them and expresses his hope and prayer for them to live in unity and peace.

# ROMANS

**Time of Writing:** During the end of Paul's third missionary journey, from Corinth (AD 55-56)

### History of the City/Paul (not) in Rome

By Paul's day, the city of Rome had become the greatest city in the Roman Empire, if not the world. It was truly a multicultural city in every sense of the word. According to ancient standards, Rome had everything from sanitation, public baths, public latrines, aqueducts, police and fire departments, monuments, theaters, public games, not to mention being the seat of government power. Simply put, the "city on seven hills" was the center of the Roman world.

Paul did not establish the church in Rome. It was begun when Jews who had accepted Jesus as the Messiah at Pentecost moved to Rome. As Gentile God-fearers were coming to accept Christ, though, there developed within the Jewish community a controversy over Jesus himself. The Jewish-Christians were claiming he was the Messiah, while the traditional Jews were claiming he was not. The controversy became so volatile that the Emperor Claudius ended up issuing the famous **Edit of Claudius** in AD 49, in which he expelled all Jews from Rome because of a conflict of a certain man named **Chrestus**, very likely a reference to Christ.

The expulsion of all Jews from Rome had significant consequences for the Church. For a number of years, the only Christians in Rome were Gentile Christians. When Jews were eventually allowed back into Rome, the Jewish Christians also returned. But in those intervening years, the Gentile Christians had developed their own church culture that was decidedly different than that of the Jewish Christians. The result was that within Rome, Gentile Christians and Jewish Christians had little to do with each other. They were "in Christ" in name only. Societal and cultural factors separated the two groups from one another.

Paul's purpose in writing his letter, therefore, was two-fold. First, he wanted to introduce himself and his gospel to the believers in Rome in order to hopefully establish a new base of operations for a future missionary journey to Spain. Second, he wanted to address the current situation among the Christians in Rome and to get the Jewish Christians and the Gentile Christians to accept each other. As far as Paul was concerned, if they couldn't worship together as the Body of Christ, then the Gospel has failed. Therefore, everything in the letter is directed toward that end.

## The Big Things to Know About Romans

A. **Paul's Gospel, Laid Out in Eight Chapters**: More than anything else in Paul's letters, Romans 1-8 crystallizes the Gospel that he preached throughout his career as an apostle.

B. **Two Ways of Living**: When it comes down to it, you can either live *according to the flesh*, which means enslavement to this world and ultimately death, or *according to the Spirit*, which means being set free from the bondage of the world and ultimately leads to experiencing resurrection life.

C. **Paul's Hope for Israel's Repentance and Restoration**: In Romans 9-11, Paul expresses his hope that his fellow Jews who had rejected Christ would see the work of the Holy Spirit among Gentile Christians and eventually come to Christ.

D. **What It Means to Live as the People of God**: The practical outworking of the Gospel is seen in Paul's appeal in Romans 12-15 for Christians from different socio-cultural and racial backgrounds to live as one, unified people of God.

## Literary Map: Romans

|  | | | | | |
|---|---|---|---|---|---|
| | **1:1-17** Greeting/Prayer Report Thesis Statement | | | | |
| **Sin Torah Righteous-ness (1:18-4:25)** | 1:18-32 All Gentiles are Sinners | 2:1-29 All Jews are Sinners | 3:1-20 Advantage for the Jew? Torah: All Unrighteous | 3:21-31 Righteousness of God comes apart from Torah | 4:1-25 The Example of Abraham |
| **How is One Righteous Without Torah? (5-8)** | 5:1-11 Last Days Worldview | | 5:12-21 Adam and Christ | | 6:1-7:6 Baptism, Slavery, Marriage Imagery |
| | 7:7-25 Paul's Former Way of Life "in the Flesh" | | 8:1-30 Walk According to the Flesh or the Spirit | | 8:31-39 Doxology and Praise |
| **What is God Doing with Ethnic Israel? (9-11)** | 9:1-5 Lament for Israel | 9:6-29 Question of God's faithfulness to his Word | 9:30-10:21 Israel's responsibility for missing out on God's Salvation | 11:1-32 Has God actually rejected ethnic Israel? | 11:33-36 Doxology Confession |
| **Living as One People of God (12:1-15:13)** | 12:1-21 Living the Life of the Holy Spirit within the Community of Faith | | 13:1-14 Living the Life of the Holy Spirit within the Pagan World: Submitting to Authority | | 14:1-15:13 Getting Jewish-Christians and Gentile-Christians to Accept One Another |
| **Personal Matters (15:14-16:27)** | 15:14-32 Personal Message and Upcoming Plans | | 16:1-23 Personal Greetings and Final Instructions | | 16:25-27 Doxology |

## A Walkthrough of Romans

### 1. Greeting, Prayer Report, Thesis Statement (1:1-18)

Paul begins Romans with a standard greeting and prayer report. In his greeting (1:1-7), Paul identifies himself as a **servant** of Christ Jesus, and as an **apostle** for the Gospel of God. As far as the Gospel that he preaches is concerned, Paul emphasizes it is about Jesus Christ, whom he describes as the **Jewish Messiah** (descendant of David) and the **Son of God** who, because of his resurrection from the dead, is **Lord**, meaning the Lord of all creation. In other words, because he demonstrated the power to defeat death, which characterizes everything in this creation, Jesus shows himself to have the power to rule all creation.

In 1:8-15 Paul tells the Church in Rome that he had been wanting to visit Rome for quite a while but had been unable to do so. Since he was not the one who founded the Church in Rome, he goes out of his way to say that he wants to visit the Christians in Rome, not only to "impart some Spiritual gift" to strengthen them, but to allow be mutually encouraged by them. Simply put, even though he didn't start the Church in Rome, he hopes to be able to come to Rome and help them spread the Gospel to more people.

At this point, in 1:16-17, Paul lays out what can be seen as the **thesis statement** of the entire letter. When it comes right down to it, the central issue is this: *"Who are the People of God?"* Paul is going to argue that the goal of God's salvation has always been to create *one people for God's Name* and that He chose Israel to be His special people in the Old Testament to be a "light to the Gentiles," so that Gentiles would come to Him and that ultimately *God's people would consist of both Jews and Gentiles*.

In other words, Israel was chosen to be the people through whom God would achieve His purpose to create one people for His Name. They weren't the fulfillment of His purpose. This, though, was not clearly obvious yet to many people in the early 60s. There was an assumption that since the Jews were "God's people," that if a Gentile wanted to become part of God's people, he would have to become a Jew. There were even some Jewish-Christians in the early Christian movement who still thought Gentiles who had accepted Christ still had to then become Jews and submit to the Torah. This is the very thing that Paul is going to argue against.

He begins in 1:16 by saying, *"I am not ashamed of the Gospel."* He isn't saying he's not *embarrassed* by the Gospel, but rather is alluding to **Psalm 24:2**: "My God, in you I trust; do not let me be *put to shame.*" He is saying the Gospel will not let him down—it is trustworthy and reliable. Furthermore, Paul says that the Gospel is, *"the power of God for salvation to everyone who has faith, for the Jew first, and also to the Greek."* Right there, he is emphasizing that it is the Gospel that has the power of salvation for both Jews *as Jews* and Gentiles *as Gentiles*. Paul continues in 1:17 by saying that it is in the Gospel that **God's righteousness** is revealed. Now, Paul explains what this means in the course of his letter (and scholars have written countless books on this), but if I was to reduce it to its simplest terms I would say that God's righteousness involves two things: (1) God's judgment of sin (He wouldn't be righteous if He let sin go unpunished), and (2) God providing a way for sinful human beings to become truly holy and righteous as Christ is holy and righteous.

The Greek word for "righteousness" is pronounced *dikaiosunae*, but the verbal form *dikaioo* is translated in English as "to justify," and the word *dikaiosin* is translated as **justification**. The problem is that when most people read their Bibles in English, they see words like *justification* and *to justify* and don't really realize how closely they are connected to the concept of **righteousness**. They see justification as more of a **legal term** and interpret it as: God is the judge and human beings are guilty sinners deserving the death penalty. Jesus accepts the punishment we deserve, and then God *declares us to be righteous*. We become what John Calvin characterized as "snow-covered dung." The problem with that view is that we aren't really actually made righteous.

If we understand justification as not just a legal pronouncement, but the actual act of God making human beings righteous, if we understand it more as a **moral term**, things make a bit more sense. In this view, God is the physician and human beings are suffering from the disease of sin that will lead to death if not treated. Jesus' crucifixion and the outpouring of the Holy Spirit, therefore, is seen as God's prescription and rehabilitation program to restore us to full Spiritual health, where we are actually made righteous, just like Christ is righteous. For that reason, perhaps instead of reading "to justify" we should read it as "to *righteousize*."

In any case, when Paul says that the righteousness of God is "revealed from faith for faith," it should obvious that we cannot understand "justification" solely in legal terms, for Paul is writing to Christians here. He's not explaining to them *how they get saved*—they already are saved. He is explaining *how one lives once one gets saved*. Thus, salvation **begins with the faithfulness of Christ**, and the righteousness that comes through the Gospel is made complete through our continued **faithfulness to Christ**. As **Habakkuk 2:4** says, "The righteous will *live by faith*." You are made righteous through faith, not by doing works of Torah.

### 2. Sin, Torah, and Righteousness (1:18-4:25)

With that, Paul now begins to methodically lay out his argument that the salvation and righteousness of the believer comes on the basis of faith alone, whether that person is a Jew or a Gentile. To do that, Paul must first show that both Gentiles and Jews are sinners in need of salvation. So, he begins in this **first part (1:18-32)** by giving a thoroughly *Jewish* understanding of the *Gentile world*. The bottom line is simple: The Gentile world is sinful and deserves God's wrath. In order to follow Paul's argument, it is important to understand the significance of the biblical understanding of God's wrath. The Greek word for wrath is *orgay*, and it is used almost exclusively to describe God's punishment of the wicked and ungodly. So here, from the Jewish perspective, what Paul says here in 1:18-32 makes complete sense, for that is how they viewed the Gentile world.

Paul then goes on to explain that the reason why the Gentile world will suffer God's wrath is because they have **rejected and suppressed the truth about God** that can be clearly seen in the natural world. Therefore, the Gentile world is **without excuse**. This failure to acknowledge the true God, led to their minds becoming darkened. Because they didn't use their God-given rational faculties to acknowledge God, they lost their ability to reason. Paul says even though they might claim to be wise, in reality they are fools, and the ultimate expression of such foolishness can be seen in the idolatry of the pagan world, where people worship objects that their own hands have made.

This gets us to a fundamental theme throughout the entire Bible: You become like what you worship. If you worship the true God in whose image you are made, you become truly human, but if you worship images that your own hands have made, you become less than human. Not only do you become blind and deaf like those lifeless idols, but you also become more beast-like and more ruled by your baser instincts and passions, because many of those idols were fashioned in images of beasts. That is why, as Paul says in 1:24-27, God gave idol-worshippers over to the lusts of their hearts. The natural consequence of idolatry is that God allows human beings to act like the beasts they have become.

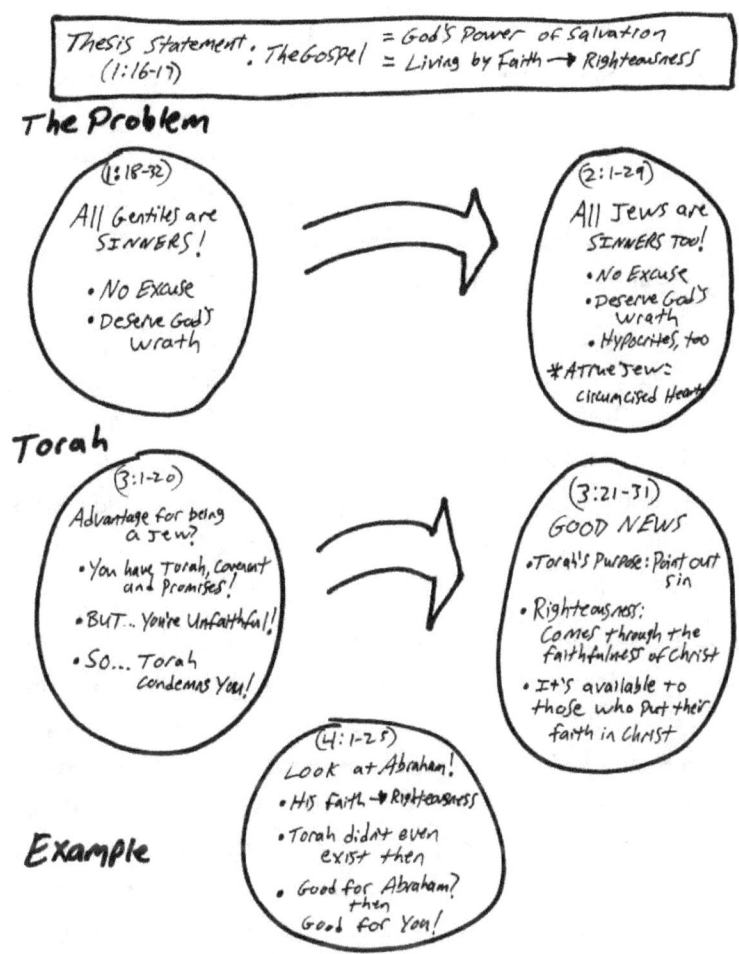

That is why Paul specifically mentions the sort of sexual libertine practices that were routinely done in pagan temples. In the Greco-Roman world, it was seen as a normal and good thing for a married man to go to a pagan temple, offer his sacrifice to a particular god or goddess, and then hire a temple prostitute (a woman, girl, man, or boy) and have sex as a part of his pagan worship. We must be clear that this is what Paul was talking about. He wasn't talking about our modern concept of *homosexuality* or *sexual orientation*.

That is not to say that Paul would ever endorse any kind of same-sex sexual activity—he almost certainly never would. The point is that here Paul is specifically highlighting pagan sexual practices associated with pagan temples. When seen in light of his argument, it isn't hard to see why. He chooses to highlight same-sex sex acts because it represents the foolishness of the Gentile "darkened mind." When it comes to the biological function of sex, same-sex sexual activity is literally unnatural and, as true back then as is today, brought about a variety of painful sexual diseases. Yet, in the pagan world, such practices *were considered a part of worship*. Paul's point is that was the natural outcome of a society that rejects the true God and turns to worshipping things made of their own hands.

Paul ends his indictment of the Gentile world in 1:28-32 by saying that God gave them over to **a worthless mind**, and then proceeding to give a laundry list of wicked and evil behavior. What Paul is saying is that the pagan Gentile world, because it has rejected the true God, is experiencing the wrath of God—God has let them suffer the consequences of their actions. The pagan world has become what it worshipped. They have become senseless and violent beasts who are ruled by their unbridled passions and lusts.

In the **second part (2:1-29)**, though, Paul then turns his attention to his fellow Jews and proceeds to argue that they are really no better than Gentiles. If the Gentile world is sinful, and if sinfulness deserves God's wrath, and if God is truly righteous and impartial when it comes to dealing with sin, then Jews, like the Gentiles, are **without excuse** and just as deserving of **God's wrath**. But Paul doesn't highlight just Jewish sinfulness, he also highlights Jewish hypocrisy. As he states in 2:1-11, the Jews were quick to condemn Gentile sinfulness, but then were all too ready to overlook their own. Because of that, they were storing up wrath for themselves on the coming **Day of Wrath**. Paul's point is simple: **God doesn't show favoritism and He will give everyone what they deserve.** Those who do good, be they Jews or Gentiles, will receive glory, honor, and peace, and those who practice evil, be they Jews or Gentiles, will receive God's wrath and anger.

In 2:12-16, Paul then emphasizes to his fellows Jews that *having the Torah* doesn't mean anything if one doesn't *keep the Torah*. Thus, Jews who don't keep the Torah are proven just as wicked as Gentiles. Paul goes on to say that the real issue is whether or not one has the Torah *written on one's heart*. He is alluding here to **Jeremiah 31:31-33**, when Jeremiah looked forward to the day when God would establish a **New Covenant**, one that wasn't written on stone tablets like the Mosaic covenant but was

**written on human hearts** by the Holy Spirit. When understood in relation to **Joel 2:28-32**, where God says a day will come when He would pour out His Spirit on all flesh, Paul is relating the fundamental worldview of the early Church: *The New Covenant has come, God's Spirit has been poured out on all flesh (even Gentiles), and thus Gentile believers, because of the empowerment of the Holy Spirit, display the righteousness that the Mosaic Torah was pointing to all along. This is true both for Jews and Gentiles.*

Simply put, having the Torah doesn't matter, truly embodying what the Torah is all about is what matters—and that only comes through the work of the Holy Spirit. Thus, Paul makes a shocking claim: *True Israel* consists of those who have had the Torah "written on their hearts" by the Holy Spirit, regardless if they were Jews or Gentiles. That means that *ethnicity is irrelevant when it comes to salvation and righteousness*. This is what Paul drives home in 2:17-24, as he attacks Jewish sinfulness and hypocrisy in the same way he attacked Gentile sinfulness in 1:18-32. Simply having Torah means nothing, because Jews who have the Torah not only don't keep it, but they actually find ways to get around the Torah. This kind of behavior, Paul says, dishonors God and **blasphemes God's Name** to the Gentile world. Simply put, the Jews give God a bad reputation.

Paul picks up on the issue of circumcision in 2:25-29 and says that it is utterly worthless if you don't actually keep the Torah and that it counts for nothing in terms of righteousness. Paul then alludes to **Deuteronomy 10:16** to show that the only kind of circumcision that matters is the **circumcision of the heart**. Obviously, this does not mean some kind of physical procedure done on one's actual heart. It is a metaphor that emphasizes the transformative work of the Holy Spirit on the person at his/her deepest level (a true "change of heart").

Therefore, it is the **circumcision of the heart by the Holy Spirit** that is the true identity marker of the people of God from all nations, not the Old Testament circumcision of the flesh. This, as we will see, is the fulfillment of the Abrahamic covenant, in which God said that He would create a great nation out of Abraham (the nation of Israel), and that *through* that nation *all nations would be blessed*. God had worked through Israel to bring about Jesus the Messiah, and the Messiah had sent the Holy Spirit to be poured out on all flesh. Paul is saying that now all nations are experiencing that blessing promised in the Abrahamic covenant.

Paul then turns his attention in the **third part (3:1-20)** to explain that just because having the Torah doesn't give Jews any advantage in terms of righteousness, they still do, in fact, have some advantages, the major one being that they were given the **oracles of God** (3:2)—*the Torah*! How can Paul say that, given what he has just said? Simple: the Torah outlines what a godly life in relationship with God looks like, and that's a good thing to know! But that advantage doesn't change the fact that, as the entire Old Testament shows, the Jews had been unfaithful to God. Paul then puts forth three objections that Jews might have to what he is saying.

- (1) **"If some Jews were unfaithful, does that mean God won't be faithful to the covenant?"** Paul responds with a resounding "No." Just because the Jews were unfaithful to the Mosaic covenant, God is still faithful to the promises He made in His covenant with Abraham and will be proven just in His judgments."
- (2) **"If Jewish unrighteousness actually ended up helping God display His righteousness, then how could God punish them?"** Paul responds with, "God would be unjust if He *didn't* punish sin. How could He punish Gentiles for their sin if He doesn't Jews for theirs?"
- (3) **"If Jewish falsehood just goes to show how truthful God is, then how could Jews be condemned as sinners?"** Basically, "I like to sin, and God likes to forgive sin! What's the problem?" To that, Paul says that is actually the sort of thing some Jews were accusing him of teaching the Gentiles. They were claiming that since he was telling Gentiles they didn't have to keep Torah and become Jews, that he was encouraging them to sin. Paul is clear—that is absurd.

Paul's point is simply that you cannot have *faith in Christ* without *faithfulness to him*. No outward show of religiosity, be it circumcision, keeping the Sabbath, or keeping the Jewish food laws, is worth anything without personal faithfulness to Christ. Paul then unleashes a slew of Old Testament quotations in 3:9-18 to prove that the Torah itself, the thing they take such pride in having, points out that throughout their history the Jews have been disobedient and rebellious. The Torah, thus, condemns Jews for their sin. And that really is the purpose of the Torah: *To bring the whole world under God's righteous indictment*. Its purpose all along was to bring a *guilty verdict*. The **works of Torah** were *never* intended to be a way to make us righteous before God. Rather, the purpose of the Torah was to *make sin known*.

To make a modern analogy, the Torah is like the **medical report** the doctor gives you that tells you that you are suffering from cancer. If you take the medical report and say, "Hey, as long as I have this medical report, I'm going to be fine," you're going to die. The medical report's purpose is simply to diagnose the problem for you. It can never make you better. That is what Paul is saying concerning the Torah. It is God's medical report that diagnoses the "cancer of sin." Gentiles were suffering from the "cancer of sin," but they didn't know exactly what the problem was. Jews were also suffering from the "cancer of sin," but God, through the Torah, had revealed to them precisely what the problem was. Nevertheless, the Torah can't do anything about the problem. A cure for that had to come from someplace else...for a medical report cannot cure cancer.

That leads to the **fourth part (3:21-31)**, where Paul lays out what exactly the cure is and where it comes from. The righteousness of God that can cure that "cancer of sin" comes to us *completely apart from Torah* (3:21). Instead, it comes *through the faithfulness of Christ*, and comes to *everyone* who puts their *faith in Christ*. In 3:23-24 Paul spells it out: Everyone (both Jew and Gentile) has fallen short of the glory of God and everyone (both Jew and Gentile) is made righteous by God's grace, through the redemption in Christ Jesus. That is the Gospel in a nutshell.

Paul then uses **Day of Atonement** imagery to further describe the significance of the work of Christ. On that day, the high priest would go into the Holy of Holies to sprinkle the blood on the Ark of the Covenant, and thus atone for the sins of the nation (**Leviticus 16**). Atonement is essentially an action that serves to correct any wrongdoing a person (or a nation) might have done. In the Old Testament, God's prescribed action for Israel was to bring a specific kind of sacrifice before Him on a specific day of the year. Paul says those actions on the Day of Atonement foreshadowed the ultimate atonement accomplished by Christ.

We must remember, though, that the ultimate purpose of the Old Testament sacrifices wasn't just to atone for sins, but ultimately to restore a right relationship with God. The fulfillment of the Old Testament sacrificial system, therefore, is found in Christ's sacrificial death. God shows Himself to be **righteous and just** by punishing sin, but then also shows that He is the one who **makes righteous** the one who has faith in Jesus. God doesn't just pardon us or acquit us. He, in fact, makes us righteous through Christ and the indwelling presence of the Holy Spirit.

Thus, the Torah can only describe what a life in relationship with God is like, it can't give you that relationship with God. Only God's grace, the faithfulness of Jesus Christ, and the indwelling Holy Spirit can do that. Still, the ultimate aim of salvation isn't just one's individual salvation. Paul emphasizes that the ultimate aim of salvation is to create **a people for God's Name**. Once we realize that is what Paul is getting at, we will see that the way in which we relate to each other is intimately tied to the way God makes us righteous.

Paul ends by answering three questions when it comes to the issues of the Torah and the relationship between Jews and Gentiles.

- (1) **"Where is boasting** (about having the Torah)?" Paul says there can't be any. The Jew cannot brag that because he does the "works of Torah" that he is more righteous than a Gentile Christian.
- (2) **"Is God only of the Jews** (or is He also the God of the Gentiles)?" Paul says of course He is God of both Jews and Gentiles, not on the basis of Torah, though, but rather on the basis of Christ. It is the faithfulness of Christ that makes you righteous, not any kind of outward show of religiosity you may do.
- (3) **"Does that mean we do away with the Torah?"** Paul says absolutely not. Rather, we do away with the *works of Torah*, namely those Jewish identity markers that distinguish them from Gentiles, because those works of Torah mean nothing in regard to righteousness. When it comes down to it, Paul is saying that there is a new Torah in town—the **Torah of faith**. It is faith in Christ that actually empowers us to live the righteous life that the Torah spells out. In that sense, faith in Christ actually confirms the Torah.

In the **fifth part (4:1-25)**, Paul talks about Abraham, the "father of the Jews," to drive home his argument about being made righteous through faith, and not through the works of Torah. He starts by quoting Genesis 15:6: *"But Abraham put his faith in God, and it was counted to him as righteousness"* in order to show that the Torah itself says that it was Abraham's faith that was counted as righteousness, not doing the works of Torah. In fact, it couldn't have been through the works of Torah, because Abraham lived over 400 years before the Torah was even given through Moses. Paul then goes on to argue that if someone "works" for something, then his wages are earned and are not a gift. By contrast, it is the one who doesn't "work," but rather puts his faith in the one who justifies the ungodly, (makes them righteous), whose faith is counted as righteousness.

For a Jew, this is a shocking statement, for Jews believed that God would justify them (make them righteous) because they did the works of Torah and thus proved that they were "godly." Essentially, they believed that if they practiced Torah, that God was *obligated* to make them righteous! God would "righteousize" the godly because they practiced Torah! But Paul has insisted that both Jews and Gentiles were equally *ungodly*, and therefore if the Jewish outlook were true, then no one would ever be made righteous because no one was truly godly. Thus, Paul insists that the ungodly person's *faith* is counted to him as righteousness, and the "godly" person's *work* counts for nothing in regard to righteousness...**because "godly" people aren't really godly.**

Paul then goes back to Abraham to make the obvious point that when Abraham's faith was counted to him as righteousness, *it was before he was circumcised.* Circumcision was simply an outward sign of a previous inward decision to put one's faith in God. Therefore, circumcision in and of itself, along with all the Torah regulations, means nothing without a decision to put one's faith in God. That is what puts Jews and Gentiles on the same level. Abraham is the father of the *circumcised Jews* who have put their faith in God, and he's also the father of the *uncircumcised Gentiles* who have put their faith in God. Paul then alludes to God's promise to Abraham that he would have a son, and that through Isaac that God would eventually bring salvation to the world and bless all nations. God made that promise to Abraham, not because he kept the Torah, but because Abraham put his faith in God.

Paul then points out that Abraham's faith in God was rooted in the conviction that God could bring life from the dead. First, he had faith that God could bring new life out from the infertile and "dead" bodies of himself and Sarah. Second, he had faith that God could somehow raise Isaac from the dead, even if Abraham sacrificed and killed him. This is why Abraham's faith was counted to him as righteousness—*it was a faith in the God who could bring life from the dead.* Paul then makes the obvious connection to Jesus, whom God literally raised from the dead. Thus, the faith that is counted as righteousness is the faith in the God who raises the dead. That is the faith of Abraham, and that is the faith that is available to both Jews and Gentiles, regardless of the Torah.

### 3. How is One Righteous without Torah? (5:1-8:39)

With the first major section of his letter done, Paul now sets out a new argument in Romans 5-8 that addresses a fundamental Jewish concern: *If you get rid of the Torah, then how can you deal with sin and how can you guarantee righteous behavior?* In other words, if you get rid of the Torah, how will you know what is right and what is wrong? How will you live a righteous life? Let's face it, that's a pretty good question! When it comes to morality, people tend to want some sort of rule book to define good and bad behavior for them, so they know exactly what the can and shouldn't do. Paul isn't going to give one, though. In fact, he's going to argue that the instinct to want a rule book actually reflects an **"old age" way of thinking** that is centered on sin, death, the "flesh," and ironically the Torah.

Instead, he's going to argue that what keeps the Christian from being dominated by sin isn't another kind of rule book, but rather a new kind of life that is characterized by the **New Age way of thinking** that is centered on righteousness, life, the Holy Spirit, faith, and grace. Simply put, he's going to argue that you don't need another rule book, because you are living out the resurrection life of the new Messianic Age and are empowered by the Holy Spirit.

The **first part (5:1-11)** acts as the first "bookend" to this section, with **8:31-39** being the second "bookend." It is important to see the "already/not yet" Christian worldview that permeates everything Paul says here. Right from the beginning, Paul speaks of what has happened **already** for Christians (*Having been 'righteousized' by faith*) and then of what has **not yet** happened that they have to continue on in faith to achieve (*Let us have peace with God through our Lord Jesus Christ*). His point is that through Christ, we are no longer God's enemies, but now have access to God's grace. Therefore, *we need to take advantage of God's grace and pursue peace with God*. What Paul means by **peace** here is to be understood in terms of the kind of peace that is instituted after a war. Paul is saying, if you will, *"The war with God is over, the hostilities have ceased! So, sign the peace treaty and live your lives in that peace with God—your former enemy, but now your beloved king!"*

In 5:2-5, Paul continues this line of thinking by encouraging the Roman Christians, *"Let us boast in the hope of glory,"* and *"Let us boast in hardships."* Boasting in the hope of glory is understandable, but what about boasting in hardships? Paul's explanation is simple: **Hardships** brings endurance, and **endurance** refines our character, and **refined character** produces that **hope that will not result in shame**. Simply put, the reason we boast in hardships is because they are the building blocks of our hope in Christ, just like an athlete goes through the "hardships" of training in order to win the prize.

In 5:6-11, Paul discusses the problem with human righteousness. It is often more like self-righteousness. The problem with a self-righteous person is that he often is not that good of a person. Much like the Pharisees, he doesn't really care for others. He sees himself as so "righteous," that he makes it a point to have nothing to do with "sinners." Of course, Paul says that Christ died for us *while we were still sinners* so that we could be made righteous. Hence, our righteousness entirely depends on God's grace, the faithfulness of Christ, and the redemption by his blood from the *wrath* to come. Given that, Paul says that if *Christ's death* has **already** reconciled us to God, Paul says, **how much more** will *Christ's life* save us from God's wrath?

In the **second part (5:12-21)**, Paul then compares and contrasts Adam and Christ in order to crystalize the two ways of life in which people can live, namely a natural, mortal existence (as characterized by **Adam**) or a Spirit-filled, supernatural existence (as characterized by **Christ**). To be clear, Paul is not trying to explain where sin came from and how it came into the world. Rather, Paul uses the figure of Adam to represent the reality of all humanity. *Like Adam, everyone sins, and like Adam, everyone dies.* In that sense, we are "in Adam." For that matter, we are just like Adam—that is the reality of our natural existence. But that is just a given. What Paul focuses on is **how much greater** the work of Christ is compared to Adam. Simply put, Paul is saying humanity in its natural state (in Adam) sins and dies, but resurrected humanity in Christ will supersede and be greater than the original, natural state.

In 5:13-14, Paul points out that everyone, *even those Jews who possess the Torah*, have sinned. Although sin was in the world before the Torah was given through Moses, it wasn't "reckoned" until the Torah, meaning (to use my medical report analogy) it was the Torah that clearly diagnosed what sin actually was—a violation of God's holy character. In any case, everyone has sinned, even if it wasn't the exact same sin of Adam, and because of that, everyone suffers death. In that sense, **death reigned** from Adam to Moses.

But, as Paul says in 5:15-17, the **gracious gift in Christ** doesn't work in the same way the **trespass in Adam** does. Simply put, as bad as sin and death in Adam is, not only is all that wiped away in Christ, but things get infinitely better. The work of Christ out-performs the work of Adam. The Age to Come will be infinitely better than the current Old Age. In this Old Age in which death reigns, we are "in Adam" and are slaves to sin. But in the New Age, life reigns through Christ's gift of grace, and we are "slaves" to righteousness, which really just means we reign with Christ.

In 5:18-21, Paul drives this point home by saying three things: (a) Sin was in the world before the Torah, (b) Torah actually had the effect of increasing transgression (because sinful people immediately want to do things they are told not to do), but (c) Christ's super-abundant grace overflowed and out-performed any effects that sin could do. Christ's work supersedes the work of Adam. Christ's grace simply doesn't *negate* the sin of Adam, it goes *over and above it*, thus bringing about something far better.

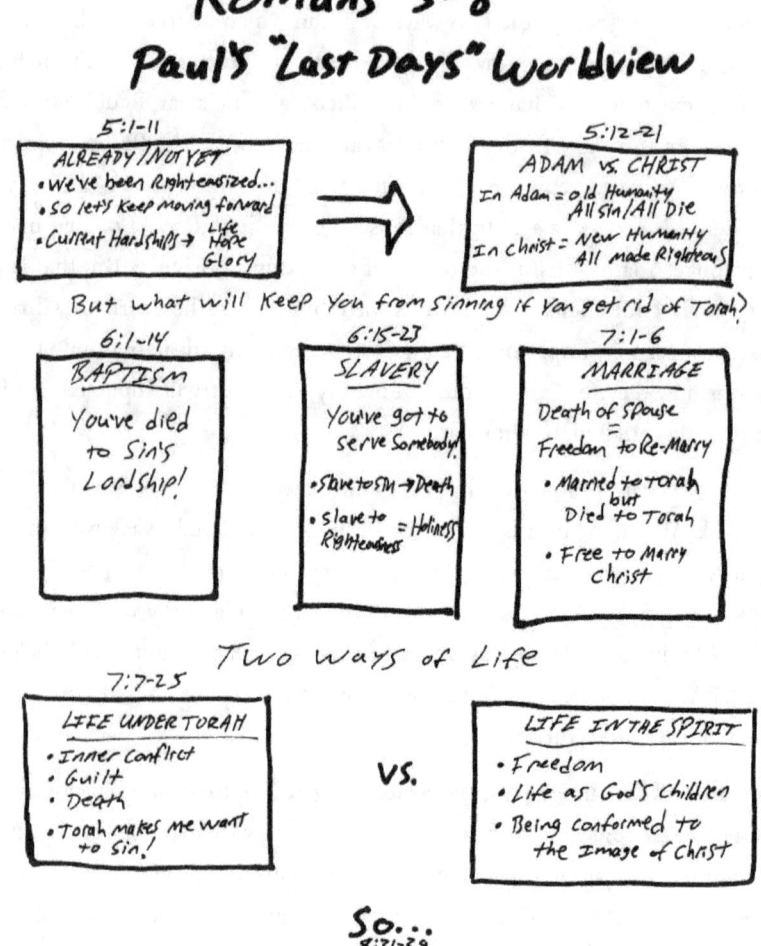

Having set up that contrast between Old Age way of life in Adam and the New Age way of life in Christ, Paul then proceeds to the **third part (6:1-7:6)**, where he answers a basic Jewish question regarding the Torah: *"What is going to keep one from sinning if you get rid of the Torah? If you get rid of Torah, and just tell people to receive grace, aren't you essentially encouraging people to sin?"* Simply put, if you get rid of the rule book, how can you guarantee Christians aren't going to just keep sinning? Paul addresses those concerns by means of three analogies.

The first analogy he gives is that of **baptism** (6:1-14). He first responds to an accusation that apparently some Judaizers were making against him, namely that he was encouraging Gentile Christians to keep sinning so that that God could show more grace. The reason why Paul was accused of this was because insisted that Gentile Christians didn't have to submit to the Torah. Paul says such an accusation is absurd. The reason Gentile Christians aren't to continue in sin is because **they've died to sin**. That is what baptism signifies: going down in the water symbolizes you dying to the "old age" way of life characterized by sin and death and coming out of the water symbolizes you being resurrected to new life, with the indwelling presence of the Holy Spirit who guides and instructs you, and who "grows you up," so that you can walk in that "newness of life."

To be clear, *Paul is not saying that Christians no longer sin*. He's saying is that Christians are no longer enslaved under the "old age" dominion of sin and death. Therefore, because they are no longer enslaved, they should not go back to their old way of life and indulge in more sin. To use an analogy, think about an alcoholic who is enslaved to alcohol. It doesn't matter if he occasionally goes for a day or two without a drink. If he is addicted to alcohol, he will inevitably continue to drink, and over time he will destroy himself. But let's say he is miraculously set free from his addiction. He has died to his old way of life and is no longer enslaved to alcohol. He is empowered to say no to alcohol, even though he still lives in a world where there are still bars and liquor stores. Therefore, it is imperative that he does not go back to visit the bars and liquor stores, or else he'll get enslaved to alcohol all over again. The more he avoids places where alcohol is made available, the more his body will heal and recover. This is what Paul is saying living as a Christian still in the "old age" is like. You've died to sin, have been empowered by the Spirit, and are no longer ruled by sin. That's why you don't choose to keep sinning. You've been set free by grace and you don't need the Torah because the Torah is there to hold people enslaved to sin to account.

The second analogy Paul uses is that of **slavery** (6:15-23). Again, he is responding to the accusation that he is telling Gentile Christians they can sin because they're not under Torah. This time, he uses the imagery of slavery to argue that *you are a slave to whomever you submit*. To quote Bob Dylan, "Don't you know you've gotta serve somebody? Well, it may be the Devil, or it may be the Lord, but you're gonna have to serve somebody!" The fact is *you are a slave—you've got to serve somebody*. Therefore, you will either be **a slave who submits to sin**, which results in death, or you will be **a slave who submits to righteousness**, which results in life. And that's the thing. Gentile Christians, before they were Christians, were slaves to sin...but they aren't anymore. They used to obey the dictates of sin, but now they obey the Gospel that Paul handed down to them.

Therefore, Paul points out the obvious. They used to offer their bodies as slaves to impurity and lawlessness (anti-Torah behavior), and that led to more lawlessness. But now they are to offer their bodies as slaves to righteousness, and that leads, not to lawlessness, but rather to holiness. With that, Paul can't resist a little bit of wordplay in 6:20-22. He says that when you were *slaves to sin,* you were technically *free of righteousness*! But the "fruit" such slavery bore were shameful things that ended in death. But now, after being *set free from sin,* you have become *slaves to God.* And the "fruit" of *that* kind of slavery is holiness, and those holy things will last into the eternal Life of the Ages. Paul then ends with the famous verse: *"The wages of sin is death, but the free gift of God is eternal life with Jesus Christ our Lord."* In other words, Paul is saying that death is well-earned. Therefore, a life of *freedom from sin* does not mean it's the *kind of freedom for sin*. The "New Age" worldview is not, "I have to be righteousness now to get God to like me!" Rather, it is, "I get to be righteous now, because God loves me and has been gracious to me!"

The third analogy Paul gives is that of **marriage and remarriage** (7:1-6). In the Torah, a woman who gets married is legally bound to her husband for as long as her husband is alive. When he dies, though, she is then free to marry another man. Paul relates that situation to the believer's relationship to the Torah. The believer is like the wife, and the Torah is like the husband. Here is where the analogy doesn't quite make sense. In order for the analogy to work, Paul would have to say, "When the Torah dies, we are now free from it." But that wouldn't really work, because the Torah can't really "die."

So, Paul says, "You have died to the Torah, and therefore are free to marry Christ!" Obviously, that really doesn't make sense—a person who has died can't remarry! But Paul's point is clear nonetheless: Through death, you are no longer bound to Torah. You are set free from Torah and are therefore free to unite yourself to Christ. Paul then extends the analogy of marriage a little further. In that "old marriage" in which you were married to the Torah, the "fruit" you bore was death. But now that you've died to Torah and have remarried Christ, the "fruit" you bear is the fruit of the Spirit.

Paul sums up his three analogies by making two points that he will expand upon in the next two parts of the letter. In 7:5, he paints a picture of **life in the "flesh" of the old age** as being a life in which sinful passions were inflamed by the commandments in the Torah and gave birth to death. By contrast, in 7:6, Paul paints a picture of the **life of the Spirit in the New Age** as being a life in which we have been released from Torah and have died to the sin and death that enslaved us.

In the **fourth part (7:7-25)**, Paul elaborates on his description in 7:5 of life in the "flesh" of the old age. It is important to realize that what Paul is talking about in 7:7-25 is not his struggles as a Christian, but rather the struggles he had as a Torah-observant Jew before he came to Christ, where he knew the Torah and tried to keep the Torah, but was so enslaved to sin, that he was utterly miserable and guilt-ridden. He includes this section, ironically, to exonerate the Torah. Up to this point, he's seemed to be very hard on the Torah, associating it with sin six times (3:20; 4:15; 5:13, 20; 6:14; 7:5). But he wants to make something clear: *The problem of sin doesn't lie with the Torah; it lies with us.* The Torah is actually "holy…righteous and good" (7:12) It is from God and is therefore spiritual. So, what happened?

Paul makes it quite clear what happened. Even though he was a Torah observant Jew, he was still a sinner who was in bondage to the old age way of the "flesh." Therefore, even though the Torah was spiritual, he, being a "fleshly" sinner, was able *to manipulate God's good Torah so he could sin even more*. Simply put, the Torah is a good thing, but it is powerless to stop sin, and therefore **sin has the ability to overpower a powerless rule book**. As soon as the Torah said, "Don't do this," Paul wanted to do it, and found ways to get around the Torah to do it. That is what Paul is getting at. For the person without Christ, a good commandment often sparks within that person all kinds of lusts and desires that wouldn't have been as strong without the commandment. You want what is forbidden.

Given that reality, Paul then asks, *"Did this good thing become death for me?"* but then answers with a resounding "No!" The problem wasn't the Torah. The problem was sin working death in me through that good, but powerless, Torah. That was Paul's dilema as a Torah observant Jew. He had the Torah, he knew it was good, he knew right from wrong, but since he was a slave to sin, he found ways to get around the Torah so he could still sin.

With that, Paul then has a field-day with wordplays on the word "law/Torah" in 7:18-23. In 7:21, he states that he sees a certain **law** (*torah*) at work: Whenever he does good, evil is right there as well. Sure, he delights in the **Torah of God** in his innermost self (7:22), but he finds within him another **law** (*torah*) warring against the **torah of his mind** (the actual Torah in which he delights). This other **law** (*torah*), though, makes him captive (a slave) to the **torah of sin** that also is within him. Given all that, what would be the response of someone who knows what is good and wants to do good, but also wants to do evil, and finds himself powerless to do the good he wants to do, and essentially "addicted" to doing evil? Paul gives that response in 7:24: *"Who will drag me out from this body of death?"* The "fleshly" experience of being an enslaved sinner living under the good Torah brings nothing but despair.

But there is good news! After all, Paul is elaborating on the Gospel he preaches. That good news is elaborated on in the **fifth part (8:1-30)**, where Paul describes what life in the Spirit is like. Those who have put their faith in Christ are no longer *"fleshly Torah-doers."* They are now *"Spirit-walkers."* Contrary to the guilt-ridden life he felt as a Torah-observant Jew, Paul now declares, "There is no condemnation for those in Christ Jesus." That's the good news: **The long-awaited New Messianic Age has dawned, and the Holy Spirit has been poured out into the hearts of those who put their faith in Christ, empowering them to live out the faith-filled righteous life that the Old Testament Torah had been pointing to all along.** That is why Paul can say in 8:2 that the **"torah" of the Spirit of Life** has freed you from the **"torah" of Sin and Death**.

Paul then lays out the fundamental contrast between the two different ways of life and says that you are either one who **walks according to "the flesh"**, or one who **walks according to the Spirit**. To be clear, when talking about "the flesh," Paul isn't talking about our literal, material bodies. He's talking about a certain kind of **mindset** that characterizes living in the present "old age" that is enslaved to sin and death. The kind of person who walks according to the flesh has a mindset of death, is antagonistic to God, disobeys Torah, and isn't even able to please God.

By contrast, the kind of person who walks according to the Spirit has a mindset of life and is at peace with God because the Spirit of God, indeed Christ himself, dwells within him. Such a person can rest in the hope that God, the one who raised Christ from the dead, will also give life to his mortal body as well because God is transforming him from a sinner enslaved to sin and death, to a Son and co-heir with Christ, the ruler of Life. Simply put, to live **according to the flesh** is to be a slave to fear and sin, and to be on the brink of death. To live, though, **according to the Spirit**, is to truly live. It is to be adopted as children of God and to call God "Abba." It is to be co-heirs with Christ, the one who will inherit and rule over God's New Creation...and as co-heirs, that is the destiny also of those who walk in the Spirit.

There is one catch, though. Paul says in 8:17 that we will be children of God and co-heirs with Christ, *provided that we suffer with him*. Indeed, we *must* suffer with Christ, so that we can also be glorified with him. You can't enjoy the Resurrection-Life unless you first go through a crucifixion. It is this very topic of suffering in relation to the Christian life, indeed to all of creation, that Paul then turns in 8:18-30. For Paul, the certain hope of us sharing in the future glory of Christ radically transforms our view of suffering itself. In other words, given the reality of Jesus Christ's resurrection as the beginning of the New Creation the Christian understanding of present suffering is seen in a whole new light.

He begins by saying that **creation itself** is looking forward to us being revealed as the children of God. This takes us back to **Genesis 1**, where mankind is made in God's image, to be according to God's likeness and to rule over and care for God's creation. Because of sin, though, not only was mankind subjected to futility and death, but so was the entirety of creation. Therefore, with the redemption and glorification of mankind to be re-created into God's image and made able to fulfill God's original purposes, so too will creation itself be redeemed and re-created—and it will finally be ruled over and taken care of the way God intended all along. Just as the corruption of humanity meant the corruption of creation, so too will the glorification of a re-created humanity mean the glorification of a re-created creation.

Paul then equates the suffering we experience within the present creation to the **labor pains** of a mother giving birth—as painful as they are, they bring about a better and fuller kind of life. Therefore, Paul says we wait patiently for the labor to be over and for the new life to begin. And because the new life is certain, our hope that we will be revealed to be sons of God, completely free from slavery to death, is sure.

Paul then addresses the **role of the Holy Spirit** in our present lives to bring about the ultimate glorification of those faithful to Christ who walk in the Spirit. In our weakness and in our pain, when we don't know what to pray for, or even how to pray, Paul reassures us that the Spirit is at work in the midst of our sighs and groanings. Just as creation "groans" in its expectation of the New Creation, the Spirit articulates and translates our desperate "groanings" to God, so that even those deep prayers that we cannot really articulate ourselves bring us closer to our future redemption and glorification. That is why Paul reassures us that *all things work together for the good of those who love God*, because the Holy Spirit is able to take even our present sufferings and make them the means by which we are transformed and glorified in Christ.

Paul ends with something that is easily misunderstood when he says, *"For those whom he foreknew he also predestined to be conformed to the image of his Son, in order that he might be the firstborn within a large family. And those whom he predestined he also called; and those whom he called he also justified; and those whom he justified he also glorified."* To be clear, Paul is not saying that God chose ahead of time the people he was going to save. Rather, Paul is saying that what God has predestined is that anyone who chooses to put their faith in Christ is guaranteed to become like Christ. It is a done deal. If you put your faith in Christ, despite any suffering you go through, you will be made righteous and you will be glorified with Christ. God is going to make good on His promises. Or, to put it in athletic terms, Paul is saying that if you choose to join Christ's team, you're going to win the championship. You have to choose to join, but once you do, Christ is going transform you into a winner, into a champion.

In the **sixth and final part (8:31-39)**, Paul just breaks out into praising God. In light of the Gospel he has just laid out in the first eight chapters, when it is clear that through Christ, God wins and nothing can stop him, Paul just lays it out there: *"Who will separate us from the love of Christ? Will hardship, or distress, or persecution, or famine, or nakedness, or peril, or sword? (As it is written, "For your sake we are being killed all day long; we are accounted as sheep to be slaughtered.") No! In all these things we are more than conquerors through him who loved us. For I am convinced that neither death, nor life, nor angels, nor rulers, nor things present, nor things to come, nor powers, nor height, nor depth, nor anything else in all creation, will be able to separate us from the love of God in Christ Jesus our Lord!"*

God wins and you're on the winning team. Not even suffering and death can separate you from the love of God. It's time to celebrate, even in the midst of your suffering.

### 4. What is God Doing with Ethnic Israel? (9-11)

In the next section of Romans, Paul answers the question, "If the people of God are those share the faith of Abraham in Christ, then what is God doing with Israel? After all, most Jews have rejected Jesus! What's going on?" That reality is why we see in the **first part (9:1-5)** Paul lamenting over the fact that his fellow Jews had rejected Jesus as the Messiah and thus missed out on the very salvation they were so long hoping for. Despite all the advantages they were given (chosen by God, witnessed His glory, the covenants, the Torah, the Temple, the promises), somehow they failed to recognized the Messiah when he came. How could that have happened? Had God failed? How could He let His "chosen" people fall away?

In response, Paul begins to answer that question in the **second part (9:6-29)**. To get right to the point, Paul says that God's people hadn't fallen away, because ethnic Israel isn't the same as True Israel! Simply put, Paul says being Jewish doesn't automatically make you part of the people of God. To prove his point, he again goes back to Abraham, who had two sons, **Ishmael** and **Isaac**. Both were children of Abraham, but only one, Isaac, was the **child of promise** who was miraculously conceived. Ishmael, though, was a **child of the flesh** who was conceived "the old-fashioned way." Clearly, Paul is using "the flesh" here in two ways. It obviously refers to the literal way Ishmael was conceived, but it also serves as a metaphor for what Paul has already said about those who "walk according to the flesh." Thus, Paul says makes it clear that the children of the flesh aren't the same as children of God. The same holds true for Jacob and Esau as well. They were actually twins, but still, God chose Jacob and not Esau.

It is important to remember here, though, that Paul is not saying that God's election of Isaac over Ishmael and Jacob over Esau was a matter of choosing who goes to heaven or hell. Paul is saying that God chose Isaac and Jacob for His purposes. He chose to work through Isaac and Jacob to bring about His promises that He made to Abraham. It was through their family line (not Ishmael's or Esau's) that God was going to bring about the Messiah. Thus, Paul is talking about how God chooses the people through whom He works—He chose them because He chose them, not because they did anything to deserve it. Paul's point is simply that bloodlines were never the determining factor in who the children of promise were. It always rested on the will of God. God is the one who chooses to use the people He uses in the way in which He determines to bring about His purposes.

In 9:14-18, in case his fellow Jews might object to that, Paul then quotes **Exodus 33:19**, where God says to Moses, "I'll show mercy to whomever I choose!" and then **Exodus 9:16**, where God says He chose to raise up Pharaoh to serve His purposes as well. It was because of Pharaoh's stubbornness that God was able to show His power over Pharaoh and the gods of Egypt. Paul's point is that God can chose to use anybody—whether they're good or bad—to bring about the fulfillment of His covenant promises. God's "election," therefore, involves how He uses each person in this world to achieve His purpose, not who gets saved or not. If God uses an evil person to further his offer of salvation, that doesn't excuse the evil that person does. The same applies to Israel. So, what's going on with ethnic Israel? Paul's answer is that God has used ethnic Israel's disobedience and rejection of Christ to bring the Gospel to the Gentiles.

This leads into the **third part (9:30-10:21)**, where Paul further ponders how such a thing could happen. Gentiles, who hadn't pursued righteousness have attained righteousness through faith, but the Jews, who had pursued righteousness through the Torah completely missed out on it! How could that have happened? Paul's answer is that they focused so much on the Mosaic Law that they forgot about the actual Abrahamic Covenant on which the Torah was based. They missed what the point of the Torah was all about and mistakenly thought that the Torah itself could produce righteousness. That is why they ended up "stumbling over the stumbling stone," Christ himself. He was the intended cornerstone, but Israel rejected the way God was going about building His New Temple. In other words, Paul is saying that unbelieving Israel is the unfaithful one. Therefore, unbelieving Israel is responsible for missing out on the righteousness of God, not God.

Paul readily admits that his fellow Jews are zealous for God. The problem was that their zeal wasn't "according to knowledge." Since they don't know the righteousness of God, and instead are trying to establish their own righteousness, they don't submit to the righteousness of God. Basically, that means they want to "do righteousness" their own way. Yet Paul makes clear that the very "end" (meaning fulfillment and goal) of the Torah is Christ. He is the fulfillment of everything God was trying to convey through the Torah. The Torah is **the pointer**, and Christ is what the Torah is **pointing to**, so if you reject Christ because you think focusing on the pointer is what God wants…you're missing the point.

Ultimately for Paul, there are only two kinds of existence. There is either **a life based on the Torah** or **a life based on faith**. They are mutually exclusive, so you can't do both. The one who insists on trying to achieve righteousness based on the Torah is going to have to do everything in the Torah all the time—and that is impossible. That is why those who think that righteousness can be obtained through our own efforts of obeying the Torah are cursed. They're doomed to fail. That kind of "Torah existence" is a curse in and of itself.

By contrast, Paul says that the one who lives a life of faith knows that since one is made righteous from faith, that he doesn't need anyone else to either "ascend to heaven" or "descend into the abyss" in order to attain righteousness for him because Christ already has done it. Because of that, the **word of faith** is already in his mouth and heart (**Deut. 30:12-14**). This leads Paul to say, "if you confess with your lips that Jesus is Lord and believe in your heart that God raised him from the dead, you will be saved" (10:9). To be clear, he's not saying that is some kind of magic formula you need to say to get saved. He's saying that anyone—Jew or Gentile—can do it because faith in Christ has been made available to everyone. Indeed, as Paul's quote of **Joel 2:32** shows, "Everyone who calls on the name of the Lord will be saved."

So, given the fact that God is able to use even the unfaithfulness of the Jews to make salvation available to the Gentiles, does that mean the Jews should be excused for their unfaithfulness? Paul's answer is a clear, "No." He then proceeds to quote a number of Old Testament verses to show that his fellow Jews had no excuse for not accepting Jesus as the Messiah because not only were they looking for the coming of the Messiah, but they preached about it from their own Bibles. The problem wasn't that they hadn't heard about God's salvation plan in Christ. The problem was their lack of obedience. Therefore, Paul says that Jews who failed to put their faith in Christ were never truly faithful or obedient to God in the first place. Paul drives his point home by quoting **Isaiah 65:2**. The reason why Israel didn't accept the Messiah is because Israel was disobedient, plain and simple, no excuses.

In the **fourth part (11:1-32)**, Paul then wants to make it clear that just because Israel had rejected God, that God hadn't rejected them. Even though Israel as a whole had rejected God, there had always been a faithful remnant. Paul points to the story of Elijah at Mount Sinai in **I Kings 19** to prove his point. When Elijah complained to God about how unfaithful Israel was, God reassured him that there were 7,000 people still faithful to Him. Hence, Paul's point is that the nation of ethnic Israel was never the real people of God. It was always the faithful remnant within the nation of Israel who were God's true people.

So, what does that mean for non-remnant Israel? Paul equates them with pagan idolaters. Paul quotes **Deuteronomy 29:3** and **Isaiah 29:10** to show that they had become "hardened" and had eyes that couldn't see and ears that couldn't hear. Like pagan idolaters, they had become like what they worshipped. Paul then quotes **Psalm 69:22-23** to show that the Jews' "table" consisted of all that God had given them (covenants, promises, Torah, Temple), but they had ended up worshipping the gifts, and not the Giver. Ironically, the ultimate "idol" of the Jews is the Torah! Instead of worshipping Christ, who fulfills the Torah, Paul is saying that the Jews ended up bowing their knee to the Torah, thus making it their idol.

Still, Paul holds out hope for his fellow Jews in 11:11-16, saying they've only stumbled and that he has still has hope that when they see Gentile Christians receiving the Gospel and experiencing the Holy Spirit, they will become so jealous that they end up choosing to accept Christ. That is why Paul says he's "glorifying" his ministry by going out to as many Gentiles as he can—he's trying to make his fellow Jews so jealous, that perhaps some of them will end up coming to Christ themselves. As Paul sees it, if their rejection of Christ means the reconciliation of the world, then if they end up accepting Christ, that would mean "life from the dead" for the nation of Israel (a clear allusion to Ezekiel's valley of dry bones.) As it turned out, though, the Israel as a nation never did accept Christ. When Paul went back to Jerusalem in Acts 21-26, his fellow Jews attacked him, and he ended up being arrested and eventually sent to Rome for trial. The hope he expresses here never was realized.

All that said, Paul then issues a stern warning to Gentile Christians in 11:17-24 by the use of the metaphor of an olive tree. The olive tree represents the people of God, the **natural branches** that are broken off are unfaithful Jews, and the **wild olive branches** grafted onto the tree are Gentile believers. Paul reminds the Gentile believers not to get too cocky because if God could break off some natural branches and have wild branches grafted on, then He can easily break off those wild branches and graft some of the natural branches back on if they repent.

Paul ends by trying to explain Israel's rejection of Christ by saying that the reason that happened was so that the Gospel could be taken to the Gentiles and so that the **full number of Gentiles** would come in and become part of God's people. That way, Paul says, "all Israel will be saved" (11:25-26). To be clear, Paul is not saying that eventually all of ethnic Israel will be saved. He's saying that true

Israel, the true people of God, consists of the faithful remnant of Jews and the full number of Gentiles.

Paul then sums up his section by saying that just as Gentiles were disobedient and were shown grace, so too does the present situation with the Jews show that the Jews are disobedient and can now be shown—and possibly accept—that same grace. With that, Paul breaks out into praise to God in the **fifth part (11:33-36)**. After laying out God's entire salvation plan seen in the Gospel of Christ, Paul can only marvel at how God doesn't need any human advisor to help Him bring together His plan of salvation.

### 5. Living as One People of God (12:1-15:13)

In the last major section of Romans, Paul turns his attention to explaining the practical application of his Gospel message to the everyday lives of the Christians living in Rome. Talking theology is all well and good (and obviously quite necessary) but living that theology out in the everyday world is what matters. If your theology isn't actually lived out, then what you have isn't faith…it's just facts and arguments.

In the **first part of this section (12:1-21)**, Paul talks about what it means to live as a Christian community. After all, God's goal of salvation is not simply to save *individuals*, so that those *individuals* can go to heaven. God's goal of salvation is to **re-create a people for His Name—the People of God**. Therefore, by virtue of being *the People of God*, Christians must take care that we *live as the People of God*. Paul begins with a very famous verse: *"Present your bodies as living sacrifices. This is your sensible act of worship."* Even though the image of a **living sacrifice** is obviously an oxymoron, Paul uses the language of the animal sacrificial system to apply it to the daily life of the believer. And since the one who offers the sacrifices is a priest, Paul is saying that believers are to offer their own bodies, just as Christ our high priest offered his, as a sacrifice that will help bring about the reconciliation of the world.

It is also important to point out a translational issue regarding Paul's description of it being a **sensible act of worship**. Some translations have **spiritual act of worship**. The Greek word in question is *logican*—it is the word from which we get the word "logic." The Greek word for "spiritual" is *pneumatikon* is not used here. Paul uses *logican* on purpose, because he is saying that sacrificing one's life for others is the *logical* and *sensible* thing for a Christian to do, and it is the complete opposite of how Paul described the *senseless thoughts* of the Gentiles back in 1:18-32, when they *worship* created things, and not the Creator.

There is also a second translational issue in 12:2. Most translations have *"Don't be conformed to **this world**,"* but it should read *"Don't be conformed to **this age**,"* because Paul is referring to the present **old age**, in contrast to the **new Messianic age** that was ushered in at Pentecost. The reason why the believer can choose to not be conformed to *this age* is precisely because he has died to the *old age way of things* and has been empowered by the Holy Spirit of the *new Messianic age*.

Not only that, but believers are also to be *"transformed by the renewing of your mind."* They must continue to walk in faith and by doing so, develop a new way of looking at things. This new **Spirit-empowered worldview** makes it possible to "discern the will of God," specifically the ability to discern *what is good*. Note that Paul doesn't say "discern *what is right*." The reason for that is sometimes, even if you are *right* about something, it is not *good* to insist on your way, because you might hurt someone else. If you knowingly hurt someone else simply because you have to prove that you are *right*, then what you've done is actually *evil*. And the aim of the Spirit-empowered worldview is to determine and *do what is good*.

The natural outgrowth of all that is articulated in 12:3-8. It comes down to having a *sober estimation of yourself* and doing everything in the context of *one another*. Having a sober estimation of yourself simply means being honest with yourself about both your strengths and weaknesses. It means not thinking too highly of yourself, but also not too critically of yourself. Then, when Paul talks about doing everything according to the "measure of faith" given to you, he simply means you should practice those things you've been gifted with for the purpose of serving others. That is why he talks about **one body, but many parts**. You are part of the **one body of Christ**, but have been uniquely gifted, so use your gifts to serve others and strengthen the body of Christ. The bottom line is that wherever you are gifted, *do that*. Do the things that God has wired you up for, and don't try to be someone you aren't.

Paul spends the second half of the chapter describing what a Spirit-empowered Christian community looks like. It is a community where people practice self-sacrificial love for one another and put the needs of others ahead of their own. It is a community that exemplifies what it means to *do what is good*: blessing those who persecute you, not cursing, rejoicing with those who rejoice, weeping with those who weep, the list goes on. Ultimately, though, Paul's description can be summed up in both 12:16 (*Live in harmony with one another*) and 12:18 (*If possible, so far as it depends on you, live peaceably with all*). Paul is clear: **A Holy Spirit community forgives wrongs and works toward peace and harmony with each other.**

As a final note, something should be said about what Paul means when he talks about **heaping burning coals** on a person's head. He's not saying, "Be nice to that person who is mean to you, so that you make him feel bad!" He's saying that when you do the Christ-like thing and repay evil with good, your "enemy" will see your goodness in response to his evil, and will hopefully find his conscience affected, and hopefully he'll respond to his conscience, repent, and come to Christ. That is why Paul ends with, *"Do not be overcome with evil, but overcome evil with good."* When you respond to evil with goodness, that person might be saved from his evil—you will have worked toward peace and will have overcome evil with good.

In the **second part of the section (13:1-14)**, Paul addresses how Christians should live their lives in relation to the pagan/secular world around them. The specific question he addresses is in regard to **obeying those in authority**. Paul wrote Romans in the first part of Nero's reign as emperor, before there was any state-sponsored persecution of Christians (although, being a unique group, Christians would undoubtedly face harassment and ridicule at the local level). Given those circumstances, Paul says in 13:1-5 that Christians are to submit to the authorities because ultimately authority is God's gift to a fallen world. In that respect, those in authority are God's servant and have the task of maintaining a just society. The law exists because people by their very nature aren't good. It is there to keep bad people from hurting society as a whole. Therefore, Paul says, if you do what is *good*, then you won't have to worry about suffering judgment and wrath by those in authority. Besides, the ultimate reason Christians are to do what is good isn't simply to avoid punishment. The reason Christians are to do good is because *of conscience*—because *you're a Christian*.

Another issue Paul addresses is whether or not Christians should **pay taxes to Caesar**. Paul says of course you should pay your taxes. If the governing authority is God's servant to promote the good, then you should pay taxes to help the govern authority promote the good. Then, playing off the idea of "owing" things, Paul says the only thing you really "owe" others is to love them, and whoever loves others *fulfills the Torah*.

Paul then encourages his readers to be **soldiers of Christ** and uses further imagery of **day** and **night** as well. He first says "the night" (the old age of the flesh) is almost over, and "the day" (the consummation of the new Messianic age) is near. Therefore, Christians should *walk in the day*, use *weapons of light*, and put off the *works of darkness*: immoral feasting, drunkenness, sexual promiscuity, perverted behavior, rivalry and jealousy. Not only are these things usually *night-time activities*, but they also represent *spiritual darkness*. Paul says, "Don't do them! Put on Christ and don't give an inch to the lusts of 'the flesh.'"

The **third part of the section (14:1-15:13)** is the goal of Paul's entire letter. It deals with **relationships within the community of faith**, and specifically concerns how Jewish-Christians and Gentile-Christians are to relate to each other. To understand this section, you have to understand that Jewish Torah observance and food laws were still an issue within the early Church, and therefore Jewish-Christians and Gentile-Christians often had nothing to do with each other. The main issue concerned eating meat from the marketplace. Jews in the Roman Empire traditionally viewed meat sold in the marketplace as being unclean because it had passed through the pagan temples. Pagan priests were basically the butchers in the Roman world who sent to the marketplace the leftover meat that was not used in pagan worship. Therefore, Jews viewed meat in the marketplace as "idol food" and refused to eat it. To Gentiles, though, it was just meat.

This cultural division between Jews and Gentiles inevitably bled over into the early Church, when both Jews and Gentiles became Christians, but still had their cultural views. On one hand, Jewish-Christians saw themselves as "extra-religious" because not only did they accept Christ, but they obeyed extra rules. Thus, they often looked down on Gentile-Christians. Gentile-Christians, though, saw the Jewish-Christians as just plain weird because they didn't eat meat and they circumcised their sons. This obviously was causing division within the Church.

So, beginning in 14:1-12, Paul encourages both Gentile-Christians and Jewish-Christians to accept each other without making these differing views a cause for division. He first encourages Gentile-Christians to accept those who are **weak in the faith**, meaning **Jewish-Christians** who place importance on Torah observance. But they shouldn't do it "for the purpose of arguing over disputed matters," meaning Gentile-Christians should not only accept Jewish-Christians who are still hung up on certain Torah regulations, but they should also not argue over those trivial things. Paul is telling them that if a Jewish-Christian has a problem with eating meat, they should accept that person and not eat meat in his presence. It isn't because the Jewish-Christian is "extra spiritual" and the Gentile-Christian has to be ashamed, but it is rather because the Jewish-Christian is actually the one who is hung up on irrelevant things, and therefore the Gentile-Christian needs to do the loving thing and not make a big deal about it. In time, hopefully, the Jewish-Christian will come around to a more mature understanding of those things, but *you can't force the issue.* Let the Holy Spirit change their heart.

At the same time, Paul tells Jewish-Christians that since God has already accepted Gentile-Christians, they shouldn't judge or condemn them as being sinners just because they eat "unclean" food. This relates to Sabbath observance and Jewish food laws in general. If Gentile-Christians work on the Sabbath, that's okay—it doesn't matter. As long as you give thanks to God, you can eat whatever you want, and if you want to abstain from certain foods and give thanks to God—that's okay too. Neither side should force the other side to change matters that simply are irrelevant. Anyone who does that is putting irrelevant issues ahead of Christ and the Gospel. Ultimately, both Gentile-Christians and Jewish-Christians belong to the Lord, so neither one should judge the other in regard to irrelevant and disputed matters. God is the one who has the right to judge a person, not us. That's actually reassuring. Since *you're* going to give account to God, *I cannot judge you.*

Paul continues in 14:13-23 to appeal to both Jewish and Gentile Christians not to judge each other. Instead, Paul says that the only thing they should "judge" to do is not set up a **stumbling block** before each other. Paul then tells them that Jesus himself said (in Mark 7) all foods were clean. Still, if Gentile-Christians eat "unclean food" in front of their Jewish-Christian brothers, then, even though the food is clean in God's eyes, *they really are not walking in love—and that is the really important issue.*

Therefore, they shouldn't let their "good" be blasphemed, because **the Kingdom of God isn't about food and drink.** It is about **righteousness, peace, and joy in the Holy Spirit**. So don't let an irrelevant thing like meat (or anything else) give the Gospel of Christ a bad name! Don't let it be used as something to turn people away from the saving grace found in Christ. Instead, Christians should pursue things that foster peace with each other within the Church and **build each other up**. They shouldn't **tear down** the work of God for the sake of food. Paul then gives a harsh challenge to both Jewish and Gentile Christians and tells them that *food is evil* if you eat it in such a way that causes a stumbling block, but *food is good* if you don't do it in order to purposely make someone stumble.

Paul then makes a final appeal in 15:1-6 specifically to Gentile-Christians and tells them that even though they are **strong in the faith** (they don't get hung up on food laws), they need to be patient and "bear the weakness" of those who aren't strong (Jewish-Christians). Instead of judging and mocking each other, Paul wants the Jewish and Gentile Christians to imitate Christ and resolve to please each other for the good of building them up. The goal is for them to glorify God the Father and the Lord Jesus Christ **together, with one voice**. The goal is the **unity of the Church**, so that the Church in Rome can truly be **the People of God in Rome**.

Finally, the conclusion of the whole argument of Romans is seen in 15:7-13. It is straightforward and simple: **Welcome one another**, just as **Christ welcomed you** for the **glory of God**. Look to Christ, who became a **servant for the circumcised** on behalf of the **truth of God**—in order to make good on the promises He made to the Patriarchs, and who became a **servant for the uncircumcised** on behalf of **mercy**—in order to glorify God.

With that, Paul unleashes a litany of Old Testament passages that serve as a final praise to God for fulfilling His promises: **Psalm. 17:50** (I will confess you among the *Gentiles*....); **Deuteronomy 32:43** (Rejoice, *Gentiles*, with His people!); **Psalm 117:1** (Praise YHWH, all you *Gentiles*....); and **Isaiah 11:10** (The one who rises to rule the *Gentiles* will be the root of Jesse, and the *Gentiles* will place their hope upon him). With that, Paul gives his benediction: "Now may the God of **hope** fill you with all **joy** and **peace** in having **faith**, in order for you to overflow in that **hope by the power of the Holy Spirit**."

### 6. Personal Matters (15:14-16:27)

The end of Paul's letter contains a number of practical concerns Paul shares with the Church in Rome. In 15:14-22, he portrays himself as a **priestly servant**, and describes his ministry in Jewish-priestly terms. The Gentiles are the offering that he is presenting to God, as if he were a priest in the Jerusalem Temple, and they are being made holy by the Holy Spirit. Of course, the true Temple of God is the Church itself. In any case, it should tell you how the early Church understood salvation. It wasn't just some abstract "Get people saved" idea. It was seen against the backdrop of the Jewish Temple—salvation was "building up" the Temple of the Holy Spirit.

In 15:23-29, Paul discusses his future plans. He wants to come to Rome, not really to stay there, but so that they can partner with him on what he hopes is a missionary journey to Spain. Then in 15:30-33, Paul mentions that he expects to encounter trouble when he visits Jerusalem to offer the Gentile gift. He realizes that he's been rejected by unbelieving Jews, but at the same time, accepted by the Jewish-Christians (saints) in Jerusalem.

Chapter 16 simply is a list of various greetings. There really are only a few interesting things to note. In 16:1-2, Paul mentions **Phoebe**, a deacon of the Church in Cenchreae. The church there meets in her house, and she is a benefactor of many Christians. Since she was going to Rome on business, Paul gave her the letter to carry to Rome. In 16:3-5, Paul mentions **Prisca** and **Aquila**. The wife (Prisca) is mentioned first—nowhere in ancient literature is this found. Paul wants his letter read in their house-church first. In 16:7, Paul mentions **Andronicus** and **Junia**, a husband-and-wife team who were considered "great among the apostles."

The rest of the letter contains mentions of various other early Christians. Paul against encourages them all to avoid divisions and stumbling blocks and ends his letter with giving praise to Jesus Christ.

# PHILIPPIANS

**Time of Writing:** During Paul's imprisonment in Rome (AD 60-63)

### History of the City/Paul in Philippi

The city of Philippi was founded by King Philip of Macedonia, the father of Alexander the Great. In 168 BC, Rome turned Philippi into a Roman colony and granted it the legal status of a Roman city. That meant they were exempt from land and poll taxes and were granted full Roman citizenship. In 42 BC, Octavius/Mark Antony defeated Brutus/Cassius in the famous battle right outside of Philippi. Philippi sided with Octavius and ended up being a city completely devoted to Caesar.

Paul visited Philippi during his second missionary journey (Acts 16:11-40), right before they travelled to Thessalonica. We know that Philippi did not have any real Jewish population, because there was no synagogue in the city. A synagogue can only convene if there are at least ten Jewish men. When Paul and Silas went out by the river to worship, it was there where they met Lydia from Thyatira, a businesswoman who sold purple cloth. She ended up becoming Paul's first covert in Philippi, and her house became the first meeting place for the church in Philippi.

It was also in Philippi where Paul cast out a *python spirit* of a fortune-telling girl. Because of this, her owners dragged Paul and Silas before the city leaders, accused them of being Jews who were disturbing the city and advocating illegal customs for Romans to practice. Paul and Silas were beaten and thrown into prison without the due process Paul, as a Roman citizen, was entitled to. That night, an earthquake shook the prison and broke open the doors. The jailer planned to kill himself because he assumed the prisoners escaped, but Paul and Silas assured him all the prisoners had stayed. He and his family then decided to become Christians. The next day, when the city leaders found out Paul and Silas were Roman citizens and that they had violated their rights, they sent a message to the prison to tell Paul that he and Silas were free to go. Paul, though, insisted that they come down to the prison and offer him and Silas a public apology. It was after that they then departed for Thessalonica.

## The Big Things to Know About Philippians

A. **Having the Mindset of Christ**: This is perhaps the biggest theological takeaway in Philippians. The goal of faith is to be transformed into the image of Christ, and that means *being like Christ* and *having the same mindset as Christ*.

B. **Your Citizenship is in Heaven**: In light of Philippi's extreme devotion to Caesar, Paul reminds the Philippian Christians that they may be citizens of Rome, but their *real citizenship* in in Heaven. They are citizens of Jesus Christ.

C. **Watch Out for Those Judaizers**: As always, Paul warns against succumbing to Jewish religious legalism.

### Literary Map: Philippians

| | 1:1-11<br>Greeting/Thanksgiving | |
|---|---|---|
| 1:12-26<br>News from Prison | 1:27-2:18<br>Citizenship in Heaven<br>Mindset of Christ | 2:19-30<br>Timothy<br>and Epaphroditus |
| 3:1-4:1<br>A Warning about the<br>Judaizers | 4:2-9<br>Final Exhortations<br>Euodia and Syntyche | 4:10-23<br>Personal Comments |

### A Walkthrough of Philippians

#### 1. The Greeting and Thanksgiving (1:1-11)

Paul begins his letter to the church in Philippi with a standard greeting, followed by a thanksgiving to God for them in which he also sets out some of the main points he is going to make in the letter. He tells them that he is constantly praying for them, that he is overjoyed because of the way they have always supported him, and that he is confident that God will be faithful and bring it to completion on the **Day of Christ Jesus** (1:6). In anticipation of that day, Paul encourages them to have **the proper mindset**. He says that even though he is in prison and wants to see them again, he is confident that they will continue to have the *right mindset* and will continue to support him and his ministry. He ends his thanksgiving by telling them again that he is praying that they increase in knowledge and insight so they will be able to discern what is the best thing to do in any given situation, and so that when that **Day of Christ** comes, they will be pure, blameless and will have received the "fruit of righteousness" through Jesus Christ.

So, what does Paul mean when he speaks of the **Day of Christ**? We tend to assume it is a reference to the **second coming** at the end of the age—and we thus assume Paul is referring to something that still hasn't happened yet. Yet we should read Paul's comments about the Day of Christ, both here and elsewhere, within that first century context. In the **Olivet Discourse** (Mark 13, Matthew 24, Luke 21), Jesus prophesied about the destruction of Jerusalem and the Temple and used the same vivid **Day of YHWH** imagery used in both the Old Testament prophets and apocalyptic writers to speak of the time when God would bring wrath upon His enemies and would save His people.

The big twist in the Olivet Discourse is that Jesus was saying God's enemies would be **Jerusalem** and the **Temple** and His people would be the followers of Jesus. But Jesus was also clear that although this would happen within his disciples' lifetime, **the end** wouldn't happen yet. This should tell us that the first-generation Christians fully expected the **Day of Christ** to happen in their lifetime and they associated it with the destruction of the Temple, that happened in AD 70. The consummation of the age, though, would not happen at that time. Thus, we should consider the possibility that when Paul talks about the Day of Christ, he is echoing Jesus' prophecy of the coming destruction of the Temple.

### 2. News from Prison and the Mindset of Christ (1:12-26)

In any case, Paul's first point in the body of his letter is to reassure the church in Philippi, despite his imprisonment, that he is doing well. In fact, his imprisonment has not only led to some of the imperial guards hearing about the Gospel, but it has emboldened other Christians in Rome to be spread the Gospel more openly. Some were speaking out in order to cause more trouble for Paul, but others were speaking out in order to support Paul. He doesn't really care what their motivations are because there really is no such thing as "bad press." Either way, Christ was being preached, and that was a good thing.

Paul says he is certain that eventually he would be vindicated and set free from prison. Still, given the possibility, however remote, that he would be found guilty and executed, Paul contemplates his death a bit in 1:21-26. Basically, he says that as long as he is alive "in the flesh" (in this old age), he knows that he will have "fruitful labor" as a minister of the Gospel, but that he knows full well that when he dies, he will be with Christ, and that is obviously a much better thing. Nevertheless, Paul reiterates that he is confident that he will be vindicated and freed, and that he would soon be able to come to see them soon.

### 3. Citizenship in Heaven and the Mindset of Christ (1:27-2:18)

Paul now switches gears to encourage the believers in Philippi to live their lives in imitation of Christ and live out their **citizenship worthy of the Gospel of**

**Christ** (1:27). Since Philippi was so loyal to Rome and the Philippians were avidly proud of being citizens of Rome, Paul's comments here are important to note. Essentially, he's saying, "You may be Roman citizens, but your true loyalty is to Christ, so live out your Roman citizenship in a way that actually brings glory and honor to Christ."

What this means is for the Church to be unified in **one Spirit** and **one soul** in the faith of the Gospel. They need to stay unified because there are those, be they Judaizers or pagans, who want to harm them. Paul tells them that the Gospel, which declares their salvation, is **a sign of destruction** for their opponents because it threatens their beliefs and declares their way of life will be judged. Nevertheless, in the meantime, Paul tells the Philippian Christians that they are bound to suffer for Christ, just as he was currently suffering for Christ in prison.

Starting in 2:1-11, Paul makes an even more fervent call for unity among them by telling them to have the **same mindset** with each other—to be united **in love, in soul, in mind, and in the Spirit**. It really boils down to putting the interests of others ahead of your own. It is the **mindset of a servant** and ultimately the **mindset of Christ himself**. With that, in 2:6-11, Paul then relates an early Christian hymn about Christ. It has a very clear and parallel structure to it. It opens with Christ equal to God, then proceeds with a "downward mobility" of Christ, to the point where he humbles himself to the point of death. At that point it then proceeds "upwards" to the point where Christ is fully exalted. We can give a visual of this chiastic structure:

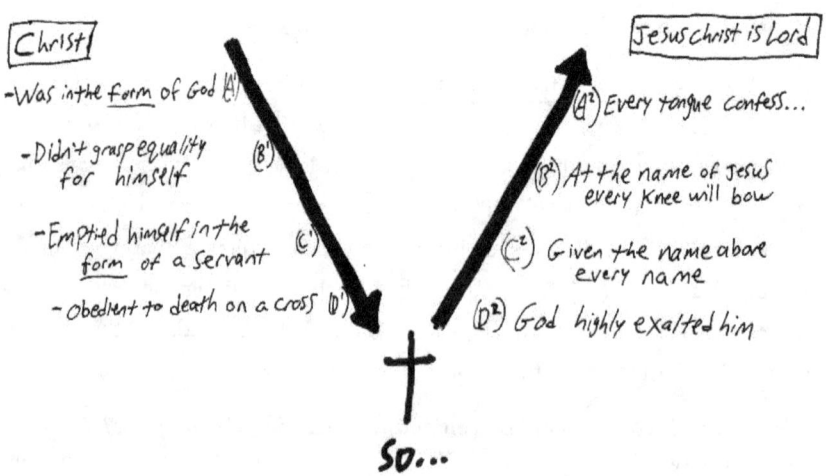

That hymn illustrates the mindset of Christ and what he chose to do in order to bring salvation to the world and become Lord of all creation. And Paul tells the Philippian Christians that that is the same mindset they are to have as well. Given that example of Christ, Paul then encourages the Philippian Christians in 2:12-18 to **work out their own salvation with fear and trembling**. To be clear, he's not saying that have to do certain things *in order to get saved*. Salvation was seen as a lifelong relationship in which the Holy Spirit slowly makes you more like Christ. Thus, Paul is essentially saying, *"You're in a saving relationship with Christ now, so be sure to keep working at that relationship."*

Here, though, is where Paul gets creative. **Jesus Christ is the Son of God the Father**. When you put your faith in him and work out your salvation, it is God (the indwelling **Holy Spirit**) who is at work within you. The full life of the Trinity thus is *at work* within your own *working out* of your salvation, so that you can be, as Paul states, "innocent and blameless **children of God**." That is the identity that differentiates you from the old age, which Paul here describes as "this crooked and perverted generation." Paul then looks forward to that **Day of Christ** and says that he knows that all his work in his ministry of the Gospel will not be in vain. Even if his imprisonment does end up in his death, Paul equates his possible death with a priestly drink offering that acts as a sacrifice in the service of the faith.

### 4. Timothy and Epaphroditus (2:19-30)

With that, Paul turns his attention to the practical matter of his sending **Timothy** and **Epaphroditus** to Philippi. Hence, in 2:19-24, Paul simply says, "I'm hoping to send Timothy to you soon. He has been a tremendous servant of the Gospel." Then in 2:25-30, Paul also mentions he is sending Epaphroditus back along with Timothy. Epaphroditus was apparently part of the church in Philippi, and the Philippians had sent him to help Paul for a time. At one point while with Paul, Epaphroditus had gotten extremely sick, and was even at the point of death, but that he had since recovered. Therefore, Paul is sending him back to Philippi so that they wouldn't have to worry about him.

### 5. A Warning Against the Judaizers (3:1-4:1)

In this next section, Paul makes it a point to warn the Philippian Christians about **Judaizers**. Apparently, they had a habit of following Paul around pressuring Gentile Christians to accept circumcision and submit to the Torah. Paul does not hold back his disgust for these Judaizers, calling them **dogs**, **evil workers**, and even **mutilators**, due to their insistence that Gentile Christians get circumcised. He then contrasts his ministry with that of the Judaizers, saying that "we" (meaning himself, his ministry, and the Gentile Christians) are the **true circumcision** and are the ones worshipping in the Spirit and boasting in Christ Jesus. Paul is thus emphasizing that the true circumcision is the one of the heart that is done by the Holy Spirit.

Nevertheless, Paul then points out his own "Jewish credentials" to show that he is just as Jewish as the Judaizers: circumcised on the 8th day, an Israelite from the tribe of Benjamin, a Torah-observant Pharisee, and so zealous that he actually persecuted the Church. But he then insists that once he encountered the risen Jesus on the road to Damascus, he realized none of those things mattered in terms of righteousness. He may have been a Torah-observant Pharisee, but he still was an enemy of God in need of the grace and forgiveness that is in Christ. That is why he says he considers all his Jewish credentials to be **scoobala**—*garbage, excrement, crap*. All that matters is the righteousness that comes through faith in Christ, and the power that makes someone righteous is the very power of Christ's resurrection. Therefore, the only way to experience that power of Christ's resurrection is to first share in Christ's suffering and death.

Paul is quick to point out that he obviously had not yet been **made perfect**. The Greek word here is **teleioo**, and it describes being made complete, whole, and **fully mature**. Simply put, Paul is saying he isn't yet fully mature in Christ—he hasn't reached the finish line yet and is still running the race. Using that metaphor of running in the Olympic games, Paul says he looks forward to when he finally receives that **upward call** and ascends the platform to receive the prize of a **victor's wreath**. Paul then says those who are **mature** should have the same kind of **mindset**. But if anyone has a **different mindset**, Paul says he is certain God will reveal the correct mindset to that person eventually.

Finally, Paul holds himself up as an example for the Philippian Christians to follow, as opposed to what the Judaizers were pressuring them to imitate. Paul calls them "enemies of the cross of Christ" (although any group that tempts them to reject Christ would be considered enemies of the cross of Christ). Paul then uses the Greek word **telos** to further describe these enemies, saying their *telos* ("end") is going to be destruction, as opposed to the *telos* of Christians, which is the resurrection from the dead and being made like Christ. He continues by saying that these enemies' minds are on **earthly things**, whereas the Christians' citizenship is in Heaven, and it is from Heaven that we are awaiting the Savior, the Lord Jesus Christ.

It should be noted that the word **savior** carries with it a priestly meaning of **one who sanctifies**. Thus, what Paul is emphasizing that Jesus is *Lord, Christ,* and a *priest*. He has the resurrection power to rule and to bring all things in subjection to him, even death—that is why he is *Lord*. But that same power enables him to, "transform the body of our humble state and conform it to the body of his glory." That is why he is a high priest who **sanctifies the mortal body** and thus **transforms** it to conform to **the body of his glory**.

Paul's talk of Heaven, therefore, shouldn't be seen as a place where bodiless spirits play harps and walk on clouds. Paul is talking about the power and reign of God being established within a transformed creation that Jesus will eventually accomplish, precisely because that power of God has been manifested in him to defeat death. That is why Paul encourages the Philippian Christians to stand firm in the Lord. Their citizenship is in the Kingdom of God, so they should imitate Paul and strive to have the same mindset of Christ, because Christ will one day bring about the New Creation and their mortal bodies will be transformed.

### 6. Final Exhortations…and Euodia and Syntyche (4:2-9)

At the end of Paul's letter, he addresses a specific problem in the Philippian Church regarding two women, **Euodia** and **Syntyche**. We don't know what the problem actually was, but Paul appeals to them to have the same mindset in the Lord. He then appeals to someone named **Syzygus** to help these women. The interesting thing about that name is that it means "loyal co-worker," so it is possible that Paul is asking Epaphroditus as his loyal co-worker to help these women (who had worked with Paul in the past, along with a man named Clement) resolve their differences. It is possible that this is the Clement that later became the bishop of Rome in the latter part of the first century and who wrote a famous letter to the Corinthians himself.

Paul then encourages the Philippian Christians to rejoice in all things, and to make their requests known to God in their prayers and thanksgivings. He reassures them that the peace of God will be with them and then gives a general encouragement that can be boiled down to this: **Set your minds on what is good, practice what we taught you, and the God of peace will be with you**.

### 7. Personal Comments (4:10-23)

Paul ends his letter by thanking them for "setting their minds on him" again. He knows they always have but didn't have the opportunity to show it. Presumably, he is referring to some kind of gift they sent him. He says he has learned to be satisfied no matter what and to find strength in all situations, but then thanks them again for "sharing in his tribulation." He then recalls that when he first left Macedonia, they were the only church to share in the giving and receiving of donations. They even sent him help twice when he was in Thessalonica. Paul tells them that he isn't looking for any gift at the moment, but that he wanted them to know he appreciated the things they sent by the hand of Epaphroditus. With that he gives a final blessing.

The last three verses of the letter were probably the part of the letter Paul wrote with his own hand. They contain final greetings to the Philippian Christians from those who are with Paul. He even can't resist telling them that the believers who are in **Caesar's household** greet them as well. It really is quite amazing to think that at that point in the early 60s, a mere 30 years after the death and resurrection of Jesus Christ, the Gospel had already born fruit to where some people in Caesar's own household had come to faith in Christ.

# EPHESIANS

**Time of Writing:** During Paul's imprisonment in Rome (AD 60-63)

### History of the City/Paul in Ephesus

Ephesus was the first and greatest city in Asia and was the home to the Temple of Artemis (Diana), one of the seven wonders of the ancient world. It was known for its library, amphitheater, gymnasium, and baths. Since it was a port city, it was involved in a lot of trade, and it sported a lucrative "tourist industry" that profited off of people visiting the Temple of Artemis.

Paul visited Ephesus during his second missionary journey (Acts 19:1-41). Paul arrived in Ephesus while Apollos was in Corinth. He spoke about the Kingdom of God and of the new movement (then known as *The Way*) in the synagogues. Those who became disciples followed Paul out of the synagogue and they met in the hall of Tyrannus. Paul performed many miracles in Ephesus; but when Jewish exorcists attempted to use the name of Jesus, the possessed man attacked them (Acts 19:11-16). After such a demonstration, many in Ephesus became believers and started to burn their "magic books." But eventually, this new movement began to threaten the local economy that depended on revenue stemming from the worship of Artemis. The local merchants started a riot, seized two of Paul's associates (Gaius and Aristarchus), and went to the theater in Ephesus, shouting "Great is Artemis of the Ephesians!" After such turmoil, Paul then left Ephesus and went on to Macedonia.

### The Big Things to Know About Ephesians

A. **Break Down the Wall**: Paul emphasizes that one of the biggest things Christ has accomplished through his death and resurrection is the breaking down of the *wall of hostility* that separated Jews and Gentiles. Simply put, the work of Christ breaks down walls that divide various people into separate and hostile groups.

B. **The New Humanity**: The goal of Christ's work is to make a *new humanity*—the true *People of God*—that is made up of Christians from all different groups, be they racial, socio-economic, or anything else.

C. **The Church's Role in Christ's Work**: Obviously, given that goal of Christ's work, that means the Church has a job to do! The Church is where this new kind of humanity should be seen.

D. **Practical Matters**: There are also practical matters for Christians who live in the Roman Empire (or anywhere, actually) to consider. Basically, how do you live as the People of God within the current systems of the world?

## Literary Map: Ephesians

|  | | | | |
|---|---|---|---|---|
| **Greeting and Thanksgiving (1:1-23)** | 1:1-14 The Greeting Spiritual Blessings in Christ | 1:15-23 Thanksgiving for the Ephesian Church | | |
| **Ephesians: Before/After (2:1-22)** | 2:1-10 Former Life of the Ephesians Now Saved Through Faith | 2:11-22 Oneness in Christ Peace Between Jew and Gentile | | |
| **The Goal of the Gospel (3:1-21)** | 3:1-6 The Mystery of the Gospel | 3:7-13 The Mission of the Church | 3:14-21 Paul's Prayer: Fulfillment of Abrahamic Covenant | |
| **Unity in Christ (4:1-5:20)** | 4:1-16 Call for Unity in Christ | 4:17-24 Put off the Old "Gentile Self" | 4:25-32 Life in the Body of Christ | 5:1-20 Walking in Love |
| **Practical Matters (5:21-6:24)** | 5:21-33 Wives Husbands | 6:1-4 Children Parents | 6:5-9 Slaves Masters | 6:10-17 Whole Armor of God |

6:18-24 Final Greetings

## A Walkthrough of Ephesians

### 1. The Greeting and Thanksgiving (1:1-23)

After giving a standard greeting, Paul immediately does a deep dive into the key focal point of the entire letter—**Christ's role in the salvation Gospel of God.** The picture here is a visual representation of what Paul lays out in these first two chapters. What we need to do, though, is a slow walkthrough of these incredibly fascinating chapters that are packed with meaning. Ephesians 1:3-14 boils down to Paul's praise of God the Father for the Gospel. It is when he proceeds to give the details of what the Gospel entails that the fireworks begin.

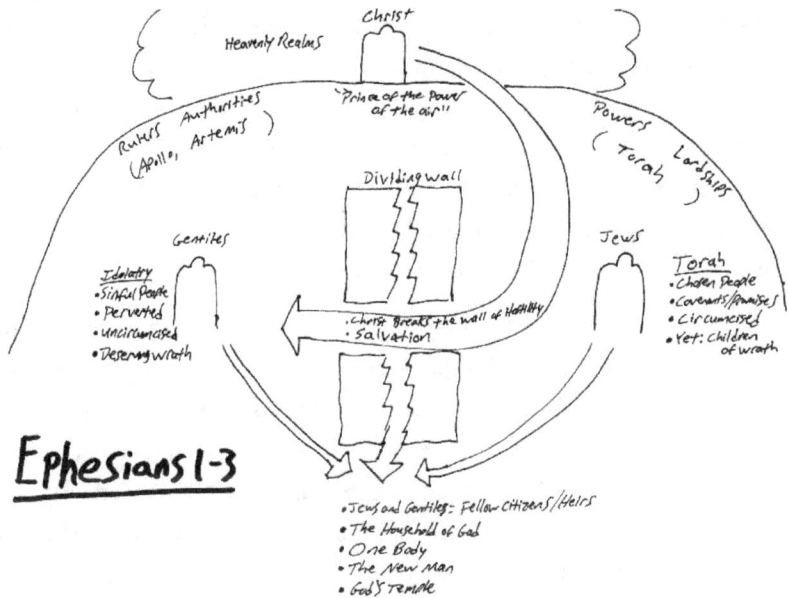

In 1:3, Paul displays his Trinitarian understanding when he praises God the **Father** because He has blessed us with **Spiritual** blessings (better understood as the blessings in the Spirit) in the **heavenly realms** in **Christ**. Now, it is important to get a firm grasp on what he means when he refers to *heavenly realms*, because he uses it a number of times in the letter. He's not talking about "heaven," but rather the *spiritual world*—the non-material side to reality, the powers that lie "behind the curtain," so to speak, that really run things in the world. For example, Paul would say Greek gods don't really exist, but there was a very real demonic power behind the worship of those gods and it was that power that was at work in trying to lead people astray and destroy them. Therefore, what Paul is going to argue is that in Christ, God the Father has poured out on the Church the

blessings of the Spirit so that we can confront and exercise authority over those powers in the heavenly realms.

In 1:4, Paul then describes the Church as those who been **called out from the present age** and **called in Christ**. When Paul says this calling was *from the foundation of the world*, he means that what God was doing in the Gospel was what He had been planning all along. The purpose of this calling was so that we could be a people who are **holy and blameless in love**. In 1:5-6, Paul says that Christians are **predestined for Sonship** through Jesus Christ, according to the **purpose and will** of the Father. In other words, God's plan has always been that those who put their faith in Christ the Son are going to eventually be like Christ the Son and hence, be a child of God Himself. Paul then explains in 1:7-8 that this has been accomplished through the blood of Christ, which has brought about forgiveness of our transgressions. Paul is actually using the **sacrificial language of the Temple** to explain salvation here, where the sacrificial death brings about reconciliation with God. All this was according to the **riches of His grace**, meaning God was gracious enough to provide a way that makes reconciliation possible.

In 1:9-10 Paul says that God the Father has made known the **mystery of His will** in Christ for the **stewardship** (or plan) **of the fullness of the times**. That "plan" is for the Church to help to **unite all things in Heaven and earth**. The easiest way to understand what Paul means is to think of God's plan in two phases. *Phase One* is the creation of the material, but corruptible created order, where human beings are made in God's image, with a special purpose and vocation, but are unable to fulfill that purpose because of sin and death.

*Phase Two* is where God transforms and sanctifies the material, corruptible creation into a new creation through the work of Christ and the empowerment of the Holy Spirit. Through Christ and the Spirit those made in God's image can be transformed into sons of God, just like the Son of God. Paul frames this **new creation language** with the **covenantal language** of Abraham in 1:11, for he says that in Christ, the Church has **obtained an inheritance**, namely the inheritance promised to Abraham's descendants—the blessing of all nations.

Paul then makes reference to both the first Jewish-Christians and the Gentile-Christians. He first says that "we" (Jewish-Christians) were first to put their hope in Christ, and then when "you" (Gentile Christians) first heard the **Word of Truth** (the Gospel), "you" put your faith in Christ and were **sealed with the Holy**

**Spirit of promise**. This is an allusion to both **Joel** and **Jeremiah**, who prophesied about God's Spirit being the evidence of the New Covenant. The Holy Spirit thus is the **guarantee of our inheritance** until we fully redeem the **possession** of the New Creation.

In light of all this, Paul tells the Ephesian Christians in 1:15-19 that he never stops giving thanks for them in his prayers. He prays that the **Father of glory,** the God of the **Lord Jesus Christ**, would give them the **Spirit of wisdom and revelation** in the knowledge of him (Christ). Paul also prays that God the Father would **enlighten the eyes** of their hearts, so that they could see two things: (1) **the hope of His calling** (the new creation), which is the **riches of the glory of His inheritance for the saints**, and (2) **the greatness of His power for the faithful**.

This power that is available to the faithful is the same power that rose Christ from the dead and seated him at the Right Hand **in the heavenly realms**. Simply put, even though demonic spirits exert authority over human beings through the power of death, Christ has overpowered death and now has authority over those spirits, and the faithful have access to that same power that has made Jesus over **every ruler, authority, power, and lordship** (1:21), subordinating everything under his feet (1:22). Now that Christ has conquered death, he has the power to remake and transform God's creation. Not only that, but the Church is Christ's body, and that means the Church has a part to play in Christ's lordship and authority (1:22-23). The Church is the means by which Christ will remake and transform God's creation. It is through the Church that God's purposes will be fulfilled.

## 2. The Ephesians: Before and After (2:1-22)

Having laid out what the Gospel entails, Paul now focuses on Gentiles and their status before and after accepting the Gospel. Even though the entire chapter focuses on Gentiles, the chapter can be broken up into two sections. In the **first section (2:1-10)**, Paul talks about the state of the Gentile Christians before they had come to Christ: "You (Gentiles) were dead in your trespasses and sins…" (2:1). He says they walked according to **the age of this world** and **the ruler of the authority of the air**. It is worth noting that most translations have **course** of this world, but the word is clearly **age**, and it reflects the Jewish and Christian worldview regarding currently living **in the old age** in which Satan ruled, and waiting for the coming **Messianic Age**, in which God would establish His rule. Obviously, the

Jews were still waiting for it, whereas Christians were saying that, because of Christ, the Messianic Age had broken into the old age.

Obviously, the ruler of the air is a reference to Satan, and Paul says this "ruler" is **the spirit that is at work in the sons of disobedience**. Given the context of the mid-first century, it would seem that Paul is talking about, Israel, his fellow Jews who had rejected Christ. So, when Paul says in 2:3 "All of us" once lived among them, he is referring to how the original followers of Christ were Jews. He further describes his former life in Judaism as living in the lusts and desires **of the flesh**, a reference to not only the Jewish practice of circumcision, but also Paul's way of pointing out that without Christ, Jews, just like Gentiles, were *living in the flesh*, under the authority of the *ruler of the air* who rules this *present, old age*. That is why Paul says that "we" Jews were once **children of wrath**, *just like the rest*—both Jews and Gentiles were in danger of God's wrath.

The good news comes in 2:4-10, where Paul declares that because God is rich in love and mercy, "we" (both Jews and Gentiles) who were dead in trespasses, are now **alive together in Christ** and have been saved by grace. Through the death and resurrection of Christ, people who had formerly been divided and were dead in their sins have now been brought together in the life of Christ. Not only that, but God has also **seated us in the heavenly realms with Christ Jesus** so that God would be able to show the surpassing riches of His grace. Thus, the Church now shares in the authority of Christ over the spiritual powers of this age and now has the power in the Spirit to take part in Christ's job of uniting all things in Heaven and earth together. In this way, the Church, by being in Christ, fulfills God's purposes for humanity as His image-bearers: *to act as priestly custodian-kings of His creation who rule His creation, who care for His creation, and who offer the creation up to Him as a form of worship.*

Paul then emphasizes something he says in most of his other letters. Salvation is a gift of God that comes through faith, and it isn't from **works**, meaning specifically **works of Torah**, as well as **pagan idolatry**, which literally is the **work of human hands**. To the contrary, Paul says "we"—Jews and Gentiles together in Christ—are **God's workmanship** and are **created in Christ Jesus** to do the **good works** that God has wanted His image-bearers to do all along. Therefore, just as Gentiles (and Jews, for that matter) once "walked" according to the age of this world, God has re-created them in Christ to do good works and "walk" in them.

In the **second section (2:11-22)**, Paul elaborates on the unity between Jews and Gentiles that has been brought about in Christ. Again, he touches upon their way of life before Christ and how they were once **Gentiles in the flesh** (2:11-12). Most translations have Paul saying that they were called "the uncircumcised" by "the circumcised," meaning Jews. The actual Greek is a bit more graphic. Jews didn't call Gentiles "uncircumcised" because to be "uncircumcised" would be to go through a surgical procedure to cover up the marks of circumcision, and Gentiles were not circumcised in the first place.

Rather, Jews called Gentiles "the foreskinned." Despite that, Paul reminds them that circumcision was nothing more than just **in the flesh made by hands**. Still, without Christ, the Gentiles had no connection with the **citizenship of Israel**, and were **foreigners to the covenants of the promise**, with no hope and without God. Simply put—Gentiles weren't part of Israel, and therefore had no hope.

The good news, though, begins in 2:13, when Paul says that now, because of Christ Jesus, they who were **once far off** have been **brought near** through the blood of Christ. Christ's death is thus described using the language of the Temple sacrificial system—because of a sacrifice, reconciliation with God is achieved. And that is precisely what Paul emphasizes when he says that Christ is **our peace**—he had made peace, not only between God and humanity, but also between Jew and Gentile. He **makes the two one** and **tears down the wall of hostility**. The irony of all this is seen when Paul says Christ did all this **in his flesh**. To highlight Paul's use of "the flesh" in this passage: (1) The Gentiles once walked *according to the flesh*; (2) Since they were not *circumcised in the flesh*, they had no connection with the citizenship of Israel; (3) But that *circumcision in the flesh* didn't mean much because Jews also lived in the *lusts and desires of the flesh*; (4) But Christ's sacrificial death tore down the dividing wall between Jew and Gentile *in his flesh*

And what was it that constructed that dividing wall? **The Torah!** Paul says in 2:15 that Christ's death in the flesh did away with the Torah, and that is what made peace between Jew and Gentile possible. Not only that, but through his death Christ can **create one man in himself**, thus making peace, to where there is now **one body**. To the point, the division is no longer between Jews and Gentiles, but between the "old humanity" in Adam and the "recreated humanity" in Christ. Thus, Jews and Gentiles together, as a part of the new humanity in Christ, have access in **one Spirit** to **the Father**.

That means that Gentile Christians are no longer foreigners but are rather **fellow citizens with the saints** and **members in God's household**, which Paul describes using Temple imagery. The "foundation" of God's house is the apostles and prophets, and the "cornerstone" is Christ. Then in 2:21, Paul mixes the metaphors of a house and a body. He says that the entire **structure** is fitted together in Christ, and that it **grows into a Holy Temple** in the Lord. Buildings don't grow, but bodies do! Still, the point is obvious: Christ's body is the Church, and the Church is God's Holy Temple; and just as God creates a new man in Christ, He also builds His House where His Spirit can dwell.

### 3. The Goal of the Gospel (3:1-21)

In chapter three, Paul focuses on three things: (A) **The mystery of the Gospel** (3:1-6), (B) **The mission of the Church** (3:7-13), and (C) Paul's prayer for the true **fulfillment of the Abrahamic Covenant** (3:14-21).

In 3:1-6, Paul says that he is currently in prison because he is doing his job as a steward to bring the Gospel to the Gentiles. He says that this **mystery** (namely, how the Gentiles would become part of God's people) was made known to him through a revelation. The mystery is simply this: **The Gentiles become fellow-heirs and sharers in the promise to Abraham through Christ Jesus, and that through Christ they become members of one body—that is what the Gospel declares**. What Paul is speaking about it the very fulfillment of the Abrahamic covenant. From Abraham would come a great nation (Israel), and through that nation all nations would be blessed. The entire history of Israel finds its culmination in Christ. He is the fulfillment of the very purpose of having an Israel in the first place. Through his death and resurrection and the outpouring of the Holy Spirit, God's promises to Abraham are achieved.

In 3:7-13, Paul reiterates that his entire job, his "stewardship of the mystery," has been to share that message to the Gentiles. And now that **wisdom of God** is made known through the Church to the **rulers and authorities in the heavenly realms** (as before in 1:3, 20-21; and 2:6-7). Once again, Paul is stressing three things: (A) Christ now has power over the "rulers and authorities in the heavenly realms," (B) The Church, as Christ's body, through the power of the Spirit, shares in Christ's power over those "rulers and authorities in the heavenly realms," and (C) thus the Church's mission is to further Christ's work of reconciliation. Because of that, the Church's confidence to do all that is rooted in Christ, and that is why Paul tells the Ephesian Christians they should not be upset that he is in prison.

What he is going through is furthering the Gospel, whose end will result in God's glory filling all the earth and bringing about the new creation and the fullness of Christ's body.

In 3:14-21, Paul ends with a prayer. By saying that he bends his knees to the Father **from whom every family under Heaven and on the earth is named**, Paul is alluding to God's covenant with Abraham, when God tells Abraham that he would become the father of many nations, and that through him, God would eventually bring blessing to all the families on the earth. In any case, Paul prays that they would be **strengthened through His (the Father's) Spirit** in the inner man (3:16) and that **Christ would take up residence in their hearts** through faith and that they would be rooted in love (3:17). The goal is for them to grasp with all the saints and to know just how much the love of Christ surpasses anything they can possibly comprehend, and "be filled with the fullness of God" (3:18-19).

### 4. Unity in Christ (4:1-5:20)

When it gets right down to it, Ephesians 1-3 says, *"This is what the Gospel is, and this is who you are in Christ,"* and Ephesians 4-6 says, *"Given that, this is how you should live your everyday lives."* In this particular section, Paul breaks his comments down in four parts. First, in **4:1-16**, Paul makes a clear appeal for the Ephesian Christians to be unified in Christ, or as he puts it, "walk in a manner worthy of your calling." That means living a life of **humility, gentleness, long-suffering, patience, love**, and a striving for **unity of the Spirit** in the **bond of peace**. After all, there is **one body** (the Church), **one Spirit** (the Holy Spirit), **one hope** (a future resurrection and new creation), **one Lord** (Christ), **one faith** (the Christian faith), **one baptism** (Christian baptism), and **one God and Father of all**, who is not only above all, but also through all and in all.

Paul then shifts to the topic of spiritual gifts and how Christians are to use them to unify and build up the Church body. He says this is possible because Christ had died and thus *descended to the lower parts of the earth* (meaning Sheol) in order to fill all things, and then *ascended to a place of authority over all creation*. As the victorious king, the gifts he gives his people are meant to work to the fulfillment of God's plan, namely, to redeem all creation to the point where God's Spirit fulfills and empowers all things.

These gifts are to be used to train up Christians, to minister to others, and to build up the body of Christ in unity of the faith and knowledge of the Son of God to **full maturity** and the fullness of Christ. We used to be **infants** who were easily deceived, sort of like **Adam and Eve** (4:14), but now we are to **grow up into Christ, who is the head**, and whose body is the Church. The entire purpose God has for human beings who are created in God's image (Adam) is that they grow up into the living image of God (Christ) and to be part of his body—the true goal God has for human beings.

Then in **4:17-24**, Paul tells the Ephesian Christians "not to walk like the Gentiles walk"—don't live like pagans anymore. He then goes on to describe the pagan way of life in the same way he did in Romans 1:18-24: Pagans live with the **futility of their mind** and a **darkened understanding** and are **alienated from the life of God** because of their **ignorance and hardness of heart**. They, though, have learned the **truth that is in Jesus** and have **thrown off their former way of life**—the old kind of man who was corrupted by the **lusts of deception** (like Adam). Now, though, they are being **renewed by the Spirit of their mind** and are **clothing themselves with the new man** (the new kind of man in Christ) who is created in true righteousness and holiness.

In **4:25-32**, Paul describes just what new life is like in the body of Christ by contrasting it with the "former way of life." Instead of lying, stewing in anger, stealing, and saying things to tear others down, the new life in Christ is about speaking truth to each other, resolving whatever is the cause for anger, working hard in order to share with those in need, and speaking only what is good for building others up. It means not grieving the Holy Spirit. It means getting rid of any kind of evil and instead trying to be kind and gracious to others, *just like God was gracious to us in Christ.*

Finally, in **5:1-20**, Paul encourages the Ephesian Christians to imitate God by **walking in love** and points to Christ as the prime example of this by giving his life on our behalf to be **a sweet fragrant offering** and **a sacrifice** to God—once again, describing Christ's death in terms of a Temple sacrifice that brings reconciliation with God. That way of life of walking in Christ-like love is in direct opposition to the kind of pagan idolatrous lifestyle that was so prominent at the time.

Therefore, in 5:3-5, Paul reminds them not to have anything to do with fornication, impurity, greed, obscenity, or foolish and vulgar talk. Paul says those kinds of people do not have **an inheritance in the Kingdom of Christ and God**. To be clear, he's not laying down some sort of legalistic purity rules that, if broken, gives you a direct ticket to hellfire and brimstone. Given the historical context of the Roman Empire in AD 60, Paul is simply saying if you routinely go to pagan temples and see pagan temple prostitutes and continue in that pagan way of life, then don't kid yourself—you're not a Christian.

If 5:3-5 is a warning about the pagan idolatrous lifestyle, 5:6-7 is a warning about Judaism. Paul warns the Ephesian Christians not to be deceived by empty words and says that is why the **wrath of God** is coming upon the **sons of disobedience**. When understood in the context of AD 60, it seems Paul is echoing Jesus' words in the **Olivet Discourse** (Mark 13, Matthew 24, Luke 21) about how Jerusalem and the Temple would soon suffer God's wrath and be destroyed because the Jews in Judea had rejected Jesus and had persecuted his followers.

In 5:8-14, Paul uses the imagery of **light and darkness** to further highlight the differences between the two ways of life. In doing so, though, Paul throws in another metaphor into the mix and thus ends up mixing his metaphors which, if one stops and thinks about it, sounds a bit odd—still, the point is clear. Paul tells the Ephesian Christians that since they have come out of the darkness of paganism into the light of the Lord, that they are to now **walk as children of the light**. But then Paul proceeds to speak of the **fruit of light**, namely goodness, righteousness, and truth. Obviously "light" doesn't bear "fruit," but Paul's point still comes across: living in the light of the Lord will lead to a certain way of life. By contrast, Paul again warns them not to have anything to do with the **unfruitful works of darkness**, but they should rather expose them...*with the light!*

He then says that what those **unfruitful works** that are done in the dark and in secret are too shameful to even speak of. Yet, when exposed by the light, those things become exposed and, as Paul says, "everything that becomes visible **is light**." Taken literally, that is absurd. If I am in a dark room and shine a flashlight onto a chair, that chair becomes visible, but that chair doesn't become light. But Paul's point is that hopefully, when people who are in darkness are exposed to the light of Christ, they will come to Christ and become part of the body of Christ. Paul then shares an early Christian saying: *"Arise, O sleeper, and rise from the dead, and Christ will shine upon you!"* With this, the whole darkness/light metaphor takes on yet another layer, that of death and resurrection, for Paul then tells them that since they have been resurrected in the light of Christ, they should *pay attention to the way that you walk*. The unwise **walk in the darkness**, whereas the wise **walk in the light**.

## 5. Practical Matters: Living Out the Gospel (5:21-6:24)

In the final section of the letter, Paul applies everything he has been saying to how it all plays out in practical ways. First, he addresses **husband-wife relationships** in **5:21-33**. His comments need to be understood against the backdrop of the very misogynistic and patriarchal Roman culture. He first says that everyone should be subject to each other in the fear of Christ. With that, Paul first speaks to wives in 5:22-24 and tells them to be subject to their husbands, because they're supposed to be subject to everyone in the Lord anyway. He tells them to treat their husbands as they would treat Christ. Paul then echoes the traditional Roman view that husbands hold authority over their wives, and thus says that the husband is the head of the wife. But he then begins to turn everything on its head by emphasizing the husband is the head of the wife, *"just like Christ is the head of the Church and the savior of the body."*

Paul then continues in 5:25-33 by addressing husbands and tells them, *"Love your wives, just like Christ loved the Church."* In Roman culture, husbands weren't even expected to be faithful to their wives. Women were second class citizens who were completely at the mercy of their husbands, and their husbands would regularly go to pagan temples to see temple prostitutes. Yet Paul is telling husbands that they are to love their wives as Christ loved the Church, even to the point of giving their life for their wives. And just as the Church is the body of Christ, husbands should love their wives as their own body.

If we put all that together, we should see how Paul has cleverly dismantled Roman patriarchy with his comments. Or perhaps a better way to say it is that Paul is showing how, when there is that kind of self-giving love in the husband-wife relationship, *any patriarchal hierarchy in the culture becomes irrelevant*. When a husband loves his wife like Christ loves the Church, there is effectively *mutual submission* between both the husband and the wife. When that happens in the love of Christ, *salvation happens*. The husband and wife love each other, sacrifice themselves for each other, and thus build each other up within the body of Christ. Paul concludes by highlighting the unity between husband and wife by quoting **Genesis 2:24: they are one flesh and one body**. Not only is that true in a marriage, Paul says that is the great mystery of Christ and the Church.

Paul then turns his attention to **parent-child relationships** in **6:1-4**. He first tells children to obey their parents in the Lord, because it is the right thing to do. If they do that, things are generally going to go well for them. But as a general rule of thumb, parents want to do what is best for their children, so if children obey their parents, they're going to grow up into well-adjusted and stable adults. What he says to parents, though, needs to be explained. Most translations have something like, *"Fathers, don't provoke your children to anger."* Paul isn't telling parents not to make their children angry. If you never make your children angry, then you're not a good parent because that means you're giving them everything they want and are spoiling them. What Paul is actually saying is, *"Don't push your children to wrath."* **Wrath** is what God brings upon rebellious people. So, Paul is telling parents not to raise their children in a way that results in them growing up into rebellious, sinful people who will incur God's wrath. Instead, parents are to discipline and train their children.

Paul then addresses the **slave-master relationship** in **6:5-9**. In the Roman world, slavery was an established institution. Although it was obviously bad, it was not the same thing as the race-based institution of slavery in Europe and America in the 18th-19th centuries. Nevertheless, Christians weren't in positions of legal authority to do anything about it, and Paul was just a travelling minister. He had to deal with the reality that some Christians were slaves and some Christians had slaves. So, here in 6:5-9, he addresses how Christians should live in that cultural context.

He first tells slaves to obey their masters, *just like you would obey Christ*. Do your service and work the best you can, not to impress your master, *but to impress God*. Basically, Paul tells them to do their work as **a servant of Christ**. Then Paul once again turns Roman cultural norms on their head by telling masters to treat their slaves in the same way their slaves treat them—basically be a servant of Christ in the way they treat their slaves. Paul tells them not to threaten their slaves or treat them poorly, because when it comes right down to it, both the slave and the master have the same Lord in Heaven. So, when Paul says that there is no favoritism with the Lord, the message is clear. In a Roman cultural context, one might be the master and the other the slave, but in the Christian context in the Church, both slave and master are on equal footing—so *be subject to one another and love one another.*

The last significant part in Ephesians is the famous **Armor of God** section in **6:10-20**. In his closing comments, Paul encourages the Ephesian Christians to be strengthened in the Lord and then tells them to "put on the whole armor of God" so they can be ready to battle against "the tricks of the devil" (6:10-11). The real battle Christians must wage isn't again "flesh and blood," but is rather against those **rulers, authorities, cosmic powers of this darkness,** and the **spiritual forces of**

**evil in the heavenly realms**—the very things he has referenced earlier in 1:20-22, 2:6, and 3:10.

Put another way, Paul is telling them that the real battle for Christians isn't with political systems, cultural conventions, or societal structures, because the real problem in the world isn't a particular party, leader, political agenda, or social more. The real battle for Christians is with the spiritual powers who work to manipulate and corrupt political systems and conventions and structures. Therefore, as Paul as emphasized throughout the letter, the love of Christ and a Christian living selflessly for others completely ignores oppressive power structures. When that happens, there is no need to actively subvert them, for they will crumble all on their own.

In any case, Paul's description of the whole armor of God in 6:13-20 is well known: *the belt of truth, the breastplate of righteousness, the shoes for the readiness of the Gospel of peace, the shield of faith, the helmet of salvation,* and *the sword of the Spirit,* which is the *Word of God.* To be clear, the sword of the Spirit and the Word of God is not the Bible. When Paul wrote Ephesians, there wasn't yet a New Testament. He is talking about the prophetic witness and empowerment of the Holy Spirit and the message of the Gospel. Obviously, the New Testament is the written canon of the testimony that the early Church preached in the first century, but it itself is not the sword of the Spirit or Word of God.

Paul ends his letter in 6:18-23 by encouraging the Ephesian Christians to pray at all times in the Spirit, thus tying the sword of the Spirit directly to their prayer life. He also encourages them to persevere in everything they are doing and to pray that he may be given the right things to say whenever he shares the mystery of the Gospel. Then after saying that he is in chains currently precisely because of the Gospel, he again asks for them to pray that he can continue to speak boldly when necessary. In his final greetings, he mentions **Tychicus**, presumably the one who has brought Paul's letter to Ephesus and tells them that Tychicus will catch them up on all that was going on with Paul. With that, Paul ends the letter by wishing peace, love, and faith from God the Father and the Lord Jesus Christ upon them all.

# COLOSSIANS

**Time of Writing:** During Paul's imprisonment in Rome (AD 60-63)

**History of the City/Paul (not) in Colossae**

Colossae was part of a tri-city area, along with Laodicea and Hieropolis. It was a city based on commerce, as well as its health resorts and medicinal springs. Like other Hellenistic cities, Colossae had its share of pagan temples and cults, one of which was the cult of goddess **Cybele**. In mythology, she compelled **Attis** to castrate himself so that he wouldn't be drawn to another lover. Therefore, during the worship of Cybele, male worshippers would sometimes castrate themselves, mimicking Attis. In general, the people of Colossae, like people throughout the Roman world, lived in fear of angelic or spiritual forces (**stoicheia**). Jews even would portray Moses and Solomon as having power over these spiritual forces. In any case, whether pagan or Jewish, it was taught that severe aesthetic practices had to be performed in order to have power over these spiritual forces.

Paul had never visited Colossae (2:1). The church had rather been founded by **Epaphrus** (1:6-7), who was a co-worker of Paul. Therefore, the church's allegiance still was to Paul. The church was made up mostly of Gentiles (1:21; 2:13). The current leader was a man named **Archippus** (4:17). Paul wrote to the church in Colossae for basically two reasons: (1) Epaphrus had visited him and had told him how the church was doing—although things were going well, there were still some problems that Paul wanted to address; and (2) Paul was about to send back with a co-worker named **Tychius** a runaway slave of Philemon's who had since become a Christian. This slave's name was **Onesimus**. Paul wrote, therefore, a second letter specifically to Philemon along with his letter to the church in Colossae.

## The Big Things to Know About Colossians

A. **Christ's Supremacy and Power to Bring About Reconciliation**: As in Ephesians, Paul emphasizes Christ's role in bringing about reconciliation, not just between human beings and God, but between formerly hostile groups of human beings (like Jews and Gentiles). Here in Colossians, though, Paul *really emphasizes* the supremacy and power of Christ.

B. **The Church's Role in Christ's Reconciliation Plan**: Again, as in Ephesians, Paul stresses that the Church is the "main vehicle" Christ uses to bring about that reconciliation.

C. **Warnings Against Pagan Philosophy and Judaism**: Again, as in Ephesians, Paul warns Christians about the dangers of falling into one of two worldviews—that of pagan philosophy and Torah-observant Judaism.

D. **Practical Matters About Living Out the New Self**: Again, as in Ephesians, Paul speaks about practical matters in everyday life concerning how to live as a Christian in the midst of the surrounding pagan culture.

### Literary Map: Colossians

**1:1-14**
Greeting/Thanksgiving

**Christ and the Church (1:15-2:7)**

| 1:15-20 | 1:21-2:7 |
|---|---|
| The Supremacy of Christ | Paul's Ministry to the Church |

**Warnings (2:8-23)**

| 2:8-15 | 2:16-23 |
|---|---|
| Warning Against Pagan Philosophy | Warning Against the Judaism of the Judaizers |

**Living the New Self (3:1-4:1)**

| 3:1-17 | 3:18-4:1 |
|---|---|
| Encouragement to Put on the New Self | Practical Instructions |

**4:2-18**
Exhortations
Final Greetings

## A Walkthrough of Colossians

### 1. The Greeting and Thanksgiving (1:1-14)

As in all his letters, Paul begins with his standard greeting in 1:1-2 in which he mentions Timothy is with him. He says the reason he gives thanks to God the Father is because he has heard about their **faith in Christ Jesus** and their **love for all the saints** because of the **hope that is stored up in Heaven**. Simply put, Paul is saying that **faith in Christ** will lead one to **love the Church**, with the end result of that faith working itself through love is **the hope of a new creation and redemption of all things**. All this started for them when they responded to the **Word of the Truth of the Gospel**.

At this point in 1:7-8, Paul mentions **Epaphras**, a leader of the church in Colossae who had come from Colossae to see him. Epaphras was the one who told Paul about them. With that, Paul lets them know he is constantly praying that they would be filled with the knowledge of God's will and all Spiritual wisdom and understanding so that they can **walk worthy of the Lord** in every good work.

In 1:12-14, Paul transitions to the next part of his letter. He thanks God the Father for making it possible for Gentile Christians to share in the portion of the **holy saints in the light** and says that God had delivered them **from the authority of the darkness** and **into the Kingdom of His Beloved Son**, and that it is through Christ the Son that we have deliverance and forgiveness of sins. As he did in Ephesians, Paul is referring to the **rulers, powers, and authorities in the heavenly realms** that are nothing more than the **spiritual powers of darkness and evil**.

### 2. Christ and the Church (1:15-2:7)

With that, Paul launches into a detailed explanation of just who Christ is and just what the role of the Church is. In the **first half of this section (1:15-20)**, Paul explains the cosmic significance of Jesus Christ. To fully appreciate how Paul describes Christ, every one of his descriptions need to be teased out.

Paul first describes Christ as **the image of the unseen God** and **the firstborn of all creation**. This hearkens back to the original creation account in **Genesis 1**. Paul is saying that Christ is the ultimate goal of creation and represents the new humanity. In Adam, original humanity is created in God's image, but since it is also naïve, immature, and sinful, that image of God is marred and tainted. Original humanity, though—natural humanity—is not the finished product. God's plan was to transform what was natural and corruptible into something supernatural and incorruptible. That transformation was made possible through Christ. So, by saying that Christ is the *image of the unseen God*, Paul is saying Christ is what God looks like in human form. But since he is also a human being, and human beings die, Christ died. But since he was God, Christ resurrected and conquered death, and in doing so, he became the **firstborn of all creation**, namely the new, transformed creation that God intended all along.

The second thing Paul says about Christ is that **everything in Heaven and earth was created in him: the seen and unseen; thrones, lordships, rulers, authorities; everything is created through him and for him**. This emphasizes Christ as the Lord of all creation. He is, in fact, the *culmination* of God's entire creation plan. Christ is the *means by which* the entirety of creation comes about. All of creation is to be *found in Christ*, that image of the unseen God, and thus, it is because of Christ that God Himself *is all in all*. Also, Paul's understanding of God's creation is not limited to just the natural world. When he speaks of that which is *seen and unseen*, and when he speaks of *throne, lordships, rulers* and *authorities*, he is speaking of what we commonly refer to as the "spiritual world"—that non-material reality that is still part of God's creation. So, Christ is Lord over all creation, and all creation consists of both the natural world and the spiritual world.

The third thing Paul says is **Christ is before all things, and all things are held together in him**. This means his resurrection from death has given him authority over all creation—he rules all creation. This also means that since Christ is the image of God, and since God existed before creation itself, then Christ too existed before creation itself, and is thus the origin of God's entire creation plan. Because of that, Paul is basically saying that Christ is the glue that holds the entire creation together.

The fourth thing Paul says is **Christ is the head of the body of the Church**. The Church here obviously is the people of God, the new humanity, those "called out" from this old age. Hence, Christ embodies the redeemed and transformed humanity.

The fifth thing Paul says is **Christ is the beginning, the first-born from the dead, so he can be above all things**. He is the origin of God's entire creation purposes. By virtue of his resurrection, he is the firstborn from the dead and is the evidence of the new creation. Also, by virtue of his resurrection, he is above all things, in that he has authority over creation and is Lord over creation.

The sixth thing Paul says is that **in Christ, all the Fullness was pleased to dwell**. This emphasizes what being the *image of the unseen God* is really about, and it has huge implications for humanity and the created order. The Fullness of God dwells in Christ, who is the image of God, and Christ's body is the Church, the people of God. Therefore, God dwells in the Church, who is Christ's body. That is how God comes to be all in all. That is how the original humanity of Adam is transformed into the new humanity—by being Christ's body, who is in the image of God.

The seventh thing Paul says is that **all things are reconciled in Christ and through Christ** and **peace comes through his blood on the cross**. The *reconciliation* and *peace* Paul is talking about isn't just reconciliation and peace between God and humanity. It is the reconciliation and peace between Jews and Gentiles within the Church, the body of Christ. Jews and Gentiles were reconciled to become that new, transformed humanity that is the Church and Christ's body, precisely because of Christ's sacrificial death on the cross.

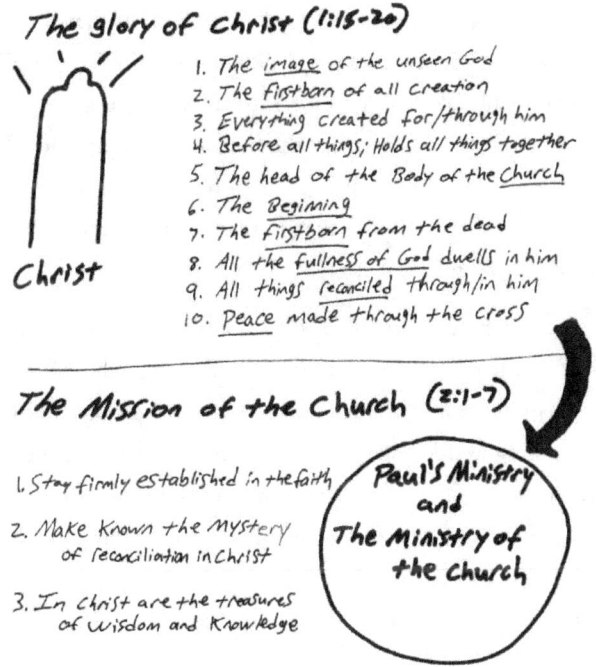

With that picture of Christ spelled out, Paul then focuses on two things in the **second part of the section (1:21-2:7)**: (1) What this means for Gentiles, and (2) His role in spreading the news about the Gospel of Christ. Gentiles used to be alienated from God and from God's people but are now reconciled is Christ's body (the Church) through Christ's death and are able to be holy and blameless as part of God's people, *if they remain firmly established in the faith* and *are not pushed out of the Gospel they heard*. In the immediate, historical context, there are basically two ways to be "pushed out" of the Gospel: Through the lure of **paganism** (2:8-15) and through the lure of **Judaism** (2:16-23).

Paul then emphasizes that he is a minister of the Gospel and proceeds to elaborate on just how he sees his own ministry. First, he sees his own suffering on behalf of the Gospel as a cause for rejoicing because he views them as "filling up what is lacking" of the tribulations of Christ, on behalf of his body, the Church. Simply put, Paul realizes that Christians are to suffer as Christ did because our suffering "fills up" and completes the suffering of Christ on behalf of the Church. Or to put it more simply: **Salvation and reconciliation come through our willingness to suffer as Christ suffered**. Second, Paul says that his job as a minister of the Gospel is to make known **the mystery** that has been hidden for generations but has now been revealed to the saints (Christians). As in Ephesians 3, this mystery was the question regarding how God would fulfill His promise to Abraham and eventually bless all nations. The answer is that it happens through the death and resurrection of Christ and the outpouring of the Holy Spirit—that is the way human beings will be made fully mature in Christ. In other words, it is through Christ and the Holy Spirit that human beings become the true image-bearers that God has intended all along.

In 2:1-7, Paul reiterates how much he is struggling on their behalf (as well as for the Christians in Laodicea, and for those in the area who have not personally met him yet). What he hopes for in his struggle for them is that they can be assured in their understanding and knowledge of that mystery of God that is revealed in Christ. He then emphasizes that true wisdom and knowledge are to be found in Christ, and not in any kind of "slick-sounding speech" that might "push them out" from the hope of the Gospel. That is why Paul urges them to stay firm in their faith in Christ and to continue to walk in him.

### 3. Warnings against Pagan Philosophy and Judaism (2:8-23)

The kind of "slick-sounding speech" Paul has in mind is articulated in this next section of 2:8-23, where Paul warns against pagan philosophy (2:8-15) and the Judaism of the Judaizers (2:16-23). He characterizes pagan philosophy as **empty deceit** that is according to the **traditions of men** and the **elements of the world**. Christ, though, is the polar opposite of those elements of the world, for he is above **every ruler and authority**. With that, Paul then emphasizes what that has meant for the Gentile Colossian Christians. They have now been "circumcised," not by the one "done by human hands" (meaning circumcision prescribed in the Torah), but rather by the one "not of human hands," meaning the circumcision of the heart done by the Holy Spirit.

In **Deuteronomy 30:6**, God promised that He would circumcise the heart, and **in Jeremiah 4:4**, He called for the people of Judah to "remove the foreskin of your hearts." Similarly, in **Jeremiah 31:31-33**, Jeremiah prophesied that God would make a new covenant with His people and would "write the Torah on their hearts." This is what Paul is getting at here when he talks about the **circumcision of Christ**. It is a reference to the promised work of the Holy Spirit that would characterize the new covenant. Therefore, the "flesh" that is removed isn't the literal foreskin that is removed in the Jewish act of circumcision, but rather it is the *old age way of life that is in bondage to the elements of the world and its rulers and authorities.*

Paul then refers to **Christian baptism** as the symbolically imitating the death and resurrection of Christ, and by doing so, signifying their "death" to the old age way of life and their "resurrection" to the new life in Christ. Paul then speaks of how the "record of the debt of trespasses" was nailed to the cross. That "record" is a reference to the Torah, which points out your sin and declares you guilty. Paul's point here is that since the death and resurrection of Christ has evoked the transforming work of the Holy Spirit, it has also rendered the Torah null and void. Not only that, but through the death and resurrection of Christ, God has **disarmed the rulers and authorities** and is now treating them like prisoners of war during a Roman victory parade. This is what he is referring to when he speaks of publicly disgracing them as prisoners in triumphal procession. Paul's point in 2:8-15 is simple: *Don't be deceived by Greek philosophy—it's the empty deceit of the spiritual powers, and through Christ, God has taken them prisoner.*

With that said, Paul then warns the Colossian Christians in 2:16-23 about the **Judaizers** who try to pass judgment on them over Jewish practices concerning food and drink, festivals, new moons, or Sabbaths. Similar to what the author of Hebrews says in Hebrews 10, Paul says these things are "shadows of things to come"—essentially the prototypes and models of the real things to come in Christ. Paul also tells them not to let anyone cheat them by taking **pleasure in humiliation**, the **worship of angels**, or about supposed visions that simply puff people in **the mind of the flesh**—again, a reference to Jewish practices. During the Intertestamental period, Judaism came to elevate the role of angels to where it might seem they were worshipping angels. The fact that we see in Hebrews the emphasis that Christ is greater than the angels indicates that in popular Judaism in the first century, angels were treated in such a way that almost evoked worship of the angels.

In any case, by describing these Jewish practices as having "the mind of *the flesh*," Paul equates them with the same kind of empty deceit of pagan philosophy and says that to follow such practices is to "not hold fast to the head" (Christ) by which the entire body (the Church) is held together. He further ties the futility of the "Old Covenant Judaism" of the Judaizers in with the empty deceit of pagan philosophy by telling the Colossian Christians that if they have died with Christ from those **elements of the world**, then why would they continue living according to that old age by submitting to those decrees of Jewish food laws that say, "Don't handle, taste, or touch"? Paul says they are decaying with use (as everything in the old age does) and are nothing more than the *teachings of men*. They might give the impression of wisdom, but in reality, they are nothing more than *the indulgence of the flesh* and only make people arrogant. Basically, Paul is addressing something that happens in virtually any religious setting, namely that tendency for people to *do certain practices* that make them look, "holier than thou." That is arrogance. That is "indulging the flesh." It may be religious, but it is operating from an old age mindset.

### 4. Living the New Self (3:1-4:1)

After warning the Colossian Christians about being sucked back into the **pagan way of life** and being suckered into the **Judaizers' way of life**, Paul encourages them to live out **the new life they received in Christ**. Since they have been raised with Christ, Paul tells them to *seek the things above, where Christ is, seated at the right hand of God*. This echoes Paul's description of Christ in Ephesians 1:20, as well as in places like Hebrews 1:3, 13, and it crystalizes a major portion of the Gospel: **Christ died, was resurrected, and then ascended to God's right hand, and now rules over the authorities, powers, and elements of the world**. Therefore, Paul's exhortation is simple: *You've died to your old way of life and were raised with Christ, so look to him and live out that "Christ-life" that rules over the elements of the world, don't submit to them anymore. You have been given a taste of that future glory by the presence of the Spirit, and when that future glory arrives and Christ is fully revealed, you will be revealed along with him.*

Paul then spells out a number of sinful behaviors that they have to "put to death" because they still tie them down. The Christian life in this old age is a work in progress, and there are parts of us that are still in bondage to the elements of the world. Paul's advice is simple: **Keep killing it. Keep nailing those things up on the cross and put them to death**. In any case, Paul tells the Colossian Christians that it is because of those types of things that the **wrath of God** is coming upon the **sons of disobedience**. Echoing Jesus' prophecy about the destruction of the Temple in the Olivet Discourse (Mark 13, Matthew 24, Luke 21), Paul is most likely referring to the Jews in Jerusalem who rejected Jesus and who persecuted the early Christians.

Paul says they used to "walk" in those very sinful behaviors when they were pagans but have now discarded that "old man," have put on the "new man," and are being **renewed in the knowledge according to the image of his creator**. The creation language is everywhere. The "old man" (Adam) has to die, so that the "new man" (Christ) can raise up from the dead, and those who put their faith in Christ are being renewed into the image of God, because Christ is that image. Therefore, Christ, along with the Church, is able to exercise authority over God's creation, truly represent God, and be the royal priestly-caretakers of God's creation. In this "new man"—the body of Christ—there is no division between Gentile, Jew, or any nationality, or even slave or free, for **Christ is all and is in all**.

Since this is what life is like in Christ, Paul encourages the Colossian Christians in 3:12-17 to live out that Christ-life. Since they are the chosen ones of God, they should "clothe themselves" with behaviors that seek to build each other up: mercy, kindness, humility, gentleness, patience, forgiveness, and love. In fact, Paul calls love the "bond of **maturity**" (the Greek word *telos*) and encourages them to let the peace of Christ rule in their hearts. After all, that is what the death and resurrection has accomplished: Not only peace between God and humanity, but peace between different groups within the human race. In Christ, believers are one body, so Paul exhorts them to love one another and be at peace with each other in everything they do. In that respect, as Paul says in 3:17, *"Whatever you do, in word or in deed, do everything in the name of the Lord Jesus, giving thanks to God the Father through him."*

With that, in 3:18-4:1, Paul gives some practical instructions for husbands and wives, children and parents, and slaves and masters. It is essentially a shortened version of what Paul says in Ephesians 5:21-6:9: Wives, be subject to your husbands, but husbands, love your wives. Children, obey your parents, but parents don't make your children resentful and discouraged. Slaves, obey your masters and do your work as if you are doing it for the Lord, but masters, treat your slaves with righteousness and fairness.

### 5. Exhortations and Final Greetings (4:2-18)

The last chapter of Colossians contains a few final exhortations and greetings. In 4:2-6, Paul asks them to pray that a door be opened for him, so he could further proclaim the Word and speak of the **mystery of Christ**. He then urges them to be smart how they appear to pagans and to be ready to "give an answer" to anyone who might ask them about their faith.

Paul's final greetings are in 4:7-18. He mentions **Tychicus**, the man who took Paul's letter to Colossae, and tells them that Tychicus will tell them all about what is going on with Paul. Paul also mentions **Onesimus** who came with Tychicus, calling him the "faithful and beloved brother." We learn about Onesimus more in Paul's letter to Philemon. Onesimus was Philemon's slave who had run away and had somehow linked up with Paul during Paul's imprisonment in Rome. Needless to say, Paul sending Onesimus back to Colossae and calling him a **faithful and beloved brother** is very important, as Paul's letter to Philemon shows.

In 4:10-11, we learn who else was with Paul at this time: **Aristarchus**, **Mark** (John Mark) the cousin of Barnabas, and a man named Jesus who went by the name **Justus**. We know these three are Jews because Paul says that they are the only ones "from the circumcision" who are co-workers for the Kingdom of God. The other people (obviously Gentiles) who are with Paul are mentioned in 4:12-14: **Epaphras** (a believer from Colossae, mentioned in Colossians 1:7), **Luke** the doctor (and author of Luke-Acts), and a man named **Demas**.

Paul ends in 4:15-18 by telling the Colossian Christians to send his greetings to the believers in Laodicea. He singles out a woman in Laodicea named **Nympha**, who leads a church in her house. Paul then tells the Colossians to make sure the letter is read to the believers in Laodicea as well. He also sends a message to a man named **Archippus**, that he should see to the ministry he received from the Lord, so he could fulfill it. Basically, Paul says, "Hey, the Lord wants you to do that thing, so get going and do it!" With that, in 4:18, Paul picks up the pen in his own hand and writes the final words of the letter, so they can recognize his handwriting and be assured that the letter is authentic: *"The greeting is in my own hand, Paul. Remember my chains! Grace be with you!"*

# PHILEMON

**Time of Writing:** During Paul's imprisonment in Rome (AD 60-63)

**Background**

Philemon was part of the church in Colossae. One of his slaves, Onesimus, had run away and somehow had ended up with Paul while Paul was in prison. Scholarly speculation is that Onesimus was not a Christian when he stole some money from Philemon and ran away. At some point, though, in the course of his time with Paul, he had come to the faith. But still, since he was a runaway slave, Paul had decided to send him back to Philemon in Colossae, with an appeal to Philemon to accept Onesimus back, not as a slave anymore, but as a fellow brother in Christ. In fact, Onesimus is mentioned in Paul's letter to Colossae. Onesimus had come back to Colossae with another co-worker of Paul, Tychicus, and in Colossians 4:9 Paul calls Onesimus "our faithful and beloved brother, who is one of you." And so, it is believed that Colossians and Philemon were sent at the same time.

**The Big Thing to Know About Philemon**

1. **What the Gospel Looks Like in Action**: The thrust of Philemon is really simple. It is a demonstration of what the Gospel looks like in the real world. Paul emphasized in all his letters how the Gospel is to bring people together in reconciliation. Here in Philemon, Paul is asking Philemon to live out that Gospel message by welcoming back a former slave, no longer as a slave, but as a brother in Christ.

### Literary Map: Philemon

| 1:1-3<br>Paul's Greeting | 1:4-7<br>Thanksgiving for Philemon's Love and Faith | 1:8-16<br>Paul's Appeal for Onesimus | 1:17-22<br>Paul's Calling Upon Philemon to Accept Onesimus | 1:23-24<br>Final Greetings |
|---|---|---|---|---|

## A Walkthrough of Philemon

Paul's letter to Philemon is a personal letter sent along with Colossians at the same time. At the end of Colossians, Paul mentions that **Onesimus** was being sent back with **Tychicus**, the carrier of the letter, and Paul specifically calls Onesimus a *faithful and beloved brother*. In Philemon, we find out that Onesimus was, in fact, a runaway slave of Philemon who had made his way to Paul in Rome and had ended up not only being saved, but also being of considerable help to Paul. Nevertheless, he still was a runaway slave. So, Paul sends him back to Colossae, to Philemon, not in order to be a slave again, but rather to demonstrate in very practical terms what the Gospel looks like in real, day to day life.

Paul addresses his letter not only to **Philemon**, but also to **Apphia** and **Archippus** and the church that meets in their home. Apphia and Archippus were probably a couple who led a house church, and Philemon was part of that congregation. After his greeting and initial thanksgiving, Paul compliments Philemon for the fellowship his has in the faith, his growing knowledge in Christ, and for his love. With that, Paul then proceeds to "ask a favor" from Philemon. It is interesting to see how Paul goes about asking for this favor, though. In 1:8-10, Paul essentially says, *"Hey, since I am an actual apostle, I could order you to do this, but I don't want to do that. Instead, I want to encourage you through love to do what I'm going to ask."* Paul then reminds Philemon that he is just an old man and a prisoner for Christ. Paul says all this to set the stage for what he's about to ask Philemon.

The actual request comes in 1:11-17. Apparently, Onesimus wasn't that good of a slave for Philemon. Paul even says that Onesimus had been useless when he had previously been with Philemon but had become very useful for Paul during his time in prison. Nevertheless, Paul is sending Onesimus back to Colossae, because it was the right thing to do. Still, Paul tells Philemon that Onesimus had become so dear to him that he calls Onesimus "my very heart." Then in 1:13, Paul says something rather sly. He tells Philemon that he wanted to keep Onesimus with him in Rome, so that he could keep serving Paul *on Philemon's behalf*. Obviously, Philemon didn't send Onesimus to Paul—Onesimus had run away. Nevertheless, Paul wants Philemon to know that Onesimus had come to him and had chosen to willingly serve him. Therefore, Paul considers Onesimus' service to him as an extension of Philemon's support for him.

After nudging Philemon to "do the right thing," Paul then says he didn't want to keep Onesimus without Philemon's knowledge, because if he did, then that would rob Philemon from being able to do the right thing. That "right thing" is to welcome Onesimus back, *no longer as a slave, but as a beloved brother* (the very way Paul describes Onesimus in Colossians 4:9). Paul ends his request in 1:17-18 by saying, "If we are in fellowship with each other" (and they were), "then accept Onesimus just as you accept me"—accept him as a fellow Christian and an equal member in Christ's body, no longer as a slave. Paul even says that if Onesimus had initially wronged Philemon in some way, he would take it upon himself to pay Onesimus' debt and repay Philemon. By doing so, Paul is putting the Gospel to work in a very practical way: *Christ paid our debts, so we should pay the debts of others.*

Paul ends his letter in 1:19-21 with a little more nudging of Philemon to do the right thing. After saying he'll repay any debt Onesimus owes, Paul drops in, *"And I won't even remind you that you really should honor this request because you owe me your very life."* Of course, by saying he won't remind Philemon of this, *Paul is actually reminding Philemon of this!* Then Paul nudges Philemon a little more in 1:21 by saying, *"I know you'll do the right thing...and obey!"* Paul began the letter by saying, "I could order you, but I won't." Then he spends the rest of the letter getting Philemon to obey without actually ordering him! In 1:22-24, Paul tells Philemon to get a room ready, because he expects to be let out of prison soon and is planning to come and visit. He then passes on greetings from **Epaphras**, **Mark**, **Aristarchus**, **Demas**, and **Luke**.

# TITUS

**Time of Writing**

Of all the letters Paul wrote, there are only two of which we do not know where or when he wrote them. We know that he wrote Ephesians, Colossians, Philippians, and Philemon while he was imprisoned in Rome (Acts 28). We also know, from the early Church historian Eusebius, that Paul, after successfully defending himself in Rome, was set free and continued on in his ministry of preaching. Eusebius then notes that after "coming a second time to the city, [Paul] suffered martyrdom under Nero. During this imprisonment he wrote the second Epistle to Timothy" (*Ecclesiastical History* 2.22.2). Because of this, many believe that I Timothy and Titus were written sometime after Paul's first imprisonment in Rome and before his second imprisonment, sometime in the early 60s.

**Background**

Titus, one of Paul's closest companions, is mentioned twelve times in Paul's letters. In Galatians, Paul says that Titus had gone with him and Barnabas when they went up to meet Peter, James and John privately, and that he was not compelled to be circumcised, even though he was a Greek Christian. Eusebius tells us that he originated from Crete and, after serving with Paul for some time, returned to Crete where he served as bishop (*Ecclesiastical History* 3.4.5-6). According to tradition, Titus lived to be 94 years old before he died.

Crete is a large mountainous island south of Greece, in the Mediterranean Sea. As it turns out, it had a horrible reputation. The ancient Greek writer Epimenides wrote in the 7th Century BC, "Cretans are always liars, evil brutes, and lazy gluttons." Paul even quotes this in his letter to Titus (1:12). Another ancient historian, Polybius, writing in the 2nd Century BC, said this of Crete: "So much in fact do sordid love of gain and lust for wealth prevail among them, that the Cretans are the only people in the world in whose eyes no gain is disgraceful" (*Histories* 6:46).

**Paul's Letter to Titus**

Paul wrote his letter to Titus because Titus was the leader of the church in Crete and was being confronted with many of the same challenges other churches were dealing with. There were some false teachings that were threatening the faith, there were false teachers who were no better than corrupt televangelists who were using their religious roles solely to make money, and, of course, there were false teachers who were promoting what Paul calls, "Jewish myths" (1:14). If we keep this in mind, reading and understanding Paul's letter to Titus will be quite straightforward and simple.

## The Big Things to Know about Titus

A. **Church Leadership**: Paul is insistent that leaders in the Church should be of the most upstanding character, not only for the sake of teaching and being a good example to their congregations, but also for the sake of maintaining a good reputation to the outside culture.

B. **Sound Doctrine**: Since Titus is the leader of the church in Crete, Paul emphasizes the importance of adhering to the sound doctrine and tradition that Jesus and the apostles have passed down.

C. **Warning Against Judaizers**: As he does in his other letters, Paul warns Titus about Judaizers who were seeking to force Torah observance on Christians.

D. **How Should Christians Relate to Secular Authorities**: Since Christianity was a "new thing," Paul gives Titus some advice on how Christians were to deal with the secular authorities.

### Literary Map: Titus

| 1:1-4 Paul's Greeting |  |
|---|---|
| 1:5-9 Qualifications for Elders | 1:10-16 Warning of Judaizing Deceivers |
| 2:1-15 Teaching Sound Doctrine within the Community | 3:1-11 Relating to Secular Authorities |
| 3:12-15 Final Greetings |  |

## A Walkthrough of Titus

### 1. Paul's Greeting (1:1-4)

Paul's greeting to Titus follows the basic pattern of most of his letters. Paul identifies himself as a **servant of God** and an **apostle of Jesus Christ**, speaks about the **faith of God's elect** and the **knowledge of the truth according to godliness**. Given Paul's history with Titus, particularly when Paul refused to circumcise him while under pressure from certain Judaizers in Jerusalem, it isn't hard to see that in the background in Paul's greeting. Paul's comments here to Titus are essentially saying, *"You know what I'm talking about—the faith of God's chosen ones—and those Judaizers who wanted you circumcised aren't!"*

Paul also mentions the Christian hope, namely the **Life of the Age** that God promised all along and revealed in the Gospel of Christ. Even though most translations have "eternal life," it literally is "Life of the Age" and it reflects the standard Jewish and Christian concept of the two ages: (A) The **current old age** was ruled by Satan and was characterized by sin and death, and (B) The **coming Messianic Age** of the Kingdom of God, in which Satan, sin, and death would be defeated, and Christ would reign with the Church. Therefore, Paul is speaking about how, with the death and resurrection of Christ, the Messianic Age had invaded the current old age, and how they were looking forward to when the Kingdom of God and the Life of the Age would be experienced fully.

### 2. Qualifications for Elders (1:5-9)

Paul's letter to Titus is straightforward advice on how Titus should oversee and organize the Church in Crete. Here in 1:5-9, Paul reminds Titus that when it comes to Church leaders (elders and the bishops), they need to be upstanding people who are beyond reproach. The things Paul lists aren't a comprehensive list—they just get to the basic point that if someone is going to be an elder or bishop in the Church, that person has to be upstanding, level-headed, compassionate, mature, and well-grounded in Church teaching.

### 3. Warning of Judaizing Deceivers (1:10-16)

The reason why was it necessary to be well-grounded in Church teaching is because, especially at the time of Paul's writing to Titus around AD 60, was that the Judaizers were still trying to convince Gentile Christians that they had to become Jews. Therefore, in that context, Paul's warning against **rebellious people** and **empty-talkers and deceivers** that were from the **circumcision group** is quite clearly a reference to Judaizers. Therefore, Paul is saying that rebellious people like that need to be refuted, and to do that, you need to know what you're talking about.

In the middle of his warning to Titus, Paul quotes the Greek philosopher-poet Epimenides to make fun of the people of Crete, and says, *"One of their very own prophets said, 'Cretans are always liars, evil beasts, and lazy gluttons.'"* In any case, Paul tells Titus to be sure to refute any false teaching that might lead people away from Christ. Again, we see that Paul specifically targets the teaching of the Judaizers when he refers to **Jewish myths** and the **commandments**, and those who are turning people away from the truth. Clearly, this reflects the rupture that was going on between the Judaism of the time and the emerging Christian movement that was coming out of Judaism. Paul is insistent that Gentile Christians were not required to submit to the Torah and become Jews. Regarding Jewish food laws, Paul says, *everything is clean for those who are clean,* but *nothing is clean for those who are defiled and unfaithful.* Not only is he saying that Jews who insist on Jewish food laws are the ones who are defiled and unfaithful, but he says they **disown God** by their actions and are **detestable, disobedient,** and **unfit for every good work**.

To be clear, the problem with the Torah isn't the Torah itself, but with those who think submitting to the Torah makes one righteous, much like modern legalists who think going to church three times a week and not smoking, drinking, or listening to secular music are the things that actually make someone righteous and holy. In reality, people with that mindset are often the most judgmental and hateful people around. Paul is adamant: *Those who are obsessed with the outward show of piety and who insist on forcing their views on others are the ones who are actually ungodly.*

### 4. Teaching Sound Doctrine within the Community (2:1-15)

In 2:1-15, Paul emphasizes how important it is to teach sound doctrine within the Church. It is interesting to note, though, that for Paul, sound doctrine really consists of two things: (A) Sticking to the basics, and (B) Living out godly behavior. That is why he says that **older men** should be of good character and be sound in faith in love (2:2), **older women** should be reverent, not gossips or lushes, and they should teach the **younger women** to be good wives and mothers (2:3-5), **younger men** should be sensible, have integrity, and be sound in their teaching (2:6-8), and **servants** should be good servants to their masters so that they can "decorate everything with the teaching of God our savior" (2:9-10). The point is pretty clear: *Teaching about Christ means nothing if the teacher doesn't live like Christ.*

Paul ends this section in 2:11-15 by highlighting the **already/not yet Christian worldview** and the Christian hope of the coming Messianic age. The grace of God *has appeared in this present age* in order to offer salvation to everyone. And because that has *already happened*, Christians are to disown the godless way of life of the *present age* and to live out *godly lives* that bear witness to Christ and that look forward to the *future "appearing of the glory of our great God and savior, Jesus Christ"* (2:11-13). We are to live our lives **between the ages** as we bear witness to Christ. And what did Christ do? He *gave himself on behalf of others*, so that he *could free people from all lawlessness* (anti-Torah behavior) and *cleanse them to be his own people who would be zealots for good works*.

In light of the conflict at the time between the Judaizers and Christians and the growing tensions in Judea with Rome that would soon result in the Jewish Revolt, Paul's comments take on extra significance. First, he says that Christ came to free people from "anti-Torah behavior," and was thus implying that when Judaizers were attempting to force those outward acts of Torah onto Gentiles, they were actually violating the whole point of Torah—to love God and love one's neighbor. Their actions of trying to force Torah observance on Gentiles were actually **anti-Torah behavior**. Second, he emphasizes that Christ cleansed **a people who were zealous for good works**. This stood in sharp contrast with what was going on within Judaism at that time, where zealotry against Rome was rising. The Jewish people of that time were becoming a people who were zealous for revolt. This, for Paul, was the antithesis of what the people of Christ were to be like.

### 5. Relating to Secular Authorities (3:1-11)

In 3:1-11, Paul turns his attention to how Christians should live in relation to the secular authorities. Paul keeps it simple: *Be good, law-abiding citizens.* Paul gives the reason to be good citizens by relating it to Christ. The stream of thought goes like this: (A) We all used to live ignorant and rebellious lives, but (B) "God our Savior" appeared, He saved us; (C) But He didn't do this because we had done anything righteous and good, but rather he did it just because of His own mercy; and so (D) This salvation happened through the "washing of rebirth" (baptism) and the renewing power of the Holy Spirit, whom God poured out on us through Jesus Christ our Savior.

The rationale Paul gives as to why Christians should be good citizens is that he wants Christians to relate to their pagan neighbors in the same way God related to them through Christ. They didn't deserve to be saved—they had been pretty bad people, just like their pagan neighbors obviously were. Rather, they had gotten saved solely because of God's mercy. So, Paul wants them to be Christ to their pagan neighbors, in the hope that they will come to salvation through the mercy Christians extend to them, just like those Christians had come to salvation through mercy that God extended to them. When that happens, when someone is "righteousized" (justified), that person is in the same position as Abraham, whose faith had made him righteous. Thus, by being righteousized (like Abraham), we are **heirs of God's promises to Abraham**, and those promises are summed up in the Christian hope of the **Life of the Age** and the renewal of all of creation in the Messianic Age.

Those are the things Paul wants Titus to emphasize to the Church in Crete, because those are the things that put everything into perspective and give the rationale for Christians to do what they are called to do. After that, in 3:9-11, Paul once again warns Titus about getting sucked into moronic debates with the Judaizers about genealogies and quarreling about the Torah ("Law" in most translations). Paul says such debates are harmful, useless, and ultimately just cause further division. Of course, that really can be tricky. On one hand, Christians must be ready to silence and refute people who are spreading false teaching and fostering divisions, but on the other hand, Christians shouldn't get sucked into useless and divisive debates.

### 6. Final Greetings (3:12-15)

Paul ends his letter to Titus with a few final greetings. He first tells Titus that when he sends Artemas or Tychicus (the person who sent Paul's letters to Ephesus and Colossae) to him, that he wants Titus to meet him in Nicopolis, a small town on the western coast of Greece where Paul was planning to spend the winter. Paul then asks Titus to make sure Zenas the lawyer and Apollos (Acts 18:24, and Paul's fellow worker mentioned in I Corinthians) are fully supplied, but to send them on their way (3:13-14). With that, Paul tells Titus that everyone with Paul sends their greetings.

# I TIMOTHY

**Time of Writing:** Possibly after one of the times Paul left Ephesus, either AD 58-59 or AD 64-65.

## Background
Timothy was one of Paul's close missionary companions throughout much of Paul's ministry. His family lived around Lystra and Iconium (central Galatia), and we even know the names of his mother, a Jewish-Christian woman named Eunice, and his grandmother, Lois (Acts 16:1). Timothy's father, though, was Greek, and therefore, even though Timothy was technically Jewish (through his mother), he hadn't been circumcised. Therefore, in order to appease the Jews of Galatia, Paul circumcised Timothy. Eventually, Timothy became the leader in the church in Ephesus.

## Paul's Letters to Timothy
During the time when Timothy was the leader in the church of Ephesus, they were struggling with false teaching. Paul wrote I Timothy to give Timothy advice on how to handle it. Chapters 1-3 deal with warnings against false speculation, and what lies at the center of the Gospel. Chapters 4-6 characterize the heresy that Timothy was facing in Ephesus and contrasts it with appropriate behavior.

II Timothy, though, is surrounded with a bit more controversy. There is a question as to whether or not it is a genuine Pauline letter. The earliest manuscript we have of Paul's letters dates from around AD 200, but that manuscript doesn't have I/II Timothy or Titus. That being said, it is an incomplete manuscript and breaks off in the middle of II Thessalonians. In any case, according to II Timothy, Paul is in prison (presumably in Rome for the second time) and is expecting to finally be executed.

## The Big Things to Know About I/II Timothy
A. **Stay Faithful to the Rule of Faith in the End Times**: Paul clearly feels the "end times" is upon them (possibly a response to the impending crisis of the Jewish War) and so he encourages Timothy to stay faithful to the Gospel.
B. **Church Leadership**: As with Paul's letter to Titus, Paul gives instructions on the qualification for anyone in Church leadership. Basically, leaders need to be of upstanding character, so to serve as good examples for their congregations and society at large.
C. **Live as a Church Community**: Paul also tends to a number of practical matters of what it means to live as a Church community.

## Literary Map: I Timothy

| | 1:1-2<br>Paul's Greeting | |
|---|---|---|
| 1:3-20<br>Avoid False Doctrine | 2:1-15<br>Instructions for Prayer | 3:1-16<br>Qualifications for Church Leaders |
| 4:1-16<br>Later Times: Avoid False Teachings | 5:1-6:2<br>Instructions for the Church Community | 6:3-19<br>Avoid False Teachings Pursue Righteousness |
| | 6:20-21<br>Closing Remarks | |

## A Walkthrough of I Timothy

### 1. Paul's Greeting (1:1-2)

Paul's greeting to Timothy is the standard type of greeting he uses in all his letters. Paul identifies himself as an apostle of Christ Jesus who has responded to the command of **God our Savior** and **Christ Jesus**, whom Paul says is our hope. As throughout the greetings in his letters, we see Paul emphasizing the equality of Jesus Christ and God the Father. He greets Timothy as **a genuine child in the faith**.

### 2. Avoid False Doctrine (1:3-20)

The first thing Paul emphasizes in I Timothy is the **importance of correct doctrine** and the **danger of false doctrine**. At this point in first century, though, doctrine was not so much the grand systematic theology that eventually developed for the centuries, as it was basic the teaching and tradition that the resurrected Jesus passed down to the apostles, who then went out and proclaimed it throughout the known world. With that said, Paul reminds Timothy of what he had told him when he left Ephesus and went off to Macedonia: *Stay faithful to the teaching and don't let people teach anything different than the Gospel that was originally handed down.* It is pretty clear that Paul is specifically warning Timothy about the false teaching of the Judaizers. He characterizes it as "myths and endless genealogies" that are more about speculation than the "stewardship of God in the faith."

At the heart of the Gospel was the proclamation that Jesus was the Messiah and the fulfillment of God's covenant with Israel, and that, by virtue of his death and resurrection, he was also now Lord of all creation and that through the Spirit God was bringing blessing to all nations so that Jew and Gentile together could be reconciled and brought together as one people in Christ. Therefore, the identity markers in the Torah that marked out Jews from the Gentiles were now irrelevant. The teaching of the Judaizers was that the way Gentile Christians could become one with the Jews in Christ was to submit to the Torah, get circumcised, *and become Jews*. Given those two doctrines, the basic question became, "Who is being the faithful stewards of God's covenant? Paul or the Judaizers?" Paul's answer is obvious: "We are, they aren't, so don't listen to them!"

Paul then says that the goal of Gospel teaching boils down to three things: **Love from a pure heart, a good conscience,** and **a sincere faith**. The Judaizers, though, had wandered off from the Gospel into "empty talk." When Paul says in 1:7 that some of them wanted to be **teachers of the law**, we need to realize that Paul is specifically talking about the **Torah**. Paul is insisting that his Gospel correctly teaches about the Torah and that the Judaizers, although they speak confidently about things like circumcision and food laws, just don't get it and don't know what they are talking about. Paul spells out the right way to view the Torah in 1:8-11 when he says that the Torah is good if one uses it in the right way, namely, to point out sin to unrighteous people in hope that they turn to Christ for salvation. What kind of sinful behavior does the Torah point out? Paul gives a quick list in 1:9-10.

Most of the list in 1:9-10 is self-explanatory, but a few words need to be said about two specific sinful acts Paul mentions, the ones that most translations have as **fornicators** and **homosexuals**. The Greek word translated as "fornicators" is *pornois*, from which we get the word *pornography*. It was used in a general way about having promiscuous sex outside of marriage, but it was also used specifically to designate the sexual promiscuous practices that took place in the pagan temples. The Greek word translated as "homosexuals" is *arsenokoitais*, and it is a difficult word to translate properly.

Technically, there are two parts to the Greek word: *areseno*, from which we get words like "arson," and *koitais*, from which we get "coitus." So, we were to be literal, we would have "burning coitus." In Paul's day, when two men engage in sexual activity, the *arsenokoitais* is the one who is penetrated by the other man. The problem with translating that word as "homosexual" is that in our day and age, "homosexual" refers to someone's sexual orientation, regardless of whether or not that person has actually engaged in sex. In the ancient world, though, no one identified as a "homosexual." In the ancient world, sex was just sex, and men would go to pagan temples to engage in sex with temple prostitutes, be they women or men, so they could enjoy the pleasures of sex without getting their wives pregnant. That is the behavior Paul is specifically condemning as sinful. He isn't even addressing the modern concept of "homosexuality" or "sexual orientation." That being said, there is very little doubt that Paul would have seen two men having sex for any reason as wrong. Still, given the context, Paul is specifically referring to the sexual libertinism promoted by the pagan world, and more specifically in the pagan temples.

After that, Paul gives a brief autobiography in 1:12-20, in which he talks about his former life as zealous Jews who persecuted the Church and then God's calling him to the ministry of the Gospel. Despite his violent past, God showed mercy to Paul because he had acted ignorantly in **unfaithfulness**, although most translations say Paul acted ignorantly in **unbelief**. What Paul is emphasizing is that his former life as a zealous Pharisee was one of ignorance of God's plan and ignorance of the point of the Torah, and therefore was a life that was **unfaithful to God's covenant as expressed in the Torah**. Simply put, Paul is saying, "I didn't get it, and that is why I was persecuting the Church! I wasn't faithful to God's covenant because I misunderstood what the point of Torah was all about!"

Paul then talks about the significance of his conversion. After saying that the grace of the Lord overflowed through the *faith* and *love* that are in Christ Jesus (1:14), Paul then says, "The *logos* (word) is *faithful* and worthy of all acceptance." Most translations have something like, "The *saying* is *trustworthy* and deserving of all acceptance." I think that is a mistake, because I think when Paul refers to the *logos*, he is referring to the word of the Gospel, as opposed to the teaching of the Judaizers. Thus, in contrast to the way he acted in ignorance and unfaithfulness as a zealous, persecuting Pharisee, it is the word of the Gospel that is faithful and that needs to be accepted—*not the ignorant and unfaithful teaching of the Judaizers*.

That **word of the Gospel** is simple: *Christ Jesus came to save sinners*, and Paul adds that he feels like he is the biggest one. Since he, the sinful, zealous, Torah-observant Pharisee, needed to receive mercy in order to be saved, that meant his zealous Torah-observance couldn't make him righteous. True righteousness is found in Christ Jesus, not in Torah observance. Christ is faithful and the Gospel that tells about Christ's faithfulness is faithful. We are saved when we put our faith in Christ the faithful one.

Paul tells Timothy he is reminding him of all this so he can "fight the good fight" and have **faith** and a **good conscience**. By contrast, Paul says that those who fail to listen to their conscience end up **shipwrecking their faith**, and he specifically names two men, Hymenaeus and Alexander. Paul doesn't elaborate on what they did, but he does say he has "given them over to Satan" so they can be disciplined not to blaspheme. By saying that, he is referring to expelling the offending person from the Church and letting him live out in the pagan world again, in the hope that person will miss the Church and repent.

### 3. Instructions on Prayer (2:1-15)

Paul then turns his attention to instruct Timothy about what he wants the men and women in the Church to do in terms of prayer. He wants them to pray for all people, and specifically for those in positions of authority. After all, if they lead well, that means Christians will be able to live a quiet and peaceful life. But ultimately, he wants them to pray for every person to be saved and to come to the knowledge of the truth in Christ. After all, that is why Paul was appointed as a preacher and apostle to teach the Gentiles. He continues on and says he wants men to pray without wrath or argument and women to present themselves with modesty, decency, and to "dress themselves" with good works, and not to get caught up in obsessing over dressing in fancy clothes or their outward looks. Paul isn't saying women aren't supposed to look nice. Rather, he is saying something that all women need to hear: It is what is on the inside that counts.

What Paul then says in 2:11-15 is one of the most misunderstood passages in Paul's letters. It seems that Paul is quite "anti-woman," telling **women to be quiet and submissive** and saying that he doesn't let a **woman have authority over a man**. But if we understand the first century context in which Paul is writing, we will see that Paul is saying something rather radical and liberal for women, namely that **women should be allowed to learn and study**. In addition, when Paul speaks of being in "submission," it is about being in submission to God and the Gospel, not specifically to men. Anyone who becomes a disciple need to be in submission to God. As for Paul's comments about not letting a woman have authority over a man, his point is that since men and women are one in Christ, they are to be equal before God. Therefore, no one should have authority over anyone based on their gender.

The reason why Paul feels the need to point this out to Timothy is because in Ephesus, where Timothy was, the pagan cult of **Artemis** had women priests who exercised authority over male worshippers. So Paul is making it clear that although he wants women to study and learn, just like men, he's *not saying* that means that they should be like the women priests in the Artemis cult. Neither men nor women should "rule the show" in the Church. The Christian proclamation was one of full equality between men and women. Given that, what Paul says about how Eve was deceived and came into transgression should make more sense. Paul is using that story to justify why women need to learn and study—*so they won't be deceived, like Eve.*

### 4. Qualifications for Church Leaders (3:1-16)

Paul turns his attention in chapter 3 to the practical matters of the qualifications for bishops and deacons. In 3:1-7, Paul focuses on **bishops**. He says that a bishop needs to be a well-respected and decent man in the community, someone who doesn't go out and get drunk, who has a bad temper, or who is always greedy for money. Paul also mentions having one wife and obedient children, but the point should be obvious: *The leader of the church needs to be above reproach.* In addition, Paul says that a bishop shouldn't be a new convert, for reasons that should be obvious: A new convert is essentially an infant in the faith and isn't yet mature in Christ.

In 3:8-13, Paul focuses on **deacons**. Deacons were assistants to the bishop who helped him carry out the duties and responsibilities of the church. The qualifications for the deacons are similar to those of bishops. They need to be upstanding in their character, above reproach, and not be the kind of people who are devious and speak out of both sides of their mouths. They shouldn't be alcoholics or greedy for money. They should be good family men whose wives have a good reputation as well. Paul also says they should *hold to the mystery of the faith* with a clean conscience. Remember, the "mystery" revealed in the Gospel is that it is through the death and resurrection of Christ that God brings blessing to the Gentiles. Paul also says they should be tested to see if they are indeed above reproach before they can become deacons.

In 3:14-16, Paul reiterates to Timothy that although he hopes to visit him soon, he just wanted to re-emphasize how leaders, and Timothy in particular, are to conduct themselves in the Church. He ends with what was probably an early Christian hymn in 3:16 that emphasizes the heart of the Gospel message: *"He was revealed in the flesh, righteousized in the Spirit, seen by angels, proclaimed among the Gentiles, so that those throughout the world may put their faith in him, and taken up into glory!"*

### 5. Living in the Later Times/Avoiding False Teaching (4:1-16)

In chapter 4, Paul returns once again to the topic of dealing with false teaching, specifically that of the Judaizers. He prefaces his comments here by telling Timothy that the Spirit says that in the **Later Times** there would be some who leave the faith and hold onto **deceiving spirits** and the **teaching of demons** because of the **hypocrisy of liars** who have **burned their own conscience** like a hot iron (4:1-2). Paul then characterizes this "teaching of demons" with two things: Forbidding marriage and abstaining from certain food that **those of the faith** can receive with thanksgiving from God.

Although we can't be sure to whom Paul is referring in regard to forbidding marriage, the fact that Paul brings up the issue of abstaining from food seems to be a reference to the food laws of the Torah and the Judaizers' attempt to get Gentile Christians to submit to the Torah. Paul responds by saying that everything God has created is good and fine to eat as long as it is received with thanksgiving. What makes it holy is the **word of God** and **prayer**. This is what Paul wants Timothy to stress to those in the Church. He then continues to warn against **silly myths**, urges Timothy to be a good minister of Christ, and equates godliness to physical training. Just like physical training "pays off" in the end, in that you get your body in shape, so too does practicing godliness "pay off" in the end—the end being the Christian hope of resurrection and a renewed creation and eternal life. Then Paul reiterates what he said back in 1:15, *"The word is faithful and worthy of all acceptance,"* and emphasizes the hope of salvation that is found in the Gospel.

With that, in 4:11-16, Paul tells Timothy to keep teaching the Gospel and to not worry about if anyone looks down on him because he was young. Instead, Paul tells him to be a good example for the faithful in terms of his conduct, love, faith, and purity. He tells Timothy to keep up with the public reading (of the Scriptures), as well as encouraging and teaching others until Paul returns. Paul also tells Timothy to not neglect his Spiritual gift that was bestowed on him at some point, with the laying on of the hands of the elders. We are not told what this Spiritual gift was, be Paul is pretty clear in telling Timothy, "Use it!" With that, Paul once again exhorts Timothy to practice these things, to be a good example, and to keep a firm grasp on **the teaching**, which again is a major focus in Paul's letter.

### 6. Instructions for the Church Community (5:1-6:2)

Paul turns his attention to more practical matters within the Church, specifically how to treat the elderly within the Church and what to do with widows.

Paul tells Timothy to honor the elderly as if they were literal family members: Elderly men like fathers, elderly women like mothers, and young women like sisters. When it comes down to the Church's care for the widows, Paul's instructions boil down to this: If an elderly woman is a widow and has family that can take care of her, then they should take care of her, so that the Church isn't overly burdened. But if a widow is truly alone, the Church should step in and essentially be her family and take care of her. To be put on the Church list, though, the widow must be at least 60 years old, have been the wife of one man, and have demonstrated good character and good work throughout her life.

In 5:11-16, Paul explains that younger widows shouldn't be put on the list for assistance, because they probably still have sexual urges and will want to marry again. Besides, Paul says, when one is young and starts accepting welfare, it becomes very easy to just be lazy all the time, and the last thing you want is a young person who is lazy and bored—they tend to get into trouble! So, Paul's advice is pretty simple: Don't give widow-welfare to young widows because they'll end up causing problems. Instead, encourage them to get remarried, have kids, and raise a family. Presumably, when Paul says in 5:15 that some young widows have **gone out after Satan**, he means that they have gone back to flirting with paganism in some way.

In 5:17-22a, Paul speaks about the elders in the Church and tells Timothy that since the elders work so hard in teaching the faithful, they are worthy of double honor and should be compensated in some way for all they do for the Church. Paul also tells Timothy to not jump to any conclusions about any accusations someone might bring against an elder in the Church. In fact, he should only consider an accusation if it is corroborated by two or three witnesses. In addition, Paul tells Timothy that if ever he does have to deal with sin within the Church, that he should do so publicly, in full view of the Church, so to make sure there is no favoritism and that everyone is treated equally.

After that, in 5:22b-25, Paul tells Timothy not to ordain anyone too quickly, but instead make sure they're really ready for the responsibility. He also tells Timothy not to share in the sins of others, but instead stay pure. He then tells Timothy to drink a little wine for his stomach and his frequent illness and gives him some wise words about both sins and good works. Things may stay hidden for a while, but eventually, a person's sins, as well as a person's good works, will come to light.

In 6:1-2, Paul also gives a quick word to slaves and masters. He says slaves should honor their masters, so that "the name of God and the teaching won't be blasphemed," meaning they should do a good job so that they won't give God or the Church a bad name. To masters, Paul says they should treat their slaves as brothers and don't look down on them, because they really are brothers in Christ.

### 7. Avoid False Teaching and Pursue Righteousness (6:3-19)

With that said, Paul turns, for a third time, to the topic of false teaching and tells Timothy that anyone who is teaching something different from the "sound words of our Lord Jesus Christ" and that goes against godly teaching, that person is **prideful, understands nothing**, and has an unhealthy urge for **controversies and quarrels**. He goes on to say that sort of false teaching just breeds divisions and arguing, and that the people who promote that sort of thing have **decaying minds**, have no handle on the truth, and are only using godliness as a means of gain. This echoes what Paul said in 1:6-7 and in 4:1-5.

Having said that such people only view godliness as a means of gain, Paul then tells Timothy that the that "great gain" of godliness is learning to be content with what one has. It has nothing to do with getting rich, which is precisely what those false teachers are ultimately trying to do. Those kinds of people just fall into temptations, snares, pride, and various lusts that will ultimately lead to their destruction. It is in that context that Paul writes that famous verse: *"The love of money is the root of all kinds of evil."* Paul says that is why some have **wandered away from the faith**, as he first mentioned in 1:6-7.

In contrast to those kinds of people, Paul urges Timothy to run away from all that, and to instead pursue **righteousness, godliness, faith, love, patient endurance,** and **humility,** and to live out the faithful word of the Gospel. He urges Timothy to "fight the good fight" and to hold tight to the Life of the Ages to which he was called and for which he made a confession. With that, Paul tells Timothy that just as Christ Jesus himself "bore witness to the good confession before Pontius Pilate," that he too must **keep the commandment** spotless and above reproach until the **appearance of our Lord Jesus Christ**.

Two things are to be noted: First, the "commandment" Paul is referring to is probably the "royal commandment" that goes back to when Jesus was asked by the scribe about the greatest commandment. He said, "Love God," and "Love your neighbor." Those two commandments sum up the entirety of the Torah. Second,

Paul's reference to the "appearance of our Lord Jesus Christ" probably relates to his comments elsewhere regarding the Day of Christ or the Coming of Christ.

In any case, Paul ends his comments by focusing on Jesus Christ as the **Blessed Ruler**, the **King of kings**, and the **Lord of lords**. Paul says Christ is the only one who **possesses immortality** and who **dwells in unapproachable light,** thus on some level, he is equating Jesus Christ with God the Father. Paul then tells Timothy to be sure to remind rich believers not to be arrogant or put their hope in their riches, and to instead be sure to do what is good, to become "rich in good works," and to be generous and liberal with their money.

### 8.   Closing Remarks (6:20-21)

With that, as Paul signs off in 6:20-21, he just can't help but warn Timothy one more time to avoid "vile and foolish conversations" and that "false knowledge" that some who have lost their way have started professing. Again, possibly a reference to the Judaizers.

# II TIMOTHY

## Literary Map: II Timothy

**1:1-2**
Paul's Greeting

| 1:3-18 | 2:1-13 | 2:14-26 | 3:1-4:8 | 4:9-18 |
|---|---|---|---|---|
| Hold Fast to the Gospel | Paul's Encouragement to Timothy | Paul's Rebuke of His Opponents | Example: Paul vs. Ungodliness | Instructions for Timothy |

**4:19-22**
Final Greetings

## A Walkthrough of II Timothy

### 1. The Greeting (1:1-2)

Paul's greeting to Timothy is typical of most of his greetings in all his letters.

### 2. Hold Fast to the Gospel (1:3-18)

Much of what Paul says in II Timothy echoes what he says in I Timothy. In this section, Paul encourages Timothy to hold fast to the Gospel. He tells Timothy that he constantly prays for him and emphasizes the importance of having a **clear conscience**. He also mentions the names of Timothy's grandmother Lois and mother Eunice. We are told a bit about Timothy's mother in Acts 16. After that, Paul encourages Timothy to "rekindle the gift of God" that was given to him through the laying on of hands (an echo of I Timothy 4:14). He doesn't want Timothy to be afraid to use his Spirit-inspired gift in power, love, and self-control. He also tells Timothy not to let himself be put to shame by the Gospel or by the fact that Paul was in prison because it is suffering on behalf of the Gospel, and the Gospel's power is seen when we imitate Christ in our own sufferings.

Paul then reminds Timothy of God's calling, and that it wasn't **according to works,** meaning the **works of Torah**. Thus, Paul wants to reassure and encourage Timothy to stay true to the Gospel and faithful to God's call because it is the Gospel that reveals God's purposes all along: *Salvation came through Jesus Christ, who abolished* *death and brought life and immortality*. It is because of this message that Paul, a preacher, apostle, and teacher of the Gospel, was currently imprisoned. So, Paul is saying, *"If I am actually in chains and not put to shame, don't let yourself be put to shame either. Instead, hold fast to the* **sound words of the faith***, to the* **love that is in Christ Jesus***, and to the* **good that has been place in his care by the Holy Spirit***."*

Paul then tells Timothy a bit of discouraging news in the personal note in 1:15-18. Apparently "everyone in Asia" had abandoned Paul during his time in prison. He even mentions two specific men, **Phygelus** and **Hermogenes**. One man, though, **Onesiphorus**, continued to support Paul throughout his imprisonment in Rome. Apparently, this man had also at one point served the church in Ephesus.

### 3. Paul Encourages Timothy to Stay Strong (2:1-13)

Despite that, Paul continues to urge Timothy to press on and to **share in the suffering**. Paul then gives three analogies in 2:3-6 to illustrate what the Christian life is like. First, there is the **good soldier** who doesn't get distracted by civilian affairs and only strives to please his commanding officer. Second, there is the **competing athlete** who competes according to the rules in order to win the crown. Finally, there is the **farmer** who engages in hard labor in the field so he can later share in the fruit of the harvest.

With that, Paul again draws Timothy's attention to the heart of the Gospel: *Jesus Christ, the offspring of David (the Messiah) died and was resurrected*. That is why Paul is in prison. A crucified Messiah is offensive to Jews and the proclamation that Jesus conquered death is a threat to every worldly power structure, particularly that of Rome. Since that is the case, Paul urges Timothy to endure any suffering that might come his way, for it is through suffering that salvation comes. After all, as he said in I Timothy 1:15, 3:1, and 4:9-10, "This word is faithful," and since the word of the Gospel is faithful, and since Christ is faithful, Christians can be confident that *if they die* with Christ that *they will also live* with him; if they *endure*, they will eventually *reign*; but if they *disown Christ*, he will *disown them*. Still, the good news of the Gospel is that even if we are *unfaithful*, Christ will stay *faithful*, because we are his, and he cannot disown himself. Apparently, there is a difference between disowning Christ and being unfaithful. To illustrate the difference, we can use a marriage analogy. If a man gives into temptation and cheats on his wife, he has been unfaithful. But if he is sorry, repents, and asks forgiveness, the marriage can be healed. That is different than if a man simply says he never loved his wife and wants a divorce.

### 4. Paul Rebukes His Opponents (2:14-26)

After encouraging Timothy to stay strong, Paul encourages Timothy to remind the Christians in Ephesus of these things and to correctly interpret the **word of truth** (the Gospel) so that they won't start **quarrelling over words**. Paul wants Timothy to avoid **vile and foolish talk** that will just lead to godlessness and will spread like gangrene. Paul then mentions two men, **Hymenaeus** and **Philetus**, who had lost their way from the truth. He mentioned Hymenaeus in I Timothy 1:19, although there he linked him up with someone named **Alexander**. Here we learn that Hymenaeus had been teaching that the resurrection had already happened. Despite what they were teaching, Paul says that the "firm foundation" of God stands and doesn't change.

To further encourage Timothy not to get caught up in **moronic and stupid controversies**, Paul uses the analogy of a house in 2:20-21. In a house, there are going to be items that are gold and silver that will be used for more honorable use, and there are going to be other items that are wood and clay that are used for more mundane things. If Timothy "cleanses himself" and avoids such quarreling and controversies, he will be a "vessel of honor." That means **fleeing youthful lusts** and to instead **pursuing righteousness, faith, love, and peace**.

Given the context, Paul is warning Timothy about fleeing from the desire to get into needless arguments and isn't really talking about sexual temptations. In fact, he insists that a servant of the Lord shouldn't get caught up in such overheated quarreling and arguments. Instead, he should be kind, put up with the other person's heated rhetoric and patiently teach that person with gentleness in the hope that maybe that person will come to their senses, repent, and come to the knowledge of the truth. In his description of that hope, Paul says that if that person does, in fact, come to his senses, then he will have **escaped from the snare of the devil**. That is interesting, given the fact that the last time he mentioned Hymenaeus, Paul said he had handed him over to Satan to be taught not to blaspheme.

### 5. Paul vs. Ungodliness (3:1-4:8)

Paul then warns Timothy of the hard times that will characterize the **last days**. After giving a laundry list of evil traits that will characterize people in the last days, Paul tells Timothy to stay away from such people, for although they will have the **outward form of godliness** but will have actually **denied its power**. Paul says such people will "snake their way" into homes and will deceive vulnerable women who are overwhelmed in sins and swayed by lusts. He says such people are always learning, but never able to come to a knowledge of the truth. He then compares such people to **Jannes** and **Jambres**, who, according to Jewish tradition, were the Egyptian magicians who confronted Moses when he was telling Pharaoh to let the Israelites go out from Egypt. Eventually, Paul says, their stupidity will be obvious to everyone.

Understanding this section really will depend on how one understands Paul's reference to the "last days." Most will automatically defer to the "end times" timeline laid out by many modern day "end times preachers" like Hal Lindsey and Tim LaHaye. The problem with that is it is obvious that Paul is talking about something that was going on *at that time*—that is why he is warning Timothy about it.

In order to understand Paul's comments about the **last days**, or similar statements of the **coming of Christ** or the **day of Christ**, we need to see them in light of what Jesus said in the **Olivet Discourse** (Mark 13, Matthew 24, Luke 21) when he prophesied that Jerusalem, along with the Temple itself, would be destroyed within a generation because Israel had, in fact, rejected him as the Messiah. When that happened, that would signal Jesus' vindication as both prophet and Messiah. That is what the **Day of Christ** meant in the early Church. Thus, the original Gospel message was both the proclamation that salvation is in Christ, as well as the prophetic word that the Day of Christ would happen soon, when God's wrath would come upon Jerusalem and the Temple because the Jews had rejected Jesus as the Messiah.

We know that in the years leading up to the Jewish Revolt of AD 66-70, that tensions in Judea and Galilee had escalated and the entire region was a tinderbox just waiting to explode in revolt. That, along with the growing tensions within Judaism over the fact that Paul was taking the Gospel to the Gentiles, should be the obvious situation Paul is addressing in passages like this. He is saying that what Jesus had prophesied in the Olivet Discourse was going to happen soon, and thus they were living in the "last days" before the Temple's destruction. That was why it is important for Paul's churches to hold fast to the Gospel and to not give in to the false teaching of the Judaizers. That is why he continues to tell Timothy to stay faithful to the Gospel and to follow his teaching, conduct, purpose, faith, patience, love, endurance, and yes, even his persecutions. In fact, Paul tells Timothy that everyone who wants to live a godly life in Christ Jesus *should expect to be persecuted* and *should expect things to get worse* because they were in the "last days" before Jerusalem's destruction.

That is why Paul tells Timothy to stand firm in the faith he had learned in the Scriptures. Paul then writes the famous verse: *"All Scripture is inspired by God and is useful for teaching, for refuting error, for correction, and for training in righteousness, so that the man of God can be fully qualified and equipped for every good work"* (3:16-17). Paul is stressing that all Scripture is inspired by God and is ultimately the work of the Spirit. But we need to understand that Paul is clearly talking about what the purpose of the Scriptures is, namely, to **teach the Gospel,** to **refute false teaching about the Gospel**, for **correcting that false teaching**, and for **training people up** to be righteous, Christ-like followers so that they can do the **good work** that God wants His image-bearers to do. He isn't saying the Scriptures speak authoritatively on science, or modern politics, or anything like that. He's saying the Scriptures are a Holy Spirit thing, and they are to be used to teach the Gospel, refute false teaching, and to train in righteousness. That lies at the heart of everything Paul has been telling Timothy in both I/II Timothy.

In 4:1-8, as if he hasn't warned Timothy enough of false teaching, Paul does it one more time. First, Paul tells Timothy that, in light of **Christ's appearing and his kingdom**, he is bearing witness before both God and Christ Jesus, who is **coming to judge the living and the dead**, that Timothy needs to keep proclaiming the word and standing firm in the Gospel. Even though some people will not put up with sound teaching, will "wander off after myths" (see I Timothy 1:4, 4:7), and will listen to teachers who only tell them what they want to hear, Timothy needs to stay faithful to his calling. Yes, he should expect to suffer as well, but Paul admonishes him to keep doing his work as an Evangelist. Finally, Paul reflects on what he expects to be his upcoming death sometime soon in the future. He first uses the sacrificial language of the Temple to say that he is being **poured out like a drink-offering**. Then he uses two other athletic metaphors and says he has **fought the good fight** and has **finished the race**. He has kept the faith and is expecting that victor's **crown of righteousness**. That crown, though, isn't just for him, but indeed is for everyone who has loved Christ's appearing.

### 6. Final Instructions (4:9-18)

Paul ends II Timothy with a number of wrap up items. He asks Timothy to try to come and see him soon, because **Demas** (Colossians 4:14, Philemon 1:24) had "fallen in love with this present age" and had gone off to Thessalonica (4:9-10). What that precisely means is unsure, but whatever the case, Demas had left Paul, and Paul wasn't too happy about it.

In addition, Paul tells Timothy that **Crescens** had gone to Galatia, **Titus** went to Dalmatia, and that only **Luke** was with him at the moment (4:10-11). Paul tells Timothy that when he does come, to pick up **Mark** and bring him along. He also tells him that he sent **Tychicus** to Ephesus (4:12). Then, almost as an afterthought, Paul tells Timothy in 4:13 to be sure to bring the cloak and the parchments he had left with a man named **Carpus** in Troas. In 4:14-15, Paul warns Timothy about **Alexander** the coppersmith, who did a few bad things to Paul. Paul says that God will repay him for whatever he had done. Nevertheless, Timothy should watch out for him, because he obviously was opposed to what Paul was doing. In 4:16-18, Paul mentions that he was entirely alone at his first defense, probably at his trial in Rome. No one had stood by him. Even though that hurt Paul, he tells Timothy that he hopes that no one holds it against them. Still, he says that he was still **rescued from the mouth of the lion**. Presumably, the trial went in his favor.

### 7. Final Greetings (4:19-22)

Paul ends his letter by telling Timothy to be sure to greet **Aquila** and **Prisca**, as well as the entire house of **Onesiphorus**. He tells Timothy that **Erstus** was still in Corinth and that he had left **Trophimus** in Miletus because he was sick. After asking Timothy to do his best to come see him before winter, Paul relays greetings from fellow Christians: **Eubulus**, **Podens**, **Linus** (who would become the bishop of Rome from 64-76 AD), **Claudia**, and the rest who were in Rome.

# THE GENERAL LETTERS

What I am calling the *General Letters* are essentially the New Testament writings outside of the Synoptic Gospels and Acts that were not written by either Paul or John. That means: *Hebrews, James, I Peter, II Peter* and *Jude*. The specifics regarding each of these letters will be addressed in their respective sections, but there is one basic thing here that needs to be pointed out about these letters and how they differ from those of Paul.

Paul's letters were addressed to the churches he had established throughout the Roman Empire that consisted primarily of Gentile-Christians. In short, Paul was "translating" the originally Jewish Gospel of Christ for a Gentile audience. Now, if we accept the traditional Church claim that James, Peter, and Jude were, in fact, the authors of these "general letters," (although the early Church Fathers admit we don't really know who wrote Hebrews), that means that these letters were written during the same time as Paul's letters. The key difference, though, is that the *General Letters* seem to be addressed to more of a Jewish/Jewish-Christian audience.

Admittedly, it really is impossible to make a clear, cut-and-dry distinction between a "Gentile-Christian" and "Jewish-Christian" audience. Like I've said many times in this reader's guide, before the Jewish War of AD 66-70, there wasn't yet a clear distinction between "Christianity" and "Judaism." Still, we can say that the make-up of Paul's churches overwhelmingly consisted of Gentiles who had come to Christ. Some had been "God-fearers" who originally had ties to the synagogue, but many had come to Christ straight out of paganism. By contrast, there simply doesn't seem to be that much of a Gentile-related focus in the *General Letters*. The over-whelming vibe in these letters is that of speaking about and presenting Jesus within a general Jewish setting still.

That doesn't mean, as some scholars have claimed, that, for instance, Paul and James were at odds with each other. If you read and study both Paul's letters and the *General Letters*, you'll be able to see that they are all presenting the same Gospel, but they are tailoring the Gospel message in different ways because they are, after all, speaking to different communities.

# HEBREWS

**Time of Writing:** Hebrews cannot be dated with any certainty. Its focus on the Levitical sacrificial system indicates that the Temple was still standing at the time of writing, and that would date Hebrews before AD 70. In addition, the fact that the writer of Hebrews mentions that the Christian community had not yet shed blood for the sake of Christ suggests it might have been written before Nero's persecutions in the mid-60s.

## Background

Not only is the date of Hebrews uncertain, so is the authorship. Traditionally, it was attributed to Paul, but even prominent early Church Fathers and historians openly admit that no one was sure who the author was. Suggestions have ranged from Barnabas, Silas, Apollos, and Priscilla among others. As for the original audience of Hebrews, the fact that virtually everything in Hebrews is refers back to the Old Testament indicates that the audience was predominately Jewish Christians. The fact that ancient commentators said Hebrews was written in Jerusalem also suggests this. At the same time, though, Gentile Christians would have been familiar with the Old Testament. In addition, 10:34 mentions that some Christians had had their property plundered and confiscated—that was something that was a threat to Gentiles who left paganism. In any case, some scholars suggest that Hebrews was written somewhere around Rome during the reign of Claudius, possibly around AD 49, when he expelled all the Jews from Jerusalem.

Long story short, when it comes to Hebrews, no one is sure who wrote it, when it was written, or to whom it was written. Still, we can tentatively say that the writer was someone in the early Christian community, that it was probably written at some point before Nero's persecutions in the mid-60s, and that the audience was probably a combination of both Jewish and Gentile Christians.

## The Big Things to Know About Hebrews

A. **Jesus' Cosmic Travels**: He was greater than the angels, made lower than the angels for a short time, made "perfect" through suffering, then exalted over all.
B. **The Exodus/New Creation Grid for the Christian Life**: Paul uses the Exodus and Creation as the primary metaphors for talking about the Christian life and ultimate hope.
C. **Jesus and the New Covenant is Greater than the Mosaic Covenant**: To show this, Paul focuses on the Torah, Temple, and Priesthood.
D. **The Faith Journey**: Using Exodus imagery, Paul speaks of the Christian journey as travelling through the wilderness of this present age, certain of what is not yet seen: the *Ultimate Promised Land*, the *Ultimate Rest*, the *New Creation*.

## Literary Map: Hebrews

|  | | |
|---|---|---|
| **Jesus: Angels (1-2)** | **1:1-2:4**<br>Jesus: Higher than the Angels | **2:5-18**<br>Jesus: Lower than the Angels for a time<br><br>Now crowned with glory and honor<br><br>"Perfected" through suffering<br><br>Offspring of Abraham Faithful High Priest |
| **Jesus: Moses (3:1-4:13)** | **3:1-19**<br>Jesus: Greater than Moses<br><br>Don't be like Exodus Israel who didn't enter into God's Rest | **4:1-13**<br>God Rested on 7th Day<br><br>Sabbath Rest for the New Creation |
| **Jesus: Melchizedek New Covenant (4:14-8:13)** | | **4:14-5:10**<br>Jesus: High Priestly Order of Melchizedek<br>Perfected Through Suffering |
| | | **5:11-6:12**<br>Don't be Lazy or Immature<br>Leave Behind "Elementary Things"<br>Go on to Maturity |
| | | **6:13-20**<br>God's Promise to Abraham<br>Christ: Order of Melchizedek in the Holy of Holies |
| | | **7:1-28**<br>Melchizedek Nature of Christ's Priesthood<br>Greater than Abraham and Levites<br>Better Covenant:<br>Eternal, Perfect, Resurrection Life |
| | | **8:1-13**<br>The New Covenant is better than the Old Covenant Promised in Jeremiah |

| | 9:1-10 | 9:11-22 | 9:23-28 | 10:1-18 |
|---|---|---|---|---|
| **Earthly vs. Heavenly Temple (9:1-10:18)** | The Earthly Temple Rituals | Christ in the Heavenly Temple  The Mediator of the New Covenant | Earthly Copies of Heavenly Realities | Christ's Sacrifice vs. Temple Sacrifices |

| | 10:19-39 | 11:1-40 | 12:1-17 | 12:18-29 |
|---|---|---|---|---|
| **Call to Faithfulness (10:19-12:29)** | Call to Hold Fast to the Confession of Faith  Remember Initial Difficulties | Past Examples of Faith  The Cloud of History | Don't Grow Weary  Present Discipline  Press On | You Haven't Come to Sinai  You've Come to Zion |

| 13:1-19 | 13:20-25 |
|---|---|
| Final Exhortations | Final Benediction |

## A Walkthrough of Hebrews

### 1. Jesus vs. The Angels (1:1-2:18)

The opening section of Hebrews comes in two parts and focuses on Jesus' relationship with the angels, namely that he is greater than the angels, but was for a short time made lower than the angels, so that he could identify with humanity and redeem them. In the **first part of the section (1:1-2:4)** focuses on Jesus' superiority to the angels. We must remember that at this point in the mid-first century, part of the early Christian proclamation was that Jesus, the prophet from Nazareth who was crucified in Jerusalem, was not only the true Jewish Messiah, but he was something much greater than a mere man. That is why the writer of Hebrews must first establish this fundamental point: **Jesus Christ, the Son of God, is greater than the angels**.

Looking back at Israel's history, the writer notes that although God had spoken in the past through the prophets, He had recently, in the first century (which the writer characterizes as the **last days**) spoken through His Son, Jesus. The writer then describes Jesus in the following ways: (1) He is appointed by God to be **heir of all things**; (2) Through him, God **made the ages**; (3) He is the **radiance of the**

**glory** and the **exact expression of God's substance**; (4) He **upholds all things by his powerful word**; (5) After establishing purification for sins, he **sat down at the Right Hand of the Majesty in the Highest Heaven**. That is why Jesus, the Son of God, is **far superior to the angels**.

With that said, the writer then lists a number of Old Testament verses to further show that the Son is greater than the angels. He is the **Son of God the Father** (Ps 2:7; II Sam 7:14); the **angels worship him** (Ps 97:7) and are **his servants** (Ps 104:4); the Son's throne (which is God's throne) **lasts into the Ages of Ages** (Ps 45:6-7); the Son is **the Lord who laid the foundation of the earth** (Ps 102:25-27), and it is the Son (not the angels) who **sits at God's Right Hand** and who is lord of all (Ps 110:1). By contrast, the angels are **ministering spirits** who serve, not just the Son, but the **ones who are about to inherit salvation**.

Right there, the writer hints that there is something more going on. As he will tease out over the course of the letter, one of the main points he makes is that Christians are **fellow sons with Jesus Christ**—He is the Son, and we are sons—and therefore the destiny and hope for Christians is that we will become as he is. Just as he is heir of all things and is the ruler of creation, our destiny as Christians is to share in that inheritance and be co-regents with Christ. That means, just as Jesus the Son is greater than the angels, so will we be greater than the angels.

That is why the writer encourages his listeners in 2:1-4 to keep holding on to the "things you have heard" (the apostolic teaching of the Gospel), so that they don't fall away. In that first generation of the Church, the biggest pitfall for early Christians was to fall back into Judaism. Therefore, it isn't surprising to see the writer focusing on that very thing when he makes an allusion to the giving of the Torah on Mount Sinai and how *that message* (the Torah) was **spoken through angels** was binding, in that it detailed the consequences for sin, namely death. So, the writer says if one falls away from *this message of salvation* (the Gospel), which was not only **spoken by Jesus the Lord**, but also even made more sure through the **power of the Holy Spirit** and the demonstration of **signs and wonders**—all one has to look forward to is the punishment for sin laid out in the Torah.

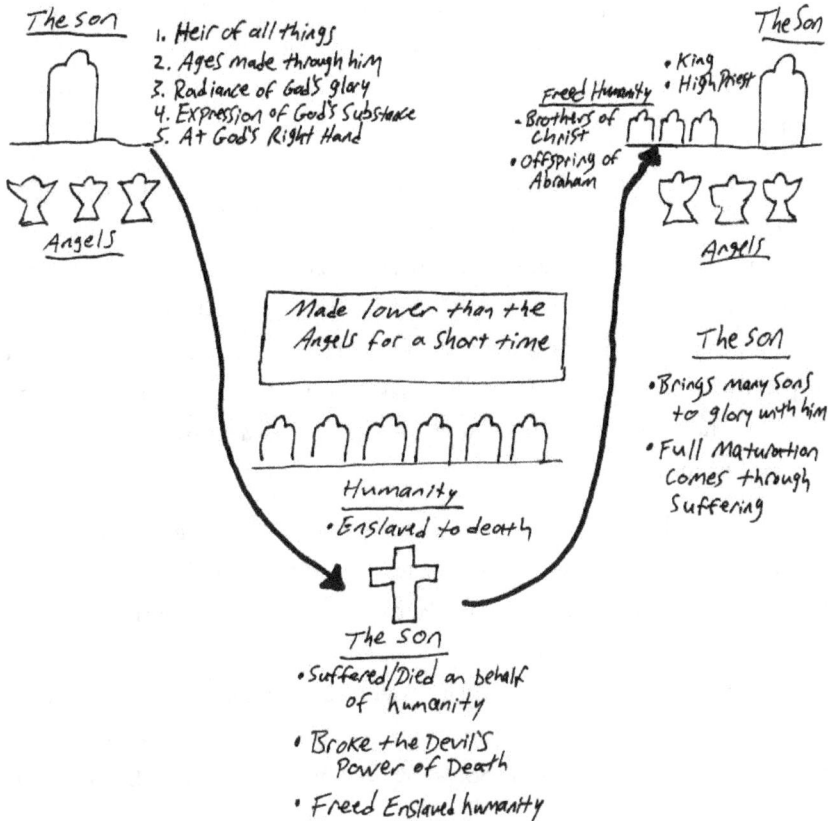

In the **second part of the section (2:5-18)**, the writer focuses on how (and why) Jesus was made lower than the angels for a short time. To understand just what is being said here, you have to first understand the basic biblical worldview that stems from **Deuteronomy 32:8**. Because of human sin and rebellion against God, He placed human beings under the authority of lesser divine beings (angels). Thus, human beings in this creation are subservient to them and are ruled by "spiritual powers." God's intention, though, is that *human beings, not just the Son*, will be rulers in the new creation and the coming world (2:5).

Simply put, in this old creation, angels rule, not humanity, but in the new creation, humanity will rule. And the way God brings that about is through Jesus the Son who enters humanity and becomes "lower than the angels," so he can transform and redeem humanity and bring them with him when he is again exalted above the angels to rule in God's new creation. This is the point of the quote in 2:6-8 of **Psalm 8:4-6**. If we can put it this way, God remembers **man** by making the **Son of Man** temporarily "less than the angels" so that he can be then resurrected, vindicated, and crowned with glory and honor as the ruler of all things—and by him doing that, human beings who put their faith in him will rule with him.

In 2:9-15, the writer says that even though at present we cannot yet see that all things are subjected to Christ, we still have the historical Jesus Christ who was a real human being who was briefly less than the angels. We know it is precisely because of his suffering and death on behalf of all that he is being crowned with glory and honor. Because of Christ, we know that the way God has chosen to **bring many sons into glory** was to make Christ the Son **perfect through suffering**. The Greek word translated as "perfect" is *telos* and has to do with achieving **full maturity**.

Therefore, what the writer is saying here can be confusing but is extremely important to understand. Basically, the writer is saying that God's goal all along was to transform the sinful humanity in bondage in this creation to a glorified humanity who rules in the new creation. In order to do that, God sent the Son into this creation (lower than the angels) to identify with sinful humanity and use suffering to accomplish God's goal to glorify humanity and elevate it to rule with the Son in the new creation. Thus, Christ the Son shows us that *salvation comes through suffering*.

The way to glory and honor *in the new creation* is the way of suffering *in this creation*. Christ the Son was glorified because he willingly went through suffering and death, Therefore, Christians need to be willing to go through suffering and death as well, if they expect to be glorified with Christ. That is why the writer says that Jesus is not ashamed to call them **brothers**, and then quotes **Psalm 22:22** and **Isaiah 8:17-18** to make the point: *Christians who suffer with Christ are called his brothers, and since he is the Son of God, that means they too are sons of God, and the coming world will be subject to Christ, and to them as well, because they are in Christ.* That is why Christ came and embraced humanity, so that, by resurrecting from the dead, he could destroy the one who has the power of death, namely the devil, and set free all those who were enslaved to the fear of death. Those who put their faith in him are thus **God's children** who will also conquer death and rule with the Son in the new creation.

With that, in 2:16-18, the writer then brings everything around to his first point about angels. The Son didn't do all that to help *angels*, but rather the **offspring of Abraham**—not so much ethnic Israel, but rather those of the faith of Abraham who put their faith in Christ. Because Christ offered his own life as a sacrifice for their redemption, the writer says that Jesus is not only **the ruler of all** but is also a **merciful and faithful high priest** who makes atonement for the sins of the people. Since he suffered, went through trials, suffered death and then resurrected, he has the power to help those who are going through trials themselves. The image of Jesus as a faithful high priest will loom large from this point forward.

### 2. Jesus vs. Moses (3:1-4:13)

In the two parts in this second section, the writer proceeds to draw a distinction between Jesus and Moses. The gist of the **first part (3:1-19)** is that the writer is warning his audience not to be like the Hebrews who were led out of Egypt by Moses during the Exodus. Now, both Jesus and Moses were faithful in what they were tasked with, but there is a key difference. Jesus is worthy of a greater glory because he, being equal with God, **is the one who built the house**—he was a **faithful Son who is over God's house**. Moses, though, was simply a **faithful servant who attended to God's house**. In other words, Moses was a great butler, but Jesus is the heir to the whole estate.

This brings the writer to 3:7-15, where he quotes **Psalm 95:7-11** and warns his audience not to like the Exodus community who was so rebellious and unfaithful to God that they weren't allowed to enter the Promised Land, but instead ended up dying in the wilderness. They had Moses and were given the Torah, but they were unfaithful and never reached the Promised Land. The writer plays upon the word "today" to emphasize to his listeners that the opportunity to enter into the **ultimate Promised Land** of the new creation is still available, as long as they don't "harden their hearts" and become unfaithful like the Exodus community.

In a sense, being baptized is the start of the Christian's own Exodus journey—not from Egypt to Canaan, but from this old age and corrupt creation to the new age and new creation. Therefore, since Christians have started on their own Exodus journey, here the writer is warning them not to waver and be unfaithful like the original Exodus community. Like he says in 3:16-19, it was the Exodus community who rebelled, whom God was angry with for 40 years, who died in the wilderness, and whom God swore that they would never enter His place of rest (the Promised Land). They didn't make it because they were unfaithful. So, the warning should be clear: *Don't be unfaithful like they were. If you become like them, you're not going to reach the ultimate Promised Land.*

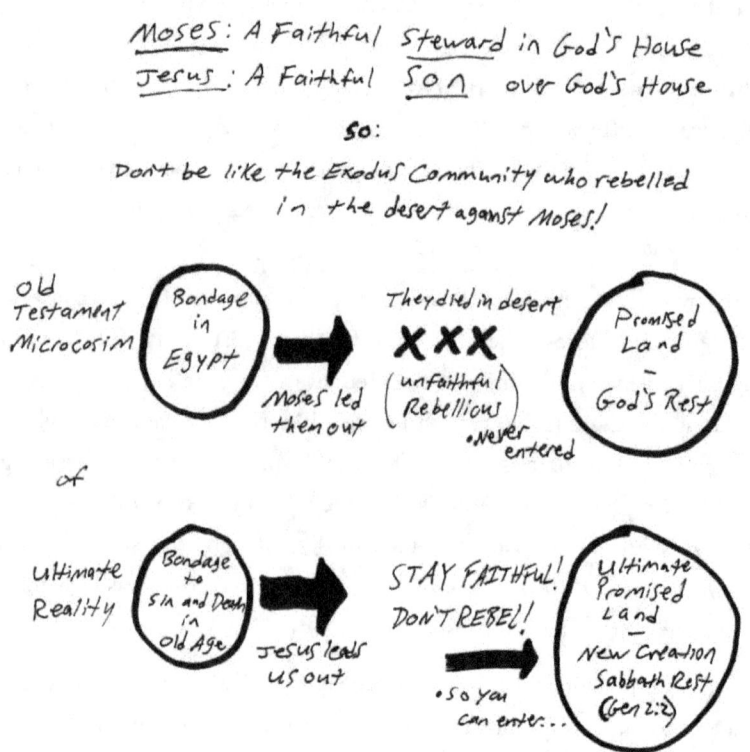

In the **second part of the section (4:1-13)**, the writer flips things around from issuing a warning to offering encouragement to his listeners to stay faithful so that they can, in fact, enter into God's rest of the ultimate Promised Land of the new creation. To do this, the writer really focuses on the term "rest" in Psalm 95:7-11. Now, in 4:2-3, the writer says something rather odd—the Gospel that those Christians in the first century heard had also been preached to the Hebrews during the Exodus, but they didn't combine hearing the Gospel with faithfulness, and that is why they never made it to the Promised Land rest.

In contrast to the Exodus community, the Christians are faithful, and that is why they were entering God's rest, meaning the new creation. Now, the writer is not suggesting that the Hebrews in the Exodus were told about Jesus of Nazareth. He's saying that God's "good news" that salvation comes through faith was available to them. If they had been faithful, they would have reached the Promised Land, but they weren't, so they didn't. Therefore, he's drawing a parallel (or rather a contrast) between the offer of salvation from Egypt, their unfaithfulness, and their failure and the offer of ultimate salvation, the Christian's faithfulness, and their assurance of the new creation.

This is where it is important to see how the writer begins using **rest**. In 4:4-7, he says that God's works have been finished ever since the **foundation of the world**, and then quotes **Genesis 2:2**, that says that God **rested from all His works** on the seventh day of creation. Therefore, the writer is saying the **Promised Land rest during the Exodus** was a foreshadowing of the **ultimate rest of the new creation**, but that that new creation was already a done deal, all worked out by God, as far back as **Genesis 2**, when God rested from all His works. Therefore, even though the Exodus community failed to enter God's rest because of their disobedience, that opportunity was still available to anyone who puts their faith in Christ—that is why **Psalm 95** used the word "today."

Ultimately, the writer is saying the Promised Land rest of Canaan was just a symbol of God's ultimate rest of the new creation. After all, he says in 4:8-9 that if Joshua's conquest had actually given the Israelites rest, then David wouldn't have talked about another rest in Psalm 95. God's ultimate Sabbath rest is the new creation—and it is available "today." To enter into that ultimate Sabbath rest of the new creation is nothing less than salvation. Then in 4:10-12, the writer draws one more contrast between Christians and Jews when he says that when one enters into God's rest, **one "rests" from one's "works."** This no doubt is a subtle allusion to Jewish Torah observance—when you enter into God's rest, there is no more need to do the works of Torah.

Hebrews 4:13 is the famous verse: *For the Word of God is living and active, sharper than any double-edged sword, able to penetrate as far as dividing soul and spirit, both joints and marrow, and able to discern the thoughts and intentions of the heart.* This verse is often associated with the Bible itself, but it is clear that, given the context, Paul isn't talking about the Bible, but rather the **Spirit of God** who is able to discern what people are really thinking. God can look past your actions and into the intentions of your heart. Nothing in creation is hidden from God's sight, so don't harbor grudges or have a disobedient heart. God knows what you're thinking already, so strive to be faithful so you can enter into His rest.

### 3. Jesus, Melchizedek, and the New Covenant (4:14-8:13)

The next section pairs Jesus up with the Old Testament figure of **Melchizedek** in order to highlight the nature of Christ's high priesthood. Thus, in the **first part**

**of the section (4:14-5:10)**, the writer stresses the connections between Jesus and Melchizedek. He begins in 4:14-18 by saying that since Jesus, the Son of God, is our **great high priest**, we should **hold fast to our confession**, meaning stay faithful to the apostolic Tradition and teaching. After all, it is because of Jesus' ability to identify with our human weakness that we can approach the **throne of grace** with **boldness** so that we can receive **mercy and grace**.

Then in 5:1-10, the writer expands on the way that Jesus' high priesthood is superior to the priesthood laid out in the Torah. First, in 5:1-4, the writer summarizes the high priesthood that is laid out in the Torah: (A) The high priest is chosen from among other men to represent the people before God and to offer sacrifices for sins on behalf of the people (5:1); (B) The high priest identifies with the sinful people and can be compassionate with them because he is just as sinful—his sacrifices aren't just for the people, but for himself as well (5:2-3); and (C) The high priest doesn't take the honor of being high priest; he is called by God (5:4).

Second, the writer then shows in 5:5-10 how Christ's high priesthood is superior: (A) Christ didn't glorify himself either; he was called "My Son" by God (Ps 2:7) and chosen by God to be a priest into the Age, not in the order of Aaron, but **in the order of Melchizedek** (Ps 110:4) (5:5-6); (B) During his life on earth, Christ offered up prayers and supplications and was saved from death because of his reverence; he learned obedience from his suffering, even though he was God's Son (5:7-8); and (C) When he was made **perfect (fully mature)**, he became the source of salvation for all who obey him, and he was designated high priest by God, **according to the order of Melchizedek** (5:9-10).

In the **second part of the section (5:11-6:12)**, the writer tells his audience they're still having a hard time understanding the Word (Gospel message) because they're still infants who need milk and who are not ready yet for solid food. He says they should be teachers by now, but they need to take "Gospel 101" all over again and re-learn the basics. Solid food is for mature grown-ups who have had their senses trained through exercise and who have the ability to *discern between good and evil*. It is hard not to see a subtle allusion to the Adam and Eve story here. They are depicted as immature children who were unable to discern good and evil. Therefore, they represent the original humanity who is not yet grown up in Christ.

That is why the writer essentially tells his audience they are like Adam and Eve and need to grow up. They need to leave behind the **beginning word about Christ** and to go on to **maturity** in Christ. He then briefly articulates what the "basics" of the Christian faith are: *Repentance from dead works, faith in God, teaching about baptism, the laying on of hands, the resurrection from the dead,* and *eternal judgment*. Regarding **repentance from dead works**, it is likely that the writer is referring to turning away from the **works of Torah**. Regarding **eternal judgment**, even though that is the way most translations have it, it literally is **judgment of the age**, and it more likely refers to Jesus' prophecy in the Olivet Discourse regarding the coming judgment of the Temple at the end of the age.

The writer then urges his audience not to fall away from the faith and give a very dire warning. He says that once one comes to the faith and has had a taste of the heavenly gift (of salvation), has shared in the Holy Spirit and has experienced the power of the Coming Age—if that person then falls away from the faith, *it is utterly impossible for that person to be renewed to repentance again*. To turn away from the faith is the equivalent of crucifying the Son of God all over again.

To be clear, the writer isn't saying that if one sins and screws up after becoming a Christian, then one is destined for hell. He is simply emphasizing that if one rejects the faith after initially accepting it, one is rejecting salvation. He then uses a land metaphor to drive his point home: Land that drinks in the rain and produces a good crop is cultivated and blessed land, whereas land that is full of thorns and thistles is just worthless and cursed—and it will ultimately be burned up.

With that warning out of the way, the writer goes back to being positive in 6:9-12 and basically tells his audience that he is confident they will remain faithful and press on to full maturity in Christ. He then exhorts them not to be lazy, but to keep pressing on in faithfulness and the endurance of suffering, for that is how they are to be imitators of those who are **inheriting the promises**.

In **part three (6:13-20)**, as soon as he mentions **inheritance** and **promises**, the writer then turns and focuses on God's covenant promises to Abraham. What does a life of faithfulness and long-suffering look like? Just look at the life of Abraham. In God's covenant with Abraham, not only did God **make a promise** to Abraham, but He also guaranteed that promise **by making an oath**. Therefore, as long as Abraham was faithful, it was a rock-solid guarantee that he would eventually reach the promise God had made to him.

Since the Christian faith is the faith of Abraham, the writer tells his audience that as long as they stay faithful that they are guaranteed to receive the inheritance that God promised and swore to Abraham. What is that inheritance? It is God's new creation. That is the Christian hope that the writer not only calls the **firm and secure anchor for the soul**, but also the **entrance into the inner place, behind the curtain**. Of course, this temple imagery isn't of the earthly temple in Jerusalem in which the Levitical priests serve, but heavenly one in which Christ, **the high priest according to the order of Melchizedek** serves.

Here in **part four (7:1-28)**, the writer takes time to elaborate further on the significance of Melchizedek. Melchizedek is mentioned in Genesis 14:18-24, where upon coming back from rescuing Lot, Abraham meets King Melchizedek of Salem, who was also a priest of God Most High. Abraham gives a tenth of the loot he took from the kings he had just defeated to this Melchizedek. To the point, the writer of Hebrews engages in a **typological argument** in which, as a way to argue that Jesus' priesthood is greater than the Levitical priesthood dictated in the Torah, he says that Jesus is like Melchizedek in that story. To be sure, the writer uses some rather creative means to highlight the typology.

In 7:1-3, the writer draws three connections between Melchizedek and Christ: (1) He was **king of Salem**, which means *peace*, therefore he was the **king of peace**; (2) The name Melchizedek means **king of righteousness**; and (3) Since Genesis 14 doesn't say anything about where Melchizedek came from or who is father and mother were, the writer of Hebrews says that in a sense Melchizedek "has no record of beginning or end." Therefore, he is like the Son of God, who is **a priest forever**.

The writer then proceeds to show in 7:4-10 how Jesus' priesthood is greater than the Levitical priesthood. His argument is as follows: In the Torah, the Levitical priests are to receive a tithe from their fellow Israelites, so that means the children of Abraham are obligated to give a tithe to the Levites. Yet in Genesis 14, Abraham himself gave a tithe to Melchizedek, who wasn't from Abraham's family, who then blessed Abraham. Therefore, the writer argues, **since** those who are inferior are blessed by those who are superior, and **since** Levitical priests all die, and **since** there is no record of Melchizedek's birth or death (hence, he still "lives"), **in a way**, the Levitical priests all pay tithes to Melchizedek **through Abraham**, since they were "in his loins" when he paid a tithe to Melchizedek. Hence, the priestly order of Melchizedek is greater than the Levitical priesthood.

Then in 7:11-19, the writer explains that the Levitical priesthood was inferior to Melchizedek's priesthood because it was inadequate and couldn't get the job done. If the Levitical priesthood was able to produce **full maturity** for God's people, there would have been no need for Christ's priesthood in the order of Melchizedek. But since Christ is a new high priest who isn't in the line of Aaron, then that change in **priesthood** means a change in **covenant**. After all, Christ didn't become a priest *according to the Torah of the fleshly commandment*, but rather *according to the power of indestructible life*. What that means is that the Levitical priesthood, the Torah, and the Mosaic covenant itself are weak and useless and aren't able to bring human beings to **full maturity**. They can't change people's hearts and can't make people righteous. That is why a better covenant and better priesthood was needed, namely **the new covenant and Christ's priesthood in the order of Melchizedek**.

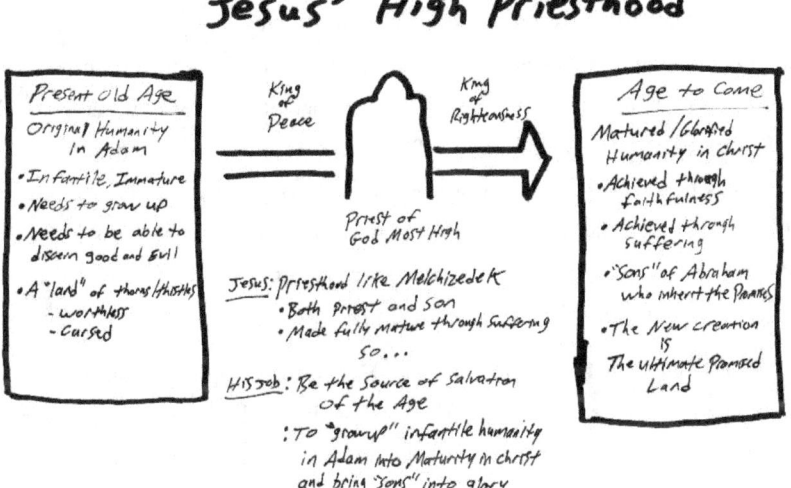

In 7:20-28, the writer expands on how Christ's priesthood is greater than the Levitical priesthood:

(1) Levitical priests become priests when they **take an oath**, but when Christ became a priest, it was **God who swore with an oath** that Christ would be a priest forever. Therefore, Christ's priesthood guarantees a better covenant.

(2) There had to be a lot of Levitical priests, **because they all eventually die**, and so new priests need to take the places of the ones who died; but **Christ conquered death** and therefore is now immortal, therefore, his priesthood is permanent.

(3) Since Jesus is blameless and undefiled and since he offered himself as a sacrifice for all, **he only had to do it once,** unlike **the daily sacrifices** Levitical priests are required to make.

(4) The Torah appoints **weak and sinful men to be high priests,** but the oath God swore came after the Torah, and with that oath He appointed a Son who had been **had reached full maturity into the ages.**

In the **fifth and final part of the section (8:1-13),** the writer drives home his argument as to why the New Covenant is better than the Old Covenant. Jesus Christ is the great high priest, seated at the Right Hand of God, who is thus the minister of the Sanctuary and true Tabernacle that God made, not man. By contrast, the **earthly tabernacle,** the **Levitical priesthood,** and the **daily sacrifices and offerings** are all just shadows and copies of the real things in Heaven—the **Heavenly Tabernacle, Christ's priesthood,** and **Christ's sacrifice** once and for all. That is why Christ's ministry is superior to that of the Levitical ministry. The New Covenant prophesied in Jeremiah 31:31-33 has come, and that means the Old Covenant is now obsolete and no longer needed. That is why, as the writer says, the old covenant, along with the Levitical ministry in the Temple, was just about gone—yet another indication that Hebrews was written shortly before the Jewish War of AD 66-70, when the Temple was, in fact, destroyed.

### 4. The Earthly Temple vs. The Heavenly Temple (9:1-10:18)

The writer of Hebrews isn't done yet with all the priesthood/tabernacle comparisons. In this fourth major section of the letter, that is what the writer focuses on. In the **first part of the section (9:1-10),** the focus is on the "two temples" themselves. The writer first focuses on the layout of the earthly tabernacle and the service of worship that was found in the Mosaic covenant:

(A) The outer tent was called the **holy place** and it held the lampstand and the table for the bread of the presence. That was where the priests performed their daily sacrifices.

(B) Behind the curtain in the holy place was the inner tent called the **holy of holies** that housed the golden censer and the Ark of the Covenant, in which was a jar that contained some manna, Aaron's rod, and the tablets of the covenant. It was only entered once a year, on the Day of Atonement, by the high priest who offered the blood on behalf of himself and the people.

After that description, the writer says that the very set up and pattern of the earthly tabernacle testifies to the fact that human beings cannot yet enter into God's Presence. As long as there is that outer tent, the way to God's Presence is still restricted. The blood that the high priest brings in once a year symbolizes the way in which God's people would one day be brought into His Presence, but it still isn't clear how that would happen. The daily sacrifices don't get the job done and don't **fully mature the conscience** of the worshipper. They point to a future reality that would accomplish that, but they themselves don't. They are **regulations for the flesh** that are required until the **time of reformation**. Basically, they acted as a placeholder until the real thing arrived—and that real thing is Jesus Christ.

In the **second part of the section (9:11-22)**, the writer focuses on the heavenly tabernacle and the service of worship of Jesus the high priest. The writer says that when Jesus the high priest appeared in the **fully matured tabernacle** that was *not made by human hands*, and *not of this creation*, that he entered the holy of holies in heaven once and for all, with his own blood, not the blood of animals, and that is what achieved the **redemption of the ages**. In the early tabernacle, the blood of goats *symbolically purified* and *sanctified* the one offering the sacrifice, but the blood of Christ was able to *sanctify our conscience from dead works*. That was why there had to be daily sacrifices and annual entrances into the holy of holies. They acted as a perpetual symbol and reminder of what God promised to eventually do, and that promise was achieved with the blood of Christ, which made the worshipper holy, so that he too could enter the holy of holies and worship in God's Presence.

That is why Jesus is the **mediator of a new covenant**, for he achieves what the sacrifices in the earthly tabernacle only symbolically foreshadowed. Through him, people can receive the promise of the ultimate inheritance in the Abrahamic covenant—the Age to Come and the New Creation. With that, the writer engages in a wordplay with the Greek word **diatheke** in 9:15-22. The word can mean both **covenant** and **will** (as in the document the articulates the inheritance after the person dies). The **covenant/will** only kicks into effect when the person dies. That is why Mosaic covenant was instituted with blood—for the blood of the sacrifices put that **covenant/will** into effect and (symbolically) purified everything in the Mosaic covenant.

In the **third part of the section (9:23-28)**, the writer points out that if the earthly copies had to be purified with the sacrificial blood of goats, that means that the heavenly things of which they were copies require the superior sacrifice of

Christ himself. At the **maturation of the age**, he offered his own blood once in the heavenly sanctuary, and it was *his sacrifice* that actually dealt with sin for real. Just like people die once and then face the judgment, so too did Christ die once in order to offer himself up for the sins of many. Since he did this, he will be seen **a second time** by those who are looking to him for salvation. This is about the future resurrection—the only way people will see Christ a second time will be if they, like Christ, resurrect.

In the **final part of the section (10:1-18)**, the writer contrasts Christ's sacrifice with the sacrifices in the Temple. His ultimate point is that the Torah and everything in the Torah (the tabernacle/priestly rites) is simply a foreshadowing of the real things that are to come, and because they are all just copies, they can never achieve God's purposes and bring **full maturation**. God's purpose for both human beings and His creation can never be achieved through the Mosaic covenant. It was just a pointer and a signpost to the way God would actually achieve His purposes. The writer then quotes **Psalm 40:6-8**, which talks about how God doesn't take pleasure in the burnt offerings and sin offerings, but instead wants His people to do His will. The point is that the Torah-mandated offerings were never God's endgame. His endgame is for His people to do His will—and through the sacrifice and blood of Christ, *the One who does God's will*, sinful people can truly be made holy so that they too can become *ones who do God's will*.

Then in 10:11-14, the writer further contrasts the Levitical sacrifices and Christ's sacrifices. They are offered daily and can never remove sins, but Christ's sacrifice is once and for all, and it does remove sin. Now that he's accomplished that, he is now at the Right Hand of God, waiting until all enemies are put under his feet. His one offering of himself has achieved the **maturation** of those who are being made holy. The writer then ends in 10:15-18 by quoting **Jeremiah 31:33**, which promises the coming of the New Covenant in which God will write it, not on tablets of stone (like the Mosaic covenant), but on His people's hearts and minds. Since Christ's sacrifice has achieved the forgiveness of sins, there is no longer any need for an more offerings or sacrifices.

| The Superiority of Christ's Priesthood over the Torah-Based Levitical Priesthood ||
| --- | --- |
| **Levitical Priesthood** | **Jesus' Priesthood** |
| • Can't bring about full maturity<br>• According to the *fleshly* commandment<br>• Levitical priests take an oath<br>• Many priests (because they die)<br>• Priests in weakness<br>• Daily sacrifices cannot bring full maturity<br>• Earthly temple made by men<br>• Old covenant/Old promises<br>• High priest goes into the Holy Place once a year with the blood of animals that can't remove sin | • Achieves full maturity<br>• According to indestructible life<br>• God Himself takes an oath<br>• One priest (who is immortal)<br>• One priest (perfected and matured)<br>• One sacrifice (himself) brings full maturity<br>• Heavenly Temple made by God<br>• New covenant/New promises<br>• Jesus entered the fully matured tabernacle in Heaven (not of this creation), once and for all, with his own blood that brings the redemption of the ages |
| • **Mount Sinai**: Darkness, Tempest, Blazing Fire, Fear | • **Mount Zion**<br>**Heavenly Jerusalem**: City of the Living God; Gathering of angels; The firstborn of Heaven; The fully matured righteous ones, with Jesus, the mediator of the New Covenant |

### 5. Call to Faithfulness (10:19-12:29)

This final section serves as the summary and conclusion to the entire letter. In the **first part (10:19-39)**, the writer begins with "Consequently." That tells you that everything the writer has been talking about for the past few chapters in regard to tabernacles, priests, sacrifices, and covenants is leading up to his main point: Christ's death opens up the way for us to come into God's Presence. The writer explains this using the extended metaphor of the Temple. Since Christ's priesthood is superior, we can now **boldly go into the holy sanctuary because of the blood of Christ**. Not only is Christ equated with the **high priest on the Day of Atonement**, but his blood is also equated with the **blood that the high priest brings** into the Holy of Holies. In addition, the writer also equates Jesus' own flesh to **the curtain** that separates the holy place and the Holy of Holies. That is why Christians can approach God with the full assurance of faith, because Jesus the high priest has sprinkled our hearts and cleansed our evil consciences. That is why Christians should **hold fast to the profession of an unwavering and confident hope** (namely the apostolic teaching of the Gospel) and keep encouraging each other to press on.

Of course, on the flip side, the writer warns in 10:26-31 about the consequences of falling away, and given the overall context of the letter, presumably back into Torah observance and Judaism. To do that is to willingly sin after coming to a knowledge of the truth, and that means there is no other sacrifice for sin that can cleanse that person. All that is left is coming judgment and wrath.

If we remember this letter was probably written at some point before the Jewish War of AD 66-70, the warning is stark: *Don't reject the Gospel and double-down on the increasingly revolutionary Judaism of the mid-first century. If you do, you're going to suffer God's wrath and judgment that is soon coming upon Jerusalem and the Temple.* That helps explain what is said in 10:28-31, namely the warning about suffering the judgment spelled out in the Torah for violating the Torah. If violating the Mosaic covenant brings about judgment, how much more judgment will you expect if you reject the New Covenant in Christ? As the writer says in 10:30: "The Lord will judge his people!"

Then in 10:32-39, the writer urges them to remember the initial persecutions and sufferings they went through when they were first enlightened (came to the Gospel). Again, given a pre- AD 70 Jewish context, the persecutions and sufferings referred to were probably the initial persecutions we read about in the early chapters of Acts, when the Sanhedrin first persecuted the Jesus movement known at that time as **The Way**. Therefore, given all they've already endured, the writer encourages them not to throw away their boldness and to keep pressing on. He then closes by quoting **Habakkuk 2:3-4**, which talks about how the **Coming One will come and won't delay**. That is why the righteous must live by faithfulness, because God won't be pleased with anyone who shrinks back to destruction.

The **second part of this section (11:1-40)** is the famous chapter about the heroes of the faith. In order to encourage his audience to press on in the faith, the writer essentially says that all the faithful and righteous people throughout Old Testament history are essentially "in the stands," cheering them on to live by faith as well. The writer first defines what he means by faith in 11:1-3: *"Now faith is the substance of things hoped for. It is the proof of things that cannot be seen, for the ancestors bore* *witness to this fact. By faith we understand that the ages were prepared by the Word of God, so that thing that are seen may come from things that are not visible."*

It is wrong to interpret these verses as saying that faith is a matter of believing certain things exist and certain things really happened, *despite the fact there is no evidence for them*, as if faith is some kind of mental assertion of some unprovable facts. Rather, the writer defines faith in terms of being certain of the Christian hope of a new creation, precisely because it is based on the reality of the resurrection of Christ, who is the "evidence" that what God promised to do will eventually come to pass. Thus, our **faith in Christ** and our **faithfulness to Christ** is rooted in the conviction and hope that what was witnessed on Easter Sunday would be experienced by all those who belong to Christ. Thus, living by faith in Christ in the present and experiencing the power of the Spirit in the present is the proof and guarantee that what God promised would eventually come to pass.

After that explanation, the writer begins with Abel and then lists all the heroes of the faith in the Old Testament as examples of faithfulness to God in 11:4-38. His point about all of them is found in 11:39-40: **They all lived by faith, but they didn't get to see the fulfillment of God's promises like you all have witnessed. What they were hoping for, you have witnessed accomplished in Christ.**

The **third part of the section (12:1-17)**, extends the metaphor of having the **cloud of witnesses** in the stands cheering us on by then encouraging us to **run the race of faith with endurance** and to look to Jesus, who is described as the one who **begins and fully matures our faith**. Since Jesus endured the suffering and shame of crucifixion in order to achieve the joy and goal of sitting down at the Right Hand of God, we should strive to be like him. In 12:4-11, the writer tells his audience that in their struggle against sin, that none of them have yet actually shed blood (suffered death) for their faith. Therefore, the writer quotes **Proverbs 3:11-12** to tell them they should view any suffering they go through as a form of God's discipline. Fathers discipline their sons so that they can grow up into fully mature and well-adjusted adults. So too is God the Father disciplining them. It shouldn't be seen as punishment for doing something wrong, but rather training to become more Christ-like and fully mature.

With that, the writer then exhorts his audience in 12:12-17 to keep pushing forward and finish the race by pursuing peace, caring for the needy, and not letting any bitterness creep into the community. He then specifically tells them not to be like Esau, who renounced his birthright for a little bit of stew to give him temporary relief from his hunger, and therefore inherit the blessing. Likewise, Christians should not forfeit the inheritance of God's new creation for some temporary relief from present suffering.

In the **final part of the section (12:18-29)**, the writer throws out one more metaphorical contrast between the Old and New Covenants by juxtaposing **Mount Sinai** (where the Mosaic Covenant and Torah was established) with **Mount Zion** (not the early Mount Zion where the Jerusalem Temple was, but the heavenly Mount Zion). In 12:18-21, he describes the situation for Israel at Sinai. The entire scene is foreboding and intimidating: *A blazing fire, a dark cloud, darkness and tempest; the commandment to not even touch the mountain or else death*. The people and Moses were completely terrified. By contrast, Mount Zion is described in 12:22-24. Christians haven't come to Sinai, where the Torah was given and where there was the threat of death. Instead, they've come to Zion, the **city of the Living God, the Heavenly Jerusalem**. They are there for a joyous celebration with angels—the celebration for the *assembly of the first born*. It is the celebration for the righteous people who have been **fully matured**. It was all made possible because of Jesus, the mediator of the New Covenant.

In 12:25-29, the writer once more exhorts his listeners to pay attention to the God speaking to them and to not reject Him. He then says that just as God **shook the earth** in the past, He will against **shake both earth and heaven**. This shaking of the earth is a reference to Sinai, and the future shaking of both earth and heaven is a reference to Christ's second coming, when God consummates the New Creation and does away with the old one. When Christ returns, this corruptible creation will be shaken and down away with, and only the incorruptible New Creation/Kingdom of God will remain.

### 6. Final Exhortations and Benediction (13:1-25)

Chapter 13 really is a "wrap-up" type chapter. In **13:1-19**, there is a final encouragement to continue in two areas. First, there is the encouragement to **continue in brotherly love (13:1-7)**. In this section, the writer encourages his listeners to keep showing hospitality to strangers—he even says that some have entertained angels without realizing it. He encourages them to remember and care for those in prison and those who are being harassed. He emphasizes fidelity in marriage and tells them to be content with what they have. Finally, he encourages them to imitate the godly conduct of their leaders. Second, there is the warning to

**be on guard against false teaching (13:8-16),** the kind that sounds a lot like Judaism, namely the food laws and the sacrificial protocol for the Levitical priests.

He then points to the practice of how the priests take bodies of the animals whose blood had been used in the tabernacle and burn them outside of the camp. He then says that Christ is sort of like that: (A) His blood was used to purify us and forgive our sins, and (B) He suffered death outside of the city of Jerusalem. Therefore, the writer tells his audience to "go outside camp" and be willing to bear the disgrace along with Christ. He then emphasizes that their "city" isn't here on earth (Jerusalem), but rather they are looking forward to the coming city (the heavenly Jerusalem). This clearly implies that the audience is Jewish-Christians still within the Jewish world and culture. In any case, the writer tells them that the kind of "sacrifices" they should be offering up to God are **sacrifices of praise** and **doing good for others**—*and not the kind of sacrifices connected with the Temple.*

In 13:17-19, the writer tells them to obey their leaders and submit to them and to pray for the writer and his people, specifically that they could be reunited soon. With that, the writer ends with a final benediction in 13:20-25, in which he prays that God, who raised up Jesus, the **Great Shepherd of the sheep** by the **blood of the Covenant of the Age**, would prepare them for everything good in accordance with His will. He also mentions in 13:23 that Timothy has been released from prison and hopefully he'll come with the writer to see them soon. He also sends greetings from those in Italy, where he obviously is.

# JAMES

**Time of Writing:** At some point before AD 62, when James was killed in Jerusalem.

## Background

James, the brother of Jesus, was known as **James the Just**. Although he was not a disciple during Jesus' ministry, Jesus appeared to James after his resurrection and James not only accepted Jesus as Messiah and Lord, but he eventually became the leader of the Jerusalem Church after the initial persecution of the apostles that began with the martyrdom of Stephen. James was eventually killed in AD 62, shortly before the outbreak of the Jewish War, when the high priest Ananus took advantage of the power vacuum that was created when the Roman governor Festus died and before the new governor arrived in Judea. The Jewish historian Josephus tells us that Ananus had James arrested, brought before the Sanhedrin, accused of breaking the Torah, and then stoned to death by a mob.

As for the letter itself, James had written it to the **twelve tribes of the Diaspora**, meaning the various Jewish communities throughout Asia Minor, Egypt, and Rome. We can say *Jewish communities* because James clearly references the synagogue in the letter. Still, the reality is that there were often Gentiles (known as God-fearers) who would attend the synagogue, and that fairly early on, the "Jesus movement" attracted a lot of those God-fearers in the synagogue and that there was not yet a clear distinction between Judaism and Christianity yet.

Therefore, what we find in James is a situation that was pretty murky—still, the predominant setting is Jewish. By contrast, Paul's churches were primarily Gentile, and the focus in his letters was on how Gentile Christians were part of God's people through faith in Christ, and they didn't have to submit to Torah and become Jewish. Since James' audience, though, was primarily Jewish, his focus was to urge his fellow Jews that **true Torah observance** consisted in keeping the **Royal Torah**—a reference to Jesus' teaching that the entire Torah hangs on the two commandments of loving God and loving one's neighbor.

It is important to realize that James and Paul were addressing two different audiences, because some people mistakenly think that they contradict each other, particularly when it comes to the issue of faith and works. In reality, James and Paul are really saying the same thing, only in different ways, given their different audiences. Paul is saying that Gentiles were saved **through faith**, that they didn't have to do **works of Torah**, and that a life of faith would be evidenced in the **fruit**

**of the Spirit.** James was telling his Jewish audience that a **life of faith** would be evidenced in keeping the **Royal Torah** that Christ taught, and that is evidenced in doing **good works**, not "works of Torah," but rather actions that reflect loving one's neighbor, which is what Paul's "fruit of the Spirit" really are about. In any case, when one reads the letter of James, it becomes quite clear that the communities he was writing to were somewhat poor and marginalized. One can go so far to say they were suffering poverty and oppression to an extent. Given that, there was a temptation for them to show favoritism to the rich and influential people where they lived in hopes of gaining some kind of material rewards.

### The Big Things to Know About James
A. **Trials "Perfect" (fully mature) Your Faith**: As one can see throughout the New Testament, James emphasizes that trials and troubles have the effect of "growing you up" to maturity in Christ.
B. **Want Wisdom? Just Ask, but Don't Discriminate**: Another major point of emphasis in James has to do with truly following the **Royal Torah**, namely loving God and loving your neighbor. His point is simple: If you want wisdom from God—if you truly love God—then you won't turn around and treat the poor among you with disdain. If you discriminate and show favoritism, you won't ever be granted God's wisdom, *because it is found among the poor and needy.*
C. **If You Love God, Prove It by Loving Your Neighbor**: Similar to the point above. You can't really love God if you hate those who are made in His image.
D. **Two Kind of Wisdom—From Below and From Above**: This is similar to Paul's distinction between the **works of the flesh** and the **fruit of the Spirit**. The wisdom from above produces peace and love, whereas the wisdom from below brings about divisiveness and judgment.

### Literary Map: James

| 1:1-15 Enduring Trials | | 1:16-27 Be Doers of the Word Pure Religion | |
|---|---|---|---|

| 2:1-7 Showing Favoritism Rich vs. Poor | 2:8-26 Faith: *Displayed in Works* Fulfilling the Royal Torah | 3:1-12 Taming the Tongue | 3:13-18 Two Kinds of Wisdom |
|---|---|---|---|

| 4:1-6 The Source of Quarrels | 4:7-17 Doer of Torah vs. Judge of Neighbor | 5:1-12 Warning to Rich Call for Endurance Coming of the Lord | 5:13-20 The Power of Prayer |
|---|---|---|---|

## A Walkthrough of James

### 1. Enduring Trials (1:1-15)

In his greeting, James identifies himself as a servant of God and the Lord Jesus Christ and addresses his letter to the **twelve tribes in the Diaspora**. This indicates that it is primarily a Jewish audience living in the Gentile world, before there was a clear-cut distinction between Christians and Jews.

The focus of James' opening section is about **enduring any kind of trials**. In fact, he says one should be joyful when one goes through tough times, because it is those tough times that grow one up and make one a more mature and complete person. They test one's faith and toughen one up to endure them, and that is what makes them more mature, to where one is not lacking in anything (1:2-4). To those who are still struggling to understand when such trials happen, James encourages them to ask God, who will give them wisdom.

At this point, he then says something in 1:6-8 that often gets misunderstood. Most translations say that when you ask God for wisdom, you should ask in faith, **without doubting**. Therefore, most people interpret this to mean that if you ask God for wisdom, but you don't *really mentally think* He will give it to you, then you're not going to get it. Consequently, it has often been twisted to mean that if your requests to God don't get answered, that it is your fault because you really doubted in your heart.

That is not what James is saying. The Greek word translated as "doubt" is *diakrinoo*, and although it can mean "doubt," it can also mean "discriminate," as in showing favoritism to people you like and neglecting people you don't like. Given the fact that one of the major themes of the letter of James is one of warning against showing favoritism, it makes a whole lot of sense to translate the word the same way here. Therefore, James is saying that if you want wisdom from God, just ask in faith, but don't go around and discriminate against the less fortunate as you try to suck up to the rich in order to get some favor from them. Since God is ready to give generously to you, you ought to be ready, willing, and able to give generously to others who need help. If you don't, then you're like someone caught in a **wave of the sea**, **a double-minded man** who is **turbulent** in all your ways. Simply put, you're not trustworthy and can't be counted on (1:7-8).

Not surprisingly, in 1:9-11, James talks about **the lowly and the rich**, by first saying the one who is lowly should **boast in his high position**. Simply put, that is because that is where Christ is, among the lowly. Secondly, James says the rich person should **boast in his low position**, for all that wealth is like a flower in a field that eventually withers up in the sun. It isn't that riches are bad, but it is that the person who puts his entire sense of self-worth in his riches is going to see his position come crashing down at some point. Hence James is articulating the very point of view in the Kingdom of God, where the poor and needy are honored and revered, and the rich are humble enough to realize that their wealth does not determine their worth.

James then takes things back around in 1:12-15 to the topic of going through trials by saying that the one who endures those trials is the one who is truly blessed, because that person will receive a **wreath of life**, as in the victory wreath of an Olympian victor, that will not wither and fade (in contrast to the rich's wealth fading like a flower in 1:11). That being said, James makes it clear that God isn't the one who puts you through trials. Rather, you go through trials because of your own **lust**. You desire something, you let that desire dance around in your mind until it basically consumes you and you do something stupid because you let that desire goad you into doing something wrong. James explains the progression by means of a birth metaphor: Lust "becomes pregnant" and eventually "gives birth" to sin; and then once sin becomes fully grown, it will eventually "give birth" to death.

### 2. Be Doers of the Word: True Religion (1:16-27)

| A Visual Guide to James |
|---|
| **Trials:**<br>Stay humble! They grow you up into maturity in Christ!<br>But remember, you bring trials upon yourself! Lusts→Sin→Death |
| **When Undergoing Trials:**<br>Ask God for *wisdom*, but don't *discriminate*. |
| *SO WHERE IS TRUE WISDOM FOUND?* |

| Hypocritical Lip Service to Torah | Living Out/Doing the *Royal Torah* |
|---|---|
| A *hearer* of the Word | A *doer* of the Word |
| Synagogue meetings that *discriminate* between the rich and the poor | Undefiled religion that cares for orphans and widows |
| Turbulent in one's ways; a double-minded person who forget what one looks like | Looks into the *fully mature Torah of Freedom* and continues to do it |
| Works in Sin/Convicted by Torah | Works out *Royall Torah* and is blessed<br>Is judged by the *Torah of Freedom* |

| Kisses up to the oppressive rich and powerful | Cares for the poor who are "rich" in the faith |
| Faith that "God is one," but no works (and hence, demonic) | Faith and Works leads to righteousness (like Abraham) |
| A tongue that blesses God, but then curses men | A tongue that is mature and blesses both God and men |
| *Wisdom from Below* | *Wisdom from Above* |
| • "Soulish" and Demonic | • Pure, Peaceful, and Gentle |
| • Jealousy, Strife, Ambitious | • Reasonable, Merciful, Good Fruit |
| • Source of Quarrels | • Doesn't Discriminate |
| • Big Talkers | • Produces Righteousness |

James made the following basic points in 1:1-15: (A) True wisdom in one's life is seen in how one treats those who are lowly, and (B) One goes through trials because one allows lust to give birth to sin, that results ultimately in death. Thus, in 1:16-18, he says that God doesn't gives us trials, but rather every **perfect/mature gift**. In other words, God has made it possible for us to grow up in Christ *through our trials*. James then refers to God as the **Father of Lights** from who there is no variation (unlike the person who discriminates). And rather than lust giving birth to sin, and sin giving birth to death, James emphasizes that God **gives birth to us by the World of Truth**, so that we can be a kind of **firstfruits** of his creatures.

That is why, as James says in 1:19-21, we should be patient and humble in times of trial—ready to listen, slow to speak, and slow to wrath, because acting out in wrath **doesn't work out** the righteousness of God. In 1:3-4, James said that the result of having one's faith put to the test is the **working out of maturity and completeness**. So here, what he is saying is that lashing out in wrath when you're going through trials won't get you to the righteousness of God. Instead, we should **receive the implanted Word that is able to save our souls**. Simply put, when you find your faith being tested, you can either ask for God's wisdom and receive the Word, so that it can bring you through that testing and make you more mature in your faith, or you can choose to act out in wrath and start discriminating and showing favoritism in order to, perhaps, find an easy way out of that trial—but it won't bring you to righteousness.

In 1:22-27, James gets to the ultimate point: **Are you going to be a mere hearer of the Word, or are you going to be an actual doer of the Word?** Merely listening to the Word is worthless if one doesn't put it into practice. It is like a man who immediately forgets what he looks like after he looks away from a mirror. That "mirror" is the **fully matured Torah of freedom**. When one looks into that "mirror" and then keeps on working it out in his life, that person will be blessed.

Since James mentions the **Torah** here, it is important tease out its significance throughout the letter. Most translations have **Law**, but given the Jewish context of the letter, we'd be best to see that James is talking about **Torah**. The biggest issue confronting the early Church at that time was the role of the Torah in the life of the community who has accepted Jesus as the Messiah. That is what James is addressing here. Simply put, the early Church, taking its cue from Jesus himself, said the entire Torah was summed up in two commandments: (1) **To love God**, and (2) **To love your neighbor as yourself**. If you do those two things, then you have fulfilled the Torah. Therefore, all the specific laws in the Torah that had to do with Jewish identity were ultimately irrelevant, now that Jesus had died, resurrected, and had commissioned his apostles to take the Gospel to the Gentiles.

Now there were many Jews, even those who had accepted Jesus as the Messiah, who insisted that Gentiles who came to faith in Christ now had to "become Jews" and observe the Torah. That view, though, was officially shot down at the Jerusalem Council in AD 50. The apostles teaching was clear: Gentiles who came to Christ didn't have to become Jews and observe the Torah. As long as they put their faith in Christ and loved both God and their neighbor, they were already observing the true Torah. This is what James is talking about when he speaks of the **fully matured Torah of Freedom**.

What he is saying here is that the one who really understands what the point of the Torah was all about and then goes out and **does the Word** (love God and love his neighbor), that person will be blessed and will become fully mature and complete in his faith. With that in mind, we can look at 1:26-27, where James says that anyone who feigns religiosity (probably Judaism in this context) but doesn't **bridle his tongue**, his religion is worthless. It isn't the **pure and undefiled religion** that looks after widows and orphans and keeps one unstained from the world. Thus, James is implying that worthless religion actually doesn't care for the lowly, but rather discriminates and speaks disparagingly against them.

### 3. Showing Favoritism (2:1-7)

In this next section, James expands what he has just said in 1:27. He begins by telling his Jewish audience that if they show **favoritism** (discriminate, treat the poor badly while sucking up to the rich), then they don't have the **faith of our Lord**

**Jesus Christ of glory**. Simply put, Jews who truly accept Jesus Christ as Lord will be **true doers of the Torah**, meaning the **matured Torah of Freedom**, which is loving God and loving your neighbor, and is therefore the **true pure and undefiled religion**. James then holds up the example of how synagogue members would fawn over a rich man who comes in, while completely neglecting, even disparaging, a poor man who comes in as well. James says that when that happens, the people who do that have **discriminated** and have **made distinctions** among themselves, and thus have become **judges with evil thoughts**. They've violated that very **Torah of Freedom** that Christ spoke of by failing to love their neighbor (the poor man) because they were too busy kissing up to the rich and influential man.

The irony of this is spelled out in 2:5-7, when James says that God has chosen the **poor in the world** to be **rich in faith** and **heirs of the kingdom**. Therefore, what those in the synagogue have done is dishonored the very people who are heirs of the Kingdom of God. Not only that, but they actually fawning over the very people who are oppressing them, dragging them into court, and blaspheming the God they claim to worship.

### 4. Faith, Works, and the Royal Torah (2:8-26)

The next section continues what James has been talking about all along. James first sets up a contrast between those who **truly observe the Torah** and those who are **transgressors of the Torah**. In 2:8, he says that the one who is **fully mature in the Royal Torah** is the one who **loves his neighbor as himself**. The Royal Torah is the same thing as the Torah of Freedom, which is Jesus' take on the Torah, namely its fulfillment is to love God and love your neighbor. By contrast, he says in 2:9 that the one who is **showing favoritism** (discriminating) is **working in sin** and is **convicted by the Torah as a transgressor**.

He then emphasizes in 2:10-11 that even if one observes all the commandments but breaks just one of them, that person is guilty of breaking the Torah, and is therefore guilty of transgressing the Torah. Given those two choices, James makes it clear in 2:12-13 that **you want to be judged by the Torah of Freedom/Royal Torah, not the "Letter of the Law" version of the Torah**. If you love your neighbor and show mercy to the poor and lowly, then God will show mercy to you and the Torah of Freedom with "judge" in your favor. By contrast, if you are merciless to the poor and lowly and if you speak badly of them and judge them, then you will not receive mercy from God and will be judged harshly by the very Torah you claim you are observing, but obviously aren't.

James further emphasizes this in 2:14-17 when he says that the kind of faith that doesn't actively work to love one's needy neighbor isn't real faith at all. Therefore, given the Jewish context, if one claims to have faith in God (and claim to observe the Torah), but then refuses to actually help those who are poor, hungry, and in need, then one's "faith" is, in fact, dead. **You can't love God if you refuse to love your neighbor who is made in God's image**. Not only that, but as he says in 2:18-20, a faith that says, "God is one" (taken from the Shema in **Deuteronomy 6:4-5**), without the actual works of loving one's neighbor, is nothing more than a mental assertion that God exists, and **that kind of "faith" is the same kind of "faith" of demons**—but it certainly isn't faith in Christ.

With that, in 2:21-26, James does something similar to what Paul does in both Romans and Galatians by appealing to Abraham as a model of faith. Although James and Paul use different terminology that have caused some to think they are arguing contradictory things, the fact is that they are arguing for the same thing. Paul, addressing a **Gentile-Christian audience**, argues that Abraham's faith was counted to him as righteousness *completely apart from doing the works of Torah*, and that a life of faith is demonstrated by the fruit of the Spirit. James, though, addressing a **Jewish audience**, argues that Abraham's faith was working together with his works—not "works of Torah," but his actual daily actions that demonstrate his faith—and that is how his faith was made **fully mature**. James quotes **Genesis 15:6**, just like Paul: "Abraham's faith in God was counted to him as righteousness" and says that faith alone, if not accompanied by works, cannot make one righteous. Simply put, both James and Paul emphasize that faith is what makes one righteous, and that faith is made evident in what Paul calls the **fruit of the Spirit** and James calls **good works**—both are referring to the same thing.

In 2:25-26, James then throws in an example of Rahab the prostitute who was made righteous by her "works" of helping the spies—indeed, those "works" is what got her spared when Joshua took Jericho. Then James uses the metaphor of the body and the spirit to drive his point home: If there is no spirit in a body, that body is dead. In similar fashion, if there are no works in a person's faith, then that person's faith is also dead.

### 5. Taming the Tongue (3:1-12)

The next section focuses on the taming of the tongue. Although it is certainly applicable to things like gossiping and swearing, given the original context of the letter, what James says ties directly into what he has been saying regarding how, if you want wisdom from God, you shouldn't be discriminating against the lowly and showing favoritism toward the rich. The fact is discrimination and favoritism are most easily seen in one's speech.

James begins in 3:1-2 by saying that not everyone should become teachers, because teachers among God's people will receive a greater judgment. If you can't control what you say and do, then your bad behavior is going to influence those whom you're teaching. That is why someone who is **fully mature** is the one who is mindful of what they say and can control what he does. Once again, James is emphasizing the idea of being fully mature. From the beginning of the letter, James emphasizes that full maturity is a result of going through trials and enduring in the faith. The one who has done that is fully mature in the Torah of Freedom/Royal Torah because his faith is accompanied with the works of loving his neighbor and not discriminating against the lowly.

Not everyone is fully mature in their faith, though, so it should not be surprising that a lot of people still have problems watching what they say, and the fact is that what one says (the tongue) often determines what that person ultimately does. Hence, in 3:3-5, James equates the tongue to a bit in a horse's mouth and a small rudder on a boat. In both examples, a very small thing is what ends up making the horse/boat go in a certain direction. The same is true of the tongue. The fact is the tongue can be a very dangerous thing that can easily get a person into trouble (3:6-8). Therefore, the tongue is like a small fire that can end up burning down an entire forest. It can enflame and corrupt the entire body with the flames of Gehenna and is (potentially) full of deadly venom.

That is why, as James says in 3:9-10, it is not right to bless God and then turn around and curse men who are made in God's image. This goes back to James' main argument in the letter: **Don't expect to be blessed by God if you discriminate against and curse men who are made in His image**. If you do that, then you are violating the Torah, namely, the Royal Torah that says one should love God and love your neighbor. In 3:11-12, James then gives the analogies of how a spring cannot produce sweet water and bitter water, a fig tree cannot produce olives, and a grapevine cannot produce figs to show that you cannot love God and hate your neighbor. You can't expect blessing from God if you discriminate against the lowly.

### 6. Two Kinds of Wisdom (3:13-18)

James transitions to the topic of wisdom he introduced in 1:6, when he said that if someone is lacking in wisdom, that person should ask God in faith, without discriminating against others. James' point is simple: The person who has wisdom and understanding will be recognized by **his works**, specifically in his gentleness toward others. James then proceeds to contrast two types of wisdom—the kind that comes **from above** (from God), and the kind that that is earthly. James calls **earthly wisdom** *soulish* and *demonic* and says that it brings about jealousy, selfish ambition and other vile deeds. By contrast, **heavenly wisdom** is pure, peaceable, gentle, reasonable, full of mercy and good fruit, and **it doesn't make distinctions or discriminate**. It sows peace and it produces the fruit of righteousness. In that respect, what James is saying is just like what Paul says regarding the fruit of the Spirit.

### 7. The Source of Quarrels (4:1-6)

Having just said that earthly wisdom brings about jealousy and selfish ambition, James then drives the point home by saying that their fights and quarrels ultimately come from their passions. This echoes what James said in 1:14-15, regarding how one is led into trials by one's own lusts. James says that when it gets right down to it, they aren't getting what they ask from God because they are **asking with the wrong motives** and are **spending everything on their passions** (4:2-3). In that respect, James says they are basically adulterers who, by trying to be friends with the world are setting themselves up to be enemies of God. After all, God opposes the proud, but gives grace to the humble (4:4-6). All this goes back to James' opening words in 1:2-9: If one wants wisdom from God, one has to ask in faith **without discriminating**, and that the one who is lowly should boast in his high position. This was precisely the problem James addressed in 2:1-7, when they were showing favoritism to the rich and discriminating against the lowly. Yet it is the lowly who are rich in faith and are blessed in the Kingdom of God.

### 8. Doer of Torah vs. Judge of Neighbor (4:7-17)

James now exhorts his Jewish audience in 4:7-10 to **submit to God** and to **oppose the devil**, so that God will draw near to them, and the devil will flee. He then calls them *sinners* and *double-minded ones* and urges them to **cleanse their hands** and **make their hearts holy**. He tells them that if they **humble themselves**, God will exalt them. All this goes back to 1:2-9. The **double-minded one** is one who **discriminates** against the lowly, the very ones who are blessed in the Kingdom of God. If they want to receive wisdom and blessing from God, they need to stop discriminating against the lowly and start identifying with them.

With that James further articulates in 4:11-12 that their problem has been they've been **speaking against** and **passing judgment** on one another—meaning they have been discriminating against each other. When they do that, they are actually speaking against and passing judgment on the Torah. For when you speak against or pass judgment on someone, you are violating Christ's commandment to **love God and love your neighbor**. Simply put, if you *judge your neighbor*, then you *judge the Torah*, and are not, therefore *doing the Torah* (namely, loving your neighbor). Since there is only one Torah-giver and Judge (God), James asks, "Then why are you *passing judgment on your neighbor*?" Basically, that's not your job! Your job is to love God and love your neighbor and leave the judging up to God.

James then points in out 4:13-17 the foolishness of big-talking people who have big plans and go about boasting about it. The truth is that people are in no position to pass judgment on others, and they are foolish to boast of all their big plans. They need to be humble and acknowledge that anything they plan to do will only be done if God allows it to be done. He then ends by saying, "Anyone who knows to do good, yet doesn't do it, that person sins."

### 9. Warning, Call, and Coming of the Lord (5:1-12)

With that, James then unloads on the kind of rich people he referred to in chapter 2, namely the kind who oppress the poor and blaspheme the Name of God (5:1-6). James' message is simple: God's judgment is coming for them on the **Last Day** because of their exploitation and oppression of the lowly and poor. In that respect, they have made themselves like fattened lambs for slaughter.

By contrast, James then speaks to those who have been oppressed (5:7-11) and hearkens back to something he said back in chapter 1, namely the topic of enduring trials. He encourages them to patiently endure and wait for the **Coming of the Lord**. That is why they shouldn't speak against each other, so that they will not be judged when the Judge comes…and the *Judge is standing at the gates*. As we've seen throughout the New Testament, beginning with the **Olivet Discourse** in Mark 13, Matthew 24, and Luke 21, it is very possible that James' comments about the Coming of the Lord is in reference to the coming destruction of Jerusalem and the Temple during the Jewish War of AD 66-70.

James then points to both the prophets, as well as Job, as examples of patient endurance and reminds them that they have seen **the ultimate purpose of the Lord** because He is compassionate and merciful. After that, James echoes Jesus' words in the Sermon on the Mount when he tells them not to swear any oath, and to rather just let their "yes" be "yes" and their "no" be "no," so that they won't **fall under judgment**.

### 10. The Power of Prayer (5:13-20)

James ends his letter with an exhortation to prayer. If you're suffering, pray; if you're cheerful, sing praises. (13). If you're sick, then have the elders of the church pray for you and anoint you with oil in the Name of the Lord (14). The vow of faith will save one who is discouraged, and the Lord will raise him up; any sin will be forgiven (15). Confess your sins to each other and pray for each other, so that you can be healed, because the prayer of a righteous person is powerful and works many things (16). Elijah is an example of the power of prayer. He prayed, and it didn't rain for 3 ½ years Then prayed again, and it rained, and the land produced fruit (17-18). Finally, James says that anyone who turns back someone who has gone astray from the truth, that person will save his soul from death and will cover over a great number of sins (19-20).

# I PETER

**Time of Writing:** Peter was executed in Rome sometime between AD 64-68. Therefore, I Peter was probably written at some point in the early-to-mid 60s, shortly before his death. There is a question, though, regarding whether II Peter was actually written by Peter, or whether it was a 2nd century letter that was attributed to Peter. The reason for this is largely due to the different writing style and terminology of II Peter, but the evidence isn't conclusive.

**Background**

Peter wrote his letters from Rome to various Christian communities throughout the Roman provinces in Asia Minor (Pontus, Galatia, Cappadocia, Asia, Bithynia). We know this because I Peter 5:13 mentions that Peter wrote the letter from **Babylon**, the nickname Christians had for Rome.

The decade of the 60s in the first century proved to be positively apocalyptic for both Christians and Jews. Within the span of about five years, James the brother of Jesus and the leader of the Church in Jerusalem was killed in Jerusalem, and both Peter and Paul were executed in Rome after Nero blamed the Christians for the great fire of Rome in AD 64 and began the first official persecution of Christians. Shortly after that, the Jewish Revolt broke out in AD 66 and the subsequent Jewish War resulted in the destruction of Jerusalem and the Temple in AD 70.

It is against this historical backdrop that we need to read I/II Peter. I Peter seems to have been written near the very beginning of the persecution. If we accept Peter as the author of II Peter, it would have been written subsequently shortly before his execution, in the midst of Nero's persecution and on the eve of the Jewish War. It is possible, therefore, to understand Peter's talk of the **last days** as referencing the upcoming Jewish War and destruction of Jerusalem. We need to remember that during the week before his crucifixion, Jesus had symbolically acted out judgment against the Temple and had prophesied that it, along with Jerusalem itself, would be destroyed within a generation.

In any case, reading I/II Peter can give us a few clues as to what the Christian communities to whom Peter was writing were like. They no doubt consisted of both Jewish and Gentile Christians from various walks of life and social classes. As should be obvious, in light of Nero's persecution and the rising tensions in Judea, the Christian communities were facing increased pressure and hostility within the Greco-Roman world.

## The Big Things to Know About I Peter

A. **Living Holy Lives in the "Last Days"**: If we are to understand the original context in which Peter is writing, we need to realize that I Peter was written in the build-up to the Jewish War of AD 66-70, when Jerusalem and the Temple were destroyed—and this was something prophesied by Jesus in the Olivet Discourse. The "last days" of which Peter (and many other New Testament writers) speaks about is, if you will, the "last days" of the Temple. In light of that impending crisis, Peter is encouraging Christians to stay committed to staying faithful to Christ and living holy lives.

B. **Demonstrating Grace by Bearing Up Under Unjust Suffering**: Given the fact that Christians were already beginning to suffer for Christ, Peter reminds them that when they bear up under unjust suffering, they are literally being Christ-like and are demonstrating the same kind of grace Christ showed us.

C. **Christ the Cornerstone in God's Temple, and You are Living Stones**: Again, when understood in the light of the impending destruction of Jerusalem and the Temple, Peter's use of Temple imagery to emphasize that the followers of Christ are God's true Temple takes on even more significance.

## Literary Map: I Peter

| | 1:1-2 The Greeting | | |
|---|---|---|---|
| **Living in the Last Days (1:3-2:10)** | 1:3-12 Salvation in Christ in the Last Days | 1:13-2:3 Call to be Holy in the Last Days | 2:4-10 Christ: Cornerstone Believers: Living Stones |
| **Living in the World (2:11-3:12)** | 2:11-17 Rulers | 2:18-25 Servants and Masters | 3:1-12 Wives and Husbands |
| **The Coming End (3:13-5:11)** | 3:13-4:6 Suffering for Doing Good Noah Example | 4:7-19 Completion of All Things Fiery Ordeal | 5:1-11 Appeal to Stand Firm in the Faith |
| | 5:12-14 Final Greetings | | |

## A Walkthrough of I Peter

### 1. The Greeting (1:1-2)

In his greeting, Peter identifies himself as an **apostle of Jesus Christ**, and he addresses his letter to those living in the **Diaspora**, specifically the regions of Pontus, Galatia, Cappadocia, Asia, and Bithynia that are located in what would today be central Turkey. By characterizing his audience as the **chosen refugees** or **elect exiles**, Peter is making a connection between the early Christians and the Exodus community in the Old Testament. Just like Israel was called out of slavery in Egypt and wandered in the wilderness like refugees before they made it to the promised land, so too are Christians called out of the bondage of this world and are currently wandering in the "wilderness" of this world (the Diaspora) before they eventually make it to the ultimate promised land of the new creation.

Peter says their calling was always part of God's plan from the beginning. Even though the actual term **Trinity** was not yet used by Christians in the first century, one can easily see the Trinitarian mindset in Peter's thinking: (1) This was **God the Father's** plan all along; (2) It was **God's Spirit** that was making them holy and set apart for that purpose; and (3) That purpose is found in obedience to **Jesus Christ** and the sprinkling of his blood. Clearly, Peter is interpreting Christ's death in light of the sacrificial system of the Temple. Just as the priests would sprinkle the blood of the sacrifice on the altar to make it holy, so too does Christ's blood make us holy.

### 2. Living in the Last Days (1:3-2:10)

In the first section of Peter's letter, he discusses how Christians in the first century were **living in the last days**. In the **first part (1:3-12)**, Peter provides an over-arching picture of what **salvation in Christ** is within the context of the **last days**. What Peter means by "last days," though, needs to be understood within that first century context, particularly in light of Christ's prophecy of the Temple's destruction in the Olivet Discourse (Mark 13, Matthew 24, Luke 21) and Peter's Pentecost sermon in Acts 2. Simply put, the "last days" were considered to be the time from Pentecost to when the coming (*Parousia*) of Christ would happen, which was connected in some way to the Temple's destruction.

Peter begins by praising God the Father for the salvation He has given us through the Lord Jesus Christ. Peter describes that salvation as beginning with a **new birth** *through* **the resurrection of Jesus Christ** *into* **a living hope** that he describes as an **imperishable, undefiled,** and **unfading inheritance** that is kept in heaven. Simply put, it is the hope of the **new creation**. Thus, the basic Christian worldview is that *this world* in *this old age* is corruptible, but because of the death and resurrection of Christ, we will be reborn into *the new creation* in *the coming new age*. In the meantime, we are like the Exodus community, traveling in between Egypt and the Promised Land, only we are traveling in between this old age and the new age. In this "in between time" that Peter calls the "last days," we are bound to go through tough times and various trials. These trials, Peter says, serve a purpose. They test and purify our faith, just like fire purifies gold in a furnace. Such trials will result in praise, glory, and honor at the **revelation of Jesus Christ.**

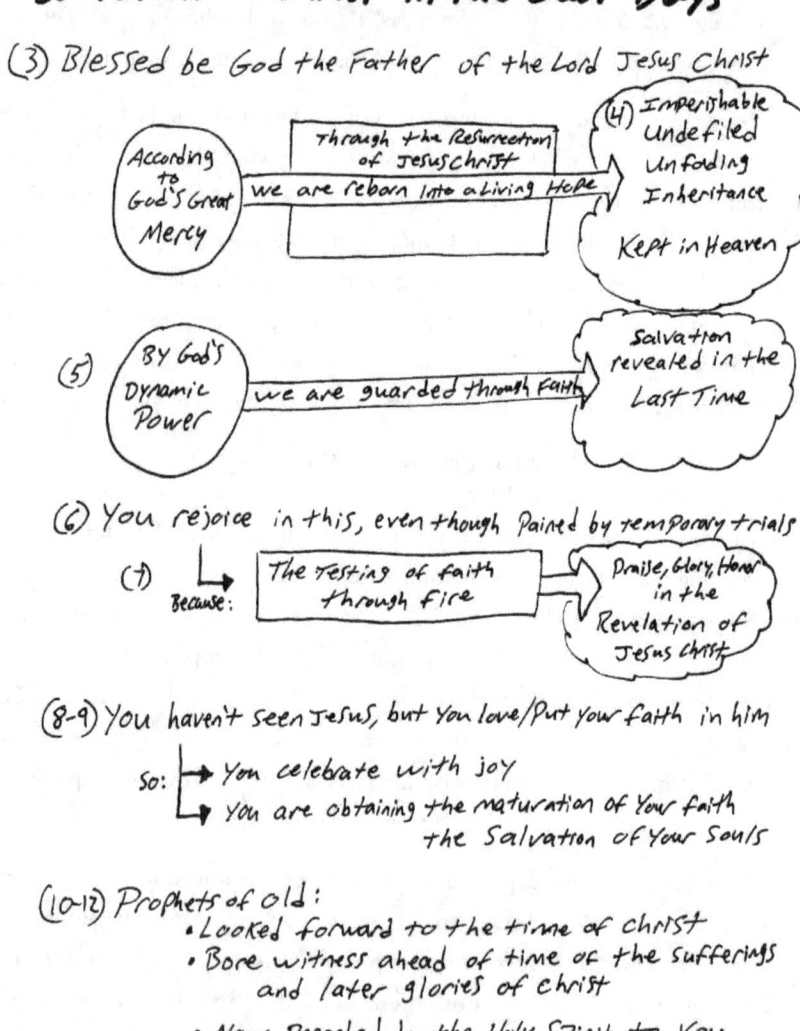

Peter then tells his audience that, although they weren't eyewitnesses who actually met Jesus of Nazareth, and even though the revelation of Jesus Christ hasn't happened yet, they still have chosen to put their faith in him and love him. That is why they are celebrating with joy—they know that through their trials, they are **obtaining the maturation of their faith, the salvation of their souls**. Two things are to be noted. First, what I have written as "maturation," most translations have as "outcome." The Greek word is *telos*, and although in a general way it means "outcome" or "goal", the gist of it is that of **full maturation**. This is important to realize because Peter isn't depicting salvation as something obtained solely in the future, but rather, as something that has already begun, that it will be brought to completion in the future. Simply put, he is emphasizing that Christian salvation is a process. Secondly, when Peter talks about the salvation of our souls, we need to interpret that in light of Adam in **Genesis 1-3**. Adam, representing natural humanity, was called a "living soul," and although he was created in God's image, he was not the "end product" or goal of God's purposes. The goal was always to take humanity in its natural state (Adam) and transform and sanctify humanity (in Christ), so that it would be reborn in God's likeness. Simply put, *salvation in Christ is the sanctification of original, natural humanity into a resurrected, Spirit-empowered humanity in Christ.*

Peter ends this part by looking back to the Old Testament prophets and saying they were looking forward to the revelation of the very Gospel the Christians were currently experiencing. In fact, he says the very **Spirit** that inspired them to prophesy about the sufferings of Christ and the glories afterward, in fact, the **Spirit of Christ**. Hence, the same Spirit of Christ that inspired the prophets of the Old Testament to prophesy about the Gospel is the **Holy Spirit** who inspired the apostles of the New Testament who preached the Gospel.

In the **second part of the section (1:13-2:3)**, Peter encourages Christians to be obedient to Christ and to live holy, Christ-like lives in the current last days. He basically tells them to stay focused on the Gospel that has been made known in Christ. They shouldn't let themselves be **conformed to ignorant lusts** that they used to live by. Instead, they are to **be holy in everything they do**, just like God Himself is holy. They are to live according to their calling and conduct themselves as refugees who have utter reverence for God.

Peter reminds them of the worthless conduct of their former lives and how they went after **perishable things like silver or gold**, and how they were saved by the **precious blood of Christ**, the **unblemished and spotless lamb**, that was sprinkled to make them obedient and holy (1:2). This was God's plan all along, and it has now been **revealed during the last times** for them. They can rest assured that their faith and hope are secure in God, because God raised Christ from the dead and then glorified him.

Because of that, Peter encourages them to keep growing up and maturing in Christ. In 1:22-23, he says that since they have **purified their souls** (1:9; 1:19—like Christ) through being obedient (1:2; 1:14) to the truth of the apostles' teaching, they are to **love one another with a clean heart**. They have been **reborn** (1:3), not from **perishable seed**, but rather **imperishable seed** (1:4, 7, 18), through the **living and lasting Word of God**. Then, in 1:24-25, Peter highlights the difference between the corruptibility of this age with the incorruptibility of the age to come by quoting **Isaiah 40:6-8**: *"All flesh is like grass, but the Word of the LORD lasts into the ages."* This **Word** that Isaiah talks about is the **Gospel** that was preached to them.

Then in 2:1-2, Peter stays with the idea of growing up and maturing in Christ. When he encourages them to put off all the bad things in the world, he equates them with **new-born infants** who are hungry for milk. Now, most translations have "spiritual" and "pure" milk, but that first word in Greek is actually *logicon*—**logical**. Hence, just as infants need milk so they can grow up into maturity, newly re-born Christians need **logical and pure milk** so they can **grow up into salvation**. Basically, if they have "tasted and seen" that the LORD is good, then Peter wants them to "keep drinking it up" so they can grow and mature in Christ (2:3).

In the **third part (2:4-10)**, Peter switches metaphors from that of an **infant growing up** to that of a **building with individual stones**. It is obvious that his use of this metaphor comes from Jesus himself (Paul also uses it as well)—and it has everything to do with the **Temple**. When confronting the Temple establishment in the days leading up to his crucifixion, Jesus told the **Parable of the Vineyard** and declared that the Temple would be destroyed as a sign of God's judgment. At that point, he ended by quoting **Psalm 118:22-23**: *"The stone that the builders rejected has become the cornerstone. It is the LORD's doing, and it is marvelous in our eyes."* Jesus' point was simple: The Temple in Jerusalem wasn't really God's House. The **real Temple** would be the followers of Jesus. He was the cornerstone of that Temple, and those who put their faith in him and followed him would be the stones in that Temple. In short, the Church, the Body of Christ, was the Temple of the Holy Spirit—it was where God would dwell with His people.

Once you realize that, you can fully appreciate what Peter says here. Jesus Christ is the **living stone** that was rejected by men, but **chosen and precious** according to God. Therefore, Christians are also **living stones** that are built together into a **Spiritual House** to be a **holy priesthood** to offer up **Spiritual sacrifices** that are acceptable to God through Jesus Christ. Notice how Peter mixes his metaphors here when he says that Christians are both a *Spiritual House* and a *holy priesthood*—both the building and the priests in the building. By calling Christians a holy priesthood, Peter is using Exodus language, specifically **Exodus 19:6**, when God says that Israel is to be a royal priesthood and a holy nation.

Peter then gives three Old Testament quotations in 2:6-8. First, **Isaiah 28:16** speaks of God laying a **chosen** and **precious cornerstone in Zion** and says that whoever puts their faith in him will never be put to shame. Second, Peter quotes **Psalm 118:22** to describe those who don't put their faith in Christ. They are like the builders who reject the stone that eventually becomes the cornerstone. Third, since he's talking about stones, Peter then quotes **Isaiah 8:14**, which speaks of a **stone of stumbling** and a **rock of scandal**. Put all these together, and Peter's point is that the Jews had rejected Christ, who is not only the cornerstone of the Church, the real Temple of God's Spirit, but is also the stone over which the Jews stumbled because the idea of a crucified Messiah was seen as scandalous. Peter makes clear, though, that the reason why they stumbled wasn't because of some honest mistake, but rather because they **disobeyed the Word**.

Peter proceeds to transfer a whole host of descriptions that were used to describe Old Testament Israel to the New Testament Church. It is the Church that is **a chosen lineage**, **a kingdom of priests**, **a holy nation**, and **a people for God's possession**. It is the Church who is to go out and proclaim the virtues of the true God who has **called them out of darkness and into His wonderful light**. Hence, not only does what Peter say here echo the Exodus community, but it also even hints at the creation story itself. What Peter says at the end of this section gives us a hint that his audience is probably a largely Gentile audience, for he says that *before* they were not a people and hadn't received mercy, but *now* they are the people of God who have received mercy.

### 3. Living in the World (2:11-3:12)

In the major section of the letter, Peter turns to very practical concerns in regard to how Christians are to live in the world. In the **first part (2:11-17)**, he focuses on how to relate to those in authority, namely rulers. Before he gets to those practical comments, though, he first reiterates in 2:11-12 the fundamental points he has made thus far: (A) They are **strangers and refugees** in the world (1:1, 17), (B) They should stay away from the **lusts of the flesh that battle against the soul** (1:14), (C) They should display **good conduct** among the nations who speak evil of them (1:15-18), so that hopefully (D) those nations will glorify God (get saved!) on the **Day of Overseeing/Visitation** (1:5, 7, 13, 20). This good conduct is then spelled out in very practical terms. It means **respecting those in human authority**, whether it is the emperor himself or any other person in governing authority (2:13-17). Peter says that the whole purpose of the governing authorities is to bring justice against those who do evil and to approve and support those who do good. Obviously, that doesn't always happen, but generally speaking, that is the purpose of government.

| 2:11-17<br>*Relating to Rulers* | • Respect those in authority—they dispense justice<br>• Good conduct toward everyone |
|---|---|
| 2:18-25<br>*Slaves and Masters* | • Show grace by bearing up under unjust treatment<br>• Imitate Christ, the Ultimate Servant |
| 3:1-12<br>*Wives and Husbands* | • Wives: Be subject to ungodly husbands—maybe they'll come to Christ<br>• Husbands: Love your wives as fellow heirs in Christ |

Peter then gives some practical advice in 2:15-16, when he says that the way God wants Christians to "shut up the ignorance of foolish men" (anyone who speaks evil against them) is not for them to use their freedom in Christ as an excuse for doing evil right back, but rather to use their freedom in Christ to be **servants of God who do good works**. That is why he says in 2:17 that they are to **honor everyone, love the brotherhood, fear God**, and **honor the emperor**. Simply put, when faced with someone who wants to hurt you or who speaks evil of you, the Christian's goal shouldn't be to hurt that person back, but rather to get that person to see God's love in your conduct, so that that person might turn to Christ.

In the **second part (2:18-25)**, Peter focuses on how Christian slaves should live their lives. What he says is similar to what Paul says in his letters, but Peter's additional comments reveal an underlying perspective that most people miss. On the surface, Peter's advice is straightforward: If you're a slave, then be subject to your masters and do a good job, regardless of whether or not the master is a kind and gentle person or a rather mean and brutal person (2:18). The theological reason for doing this, though, is spelled out in 2:19-20. Unfortunately, most translations translate Peter as saying that it is *commendable*, or *a credit to you*, or *finds favor*. The ESV comes closest when it says, "It is a *gracious thing*, when mindful of God, one endures sorrow while suffering unjustly." The Greek word in question is *charis*, and it literally means **grace**.

Peter's point is that if you are a slave and are suffering unjustly because of a bad master, bearing up under that unjust treatment isn't just "commendable," or "a credit" to that Christian slave, but it is actually **grace in action**. Peter isn't just telling Christian slaves who suffer unjustly, "Hey, good for you! I'm impressed!" He's telling them that when they bear up under that unjust suffering, they are displaying the very same grace Jesus displayed and are literally imitating Christ and following his example. Thus, in their suffering, they are making grace and salvation available to those who are guilty of that injustice. Simply put, bearing up under unjust suffering is grace and opens the door to salvation.

This is why Peter proceeds in 2:22-23 to quote from **Isaiah 53:5-9**. In its original context, **Isaiah 53** was about the returning remnant of Israel coming out of the Babylonian Exile. The idea was that the returning exiles were God's purified remnant and God's servant through who God would eventually fulfill His covenant promise to Abraham, namely that through the great nation that came from Abraham (Israel), He would bless all nations and redeem the world. The Christian declaration was that Christ was the **Ultimate Servant**, in that he succeeded in being faithful and righteous, whereas Israel, even after the exile, obviously failed to be.

Therefore, Christ was the fulfillment of God's purposes and plan for Israel. The point made here is that Christ is held up as the example of bearing up under unjust suffering in order to bring about salvation for those who have gone astray. As Peter quotes Isaiah 53:5, *"By his wounds you have been healed."* By extension, he is telling Christian slaves that if they are unjustly treated and bear up under that suffering, then they are being like Christ and are offering a chance of healing and salvation to their cruel masters.

Peter ends this section in 2:24-25 by quoting **Isaiah 53:5** and reminding them that they *"were like sheep led astray,"* but they have been brought back to Christ, the **shepherd and overseer of your souls**. Thus, they have an opportunity to lead other "straying sheep" to Christ the Shepherd if they imitate Christ, bear up under unjust suffering, and show grace to others. The Greek word *episkopos* is usually translated as either "bishop" or "overseer," but the easiest way to understand it is in terms of being a **caretaker**, as a shepherd is of the sheep.

In the **third part (3:1-12)**, Peter addresses wives and husbands, echoing some of the same things Paul says in his letters. In 3:1-6 he says to wives that they should *be subject to their husbands*, even if their husbands disobey the Word (don't follow Christian teaching), for the same reason that slaves should bear up under unjust suffering from their masters—good and godly conduct might win the person over, and he might be saved. Peter then stresses in 3:3-4 the importance of inward beauty over outward beauty. He isn't telling women they shouldn't try to look nice, but rather to not obsess over their looks. Displaying a gentle and quiet spirit is infinitely more important than physical beauty in God's eyes. In 3:5-6, Peter refers to women like Sarah in the Old Testament as examples women should pattern their lives after.

Peter's comments to husbands are in 3:7. It is short and sweet, but make no mistake, what Peter says here would sound like insanity in the Roman world and culture, for he says that husbands are supposed to actually *live with, protect,* and *honor their wives as fellow-heirs in Christ.* Simply put, Peter tells husbands to treat their wives as equals and to treat them with love and respect. That idea was simply foreign in the Roman world. Peter ends with some general advice in 3:8-12. Since the goal of every Christian should be unity in Christ, every Christian should strive to be **like-minded, sympathetic, brotherly love, tender-hearted, humble**, and **not repay evil with evil**. In short, the only way to achieve true, Christian unity is to imitate Christ in all things, even when one suffers at the hands of others. If you repay evil with grace and blessing, you will inherit a blessing—that of salvation and a new creation. With that said, in 3:10-12, Peter then quotes **Psalm 34:12-16** to emphasize the point that Christians are to refrain from the bad, and to instead pursue peace instead.

## 4. The Coming End of All Things (3:13-5:11)

In the final section of the letter, Peter elaborates on how Christians should live in light of the "coming end of all things." In the **first part of the section (3:13-4:6)**, he elaborates further on the topic of suffering because one does what is good. Granted, generally speaking, not too many people are going to object or treat you badly if you are doing something good. Nevertheless, when that does happen, Peter says you should consider yourself blessed, because you have an opportunity to imitate the example of Christ and display the grace of God in that situation. Then Peter adds that if someone is impressed by how you bear up under unjust suffering, you should be able to be ready to give an account and explanation for your faith. Who knows? That person who asks might become a Christian and the person who was harassing you will be put to shame.

Peter reiterates in 3:17-18 what he told Christians slaves earlier: It is better to suffer for doing something good than to suffer for doing something bad—in that case, you'd obviously deserve it! But if you suffer for doing good, then you are being like Christ, the **Righteous One,** who also suffered for the sins of the unrighteous (of whom you once were), so that he could lead them to God. Simply put, **suffering in the flesh** opens the door to **life in the Spirit**. That's what Christ did for you, and that is what you can do for others.

At this point in 3:19-22, Peter alludes to the story of Noah and the flood to drive his point home about what Christ was able to accomplish through his suffering. Peter begins by working off of what he just said in regard to Christ bringing us to life in the Spirit. Peter then says that, in that same Spirit, Christ went to proclaim to the **spirits in prison** who disobeyed before the days of **Noah** and the **construction of the ark,** in which **only eight souls** were saved **through water.** Peter's point seems to be that Christ's sacrificial death on the cross not only was able to make salvation available to the people at that time who had heard the Gospel message, but it somehow also made salvation available to those who sinned and died before the time of Christ.

In any case, Peter brings up Noah's flood in order to draw a parallel with **Christian baptism**. Just like Noah and his family were saved *through water,* while others died in that same water, baptism symbolizes the believer's "death" in the water, and then "resurrects" him to salvation *through that same water of baptism.* So, in addition to being paralleled to Noah's flood, baptism is also a reenactment of the resurrection of Jesus Christ that makes it possible for the believer to have the same mindset of Christ. Of course, the resurrection and being saved from death isn't the ultimate goal, for Christ hasn't just been resurrected, but he has been glorified at **the right hand of God**, with the **angels, authorities,** and **powers** made subject to him—*and that is the destiny of any Christian who has been baptized into Christ*. Not only can one look forward to defeating death at the resurrection, but one can look forward to ruling with Christ and having authority over the spiritual powers of evil as well.

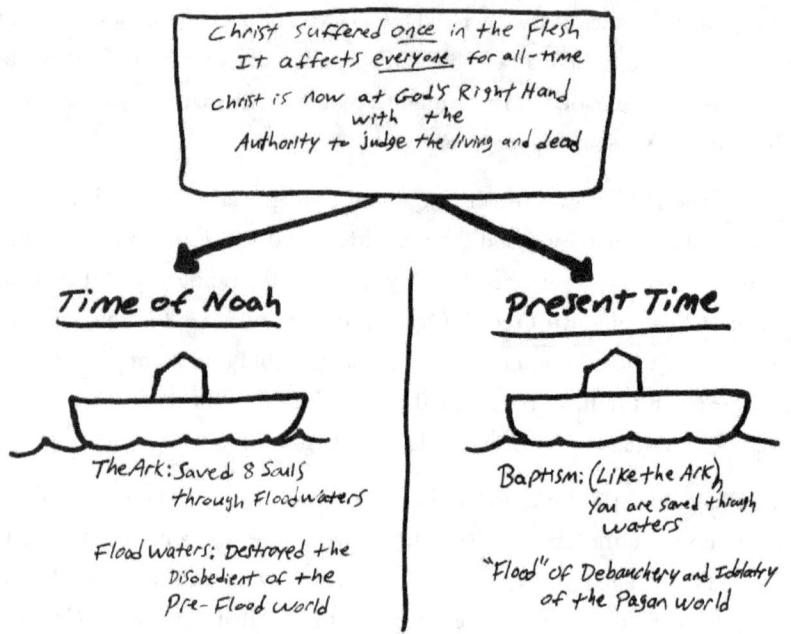

But Peter isn't quite done with playing a bit with the imagery of Noah's flood. In 4:1-6, Peter once again emphasizes that if you suffer in the flesh like Christ suffered in the flesh, and if you have the same mindset of Christ, then you will keep yourself from sin and will live out the rest of your life in this world, not according to the **lusts of men**, but rather according to the **will of God**. This is where Peter then brings it back to Noah by telling his audience that they already spent too much of their lives (before they came to Christ) living in the perverted behavior of the pagan Gentiles. Now that they no longer do that stuff, their pagan neighbors are shocked and can't understand why they don't join them in their **blaspheming flood of debauchery** anymore.

And why don't the Christians join them? *Because, like Noah, they have been saved through those "waters"—that is what their Christian baptism signifies.* Their pagan neighbors, though, are going to find themselves in the same situation as the people who died in Noah's flood and are going to have to give an account to the one who judges the living and the dead, namely Christ. That is why Peter said that Christ went in the Spirit to preach to the spirits in prison—the Gospel was shared to everyone who has ever lived, so that, although everyone literally dies **in the flesh**, the power of Christ makes it possible for everyone to **live according to God in the Spirit** (4:6).

In the **second part of the section (4:7-19)**, Peter talks about how the **end of all things** is near. We in 21st century America who've grown up with the *Left Behind Series* immediately jump to that kind of "end times" speculation. That is not what Peter is talking about, though. In the context of the first century and light of Jesus' prophecy about the Temple's destruction in the **Olivet Discourse** (Matthew 24, Mark 13, Luke 21), it is more likely that Peter, writing somewhere in the early 60s, shortly before the outbreak of the Jewish War of AD 66-70 that resulted in the destruction of Jerusalem and the Temple, saw the hand-writing on the wall and was simply saying that everything Jesus had prophesied was about to happen and the destruction of Jerusalem and the Temple was at hand.

Therefore, given the impending crisis, Peter tells his audience in 4:8-11 to keep their heads on straight, commit themselves to prayer, continue to love each other and show hospitality to each other, and get busy serving others with whatever gift God had given them...because things were about to get really tough. This is precisely what Peter is getting at in 4:12-19 when he says that they shouldn't be surprised at the **fiery ordeal** that they were beginning to experience, because that fiery ordeal was going to test them, like gold being purified in a furnace. That is why they should be rejoicing in the ordeal, because they will be **sharing in the sufferings of Christ**. If they do, in fact, end up suffering because they are Christians, they can be certain that they won't be put to shame. Their suffering will result in glory to God.

Peter ends by telling his audience that the **time of judgment is to begin with the House of God**. After reassuring them that in the end, Christians will be vindicated, glorified, and will rule with Christ, Peter then asks a question by quoting **Proverbs 11:31**: *"If the righteous one barely is saved, where will the wicked one and the sinner appear?"* If Peter is, in fact, talking about the impending Jewish War of AD 66-70, we can assume he is talking about Jerusalem and the Jews who had rejected Jesus and persecuted the Church for the previous thirty years. Thus, the "righteous one" would be Christians and the "wicked ones" would be the Jews of Judea. What this all comes down to is this: *If you're suffering for doing good, then keep doing good and commit yourself to God—you will not be put to shame; but if you're suffering for doing evil, well you deserve what is coming to you.*

In the **third part of the section (5:1-11)**, Peter concludes with some final comments directed to both his fellow elders as well as any new Christians. Once again, he emphasizes the theme that has run throughout the letter, that of **suffering** and **glory**. He says that not only is he a **witness of the sufferings of Christ**, but that he also **shares in the glory that is about to be revealed**. As far as the claim of witnessing the sufferings of Christ is concerned, we can take it in two ways: (1) That he was an actual witness to the sufferings Jesus went through, throughout his ministry in general and during his crucifixion in particular; or (2) That he personally has undergone sufferings as a Christian. Of course, both could be true.

With that, Peter speaks to the elders in 5:2-4 and tells them to **shepherd the flock of God** and **oversee it**. This hearkens back to how Peter described Jesus as the **Shepherd** and **Overseer** of their souls. In a sense, Peter is telling the elders to "be Jesus" for the people. He further tells them to use their authority to truly care for the flock, and not to lord their authority over the flock. They are to be an example to the Christians in their care, just as Christ is an example for them. If they do that, Peter tells them that they will receive an **unfading wreath of glory** when the **Chief Shepherd is revealed**. As for the new Christians, Peter tells them to be subject to the elders. After all, if the elders are imitating Christ and serving as an example to the flock, that advice is warranted.

Peter then addresses everyone with a few final words: **Humble yourselves**—God will exalt you in time; **Cast your anxiety on Him**—because He cares for you; **Stay sober and awake**—for times are tough and the Devil is on the prowl, like a lion; and finally: **Stand firm in the faith**—and realize that the current sufferings they are going through will soon be **brought to full maturation**. After a little suffering, God, who called them into His **ageless glory in Christ Jesus**, will heal and strengthen them.

### 5. Final Greetings (5:12-14)

We find out in these last two verses that Peter wrote this through Silvanus, who acted as the scribe. Peter tells them that he has written to them in order to encourage them to stand firm in the faith and that she who is in Babylon, chosen with you, sends greetings, along with Mark (whom Peter calls his son). Since

"Babylon" was the nickname Christians gave Rome, we can be fairly certain that Peter is writing from Rome, and that he is telling his audience that the Church in Rome sends greetings. Concerning Mark, he is the same Mark who wrote the Gospel of Mark, who, according to Church tradition, wrote it in Rome with Peter. Peter ends by telling them to greet each other with a kiss of love and wishing peace to all who are in Christ.

# II PETER

## The Big Things to Know About II Peter and Jude

A. **Don't Have Anything to do with False Prophets and Teachers**: If we read II Peter as being authored by Peter, and thus dated to shortly before the outbreak of the Jewish War of AD 66-70, we can see that Peter feels an urgent need to implore Christians not to be deceived by any false prophets and teachers (the kind Jesus himself warned his disciples about in the Olivet Discourse).

B. **Living in the "Last Days"/The Day of The Lord's Coming**: As mentioned before, we should consider the possibility that the talk of "last days" and the "day of the Lord" was related to the upcoming Jewish War and the destruction of Jerusalem and the Temple.

## Literary Map: II Peter

|  | 1:1-2 The Greeting |  |
|---|---|---|

| 1:3-11 Make Your Kingdom Calling Firm | 1:12-21 Peter's Coming Death / Remembering the Transfiguration | 2:1-22 Warning of False Prophets and Teachers | 3:1-7 Warning of Scoffers in the Last Days | 3:8-17 The Day of the Lord is Coming |
|---|---|---|---|---|

## A Walkthrough of II Peter

### 1. The Greeting (1:1-2)

In the greeting, Peter identifies himself as an apostle of Jesus Christ and addresses his letter to those who have **received a faith,** just as equal as the faith of the apostles. This faith is in the **righteousness of God and Savior Jesus Christ**. He wishes his audience **grace** and an increase of **peace** in the **knowledge of God** and **Jesus our Lord**.

### 2. Make Your Kingdom Calling Firm (1:3-11)

Peter first tells his audience that Christ's divine power has given them everything for **life** and **godliness**, through the **knowledge** of the one who calls us (God) to be His own in **glory** and **virtue**. It is through that power and knowledge that God has given us the **precious and great promises**, so that through it they can become **fellow partners of the divine nature** and escape the **corruption in the world because of lust**. Given that, Peter then calls upon them to supply their faith with virtue and shows how that will lead to a sort of "domino effect" in the life of a Christian: Faith + Virtue→ Knowledge→ Self-Control→ Patient Endurance→ Godliness→ Brotherly Love→ Love.

Peter says these things will keep them from being lazy and unfruitful in the knowledge of the Lord Jesus Christ. Or, as Peter puts it in 1:9, if you don't have those things, then you're blind and near-sighted, and you've forgotten that your old sins have been already cleansed. With that, Peter exhorts his audience to make their **calling** and **election** firm by striving to develop all those things in that "domino effect." If you do that, you won't stumble in your faith and you'll gain entry into the **Kingdom of the Ages** of the **Lord and Savior Jesus Christ**.

### 3. Peter's Coming Death (1:12-21)

In this section, Peter recalls the event of Jesus' transfiguration (in Mark 9). Peter begins, though, by telling his audience that as long as he is still alive, he is going to keep reminding them of the apostolic teaching and tradition, even though he knows full well that they are firmly established in their faith. He speaks of his own body as a **tabernacle**, obviously an allusion to the Exodus, and says he knows that the time of his "departure" is near. Simply put, he knows he's going to die soon and go on to that "ultimate Exodus" to heaven.

He then tells them that he and the apostles have not followed **wise-sounding myths** when they shared the Gospel with them, specifically mentioning the **power** and **coming** (*Parousia*) of the Lord Jesus Christ. Simply put, they didn't make the Gospel up. In fact, they were actual eyewitnesses who got a glimpse of Jesus in his glory at the **transfiguration on the holy mountain**. Not only did they *see it*, but they also *heard the voice of God the Father*, when He said, "This is my Son, my Beloved One, in whom I am well-pleased!"

Given that historical encounter, Peter then says that the **prophetic word** they have preached is even **more certain**. The prophets of old had prophesied about a coming Messiah, but exactly how it would come about was still unclear. By contrast, the prophetic word of the apostles is, in fact, more certain, precisely because Peter, James, and John got a "sneak peek" and personally witnessed Jesus in his glory. That is why Peter tells his audience that they would be smart to pay attention to it and keep their "lights shining in a dark place" until the **day dawns** and the **morning star rises in their hearts** (presumably a reference to the Coming of Christ). Peter then says in 1:20-21 that every **prophetic message of Scripture** is not just a matter of someone's **interpretation** or random opinion. They are, in fact, inspired by the **Holy Spirit**. In some mysterious way, biblical prophecy comes from the Spirit of God, although it is spoken through men.

### 4. Warning of False Prophets and Teachers (2:1-22)

The next section can be summed up very easily: *Beware of false teachers! They're bad!* Peter begins by stating in 2:1-3 that false prophets and teachers have, indeed, cropped up within the Church and have caused divisions within the community by bringing in **destructive heresies**. Peter doesn't detail what these false prophets taught, but he does say that they were "denying the Master" who redeemed them. Therefore, we can assume they were denying the basic apostolic teachings about Jesus. In any case, Peter says that those people were bringing destruction upon themselves.

This brings us to 2:4-10, where Peter equates these false teachers with a number of figures from the Old Testament: (A) The **angels who sinned**, who were put in chains of gloom in Tartarus and kept until the judgment; (B) The **godless people in Noah's day**, who perished in the flood (though Noah and 7 others survived); and (C) The **godless people of Sodom and Gomorrah** who were reduced to ashes (though Lot was saved). Peter's point is obvious: God will deliver godly people from judgment, but the unrighteous will be punished on the Day of Judgment.

Although the stories of Noah and Sodom and Gomorrah are generally known, not too many people know about the **angels chained in Tartarus**. What Peter is alluding to here is the book of **I Enoch**, which interprets Genesis 6:1-4 (the story about how the **sons of Elohim** had sex with the **daughters of man**, who gave birth to the **Nephilim**) as being about how angels had sex with women and fathered a race of giants. For that sin, I Enoch says God bound those angels in chains of gloom and threw them into Tartarus (Hades, or Hell), where they are being kept until Judgment Day. All that said, Peter's simple point is that the false prophets among them were like those sinful angels, the pre-flood people, and the people of Sodom and Gomorrah. All of them are sinful and perverse, and all of them will suffer judgment and destruction.

With that, Peter then proceeds to really take it to the false prophets in the rest of the section. He says they are **bold and arrogant**, and that they **blaspheme the glorious ones**. It is unclear who Peter is referring to with the term "glorious ones." Some think it is a reference to possibly something like archangels, or else Christians themselves. In any case, Peter says that not even the angels utter such **blasphemous judgment** on the "glorious ones" before the Lord. He goes on to say that these false prophets are like **unreasoning animals** who just act on instinct and are just waiting to be caught and destroyed.

Peter then says in 2:13 that these false teachers are going to get "paid" for doing certain unrighteous things. By Peter's description, it sounds like basic debauchery and partying. He says they are **blots and blemishes** while they feast with the Christians, so perhaps these false teachers were corrupting the Eucharist meal in some way. In any case, Peter thoroughly condemns them in 2:14-19: (A) They have eyes for adultery and a desire for sin; (B) They are unsteady souls with greedy hearts, (C) They are accursed children, (D) They forsook the right way and were led astray on the path of Balaam—(Balaam was known for encouraging King Balak of Moab to send Moabite women into the Israelite camp to lead them stray into immoral pagan worship); (E) They are waterless springs, fog driven by a storm, and only have gloom and darkness waiting for them; (F) They promote haughty nonsense and perverted lusts of the flesh; and (G) They may promise freedom, but they are slaves to corruption.

What Peter says in 2:20-22 indicates that these false prophets and teachers were originally part of the Christian community and were indeed saved at one point. For Peter says that *if anyone escapes* the shameful deeds of the world through the knowledge of the Lord and Savior Jesus Christ, but *then gets mixed up again* in the world, then that person is actually worse off than before. It would have been better to have never known the way of righteousness, than to have found it, only to wander off from it and act like a dog that returns to its vomit, or a washed pig that goes right back to wallowing in the mud.

### 5. Warning of Scoffers in the Last Days (3:1-7)

As with a number of other New Testament letters, II Peter warns his audience of the **last days**. Peter says the reason for this second letter is to remind his audience of the *words of the holy prophets* and to tell them to remember the *commandment of the Lord and Savior that was spoken by the apostles*. It was important to hold fast to the apostolic tradition because these **scoffers** in the **last days** who were going about in their **own lusts** and questioning whether or not the ***Parousia* of Christ** would come. Evidently, they were saying that some "fathers" (meaning original Church leaders) had died, the *Parousia* hadn't happened yet, and that things were just going as they always have gone, ever since the beginning of creation. It is obvious that

Peter thinks they, at that time in the first century, were currently living in those last days, and these scoffers are the same false prophets in chapter 2.

Peter responds to their objection by drawing a distinction between the pre-flood world (of Genesis 1-8) and the current world. He first points out that the heavens existed long ago by means of the Word of God, and that the earth was formed out of water and through water. That original world, though, was destroyed in the waters of the flood. By contrast, Peter says the present heavens and earth were being kept by that same Word of God for the fire of the Day of Judgment, when the godless men will be destroyed.

### 6.  The Day of the Lord is Coming (3:8-17)

Peter then stresses that that future Day of Judgment—the Day of the Lord—indeed was coming. Although it might seem like a long wait, one day with the Lord is like a thousand years, and a thousand years is like a day for the Lord. God wasn't running late. He's delaying because He's being patient and giving a chance for more people to repent so they can avoid the coming destruction. But make no mistake, Peter says in 3:10, the *Day of the Lord is coming*, and when it comes, it is going to come **like a thief** and is going to catch a lot of people off guard. When it comes, **the heavens will pass away, the elements will be dissolved,** and **the world and its works will be exposed**. This description is very similar to what Jesus says in the Olivet Discourse (Mark 13, Matthew 24) when speaking about the destruction of the Temple in relation to the Coming of the Son of Man.

Given that, Peter gives a simple question and answer in 3:11-13, "How should you live your lives?" The answer? You should live your lives in holy conduct and godliness, and you should look for the **coming Day of God**, when the heavens will burn up and the elements will be dissolved. That shouldn't upset Christians, though, because the Christian hope isn't in this current heavens and earth. Rather, according to the promise, it is in the new heavens and earth, where righteousness is at home. Indeed, as they are longing for that new heavens and earth while still living here, they are to be **spotless**, **blameless**, and **at peace**. The seeming delay was simply God extending the opportunity of salvation for more people.

Peter then reminds them in 3:15b that the apostle Paul had written about the same things in his letters, according to the wisdom that God had given him. Peter acknowledges that some of what Paul says is hard to understand. Still, some ignorant and unstable people have twisted Paul's words, but it is to their own destruction. It is interesting to note that Peter says these people twist Paul's letters, *as they do with the rest of the Scriptures*. That implies that already Paul's letters were taken as being on the same level of Scripture.

In any case, Peter ends by saying that since they already are aware of that, they need to be on their guard against such unprincipled and lawless people, so they don't get carried away and lose their own firm footing. With that, Peter exhorts them to continue to grow in the **grace** and **knowledge** of our Lord and Savior Jesus Christ. And he ends with, "To him be the glory, both now and the **day of the age**! Amen!"

# JUDE

**Time of Writing:** At some point during the Mid-First Century.

**Background**

Jude was the brother of James the Just, and hence also one of Jesus' brothers. In this short letter, we find that Jude had intended to write to the churches in Palestine about their "shared salvation," but that he instead felt impelled to write a response to certain false teachers who were obviously causing trouble and confusing people. In his response, Jude makes a number of references and allusions to, not only various stories in the Old Testament, but also to certain apocryphal works like *I Enoch* and *The Assumption of Moses*. What this tells us is that these works, although not necessarily considered inspired scripture, were still known well enough that Jude was able to use them in his argument.

## The Big Things to Know About Jude

A. **Don't Have Anything to do with False Prophets and Teachers**: Just as with II Peter, if we date Jude to shortly before the outbreak of the Jewish War of AD 66-70, we can see the urgent need to implore Christians not to be deceived by any false prophets and teachers (the kind Jesus himself warned his disciples about in the Olivet Discourse).

B. **Living in the "Last Days"/The Day of the Lord is Coming**: Again, as with II Peter (and most other works in the New Testament), we should consider the possibility that the talk of "last days" and the "day of the Lord" was related to the upcoming Jewish War and the destruction of Jerusalem and the Temple.

### Literary Map: Jude
*Current False Teachers and the Judgments of the Past*

| 1:1-4 Greeting |
|---|

| 1:5-16 Current False Teachers Judgments of the Past | 1:17-23 Final Exhortations: Stand Firm in the Last Time |
|---|---|

| 1:24-25 Benediction |
|---|

## A Walkthrough of the Letter of Jude

### 1. The Greeting (1:1-4)

In his greeting, Jude identifies himself as a servant of Jesus Christ and the brother of James, who eventually became the leader in the church in Jerusalem at some point early on. The letter itself is simply addressed to those who are **called**, who are **loved of God**, and who are **kept for Jesus Christ**—obviously, to Christians.

We always have to remember, though, that at this point in the first century, that line between Jews and Christians was not yet completely clear. Therefore, we need to read Jude as addressing almost an **inner-Judaism conflict** between (A) Jesus' followers who were proclaiming Jesus was the Messiah and that through the Holy Spirit, salvation was now being extended to Gentiles, and (B) Jews who may have initially been attracted to the Jesus movement and were indeed part of it, but who insisted on Torah observance.

In any case, Jude says his purpose in writing the letter was (A) to encourage them to keeping **fighting for the faith** that was given to the saints, and (B) to warn them about **false teachers**. Jude refers to this faith as the one that was **given to the saints**, namely the **holy tradition** and the **rule of faith** that the resurrected Jesus passed on to the apostles. Thus, it was obviously different from the traditional Judaism of that time and is thus the reason for Jude's warning against **false teachers**.

The way Jude describes these false teachers implies that they were Judaizers who claimed (at least originally) to be followers of Jesus, but who then insisted on imposing Torah observance as a requirement for righteousness. That being said, what Jude says about these false teachers is easily applicable to any kind of false teachers, not just Judaizers. But Jude is clear, whoever these false teachers were, they originally seemed to be a part of the early Jesus movement. As was stated in II Peter, Jude says they had "snuck in," yet were **perverting God's grace into sensuality and denying that Jesus was the only Master and Lord.**

### 2. Current False Teachers and the Judgments of the Past (1:5-16)

Like II Peter, most of the letter is directed to equating these false teachers with really bad figures from the Old Testament and essentially saying, *"Those false teachers are going to suffer God's judgment, just like these Old Testament figures did!"* Jude first points out that even though God had saved the **Hebrews** out of Egypt during the Exodus, most of them were nevertheless destroyed in the desert because they were unfaithful to God. In the same way, Jude says that even though these false teachers may have been originally part of the early Jesus movement, their unfaithfulness to the apostles' teaching meant that they would eventually be destroyed as well.

Jude then equates these false teachers to **fallen angels** who didn't stay within their prescribed positions of authority and who were thus bound in "everlasting chains of gloom" until Judgment Day. Jude is alluding to an interpretation of Genesis 6:1-4 found in **I Enoch** that equated the "sons of God" with fallen angels who corrupted humanity by having sex with women and teaching mankind various forbidden arts and magic. For that sin, God bound them up in chains of gloom, where they had to wait until Judgment Day. Understanding this helps us make sense of what Jude then says when he further equates these false teachers with the **Sodom and Gomorrah** story in **Genesis 14**, where the people of Sodom and Gomorrah pursued unnatural and perverted sexual behavior and suffered God's judgment. This sexual immorality "after other flesh" relates both to the sin of Sodom and Gomorrah as well as to the sin of the fallen angels in **Genesis 6:1-4** who had unnatural sex with women.

Jude then comes full circle back to the false teachers, whom he called "so-called visionaries," when he says that not only do they **defile the flesh**, but they **reject lordly authorities and blaspheme the glorious ones**. Evidently, these false teachers were promoting some kind of sexual perversion (hence the references to the fallen angels and to Sodom and Gomorrah). In addition, their rejection of "lordly authorities" might mean they were almost kind of an anarchist movement—this would seem to fit with what Jude says in 1:4, that they denied Jesus was the only Master and Lord. Finally, their blaspheming the "glorious ones" seem to be a reference to how their perversions were giving Christians a bad name and ruining their reputation.

As it turns out, 1:8 is a bit of a transitional verse. Since it ends with the statement that these false teachers were blaspheming the glorious ones, that allows Jude to refer to another apocalyptic Jewish work of that time, **The Assumption of Moses** in 1:9. Jude refers to a scene when Michael the archangel is arguing with the devil over the body of Moses. Apparently, the devil's attempt to claim Moses' body was considered blasphemous, but in response, Michael didn't bring judgment upon the devil for it. Instead, he said, "May the Lord rebuke you!" Therefore, Jude is saying that it isn't the job of Christians to bring judgment on the false teachers for their blasphemy. Instead, the Christians should leave the judgment up to God.

After that, Jude says these false teachers blaspheme what they don't understand, namely, the Gospel. Their inability to understand it just shows that they are like **unreasoning animals** who are driven by their instincts. Jude says they walk down the way of **Cain**, that they, like **Balaam**, sold themselves out for money, and that they will eventually perish, just like those who perished in the **rebellion of Korah**, who led a rebellion against Moses. Jude then says that these false teachers are **blemishes in the Christian love-feasts**. This is further evidence that whoever these false teachers were, they were, at one point, considered part of the early Christian community.

In any case, Jude then calls them **waterless clouds** that are carried away by the winds, **late autumn trees** that don't produce fruit and are thus uprooted, **wild waves of the sea**, and **wandering stars** that are destined for the gloom of eternal darkness. By being **waterless clouds**, these false teachers don't bring any Spiritual refreshment to God's people, but instead are carried away by any "wind of doctrine." When Jude calls them **late autumn trees** that don't produce fruit and are thus uprooted, one cannot help but think of Jesus' cursing of the fig tree because it didn't produce fruit—and that action was prophetically signaling the destruction of the Temple. The false teachers are like the **waves of the sea** that "splash up" their shameful deeds—plus, the sea is often seen in light of the Sea of Chaos. Finally, by calling them **wandering stars** that are destined for the gloom of darkness, Jude once again equates these false teachers with the fallen angels in 1:6.

Jude ends this section with a few words about **Enoch**, the seventh in line in the genealogy of Adam (Genesis 5:21). Jude says that Enoch prophesied about the judgment that was coming upon godless sinners like the false teachers who were engaging in godless works. Jude calls them **grumblers and complainers** who walk about in their own lusts and who talk big and flatter people in order to get some kind of advantage for themselves. Thus, the basic point of this entire section is this: *These false teachers are bad news. Judgment will soon come for them.*

### 3. Final Exhortations (1:17-23)

In the next section, Jude again appeals to his audience to remember the words that the apostles of the Lord Jesus Christ handed down to them and reminds them that during the **last time** there would be mockers who walk about in their own lusts and ungodliness and who cause only divisions. Again, we need to consider that when the New Testament writers talked about the **last days**, that they were echoing Jesus' prophecy in the **Olivet Discourse** (Matthew 24, Mark 13, Luke 21) about the destruction of the Temple in relation to the Coming of the Son of Man.

Jude characterizes these mocking, godless, false teachers as **soulish ones** who don't have the Spirit. Many translations have "worldly people" who are devoid of the Spirit, but that tends to be too general. We need to see this description in light of the figure of Adam in Genesis. When God created Adam, he became "a living soul." Paul also contrasts Adam and Christ in I Corinthians 15 by saying that Adam was a man of the dust and was a soul, but that Christ was the man from heaven who became a life-giving Spirit.

Finally, in 1:20-23, Jude again exhorts his audience to stand firm, build themselves upon their holy faith, and to pray in the Holy Spirit (because they have the Holy Spirit, unlike those "soulish" false teachers). He tells them to stay in the love of God and to wait for the mercy of the Lord Jesus Christ that leads into the Life of the Age. He also encourages them to show mercy to those wavering in doubt and to try to "snatch them from the fire." The comment regarding "hating the garment stained by the flesh" isn't so much a hatred for the physical body—after all, the point of the resurrection is that God's creation is good and that He will redeem and transform our physical bodies. Rather, Jude is commenting on hating the kinds of perversions these false teachers were inflicting on their physical bodies.

### 4. The Benediction (1:24-25)

Jude ends the letter with a benediction, in which he emphasizes that God has the power to keep them from stumbling and to make sure that they will stand before His glory "without blemish" and with great gladness. He calls God "our Savior" and Jesus Christ "our Lord."

# THE WRITINGS OF JOHN

The writings of John deserve their own section. Obviously, in most (if not all) Bibles, the Gospel of John is placed between Luke and Acts, because it is, after all, a Gospel, and an argument can be made for putting it with the other three Gospels. Still, by placing it between Luke and Acts, not only does that break up the clear narrative continuity between Luke and Acts, but it also divorces the Gospel of John from the other writings of John, with which it shares several literary and narrative connections.

In any case, according to Church tradition, the Apostle John eventually travelled Ephesus in Asia Minor (modern day Turkey) and became a leading figure of the Christian communities there. That being said, there is speculation that the John of these writings was not **John the Apostle**, but rather a different man known as **John the Elder**. Although not one of Jesus' twelve apostles, it is believed John the Elder was a disciple of Jesus throughout his ministry who lived in Judea (as opposed to Galilee) and who was in some way connected to the Temple priesthood. That would explain why the bulk of material here in the Gospel of John takes place in and around Jerusalem, as opposed to how much of the material in the Synoptic Gospels takes place in Galilee. So, even though we cannot be certain whether the author of these writings is John the Apostle or John the Elder, most agree that this John had close ties with Jesus during his ministry years.

# I/II/III JOHN

**Time of Writing**: I John was probably a general treatise that was meant to be distributed among various churches. II John and III John, though, are personal letters. We don't know precisely when any of them were written, but the general consensus is that they were written sometime between AD 70-90.

**A Few Details**:

I John itself is somewhat hard to map out. Unlike Paul's letters, I John doesn't have clear and discernable sections that go from point to point. Instead, I John contains a handful of metaphors, key concepts, and phrases that John weaves together throughout the course of his letter. But as it stands, I've mapped out I John in three general sections that should help get a better grasp on the letter itself.

It is worth noting that after Jerusalem and the Temple were destroyed in AD 70, the "divorce" between Judaism and Christianity was pretty much complete, and the Christian communities in the latter part of the first century were faced with new challenges. Consequently, one of the main emphases in John's letters is the importance of holding fast to the teaching and tradition that had been taught from the very beginning and maintaining the fellowship of the Christian community. In addition, much of the language and imagery in John's letters are directly related to the language and imagery in John's Gospel.

## The Big Things to Know about I/II/III John

A. **The Same Word from the Beginning**: Fellowship and love with each other equals fellowship and love with Christ.

B. **Love God? Then Keep His Commandments**: As is similar to what is found in James, John here emphasizes what we would deem as the **Royal Commandment**—those two commandments Jesus said fulfilled the entire Torah: *Love God* and *love your neighbor as yourself*.

C. **Watch Out for Antichrists—Yes, That's Plural**: John warns Christians to be on the lookout those who deny Jesus is the Son of God and those who deny Jesus has come in the flesh. He is quite clear that those who deny either one of those two claims about Jesus is an "antichrist." Therefore, there will be many.

## Literary Map: I John

| The Message from the Beginning (1:1-2:17) | 1:1-4<br>The Word of Life | 1:5-10<br>God is Light | 2:1-6<br>Christ is Our Advocate | 2:7-17<br>A New Commandment |
|---|---|---|---|---|
| Last Hour Coming of Christ (2:18-4:6) | 2:18-27<br>Last Hour Antichrist | 2:28-3:10<br>Children of God | 3:11-24<br>Loving One Another | 4:1-6<br>Testing the Spirits |
| Love God Keep the Commandments (4:7-5:12) | 4:7-21<br>Love is of God | 5:1-12<br>Christ who Conquers the World | 5:13-21<br>Parting Comments | |

## Walkthrough of I John

### 1. The Message from the Beginning (1:1-2:17)

This first major section of I John can be divided up into four smaller subsections. The **first part (1:1-4)** begins in a similar way that the Gospel of John begins, introducing us to **The Word**, namely Jesus Christ. In Greek philosophy it was taught that there was a unifying rational principle by which the unknowable God created the universe. That rational principle was called the **Logos**, the Greek word that we translate as **The Word**. In Intertestamental Judaism, that concept of the **Logos** was used to describe the act of God's creating of the universe by speaking it into existence and was thus identified with **God's Wisdom**.

Therefore, when God spoke the universe into existence, He created the universe by His **Wisdom/Word**. Since the Jews believed that God chose them to be His special people, they further claimed that God's **Wisdom** was revealed in the **Torah of Moses**. Thus, the Torah was the thing that provide the Jews with their distinct identity and arena of fellowship with each other. What John does here is he takes all of that and reconfigures it all around Jesus Christ, whom he says is **God's Word come in the flesh**. Thus, since Jesus is the **Word of God**, it follows that God created the universe *through Christ*. And since that means Jesus is also **God's Wisdom**, it means that the true fellowship of God's people is to be found in him, and not in the Torah.

Given all that, John's comments about how he is going to present what has been there *from the beginning* are very interesting. On one hand, he's clearly alluding to the **creation account in Genesis**. At the same time, though, John *is really* talking about the **Gospel of Jesus**, for he talks about having actually borne witness to the **Word of Life**, namely Jesus. He further elaborates on this in 1:2, when he talks about how the **Life of the Ages** was with the Father, had now been made clear to the followers of Christ, and *that* is the Gospel that they are now proclaiming. *Simply put, the Gospel is about Jesus Christ, and Jesus Christ is the beginning of the New Creation.*

After that, John states that they are proclaiming the Gospel so that people can have **fellowship** with them, and that fellowship is the same fellowship they have with God the Father and His Son Jesus Christ. Hence, it is not the Torah that is the basis of identity and fellowship of God's people, but rather Jesus, the **Living Word**. Therefore, not only do Christians have fellowship with one another in Christ, but since they are in Christ, they have fellowship with God the Father as well.

In the **second part (1:5-10)**, John elaborates on just what the message of the Gospel is by means of using the same metaphors of light and darkness that he uses in the prologue to his Gospel: *God is light, and in Him there is no darkness*. Ultimately, John's point is this: (A) Walking in the light means forgiveness, truth, and fellowship with God and His people, whereas (B) Walking in the darkness means lying, sin, and no fellowship with God. To drive this home, he ties the metaphors of light and darkness in with the concepts of **fellowship, truth/lying,** and **sin/forgiveness**, all within five separate hypothetical "if/then" type of sentences:

*If we say we have fellowship with Him,* **yet** *walk in darkness,* **then** *we are liars (1:6)*

*If we walk in the light,* **then** *we have fellowship with each other* **and** *the blood of Jesus cleanses us of sin (1:7)*

*If we say we don't have sin,* **then** *we're fooling ourselves and the truth isn't in us (1:8)*

*If we confess our sins,* **then** *He is faithful and righteous and will forgive our sins and cleanse our unrighteousness (1:9)*

*If we say we haven't sinned,* **then** *we make Him out to be a liar, and* **His Word isn't in us** *(1:10)*

In the **third part (2:1-6)**, John develops the idea of forgiveness of sin in Christ from 1:9 and links it up to another major theme in the letter: **The knowledge of God and the Love of God is demonstrated in the keeping of His commandments**. He begins by saying he hopes his audience doesn't sin, but even if they do, they can rest assured that Jesus Christ, the **Righteous One**, is our **Advocate** before the Father, and that he has the ability to forgive, not just their sins, but the sins of the entire world. Then in 2:3, John introduces the theme of keeping the commandments by saying that our **knowledge of Christ** is seen in our keeping of his commandments. John then uses two more "if/then" sentences to make his point in 2:4-5:

*If one says he know him,* **but** *don't keep his commandments,* **then** *that person is a liar, and the truth isn't in him.*

*But* **if** *one keeps Christ's word (commandment),* **then** *the love of God is made perfect in him.*

John then sums it all up in 2:6: You know you're in Christ and you **remain** in Christ if you walk as he walked. In any case, two things need to be addressed. First, when John speaks of "keeping Christ's commandments," he is referring to what Jesus said in **Matthew 22:34-40**. When asked what the greatest commandment was, Jesus said that the entire Torah was summed up in the two commandments to **love God** and **love your neighbor as yourself**. Throughout the New Testament, those two things are considered Christ's commandments, or as said in James, the "royal Torah."

Second, when John speaks of being "made perfect," the Greek word there is *teleioo*, and it conveys more the idea of reaching full maturity than some concept of a static stat of "perfection." The goal of the Christian life is to be like Christ and to grow into the fullness of Christ, particularly in relationship with the Father—to be fully remade into God's image. Therefore, John's point is that if you love God and love your neighbor, you're keeping Christ's commandment and you are being remade to that fully mature image of God.

In the **fourth part (2:7-17)**, John emphasizes a **new commandment**, that really isn't a new commandment at all. It is the old one that was there *from the* *beginning*, and that **old commandment** is the **Word** that they have heard from the apostles, namely the Gospel—and that commandment/Word is true. Simply put, John is saying that what God wanted for mankind ever since the beginning was for people to love Him and love one another—and the ability to do just that is to be found in Jesus Christ. With that, John teases out the light/darkness metaphors even more. Since God is **light**, and since Christ the Word is **true**, then that means that **the true light is already shining**, and that **the darkness is passing away** (2:8b). Therefore:

*If one says, "I'm in the light,"* **but** *hates his brother,* **then** *that person still is in the darkness (2:9)*

*If one loves his brother,* **then** *that person* **remains** *in the light (2:10)*

**But** *the one who hates his brother is/walks in the darkness, and doesn't* **know** *where to go; he's blind (2:11)*

Then in 2:12-14, John writes what seems to be some kind of poem, or some kind of poetically structured stanza, addressed to (A) little children, (B) fathers, and (C) young men, in two successive triplets. They emphasize the same points John has made up to this point: **forgiveness of sins, knowledge of God/Christ**, that which was **from the beginning**, and **the Word of God** that **remains** in them. In addition, John tells them that they have **conquered the evil one**. This is something new that he introduces here that he will elaborate on in the next section.

John ends this section in 2:15-17 by warning his audience not to love the world or anything in the world. If they do, then that means the love of the Father isn't in them. To be clear, he's not talking about hating God's material creation, but rather hating the **current old age world order**. This is what he means when he mentions the lust of the flesh, the lust of the eyes, and the pride of life. These things are characteristic of a world that is subject to corruption. That is why John says it is passing away. By contrast, the one who does the will of God and keeps Christ's commandments will overcome death, just like Christ, and will live on into the **Life of the Ages**. Simply put, it is through the love of Christ that we, the image-bearers of God become fully mature in God's likeness.

# I John 1:1-2:17
## The Message from the Beginning

The Word of Life: From the Beginning
- A **New** Commandment: Really the <u>old</u> one from the Beginning
  - Love God = Love one Another, So...

```
┌─────────────┐     ┌─────────────┐     ┌─────────────┐
│ Fellowship  │     │ Fellowship  │     │ Fellowship  │
│with each other│ →  │with Christ  │  →  │    with     │
│      =      │     │(who commanded│    │ the Father  │
│  Love one   │     │  us to love │     │             │
│   Another   │     │ one another)│     │             │
└─────────────┘     └─────────────┘     └─────────────┘
```

Walking in ↔ Christ the word ↔ God is Light
the Light      is              No Darkness in him
               The Light of the world

| The Love of God is made fully Mature in the one who • Keeps Christ's Word • Loves his brother | Christ the Advocate's blood cleanses us from Sin |

**2. The Last Hour and Coming of Christ (2:18-4:6)**

This second major section of I John can also be divided up into four smaller subsections. In the **first part (2:18-27)**, John talks about how it is the **last hour** and about how the **antichrist** is coming. We have to remember that when John was writing this letter in the latter part of the first century, he was writing to real people in a real historical situation. Therefore, this talk about the **last hour** and **antichrist** had to have meant something to them. Therefore, we need to realize that when John tells his audience at that time, "It is the last hour," he's saying it was already at hand.

In addition, when he talks about the coming antichrist, that he says, in fact **many antichrists** exist. These antichrists, John says, "came out from us" but never were really "of us." This indicates that John is saying these antichrists were in some way, originally part of the early Christian movement. Despite the deception from those antichrist people, John reassures his audience that they, in fact, have the **anointing of the Holy One** and **know the truth** and haven't been suckered by the lies that the antichrists were peddling.

So, what lie were these antichrists peddling? John answers that question by saying anyone who denies that Jesus is the Christ and is the Son of God the Father is a lying antichrist. Since the Greek word **Christos** relates to the Hebrew word for **Messiah**, it seems that John might very well be speaking of Jews who have rejected Jesus as the Messiah and as God's Son. The very linkage of Jesus and God in terms of a Father-Son relationship shows that from very early on in the Christian movement that the followers of Jesus proclaimed that he was more than just a man and that he shared a unique relationship with God.

John goes on to solidify the Father-Son connection between Jesus and the God of Israel by hearkening back to the creation language from earlier in his letter. If you remain in the word of the Gospel that you've heard from the beginning and if you confess the Son, then you will remain in the Son and in the Father, and you will enjoy the Life of the Ages He had planned from the beginning. John then summarizes everything in 2:26-27: (A) You have the anointing of Christ, (B) It remains in you and continues to teach you, so you don't need anyone else to teach you anything different, and (C) Since it is true and not a lie (like what the antichrists are trying to teach), just remain in Christ by keeping to the teaching.

In the **second part (2:28-3:10)**, John really teases out the idea that Christians are children of God. He begins by addressing them again as little children and tells them that if they remain in Christ, they will have boldness and won't be put to shame **at his coming when he is revealed**. As has been discussed throughout this reader's guide, we need to seriously consider, given a pre-AD 70 context, that when we find talk of **Christ's coming** (or the **Day of Christ**) in the New Testament, it was connected in some way to the destruction of Jerusalem and the Temple in AD 70.

John then teases out the children of God metaphor even more by saying that since Christ is righteous, everyone who does righteousness is **born of him**. With that, John launches into an elaboration in 3:1-10 regarding what it means to be children of God. In 3:1, he emphasizes the love that God the Father has given so that we can be called **children of God** and says that the reason why the world doesn't know us is because it doesn't know **God the Father**. Still, even though we are already children of God, what *we will be* hasn't been revealed yet, and when it is, we will be in the **likeness of God** and will **see Him as He is** (3:2). In the meantime, those who have put their hope in God are currently in the process of purifying themselves, and thus are becoming more like God even now (3:3).

All this relates back to **Genesis 1:26-27**, when God creates man **in His image** to be **according to His likeness**. Simply put, what this means is that God's plan all along was to come in two phases. The first phase was to create humanity in His image, as a sculptor would fashion a statue. This is what the creation of Adam depicts. He is in God's image, but nevertheless is still susceptible to sin, corruption, and death. He isn't the finished product. The second phase was to bring that statue to life so that that statue truly becomes like the sculptor. This is what the Gospel of Christ reveals. Through the death and resurrection of Christ and the outpouring of the Holy Spirit, God's image-bearers can become truly like God. As **Athanasius of Alexandria** said back in the fourth century, *"God became man, so that man could become like God."*

In 3:4-6, John focuses on the topic of sin in relation to both **Christ** and the **Torah** (the Law). He first says that the one who sins is doing something against the Torah, because sin is basically anti-Torah (lawless) behavior. But Christ, who was sinless, was revealed so that he could take away sins. So, now that Christ has accomplished this, the Torah becomes irrelevant. If the Torah points out sin, and if your sin is taken away, then the Torah has nothing else to do. That is why John says that those who remain in Christ don't sin, because Christ has taken away their sin and they are no longer under the jurisdiction of the Torah. By contrast, John says that those who do sin, don't see because they don't know Christ.

John takes things up a notch in 3:7-10 when he says that those who are doing righteousness **are righteous because Christ is righteous**. Simply put, there is a cause-and-effect going on here: *If you know Christ, then you have him, and you do righteousness, because that's what Christ does. By contrast, if you don't have Christ, then you sin because you don't know Christ.* In fact, as John says, you are *from the devil!* Why? Because that's what the devil does—he sins, and he's been doing it from the beginning. That is why the Son of God was revealed—to abolish the sinful works of the devil.

John ends by spelling it out in even plainer language: *If you're born of God, then you don't sin because* **God's seed** *remains in you, so you can't sin.* Although John doesn't fully spell it out, he says the same idea holds true if you're a child of the devil. If we look back at God's cursing of the serpent in **Genesis 3:15**, where He says there would be enmity between the seed of the serpent and the seed of the woman, we can tease out what John implies here by saying this: **If you're a child of the devil, then you do sin, because you're of the serpent's seed.** Ultimately, if you don't do righteousness and don't love your brother, then you're not from God.

In the **third part (3:11-24)**, John focuses on the importance of loving one another by alluding to the **creation account in Genesis** and saying that the message he is teaching is the same message they have heard from the beginning: *They are to love one another.* To highlight the importance of loving one another, John alludes to the story of Cain and Abel in **Genesis 4**: Cain's works were evil because he was from the **evil one** (from the serpent's seed) whereas Abel's works were righteous (because he was from God's seed). Therefore, they are to be like Abel, not Cain. John then relates Cain and Abel to their present situation, where Cain's hatred of Abel is like the world's hatred of the Christians. Of course, John's parallel only goes so far, because Abel was killed and is dead, whereas Christians, by virtue of following Christ, have **crossed over out of death and into life**. The evidence of this is that Christians love their brothers and sisters (unlike Cain).

In 3:14b-15, John then pushes the Cain analogy a bit more by saying that if you don't love your brother, if you actually hate your brother, then you are effectively a murderer, like Cain. You remain in death and the Life of the Ages doesn't remain in you. By contrast, Christians have known the love precisely because Christ has laid down his soul for us. Since that act of self-sacrifice has opened the door to knowing God's love, Christians are then called to imitate Christ and lay down their own souls so that others may come to a knowledge of God's love. Thus, the love of God is evidenced in the way Christians love their neighbor. After all, as John asks, *"How can the love of God remain in anyone who sees his brother in need, but doesn't help him?"*

In 3:18-24, sums up his point in this third part by urging his "little children" to show their love, not just in words, but in actual actions—in their works and the truth of what they say. Not that they should worry about whether or not they are doing enough, though. John reassures them that whenever their heart tries to condemn them, they need to remember that God is greater than those doubts and He already knows everything. If you remember that, then your heart won't condemn you, and you can have that boldness before God. As long as you are striving to keep His commandments, He is going to be pleased with you. Ultimately, it all comes down to two things: (1) Put one's faith in God's Son, Jesus Christ, and be faithful to him, and (2) Love one another. It all comes down to what Christ said when the scribe asked him what the greatest commandment was: *Love God and love your neighbor as yourself.* If you do that, then you will remain in Christ and Christ will remain in you through the indwelling of the Holy Spirit.

The **final part (4:1-6)** jumps off from the last thing John said in 3:24 about the indwelling of the Holy Spirit. Since Christians have the Holy Spirit, they shouldn't immediately *believe every spirit*, but are to *test the spirits* to see whether or not they are truly from God, because many false prophets have gone out into the world. Simply put, John is warning against false teachers who claim to be prophets who have the Spirit. His basic test to see if a teacher truly has the Spirit or not is simple: *Those who confess that Jesus Christ was a real human being are speaking with the Spirit of God, whereas those who don't confess that are not of God.* In fact, John says they are denying Christ and are therefore speaking with **a spirit of the antichrist**. John adds that this antichrist, the one they "have heard is coming," is, in fact, already in the world. Or in other words, he is saying there is ultimately **one spirit of the antichrist**, but that one spirit is manifested in **many false teachers** who, by virtue of denying Christ in the flesh, show themselves to be antichrists themselves.

In any case, John then contrasts his Christian audience with those antichrist false prophets. Christians are not of the antichrist. They are, in fact, God's children who have conquered "the one who is in the world" (the antichrist). Those false prophets have that spirit of the antichrist and that is why the world listens to them—they are spouting the nonsense coming from "the one who is in the world." Christians, though, are of God and listen to the teaching of the apostles, as opposed to those of the antichrist, who obviously don't. That is the fundamental difference between the Spirit of truth and the spirit of error. We can put it this way:

*The apostles' teaching* → *Christ in the flesh* → *The Spirit of truth* → *Of God, In Christ*

*False prophets' teaching* → *Deny Christ in the flesh* → *The spirit of error* → *antichrist*

### 3. Love God and Keep His Commandments (4:7-5:12)

The third major section of I John can be divided up into two smaller subsections. The **first part (4:7-21)** is pretty much an elaboration on John 3:16. John begins by exhorting his audience to love one another because love comes from God. He says if you love one another, then that means you are **born of God** and you **know God**. By contrast, if you don't love others then you don't know God. John then holds up Christ as the revelation of the love of God, and in doing so he echoes John 3:16—*God sent His Only-Begotten Son into the world as an atoning sacrifice for our sins so that we could live through him*. If you want to know what the love of God looks like, look at Christ. Therefore, Christians are to love one another like God loves us, and that means being willing to sacrifice oneself for the salvation of others. Even though no one has actually seen God, John says that God remains in us if we love one another, and His love is **made mature** in us when we do.

John describes Jesus here in two ways. First, he says Jesus is God's **Only-Begotten Son**. This is an allusion to Psalm 2, a royal psalm that celebrates the king of Israel as God's son—therefore, John is describing Jesus as the true king of Israel, the Messiah. Second, he says that Jesus' death was an **atoning sacrifice for sins**. This is the language of the Temple sacrificial system that was set up to manage God's covenantal relationship with His people. When Jews offered sacrifices at the Temple in Jerusalem, they weren't doing it because they were afraid God would hate them and squash them if they didn't pay him off. They were doing it because they were in a covenantal relationship with God. After the priest performed the sacrifice and took a portion on behalf of YHWH, he would then give a portion back to the one who brought the sacrifice, and that person (and those with him) would then have a meal on the Temple grounds that celebrated YHWH's forgiveness of their sins and the reconciliation of their relationship with Him. That is the idea John is getting at when he calls Jesus the "atoning sacrifice for our sins." Using the Temple metaphor to explain the significance of the atonement, John is emphasizing God's love for us and His providing a way for us to be reconciled to Him.

The rest of 4:13-21 repeats many of John's earlier points. It helps to just see them in bullet-point fashion:

- *4:13: We **know** we **remain** in Him because He has given His **Spirit**.*
- *4:14: John (and the apostles) **bear witness** that the Father has sent the Son as the **Savior** of the world.*
- *4:15: If you **confess** that Jesus is the Son of God, then God **remains** in you, and you **remain** in God.*
- *4:16: We **have known** and **have put our faith** in the **love of God**.*
- *4:17: Love is **made mature** in us, so we can have **boldness** on the **Day of Judgment**.*
- *4:18: There's no fear in love; **mature love** casts out fear, because fear has to do with punishment. If you fear, then you haven't been **made mature in love** yet.*

- ***4:19:*** *We love because God* **first loved us.**
- ***4:20:*** *If you say, "I love God," but then hate your brother, then you're a liar. If you can't love your brother, then you can't love God.*
- ***4:21:*** *Keep the commandment to* **love God** *and to* **love your brother.**

In the **second part (5:1-12)**, 5:1-5 acts as a transition between 4:7-21 and 5:6-12. If the main focus on 4:7-21 is that of **love** and the main focus in 5:6-12 is **Christ**, then 5:1-5 really does bring those two things together. Truth be told, what John says in 5:1-5 is a repeat of the same things he has said throughout the letter:

- ***5:1a:*** *If you have faith that Jesus is the Christ, then you are* **born of God.**
- ***5:1b:*** *If you love the* **one who gives birth** *(God), you'll love the* **one who is born** *(those in Christ).*
- ***5:2:*** *We* **know** *we* **love God's children** *when we* **love God** *by* **doing His commandments.**
- ***5:3:*** **Loving God** *means* **keeping His commandments.**
- ***5:4:*** **Keeping his commandments** *are not hard because if you're* **born of God**, *then you've* **conquered the world,** *and your* **faith is the victory** *that conquers the world.*
- ***5:5:*** *Who conquers the world? The one who has* **faith** *that* **Jesus is the Son of God.**

With all that, John concludes the main body of his letter in 5:6-12 by elaborating on Jesus Christ. He first says that Jesus Christ **came through water and blood**, and that the **Spirit bears witness** to this, because the Spirit is the truth. He then says that the water (of baptism), the blood (of Christ on the cross), and the Spirit all bear witness and are in agreement. Since we accept the **testimony of men**, then we should obviously accept the **testimony of God**, because it is greater. John then says that anyone who has faith in the Son of God has God's testimony **within himself**, meaning he has God's indwelling Spirit who bears witness. The one who doesn't have faith in God, though, has made God out to be a liar, precisely because that person has rejected the testimony of God regarding His Son, Jesus Christ. Finally, in 5:11-12, John spells out just what that testimony is: **God gave the Life of the Ages to us, and that Life is found in the Son**. Therefore, if you have the Son, then you have that Life, and if you don't have the Son, then you don't have that Life.

### 4. Parting Comments (5:13-21)

In his parting comments, John tells his audience that the reason he wrote the letter was so that they could **have faith in the name of the Son of God** and so that they could **know that they have the Life of the Ages**. Simply put, it was to reassure and encourage those first century Christians as they continued in the faith.

With that encouragement, John reminds them they can be bold before God to ask things according to His will. So, for example, if a Christian commits a **sin that doesn't lead to death**, then other Christians can ask God to forgive that person and God will **give life** to that Christian. Still, John then says there is, in fact, a **sin that leads to death**, and that Christians should not ask God concerning those types of sins. Given the context of what he has said about the false teachers, presumably it has to do with denying Christ in the flesh. With that, John ends by once again repeating the main points of his letter:

- *5:18: If you're* **born of God**, *then you* **don't sin;** *God protects you so the* **evil one can't touch you.**
- *5:19: Christians are* **of God**, *whereas the world* **lies in the evil one.**
- *5:20: The* **Son of God has come** *and has given us* **a mind of understanding** *to know the True One, and we are in the True One*—**God's Son, Jesus Christ.** *Not only that, but Jesus Christ, the Son of God,* **is the true God** *and the* **Life of the Ages.**

John ends with a final warning to **be on your guard from idols**.

## Literary Map: II John

| 1:1-3 | 1:4-6 | 1:7-11 | 1:12-13 |
|---|---|---|---|
| The Greeting | A New Commandment: Love One Another | A Warning Against Anti-Christs | Final Greetings |

## A Walkthrough of II John

II John is a mere thirteen verses, and although it obviously addressed to a different audience than I John, the topic and points of emphases are the same. John addresses the letter in **1:1-3** to **the chosen lady and her children**. John clearly has a close relationship with this church, for he says he loves them in truth. He further repeats something he said in I John: Because of their love for each other, the truth remains in them and will continue to be with them **into the Age**. In any case he greets this church in the grace, mercy, and peace from both God the Father and Jesus Christ the Son...of course, in truth and love.

Then in **1:4-6**, and just like he said in I John, John talks about the **commandment to love one another**. After telling them that he is overjoyed to know that this church is walking in the truth (staying faithful to the apostolic teaching), he encourages them all to continue to walk in the **commandment from the Father** that has been there **since the beginning**—and that commandment is **to love one another**.

In **1:7-11**, just like he said in I John, John warns the church about **antichrists** who are out to deceive people. That "antichrist deception" boils down to denying that Jesus Christ is coming in the flesh. He warns them so that they don't destroy everything they've worked for and can receive their full reward (at the **Coming of Christ**). John also emphasizes the importance of **remaining in the teaching of the apostles**. That is the essential litmus test: *If you stay true to the apostles' teaching, then you have the Father and the Son; if you don't, then you have neither and you should have no fellowship with the Church*. In fact, John explicitly says that if anyone comes to them who doesn't hold to the teaching of the apostles, then they should refuse any kind of fellowship with him.

John ends with some final greetings in **1:12-13**. In his final words, John tells the church that although he has a lot more to write to them, he'd much rather tell them face to face, and in fact, he is planning to come and visit them soon. He also tells this church that the **children of your chosen sister** (presumably another church) greet them.

### Literary Map: III John

| 1:1 | 1:2-8 | 1:9-10 | 1:11-12 | 1:13-15 |
|---|---|---|---|---|
| The Greeting | Well Wishes to Gaius | A Word About Diotrephes | Testimony Concerning Demetrius | Final Exhortation to Gaius |

### A Walkthrough of III John

III John, although just about as short as II John, is not addressed to a church, but rather to a specific person. In his greeting in **1:1**, John identifies himself as **the elder** and he addresses his letter to a man named **Gaius**, whom he calls his beloved brother.

He then proceeds in **1:2-8** to express his well wishes to Gaius. John says he prays that Gaius is in good health and how overjoyed he was to learn from some of the brothers and sisters (Christians) that Gaius was staying true to the faith (walking in the truth). John commends Gaius for working for the brothers and sisters even though they were **foreigners**. Perhaps these are the same brothers and sisters from 1:3-4 who had come to John.

In any case, they certainly gave a glowing report about Gaius to John, so he congratulates Gaius for doing such a good job with these foreigner brothers and sisters by saying that he did well in sending them off **in a manner worthy of God**. When they "went out" they went out "on behalf of the Name" and didn't take anything from the **Gentiles** (pagans). John then says that "we" should support people like this so "we" can become **co-workers in the truth**.

In **1:9-10**, John says a few things about a man named **Diotrephes**. Apparently, this man was trying to be a leader in the church but refused to recognized John as a proper apostolic authority. Not only that, but he was refusing to recognize the **brothers and sisters** (perhaps the same ones from 1:3-4) and was throwing anyone who was accepting and recognizing of these brothers and sisters out of the church. Needless to say, John says that when he visits, that he will "remember the works" Diotrephes was doing and really deal with him.

In **1:11-12**, after encouraging Gaius to imitate what is good and to avoid doing what is bad (because the one who does good is from God, but the one who does bad has never seen God), John mentions a man named **Demetrius**. He says that everyone has borne witness for this man, including himself, and that Gaius should rest assured that their testimony about Demetrius is true. After that, in **1:13-15**, John tells Gaius he has more to tell him, but he'd rather do it face to face, rather than in a letter. He concludes by passing along the greetings from the friends with John.

# THE GOSPEL OF JOHN

**Time of Writing**: As with the other writings of John, we really don't know for certain when it was written. That being said, the general consensus is that it was written after the destruction of the Temple in AD 70 yet before the turn of the century. All in all, probably sometime between AD 80-100.

**Authorship/Style**: Either John the Apostle or John the Elder. A number of early Church Fathers characterized John's Gospel as a "Spiritual Gospel," due to the fact that it was clearly different in style and content than the other Gospels. Simply put, there is a lot more highly symbolic language and imagery in John's Gospel.

**Distinctive Features:** John's Gospel is structured in a very different way than that of Matthew, Mark, and Luke. For example, if all we had were Matthew, Mark, and Luke, we could easily be under the impression that Jesus' ministry lasted no more than a year, for those Gospels tell of only the one Passover when Jesus was crucified. John, on the other hand, tells of Jesus' time at three different Passovers, and that is why most people believe Jesus' ministry was closer to three years.

In terms of actual literary composition, John's Gospel has a lot of "sevens" in it. First, in the very first section of 1:19-2:12 is laid out in the course of seven days, echoing the **creation week in Genesis 1** and thus symbolically presenting the beginning of Jesus' ministry as the beginning of God's new creation.

Second, John also weaves into his narrative **seven different I AM statements**. When God reveals himself to Moses at the burning bush in **Exodus 3**, He says His name is **YHWH**, translated to mean, "I Am that I am." In the Septuagint, the Greek translation of the Hebrew Bible, that name was translated as *Ego eimi*, literally "I am." At seven different times in John, Jesus identifies himself using *Ego eimi* and a certain metaphor: (1) I AM the **bread of life** (6:35, 41, 51); (2) I AM the **light of the world** (8:12); (3) I AM the **door of the sheep** (10:7, 9); (4) I AM the **good shepherd** (10:11, 14); (5) I AM the **resurrection and the life** (11:25); (6) I AM **the way, the truth, and the life** (14:6); and (7) I AM the **true vine** (15:1, 5). In addition, in the middle of a dispute with some Jews in Jerusalem, there is the shocking statement in which Jesus says, "**Before Abraham was, I AM** (8:58), thus making a direct claim of his equality with God.

Third, John also has in his narrative **seven distinct signs** during Jesus' ministry. Like the I AM metaphors, these signs also speak to his true identity. They are the following: (1) **Turning water into wine at the wedding at Cana** (2:1-12); (2) **Healing the royal official's son** (4:46-54); (3) **Healing the paralyzed man at the pool of Bethesda in Jerusalem** (5:1-15); (4) **Feeding the 5,000** (6:5-14); (5) **Walking on the water on the Sea of Galilee** (6:16-21); (6) **Healing the man born blind** (9:1-7); and (7) **Raising Lazarus from the dead** (11:1-45).

Finally, although not limited to seven instances, John's Gospel repeatedly makes use of the concept of **the coming hour of Jesus**. The "hour" is of Jesus' glorification, which ironically is that of his crucifixion. Throughout John's Gospel, the recurring reference to the "coming hour" serves as a way of building up the anticipation for the climactic even of the crucifixion.

| Wedding at Cana (2:4) | Jesus to Mary: *"My hour has not yet come."* |
| --- | --- |
| Samaritan Woman (4:21-23) | Jesus to Samaritan Woman: *"The hour is coming when the true worshippers will worship the Father in Spirit and truth."* |
| Crowds in the Temple (5:25-28) | Jesus to the Crowds: *"The hour is coming, and is here now, when the death will hear the voice of the Son of God and live."* |
| Feast of Tabernacles (7:30) | Temple Authorities try to arrest Jesus, but *"his hour had not yet come."* |
| Feast of Tabernacles (8:20) | Temple Authorities try to arrest Jesus, but *"his hour had not yet come."* |
| Requested Meeting with Some Greeks (12:23-27) | Jesus: *"The time is coming for the Son of Man to be glorified. Can I say, 'Save me from this hour?' I came to this hour for this."* |
| The Last Supper (13:1) | *"Jesus knew that the hour had come for him to go away from this world to the Father."* |
| The Last Supper (16:2-4) | Jesus to the Disciples: *"The hour is coming when you are going to be persecuted."* |
| Last Supper (16:21) | Jesus equates his coming crucifixion and resurrection with a woman in labor who gives birth. |
| The Last Supper (16:25) | Jesus to the Disciples: *"The hour is coming when I speak plainly to you."* |
| The Last Supper (16:32) | Jesus to the Disciples: *"The hour is coming, and is already here, when you will be scattered."* |

| The Last Supper (17:1) | Jesus to the Father: *"Father, the hour has come; glorify your Son so that the Son may glorify you."* |

**The Big Things to Know in the Gospel of John**
A. **The Logos is God's Wisdom is Jesus in the Flesh is the Light of the World**: Using the Greek philosophical concept of the *Logos* and the Old Testament concept of *God's Wisdom*, John repeatedly emphasizes that Jesus is the literal, physical manifestation and embodiment of God's Wisdom.
B. **Jesus is Greater than Moses and is the Fulfillment of the Torah**: John also hammers home throughout his Gospel that not only is Jesus greater than Moses, but that everything in the Torah, and Judaism as a whole, had pointed to Jesus all along, and therefore the coming of Jesus signaled the fulfillment of the Torah and the Old Testament Jewish hopes.
C. **Jesus the Son is in Equal Unity with God the Father**: As the I AM statements show via metaphor, John proclaims that Jesus, in some albeit mysterious way, shares equality with God the Father.
D. **Want to be Like Christ? Then be a Servant**: This is emphasized throughout the New Testament as well: To be a follower of Christ is to be like Christ, and Christ made himself a servant to all.
E. **The Coming and Empowerment by the Holy Spirit to Guide Us**: John also emphasizes that John told his disciples that after he was to leave, that the Holy Spirit would come and guide them in all truth.

## The Gospel of John: Story Chart

|  | | | | | |
|---|---|---|---|---|---|
| **The Prologue** (1:1-18) | **1:1-18** The Word Became Flesh | | | | |
| **"First Week"** (1:19-2:12) | 1:19-28 Testimony of John the Baptist *(Day 1)* | 1:29-34 John: Jesus is the Lamb of God *(Day 2)* | 1:35-42 Jesus Calls His First Disciples *(Day 3)* | 1:43-51 Jesus Calls Philip and Nathanael *(Day 4)* | 2:1-12 The Wedding at Cana *(Day 7)* |
| **Passover to Galilee** (2:13-4:54) | 2:13-25 Jesus Trashes the Temple | 3:1-21 Jesus and Nicodemus | 3:22-36 John the Baptist Exalts Jesus | 4:1-45 Jesus and the Samaritan Woman | 4:46-54 Jesus Heals Official's Son in Cana |
| **Feast of Jews to Galilee** (5:1-6:71) | 5:1-18 Jesus Heals Invalid at Pool of Bethesda | | 5:19-47 Authority of the Son | | 6:1-15 Jesus Feeds 5,000 |
| | 6:16-21 Jesus Walks on Water *Capernaum* | | 6:22-59 I Am the Bread of Life *Capernaum* | | 6:60-71 Jesus' Words: Eternal Life *Capernaum* |
| **Feast of Tabernacles** (7:1-10:21) | 7:1-36 Jesus at the Feast of Tabernacles | | 7:37-53 Last Day of the Feast Rivers of Living Water | | 8:1-11 Woman Caught in Adultery *Temple* |
| | 8:12-59 *I Am* the Light of the World Truth Will Set You Free Who is Your Father? | | 9:1-41 Jesus Heals a Man Born Blind Pool of Siloam | | 10:1-21 *I Am* the Gate *I Am* the Good Shepherd |

# Gospel of John | 465

|  | | | |
|---|---|---|---|
| **Feast of Dedication to Passover Conflict** (10:22-12:50) | 10:22-42 I and the Father are One | 11:1-57 Raising Lazarus *I Am* the Resurrection | 12:1-11 Jesus Anointed Plot to Kill Lazarus |
| | 12:12-19 Untriumphal Entry | 12:20-36 Greeks Seek Jesus | 12:37-50 Isaiah 6: Blinded Eyes |
| **The Last Supper** (13:1-38) | 13:1-20 *Passover* Jesus Washes Disciples' Feet | 13:21-30 Judas Agrees to Betray Jesus | 13:31-38 A New Commandment Jesus Foretells Peter's Denial |
| **Last Supper Teaching** (14:1-17:26) | 14:1-14 *I Am* the Way, the Truth, and the Life | 14:15-31 The Coming Spirit | 15:1-17 *I Am* the True Vine |
| | 15:18-16:4 The Coming Spirit of Truth | 16:5-15 The Work of the Holy Spirit | 16:16-33 I've Overcome the World |
| | 17:1-26 Jesus' High Priestly Prayer | | |
| **Betrayal to Burial** (18:1-19:42) | 18:1-11 Betrayal and Arrest of Jesus | 18:12-27 Before Sanhedrin Peter's Denial | 18:28-40 Before Pilate |
| | 19:1-16a Jesus Delivered to be Crucified | 19:16b-37 Crucifixion of Jesus | 19:38-42 Burial of Jesus |
| **Resurrection and Post Resurrection Appearances** (20:1-21:25) | 20:1-18 Resurrection Morning | 20:19-29 Jesus Appears to the Disciples | 20:30-31 The Purpose of the Book |
| | 21:1-14 Jesus Appears to Seven Disciples *Sea of Tiberias* | 21:15-19 Jesus and Peter | 21:20-25 Jesus and the Beloved Disciple |

# A Walk Through of the Gospel of John

## 1. The Prologue (1:1-18)

The Gospel of John begins with a **prologue (1:1-18)** that lays out a number of themes that run throughout the Gospel. In his initial presentation of Christ, John draws upon an Intertestamental Jewish work known as ***The Wisdom of Ben Sirach***, specifically chapter 24. *Sirach* 24 is a poem that personifies God's Wisdom through which He created the world as Lady Wisdom. *Sirach*, though, is actually a response to the prevailing Greek philosophy of the time that taught that the entire created order came about through the work of an all-encompassing universal reason and wisdom. The Greek word to describe this universal reason and wisdom was the *Logos*, translated as the **Word**. *Sirach*, therefore, argued that the *Logos* was actually God's Wisdom, and that God not only created the world through His Wisdom, but that He revealed His Wisdom in the Torah given to Moses. John, though, takes it the next step further by saying that the *Logos*—universal reason, the very wisdom of God—actually became a human being, Jesus Christ, and that it is in him that the fullness of God's Wisdom has been revealed.

Therefore, in 1:1-5, John begins his Gospel with, *"In the beginning,"* an obvious allusion to **Genesis 1:1**, emphasizing what Greek philosophers and Jews would have generally agreed upon: The *Logos/God's Wisdom* is the means by which the world was created and is the source of life. John then introduces the metaphors of **light** and **darkness** by equating the life that is in the *Logos* with the "light of wisdom" that is among mankind and contrasting that with the "darkness" that is among mankind as well. Depending on the translation, John says in 1:5 that this "light of the *Logos*" cannot be *comprehended/overcome* by the darkness.

The Greek word here is *katalambanoo*. The main verb, *lambanoo*, basically means "to hold/grasp," and the prefix *kata* emphasizes something like "down." Therefore, depending on the context, *katalambanoo* means either to "mentally grasp" or to literally "physically hold down." Here in John, it sort of means both. As we will see in the course of John's Gospel, Jesus' fellow Jews *don't understand* who he truly is, and because of that they *do try to take him down*. Since John is dealing with the **light/darkness** metaphor, though, I think the best way to understand it is by means of a visual picture of a shining a flashlight in a dark room. It breaks through the darkness and the darkness simply cannot swallow up the light. That is what John is getting at: *The light of the Logos has broken into the darkness of the world, and that* *darkness simply cannot stop him.* That is going to be a major theme throughout the Gospel.

After that, John introduces us to John the Baptist in 1:6-10. This gist of these verses is that John the Baptist bore witness to the *Logos* as the light that was coming into the world. Shockingly, though, we are told that the world, the very world that was created through the *Logos*, doesn't know or recognize the *Logos*, because the world is blind and in darkness. Then in 1:11-13, John makes a further connection to *Sirach*. In *Sirach* 24, it is said that God's Wisdom found a dwelling place among God's people (the Jews) in Jerusalem. Here, though, John flips that on its head and says that when the *Logos* came to his people (the Jews), they *didn't receive him*—the word here being *paralambanoo*, a further wordplay involving *lambanoo*. Still, the ones who *do receive him* and put their faith in him get the right to become **children of God**. John then emphasizes this kind of sonship doesn't come through bloodlines, the will of the flesh, or the will of man, but rather is the result of being **born of God**. By saying that, John is saying that being an ethnic Jew doesn't make one a child of God. A true child of God is one who puts his faith in the *Logos* and is re-born by the Holy Spirit. One's ethnicity is completely irrelevant.

In 1:14-18, John brings his prologue home with the bold statement in 1:14: **The *Logos* became flesh** (meaning a human being) **and dwelt among us**. The Greek word here for "dwelt" is the verb used to describe the presence of YHWH *dwelling among His people* in the tabernacle during the **Exodus**. Therefore, it would be better to translate it as, "The *Logos* became flesh and *tabernacled* among us." At this point, we should realize that John has not specifically mentioned Christ yet. He has simply said the following about the *Logos/God's Wisdom*:

(A) He is equal with God and is God;

(B) The created order came through him;

(C) The world did not recognize him when he came into the world;

(D) The Jews didn't receive him when he came to them;

(E) Those who did receive him became children of God by being born of God;

(F) The *Logos* became a human being and "tabernacled" among human beings (just like YHWH "tabernacled" among the Hebrews during the Exodus).

With that, John then says that "we" (meaning the original followers of Christ) had actually seen the glory of the *Logos* as the **Only-Begotten of God, full of grace and truth**. Thus, the relationship between this *Logos* and God is that of a Father and Son, which makes sense because John has just said that it is through faith in the *Logos* that human beings can be **born of God** and thus be **children of God**.

After re-emphasizing the testimony of John the Baptist in 1:15, and how we have received grace through the fullness of the *Logos* in 1:16, John finally comes out and identifies the *Logos* with Jesus Christ in 1:17. He does this, though, by drawing a parallel between Christ and Moses—and this ends up being a major theme that runs throughout his Gospel. It is quite simple: **The Torah was given through Moses, but grace and truth came through Jesus Christ, the *Logos* made flesh**. Thus, John is saying that the Torah had its place and played an important role in God's salvation plan, but **Jesus Christ, because he is equal with God and has actually made God known, supersedes the Torah. And now that Christ has come, the Torah has served its purpose**. This theme of Jesus being greater than the Torah plays out in numerous episodes in John's Gospel, as we can see in the following chart:

| | |
|---|---|
| **Wedding at Cana** (2:1-12) | Jewish Water Purification Jars vs. Wine of the Messianic Banquet |
| **Temple Trashing** (2:13-25) | Temple in Jerusalem vs. The "Temple" of Jesus' Body |
| **Moses' Serpent** (3:14-15) | Moses' Lifting up the Bronze Serpent vs. Jesus Lifted Up on the Cross |
| **Samaritan Woman** (4:1-45) | Water from Jacob's Well vs. The Living Water that Jesus Gives |
| **Pool of Bethesda** (5:1-18) | After Jesus' Healing: Obey the Torah vs. Obey the Word of Jesus? |
| **Feeding the 5,000** (6:1-15) | Bread of Heaven (Exodus) vs. Jesus' Body/Blood as the Bread of Heaven |
| **Feast of Tabernacles** (7:37-53) | Water Ceremony at Pool of Siloam vs. Living Water from Jesus |
| **Feast of Tabernacles** (8:12-20) | Lighting of the Menorah vs. Jesus as the Light of the World |
| **Pool of Siloam** (9:1-41) | After the Healing of a Blind Man at the Pool of Siloam (Light/Water): Obey the Pharisees or Obey Jesus? |

| | | Celebration of Passover Sacrifice and Freedom from Egypt vs. |
|---|---|---|
| | **Passover** (13-17) | Redefinition of Passover-Christ's Sacrifice for Freedom from this World |

### 2. The "First Week" (1:19-2:12)

The **second section (1:19-2:12)**, is set up as a subtle allusion to the creation week of **Genesis 1**. After all, since John begins his prologue with the words, "In the beginning," it shouldn't be that surprising to see an allusion to the seven days of creation here in the next section. The point is to show that in Christ, the new creation has come. In any case, the narrative movement begins in Judea and moves to Galilee.

On the **first day (1:19-28)**, we are told of the testimony of John the Baptist near Bethany, as he was baptizing people in the Jordan River. When the Pharisees of Jerusalem send some priests and Levites to find out who John the Baptist is, John tells them he isn't the Christ, Elijah, or the prophet (meaning the prophet like Moses mentioned in **Deuteronomy 18:15**). Instead, John identifies himself with the **voice in the wilderness** in **Isaiah 40:3**. Isaiah 40 was a prophetic call for the Jews to come out from the Babylonian Exile, and thus their return to the land was seen as a **second Exodus**. When the Jews returned to the Promised Land, they had hopes that God would fully restore them, but that full restoration had never happened. So, as of the first century, they were still waiting for that restoration to happen.

Thus, John was announcing that the long-awaited restoration was at hand, with his baptism in the Jordan River signifying not only the symbolic washing away of the nation's sins, but also serving as a precursor to the baptism of the Holy Spirit that the one coming after him would bring. Not only that, but John's baptism in the Jordan River also served as a re-enactment of Joshua's entry into the Promised Land at the end of the first Exodus. Put that all together, and John's testimony was basically that God's restoration and the end of their spiritual exile was at hand.

On the **second day (1:29-34)**, John the Baptist identifies Jesus as the **Lamb of God who takes away the sins of the world**. He also says the purpose of his own baptism was to **bring Christ to light in Israel**, obviously echoing the prologue's statement about how the light of the *Logos* came to his own people. Interestingly enough, there is no actual account of Jesus' baptism by John. It just says that when John saw Jesus, that the Spirit came down in the form of a dove upon Jesus. John then declares that Jesus is the one who will baptize in the Holy Spirit, and he testifies that Jesus is, in fact the Son of God.

On the **third day (1:35-42)**, John the Baptist again calls Jesus the Lamb of God and two of his disciples go and follow Jesus, one of them is Andrew. After they meet with Jesus, Andrew finds his brother Simon, tells him they had found the Christ, and introduces him to Jesus. Upon meeting Simon, Jesus tells him that he will call him **Cephas**, which is the Aramaic name for **Peter**, meaning "rock."

On the **fourth day (1:43-51)**, Philip and Nathanael become disciples of Jesus. One clear sign that John is actually claiming all these events happened within a literal span of seven days is that he says here that "on the next day" Jesus went to Galilee. Travelling from Jerusalem to Galilee takes many days. It is impossible to walk to Galilee from Jerusalem in one day. In any case, when Philip becomes Christ's disciple and then tells Nathanael that he's found the Christ. When Nathanael learns that Jesus was from Nazareth, he mockingly says, "How can anything good come from Nazareth?" Nevertheless, he goes with Philip to meet Jesus.

What transpires next is difficult to interpret. Jesus calls Nathanael a **true Israelite** in whom there was no deceit. Then, when Nathanael asks Jesus how he knows him, Jesus tells him that he saw him under the fig tree. In response, Nathanael calls Jesus the **Son of God** and the **King of Israel**. To that, Jesus essentially replies, "You're that impressed just because I said I saw you under the fig tree? You're going to see a lot more than that!" His reference to seeing angels ascending and descending on the Son of Man hints at just what Nathanael will see, namely how Jesus will be the one who will be glorified and will bring heaven and earth together in himself.

With that, John skips ahead three days to the **seventh day (2:1-12)**, where Jesus turns the water into wine at a wedding in Cana. In many respects, this is the first real story in John's Gospel. When the wine runs out, Jesus' mother tells him to do something, and despite his initial protest, he agrees, and his mother tells the servants to do whatever he tells them. He has them fill up some jars with water, draw some water out, and take it to the head steward. Not only is it wine, but it is better than the original wine of the wedding! John then tells us that this was the **first sign** Jesus performed that revealed his glory. After the wedding, Jesus then goes to Capernaum.

There are a couple of significant things to note in this story. First, there is the fact this takes place at a wedding, for one of the ways in which the Jewish Messianic hopes were expressed was the use of the imagery of a **great Messianic wedding banquet**. When the Messiah comes, it will be like a joyous wedding celebration. Therefore, the fact that Jesus' first sign takes place at a wedding banquet is sending the clear message that the Messianic wedding banquet had come, or was indeed coming, even though the "hour" of Jesus' own sacrificial death had not yet come.

Secondly, there is the way in which Jesus turned the water into wine. He had the servants fill up **six stone water jars that were used for the purification of the Jews**. This helps to highlight one of the major themes in John's Gospel, namely, how Jesus supersedes Moses and the Torah. The purification guidelines are spelled out in the Torah and was part of the Old Covenant. They, like everything in the Torah, were done in anticipation of God's future salvation and the coming the Messiah. Of course, with the coming of Jesus, that future salvation is now. Therefore, Jesus turns the water of purification that is outlined in the Torah into the wine of the great Messianic wedding banquet. That is the sign: *The Messianic wedding banquet is now here! Come and celebrate and drink its wine.* What that also means, though, is that the old way of doing things in the Torah has now passed. It is time to put the old ways behind and step out into God's new creation. After all, it's the seventh day.

### 3. From Passover to Galilee (2:13-4:54)

The **third section (2:13-4:54)** repeats the narrative movement of the previous section, beginning in Judea, specifically Jerusalem, and then moving into Galilee, back to Cana. In the **first scene (2:13-25)**, Jesus is in Jerusalem for Passover, during which time he trashes the Temple. In the Synoptic Gospels, this famous scene takes place during the final Passover week of Jesus' crucifixion. Here in John, though, it is set during an earlier Passover. What could account for this? Maybe Jesus performed this Temple action at two different times, and it was the second time that led to his crucifixion. Or maybe, for his own literary reasons, John decided to tell of Jesus' Temple action here near the beginning of his account of Jesus in order to further highlight his main theme that Jesus supersedes Old Covenant Judaism, be it seen in his reference to the Torah (1:17-18) or here with the Temple.

In any case, Jesus drives out the oxen and sheep that were being sold for sacrifices in the Temple and chastises the people there for turning his Father's House (the Temple) into a marketplace. This is slightly different than in the

Synoptic Gospels, where Jesus condemns the Temple for having become a *hideout for revolutionaries*. We have to remember that the Synoptics were written right around the time of the Jewish War of AD 66-70, when, in fact, zealot revolutionaries revolted against Rome and eventually turned the Temple complex into their revolutionary headquarters. In light of that reality, the Synoptics were commenting on how the very reason why Jerusalem and the Temple had been destroyed was because the Jews had rejected Jesus as their king and instead embraced the way of revolution. By the time John wrote his Gospel, the Jewish War was a good 20 years in the past, so John has changed the focus and significance of the Temple action from the specific condemnation of the revolution to a more general condemnation of the overall corruption of the Temple establishment.

At this point, we are told that "the Jews" demand that Jesus show them a sign that proves he has the authority to do what he did. In response, Jesus says, "Destroy this Temple and I will raise it up in three days!" They, along with the disciples at that time, think he is talking about the physical building of the Temple, but John tells us he was speaking about his body and his future resurrection. As we saw with the wedding at Cana, Jesus is being presented as being superior to traditional Judaism. In the prologue, **Jesus is greater than the Mosaic Torah**; at Cana, **Jesus' wine is better than the water of Jewish purification jars**; here, **Jesus is the true Temple of God and is therefore greater than the entire Temple and its sacrificial system**. John tells us that Jesus performed many signs at that time and that many people put their faith in him, but he did not trust them. Clearly, many people may have been initially attracted to him and thought he might be the Messiah, but the problem was that their Messianic expectations did not match Jesus' own Messianic mission, and he knew it.

A comment needs to be made concerning **John's characterization of the Jews** in his Gospel. Obviously, throughout the centuries, this characterization in John's Gospel has been used to justify anti-Semitism and persecution of Jews as Christ-killers. We have to remember, though, that John himself was Jewish, as was Jesus and the earliest followers. Therefore, we need to realize that John is not necessarily saying what we might think he's saying. First of all, given John's clear distinction between Jesus' time in Judea, as opposed to Galilee, it is entirely possible that what is translated as "the Jews" should rather be "the Judeans." Thus, John was making a distinction between Jews who lived in Judea (Judeans) and Jews who lived in Galilee (Galileans).

At the same time, we should realize how monumental the Jewish War of AD 66-70 had been. Up to that point, as we see in much of the New Testament, the early Jesus movement was seen in connection in some way with Judaism. Even when Paul took the Gospel to Gentiles, there still was a question regarding the relationship between this new "Christian" community and Judaism as a whole, although it was obvious there was a slow divorce going on. After the Jewish War, that divorce was pretty much final, and "Christianity" was seen as a religion quite distinct from "Judaism." Therefore, by the time John wrote his Gospel, his use of "the Jews" just reflected that split. It would be like when Americans referred to "fighting the Germans" in WWII. Obviously that reference was to Nazis specifically, and not every human being of German descent.

The **second scene (3:1-21)** involves the famous discussion between Jesus and Nicodemus. It is still set at the time of that Passover. Nicodemus, a Pharisee and a Jewish leader of some sort, comes to Jesus **during the night**. We can take this both literally as well as symbolically: *Jesus, the Light of the World, is shining in darkness*, and Nicodemus, for his part, is responding to it. Jesus' discussion with Nicodemus reinforces some of the major themes that are laid out in the prologue. Not only is there the **light/darkness imagery**, but in 3:1-8, Jesus also speaks of how only those **being born again, from above, and by water and the Spirit** will see the Kingdom of God. This obviously alludes back to both John the Baptist's baptism in water, and to Jesus' baptism of the Holy Spirit. Jesus' distinction between **being born by the will of the flesh** and **being born of the Spirit** echoes John 1:13 as well. Finally, Jesus' comment about how those who are **born of the Spirit** are like the wind, in that it goes where it wants, further implies that this new birth by the Spirit isn't going to be limited solely to the Jews.

John 3:9-15 further elaborates on a number of items from the prologue. The main focus is that of **bearing witness**. Just as John the Baptist bore witness to Jesus, so too does Jesus bear witness to God the Father, the one who sent him from Heaven. Jesus then draws another parallel between himself and Moses. In Numbers 21, Moses made a bronze serpent, put it on a pole, and told the Israelites who were suffering from serpent bites as punishment for their disobedience that if they looked upon the bronze serpent that they would be healed. Jesus tells Nicodemus that something similar will happen with himself. He, too, will be "lifted up" (foreshadowing his crucifixion on a cross) and, just like those who looked upon the bronze serpent were healed, so too will those who put their faith in him will be given the **Life of the Age**. To translate this as "eternal life" is, in my opinion, too general. The Jewish and Christian worldview entailed a belief that this current age was one in which sin and death reigned, and that when the Messiah would come and usher in the Kingdom of God, that would mark the beginning of a new age. Therefore, Jesus is speaking here about being given that life of the coming Messianic age, not just some overgeneralized concept of "eternal life." Finally, 3:16-21 reinforces what John has laid out in the prologue: *The Only-Begotten Son was sent into the world to save the world, not to judge it. And those who put their faith in him will be given the Life of the Age*. Unfortunately, the "judgment" of the Son's coming into the world is that even though the Son, **the Light of the World**, has come into the world, the world prefers the **darkness** and doesn't like to have its evil deeds exposed by that Light.

In the **third scene (3:22-36)**, we are told that Jesus and his disciples start to baptize in the region of Judea. (In John's timeline, they went to Jerusalem for Passover and stayed in Judea to baptize followers). Pretty soon, Jesus starts gaining more followers than John the Baptist. (At this point, John tells us, John the Baptist had not yet been arrested). In response to Jesus' growing following, John the Baptist explains that he doesn't have a problem with it, because he realizes Jesus is the **Bridegroom**, the one for whom John was preparing the way and to whom he was bearing witness. Of course, by calling Jesus the Bridegroom, not only does John the Baptist use the language of the Messianic wedding banquet, but John the author clearly wants us to see the connection to Jesus first sign at the wedding in Cana. Now that Jesus the Bridegroom had come, John the Baptist clearly saw that his own ministry would wind down. He had done his job and now must give way to the coming of the Bridegroom. John's speech ends with what the basic "game plan" is now. There are two choices people can have: *Either put their faith in the Son and have the* **Life of the Age** *or disobey the Son and incur the* **wrath of God**.

The **fourth scene (4:1-42)** is the story of Jesus and the Samaritan woman. John tells us that when Jesus found out that the Pharisees in Judea had become aware that his ministry was growing larger than John the Baptist's, he and his disciples went back to Galilee in the north. To get to Galilee from Judea, though, one had to travel through the central region of the land known as Samaria. Jews hated the Samaritans and viewed them essentially as heretical half-breeds whose came from the idolatrous Israelites of the northern kingdom who had intermarried with the foreign people whom Assyrians had moved into the area after they had destroyed that kingdom in 721 BC. Given that history and given the fact that Jesus talks to a woman, the story is scandalous from beginning to end.

The story begins when Jesus and his disciples stop by the town of Sychar, and he rests at **Jacob's well** while his disciples go into town to get food. The well provides the basis for the entire scene: (A) The Samaritan woman shows up to draw water and Jesus asks her for a drink; (B) Jesus tells her if she knew the gift of God and who he was, she'd be asking him for living water; (C) She asks him if he thinks he's greater than Jacob, to which he replies by telling her that anyone who drinks from Jacob's well will be thirsty again, but whoever drinks from the **living water** he gives will find that it becomes a spring of living water within him that will flow over into the **Life of the Age**; (D) When she asks (I think sarcastically) Jesus for this water, Jesus tells her to go get her husband, and when she says she doesn't have a husband, he tells her he knows she has, in fact, had five husbands and was currently living with a man who wasn't her husband; (E) At that point, she acknowledges Jesus must be a prophet and asks him if the proper place to worship God was either "this mountain" (Mt. Gerizim) or in Jerusalem. Jesus responds by telling her that the true worshippers of God will **worship in Spirit and truth** (therefore, making the physical location irrelevant); (F) She then says that she believes when the Messiah comes, that he will proclaim everything to them. At that point, Jesus tells her he is, in fact, the Messiah; (G) As the disciples return, she leaves her water jar behind to go back to town to tell others about Jesus.

Given these details, a few key things need to be pointed out. First, the recurring theme that Jesus supersedes the Old Testament is there: Jesus is doing something new, so therefore the old must go. That is the significance of the woman *leaving her water jar behind*. Jesus is greater that Jacob, and Jacob's well isn't going to bring about the Life of the Age. Only the living water Jesus gives will do that.

Secondly, there is a really neat marriage motif going on in this story. To get it, though, you have to realize that there are a number of stories in the Old Testament that involve a **man coming to a well in a foreign land** and **finding a wife**: Abraham sends his servant back to Aram to find a wife for Isaac, and the servant meets Rebekah at a well, who has come to draw water; (B) Jacob flees from Esau, goes to Aram, and encounters Rachel at a well, coming to draw water; and (C) Moses flees Egypt, goes to Midian, sits down by a well, and meets his wife-to-be Zipporah, who has come to draw water. If you know your Old Testament, anytime you read about a man in a foreign land who meets a woman at a well, you expect a marriage to happen in the near future.

This story follows that same narrative, but then has a twist to it at the end. Jesus is traveling through foreign territory, he comes to a well, and he meets a woman who has come to draw water. In this case, though, Jesus doesn't literally marry her, of course, but he does show himself to be the **Bridegroom** of whom John the Baptist spoke (3:22-36) who is bringing the **Messianic wedding banquet** (2:1-11) to someone beyond the boundaries of Judaism. Simply put, the marriage happening here is the one between the Messiah-Bridegroom and his Church, and the shocker is that it is going to include, of all people, *Samaritans*. The people of the Messiah will come from all peoples and ethnicities and won't be confined to ethnic Jews.

The story ends with Jesus telling his disciples that the **fields are white for harvest**, and he's sending them out into the fields to reap what he is sowing. That is what their job is. We are then told that some of the Samaritans from Sychar came to the well to meet Jesus. The living water was accepted, the Bridegroom's Messianic wedding banquet was extended beyond the Jews, and the harvest was beginning to be reaped.

The **fifth and final scene (4:43-54)** takes place a couple of days later, in, of all places, **Cana of Galilee**. Here, a royal official asks Jesus to come to Capernaum and heal his sick son. Jesus says that people won't put their faith in him unless they see signs and wonders, meaning he feels that people are more interested in seeing "magic tricks" than seriously following him. The man pleads with Jesus to heal his son, and so Jesus tells him to go home and that his son will live. We are told that the man put his faith in Jesus and went home. The next day, his servant comes to meet him as he is returning home and tells him that his son's fever had broken around 1:00 pm the previous day, the exact time when Jesus had told him that his son would live. John ends by telling us that Jesus' healing of the official's son was the **second sign** he had done since coming to Galilee from Cana. John tells us that this was the **second sign** Jesus had done, the **first sign** being turning the water into wine during the wedding at Cana in 2:1-11.

### 4. From the Feast of the Jews to Galilee (5:1-6:71)

The **fourth section (5:1-7:1)**, like the previous two sections, follows the same narrative pattern, in that it begins with a feast in Jerusalem and ends back in Galilee.

The **first scene (5:1-18)** takes place at another "feast of the Jews" in Jerusalem, where Jesus encounters a 38-year-old lame man at the Pool of Bethesda. Apparently, there was a belief at that time that from time to time an angel would come down and disturb the water of the pool, and when that happened, the first person who got into the pool would be healed. Of course, since this man was lame, he could never get in first. Jesus, though, heals the man and tells him to carry his mat home.

It turns out, though, that the day on which Jesus healed the man was the Sabbath. And so, "the Judeans" saw the man carrying his mat and accused him of violating the Torah by working on the Sabbath. The man told them that he was only doing what the man who healed him told to do. This highlights the real point of the story: *After Jesus' restorative and healing work has come, do you continue to observe the Torah or do you start to obey the word of the Messiah?* In any case, the man didn't know who Jesus was until they happened to meet in the Temple a short time later. Jesus tells him to not to sin anymore, so that nothing more evil would happen to him. When the man starts to tell people that it was Jesus who healed him, John tells us that is when "the Judeans" began seeking to persecute and kill Jesus. Not only was he healing on the Sabbath (a supposed violation of the Torah), but he was also calling God his Father, and was thus claiming equality with God. This leads into the subsequent dialogue in the next scene.

The **second scene (5:19-47)** is an extension of the first scene and involves a long speech by Jesus in which he focuses on three issues: The **authority** of the Son (5:19-30), the **testimony** of the Son (5:31-37a), and the reason why the "the Judeans'" **reject him** (5:37b-47). What Jesus says regarding his **authority** can be boiled down to these four points: (1) His authority as the Son comes from the Father—the Son does what the Father does, and to honor one is to honor the other; (2) If you listen to the word of the Son and put your faith in the Father, you'll have the Life of the Age and won't come under judgment; (3) The power of resurrection is already available now to give life; and (4) The Son not only offers life, but he also has the authority to execute judgment.

When it comes to the issue of his **testimony**, Jesus first points to the testimony of John the Baptist as bearing witness to him. He then says his own testimony is actually greater than the testimony of John the Baptist, because he is bearing witness to the Father. Not only that, but the **works** he is doing were given to him by the Father for him to complete, so that they could bear witness that the Father had sent him. Simply put: John the Baptist testified he was the coming one, and the works he is doing is further testimony that the Father had indeed sent him.

Jesus then says the reason they refuse to accept him is because they never really have seen or known the Father—and that is why they don't put their faith in him, the Son. They search their **Scriptures** (the **Torah**), thinking they contain the **Life of the Age**, but they don't realize their Scriptures actually bear witness to him. In other words, the Torah is the pointer to the coming Savior who gives life, but the Torah itself isn't the Savior and it can't give life. And that is why Jesus tells them that **their accuser is Moses**—if they had really believed Moses, they would have realized that the Torah points to Jesus and would then put their faith in him.

The **third scene (6:1-15)** tells of Jesus feeding the 5,000. Here in John, Jesus is now back in Galilee and goes to the other side of the Sea of Galilee (the Sea of Tiberias), which is essentially Gentile territory. John also tells us that the **Passover** was near. The significance of this should be obvious: God's salvation is going to extend beyond the borders of Israel to Gentiles. The fact that Jesus goes **up a mountain** is yet another allusion to the Exodus, in that after the Hebrews left Egypt during the Passover, they made their way to **Mount Sinai**. Thus, Jesus is presented as a "new Moses." In any case, Jesus feeds the 5,000 with some loaves and fish and there are twelve baskets of leftovers. In response, the people recognize this as **a sign** and declare that Jesus is a prophet. This is the third sign John points out—the first being changing the water to wine (2:1-12) and the healing of the official's son (4:43-54). Jesus, though, withdraws from them because they wanted to make him a king.

The **fourth scene (6:16-21)** is that of Jesus walking on the Sea of Galilee, the night after he feeds the 5,000. The disciples cross back over the Sea of Galilee in the boat back to Capernaum, but Jesus stays behind. When a storm kicks up on the sea and they are in clear danger, Jesus comes walking to them on the water and says, "I am! Don't be afraid!" He then gets into the boat and they arrive on the shore. The point of this is not just to show that Jesus can do a magic trick. The point is to give us a clue regarding Jesus' identity. Who is it that has power and authority over the sea? God, of course. And here, we see Jesus demonstrating that same power and authority over the sea. Jesus the Son shares equality with God the Father.

The **fifth scene (6:22-58)** takes place the next day in Capernaum. The people from the 5,000 find Jesus and ask him how he got there. This begins a dialogue regarding the significance of the feeding of the 5,000. Jesus focuses on the imagery of the bread and tells them they aren't seeking him because of any signs he did, but because they had a "taste" of the kind of bread he offers and they want the kind of **bread that lasts into the Life of the Age**. When they ask Jesus what they have to do, he tells them they have to put their faith in the one whom God sent, the Son. In an ironic response, given the fact that they had just been miraculously fed by Jesus, they ask Jesus **what kind of sign** he'll do to convince them, and even bring up the Exodus account of God sending **manna from heaven** as an example. Thus, the contrast between the new and old, between Jesus and Moses comes up once again.

Jesus tells them the manna in the wilderness wasn't the true bread from heaven; **he himself was the true Bread from Heaven** who gives **life to the world**. As the **Bread of Life**, he would raise up what the Father has given him on the Last Day (the future resurrection). So, if they put their faith in the **Son of Man**, they will have the **Life of the Age** and will be **raised up on the Last Day**.

After "the Judeans" complain, Jesus repeats what he just said and then adds that his own flesh was the Bread of Life, and that everyone who **eats his flesh** and **drinks his blood** would be raised up on the Last Day. We understand this to be a foreshadowing of the Christian Eucharist, but at that time, Jesus' words would have seemed insane. The reaction of "the Judeans" illustrates that very thing. Still, if we understand Jesus' comments in light of the clear Exodus/Passover imagery in throughout chapter 6, we can see (as he later does at the Last Supper) he is alluding to the sacrificial lamb and the wine in the Passover meal.

The **sixth scene (6:59-71)** continues the dialogue from the previous scene. Here, Jesus is teaching in the synagogue in Capernaum, and his teaching is just too tough for many who were there. Consequently, some of his followers leave him. They thought he might be a prophet, perhaps the Messiah, but the talk of eating his flesh and drinking his blood proved just too much. Jesus' response is, "The Spirit gives life, but the flesh counts for nothing." When Jesus asks the Twelve if they are going to leave too, Peter responds with, "Where would we go? You have the **Life of the Age**. Our faith is in you, for you are the Holy One of God." Jesus responds with, "I've chosen you, but one of you is the devil" (a reference to Judas Iscariot). Clearly, this scene further highlights what was first said in the prologue—namely, that **Christ the Logos** had come to his own people, and that some refused to receive him.

### 5. The Feast of Tabernacles (7:1-10:21)

The **fifth section (7:1-10:21)** finds us back in Jerusalem for the **Feast of Tabernacles**, the celebration of the wilderness wanderings of the Exodus. Everything in this relates in some way to the main symbolism surrounding the Feast of Tabernacles. In the **first scene (7:1-36)**, opens in Galilee with the Feast of Tabernacles drawing near. In 7:1-10, Jesus' brothers (who do not yet believe him) tell him he should go down to Jerusalem for the feast and reveal himself to the world. Jesus responds, though, by saying that **his time hadn't come yet**. This is a recurring theme in John's Gospel. At the wedding at Cana (2:1-12), when Jesus' mother tells him to address the problem with the lack of wine, Jesus tells her **his hour had not yet come**. Then in Samaria when talking to the Samaritan woman at the well (4:1-42), Jesus tells her that the **hour is coming, and is now here,** when the true worshippers of God will worship the Father in Spirit and truth.

After his brothers go to Jerusalem for the feast, though, Jesus decides to go after all, but "in secret." This can be a bit confusing because, as we will see, when he gets to Jerusalem, he openly teaches in public and has quite the confrontation with certain people there—hardly something that can be characterized as "in secret." Therefore, we should realize that what John is getting at is that when Jesus went to Jerusalem, he didn't go to reveal his true glory yet—after all, his "time" had not yet come.

In any case, what we see in the rest of this scene (7:11-36), as well as throughout the entire fifth section, is a rather long, meandering confrontation between Jesus and the Jewish religious authorities in Jerusalem during the Feast of Tabernacles. The easiest way to grasp what is going on is to picture **Jesus** on one side and the **Jewish authorities** on the other side, with the **crowds** in the middle, trying to make up their mind about Jesus—do they believe what Jesus says or what the Jewish authorities say? Is Jesus a good man or is he leading people astray? In the course of this back and forth, a number of points should be noted:

(1) There is a clear **fear of the Jews** on the part of the crowds. The fact this scene takes place *in Jerusalem*, though, should make it clear that the "crowds" are, in fact, Jewish, so it wouldn't make sense to interpret "fear of the Jews" as them being afraid of themselves. Rather, we would be better served to realize that the crowds are afraid of the Jewish religious authorities in Jerusalem who clearly are antagonistic to Jesus. Therefore, many in the crowds don't want to publicly show

their support of Jesus for fear of incurring the wrath of the Jewish religious authorities.

(2) There is the issue of **Jesus' teaching and training**. Despite having no formal training, Jesus clearly knows the Scriptures, and this shocks "the Jews" (probably the Jewish religious authorities).

(3) There is the **open confrontation** between Jesus and the Jewish religious authorities. Jesus first claims his teaching came from the **one who sent me**, namely God the Father Himself. Second, he accuses the Jewish religious authorities of not only not practicing the **Torah of Moses**, but also of seeking to kill him. Third, he confronts them on their opposition to him healing people on the Sabbath, saying if it is okay to circumcise on the Sabbath, then there's nothing wrong with healing on the Sabbath either.

(4) There is a **clear division among the crowd**. Some accuse Jesus of having a demon and think he's crazy for saying that anyone is trying to kill him, whereas others are amazed that Jesus is speaking so openly to the very leaders who are trying to kill him and are wondering whether or not he really is the Christ (Messiah). Some, in fact, do put their faith in him.

(5) There is the **question of where Jesus is really from**. They know Jesus is literally from Galilee, but he says he is really from the **one who sent me** (God the Father), and that not only He is true, but they don't know Him.

(6) There is the **failed attempt** by the Jewish religious leaders to arrest Jesus because Jesus' **hour had not yet come**.

(7) There is the **foreshadowing of Jesus returning to the Father** and the eventual **taking of the Gospel to the Gentile world**. When they come to arrest him, he says he is only going to be there a little while longer, and that when he returns to the Father, they won't find him and they won't be able to come. They then wonder if he is talking about going out to the Diaspora, to the Greeks.

The **second scene (7:37-53)** takes places on the last day of the Feast of Tabernacles. To understand what is going on in this scene, you have to know about the water-drawing ceremony that would happen on the last day of the Feast of Tabernacles. Priests and Temple elders would make a procession from the Temple to the Pool of Siloam, draw water out from the pool, then proceed back to the Temple and pour water out upon the altar, symbolically re-enacting the description of how the River of Life flowed out of Eden to water all the earth. The Temple was thus seen as the navel of the world, and the point of the ceremony was to affirm that the place of God's dwelling was the center of His creation and the source of its life.

On that last day of the feast, Jesus exclaims that *whoever is thirsty should come to him and drink*, and that when he does, *"rivers of living water will flow from his belly."* First, this is a clear echo of what he said to the Samaritan woman at the well. Second, as is also emphasized with the Samaritan woman, the "water" of which Jesus speaks is a reference to the future **outpouring of the Holy Spirit**, of which John points out had not yet come yet. Third, again similar to what he told the Samaritan woman, we cannot miss the significance of what he is saying. The source of this "living water of the Spirit" *is not going to be the Temple*. It is going to come from within those who come to Christ. With the outpouring of the Spirit, the true worshippers of God won't be limited to worshipping at the Temple. *The Spirit will overflow throughout the world.*

Not surprisingly, such a declaration caused further division among the crowds. Some believed he was the coming prophet like Moses, some believed he was the Christ, but some rejected that notion because the Christ was to be the offspring of David, and therefore from Bethlehem. In any case, the Temple officers who were sent to arrest Jesus return to the chief priests and Pharisees empty-handed and declare that no one has ever spoken like Jesus before. The chief priests and Pharisees, though rebuke the officers and are quick to point out that none of them—the educated religious elite—had put their faith in Jesus. It was only the uneducated crowds who didn't know the Torah and who were therefore accursed, who had gone after him.

At that point, Nicodemus, the one who had privately come to talk with Jesus at night in chapter 3, speaks up and tries to defend Jesus a bit by saying that the Torah doesn't allow for a man to be judged unless he is at least given a hearing first. He gets shouted down rather quickly, though, when they mockingly ask him if he was from Galilee and unequivocally say that prophets don't come from Galilee. This shows just how much the "big city religious elites" of Jerusalem looked down on what they considered to be the low class, uncultured country bumpkins of Galilee.

The **third scene (8:1-11)**, the story of the woman caught in adultery, actually is not found in our earliest manuscripts of John. (The earliest manuscript that does have it is dated to around AD 400). Nevertheless, as it stands here in John 8, it takes place the next day in the Temple. Since the Temple officers failed to arrest him, the scribes and Pharisees decide to try to expose Jesus for not being as learned in the Torah as they were. So, they bring to him a woman who had been arrested for committing adultery and basically ask him if he agrees with the Torah that clearly commands that anyone caught in adultery should be stoned to death. As we have already seen, a recurring theme in John's Gospel is how Jesus is greater than Moses and the Torah. In addition, John has also highlighted the confrontation between Jesus and the Temple authorities from the very beginning of his Gospel.

In any case, Jesus responds by writing something in the ground with his finger and then telling them that the one who has never sinned should be the one to cast the first stone. Soon, all of them, beginning with the elders, leave. At that point, Jesus asks the woman where her accusers went, to which she replies that they all left. With that, Jesus says he doesn't judge her either and then tells her to go and sin no more. Many speculate as to what Jesus might have been writing, but it really isn't important. Instead, the significance of him writing in the ground goes back to that theme that he is greater than Moses and the Torah. In effect, the point is that *his writing* and *his authority* is greater than that of the Torah. Like John said in 1:17, the Torah might have been given through Moses, but *grace and truth* came through Jesus Christ.

The **fourth scene (8:12-59)** is a long, rambling dialogue between Jesus and the Jews in Jerusalem that takes place in the treasury of the Temple. The setting is still the Feast of Tabernacles, and just as Jesus' invitation to come to him to drink related to the water ceremony, so does his first comment here about being the **light of the world** correspond to the Temple illumination ceremony at the Feast of Tabernacles, where the giant lampstand in the Court of Women was lit, symbolizing the pillar of fire that led the Hebrews out of Egypt during the Exodus. It also echoes John 1:4-5, that talks about Jesus, the Logos made flesh, being the light of the world.

It is during this illumination ceremony that Jesus declares, *"I AM the Light of the World."* Upon saying this, Jesus gets into a debate with the Pharisees regarding his testimony, and that spills over into a larger debate with "the Jews" there over a number of related things:

When the Pharisees say Jesus' testimony isn't true because he alone is making the claim, Jesus tells them that his testimony is, indeed, true because both the Torah and God the Father—the one who sent him—serve as two witnesses to his claim.

Jesus then accuses the Pharisees of acting and judging **according to the flesh**, and says he knows where he's from and where he's going, and that when he goes away, they cannot come. At this point, "the Jews" ask if Jesus was planning to kill himself, but in response, Jesus tells them they are of "this world," but he is not, and that is why they will die in their sins.

At this point, they basically say, *"Who do you think you are?"* to which he says he's told them already. He is simply saying and doing what the one who sent him has told him to do, and that when they **lift up the Son of Man**, then they will understand who he is and that he had come from the Father.

When some put their faith in him, he tells them that if they if they remain his disciples, that the truth would set them free. But in response, some of "the Jews" (who clearly did not put their faith in him) object and say that they are **offspring of Abraham** and have never been slaves to anyone (which is ironic, given the fact that the entire Exodus story begins with their ancestors being slaves in Egypt!).

Jesus responds by telling them that are **slaves to sin**, and that it was the Son, (and those whom the Son frees), not the slaves, who would "remain in the household *into the Age*." Most translations have "remain in the household *forever*," but to translate it that way is to miss the Jewish eschatological worldview that looked forward to the coming *Messianic Age*.

He then says if they were truly children of Abraham (not just ethnic Jews), if Abraham truly was their father, they would do the works Abraham did. Instead, the works they are doing are looking for a way to get Jesus killed, and those are the works of their true father. When they retort by alluding to the fact that Jesus was conceived out of wedlock *("We weren't born from fornication!")* and claiming God is their Father, Jesus responds by openly saying that their real father is the devil and that they were not of God.

At that point, "the Jews" further accuse Jesus of being a Samaritan and of being demon-possessed, to which Jesus responds by saying that he honors his Father (God), but that they are dishonoring him.

Jesus doubles-down on what he said earlier and says anyone who keeps his word would "never see death *into the Age*." When they again accuse him of having a demon, they ask him if he thinks he is greater than Abraham, Jesus tells them that Abraham was overjoyed to see his day. When they (sarcastically, I think) ask him how it is possible for him to have seen Abraham, when he himself isn't even yet fifty years old, it is then that Jesus ushers yet another "I Am" statement: *"Before Abraham was, I AM!"*

Upon saying that, "the Jews" realize he is claiming to be equal to God, so they try to stone him, but Jesus escapes and gets out of the Temple.

The **fifth scene (9:1-41)** tells about Jesus healing a blind man at the Pool of Siloam and the man's subsequent run-in with the Pharisees. Since there is no narrative cue that Jesus went back to Galilee, the setting is still in Jerusalem, presumably still around the time of the Feast of Tabernacles. Upon seeing the blind man, the disciples ask Jesus whose fault it was (who sinned?) that the man was born blind—his or his parents? Jesus tells them neither, and says the reason the man was born blind was so that the work of God could be revealed in him. Simply put, Jesus is saying that the reason why some people are blind, or deaf, or lame, or sick, etc., is so that other people can participate in God's work by bringing healing to the least of these. *Instead of wondering whose fault it is for a certain person's plight, followers of Christ should simply get busy in the work to care for that person.*

In any case, after reiterating that he is the "light of the world" (9:5) and encouraging his followers to do the work of God "during the day," Jesus spits on the ground to make some mud, puts it on the man's eyes, and then tells him to wash it off in the Pool of Siloam, *the very pool from which the Jews drew the water for the water ceremony during the Feast of Tabernacles.* The man obeys, washes in the Pool of Siloam, and is able to see. Because he has done this on the Sabbath, though, he is brought before the Pharisees for questioning. They tell the man that Jesus is not from God because he doesn't keep the Sabbath. Other Pharisees, though, ask how Jesus could be a sinful man and still have the power to do such a sign as healing a man born blind. When they ask the former blind men what he thought, he says Jesus must be a prophet.

The Pharisees can't believe the man really had been born blind, so they call in his parents and ask them. They tell them that he really was born blind, but they don't know now he was healed. John tells us that they were "afraid of the Jews," because "the Jews" had already begun to kick anyone who professed Jesus to be the Messiah (Christ) out of the synagogue. The fact that these parents were, in fact, Jews, and that they were speaking before the Pharisees should tell that when John uses the term "the Jews," more times than not he is specifically referring to the Jewish religious authorities, particularly those in Jerusalem, and not the Jewish people as a whole.

Since the man's parents would say nothing more, the Pharisees call the man back in, declare Jesus to be a sinner, and tell him to give glory to God. The man responds by saying that he doesn't know anything about Jesus, but all he knows is that he was blind, but now was able to see. When, they then ask him again *exactly how Jesus healed him*, the man (presumably exasperated) asks them if they want to become Jesus' disciples. This question, though, clearly offends the Pharisees, so they berate him and accuse him of being a disciple of Jesus. They tell him they are disciples of Moses (not Jesus!), and that they know God spoke through Moses, but they don't know where Jesus was even from. At that point, this lowly, formerly blind man, finds the courage to stand up to these religious authorities and (presumably sarcastically) says, *"You don't know where he's from, and yet he opened my eyes? If he wasn't from God, he wouldn't be able to do anything!"* As soon as he says that, they accuse him of being an utter sinner (born in your sins) and throw him out (presumably of the synagogue).

When Jesus finds out what had happened to the man, he finds him and asks him if he will put his faith in the Son of Man. When the man asks who the Son of Man is, Jesus tells him that he is—the very one who the man is looking at. The man does put his faith in Jesus and Jesus says, *"I came into the world for judgment, so the blind can see and those who see can become blind."* Some Pharisees hear him say this ask, "We're not blind, are we?" To which Jesus tells them that if they were blind, they wouldn't be guilty of sin, but since they claim to see, their sin remains.

The **sixth and final episode (10:1-21)** consists of a speech by Jesus (still set during the time of the Feast of Tabernacles, and perhaps a continuation of what he has just said to the Pharisees) in which he identifies himself as the Gate and as the Good Shepherd. The metaphors of both the gate and the good shepherd are pretty self-explanatory. The first metaphor is that of the **gate to the sheepfold**. The sheep in the sheepfold represent the people of God and the gate represents Jesus. One only gets into the sheepfold through Jesus, and anyone who tries to get in another way is a **stranger** and a **thief** who wants only to steal or kill the sheep.

The second metaphor, obviously related to the first, is that of the **good shepherd** (also Jesus) who comes and goes in through the gate, who cares for the sheep, and lays his life down for the sheep, unlike a **hired hand** who will flee to save his own life when a wolf comes. Furthermore, Jesus says that the sheep and the good shepherd know each other just like he and the Father know each other, and that he has **other sheep** who are **not of this sheepfold**. He will bring them in too, and that way there will be **one flock** and **one shepherd**. Jesus is not only hinting at the inclusion of the Gentiles into the people of God, but when he speaks of having the authority to lay down his life and take it up again, he is also hinting that the way in which he will bring the Gentiles in will be through his death and resurrection.

The reaction to what Jesus says, not only here, but to everything he has said in this section set during the Feast of Tabernacles, is that there is division among "the Jews," in this context, probably not just the religious leaders, but the Jews as a whole. Some think he is crazy or has a demon, while others clearly see that a demon-possessed man wouldn't be saying what Jesus was saying and would be able to open the eyes of the blind.

### 6. Feast of Dedication to the Passover Conflict (10:22-12:50)

The **fifth major section (10:22-12:50)** spans the time from Hanukkah, also known as the Feast of Dedication (which happens in December), to the time of the Passover (which happens in April), at which Jesus will be crucified. Therefore, if we were to plot these events on a timeline, these events would have happened between Hanukkah of AD 29 up to Passover of AD 30.

The **first episode (10:22-42)** is set during **Hanukkah** and tells of yet another confrontation between Jesus and "the Jews" in Jerusalem. Once again, Jesus is in the Temple, specifically in the Portico of Solomon, the place that Luke tells us in the Book of Acts, where the early followers of Jesus would meet after the events of Pentecost, before the first real persecution of the Church took place after Stephen's martyrdom. At this time, "the Jews" challenge Jesus to openly declare he is the Christ (the Messiah). Jesus' response, though, isn't exactly straightforward, and he reiterates some of the things he has said earlier in John's Gospel. He says he's told them already, but they don't put their faith in him. He's told them through the works that he has done in the name of his Father—those works bear witness to who he is. They, though, don't put their faith in him because they aren't his sheep. His sheep know his voice and follow him, and they will be given the Life of the Age and won't be destroyed, because no one has the power to snatch them from his Father's hand, because **he and the Father are one**.

As soon as he claims to be one with God, "the Jews" want to stone him and tell him it isn't because of anything he has done, but because he has made himself out to be God—clearly blasphemy. In response, Jesus engages in some creative biblical interpretation by referring to **Psalm 82:6**, in which God says to human beings, *"I said you are 'gods.'"* In the original context, it seems God is condemning human rulers, saying that even though He has set them up in positions of power (and in that sense "gods" in a way), that they will suffer judgment and die like mere men. Jesus' point is that if Scripture itself refers to human beings as "gods," then how could they accuse him of blasphemy when he said, "I am the Son of God"?

Interestingly enough, it is clear when one reads Psalm 82 is that the reason God is condemning these human rulers ("gods") is that they were failing to do His work by caring for the lowly and needy but were instead siding with the wicked. In short, they were supposed to be doing God's work, but were instead letting themselves be corrupted by wicked men. Given that context, what Jesus says next makes more sense, when he tells them that if he isn't **doing his Father's work**, then they shouldn't put faith in him, but if he is doing his Father's work by caring for the lowly and needy (and as we've seen throughout John's Gospel, he most certainly is doing just that), then they should recognize that and understand that the Father is in him and he is in the Father. Not surprisingly, "the Jews" try to arrest him, but he escapes and gets across the Jordan River, to another jurisdiction where those in Jerusalem couldn't arrest him. John tells us that Jesus goes the area where John the Baptist had started baptizing and that more people put their faith in him there.

The **second episode (11:1-57)** is the story of the raising of Lazarus from the dead. We are not told exactly when this happened, but according to the timeline of the narrative, it happened sometime between Hanukkah and Passover. At the time of Lazarus' death in Bethany, Jesus and his disciples are back in Galilee. In any case, we are told that Lazarus is the brother of Mary and Martha, and that Mary was the one who anointed Jesus with perfume and wiped them with her hair. Admittedly, this is an odd place to put this bit of information, given that Mary's anointing of Jesus doesn't take place until the next episode in chapter 12.

In any case, we are told in 11:1-16 that when Lazarus falls sick, Mary and Martha send word to Jesus, but he doesn't immediately head off to Bethany.

Instead, he says that Lazarus' sickness won't result in death, but that it happened for the glory of God and so that the Son of God would be glorified through it. Two days later, Jesus finally tells his disciples that they are going to go back to Judea, but they warn him that "the Jews" were still looking to stone him. Jesus responds by echoing both what John says in his prologue about him being the light of the world and what Jesus himself said when he healed the blind man.

The point of the imagery is obvious. In Jesus, *the Logos made flesh*, was life, and that life was *the light of men*. So even though by going to Judea he was risking his life, since he was, in fact, the *light of the world*, he was going to go bring the *light of life* back to Lazarus. He first says he's going to wake Lazarus up, but when his disciples don't get it, he comes right out and tells them that Lazarus was dead and that he wants to go to him. Thomas, then (sarcastically), says, "Let's all go die with him!"

The episode shifts in 11:17-44 to Bethany and Jesus' raising of Lazarus. By the time Jesus gets to Bethany, Lazarus has been dead for four days. John tells us that Bethany was just two miles outside of Jerusalem and many Jews from Jerusalem had come to console Martha and Mary. When Jesus gets there, Martha tells him that if he had gotten there earlier, that Lazarus wouldn't have died. When Jesus tells her that Lazarus would resurrect, Martha says she knows that would happen on the **Last Day**, echoing the Jewish belief that the righteous dead would resurrect when the Kingdom of God arrives. It is at this time, though, that Jesus says yet another "I Am" statement, when he tells Martha, *"I am the resurrection and the life. The one who puts his faith in me, even if he dies, will live."* When he asks Martha if she has faith in this, she says yes, and declares that she believes he is the Christ, the one coming into the world. This episode thus echoes John the Baptist's initial declaration of the coming one when he was baptizing near Bethany in chapter 1.

In any case, when Mary learns that Jesus had come, she, and many of the Jews who had come to console her, go to him. As they get to the tomb, Jesus begins to cry. Some Jews realize just how much he loved Lazarus, while some others cynically say that if he had the power to open the eyes of the blind man, why couldn't he have the power to keep Lazarus from dying. Once at the tomb, when Jesus orders them to take the stone away, both Martha and Mary object and say that he had been dead for four days, but Jesus tells them that if they put their faith in him, they would see the glory of God. It is then that Jesus openly thanks the Father for hearing him, and then commands Lazarus to come out…and he does.

The episode shifts again in 11:45-57 to Jerusalem. As a result of Jesus' raising of Lazarus, many of the Jews who had come to console Mary and Martha ended up putting their faith in him. Some, though, went back to Jerusalem and told the chief priests and Pharisees what had happened, and this created a debate in the Sanhedrin as to what to do about Jesus. They were afraid that if more people started following him that the Romans would eventually try to crush Jesus' messianic movement, and when they do, they would destroy both the Temple and the nation itself. It is at that point that Caiaphas the chief priest said that it was better for one man to die on behalf of the people, so that the nation wouldn't be destroyed.

In other words, it is better to make sure Jesus dies so the Jewish nation won't be destroyed. The irony, as John says in 11:51-52, was that Caiaphas' suggestion actually was prophetic in a way that Caiaphas himself probably wasn't aware off. After all, Jesus *would die* on behalf of the nation, but not to save the Jewish nation from destruction (that ended up happening in AD 70), but rather to open the door to gathering the scattered children of God into one people. This comment not only echoes what John says in his prologue regarding who the true children of God are (1:11-13), but also Jesus' words about gathering sheep from other sheepfolds (10:16).

As a result of all this, Jesus no longer goes out in public in Judea. Instead, he stays out in the countryside, near the wilderness, near a town called Ephraim. Still, Passover is coming, and many were wondering if Jesus would dare come to Jerusalem. After all, the chief priests and Pharisees had ordered that if anyone knew where Jesus was, they should alert them so they could arrest him.

The **third episode (12:1-11)** takes place in Bethany, six days before Passover. Jesus and his disciples are visiting Lazarus, Mary, and Martha, when Mary takes a bottle of perfume, anoints Jesus' feet with it, and then dries his feet with her hair. Judas Iscariot objects and says the perfume should have been sold and the money be given to the poor. John, though, tells us Judas would steal money from the money bag and just wanted to sell the perfume so he could get more money for himself. Jesus defends Mary and says she had kept the perfume for the day of his burial, and that they would always have the poor to help, but they wouldn't always have him.

The reason this is significant is that many Jews believed Jesus was the Messiah, and their belief that the Messiah was *anointed to be the next king and to defeat their oppressors*, namely Rome. But here, Jesus is making it clear that he is a different kind of Messiah—he is *being anointed for burial*. In any case, John tells us that many people in Judea came to see, not only Jesus, but also Lazarus, and that because of Jesus' raising of Lazarus, more were putting their faith in Jesus. As a result, in a truly twisted move, the chief priests planned to kill, not only Jesus, but Lazarus as well.

The **fourth episode (12:12-19)** is somewhat similar to the accounts in the Synoptics. John tells us Jesus' entry into Jerusalem happened the **next day** after Mary anointed his feet in Bethany. John's description of Jesus' entry is similar to that of the Synoptics, in that we are told that people went out to meet Jesus, waving palm branches and singing **Psalm 118**, particularly 118:25-26: *"Hosanna! Blessed is the one who comes in the Name of the LORD! The King of Israel!"* In addition, we are told that Jesus rode in on a donkey and that served as an allusion to **Zechariah 9:9**. John tells us, though, that at the time, the disciples didn't make that connection, and that it was only after Jesus was glorified that they really got the significance of that action.

What John tells us next, though, is not in the Synoptics. In 12:17-19, John tells us that the people who had witnessed Jesus' raising of Lazarus earlier had been telling everyone what Jesus had done, and that precisely was the reason why so many in Jerusalem came out to see Jesus—they recognized Jesus' raising of Lazarus as a sign. In response, the Pharisees are exasperated and say in a hyperbolic, but also highly ironic, fashion, "Look! The world has gone off after him!"

The **fifth episode (12:20-36)** tells us of an encounter Jesus has with his disciples, Andrew and Philip, about certain Greeks who had expressed a desire to meet him. At first, it might seem that Jesus' response doesn't have anything to do with the request to meet with him. Let's break down what he says though. First, instead of a clear yes or no, Jesus says that the **time has come for the Son of Man to be glorified**. He then says that a **grain of wheat must fall to the ground and die** in order to bear much fruit, and that the one who loves his own soul will destroy it, whereas the one who hates his own soul in this world will keep it into the **Life of the Age**. Simply put, Jesus declines to meet with the Greeks, but hints that the Gospel would eventually go out to them. It is interesting to see that Jesus equates his glorification with his death and points to the fact that his death is the necessary prerequisite to his glorification and to the Gospel going out to the Gentiles. Accepting suffering and death in his age/world is the key to the salvation of one's soul in the life of the age to come.

Second, that is why Jesus then says that to serve him means to follow him, even into death. If one does that, the Father will honor that person. That is why, even though Jesus might be tempted to ask the Father to **save him from this hour** (of his upcoming death), he realizes his entire purpose was to come to **this hour** and sacrifice his life so that the Father's Name would be glorified. At that point, John says that a voice from Heaven said, *"I have glorified it, and I will glorify it again."* Some think it was only thunder, while others think an angel had spoken to him. Jesus tells them that the voice was for their sake, and that the **judgment of this world** was about to happen, when the **ruler of this world would be cast out**. He further says that when he is **lifted up**, that he would **draw everyone** to himself.

It is clear that all of Jesus' talk throughout the Gospel about how "his hour had not yet come" was a reference to his crucifixion. We see here that it is through Jesus' crucifixion that God would be glorified, that the judgment of the world would be realized, and that the ruler of the world (Satan) would be cast out and lose his grip and authority over God's creation. It is through Jesus' crucifixion (as the Good Shepherd who lays his life down for his sheep) that everyone from all peoples and nationalities would be drawn to him (the sheep from other sheepfolds).

In addition to all that, the last part of what Jesus says in this episode also echoes what he told Nicodemus in chapter 3: (A) How he would be "lifted up" and would draw everyone to him; (B) How those who follow him/put their faith in him would receive the Life of the Age; and (C) How the judgment of the world was at hand, and how light had come into the darkness, but that people loved darkness more than the light, and therefore showed themselves to be judged already.

Clearly, though, the crowd does not "get" what Jesus is saying about the necessity of his death. They say that since the Torah speaks of Christ **remaining into the Age**, then why would it be necessary for the Son of man to be **lifted up** (crucified). In response, Jesus implores them to **walk in the light** while they still have it, so that the **darkness wouldn't take them down**, and to **put their faith in the light** while they still have it, so that they could become **Sons of light**, because the light (he) wouldn't be around much longer. After saying that, Jesus goes off and hides from them. This is actually the last time he is seen in the public at large.

It is hard to explain what Jesus is saying here, just as it would be hard to "explain" the artistic beauty of a Van Gogh painting. But if we recognize the same images and themes that John has been teasing out throughout his Gospel, we should be able to appreciate the message being conveyed through these images and metaphors: *Christ is the light of the world that has come into darkness to open people's eyes, so they could put their faith in him and walk in the light. He draws all people to him by being lifted up on a cross, being buried, but then resurrecting. Therefore, to walk in his light means to follow him into death, like a grain of wheat going into the ground, but then raising up and resurrecting into the Life of the Age, becoming Sons of light who bear much fruit that goes beyond the borders of ethnic Israel.*

The **sixth episode (12:37-50)** tells of the mixed reaction of the Jews to Jesus. John tells us that many of "the Jews" don't put their faith in him, despite all the signs he had done. John also says that their rejection of him was a fulfillment of **Isaiah 53:1**, which asks, *"Lord, who has put their faith in our report? To whom has the arm of the Lord been revealed?"* In other words, Jesus had clearly presented his message to his fellow Jews and had revealed it to them, but most didn't put their faith in him. John says the reason they didn't could be seen in Isaiah 6:10—God had blinded their eyes and made their hearts hard so that they wouldn't respond in faith. It is important to know, though, that in the original context of Isaiah 6, God has called Isaiah to prophecy to the people of Judah, but He tells Isaiah they wouldn't listen in Isaiah 6:9-10 precisely because they had become like the idols they worshipped. They had eyes, but couldn't spiritually see, and had ears, but couldn't spiritually hear. Thus, God had "blinded their eyes" in the sense that He allowed them to become like the things they worshipped. That is the same thing John is saying about the Jews of Jesus' day. *Most of them were spiritually blind and calloused because they were, for all practical purposes, idol-worshippers who had made the Torah itself into their own idol, and therefore couldn't see that the Torah was pointing to Jesus all along.*

John does say, though, that many of the Jewish religious leaders did put their faith in Jesus but kept quiet about it because they were afraid of the Pharisees and didn't want to be banned from the synagogue. As should be obvious by now, John is using the term "Pharisees" as a general statement for the Jewish religious leaders of the time. In Jesus' actual day, the Pharisees were a religious sect who were quite distinct from the Sadducees, who were in charge of the Temple and essentially ran the Sanhedrin.

John hasn't mentioned the Sadducees once, though, and gives the impression that the Pharisees ran the Temple, along with the chief priests. The reason he does this can be explained when you realize that John wrote his Gospel closer to AD 90, a good 20 years after the destruction of the Temple in AD 70, when the slow "divorce" between the Jesus movement and traditional Judaism that had been going on from AD 30 to AD 70 was finalized to the point where there were now two distinct religions: Christianity and Judaism. After the destruction of Jerusalem and the Temple in AD 70, the only two Jewish sects that survived were Pharisaism, which evolved into what became Rabbinic Judaism and from which modern Judaism descended, and the Jesus movement, which obviously became known as Christianity. That is why John uses the term "Pharisees" to denote most everything Jewish in Jesus' day—because in John's day, outside of Christianity, Pharisaism was the only thing left of pre-AD 70 Judaism.

In any case, after pointing out that the reaction of "the Jews" to Jesus was divided in 12:37-43, John ends this episode (and indeed the first part of his entire Gospel: **The Book of Signs**) with the words of Jesus that really do summarize the main points that were made throughout John 1-12:

(1) The one who puts his faith in Jesus, puts his faith in the **one who sent Jesus**.
(2) The one who sees Jesus, sees the **one who sent Jesus**.
(3) Jesus is the **light of the world**, and the one who puts his faith in Jesus **won't stay in the darkness**.
(4) Jesus **doesn't judge** the one who doesn't keep his words, but rather **has come to save the world**.
(5) The one who rejects Jesus will be judged **someone else on the Last Day**.
(6) Jesus has spoken what the Father has commanded him to say, and His commandment is the **Life of the Age**.

### 7. The Last Supper (13:1-38)

The **seventh section (13:1-38)** is the account of the Last Supper and is directly tied in with the subsequent section of chapters 14-17 that consists of a long monologue by Jesus on the night of the Last Supper. In this section, though, there are four episodes. The **first episode (13:1-20)** tells of Jesus' act of washing his disciples' feet and then his explanation of why he did it. The episode opens by telling us that the **hour had come** for Jesus to go away from the world to the Father. All throughout John's Gospel, beginning at the wedding at Cana, there have been mentions of Jesus' hour having not yet come. Here, on the eve of Passover, is when his hour finally comes. Indeed, John tells us that the **devil had already entered the heart of Judas Iscariot** and that Judas had already decided to betray Jesus.

Interestingly enough, unlike the Synoptics, John does not tell of Jesus' actions with the bread and the wine. Instead, he chooses to focus on Jesus' washing of the disciples' feet. When he comes to Peter, though, Peter objects because, after all, it wasn't proper to have a leader wash the feet of his followers. Jesus tells Peter, though, that if he didn't let him wash his feet, then he would have no share in him. After Peter hyperbolically asks Jesus to wash not just his feet, but his hands and head as well, Jesus reassures both him and the other disciples that they were clean, with the exception of one person (whom we the readers already know is Judas Iscariot).

After this action, Jesus then explains its significance. It boils down to this: He is their teacher and Lord, and therefore they should try to imitate him. Therefore, if he took the form of a servant and washed their feet, if they want to be like him, they needed to become servants and "wash the feet" of others. Obviously, this is more about than just washing people's feet, but about humbling themselves and serving others in order to make Christ known. The episode then ends by Jesus telling them that he knows which one of them would "lift up his heel" against him. He says he is telling them of it ahead of time, so that when it, in fact, happens, they would maintain their faith in him.

The **second episode (13:21-30)** dovetails from what Jesus just has said when he comes right out and tells them he knows that one of them is going to betray him. When Peter gets the "disciple whom Jesus loved" to ask Jesus who it is, Jesus tells him it is the disciple to whom he gives the bread to after he dips it—that disciple is Judas. John then tells us that when Jesus gives Judas the bread, he essentially tells Judas to get it over with and do what he was going to do quickly. Satan "went into Judas" and Judas quickly left. John tells us that the other disciples thought Jesus was just sending Judas out to buy some things they needed for Passover, or perhaps to give some money to the poor. Interestingly, John makes it a point to say that when Judas left, **it was night-time**. Not only was it literally night, but it further highlights the light/darkness imagery John has employed throughout his Gospel.

The **third episode (13:31-38)** covers what happens at the Last Supper after Judas leaves. Jesus tells his disciples that he, the Son of Man, has been glorified, and that God has been glorified with him—again, emphasizing Jesus' equality with God. He then tells his disciples that he will be with them only a little while longer and that when he goes away that they won't be able to come. This is pretty much what Jesus had told "the Jews" in 8:21-33. In any case, Jesus then gives his disciples a **new commandment**—to love one another. When Peter presses Jesus on where he is going, Jesus simply tells Peter that he won't be able to follow him right now, but that eventually he would. When Peter insists that he would be willing to lay down his life for Jesus, Jesus tells them that one day, in fact, he would end up doing just that, but that in the immediate future, by the next morning actually, before the rooster crows, Peter would deny Jesus three times.

### 8. Last Supper Teaching (14:1-17:26)

The **eighth section (14:1-17:26)** consists of four chapters of an extended speech by Jesus on the night of his arrest. The purpose of the extended speech is obviously to highlight many of the theological points John has made throughout his Gospel. All in all, there are six different parts in the extended speech. In the **first part (14:1-14)**, Jesus emphasizes the following points: (1) **His being equal to God the Father**: He tells his disciples to have faith in God and in him. When Philip asks Jesus to show them the Father, Jesus tells Philip that if he's seen Jesus, he's seen the Father, and that he is in the Father and the Father is in him. (2) **His going away and his returning**: Jesus talks about going to "prepare a place" for them in his Father's house and coming back to get them. (3) **Another "I Am" Statement**: When Jesus tells them they know the way to where he is going, Thomas says, "No we don't!" In response, Jesus says, *"I am the way, the truth, and the life. No one comes to the Father except through me."* What Jesus is getting at in this part is that the way to full reconciliation with God the Father, the way to being glorified, is the way of putting one's faith in him and following him.

In the **second part (14:15-31)**, Jesus then tells them about the coming Holy Spirit, who will empower them to do all the things he has commanded them to do. He makes the following points: (1) **To love him is to keep his commandments**. (2) **The coming of the Encourager, the Spirit of Truth**: Since Jesus will be going away, he tells them that the Holy Spirit will be with them *until the end of the age*. He will teach them and remind them of everything Jesus had told them until Jesus returns in glory at the end of the old age and the consummation of the new age. (3) **His going away and his returning**: Again, he is going away, but will return at the end of the age, at which time he and the Father will dwell with His people. (4) **The unity of the Church in Christ**: Not only does Jesus reiterate that he is in the Father and the Father is in him, but he then takes it a step further and tells them that they are in him, and he is in them—through Christ, the Church is taken up into the life of God. (5) **His upcoming death**: Jesus tells them he doesn't have much longer with them because the "ruler of the world" is coming, meaning Satan.

In the **third part (15:1-17)**, Jesus makes another "I Am" statement, this time using the extended metaphor of the **vine and branches**: Jesus is the vine, the Father is the farmer, and his followers are the branches. Jesus tells them that God will cut off any branches that don't bear fruit and will prune those that are bearing fruit, so that they can bear even more fruit. Therefore, they need to remain in him if they are to continue bearing fruit. If they don't, then they will be cut off, gathered up, and burned. And the way to bear fruit, the way to remain in him, is to keep his commandment, and it really is just one commandment: **love one another, like I have loved you**. He has already shown them what this means by becoming a servant and washing their feet, and he will fully show them what this means when he lays down his life and allows himself to be crucified. That is why he tells them that there is **no greater love than to lay down one's life for his friends**. With that, he tells them they are no longer servants, but his friends…if they do what he commands and love each other. If they do that, they will **bear much fruit**, and that fruit will last.

In the **fourth part (15:18-16:15)**, Jesus warns about coming persecution and how the coming **Spirit of Truth** will be with them during persecution. Much of what he says echoes the very beginning of John's Gospel, where we were told about how the **Logos/Light of Life** came into the world, to his own people, and how they rejected him. Here, Jesus tells his disciples, "That happened to me, and that is what is going to happen to you too. They'll hate and persecute you, just like they hated and persecuted me." In saying this, Jesus again emphasizes his oneness with the Father, for to hate him is to hate the Father. In any case, because he had come and done the works the Father had sent him to do, their rejection of him reveals their guilt and sin.

Jesus then again tells them of the coming Holy Spirit who, through them, will bear witness to him. They, though, will be "thrown out of the synagogue," meaning they'll be cast out of Jewish society. They'll also be persecuted and killed by their fellow Jews who will think they're serving God by doing so—this was exactly the situation with Paul before his Damascus Road experience. Jesus then tells them again that it is better that he goes away, so that the Holy Spirit could come and expose the world of sin (those who don't put their faith in Christ), righteousness (Jesus' going to the Father), and judgment (the ruler of this world has been judged). Jesus says he wants to tell them more but isn't able to do so. But when the Spirit of

Truth comes, he'll guide them in all truth, glorify Jesus, and will tell them everything that comes from Jesus—and everything the Father has is his.

The **fifth part 16:16-33** is a bit more of a dialogue between Jesus and his disciples. Once again, he tells them that they soon won't see him anymore, but then later on they will see him again. Obviously, they don't understand what he's talking about, because they aren't expecting him to be killed, let alone resurrected a few days later. But Jesus is telling them this ahead of time, because he knows what will soon happen and how traumatic it will be for them. That is why he tells them they are going to weep and mourn as the world rejoices (meaning, over his crucifixion), but that soon after that, their sorrow will turn to joy (at the resurrection). Jesus then equates his upcoming death and resurrection with a woman giving birth—there is tremendous pain at the hour of birth, when the labor pains begin, but then once the baby is born, there is tremendous joy. Once that happens, "on that day," Jesus tells them that whatever they ask the Father in Jesus' name will be given to them.

Jesus realizes that they don't fully understand what he's telling them, but he says soon it will be clear. He then reassures them that the Father loves them *as friends* because they have loved Jesus *as a friend*—again, there is that emphasis on the equality of Jesus and God the Father. Jesus then again tells them that he is leaving the world and going to the Father. In response, the disciples reiterate their faith in him, but Jesus responds by telling them that the **hour has come for you to be scattered** and for him to be left alone, of course, he won't really be alone because the Father is with him. He then tells them that they are going to suffer tribulation in this world, but they should take courage, because he has conquered the world (ironically, through his death…and resurrection).

The **sixth part (17:1-26)** is known as Jesus' **high priestly prayer**. It is the last thing he says before he is arrested, tried, and crucified. Much of the prayer is just a reinforcement of many of the things he has said throughout John's Gospel. Here, on the night of his arrest, he says that the **hour has come**—it is in the events of the crucifixion and subsequent resurrection that the Father will glorify the Son and the Son will glorify the Father. It is through his death and resurrection that the Son is given **authority over all flesh**, and that authority is what empowers him to **give the Life of the Age** to those whom the Father has given him, to those who put their faith in him. The way Jesus defines the **Life of the Age** is interesting to note. It is **to know the true God, and the one whom God sent, Jesus the Christ**.

Jesus then declares that he has done everything God has given him to do, so now is the time for the Father to glorify Himself in Christ.

After that, Jesus declares he is coming to the Father, and he prays that the Father will keep his followers in His name so that **they will be one just like the Son and the Father are one**. He declares that only Judas, the "son of destruction," has been lost, and he prays that the Father keep his disciples from the Evil One. He then says he is sending his followers into the world, just like the Father had sent him into the world. He says he made himself holy for them, so that they could be made holy in the truth. Again, he prays that his followers **be one as he and the Father are one**, so that the world may have faith that the Father had sent Jesus the Son. He then states that he has given his followers the glory that the Father had given him, for the purpose of them **becoming fully matured into one**.

The world didn't know the Father, but Jesus the Son knows the Father, and his followers know that he knows the Father and that the Father sent him.

### 9. Betrayal to Burial (18:1-19:42)

The **ninth section (18:1-19:42)** tells of Jesus' arrest, trials, crucifixion, and burial. Although the basic parts of the account are similar to that of the Synoptics, John includes a number of different elements. The **first episode (18:1-11)** is that of the arrest in Gethsemane, although John doesn't actually identify the garden as Gethsemane—he only says it was a garden across the Kidron Valley. John tells us that the group who came to arrest Jesus came from the chief priests and Pharisees. It is important to note that it was not Roman soldiers who came to arrest Jesus. This was entirely done by the Temple establishment. Only later, in the morning, do they take Jesus to Pilate. When they come to arrest Jesus, even though Judas leads them to the place, John does not include Judas' kiss as a way to identify Jesus. Instead, Jesus asks them who they are looking for, and when they say, "Jesus of Nazareth," he responds (keeping in line with the "I Am" statements throughout John), "I am!" and tells them to leave the disciples alone and only take him.

At that point, John tells us that Peter draws his sword and cuts off the ear of Malchus, a servant of the chief priest. Although Mark tells of this as well, he leaves out Peter's name. According to Church tradition, Mark got his information for his Gospel from Peter, so one can see how when Peter was telling Mark about that night, he conveniently left out the part where he was the one who cut off the ear! John, though, has no qualms about who it was—Peter! John also gives the name of the servant who was struck, although he doesn't mention that Jesus healed the servant's ear. In any case, Jesus tells Peter to throw down his sword and insists that he must "drink the cup" that his Father had given him to drink.

The **second episode (18:12-27)** is that of Jesus' night trial, along with Peter's denial that happened in the courtyard, outside of the house of the chief priest. John's account is a bit different, in that whereas the Synoptics tell us that the other members of the Sanhedrin are gathered against Jesus, here in John it just seems to be the chief priest, along with the arresting officers, who question Jesus. More specifically, it is **Annas, the father-in-law of Caiaphas**, the chief priest for that year. Annas questions Jesus about his teaching and Jesus responds by saying he had always taught in public, so Annas could just ask anyone who had heard him teach in public. One of the officers feels Jesus is being disrespectful, so he slaps Jesus, but Jesus challenges the officer to explain exactly what he had said that was bad. After that, Annas sends Jesus to Caiaphas, but John does not tell us anything about that encounter.

While all of this is happening inside the house of the chief priest, Peter and the "other disciple" (generally assumed to be the author of the Gospel) wait out in the courtyard. John tells us that this "other disciple" knew the chief priest, and that is why he was able to talk to the gatekeeper to let Peter in the courtyard as well. John's account of Peter's denial is slightly different than the accounts in the Synoptics. Here, there is no buildup of denying Jesus three times. Instead, the crowd outside ask him if he was one of Jesus' disciples, which he denies, and then a relative of Malchus (the servant whose ear Peter cut off), who apparently was there in the garden at Jesus' arrest also claims to have seen Peter in the garden, and again Peter denies it. At that point, the rooster crows.

The **third episode (18:28-19:15)** takes place the next morning. For some reason, John skips over the confrontation between Jesus and Caiaphas and the Sanhedrin that the Synoptics tell us about. Instead, he just gets to the next morning, when Caiaphas and his group take Jesus before Pilate in the praetorium. At first, when Pilate asks them what the charges are, they evade the question and just say, "If it wasn't bad, we wouldn't be handing him over to you." Pilate, clearly not impressed, tells them to deal with it themselves, but then they tell him they weren't allowed to kill anyone.

At that point, Pilate questions Jesus, and his questioning makes it obvious that the chief priest's people had told Pilate that Jesus was claiming to be the king of the Jews, for that is what Pilate asks Jesus. In response, Jesus makes it clear that although he is a king, his kingdom is not of this world. Simply put, it was clear that Jesus didn't consider himself a king in any political sense that would be deemed a threat to Caesar. When he tells Pilate that he had come to bear witness to the truth, Pilate cynically asks, "What is truth?"

In any case, it is clear to Pilate that Jesus wasn't guilty of anything and that for some reason the chief priest wanted Jesus dead. Since Pilate made it a habit as governor to irritate the Jewish religious leaders every chance he got, he told the chief priest that he couldn't find any accusation against Jesus. But (presumably because it was Passover?) he told them he'd give them a choice—he could release either Jesus, the so-called "King of the Jews," or Barabbas, who was a violent revolutionary. The choice is very telling, especially given the reality of what eventually happened during the Jewish War of AD 66-70. The choice of the chief priest's people to release Barabbas instead of Jesus foreshadows the Jews choosing the way of zealotry and rebellion against Rome that sparked the Jewish War and led to the complete destruction of both Jerusalem and the Temple.

Pilate decides to flog Jesus in an attempt to appease the chief priest's people. In typical Roman fashion, Jesus is not only flogged, but he is forced to wear a crown of thorns and a purple robe, while the Roman soldiers mockingly hail him as the king of the Jews. Pilate assumes such a punishment would be enough, but the chief priest's people insist that Jesus be crucified. When Pilate again insists that there was no valid charge against Jesus, the chief priests let the cat out of the bag and tell Pilate they want him crucified because he claimed to be the Son of God. That gets Pilate worried, so he calls Jesus back in and asks who he is, but Jesus doesn't respond. Exasperated, Pilate tells Jesus that he has the authority to either crucify him or let him go, to which Jesus responds by telling him that he wouldn't have any authority if it were not given to him from above, and that the chief priests and their people were, in fact, guilty of the greater sin.

One more time, Pilate goes out to the chief priests and their people and attempts to release Jesus. At that point, though, the chief priests pull their trump card and warn Pilate that if he does let Jesus go, that he was **no friend of Caesar**. That was essentially a threat that said, *"If you release Jesus, we will send word to Caesar himself that one of his governors let a guy who claimed to be a king (and hence a threat to Caesar)* *walk, and Caesar will not be happy, and you will be in big trouble."* With that, perhaps Pilate decides Jesus isn't worth the hassle, and so he sits on the judgment seat and tells them, "Here is your king!" When they continue to call for Jesus' crucifixion, Pilate asks them, "Do you want me to crucify your king?" to which they shockingly reply, "We have no king but Caesar!"

The **fourth episode (19:16-37)** tells of the crucifixion. Pilate hands Jesus over to be crucified and they take him to Golgotha (the Place of the Skull) to be crucified with two other men. The sign Pilate orders to be placed above Jesus' head on the cross is: **Jesus the Nazarene: The King of the Jews**. The chief priests object and tell Pilate to have it say, "This man said, 'I am King of the Jews,'" but Pilate refuses to change it. They got what they wanted. He was done capitulating to their demands.

As far as the crucifixion itself is concerned, John tells of the soldiers' dividing Jesus' garments and cast lots for his tunic, and how that fulfilled **Psalm 22:18**. John also tells us that Jesus' mother, his aunt, Mary the wife of Clopas, and Mary Magdalene were there to witness his crucifixion. It is then Jesus tells the "beloved disciple" to take his mother in and to care for her. A short time later, Jesus says he is thirsty, so they fill a sponge with sour wine, and after he takes a drink, he says, *"It is fulfilled!"* and died.

Since it was Preparation Day for the Passover, "the Jews" want the bodies down and taken away, so that they wouldn't be up on the crosses over the Sabbath. So, Pilate orders the soldiers to break their legs to speed up their death, but when they come to Jesus, he was already dead. To make sure, they pierce his side and blood and water come out. John adds his own editorial note to tell his readers that he actually saw this happen and that he is telling the truth so that his audience could have faith. He then says this happened to fulfill the scripture (found in **Psalm 34:20, Exodus 12:46,** and **Numbers 9:12**), *"Not one of his bones will be broken,"* and (**Zechariah 12:10**), *"They will look on the one they have pierced."*

The **fifth episode (19:38-42)** tells of Jesus' burial. At that point, Joseph of Arimathea and Nicodemus, whom John calls "secret disciples," ask Pilate for the body. John has already told us that Nicodemus was a "ruler of the Jews" and we know from the Synoptics that Joseph of Arimathea was a member of the Sanhedrin, so we can reasonably assume that both men did not approve of what the chief priest and Temple authorities had done, but were too afraid to say anything at the time, but now that Jesus was dead, they summoned their courage to at least give Jesus a proper burial. They wrapped Jesus' body in linen cloths and brought myrrh and aloes to prepare the body. Since it was late in the day, though, they placed Jesus' body in a nearby, new tomb.

### 10. Resurrection and Post-Resurrection Appearances (20:1-21:25)

The **final section (20:1-21:25)** of John's Gospel is that of Jesus' resurrection and a number of post-resurrection appearances. The **first episode (20:1-10)** is of resurrection morning, when the women, and later Peter and the "beloved disciple" go to the empty tomb. On the first day of the week (that would be Sunday morning), when Mary Magdalene goes to the tomb, she finds the stone rolled away and the body of Jesus missing, so she immediately goes and tells Peter and the "beloved disciple" that the body is missing. It is interesting to note that John' account here is different than that of the Synoptics in two basic ways. First, John mentions only Mary Magdalene, and not the other women that Matthew, Mark, and Luke mention. Second, unlike what we read in the Synoptics, there are no angels in the tomb at the time Mary discovers the empty tomb.

John's resurrection account continues in ways that are different than what we find in the Synoptics. After discovering the empty tomb, Mary Magdalene goes and tells Peter and the "beloved disciple" about it. They both race to the tomb (John adds the odd note that the "beloved disciple" beat Peter to the tomb), look inside, and see the linen sheets and face cloth lying there. John then tells us that when the "beloved disciple" saw this, he had faith, and *up to that point* the disciples had not understood from Scripture that it was necessary for Jesus to rise from the dead. This implies that it was the "beloved disciple" who first "got it."

Now, neither Matthew nor Mark say anything about Peter and the "beloved disciple" visiting the tomb, and Luke only briefly mentions that Peter went to the tomb. On top of that, because all three other Gospels have the women's encounter with the angels at the moment they first discover the empty tomb, their message to the disciples is clearly different. In the Synoptics, the message is that angels had appeared to them and told them that Jesus was resurrected. Here in John, though, since Mary has no initial encounter with angels, her message to Peter and the "beloved disciple" is nothing more than the body was missing.

In any case, once Peter and the "beloved disciple" leave, it is then that John has Mary encounter **two men in white** (angels). She stays behind, outside the tomb, crying. At that point, she looks inside the tomb again and see these two men in white. She evidently doesn't get they are angels, because when then ask her why she's crying, she says, *"They took the body, and I don't know where they've put him!"* She then turns around and bumps into Jesus himself—still, though, she doesn't realize that it is Jesus. In fact, John tells us that she thought it was the gardener. When Jesus asks her why she's crying, she asks him if he had taken the body, and if so, to tell her where he put it. At that point, Jesus says, "Mary!" and she immediately recognizes him and hugs him. Jesus then tells her to let him go because he hasn't yet **gone to the Father**. Instead, he tells her to go tells **his brothers** that he is going to *"my Father and your Father, my God and your God."* It is then that Mary goes to the disciples (not just Peter and the "beloved disciple") and tells them that she had seen the resurrected Jesus.

The **second episode (20:19-29)** tells of Jesus' appearance to the disciples on that Sunday night, without Thomas being present, and then a second appearance to the disciples, with Thomas present, eight days later. That night, he appears to them as they are in a room with locked doors, because they were afraid of "the Jews." When he appears, he shows them his hands and his side to prove to them that he had really physically resurrected from the dead. He then tells them that he is going to "send them" just as the Father had "sent him," and he **breathes on them**, and they **receive the Holy Spirit**. He then tells them that if they forgive sins, those sins are forgiven, and if they withhold forgiveness, then it is withheld.

For some reason, Thomas was not there that night, so he didn't encounter Jesus. When the other disciples tell him about what had happened, he refuses to believe it. Assuming that they told him that Jesus showed them his hands and his side, Thomas says that unless he personally witnesses it, he won't believe it. So, **eight days later**, Jesus appears to the disciples, along with Thomas, in that same room. Jesus invites Thomas to inspect his hands and his side, and then encourages him to put his faith in him. Thomas responds with, "My Lord and my God!" This echoes a bit of what Nathanael says back in chapter 1, when he says that Jesus is the Son of God and the King of Israel. Back then, Jesus told Nathanael that he would see greater things still, and here Jesus tells Thomas that even though he has believed after seeing, that those who believe without seeing are blessed.

The **third episode (20:30-31)** is hardly an episode at all. It is just an editorial comment by John in which he tells us about the purpose of his book. He first says that Jesus did **many other signs** that he didn't include in the book, and then says that the purpose of the book was so that people could have faith that Jesus is the Christ, the Son of God, and that through faith in him life in his name was possible.

The **fourth episode (21:1-14)** takes place at some later time, when Jesus revealed himself a third time to some of the disciples (Peter, Thomas, Nathaniel from Cana, James, John, and two other disciples) by the Sea of Tiberias, up in Galilee. They had been fishing all night but had caught nothing. At daybreak, Jesus appears on the beach and calls out to them and asks them if they caught anything. When they tell him no, he tells them to drop their nets on the other side of the boat. When they do, they haul in a great catch of fish. Peter then realizes it is Jesus, so he dives in the water and swims to the shore, while the other disciples drag the net in. By the time they get to shore, Jesus already has a fire going, along with some fish and bread. John tells us that the catch of fish totaled 153 fish, but the net wasn't torn.

The **final episode (21:15-23)** takes place that same morning, after breakfast, when Jesus has a private conversation with Peter. Three times Jesus asks Peter if he loves him. The first two times, Jesus uses the Greek word *agapeo*, which conveys a deep love and loyalty to someone, and Peter responds those two times by saying yes, but using the Greek word *phileo*, which conveys brotherly love. The two words are obviously similar, but it is striking that Peter doesn't use the word Jesus uses. In both of those cases, Jesus responds by telling Peter to "feed my lambs" and "shepherd my sheep." The third time, when Jesus asks Peter if he loves him, though, Jesus uses *phileo*, and Peter responds by saying, "You know everything. You know I do." And to that, Jesus again tells him, "Feed my sheep." But then Jesus essentially tells Peter that one day he will suffer martyrdom when he tells Peter that when he gets older, he will stretch out his hands and someone will take him where he doesn't want to go. Nevertheless, Peter is to follow him. John tells us that this was to indicate what kind of death with which Peter would glorify God. According to Church tradition, Peter died in Rome at some point in the mid-60s, during Nero's persecutions, when Peter was crucified upside down.

In any case Peter then notices the "beloved disciple" following him and Jesus, so he asks Jesus about what would happen to him. Jesus tells Peter that if he wanted to keep the "beloved disciple" alive until he came back, what business of that was his? All that Peter had to worry about was following Jesus. John adds a bit of an editorial comment to clarify what Jesus meant, because apparently, there was a rumor in the early Christian community that the "beloved disciple" would never die, but John makes it clear that Jesus didn't actually say that but was only giving a hypothetical.

John ends with a **two-verse epilogue (21:24-25)** in which he says that he, the writer of the Gospel, is the "beloved disciple" and that he bears witness that everything he wrote in his Gospel is true. He tells us Jesus many more things, but that if everything Jesus had done had actually been written down, that the world wouldn't be big enough to hold all the books (clearly a hyperbolic statement).

# REVELATION

**Time of Writing**: The book of Revelation was written by John (either John the Apostle or John the Elder), who was exiled on the island of Patmos around AD 95. He was writing to seven specific churches in Asia Minor (modern day Turkey) during a time of empire-wide persecution of Christians by the Roman emperor Domitian.

**Background**:

Because Revelation is so unique, it is important we spell out exactly what it is up front. If you want to really understand Revelation, you have to put aside many of the "end times" assumptions most people have picked up from things like the *Left Behind Series*. John was a real person who wrote to real people at the end of the first century, therefore Revelation **meant something to them**. Whatever the original message was to them, *that is the inspired message we need to try to understand*. Therefore, the place to begin is a few words about the genre, or more properly, *genres*, of Revelation.

First, Revelation is **an apocalypse**. Apocalypses were a distinct genre of literature that was very popular among both Jews and Christians from between the years 200 BC to AD 200. We in the 21st century simply don't have this kind of literature today—that's why Revelation sounds so weird to us: we have no reference point for it. Apocalypses were mostly written during times of persecution, and they looked forward to a time when God would finally fulfill His promises to His people. Like any genre of literature, apocalypses had certain defining characteristics:

1. It was concerned with the **salvation** of God's people and the **judgment** of God's enemies.
2. They were almost always written during times of **persecution**.
3. They no longer looked for God's salvation and vindication to happen **within history**, but rather looked for God to bring a violent **end to history**.
4. They were **literary works**, meaning they weren't like the prophets who proclaimed their prophecies orally, only to have them written down later on.
5. They contained **highly symbolic language**: dreams, visions, strange-looking beasts.
6. Within the works of almost all apocalypses was a command that they be **"sealed up"** until the end of time. Therefore, when they were written down and read, the implication to the reader obviously was, "Yes, the end is here—this has been unsealed, so read it!"

Second, Revelation is unique among apocalyptic literature in that it also claims to be **a prophecy** as well. We need to remember, though, that prophecy does not simply mean a prediction of future events. First and foremost, it means that God is speaking directly to the present situation. In the case of the book of Revelation, the present situation was one of Christians being persecuted by Rome. Since Revelation claims to be a prophecy, that entails another difference between it and other apocalypses. One of the typical features in apocalyptic literature was that they were written in a time of spiritual dryness, and they looked forward to a time when God would finally "pour out His Spirit" on His people.

John, though, claims that Revelation is, in fact, the product of God's pouring out of His Spirit. That is why Revelation claims to be a **Spirit-inspired message** to God's people. It was a prophecy that revealed to them what was really going on "behind the scenes," if you will. The early Christians were suffering persecution at the hands of the Roman Empire. Why? Where was Christ in all of this? The book of Revelation is a Spirit-inspired prophecy that speaks to those very real events.

Third, Revelation is **a letter** John wrote to seven actual churches in Asia Minor. Its message, even though it is an apocalypse, was not mean to be "sealed up until the end of time," because for John and the early Christians, *the end times had already begun with the resurrection of Jesus and the out-pouring of the Holy Spirit at Pentecost*. Since Revelation is a letter, it was written to address very real concerns of the actual historical situations of these seven churches. Therefore, the ultimate purpose of Revelation was to encourage these seven churches who were being victimized by the first empire-wide persecution of Christians. Since that's the case, we must do our best to understand the historical context of that situation which John was writing about.

## The Big Things to Know About Revelation

A. **What's Being Revealed?** What God is doing in the course of history. The bulk of Revelation is not about "telling the future" regarding what will happen at the end of time. Revelation is revealing to Christians in AD 95 how their current sufferings played into God's plan to bring about salvation and the New Creation.
B. **A Warning to Christians Tempted to Get in Bed with the Whore:** Revelation also warns Christians about "getting too comfy" with the seductiveness of the Roman Empire. This also applies to Christians today.
C. **Call to be Faithful Witnesses, even to the Death:** When Christians are faced with suffering, Revelation challenges them to stay faithful to Christ. For when you suffer like Christ suffered, you bear witness to the truth of the Gospel. And that is how Christ's victory is achieved—*through suffering and death, and then out the other side in glory*.
D. **Contrasts Galore**: The Whore vs. the Bride; Rome/Babylon vs. New Jerusalem; The Woman's Offspring vs. the Dragon's Offspring; The Beast vs. the Lamb; The

Imperial White Horse vs. Christ on the White Horse; The Wasteland vs. the New Eden

**E. Tribulation and Wrath**: Tribulation is what Christians should expect to encounter. Wrath is what those who inflict tribulation on Christians will receive as punishment from God.

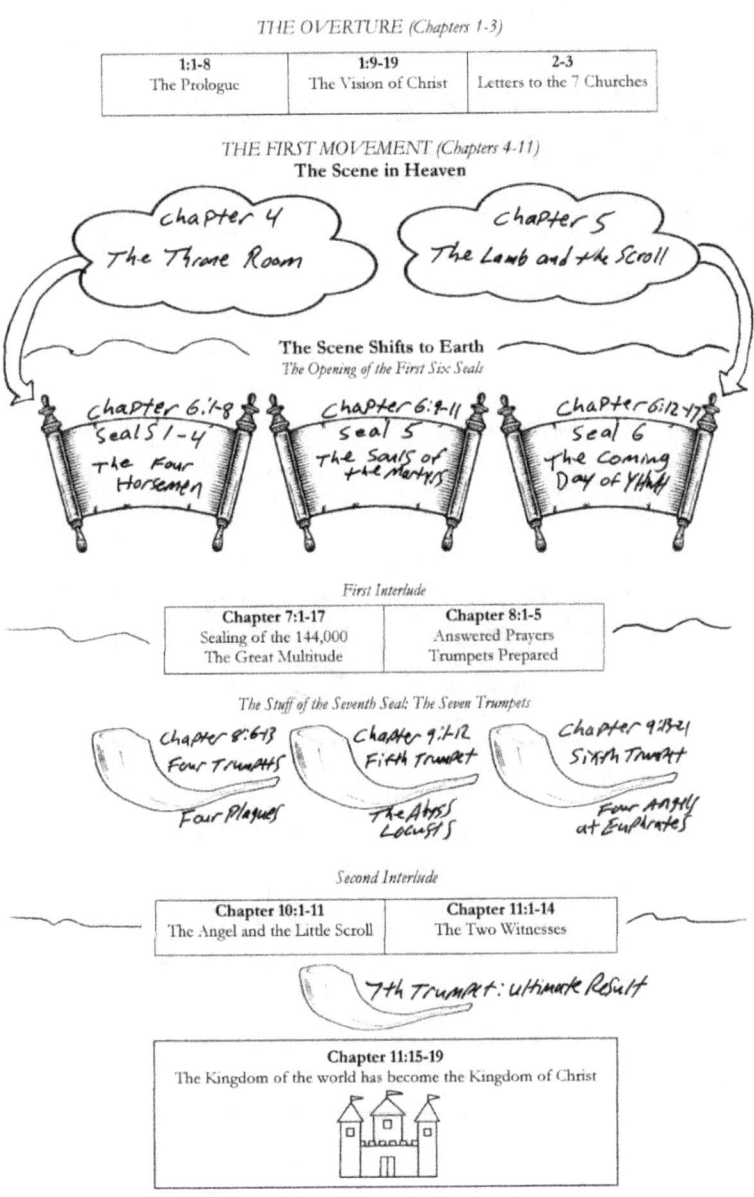

510 | Reader's Guide to the New Testament

# The Symphony of Revelation

**THE SECOND MOVEMENT** *(Chapters 12-22)*
**The Scene in Heaven**

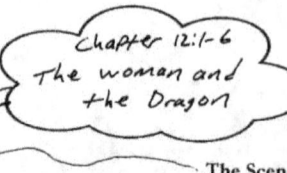

Chapter 12:1-6
The woman and the Dragon

Chapter 12:7-12
The War In Heaven

The Scene Shifts to Earth

Chapter 12:13-13:1
Dragon → Woman

Chapter 13:2-10
Sea Beast

Chapter 13:11-18
Land Beast

*First Interlude*

| Chapter 14:1-20 | Chapter 15:1-8 |
|---|---|
| Mount Zion: | The Ultimate Exodus |
| The Lamb and the 144,000 | The Seven Bowls of Wrath |
| The Harvest of the World | Prepared |

*The Seven Bowls of God's Wrath*
Chapter 16:1-21

  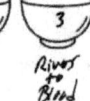    

1. Painful sores
2. Sea to Blood
3. Rivers to Blood
4. Scorching sun
5. Beast's Throne Darkness
6. Army at Euphrates
7. It is Finished!

*Second Interlude*

| Chapter 17:1-18 | Chapter 18:1-19:10 | Chapter 19:11-21 | Chapter 20:1-15 |
|---|---|---|---|
| The Whore of Babylon | Call to Come Out Lament of the Nations Rejoicing in Heaven | War with the Two Beasts Defeat of the Two Beasts | War and Defeat of the Dragon Judgment of the Dead |

*Ultimate Result*

| Chapter 21:1-22:6 |
|---|
| New Heaven and New Earth |
| The New Jerusalem |
| The Return to Eden |

| Chapter 22:7-21 |
|---|
| The Epilogue |

## A Walkthrough of Revelation

The easiest way to understand how Revelation is to think of it in terms of a symphony. **Chapter 1**, John's vision of Christ acts like the **program** to the symphony that gives us a glimpse of the symphony to come. **Chapters 2-3** act like the **overture** that introduces us to the main themes of the symphony. **Chapters 4-11** is the **first movement** of the symphony, with the focus really on the present-day challenges Christians were having in the Roman Empire. **Chapters 12-22** is the **second movement** of the symphony, where music of the first movement is amplified and expanded and the curtain is pulled back, so to speak, where the focus is on spiritual battle between Christ and Satan. As one can see in the *Symphony Chart*, the second movement of chapters 12-22 follows the same narrative pattern as that of the first movement of chapters 4-11.

### 1. The Program (Chapter 1)

Since Revelation is a letter, what we have in **1:1-8** is John's greeting to the seven churches in Asia Minor in which he already begins to lay out some of the major themes in Revelation. He begins by describing God as "The One who was, who is, and who is coming," a clear allusion to the way God revealed Himself to Moses at the burning bush, as the great I AM. John also mentions the **seven spirits** around God's throne, seven being God's number, as it is the number of completion, an allusion to God resting on the seventh day of the creation account.

John also describes Christ in a number of ways that emphasize his Lordship over all creation. He is the **Faithful Witness**, who was faithful to his calling, bearing witness to the point of death. He is the **Firstborn from the Dead**, because he had risen from the dead. He, by virtue of his conquering of death, is also the **Ruler of the kings of the earth**. All of this directly speaks to the situation the early Christians were facing at the time, that of the threat of Roman persecution. John is thus encouraging them to be faithful witness like Christ, even if it means death, because they have the assurance that they will rise from the dead as well, just like Christ, and will share in his authority over all creation.

John goes on to describe Christ as the one who **freed us from our sins** and who **made us a kingdom of priests** to God the Father. This not only is an allusion to the Exodus community, whom God freed from Egypt to be a kingdom of priests who bear witness to Himself, but it also alludes back to the creation of Adam, in that the God's original purpose of humanity was to have them rule His creation **as**

**kings**, but also to act **as priests** who offer up creation to God in an act of worship. Therefore, in Christ, God's purposes for humanity are realized.

John also describes Christ as **the one coming in the clouds**. This is an allusion to **Daniel 7**, in which Daniel has a vision of four beasts coming up out of the sea, each one corresponding to various empires. On the last beast, a "little horn" springs up and makes war with the saints (Jews in the original context, but John is now applying it to Christians who are being persecuted by Rome). It is then that Daniel sees one like the Son of Man coming on the clouds of heaven, who ascends to God's throne to rule over the earth and to defeat the little horn. Thus, John is reassuring the seven churches that Jesus is indeed ruling and will indeed defeat those who are currently persecuting them. John ends by once again calling God **the One who was, who is, and is to come**, as well as **the Almighty**. The Greek word here is *pantokrator*—one who is all-powerful and who holds everything in his hand. This title is used seven times in Revelation (1:8; 4:8; 11:17; 15:3; 16:7; 19:6; and 21:22) to emphasize that God is all-powerful and Christ reigns over all.

With that, John then begins to give a vivid description in **1:9-20** of Christ in his full glory as the cosmic ruler of all in order to serve as an encouragement for the churches that were facing persecution at the hands of Rome. He begins by reminding them he is a partner with them in the **tribulation, kingdom**, and **patient endurance in Jesus**. Depending on the translation, the Greek word, *thlipsis*, is rendered either as tribulation, persecution, or suffering. It is important to realize, though, that throughout the New Testament, *thlipsis* is almost always used to describe what Christians should expect to go through, not something that God will rescue them from. The message in the New Testament is consistent: *If you put your faith in Christ and follow Him, you will suffer tribulation because that is what following Christ means—sharing in his sufferings and living in the hope that you will then share in his resurrection as well.* By contrast, as will become evident in Revelation, the Greek words, *orgay* and *thumos* are words that describe God's judgment on the evildoers who inflict *thlipsis* on God's people. Christians suffer **tribulation**, but they are saved from God's **wrath**.

In any case, since John is a partner in the tribulation they are enduring, he wants to encourage them by giving them a picture of Jesus as the cosmic king of creation. Each description will be picked up and highlighted in his seven notes to the seven churches in chapters 2-3. John's description of Christ sounds odd, containing the following elements:

- He is walking among seven golden lampstands
- A golden sash is around his chest
- His hair is white like wool, like snow
- His eyes are like flames of fire
- His feet are like burnished bronze from a furnace
- He has a voice like the rushing of many waters
- He is holding seven stars in his right hand
- A sharp double-edged sword is coming from his mouth
- His face is shining like the sun

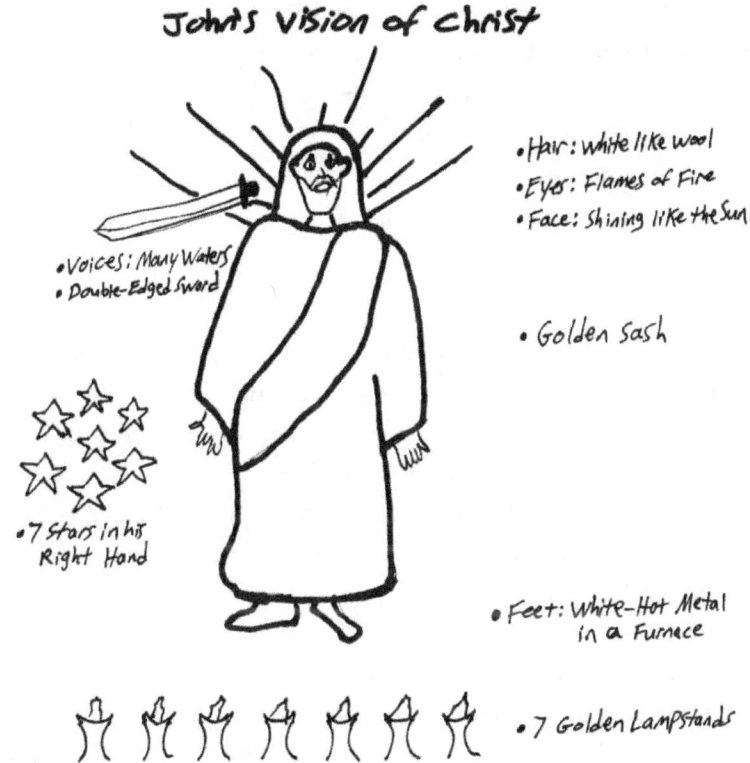

Obviously, John is not saying Jesus literally looks this way. It is a symbolic description of Christ to emphasize his glory and majesty. We will expand on these descriptions as they are brought up in chapters 2-3. In any case, John ends his description with Christ calling Himself **the First and the Last** and **the Living One** who was dead, but is now alive forever, and who **has the keys of Death and Hades**. All of this drives home one obvious point: Christ has conquered death itself. He then tells John to write to the seven churches, which John then proceeds to do.

## 2. The Overture: The Letters (Chapters 2-3)

Chapters 2-3 consist of seven messages John writes to the seven churches: Ephesus, Smyrna, Pergamum, Thyatira, Sardis, Philadelphia, and Laodicea. What we find when we read these seven messages is that various churches were faced with various problems. Some were being persecuted, some were being led astray by false teaching, some were getting rich, arrogant and seduced by the things of the world, and some were just stale and lifeless. John fashions his seven messages using a basic formula for each one. Each message is laid out in the following manner:

- **A description of Jesus** that corresponds to John's vision in chapter 1
- **An encouraging word** to the church for something good
- **A reproof** to the church for something bad
- **A warning** and/or **instruction**
- **A promise** to those who "conquer" and remain faithful
- **A final statement**: "He who has an ear, listen to what the Spirit says to the churches."

### Ephesus (2:1-7)

In John's message to Ephesus, Jesus is depicted as the one **holding the seven stars** and **walking among the seven golden lampstands**. John congratulates them on their toil and patient endurance, the fact they don't put up with "evil-doers," and that they guard against false teaching. They are still standing strong, even in the face of some resistance. Still, John says that they have **abandoned the love you had at first**, and he calls them to repent. John congratulates them for hating the works of the **Nicolaitans**. Some speculate that since the word Nicolaitans is derived from the Greek word *nike*, which means "to conquer," or "victory," this group might have been preaching some ancient form of what we might call the "health and wealth gospel." The promise John gives to Ephesus is that to the "one who conquers" will be allowed to **eat from the Tree of Life in the garden of God**. This foreshadows the end of Revelation when John sees the Tree of Life in the New Jerusalem.

### Smyrna (2:8-11)

In John's message to Ephesus, Jesus is depicted as **the first and the last, who was dead and came to life**. Smyrna is the one church the John has nothing bad to say about. The only word he gives to them is positive. Even though they were undergoing affliction and poverty, John says they are truly rich. We learn that there was a group of Jews in Smyrna who were slandering the church. John goes so far as to call them the **synagogue of Satan** because they were being actively hostile to the Christians in Smyrna. In any case, John tells them not to be afraid of the coming suffering, and that some of them would be thrown in prison. If they stay faithful even to death, John says they will be given the **crown of life**. The promise John gives to Smyrna is that the "one who conquers" will **not be hurt by the second death**. By the end of Revelation, it becomes clear that this "second death" is a reference to the Lake of Fire.

**Pergamum (2:12-17)**

In John's message to Pergamum, Jesus is depicted as **the one with the sharp, two-edged sword**. John says that Pergamum is where **Satan's throne**, probably a reference to the Roman authority in Pergamum. Nevertheless, he congratulates the church for holding fast to Christ, even **in the days of Antipas my witness**, evidently a church member who was martyred there. Nevertheless, John says some of them are holding to the **teaching of Balaam**. In the book of Numbers, Balaam gave advice to King Balak of Moab to send his women into the camp of Israel and entice the Israelites to sleep with them and worship their gods. Therefore, it seems that some Christians were still frequenting the pagan temples in Pergamum. In addition, some in Pergamum were also enticed by the teaching of the **Nicolaitans**. The promise John gives to Pergamum is that the "one who conquers" will be given **hidden manna** and will be given a **white stone** with a new name written on it. The manna is clearly a reference to the Exodus. As for the **white stone**, in the ancient world, the giving of stones was part of the judicial system—that's how verdicts were handed down. Basically, John is saying that God will judge in their favor.

**Thyatira (2:18-29)**

In John's message to Thyatira, Jesus is depicted as the **Son of God** who has **eyes like fire** and **feet like burnished bronze**. After commending Thyatira for their love, faith, service, and patient endurance, John spends most of his time with what's wrong in Thyatira. It has to do with a woman named **Jezebel** (an allusion to the Jezebel of the Old Testament). Like in Pergamum, some were indulging in fornication and idol food, and apparently this Jezebel was someone in the church of Thyatira who was encouraging it. John says that she is going to be punished, and when that happens, anyone with her will be punished too. Whatever this teaching of Jezebel was, John calls it the **deep things of Satan**. He then tells the rest of the Christians there to hold fast until Christ comes. The promise John gives to "the one who conquers" is that he will be given **authority over the nations** (an allusion to **Psalm 2:8-9**), and he will be given **the morning star**.

### Sardis (3:1-6)

In John's message to Sardis, Jesus is depicted as the **one who has the seven spirits of God and the seven stars**. John, though, says nothing positive about it. Although they have a reputation for being alive, John says they really are dead. He calls them to repent and remember what they had been taught. If they don't, John says that Christ will come **like a thief in the night**. That being said, John does say that there are some in Sardis who are still faithful who, as John says, **have not soiled their clothes**. The promise John gives to "the one who conquers" is that he will be **clothed in white** and will **not have his name be blotted out from the Book of Life**. Again, this reference foreshadows what comes at the end of Revelation, where the Book of Life is mentioned again.

### Philadelphia (3:7-13)

In John's message to Philadelphia, Jesus is depicted as **the holy and true one who has the key of David**, who **opens what no one will shut**, and who **shuts what no one will open**. Philadelphia gets only good words from John. It was a small church with little power, but they had remained faithful and hadn't denied the name of Christ. As in Smyrna, there is a **synagogue of Satan** in Philadelphia making trouble for the church. John says that Christ will make them eventually bow down at the feet of the church in Philadelphia. Because they have remained faithful, John tells them Christ will spare them from the **hour of trial** that is coming on the whole world, probably a reference to Domitian's empire-wide persecution of Christians. John's promise to "the one who conquers" is that he will be made **a pillar in the temple of God**, have the **name of God written on him**, along with the **name of the New Jerusalem** that will come down from heaven. Once again, this foreshadows the last few chapters of Revelation.

### Laodicea (3:14-22)

In John's message to Laodicea, Jesus is depicted as **the Amen, the faithful witness, and the origin of God's creation**. Laodicea was a commercially successful city known for its banking industry, its textile and wool trade, and even a medical school that developed an ear and eye ointment. Basically, it was a city known for money, clothes, and eye medicine. Yet, John only has negative things to say about the church. He says they are **poor, naked**, and **blind**. John also says they are lukewarm, and that Christ will soon spit them out of his mouth. This is interesting because there was a nearby city called Hieropolis that was famous for its hot springs and another nearby city called Colossae was famous for its cold springs. Laodicea, by contrast, produced only lukewarm, tepid water. It is here, in the message to Laodicea that we find a famous verse: "I stand at the door and knock. If you hear my voice and open the door, I will come in and eat with you and you with me" (3:20). This verse serves as the transition to the next section of Revelation—the beginning of the symphony, if you will. In any case, John's promise to "the one who conquers" is that he will be given **a place on Christ's throne**.

### 3. The First Movement (Chapters 4-11)

With the beginning of chapter 4, we have the "first movement" of the symphony of Revelation. This is where the main concert begins. The first movement is comprised of chapters 4-11 and has a distinct literary structure to it. The second movement is comprised of chapters 12-22, and it repeats that same basic literary structure. In that sense, Revelation is a little like Ravel's *Bolero*. What you notice when you listen to that musical piece is that the same, basic musical theme is repeated over and over again. But each time the theme is repeated, more and more instruments are added and the music intensifies, so that what started out with only one or two instruments ends up with an entire orchestra.

The first movement of Revelation 4-11, therefore, focuses on the this-worldly "battle" between Christians the oppressive kings of *the earth*, specifically Rome, where Christians are asking, "Why is this happening?" and waiting for God to act. In the second movement of Revelation 12-22, though, John takes up this basic theme, expands and intensifies it, and shows the eternal and cosmic significance of the Christians' earthly struggle. The real problem isn't simply Rome, but rather Satan, the Great Dragon.

### A. The Scene in Heaven (Chapters 4-5)

The "symphony" begins with John's vision of the very throne room of God in Heaven in chapter 4. As with John's vision of Christ in chapter 1, the purpose of this vision of God's throne room is to remind Christians suffering under Rome just who the true King of the universe is. Someone who is bloodied in battle has to be given a reminder of who and what he is fighting for. In any case, John's vision of the throne room of God is loaded with Old Testament imagery. He first describes the throne itself as being encircled by an **emerald rainbow**, in front of which is a **sea of glass**. The rainbow alludes to the rainbow after the flood in Genesis 9:13-17, the fact that it is essentially various shades of green perhaps emphasizes life itself. As for the sea, it is hugely symbolic throughout the Bible: (1) God creates dry land out of the *Sea of Chaos* (**Genesis 1**); (2) God saves Noah from the flood, and brings the ark to rest on dry land (**Genesis 6-9**); (3) God saves Israel by bringing them through the *Red Sea* (**Exodus 14**); and (4) Throughout the Old Testament in places like **Psalms 74** and **89**, and **Isaiah 27**, God's salvation of His people is spoken of using the mythological language of God crushing Leviathan in the Sea.

Secondly, there are the **24 thrones** and the **24 elders** on the thrones, clothed in white and wearing crowns. Numbers in Revelation are very significant and symbolic. Here we have to realize that 12+12=24. Twelve stands for both the **12 tribes of Israel** and the **12 apostles** who go out to the Gentiles. Simply put, this is John's way of emphasizing that there is one people of God, consisting of both Jews and Gentiles.

Thirdly, there is the description of **lightning**, and **rumblings and peals of thunder** bursting forth from the throne. This description hearkens back to Mount Sinai (**Exodus 20:18**) and emphasizes that God is acting. Therefore, when John mentions lightning and thunder in Revelation, he is not describing literal natural phenomena. Rather, it is his creative way of saying, "God is on the move and is acting on the behalf of His people!" Finally, there are the **four creatures** around the throne. This is an allusion to both Isaiah's vision of God's throne in **Isaiah 6**, as well as Ezekiel's vision in **Ezekiel 1**. These are angelic creatures who bear witness to the glory of God. (The picture below was actually an art project I did as a 16-year-old in high school!).

Something happens in chapter 4 that carries over into chapter 5 is what I call the **ripple effect of praise**. Picture this scene as four concentric circles around God's throne: (A) the four creatures around the throne; (B) the 24 elders around them; (C) the many angels around them; and then (D) the entirety of creation. The praises begin with the four creatures (4:8), and they continue with the 24 elders (4:11). They are praising God for being the Ruler of all, the great I AM, and for being the Creator.

Before this ripple effect of praise continues, we see that the One sitting on the throne (God the Father) has a **sealed scroll** in His hand, and we learn that no one is worthy to open it. As will become evident, this scroll contains God's judgment against the oppressors of His people. That is why John weeps when he learns that no one was worthy enough to open the seals. If they aren't opened, God's people won't be vindicated, and God's enemies won't be punished. John is told, though, that the **Lion of Judah** is worthy to open the scroll. This is clearly a reference to the Davidic Messiah.

To John's surprise, he looks and sees a **lamb that has been slaughtered**, standing in the center of God's throne. This is the very paradox of Christ: he is a crucified Messiah, a slaughtered lamb who is a king, a lion. When the Lamb takes the scroll, all of Heaven that had just been worshipping God the Father now worships Christ the Lamb, and the ripple effect of praise begins again. The four creatures and the 24 elders proclaim He is worthy to take the scroll, because He was slaughtered, and because it was through His blood that God was able to make a **kingdom of priests** from among **all tribes, languages, peoples, and nations**. Then the thousands of angels in Heaven join in, and then finally all of creation joins in the praise of the Lamb. Once that praise hits all of creation, the four living creatures around the throne say, "Amen!" And with that, the seals begin to be opened.

### B. The Scene Shifts to Earth: The First Six Seals (6:1-17)

Here in chapter 6, as the Lamb breaks each seal, the scene shifts to earth. What Christ opens in Heaven is seen unfolding on earth. The **first subsection (6:1-8)** tells of the breaking of the first four seals and the **four horsemen** of the apocalypse. They aren't predictors of things that will happen *in the future*, as they are revelations of what was happening *at that time* in the world. Each horse that comes out with the first four seals has a certain color and a certain description:

- **The White Horse**: The rider has a bow and crown and goes out to conquer.
- **The Red Horse**: The rider is given a great sword, takes peace away, where people slaughter each other.
- **The Black Horse**: The rider has balances in his hand; the voice describes high prices and lack of food.
- **The Pale Horse**: The rider is Death, with Hades behind him; he kills ¼ of the earth.

Taken as a group, we can see that the four horsemen symbolize the self-destructive and war-like nature of this fallen world, in particular that of the ancient Roman empire. The **white horse** thus symbolizes the imperialistic and conquering nature of empires, notably Rome. The **red horse** is thus the logical consequence of the white horse. When empires like Rome are bent on conquest, they bring about war. The **black horse** shows the result of war, namely the economic ruin and poverty of the conquered country. Finally, the **pale horse** is the ultimate consequence of all this: death and the grave. Taken together, these first four seals reveal the state of the human race in general, and the destructive forces of Rome in particular.

The **second subsection (6:9-11)** tells of the breaking of the fifth seal. When it is broken, John sees the **murdered saints** under the **altar of souls** in Heaven, who have been martyred because of their witness to the Word of God. It is important to realize that the altar is Jerusalem was the place where priests made atoning sacrifices to YHWH on behalf of Israel. Atonement basically means to make peace with God. We have always been told that Christ's death has reconciled to God. The fifth seal shows something most people don't realize, though. The saints (the Christians) because they bore witness to Christ, are sharing in Christ's sacrifice. If that isn't shocking enough, when the souls under the altar ask how long God will wait to avenge their blood, God's response is to give them white robes (which symbolize being cleansed of their sins) and to tell them they have to wait **until the complete number of their fellow servants are killed**. In other words, *"Wait, I'm going to let more of you be killed."*

The fifth seal, therefore, gives a stark picture of the reality of what it means to follow Christ. Yes, Christ died for the sins of the world and his death was the atoning sacrifice that made peace with God possible. But Christians also share God's grace and salvation through their own sacrifice and persecution. The world comes to a knowledge of God's grace when Christians imitate Christ and accept unjust suffering, persecution, and possibly death without resistance. To follow

Christ means to pick up one's cross and share in his sacrificial sufferings. Therefore, John's message is admittedly hard: Be prepared to imitate Christ unto death. Salvation only comes through suffering.

The **third subsection (6:12-17)** tells of the breaking of the sixth seal. Simply put, it gives a picture of the **coming day of God's wrath** upon the evildoers of the world who have persecuted God's people. The images of a **great shaking of the land**, the **sun turning black**, and the **moon turning to blood**" are all images that the Old Testament prophets used to talk about when God would finally come and redeem His people, avenge their suffering, and judge the evil people of the world. It isn't describing future, literal natural phenomena. It is metaphorical language to describe God's actions to bring wrath upon the wicked. Not only that, but the imagery alludes back to the description of God's throne in chapter 4, and is thus saying, "God is acting from His throne!" Since that is the case, we need to realize that the sixth seal is the answer to what the martyrs under the altar of souls have asked for: God is getting ready to answer their prayers.

The final verse of 6:17 is quite interesting. As the kings of the earth see the Day of the Wrath of the LORD coming, they ask, "Who can stand?" To them, it is obvious that none of them are able to stand. The answer to that question, though, comes in the very next verse that begins chapter 7.

### C. First Interlude (7:1-8:5)

"Who will be able to stand?" In the **first subsection of 7:1-17**, we find out. **Four angels are standing**, then another angel comes forth to seal the 144,000 servants of God. John sees a **great multitude standing before the throne of the Lamb**. Then we find that all the angels, the elders, and the four living creatures **are standing before the throne**, worshipping God. Now, there is quite a lot of debate over the identity of the 144,000 and the great multitude, and the meaning of the **great tribulation**. In dispensationalist theology, the 144,000 and the great multitude are two different groups, with the 144,000 being the number of Jews who are saved during a literal 7-year tribulation period, and the great multitude being the believers who are raptured to Heaven either before, during, or after the great tribulation. Such a view, though, is simply wrong.

In 7:3, we are told the 144,000 are the servants of God. Yes, in the Old Testament, that would have been the Jews, but with the coming of Christ, the Gospel proclamation was that true Israel was to be made up of both Jews and

Gentiles, for it was the fulfillment of God's covenant promise to Abraham. Therefore, these servants of God are the True Israel in Christ—Jewish and Gentile believers together as one people of God. That explains the significance of the number 144,000. The number is symbolic of the full number of the chosen people of God: 12 tribes (Jews who put their faith in Christ) x 12 apostles (who went out to proclaim the Gospel to the Gentiles) x 1,000 (a symbolic number of completion). The reason why Jesus named 12 apostles was because he was making a statement that he was redefining who the True Israel was. Therefore, 12 x 12 = 144 (Jews and Gentiles together) then multiply it by 1,000 (God's number of completion) and voila: the 144,000 are the full number of believers from the Jews and Gentiles together, fulfilled in Christ.

If we realize this, we should also see that the great multitude John sees is not a second group, distinct from the 144,000, but rather is the same group. After John **hears** the number 144,000, he then **looks and sees** a great multitude from every nation, tribe, people, and language. True Israel is comprised of Christ followers from all nations. It is also important to note that they are wearing **white robes**, for it connects this great multitude with the martyrs under the altar of souls in the fifth seal, when God tells them that they had to wait until the **full number of their fellow servants** are killed. Here is that full number. These are the one who will be able to stand on the Great Day of the Wrath of YHWH.

This also helps us make sense of the angel telling John that this great multitude are those who have come out of the **great tribulation**. He doesn't tell John they escaped or were raptured away to avoid the great tribulation, but rather they have *come out of the great tribulation*, meaning they went through it. That shouldn't be surprising, because the New Testament witness is clear that **Christians go through *thlipsis*.** Therefore, in the context of the Revelation 6-7, the picture John gives is of Christians who were martyred and who went through that great tribulation. They may have been killed by Rome, but John is declaring that they are standing before the throne of the Christ the Lamb, the one who has conquered death itself. They are in God's Temple, and Christ the Lamb is their shepherd.

The **second subsection (8:1-5)** sets the stage for the next scene about to take place. When the Lamb opens the seventh seal, the next round of seven emerges, that of the seven trumpets. Simply put, the seven trumps are the stuff of the seventh seal. But before they are blown, we are told that as soon as the seventh seal is opened, there is silence in Heaven for about a half an hour, during which time an angel with a golden censer is **at the altar** (the altar of souls from the fifth seal), filling the censer with **the prayers of the saints** (the martyred saints who are under the altar). The incense from the altar is therefore symbolic of the prayers of the martyred saints, rising up to God. That is why there is silence in Heaven—God is listening to their prayers. After that, the angel then takes the censer, fills it with fire from the altar, and hurls it down to earth. When he does, we are told that there came **peals of thunder, rumblings, flashes of lightning,** and a **great earthquake**. God is now about to answer the prayers of the saints. He is about to act from His throne.

### D. The Stuff of the Seventh Seal (8:6-9:21)

With that, the next cycle of the seven trumpets begins, following the same pattern as we saw with the seven seals. The **first subsection (8:6-13)** gives us the first four trumpets, the descriptions of which echo God's past judgments upon evil nations who had oppressed Israel in the Old Testament, namely Egypt and Babylon.

- **First Trumpet**: Hail and fire mixed with blood is hurled down to the earth.
- **Second Trumpet**: A blazing mountain is thrown into the sea.
- **Third Trumpet**: The great star Wormwood is thrown down from Heaven and turns the waters bitter.
- **Fourth Trumpet**: One-third of the sun, moon, and stars are darkened.

What these trumpets reveal is that God will indeed answer the prayers of His servants and will bring His wrath and judgment upon the evildoers of this world, just as He has done in the past. To be clear, the first trumpet echoes the plague of hail in Egypt (**Exodus 9:13-16**); the second trumpet alludes to Jeremiah's prophecy of Babylon's destruction (**Jeremiah 51:25, 42**); the third trumpet recalls Moses' turning the Nile to blood (**Exodus 7:14-24**), as well as his turning the water bitter after the Israelites were caught worshipping the golden calf (**Exodus 32:20**); and the fourth trumpet echoes the plague of darkness in Egypt (**Exodus 10:21-23**) and is similar to the prophecy of Joel concerning the Coming Day of YHWH (**Joel 2:30-31**).

The **second subsection (9:1-12)** tells us of the fifth trumpet. When it is blown, we see a **fallen star** from heaven come down to earth with a key to open the shaft to the **Abyss**, out of which comes swarms of **locusts**. We are then told that the king of the locusts is the **angel of the Abyss**. His name in Hebrew is **Abaddon** and means "destruction," and his name in Greek is **Apollyon** and means "**Destroyer**."

Traditionally, the Abyss is identified with the waters of chaos from ancient Near Eastern mythology. In **Genesis 1**, they are the waters that God caused to recede in order to bring forth the land on which mankind can dwell. Throughout the Old Testament, God is shown as the God who brings order out of chaos. Here in Revelation, we see the power of that chaotic Abyss being unleashed into the world, with evil "flooding over" the world, if you will. The **fallen star** is a reference to Satan. Although God allows him to open the Abyss, God is still ultimately in control. God can even allow evil, in order to bring about His divine purpose of salvation.

As for the **locusts**, if we are to understand why they refer to, we have to look again to the Old Testament. First off, they echo the plague of locusts during the Exodus (**Exodus 10:1-19**) and are thus the instruments of God's judgment on the enemies of His people. Secondly, they also allude to the plague of locusts from Joel 1:4-13, in which Joel warns Judah of YHWH's coming judgment in the form of a foreign army to punish unfaithful Judah. Therefore, here in the fifth trumpet, these locusts give us a picture of God's coming judgment on the oppressors of the servants of God, which in the first century context would refer to God's judgment upon Rome for its persecution of Christians.

That brings us to the identity of the **Destroyer**, the **king of the Abyss**. Before we assume it is Satan (although to a certain extent it is), we need to consider something else. Specifically, the Greek word *Apollyon* is related to the Greek god **Apollo**, and the cult of Apollo used *the locust as its symbol*. Furthermore, a number of Roman emperors like Caligula and Nero identified themselves with Apollo. The Emperor Domitian even claimed to be the incarnation of the god Apollo himself. Therefore, John is saying here that the king of the Abyss, the one responsible for the destruction and torture in their world, the embodiment of the destructive power of Satan himself…*was none other than the Roman Emperor.*

The **third subsection (9:13-19)** tells us about the six trumpet and gives us a picture of an invading army from beyond the Euphrates River. The four angels at the Euphrates River refers back to the four angels in 7:1 who were told to wait until the servants of God sealed. Here, with the sixth trumpet, they are released to kill one-third of mankind. Incidentally, as seen in the fourth trumpet, the "fraction of destruction" associated with the trumpets is **one-third**, whereas the fraction associated with the seals is **one-fourth**.

In any case, the significance of the Euphrates River is that it acted as the boundary between Israel and the world empires. Any empire, be it Babylon or Assyria, would have to cross the Euphrates River if it were to make its way to Israel. The threats, therefore, to Israel always came from beyond the Euphrates River. In the first century, though, Rome's chief rival was the **Parthia**, which was also from beyond the Euphrates River.

John says that this army from beyond the Euphrates totaled 200 million troops. In Greek, the actually rendering is "two myriads of myriads" (or "twice 10,000 times 10,000"). The number relates back to Psalm 68:17 (which gives the number of chariots at Sinai), and to Daniel 7:10 (which gives the number of angels attending God on His throne). This army from beyond the Euphrates River then is seen as God's instrument of judgment. Like the locusts of the fifth trumpet, it is a destroying army that is used by God to execute His wrath. If we consider the fifth and sixth trumpets together, John's cryptic message is nevertheless clear, once you understand the symbolism: The way in which God is going to answer the prayers of the saints and bring His wrath upon the Roman Empire was through the destructive actions of both the Roman Emperor himself and foreign powers. At the end of the sixth trumpet, though, we are told that the rest of mankind still **did not repent and did not stop worshipping idols**. That sets the stage for what happens next.

### E. Second Interlude (10:1-11:14)

Just as chapter 7 was an interlude between the 6th and 7th seals, this next section also serves as an interlude between the 6th and 7th trumpets. In both instances, something special must be done before the opening of the 7th seal and the sounding of the 7th trumpet. The **first subsection (10:1-11)** begins with a mighty angel coming out of Heaven and holding a little scroll. With his right foot on the sea and his left foot on the land, he cries out and the **seven thunders spoke**. John was going to write down what they said, but a voice from Heaven tells him to seal them up and not to write down what they said. Instead, the mighty angel cries out that there isn't any more time and that the mystery of God would now be fulfilled. Therefore, the seven thunders are skipped. As we've noted, there is somewhat of an intensification in judgment in the course of Revelation. The seven seals affect one-fourth of creation; the seven trumpets affect one-third of creation; and as we will see later on, the seven bowls affect all of creation. Therefore, it is logical to assume that if the seven thunders had been written down, they would have affected one-half of creation—to coincide with the progression throughout the book.

In any case, we are told that the mystery of God will be fulfilled at the sounding of the seventh trumpet. But *how* will the mystery of God be accomplished. Or, for that matter, *what* is the mystery of God in the first place? That is answered by the end of chapter 11. For now, though, something else happens first. The mighty angel gives the little scroll to John and tells him to eat it. When John does, he finds that it is **sweet as honey** in his mouth, but it turns **bitter in his stomach**. He then is told to prophesy again about many peoples, nations, languages and kings.

This scene calls to mind similar instances in **Ezekiel 2:10** and **Jeremiah 15:16**. In all three instances, the message that although the Word of God is a delight to receive, it causes pain when its grim nature is fully understood and declared. Simply put, John's prophetic message is "hard to swallow" because it says that being a Christian costs you your entire life. There are no half measures with salvation. A Christian who doesn't suffer, or who doesn't share in the suffering of others, is like a fish who doesn't swim because it is afraid of the water. The result is that fish is going to die. The fact is that it is through suffering that the Gospel is spread. It is through suffering that God's grace is made visible and available to others. It is because of suffering and death that eternal life in Christ is possible.

That brings us to the **second subsection (11:1-14)**, in which we are told how the "mystery of God" will be accomplished. He going to bring salvation to the world through the suffering, death, and resurrection of his two witnesses. But before John mentions the two witnesses, he is told to measure the **Temple of God**, along with the **altar**, and to count the **worshippers** there. He is told to exclude the outer court of the Temple, "because it has been given to the Gentiles" and that they will **trample the holy city for 42 months** and that **God's two witnesses will prophesy for 1,260 days, dressed in sackcloth.**

The reference to 42 months and 1,260 days is an allusion to **Daniel 9:24-27**, where Daniel is told that an "evil prince" will come and destroy the city and the sanctuary of Jerusalem. Daniel is told that for "one week" this prince would make a "strong covenant" (7 days was understood to stand for 7 years, so "one week" meant "7 years"). Halfway through that "week," he would make sacrifice and offering cease, and would instead set up the "abomination of desolation." After that, the end would come, and the "desolator" would be destroyed.

In its original context, Daniel 9:24-27 pointed forward to the actions of Antiochus Epiphanes IV, and his attempt to wipe out Judaism in the mid-second century BC. Essentially, it was a prophecy about a horrible Gentile ruler attacking God's people, Israel. John is taking that context and re-contextualizing it to fit the situation of the first century Christians who were being persecuted. Therefore, the "Gentiles" in Revelation 11:2 aren't literally Gentiles, but rather the enemies of God's chosen people, the "True Israel"—Christians. The "trampling of the holy city," therefore, corresponds to the suffering and persecution of the Christians. So, why 42 months? It shows that God is allowing suffering for a time, but He is still in control: the "trampling" is only for a time.

Given that, John proceeds to speak of **God's two witnesses** who prophesy during those 1,260 days. First, the reference to them being the **two olive trees** and **two lampstands** is a reference to a prophetic vision in **Zechariah 4:3-13**, where "two anointed ones" (Zerubbabel the governor and Joshua the high priest) stand before the Lord and God tells them that the Temple was to be rebuilt after the exile and that salvation would come, not by might or by power, but by the Spirit of God. Secondly, **sackcloth** was understood to be a sign of mourning and repentance. Thirdly, the two witnesses are clearly associated with **Moses** and **Elijah** (Moses turned the waters to blood in Exodus 7:14-24 and Elijah shut up the sky in I Kings 17:1). Moses and Elijah also came to represent the Torah and the Prophets in the Old Testament. That is why, when Jesus speaks of how the Torah and the Prophets bear witness to him, the figures of Moses and Elijah are often referred to (as on the Mount of Transfiguration). Put all that together, the two witnesses represent the prophetic Christian witness to Jesus Christ. During their tribulation, Christians who bear witness to Christ do so in the power of Moses and Elijah.

Shockingly, John says that the two witnesses are overpowered and killed by the **beast that comes up from the Abyss**, that their bodies lay in the street of the **great city** (which called **Sodom**, **Egypt**, and is the place their Lord was crucified—**Jerusalem**), and that people from the entire world celebrate their deaths. First, the beast has to be seen in light of Daniel 7:1-14, where Daniel sees a vision of four beasts coming up out of the watery chaos. The fourth beast wages war against God's people but is eventually judged and destroyed by the Son of Man, who is given the power of God Himself. This beast in Revelation, therefore, represents the ultimately satanically-inspired kingdoms of the world that oppress and persecute God's chosen people. In the first century context, that beast would be seen as the Roman Emperor himself.

Secondly, we need to understand the connection between Jerusalem (the great city) and Sodom and Egypt. Sodom was the city destroyed by God for its wickedness, and Egypt was the nation that first enslaved and oppressed God's people. Jerusalem was now seen to be just as evil and wicked as Sodom and Egypt because the Jews as a nation had rejected Jesus as the Messiah and had been the first persecutors of his followers. Therefore, they were no longer God's people. So, when John tells us that men from every people, language, tribe and nation celebrate the death of the two witnesses, he is making it clear that the whole world, *Gentiles as well as Jews*, shares in the guilt of persecuting God's chosen people. To persecute God's people is to persecute Christ, and to do that is to show yourself to be an enemy of God.

After 3 ½ days, though, John says that the two witnesses are resurrected by the breath of God and ascend to Heaven. Because they suffered and died like Christ, they now ascend to Heaven to rule with Christ. It is then that there is a severe earthquake, one-tenth of the city collapses, and 7,000 people are killed. The result is that the survivors end up **giving glory to the God of Heaven**. This needs to be seen in light of the end of chapter 9, when we are told that after the first six trumpets there was still no repentance. Simply put, God's wrath brings judgment and punishment, but not repentance.

What is revealed here in chapter 11 is that it is the suffering of Christians as they bear witness to Christ that will bring about the repentance of the world. That being said, the mention of one-tenth of the city being destroyed and 7,000 killed is a bit foggy. A possible explanation is that they are allusions to Amos 5:3, Isaiah 6:13, and I Kings 19:18. All three verses deal with the **faithful remnant** in Israel. Therefore, what John is emphasizing is that the true remnant of God's people must be willing to be sacrificed in order to bring about the repentance of the entire world.

### F. The Ultimate Result (11:15-19)

When the seventh trumpet sounds in 11:15-19, the angels in Heaven break out into praise and say, *"The kingdom of the world has become the kingdom of our Lord and of His Christ!"* Then the 24 elders praise God, calling the Lord, *"the one who is and who was,"* but no longer, *"who is to come."* Now they sing, *"He has come."* The wait is over.

They also say the time has come for God to *"destroy those who destroy the earth."* God's judgment has come.

Finally, in 11:19, we have the climax of the first movement of the symphony of Revelation: **God's Temple** in Heaven is opened, the **Ark of the Covenant** is seen, and there is **lightning**, **thunder**, an **earthquake**, and a **hailstorm**. God's presence is with his people and God's covenant promise to Abraham has been fulfilled. The thunder and lightning is not a picture of dread, but of the Glory of God, almost like the grand finale to a Fourth of July fireworks display. The celebration in Heaven has started because God has answered the prayers of His saints. He has brought judgment on the wicked, and through the sacrifice and suffering of His chosen people, He has brought repentance and salvation to the world.

Thus ends the first movement in the symphony of Revelation. As we will see, the second movement in chapters 12-22 will follow the same narrative structure and "play the same theme," so to speak, but on a much greater scale.

### 4. The Second Movement (Chapters 12-22)

This second movement in the symphony of Revelation follows the same overall literary structure to the first movement, only this time, the curtain is pulled back, so to speak, and John reveals that the real battle isn't really just between Rome and the Christians, but ultimately between Christ and Satan on a cosmic scale.

#### A. The Scene in Heaven (12:1-12)

The second movement of Revelation opens in **12:1-6** with another scene in Heaven. This time, though, it is not of God's throne room, but rather of a confrontation between a **woman clothed with the sun** who is giving birth, and a **great red dragon** with 7 heads, 10 horns, and 7 crowns, who intends to devour the **child** as soon as he is born. The child, though, is snatched up to God, and the woman flees to the wilderness and is cared for by God for 1,260 days. To understand all this, we need to make sure we understand who the woman, the dragon, and the child are.

First, the woman clothed with the sun is symbolic the **Heavenly Zion**, of which **Old Testament Israel** represented. Her crown of 12 stars alludes to the 12 tribes of Israel. She also echoes the **woman in Genesis 3**, specifically 3:15-16, who is the mother of all the living and who gives birth to the offspring who eventually strikes the serpent's head. Secondly, the great dragon is obviously Satan, portrayed as the ancient mythological sea serpent (referred to in various Old Testament passages like **Job 3:8; 41:1; Psalm 74:4; 89:10; Isaiah 27:1; 51:9**) whom God promises to one day kill. He is the dark power behind the empires like Egypt and Babylon (and Rome in the first century) who oppressed God's people, be it Old Testament Israel or the first century Christians.

The dragon echoes the serpent in **Genesis 3:15-16** as well. After the man and woman eat the fruit, God declares that there would be a war between the woman and the serpent and the **woman's offspring** and the **serpent's offspring**, and that the serpent would strike the heel of the woman's offspring, but that he would crush the serpent's head. Therefore, what we see in 12:1-6 is the ultimate cosmic battle to which Genesis 3:15-16 refers. This also helps us better understand the child to whom the woman gives birth. Obviously, it is Jesus Christ, the promised Messiah. The mention of the fact that he will **rule all the nations with a rod of iron** is a reference to **Psalm 2:7**, which looks forward to the coming Messiah. Early Christians would have easily seen the child being taken up to God's throne as a reference to the ascension, vindication, and glorification of Christ.

With that, we are told in **12:7-12** of a great war in Heaven, where the angelic legions of Heaven, led by Michael, defeat the dragon and his legions and cast them down to earth. It is then that a voice in Heaven declares, *"Now have come the salvation and the power and the kingdom of our God, and the authority of His Christ,"* meaning that with Christ's life, death, resurrection and ascension, the decisive battle in Heaven has been won and the Kingdom of God had now come to earth. Satan's defeat has come about by the **blood of the Lamb** (Christ's saving work on the cross) and the **witness and faithfulness of the saints** (even to the point of death). Still, even though the victory is already secure in Heaven, that war between the dragon and the woman, between the serpent's offspring and the woman's offspring, has to still be played out on earth.

### B. The Scene Shifts to Earth: The Dragon and Two Beasts (12:13-13:18)

As the scene shifts to earth, the **first subsection (12:13-17)** contains a re-playing of 12:1-6, but now on the earth. The dragon pursues the woman, but she is given two wings like an eagle and flies into the wilderness, where she is cared for by God for **a time, times, and half a time**, even though the dragon tries to sweep her away in a flood. This is another way to say 1,260 days, or 42 months, or three and a half years—the same time period expressed in Revelation 11 concerning the two witnesses. It is also an allusion to **Daniel 9:26-27**, which speaks of an evil prince who will try to bring destruction on God's people and God's city like a flood.

Therefore, John is combining this allusion to Daniel 9:26-27 with the "war of the offspring in **Genesis 3:15-16** to articulate for his audience who they are and what they are experiencing. Simply put, he's telling them that although Christ has defeated Satan, and the ultimate victory is certain, they were currently living in that time, as he says in 12:17, when Satan is **making war with the rest of the woman's offspring**. The *ultimate offspring*, if you will, is Christ. The *rest of the woman's offspring* is the Church.

Chapter 12 ends with the dragon standing on **the shore of the sea**. This sea is the Sea of Chaos. Here in the **second subsection (13:1-10)**, John introduces us to essentially his offspring (the *serpent's offspring*)—the **beast from the sea**. Given that first century context, Christians would have easily seen the sea beast as a reference to the Roman Emperor Domitian. The way John describes the sea beast gives it away. First, he says there were **blasphemous names on its heads**. One of the major points of conflict between the early Christians and Rome was the fact that the Roman emperors were called by such titles as *Lord and God*, or *Lord and Savior*. To Christians, such titles belonged only to Christ, so they wouldn't address the emperor that way. To do so was blasphemous. Caesar isn't Lord and Savior, Christ is.

Second, John says the beast **had a fatal wound that was healed**. In AD 68, when it was reported that Nero had commit suicide, many Romans couldn't believe that the tyrant was really dead. Conspiracy theories arose that said Nero really wasn't dead, and consequently, certain people played on those fears. Imperial edicts were issued in Nero's name, as though he were still alive, and no less than three men claimed to actually be Nero. One led a rebellion in Rome in AD; another was welcomed by Rome's major enemy, the Parthians, in AD 80; and one nearly persuaded the Parthians to march with him against Rome in AD 88.

By the mid-90s, the conspiracy theory evolved, and some people thought that although Nero had died, he would return from the dead and lead armies against Rome. Needless to say, Christians had deep fears about Nero. He was the first emperor to savagely persecute Christians, although it was limited to Rome itself. So, in AD 95, when Domitian unleashed the first empire-wide persecution of Christians, many Christians saw him sort of a "second coming of Nero."

Third, John says the sea beast had **dominion over every tribe, people, language and nation**, and that the entire world followed the beast and worshipped the dragon. The only person in AD 95 would had dominion over the known world would have been Domitian. John furthers says the sea beast, the very embodiment of the dragon's evil, would be allowed to exercise his authority for **42 months**, the time during which the dragon was allowed to make war with the rest of the woman's offspring. Once again, we see this particular time period associated with a time of persecution for Christians.

Coupled with that is when John says that all the inhabitants of the earth will worship the beast (presumably during that same time). Therefore, the line of demarcation is no longer Jews vs. Gentile oppressors, but rather Christians, who are citizens of Heaven whose names have been written in the Lamb's book of life, vs. the worshippers of the beast, who are citizens of the land, whose names are not in the book of life. The saints live in Heaven and worship the Lamb, whereas the inhabitants of the earth worship the beast, and ultimately the dragon himself.

In any case, John ends this subject in 13:10 with a chilling statement: *"He who has an ear, let him hear! If anyone is to go into captivity, into captivity he will go. If anyone is to be killed with the sword, with the sword he will be killed. This calls for patient endurance and faithfulness on the part of the saints."* In other words, John is telling these churches that some of them are going to die, so they had better be prepared to be either killed or uprooted from their homes, because that is what is meant to follow Christ. Things are going to get bad, so endure and be faithful to Christ.

In the **third subsection (3:11-18)**, there is another beast from the land. It has two horns like a lamb, but it spoke like a dragon; it made the citizens of the earth worship the sea beast; it performed miraculous signs to deceive people; it made an image of the sea beast and made it talk; it killed anyone who didn't worship the image; and it made everyone take a mark on their foreheads or hands in order to buy and sell. Clearly, its main job was to get people to worship and serve the sea beast.

When seen in the context of the first century Roman Empire, this beast is a reference to the official **Imperial Cult**—the state-sponsored worship of the Roman Emperor as a god, as the "Lord and Savior" of the world. Not only did Domitian demand to be addressed as "Lord and God," but throughout the Roman Empire, it was common to have the huge images of various gods (and presumably god-emperors) that were set up in pagan temples to have hollowed out heads, so that the priests could actually climb inside these idols and give the impression that the image of the "god" actually spoke.

As far as the **mark of the beast** is concerned, many Roman coins had the title of the emperor on them, and undoubtedly many Christians would have a big problem buying something with a coin that said, "Caesar is Lord and Savior" on it. The reason why John says the number is **666** has to do with the numerical value of the name "Nero Caesar." Therefore, it is likely the early Christians would have identified 666 as referring to Nero or the "second coming of Nero," namely Domitian. In addition, 666 is a triple failing of 777, 7 being the divine number of God.

It is no wonder why Domitian persecuted Christians. They didn't acknowledge him to be a god. Indeed, John saw this emperor worship as the work of Satan himself. The Roman emperor had become the "lamb of the dragon" so to speak. Hence, the reference to having two horns **like a lamb**, yet speaking **like a dragon**. It was the reason why he was seen as the **anti-Christ**. The persecuting emperor and the Imperial Cult embodied Satan's war against the woman's offspring.

### C. The First Interlude (14-15)

We now come to the first interlude in the second movement, just as there was a first interlude in the first movement. Back in chapter seven, we saw the 144,000—the full number of saints who went through the great tribulation. Here in chapters 14-15, we meet the 144,000 again. In this **first subsection (14:1-20)**, John sees the **144,000 standing with the Lamb on Mount Zion**, with the name of the Lamb and his Father on their foreheads. They have been redeemed from the earth, and John says that they have not defiled themselves with women and had kept themselves pure. Indeed, they were purchased from among mankind and were offered as firstfruits to God and the Lamb. No lie was found in their mouths, and they were blameless.

The first thing we notice is that they have the name of the Lamb on their foreheads, not the mark of the beast. Secondly, the comment regarding not defiling themselves with women is not a claim that there will be a special group of 144,000 literal virgin men. It is a foreshadowing regarding the description of the **Whore of Babylon** in the next chapter who represents the seductions of the city of Rome. Throughout the Old Testament, Israel is accused of being unfaithful to God when it "whored" after other gods. Simply put, idolatry was spiritual adultery. In AD 95, the big temptation was to commit spiritual adultery with the Roman Empire and to engage in its debauchery and perversion and to worship any one of its gods, particularly the emperor. These 144,000 have refused to do that and are now seen on Mount Zion as a great army. In ancient Israel, the men had to be ritually pure and not have sex with women before a holy war (**Deut. 23:9-14; I Sam. 21:5; II Sam. 11:9-13**). That same idea is found here. Before the final holy war with Satan, the followers of the Lamb must be pure.

Thirdly, these 144,000 are called **firstfruits**. Remember, they are the full number of those who were to be martyred. That is why they are called firstfruits, for the firstfruits were offered to God before the harvest was reaped to ensure a good harvest. By virtue of being martyred for the sake of Christ, they are the ones sacrificed before the full harvest of the world.

After John describes the 144,000, three angels make declarations that set the stage for what comes later on in Revelation. The first makes a call to those who live on the earth (unbelievers) to fear God and give Him glory. In short, it is a call to repentance. The second angel makes the first reference to a very important figure in the rest of the book: **Babylon the Great**. The angel accuses her of making the nations drunk with the wine of her adulteries. Finally, the third angel declares that anyone who worships the beast and his image will drink the **wine of God's wrath**.

After the 144,000 have just been called the firstfruits and the angels have made a reference to the wine of God's wrath, John then describes the **harvest of the earth**, specifically a **grain harvest** and a **grape harvest**. The grain harvest is essentially the full harvest of Christians whom the 144,000 are the firstfruits. That is why the one doing the reaping is **one like the Son of Man**—Jesus Christ himself. It is not a harvest of judgment, but rather salvation. By contrast, the grain harvest is something quite different. An angel gathers the grapes and throws them into the **great winepress of God's wrath**. They are trampled in the winepress outside the city, and the blood flows out of the press, rising as high as the horses' bridles for a distance of 1,6000 stadia.

To understand this, one has to see how John weaves in a number of metaphors. First, all through the Bible there are references to the gathering and trampling of the chaff—the useless stuff left over from the grain harvest (**Jer. 51:33; Micah 4:12-13; Hab. 3:12; Hosea 13:3; Matthew 3:12; Luke 3:17; Psalm 1:4-5; 35:5; Isaiah 17:13; 29:5; Daniel 2:35**). What John does here, though, given all the images of blood, Babylon's adulterous wine, and the cup of God's wrath, John transforms the trampling of the rejects of the grain harvest into a trampling of grapes in order to speak to Rome's shedding of the blood of Christians, as well as God's judgment on Rome that will be shown in the next few chapters. Essentially, what plays out will be this: *Because Rome tramples upon Christians and sheds their blood, that shed blood will used to make the wine in the cup of God's wrath that Rome will be forced to drink.*

Stemming from the grape harvest, the **second subsection (15:1-8)** gives us a picture of the seven bowls of God's wrath being prepared. John says that after they are poured out, God's wrath will be completed. The overall picture in this chapter, though, is an allusion to Israel during the Exodus, just having crossed the Red Sea, just after God had delivered them from the Egyptian army. This scene, though, is in Heaven. This is the heavenly perspective of the redemption of the Christians, seen in the light of the Exodus. John sees the saints who had been victorious over the beast **standing beside the sea** and **singing the Song of Moses (Exodus 15:1-18)**. This sea though is not the Red Sea, but is the Sea of Chaos, and these are the saints who were victorious over the beast by means of their being killed by the beast. Like Christ, they were victorious through their suffering, martyrdom, and eventual resurrection. The beast killed them, but they were resurrected and defeated death itself, just like Christ. A crucified Messiah is the savior of the world; and his followers overcome the beast by letting themselves be conquered by him—and this is how salvation comes to the world.

The chapter ends with a picture of the Temple in Heaven, filled with the glory of God's Presence. It thus echoes all the Old Testament references to how God's Presence dwelled in the Tabernacle in the wilderness and how God's Presence dwelled in the Temple in Israel. Here, once again we get a glimpse of God's glory, but things are not yet complete. God has trampled the grapes of wrath and the bowls of wrath have been prepared. It is now time to pour them out.

### D. The Seven Bowls of God's Wrath (16:1-21)

The seven bowls of God's wrath here in chapter 16 are very similar to the seven seals and the seven trumpets. The only thing to point out here is that whereas the seven seals affected one-fourth of creation, the seven trumpets affected one-third of creation, and the seven thunders (which were passed over) would have affected half of creation, here the seven bowls affect all of creation. As for the first five bowls, they easily correspond to the plagues of Egypt during the Exodus:

- **First Bowl**: Painful sores (**Ex. 9:8-12**)
- **Second Bowl**: The sea turning to blood (**Ex. 7:14-24**)
- **Third Bowl**: The rivers turning to blood (**Ex. 7:14-24**)

- **Fourth Bowl**: The sun scorches people with fire (**opposite of Ex. 10:21-29**)
- **Fifth Bowl**: The throne of the beast is plunged into darkness (**Ex. 10:21-29**)

One interesting translational issue is in 16:5-6, when the angel of the waters says in 16:5-6 says that those who have shed the blood of the saints and prophets *deserve the blood* (God's wine of wrath) that God has given them to drink. A better translation of 16:6 would be: "Because they poured out the blood of the holy ones and the prophets, you have also given them blood to drink! *That is what they are worthy of.*" Although it is a minor point, translating the word as *worthy* helps us see the connection to 5:2, where another angel asks, "Who is *worthy* to open the scroll?" The point is that just as Jesus is the only one worthy to open the scroll, the only thing those who persecute Christ's followers are "worthy" of is God's wrath.

Another thing to point out is that at the end of both the fourth and fifth bowls, the result is that *the people cursed God and refused to repent*. It is ironic that they curse God for the judgment that they brought upon themselves. Just as in the Exodus, when Pharaoh brought the plagues upon himself by not letting the children of Israel go free, so do the worshippers of the beast bring judgment upon themselves by persecuting and killing the saints.

The **sixth bowl** (like the sixth trumpet) gives a picture of a great army coming from the Euphrates River. If the sixth trumpet hinted this army was ultimately Satanic, here with the sixth bowl there is no doubt. The army is to be gathered by the **three evil spirits** (that look like frogs) that come out of the mouth of the **dragon**, the **beast from the sea**, and the **false prophet** (the beast from the land). They are getting readying for the **battle on the great day of God Almighty**. Throughout the Old Testament, this signified when God would come to redeem His people and bring His wrath upon His enemies. At this point, John writes in 16:15, *"Behold, I come like a thief! Blessed is he who stays awake and keeps his clothes with him, so that he may not go naked and be shamefully exposed!"* This declaration, similar to other warnings in the New Testament about the coming day of the Lord (**Matt. 24:3-25:13; I Thess. 5:2; II Peter 3:10**), essentially tells Christians to not be caught off guard when trouble arises and to be prepared to face the challenge.

In 16:6, John says that this Satanic army gathered at Armageddon. In Old Testament Israel, Armageddon was strategic place in during war time (**Judges 5:19; II Kings 9:27; 23:29; II Chron. 35:22-25**). Anyone invading Israel from the north had to pass through a narrow plain near the town of Megiddo. That is why John uses it as a symbolic reference to the ultimate confrontation between God and Satan, between the offspring of the woman and the offspring of the serpent.

The **seventh bowl** is the consummation of God's wrath, for it is poured out on the very air and every living, breathing thing is affected. The words, "**It is finished!**" echo the words of Christ on the cross and the **lightning** and **thunder** have been images associated with the throne of God throughout Revelation (4:5; 8:5; 11:19). In addition, the **earthquake** is not only associated with the great Day of YHWH in the Old Testament (**Ezekiel 38:18-19; Haggai 2:6-7**), but there was also an earthquake at the time of Christ's crucifixion, the "first tremor" of the ultimate earthquake of God's coming day of wrath. Finally, we learn that the **great city Babylon** is split into three parts, the **cities of the nations** that followed Babylon collapsed, and **great hailstones** (another echo of the Exodus plagues) fell upon the people, who then blasphemed God. This description of God's wrath coming upon Babylon sets the stage for the next few chapters, where the city of Babylon (Rome) is personified as the great whore.

### E. The Second Interlude (17:1-20:15)

At the end of chapter 9, after the blowing of the sixth trumpet, we were told that the people refused to repent, and that is what leads to the second interlude in chapters 10-11 regarding the angel and the little scroll and the two witnesses. At the end of chapter 16, after the seventh bowl is poured out, we are told that the people associated with Babylon continued to blaspheme God. That leads to this second interlude here in this second movement of the symphony of Revelation.

It begins with the **first subsection of 17:1-18**, where an angel shows John the **great whore who sits on many waters**. The ancient city of Babylon stood on the banks of the Euphrates River and was known as the city that sat on many waters. In imagery of the waters also relate to the fact that the sea beast was called out, obviously, from the Sea of Chaos, and is thus satanic in its origin. When John is taken to see the woman, though, he is taken **into the wilderness**. This is a bit odd, given the fact the only other woman in the wilderness was the woman clothed with the sun from chapter 12. We should not think it is the same woman, though, for as we'll see in these last few chapters, John takes great pains to set up a clear contrast between the **New Jerusalem** and **Babylon** and between the **Bride** and the **Whore**.

Instead of being clothed with the sun, this woman is dressed in **purple** and **scarlet**, glittering with **gold, precious stones**, and **pearls**. She holds a **golden cup** filled with the filth of her adulteries, and she is **drunk on the blood of the saints**. She is seductive, alluring, drunk, and deadly. She is also sitting on a **scarlet beast** that is covered with **blasphemous names**. Given the beast's description (seven heads, ten horns), it is clear that it is the sea beast, the Roman Emperor Domitian. We are told that the beast **once was, now is not, and yet will come**. This is parody of the description of God as the one "who was, who is, and is to come (Rev. 1:4, 8; 4:8) shows this beast is the antichrist. Not only that, it speaks to the idea that Domitian was sort of a "Nero 2.0," in that Nero was, then committed suicide, but then in a sense "comes back" in the person of Domitian.

We are also told that the beast comes up **out of the abyss** and **goes to his destruction**—this not only spells out his satanic origins and his ultimate end, but it also associates him with the **king of the abyss** from the fifth trumpet, whose name means "destruction" and "destroyer." Finally, we are also told that the woman who is sitting on the beast is the one who **sits on seven hills**. These seven hills represent the city of Rome, which was built on seven hills. Put all this together, and the picture is that of Rome and the emperor and helps explain why the angel tells John it is God's purpose that the beast will hate the whore, bring her to ruin, and leave her naked. This echoes the way God allows Jerusalem to be destroyed by Babylon in **Ezekiel 23:25-31**. Because she whored with other nations, God will allow Babylon to strip her naked and expose her shame, and God will give her His cup of wrath to drink. John thus says that this is how God dealt with unfaithful Jerusalem in the Old Testament, and this is how He will soon deal with Rome.

With that, the **second subsection (18:1-19:10)** consists of four sets of declarations. The first declaration (18:1-8) is of Babylon the Great's fall, coupled with God's calling for His people to come out of her and have nothing to do with her. The declaration of Babylon's fall echoes many passages in the Old Testament (**Isaiah 13:1-14:23; 21:1-10; Jeremiah 25:12-38; Jeremiah 50-51; Ezekiel 26-28**). The call to come out of her also echoes passages like **Isaiah 48:20** and **Jeremiah 51:45**. In both passages the declaration of God's judgment on Babylon is coupled with a call of redemption for God's people. The declaration to the seven churches is the same: Rome will eventually be laid waste, and the children of God will be vindicated and redeemed from this evil world, so have nothing to do with Rome's sins.

The second set of declarations (18:9-19) consists of the laments by the **kings of the earth**, the **merchants of the earth**, and the **sailors of the sea**. They all *weep and mourn, stand far off*, and are *terrified* by Babylon's torment because they were the ones who had "gotten in bed with her," so to speak and had prospered in the commerce and materialism of the empire. The fall of Babylon meant the destruction of their fortunes. It is worth noting in the list of the cargoes of the merchants in 18:11-13, that the last cargo mentioned is the bodies and souls of human beings. Not only is it a direct condemnation of the actual institution of slavery, but we can also see it as a reference to the dehumanizing effect materialism and commercialism has on society. Back then, there wasn't just slavery, but also forced prostitution in pagan temples and gladiator games in the coliseums.

In the third declaration (18:20-24), a strong angel hurls a great millstone into the sea and declares that Babylon, the great city, will be thrown down with violence, never to be found again, and that all the voices within her will be silenced. The reason for her destruction is because the **blood of the prophets, holy saints**, and **everyone who was slaughtered** was found in her. Simply put, because Babylon brought about destruction, it will be destroyed.

In the fourth set of declarations (19:1-10) is that of the rejoicing in Heaven over Babylon's destruction (19:1-4) and a declaration of the wedding preparations for the **Marriage Supper of the Lamb** (9:5-10). The **bride of the Lamb** is clearly the Church (the saints) and the way she is dressed serves as a clear contrast of the whore of Babylon, for the bride is clothed in fine linen, pure and bright, representing the righteous acts of the saints. This Marriage Supper of the Lamb is the fulfillment and consummation of a number of meals throughout the entire Bible:

- (1) Adam and Eve eating in the Garden of Eden.
- (2) The Passover meal that celebrated God's freeing of His people.
- (3) The Temple meals that celebrated reconciliation between God and His people.
- (4) Jesus' sharing meals with all kinds of people, celebrating the coming of God's Kingdom.
- (5) The Last Supper, that commemorated Jesus' own sacrifice that would bring about salvation and reconciliation with God.

All of these foreshadow the future Marriage Supper of the Lamb and the consummation of God's redemption of all creation.

The **third subsection (19:11-21)** gives us the picture of the defeat of the beast and the kings of the earth at the hands of Christ. Christ's description in 19:11-16 not only echoes John's description of him in 1:9-20, but his depiction of being a rider on a white horse is a direct contrast to the rider on the white horse from the first seal, which was that of imperialistic Rome. In addition, John tells us the rider's name is the **Word of God**, a clear echo of his depiction of Jesus in John 1:1-18 as the **Word made flesh**. John further says that the **armies of Heaven** are following him—the fact they are dressed in fine linen connects them to the martyrs under the altar of souls, the 144,000 (from both 7:1-17 and 14:1-5), and the bride of the Lamb. He says that rider strikes down the nations with a sharp sword from his mouth, namely the power of the Holy Spirit, and that he is the one who **treads the winepress of God's wrath** (14:17-20).

With that, 19:17-21 gives us a picture of a far different meal than the Marriage Supper of the Lamb. This **Great Supper of God** (echoing Ezekiel 39:17) is one in which the birds of mid-heaven are called together to feast on the flesh of the kings of the earth who had allied themselves with the sea beast. Indeed, John then says that the two beasts are captured and thrown into the **Lake of Fire**, while the kings of the earth are killed by the sword that comes out of the mouth of the rider on the white horse, and the birds gorge themselves on their flesh. Those who oppressed God's people are dead. All that is left to deal with is the great dragon himself.

The **fourth subsection (20:1-15)** is perhaps the most puzzling chapters in all the Bible. Ultimately, it is about the final war and defeat of the dragon. But there are also a number of things that continue to perplex people. It begins in **20:1-6**, where we are told of two things happening during the same time: (1) Satan is bound and thrown into the abyss for 1,000 years, while (2) The martyred saints are resurrected in the first resurrection and reign with Christ during that time. Then in **20:7-10**, there is a final battle between God and His people vs. Satan and Gog and Magog, where Satan is thrown into the Lake of Fire. This is followed in **20:11-15**, where we are told of the second resurrection and the Great White Throne judgment, where the dead are judged according to their works and where Death and Hades, along with those whose names weren't in the Book of Life, were thrown into the Lake of Fire.

One should be able to recognize the echoes of other things in Revelation, but the pressing question here is, *"What does the 1,000 years stand for and what exactly is the correct 'timeline' of all this?"* This gets us into the question of **millennialism**. There are four general views: *Historical Premillennialism, Dispensationalist Premillennialism, Postmillennialism,* and *Amillennialism*. Books have been written about these views, but for our purposes, I want to try to understand it against the backdrop of the prevailing Jewish apocalyptic views concerning God's kingdom were during the time of John.

Generally speaking, Jewish apocalypticism tended to see history as a repeating of the seven days of creation, with each day representing 1,000 years. Since the six days of divine work were followed by God's Sabbath rest, so it was believed that the "six days" of human history would be followed by a Sabbath of the Messiah's kingdom, which in turn would give place to an "eighth day" without end—the Age to Come and new creation in the Kingdom of God. Therefore, many viewed history as 2,000 years from creation to Moses, 2,000 years from Moses to the Messiah, 2,000 years of the Messiah's kingdom, followed by 1,000 years of Sabbath for the world.

John, though, has patterned Revelation 20-22 after **Ezekiel 36-48**, where there is the following unfolding of events: (1) A **resurrection of Israel** and the **restoration of the nation** to its land under the rule of a **new David** (36-37), then after an unspecified time, (2) A **rebellion of Gog and Magog** (mythological nations that represent the spiritual forces of Satan) of and their defeat (38-49), followed by (3) The promise of a **new Jerusalem** with a **new Temple** in a **sanctified Promised Land** (40-48). As we will see, John uses this narrative pattern from Ezekiel, but then takes the idea of a 1,000-year Sabbath rest from general Jewish apocalyptic thought and makes that the unspecified time between the resurrection of God's people (the first resurrection) and the final rebellion of Satan, along with Gog and Magog.

The result of all this is that John seems to be telling the seven churches the following things: (1) God would soon act and their tormentors, the whore of Babylon (Rome) and the beast (the emperor), would be destroyed and (2) those who had been killed by Rome would be resurrected and would reign with Christ in during a "Sabbath rest." Still, (3) That wouldn't be the end of the story, because the final defeat of Satan, Death, and Hades themselves was yet to come. Simply put, the end of their current persecution would soon come, their martyrs would be reigning with Christ, yet there was more history to play out before the ultimate end of the old age and the full consummation of the new creation.

### F. The Ultimate Result (21:1-22:5)

Of course, the New Creation is the focus of this final section in Revelation. Not only is it the climax of Revelation, or even of the New Testament. *It is the climax of the entire biblical story itself—the climax of God's entire creation project, from beginning to end.* The **first subsection (21:1-8)** is a picture of the New Heaven and New Earth. John tells us that the first heaven and earth was no more and that there was **no longer any sea**, namely the Sea of Chaos, because Christ had defeated death. John also sees the **New Jerusalem**, coming out of Heaven like a **bride**. This picture of the heavenly city of the New Jerusalem as a bride stands in contrast to the earthly city of Babylon, the great whore.

Then a voice from the throne declares that God's dwelling will now be with His people. This has been God's goal from the beginning of creation. Adam and Eve were cast out of God's presence because of sin. God dwelled in the tabernacle in the wilderness with Israel, then in the Temple in Jerusalem, but there was always still a separation, and the high priest was only allowed into the Holy of Holies once a year. Yet here, John declares that in the New Heaven and Earth, God's presence would fully dwell with His people. It is then in 21:5-8 that Christ, the Lamb of God, speaks from the throne. He calls himself the **Alpha and Omega**, thus speaking to his equality with God the Father. He also invites everyone to come to him, promising them the **water of life**, a clear allusion to the river in Eden, his conversation with the Samaritan woman in **John 4:7-15**, as well as his statement at the Feast of Tabernacles in **John 7:37-39**.

He then says that those who **conquer** (echoing the promises in chapters 2-3) will **inherit the Heavenly Jerusalem**. This language of inheritance goes all the way back to God's covenant with Abraham, where He promised that Abraham's descendants would inherit the Promised Land. Here, the New Creation and Heavenly Jerusalem are the ultimate inheritance and ultimate Promised Land for God's people. Coupled with the promise of inheritance is the declaration that those who conquer will become **God's son**. Obviously, this includes both men and women, and hence "children" of God, but the use of "God's son," emphasizes the unity Christians have in Christ and how it is through Christ that we become **co-heirs and children of God Himself**.

The **second subsection (21:9-27)** gives us a picture of the Heavenly Jerusalem, who is called the **Bride** and the **wife of the Lamb**. John tells us that the city shone with the glory of God, meaning God's presence filled the city, an allusion to when we are told in the Old Testament that God's presence filled the Tabernacle or the Temple. He also describes the **twelve gates** as having on them the names of the **twelve tribes of Israel**, and that on the foundation, there are the names of the **twelve apostles**. The city is thus shown to be the home of God's people, comprised both of Jews and Gentiles.

In 21:15-21, John tells us about the walls of the city. Basically, the city is described as the shape of a cube: 12,000 square stadia. The reason for this is because it is an allusion to the Holy of Holies in both the Tabernacle in the wilderness and the Temple in Jerusalem. John is thus saying that in new creation and Heavenly Jerusalem *everything will be as holy as the Holy of Holies*. The 12,000 stadia measurement of the city is obviously a symbolic number: 12 x 1,000, with 12 being the people of God and 1,000 being God's number of completion. In addition, John says the walls themselves were 144 cubits think. As with the 24 elders and the names of the 12 tribes and the 12 apostles (not to mention the 144,000 thousand), 144 is a symbolic number: 12 (tribes of Israel) x 12 (apostles to the Gentiles) = the full people of God.

In 21:22-27, John tells us that there was no Temple in the city because God Himself and the Lamb were its Temple—He now fully dwells with His people. He further says that the nations will walk by its light and the kings of the earth will bring their splendor into it. This echoes a constant theme in the Old Testament, that when God restores the fortunes of His people, that His people will be a light to the nations, thus fulfilling God's promise in the Abrahamic covenant that through the nation that comes from him, all nations will be blessed (**Isaiah 2:2-4; 60: 3, 5, 11; Micah 4:1-3; Zechariah 8:20-23; 14:16**).

In the **third subsection (22:1-5)**, John takes us into the city to bring the entire biblical story full circle, for when we get into the city, we find a full reversal of the curse and the fall in **Genesis 1-3**. There is the **River of the Water of Life**, which, obviously, brings life. There is access to the **Tree of Life** for the healing of the nations. And there is **no more curse**. Indeed, the creation that was subject to decay is now renewed and the paradise that was lost is now restored. God's promise to redeem a suffering people is fulfilled and His promise to defeat death and evil is now accomplished. All that was broken and cursed is now made new and healed. This is John's way of saying that in the end, God wins, and we will see His face. We will be brought home out of our exile. That is what we long for.

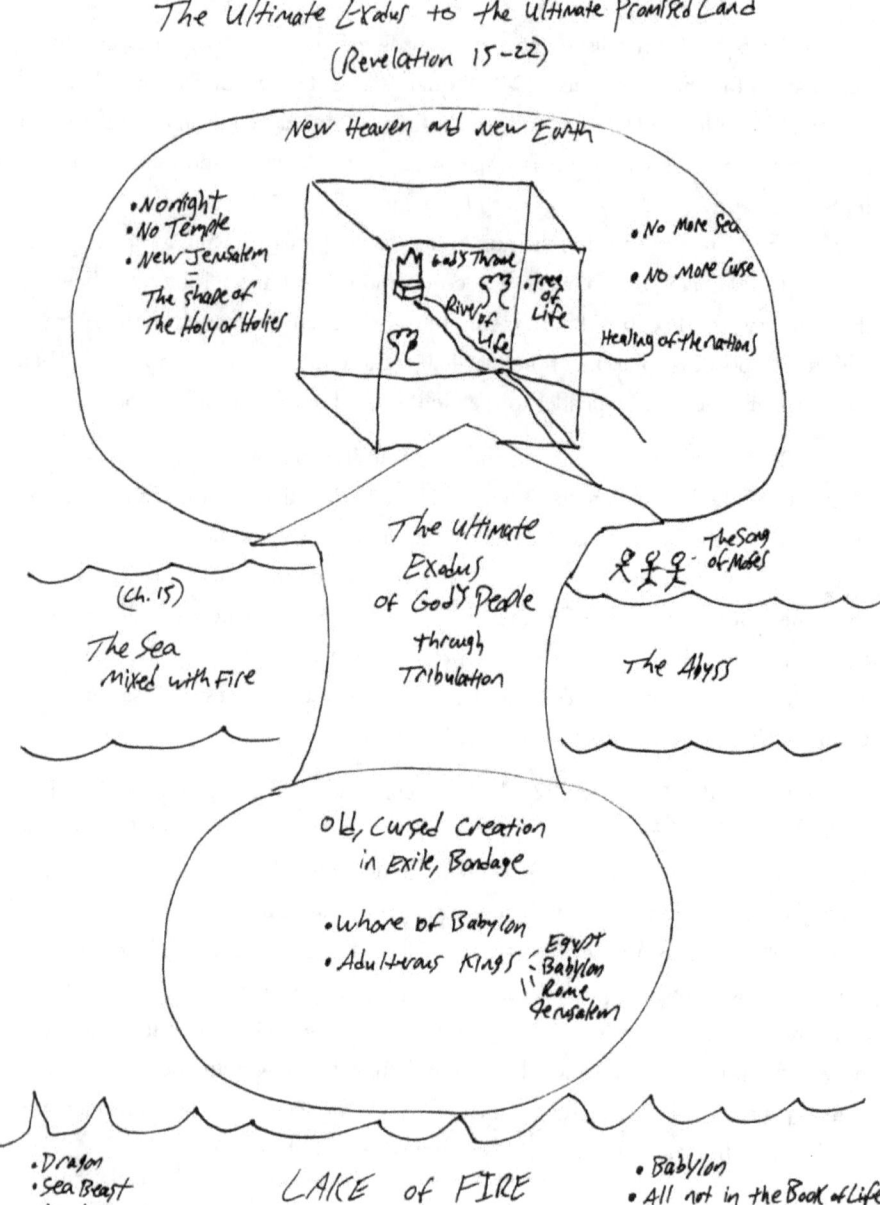

## 5. The Epilogue (22:6-21)

With John's apocalyptic symphony finished, he now gives some concluding comments in the epilogue. He begins by saying that anyone who keep the "words of the prophecy in this book" is blessed. Simply put, it is a challenge to live out the message of Revelation. Live as the Bride of the Lamb and don't get in bed with the Whore of Babylon. Live as a co-heir of Christ and as the offspring of the woman and don't ally oneself with the offspring of the serpent. *Above all, stand firm, keep the faith, and realize that your participation in the suffering of Christ is the means by which Christ redeems the world.*

John is told by the angel to **not seal up the words of this prophecy**, because the **time is near**. In most apocalypses, the "writer," a character from Israel's past, is told to "seal up" the apocalyptic vision. The effect is that the actual writer who is writing much later is thus giving the impression that the apocalyptic vision given, to let's say Daniel around 550 BC, had been sealed up for centuries, only to be unsealed in his day (probably around 170 BC, and the time of the Maccabean Revolt). John, though, is not writing with a pseudonym of some figure in Israel's past. He's writing as himself, there in AD 95, to that present situation confronting Christians in the late first century. Therefore, he is saying that Revelation isn't to be "sealed up" until the last days, *because the last days were now.* From the Christian perspective, from the time of Christ's ascension until he comes again are the **last days**.

In 22:18-19, John then warns is audience to not add or subtract anything from the book of Revelation, basically saying, "Don't change anything I've written here." Therefore, we should avoid two tendencies people have when confronted with Revelation. First, we shouldn't try to obsess over Revelation like some "far-off future prediction" of a time when God will *take Christians away from tribulation.* Revelation, indeed, the entire New Testament is crystal clear: If you are a Christian, expect tribulation and realize your suffering is a participation in the sufferings of Christ by which God redeems the world and puts an end to sin and death. At the same time, we shouldn't ignore Revelation because it just seems too weird, for its message directly speaks to Christians of any time. John warns us not to take those difficult parts out, because that is how the script has been written. Those difficult parts are the means by which Christ saves the world. To change the script is to reject Christ's plan of salvation.

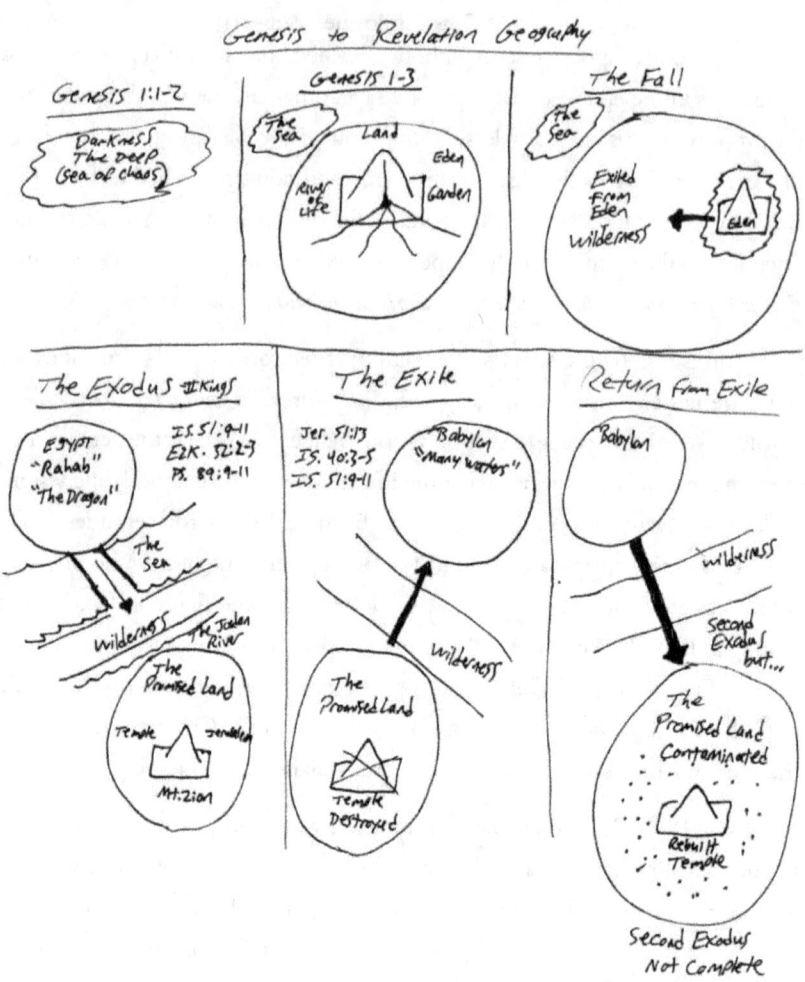

It should be obvious that Revelation is an explosive and dangerous book. Adding or subtracting from it easily perverts the Gospel that Christ preached, and that Christians are called to live out. That is why it is so important to read Revelation in its historical and literary context. That is why it is so important to understand what it originally meant. Only after we understand the original and inspired meaning of Revelation can we begin to relate its message to our lives today.

## Chart of the "Sevens" in Revelation

|   | Seals (1/4) | Trumpets (1/3) | Thunders (1/2) | Bowls (Complete) |
|---|---|---|---|---|
| 1 | White Horse | Hail and Fire mixed with Blood<br><br>Land | X | On the Land<br><br>Sores upon Worshippers of the Beast |
| 2 | Red Horse | Blazing Mountain into the Sea<br><br>Sea to Blood | X | Into the Sea<br><br>Sea to Blood |
| 3 | Black Horse | Star Wormwood into Rivers<br><br>Bitter Waters | X | Into the Rivers<br><br>Rivers to Blood |
| 4 | Pale Horse | Sun, Moon, Stars<br><br>Light Affected | X | Onto the Sun<br><br>Scorched People |
| 5 | Souls of the Martyrs under the Altar | Locusts out of the Abyss | X | Onto the Throne of the Beast<br><br>Kingdom shrouded in Darkness |
| 6 | Coming Day of the Lord | Army Beyond Euphrates | X | On the Euphrates<br><br>The Coming of the Kings of the East |
| 7 | Reveals the Trumpets | Kingdom of the World now the Kingdom of Christ | X | Onto the Air<br><br>"It is Done" |

www.ingramcontent.com/pod-product-compliance
Lightning Source LLC
Chambersburg PA
CBHW062056280426
43673CB00073B/207